South Australia

Denis O'Byrne

D0318298

LONELY PLANET PUBLICATIONS
Melbourne • Oakland • London • Paris

NORTHERN
TERRITORY

Kulgera

WITJIRA
NATIONAL
PARK

Great Victoria Desert

Aboriginal
Land

Mintabie   Marla

Cadney
Homestead

COOBER PEDY
Opal-mining centre with
lunar landscapes and
underground houses

Great Victoria Desert

Unnamed
Conservation
Park

Tallaringa
Conservation
Park

Coober
Pedy

Jubilee
Lake

WESTERN
AUSTRALIA

Lake Maurice

Nullarbor Plain

Woomera
Prohibited
Area

Aboriginal
Land

Maralinga (Abandoned)

Nullarbor Plain

Trans Australia Railway

Tarcoola

Nullarbor
Regional
Reserve

Yellabinna Regional
Reserve

Rawlinna   Loongana

Nullarbor Roadhouse

Aboriginal
Land

Yalata

Yumbarra
Conservation
Park

Eucla

Penong

Eyre
Ceduna

Highway

Madura Pass
Roadhouse

NULLARBOR
NATIONAL
PARK

Cocklebiddy

Streaky Bay

Eyre Highway

Caiguna

HEAD OF BIGHT
A prime spot to watch southern
right whales in the world's
second largest marine park

Venus Bay

Flinders Island   Ellisto

Great
Australian
Bight

PORT LINCOLN
Magnificent coastline,
sandy dunes and
rugged islands

Eyre Peninse

YORKE PENINSULA
Home of the Kernewek
Lowender Cornish Festival

FLEURIEU PENINSULA
Good wineries and whale
and penguin watching

SOUTHERN
OCEAN

KANGAROO ISLAND
A relaxing place with a scenic
coastline, friendly people
and abundant wildlife

ELEVATION

1500m
1000m
500m
200m
0

0   50   100 km

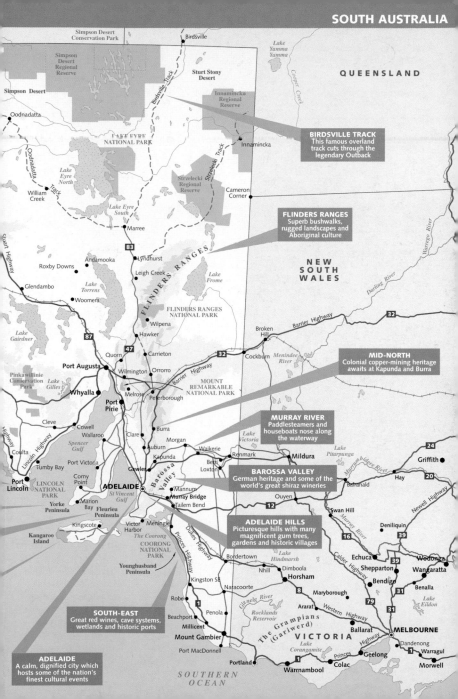

Simpson Desert
Conservation Park

Birdsville

Simpson
Desert
Regional
Reserve

QUEENSLAND

Lake
Yamma
Yamma

Copper Creek

Simpson Desert

Sturt Stony
Desert

Innamincka
Regional
Reserve

Oodnadatta

LAKE EYRE
NATIONAL PARK

Lake
Eyre
North

Innamincka

BIRDSVILLE TRACK
This famous overland
track cuts through the
legendary Outback

William
Creek

Oodnadatta Track

Strzelecki
Regional
Reserve

Cameron
Corner

Marree

Lake
Eyre
South

Lake
Frome

FLINDERS RANGES
Superb bushwalks,
rugged landscapes and
Aboriginal culture

83

Lyndhurst

Roxby Downs

Andamooka

Leigh Creek

Warrego River

Stuart Highway

Glendambo

Lake
Torrens

Woomera

F L I N D E R S   R A N G E S

Wilpena

Hawker

FLINDERS RANGES
NATIONAL PARK

N E W
S O U T H
W A L E S

Darling River

Lake
Gairdner

87

Pinkawillinie
Conservation
Park

Quorn

47

Carrieton

Orroroo

Broken
Hill

Barrier Highway

32

Lake
Gilles

Port Augusta

Wilmington

Cockburn

Menindee
River

MID-NORTH
Colonial copper-mining heritage
awaits at Kapunda and Burra

Melrose

Barrier Highway

32

Whyalla

Port
Pirie

Peterborough

MOUNT
REMARKABLE
NATIONAL PARK

Cleve

Cowell
Wallaroo

Clare

Burra

Morgan

Waikerie

MURRAY RIVER
Paddlesteamers and
houseboats nose along
the waterway

Lake
Victoria

24

Griffith

Highway

Coulta

Lincoln Highway

Port Victoria

Auburn

Kapunda

Renmark

Berri

Loxton

Mildura

Lake
Pitarpunga

Murrumbidgee River

Hay

20

Tumby Bay

Gawler

Barossa
Valley

Balranald

Newell Highway

Port
Lincoln

LINCOLN
NATIONAL PARK

Corny
Point

ADELAIDE

St Vincent
Gulf

Spencer
Gulf

BAROSSA VALLEY
German heritage and some of the
world's great shiraz wineries

Ouyen

12

Swan Hill

Deniliquin

39

Yorke
Peninsula

Marion
Bay

Fleurieu
Peninsula

Mannum

Murray Bridge

Tailem Bend

ADELAIDE HILLS
Picturesque hills with many
magnificent gum trees,
gardens and historic villages

Murray River

Echuca

39

Wodonga

Kingscote

Victor
Harbor

Meningie

Princes Highway

Dukes Highway

16

Swan Hill

Calder Highway

Shepparton

Bendigo

Wangaratta

Benalla

31

Kangaroo
Island

The Coorong

COORONG
NATIONAL PARK

Bordertown

Lake
Hindmarsh

Nhill

Dimboola

Horsham

Maryborough

Lake
Eildon

Younghusband
Peninsula

Kingston SE

Naracoorte

8

Ararat

Western Highway

79

31

MELBOURNE

Robe

Penola

Glenelg River

Rocklands
Reservoir

The Grampians
(Gariwerd)

Ballarat

Highway

Dandenong

1

Warragul

SOUTH-EAST
Great red wines, cave systems,
wetlands and historic ports

Beachport

Millicent

Mount Gambier

Port MacDonnell

VICTORIA

Lake
Corangamite

Princes
Highway

Geelong

Morwell

ADELAIDE
A calm, dignified city which
hosts some of the nation's
finest cultural events

Portland

Warrnambool

Colac

*SOUTHERN
OCEAN*

South Australia
2nd edition – October 1999
First published – September 1996

Published by
Lonely Planet Publications Pty Ltd A.C.N. 005 607 983
192 Burwood Rd, Hawthorn, Victoria 3122, Australia

Lonely Planet Offices
Australia PO Box 617, Hawthorn, Victoria 3122
USA 150 Linden St, Oakland, CA 94607
UK 10a Spring Place, London NW5 3BH
France 1 rue du Dahomey, 75011 Paris

Photographs
Many of the images in this guide are available for licensing from
Lonely Planet Images.
email: lpi@lonelyplanet.com.au

Front cover photograph
Remarkable Rocks, Flinders Chase National Park (Paul Sinclair)

ISBN 0 86442 716 6

Printed by Craft Print Pte Ltd, Singapore

Contents – Text

MAP LEGEND   back page

METRIC CONVERSION   inside back cover

Contents – Maps

MAP INDEX

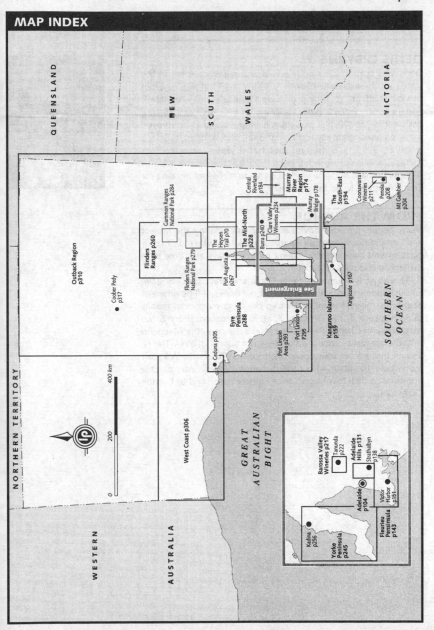

QUEENSLAND

NEW

SOUTH

WALES

VICTORIA

NORTHERN TERRITORY

WESTERN

AUSTRALIA

Outback Region
p310

Coober Pedy
p317

West Coast p306

Gammon Ranges
National Park p284

Flinders Ranges p260

Flinders Ranges
National Park p279

The
Heysen
Trail p70

Port Augusta
p267

Ceduna p305

Eyre Peninsula
p288

Port Lincoln
Area p293

Port Lincoln
p295

Central
Riverland
p184

Murray
River
Region p174

Murray
Bridge p178

The Mid-North
p228

Clare Valley
Wineries p234

Burra p240

See Enlargement

The South-East
p194

Coonawarra
Wineries
p211

Penola
p208

Mt Gambier
p204

Kangaroo Island
p159

Kingscote p167

SOUTHERN
OCEAN

GREAT
AUSTRALIAN
BIGHT

0   200   400 km

Barossa Valley
Wineries p217

Tanunda
p222

Adelaide
Hills p131

Strathalbyn
p138

Adelaide
p104

Victor
Harbor
p151

Fleurieu
Peninsula p143

Kadina
p256

Yorke
Peninsula
p245

The Author

DENIS O'BYRNE

Denis was born in the Adelaide Hills and raised at Robe, in the state's south-east. He left South Australia at 17 but returns often to visit relatives, go fishing on Eyre Peninsula and – of late – update Lonely Planet books. He describes his career as a zig-zag path leading nowhere in particular, having worked as a surveyor, mine planner, plant operator, national park ranger, builder's labourer, building consultant and travel writer, among other things. Denis isn't sure whether Lonely Planet represents a zig or a zag or perhaps both; he worked on *Vanuatu* before heading for South Australia to do this update.

FROM THE AUTHOR

Many people provided advice and assistance during the project and I'm grateful to them all – particularly Mum, who didn't complain when I took over her dining room for days at a time with my laptop and piles of paper.

As always, Phil Brennan, Peter Caust and Brett Knuckey gave enthusiastic support and even bought *me* drinks. It'll be different next time, fellers, I promise. I'd also like to give a special thanks to Bronte Leak of the Office of Sport & Recreation, Barry & Jan Matthew and Cheryle Pinkess from the Barossa, Kathy Machado of the Clare Valley tourist office, Heather Simms of YHA Travel, and all those other tour operators, tourism officers, NPWS staff etc around the state who patiently answered my interminable questions. A final thanks goes to Sr Patricia Keane and to Corrine Cartwright.

This Book

Denis O'Byrne researched and authored both the 1st and 2nd editions of Lonely Planet's *South Australia* guide. Additional information for disabled travellers was provided by Bruce Cameron, and Adam Marks brought his palate to bear in authoring the boxed text 'Wine Tasting'.

From the Publisher

South Australia was produced in Lonely Planet's Melbourne office. Editing was coordinated by Hilary Ericksen, who was ably assisted with editing, proofing and indexing by Arabella Bamber, Tony Davidson, Lyn McGaurr and Cherry Prior. Mapping and design was coordinated by the incurably cheerful Barbara Benson, and Pablo Gastar turned a discerning eye to the book's colour wraps. Thanks to LPI for providing the images. Leanne Peake, Tony Fankhauser and Chris Lee Ack assisted with the mapping; Leanne drafted the colour map of South Australia. The superb cover was designed by Guillaume Roux, and Matt King was central in producing the book's illustrations. Tim Uden provided expert knowledge of QuarkXPress (and on occasion chocolate biscuits too). The seasoned advice of Mary Neighbour and Jane Hart was invaluable in putting this book together. Martine Lleonart and Mark Griffiths also gave advice during production.

Our thanks to Phillip Brownscombe and Sara Martin for their tactical approach to impromptu research assistance.

Acknowledgements

Finally, Lonely Planet thanks the travellers who used the 1st edition and wrote to us with useful tips and advice:

Paul Anderson, Gilbert C Aue, Joy Behennah, Kathy Bowden, Roger Boyes, T Davies, Jane Dunn, Chris Gibson, Jesse Grainger, Dianne Groves, Robert Hia, DR Howlett, Heather K James, Stuart Kelly, Robina von Kolczynski, Carla Lathe, John & Debbie Lawrence, Milton Lever, Angela McKay, Chris McLaughlin, Maxwell Millowick, Trudy Mooy, Michiel & Monique, Sherrill Pinney, Carol & Sean Richardson, Elisabeth Richmond, Ann Schioldann, John Silby, Martin J Smith, Cindy & Greg Strauss, Kathy Strauss, Dr Klaus Truoel, Craig Walsh, Margaret Web, Jeff M Weeks, Fred Wilson and Gaynor Wood.

Foreword

ABOUT LONELY PLANET GUIDEBOOKS

The story begins with a classic travel adventure: Tony and Maureen Wheeler's 1972 journey across Europe and Asia to Australia. Useful information about the overland trail did not exist at that time, so Tony and Maureen published the first Lonely Planet guidebook to meet a growing need.

From a kitchen table, then from a tiny office in Melbourne (Australia), Lonely Planet has become the largest independent travel publisher in the world, an international company with offices in Melbourne, Oakland (USA), London (UK) and Paris (France).

Today Lonely Planet guidebooks cover the globe. There is an ever-growing list of books and there's information in a variety of forms and media. Some things haven't changed. The main aim is still to help make it possible for adventurous travellers to get out there – to explore and better understand the world.

At Lonely Planet we believe travellers can make a positive contribution to the countries they visit – if they respect their host communities and spend their money wisely. Since 1986 a percentage of the income from each book has been donated to aid projects and human rights campaigns.

Updates Lonely Planet thoroughly updates each guidebook as often as possible. This usually means there are around two years between editions, although for more unusual or more stable destinations the gap can be longer. Check the imprint page (following the colour map at the beginning of the book) for publication dates.

Between editions up-to-date information is available in two free newsletters – the paper *Planet Talk* and email *Comet* (to subscribe, contact any Lonely Planet office) – and on our Web site at www.lonelyplanet.com. The *Upgrades* section of the Web site covers a number of important and volatile destinations and is regularly updated by Lonely Planet authors. *Scoop* covers news and current affairs relevant to travellers. And, lastly, the *Thorn Tree* bulletin board and *Postcards* section of the site carry unverified, but fascinating, reports from travellers.

Correspondence The process of creating new editions begins with the letters, postcards and emails received from travellers. This correspondence often includes suggestions, criticisms and comments about the current editions. Interesting excerpts are immediately passed on via newsletters and the Web site, and everything goes to our authors to be verified when they're researching on the road. We're keen to get more feedback from organisations or individuals who represent communities visited by travellers.

> Lonely Planet gathers information for everyone who's curious about the planet – and especially for those who explore it first-hand. Through guidebooks, phrasebooks, activity guides, maps, literature, newsletters, image library, TV series and Web site we act as an information exchange for a worldwide community of travellers.

Research Authors aim to gather sufficient practical information to enable travellers to make informed choices and to make the mechanics of a journey run smoothly. They also research historical and cultural background to help enrich the travel experience and allow travellers to understand and respond appropriately to cultural and environmental issues.

Authors don't stay in every hotel because that would mean spending a couple of months in each medium-sized city and, no, they don't eat at every restaurant because that would mean stretching belts beyond capacity. They do visit hotels and restaurants to check standards and prices, but feedback based on readers' direct experiences can be very helpful.

Many of our authors work undercover, others aren't so secretive. None of them accept freebies in exchange for positive write-ups. And none of our guidebooks contain any advertising.

Production Authors submit their raw manuscripts and maps to offices in Australia, USA, UK or France. Editors and cartographers – all experienced travellers themselves – then begin the process of assembling the pieces. When the book finally hits the shops, some things are already out of date, we start getting feedback from readers and the process begins again …

WARNING & REQUEST

Things change – prices go up, schedules change, good places go bad and bad places go bankrupt – nothing stays the same. So, if you find things better or worse, recently opened or long since closed, please tell us and help make the next edition even more accurate and useful. We genuinely value all the feedback we receive. Julie Young coordinates a well travelled team that reads and acknowledges every letter, postcard and email and ensures that every morsel of information finds its way to the appropriate authors, editors and cartographers for verification.

Everyone who writes to us will find their name in the next edition of the appropriate guidebook. They will also receive the latest issue of *Planet Talk*, our quarterly printed newsletter, or *Comet*, our monthly email newsletter. Subscriptions to both newsletters are free. The very best contributions will be rewarded with a free guidebook.

Excerpts from your correspondence may appear in new editions of Lonely Planet guidebooks, the Lonely Planet Web site, *Planet Talk* or *Comet*, so please let us know if you *don't* want your letter published or your name acknowledged.

Send all correspondence to the Lonely Planet office closest to you:

Australia: PO Box 617, Hawthorn, Victoria 3122
USA: 150 Linden St, Oakland, CA 94607
UK: 10A Spring Place, London NW5 3BH
France: 1 rue du Dahomey, 75011 Paris

Or email us at: talk2us@lonelyplanet.com.au

For news, views and updates see our Web site: www.lonelyplanet.com

HOW TO USE A LONELY PLANET GUIDEBOOK

The best way to use a Lonely Planet guidebook is any way you choose. At Lonely Planet we believe the most memorable travel experiences are often those that are unexpected, and the finest discoveries are those you make yourself. Guidebooks are not intended to be used as if they provide a detailed set of infallible instructions!

Contents All Lonely Planet guidebooks follow roughly the same format. The Facts about the Destination chapters or sections give background information ranging from history to weather. Facts for the Visitor gives practical information on issues like visas and health. Getting There & Away gives a brief starting point for researching travel to and from the destination. Getting Around gives an overview of the transport options when you arrive.

The peculiar demands of each destination determine how subsequent chapters are broken up, but some things remain constant. We always start with background, then proceed to sights, places to stay, places to eat, entertainment, getting there and away, and getting around information – in that order.

Heading Hierarchy Lonely Planet headings are used in a strict hierarchical structure that can be visualised as a set of Russian dolls. Each heading (and its following text) is encompassed by any preceding heading that is higher on the hierarchical ladder.

Entry Points We do not assume guidebooks will be read from beginning to end, but that people will dip into them. The traditional entry points are the list of contents and the index. In addition, however, some books have a complete list of maps and an index map illustrating map coverage.

There may also be a colour map that shows highlights. These highlights are dealt with in greater detail in the Facts for the Visitor chapter, along with planning questions and suggested itineraries. Each chapter covering a geographical region usually begins with a locator map and another list of highlights. Once you find something of interest in a list of highlights, turn to the index.

Maps Maps play a crucial role in Lonely Planet guidebooks and include a huge amount of information. A legend is printed on the back page. We seek to have complete consistency between maps and text, and to have every important place in the text captured on a map. Map key numbers usually start in the top left corner.

Although inclusion in a guidebook usually implies a recommendation we cannot list every good place. Exclusion does not necessarily imply criticism. In fact there are a number of reasons why we might exclude a place – sometimes it is simply inappropriate to encourage an influx of travellers.

Introduction

South Australia (SA) epitomises the 'sun-burnt country' and 'wide brown land' of the nation's literature and legend. It's by far the driest state, and as for space ... 80% of its vast area is home to only 1% of its population. There are few better places to experience Australia's legendary Outback.

But there's a lot more to SA than wide horizons. Its 3700km coastline varies from sheltered bays to some of the country's finest surf beaches. Inland is the stunning scenery of the 800km-long Mt Lofty and Flinders ranges, made famous by local artist Hans Heysen. And meandering through the state on its final 650km to the sea is the mighty Murray, which has all the romance and atmosphere of big rivers anywhere.

Paddle-wheelers still ply what was once the inland highway of Australia.

In terms of outdoor activity, you can do just about anything in SA (even ice-skating, snow-skiing and tobogganing, at a huge facility in Adelaide). You can walk in forested hills, among arid ranges and along pristine coastline. You can climb soaring cliffs in the Flinders Ranges, cycle the 800km Mawson Trail and go wilderness camping far (and I mean *far*) from the sight and sound of civilisation.

If you prefer the water, there's swimming, windsurfing, scuba diving, fishing, canoeing and sea kayaking, and surfing at places like world-famous Cactus Beach. If it's wildlife you want to see, there are

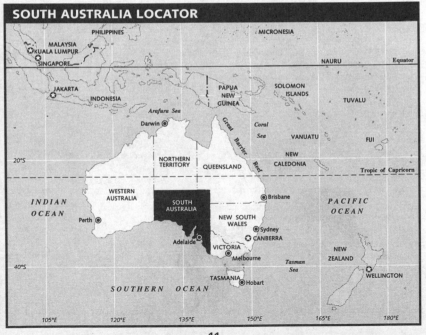

SOUTH AUSTRALIA LOCATOR

whales, seals, penguins, koalas, kangaroos, emus, parrots and many, many more critters, all in their natural habitats.

You can enjoy most of these activities in conservation areas; 21% of SA's land area is under some form of official conservation management. These range from national parks to game reserves, where you can go hunting in season. Perhaps best known is the Flinders Ranges National Park, which includes Wilpena Pound. It's a respectable size at 94,500 hectares, but small compared with the huge reserves in the state's far north.

Conveniently close to the state's capital is the Barossa Valley, one of Australia's premier wine districts – it's a world-class producer of shiraz. Other excellent wine districts include Coonawarra, the Clare Valley, McLaren Vale and the Adelaide Hills. Complementing this is a wealth of fine restaurants, all selling fresh local tucker.

South Australia's rich cultural heritage includes Aboriginal rock engravings (the oldest in the world) and the traditions of early German and Cornish settlers. Thanks to events such as the biennial Adelaide Festival of Arts, Adelaide is recognised as one of Australia's cultural capitals. The city has many wonderful Victorian buildings that have escaped redevelopment, as well as a lively visual and performing arts scene.

Allow plenty of time to look around this big state with its many diverse attractions. South Australia is a great place. Enjoy it!

Facts about South Australia

HISTORY
Aboriginal Settlement

Australian Aboriginal (which literally means 'indigenous') society has the longest continuous cultural history in the world. Although mystery shrouds many aspects of Australian prehistory, it is almost certain that the ancestors of today's Aborigines came across the sea from South-East Asia at least 50,000 years ago.

Although much of Australia is now arid, those early migrants found a much wetter continent, with vast forests and lakes teeming with food resources. The fauna included giant flightless birds, 3m-tall kangaroos, and wombat-like mammals the size of beef cows. Apart from a few carnivorous predators and poisonous snakes, the environment was relatively non-threatening to the continent's first people.

Because of these favourable conditions, archaeologists suggest that within a few thousand years the Aboriginal people had populated most of the continent except the drier central regions, which were occupied 25,000 years ago. The earliest known relics of the Aboriginal occupation of South Australia (SA) are rock carvings near Olary which have been dated at 43,000 years (16,000 years older than the Neanderthal carvings of Europe).

Aboriginal Society

At the time of European settlement, SA is thought to have been populated by between 10,000 and 15,000 Aboriginal people living in 43 tribal groups. About half of these people lived in the temperate, well-watered area between Gulf St Vincent and the Victorian border.

While the arid inland was sparsely populated, few parts were permanently uninhabited. Even the hostile Simpson Desert in the far north-east was occupied on a year-round basis. Here the people survived thanks to water obtained from scattered permanent wells, along with an encyclopaedic knowledge of the desert's resources.

Aborigines lived in extended family groups, or clans, within defined areas of land. Contrary to popular belief they did not wander aimlessly in search of food and water. Rather, almost every facet of their lives was governed by millennia of ritual and tradition, with religious requirements a powerful influence. In fact, the overwhelming force in Aboriginal life was the obligation to observe laws handed down by spirit ancestors who had created the landscape and all life during the so-called Dreamtime.

The traditional role of men was that of hunter, tool-maker and custodian of male law. The women gathered and prepared food, reared the children, and were responsible for women's law and ritual. The observation of a complex system of law and custodianship has ensured the continuation of fundamental traditions of Aboriginal culture.

Knowledge and skills developed over thousands of years enabled Aboriginal people to utilise their environment to the fullest. An intimate understanding of animal behaviour and plant ecology ensured that serious food shortages were rare. On the Murray River and associated wetlands, food sources were harvested using canoes made from the bark of river red gums; so-called 'canoe trees' – those showing the huge scars of bark removal – are still common in these areas.

The only major modification of the landscape was the seasonal and selective burning of undergrowth in the forests, dead grass on the plains and perennial tussock grasses of desert areas. This promoted the growth of fire-dependent food plants, while new shoots attracted game animals such as kangaroos. It also reduced the likelihood of large-scale fires and made the country easier to travel over.

Various hunting techniques were employed. For example, on the Coorong wetlands long crescent-shaped lines of rock were built from the shore to catch fish as the water level receded. On Eyre Peninsula, the men went spear fishing at night in shallow water using burning brands as torches. In the South-East bird snaring was carried out from wickerwork hides.

Aborigines also traded goods across Australia, using routes that followed the paths of Dreamtime ancestors. One trade route ran from Lake Alexandrina through the Flinders Ranges and south-west Queensland to the Gulf of Carpentaria. Many of the items traded had great spiritual significance. Others were practical commodities such as *pituri* (a drug) and certain types of stone and wood for making tools or weapons. The longer routes passed through 'exchange centres', where not only goods but songs and dances were traded.

The Europeans

History suggests that the first non-Aborigine to see SA's coast was the Dutch navigator Francois Thijssen aboard *Gulden Zeepaard*, in 1627. While on his way from Holland to Batavia (present-day Jakarta), he detoured to explore the coast as far east as Nuyts Archipelago, south of Ceduna.

The French ships *Recherche* and *L'Esperance*, under Rear-Admiral Bruni d'Entrecasteaux, arrived in 1792, and were likewise confined to the far west coast. D'Entrecasteaux described the region as so sterile and uniform 'that the most fertile imagination could find nothing to say about it'.

The first British explorer on the scene was Lieutenant James Grant, in 1800. He sailed along the far south-east coast and named several key features, including Mt Gambier and Mt Schank. This still left most of the SA coast unknown as far as Europeans were concerned.

Matthew Flinders The English were very keen to beat the French in charting the huge unknown chunks of Australian coastline. They chose young Royal Navy lieutenant Matthew Flinders to undertake the daunting task.

Flinders left England in mid-1801 in command of the *Investigator* and reached Fowlers Bay, 125km west of Ceduna, the following January. From there he sailed east, charting and naming Spencer Gulf, Gulf St Vincent and Kangaroo Island; he failed to recognise the mouth of the Murray River, which was masked by sandbars and surf. Generally, his surveying work proved so accurate that much of the data he collected is still in use today.

On 8 April 1802, Flinders unexpectedly met the French ship *Le Géographe* anchored in a bay – which he called Encounter Bay – just west of the Murray River mouth. The French, under Captain Nicholas Baudin, had sailed from the east, examining the coast as they went. Like Flinders, they had unknowingly passed the Murray's outlet, which remained a mystery until Charles Sturt revealed it 28 years later.

Flinders informed sealers of the abundant wildlife he'd seen on Kangaroo Island, and in 1803 the hunting of kangaroos, wallabies and seals for their skins commenced. He had ended speculation of a north-south channel through Australia. However, the prospect of an inland sea in the vast Outback fuelled debate and lured expeditions for decades to come.

Charles Sturt Determined to unravel the riddle of the westward flowing rivers, Captain Charles Sturt left Sydney for the inland late in 1829. At the Murrumbidgee River he assembled a whaleboat and took to the water, rowing downstream until he met a large waterway he called the Murray. Continuing for a further 26 days, he arrived on the shores of Lake Alexandrina. Here he landed to survey the area, rhapsodising over the country around him.

Referring to the area near the future site of Adelaide, Sturt wrote: '... the colonist might venture with every prospect of success, and in whose valleys the exile might hope to build for himself and for his family a peaceful and prosperous home.'

Such comments attracted the attention of the National Colonisation Society, a radical

Explorer Charles Sturt (1795-1869)

group of English colonial reformers. Their opinion was that previous British colonies had been poorly founded, mainly because of problems with convicts and land distribution. They proposed that a colony should be based on planned immigration with land sales, rather than with free grants of land.

The theorists believed that by controlling the sale of land – it would be surveyed before being sold – they could balance the flow of labour and capital, thus avoiding an unproductive and unseemly free-for-all. Money from land sales would be used to pay for public works and the passage of poor but energetic young migrants, who would be supported by the fund until they found employment. In this way, such a colony would be self-supporting, with no need for subsidy from the British government. From the reports of Flinders and Sturt, it seemed SA was an ideal place to put these theories into practice.

Colonisation

In 1834 the British Parliament passed the SA Colonisation Act, which had been in-spired by the ideas of the colonial reformers. It allowed the settlement of around 800,000 sq km, but convicts would not be admitted under any circumstance. This made SA the only Australian colony to be established entirely by free settlers.

However, the British government refused to take any responsibility for the new colony in terms of its financial backing or reformist charter. A board of commissioners was set up to control immigration and land sales, and to undertake the colony's planning. In its first six years SA had a hybrid government made up of representatives of the board and the British government.

The first official settlement was established in 1836 at Kingscote on Kangaroo Island. However, colonial surveyor-general Colonel William Light rejected Kingscote and several mainland sites for the capital, selecting Adelaide instead. The first governor, Captain John Hindmarsh, landed at present-day Glenelg (a suburb of Adelaide) on 28 December 1836, and proclaimed the Province of SA that day.

Despite its optimistic beginning, the colony was on the verge of collapse two years later. Immigrants were unemployed and farming had barely started owing to the lack of surveyed land.

The colony's second governor, Lieutenant George Gawler, arrived in 1838, and, being more energetic than his predecessor, instigated a vigorous program of land surveys. By 1841 about 1000 sq km had been

What's in a Name?

South Australians are often referred to as 'Crow-eaters' by people of other states. The reason has been lost in time, but it may have had something to do with the hardship SA experienced in its infancy. Perhaps neighbouring Victorians joked that the colonists were so poor that they were reduced to eating crows!

Denis O'Byrne

made available for settlement, while Adelaide had grown from a collection of huts into something approximating a town. However, the construction of numerous public buildings and other works had had a disastrous effect on colonial coffers.

Gawler was recalled in 1841 and replaced by George Grey, who immediately made himself unpopular by tightening the purse strings and reducing the salaries of public servants. Supported migration ceased, employment was hard to come by and SA plunged into its first recession.

But Grey's parsimonious ways had the desired effect and economic life was improving by 1843. Some wool was being exported and wheat farms were producing a surplus, although harvesting labour was in short supply. Immigration recommenced and the population rapidly increased; the 1844 census showed that SA had a European population of 17,366. Discoveries of rich copper lodes at Kapunda and Burra around this time were a tremendous boost to both confidence and the economy.

By the time Grey departed in 1845 the infant colony was at last on its feet. Because the land was largely owned by South Australians, the profits stayed in the colony and contributed to community wealth.

A decade later things were looking good and getting better. The colony was one of the world's major producers of copper, and pastoral leases had reached the northern Flinders Ranges. In 1850, SA produced 18,200 tonnes of wheat and 4700 tonnes of copper metal; 26,000 hectares were under cultivation and there were one million sheep and 100,000 cattle. A year later, the European population was 63,700, a quarter of whom lived in Adelaide.

Early Immigrants

The first immigrants to arrive in SA were mainly poor English, Scots and Irish with agricultural or trade experience. About 12,000 immigrated to SA in the first four years of settlement. There was a deliberate policy of selecting young married couples to encourage natural population increase

and foster interest in the colony's future. Throughout SA's history, most of its immigrants have come from the UK and Ireland.

Another important group were the 800 German farmers and artisans who arrived between 1838 and 1841. They were mainly Lutherans who disapproved of what was happening to their Church in Prussia, and who had come to SA to escape persecution. One of their first villages was Hahndorf, in the Adelaide Hills.

A second group of 5400 hard-working Germans had arrived by 1850, with many more arriving through the following decade. They settled mainly in the Adelaide Hills and the Barossa Valley, where the soil and climate were similar to the wine-growing areas of their homeland. Vineyards were established and the SA wine industry was born.

Thousands of Cornish people came to SA following the discovery of copper at Kapunda and Burra in the 1840s, and at Moonta and Kadina around 1860. They were skilled miners and builders, and developed a strong subculture in the areas they settled.

Second-Wave Explorers

SA's first 30 years saw a number of important exploring achievements. Between 1839 and 1841 Edward John Eyre made the first traverse of the Flinders Ranges; his enthusiastic reports of potential agricultural land in the Mid-North gave impetus to the settlement of that region. In 1840 he set out from Port Augusta to explore the west coast, suffering appalling hardship in the five months it took him to reach Albany in Western Australia (WA).

In 1839, Charles Bonney drove the first herd of cattle from Melbourne to Adelaide via Mt Gambier, establishing a safer alternative to the Murray River stock route from New South Wales (NSW) – where bloody clashes between drovers and Aborigines were common. It also opened up the lower South-East, which became one of the colony's finest agricultural areas.

Five years later, Charles Sturt set off to look for the inland sea. With the courage of his convictions he took along a whaleboat, but after 18 months of terrible privation he abandoned it in a waterless red sea of stones and sandhills. If nothing else he had discovered the Simpson Desert, one of Australia's most inhospitable regions.

Perhaps SA's greatest explorer, John MacDouall Stuart made several epic forays into the interior between 1858 and 1862. His most famous feat took place in 1862 when he succeeded in crossing the continent from south to north. Stuart's heroic efforts opened up a route for a telegraph line between Adelaide and Darwin, and led to SA taking control of the Northern Territory (NT) in 1863.

The Copper Rush

Copper has been mined in about 300 locations in SA, but only a handful of these have had any economic significance. The four most successful helped save SA from bankruptcy on more than one occasion.

Mines were developed on rich deposits at Kapunda (1844), Burra (1845), Moonta (1859) and Kadina (1861). Other ore bodies were worked in the Flinders Ranges (the Blinman mine was significant) but the lack of water, isolation and distance from the sea made them generally marginal propositions.

By the 1870s, SA had replaced Cornwall as the leading copper producer in the British empire – a major reason why so many Cornish miners immigrated to the colony. Although Kapunda and Burra both closed in the late 1870s, Moonta and Kadina were worked until 1923. The latter were big mines by world standards of the day, and they supported the largest towns in the colony outside Adelaide. The thousands of Cornish families who lived there gave the area the nickname 'Little Cornwall', which has stuck to this day.

Copper made many people in SA rich. It also left a legacy of fine public buildings in mining towns and in Adelaide. One beneficiary was the University of Adelaide, founded in 1874 with grants made from mine profits.

Wheat & Wool

In 1865, SA had half of all land under wheat in Australia. However, overcropping had al-

ready begun to exhaust the soils in the Adelaide Hills and Fleurieu Peninsula. When more land was opened in the 1870s, there was a mass exodus from these regions. It wasn't until 1897 that another Australian colony (Victoria) sowed more wheat than SA.

Wheat was perceived as a solid foundation for the colony's prosperity, and there was much public debate on the wisdom of allowing large estates to outbid and thus limit settlement by small farmers. The Strangways Act of 1869 eased this situation by allowing land to be purchased on credit terms; previously, the price of a block of land had to be paid in full at the time of purchase.

The Strangways Act ushered in a wheat boom which resulted in the creation of many towns, particularly in the Mid-North and southern Flinders Ranges. It also fostered the development of new railway and port facilities. By 1880 the Willochra Plains in the central Flinders Ranges were under the plough, and there was enthusiastic trumpeting of 'a rich golden harvest' extending all the way to the NT. Sanity returned with the onset of drought in the mid-1880s.

If wheat was SA's foundation, wool was its wealth, at least for a large number of colonists. Generally it was sheep farmers who opened up the country for settlement, particularly in areas distant from Adelaide.

As with wheat growers, the first pastoralists had little if any understanding of the natural environment. They had a tendency to overestimate carrying capacity, which led to gross overstocking. The fact that no pasture was kept in reserve brought ruin to many in the 1865 drought.

The wool industry, then as now, was based on merinos; starting in the 1840s, South Australian breeders have developed a strain that is better suited to semi-arid conditions, while retaining the fineness of fleece for which merinos are famous.

Goyder's Line As silly as it now seems, the early wheat farmers were convinced that 'rain follows the plough'; all they had to do was clear the native vegetation and till the soil, and rainfall would increase. Talk about wishful thinking! Still, a run of good seasons in the 1850s and early 1860s confirmed their belief as the farming frontier pushed northwards.

Unfortunately, reality was about to rear its ugly head in the form of the 1864-65 drought, which devastated pastoralists and wheat growers alike. Sent to report on the disaster, colonial surveyor-general George Goyder drew a line on the map which showed the northern limit of rainfall in 1865. As it happened, this 'line of rainfall' approximated the 250mm isohyet.

After further droughts, particularly in the 1880s, 'Goyder's Line' was generally accepted as the demarcation between cereal farming and pastoral regions. In recent times, however, new hardier varieties of wheat have allowed farms to push closer to the 200mm isohyet.

Self-Government to Federation

South Australia was initially governed by a body made up of representatives from the colony's Board of Commissioners and the British government. However, the financial problems of the early 1840s upset the British government, which had to pay off the debts. As a punitive measure, it abolished the board in 1842 and made SA an ordinary Crown colony.

In 1856 a new act created the SA Parliament (with executive ministers responsible to the elected representatives) and gave SA the most democratic constitution of any Australian colony.

Recession returned in the mid-1860s and once again copper helped stave off bankruptcy. Apart from this hiccup, prosperity continued right through the 1850s until the 1880s. This was reflected in the growth of the transport and communications system.

By 1860 a steam railway had opened to Kapunda; 30 years later SA had 2700km of railway connecting Adelaide to places such as Oodnadatta in the north, Melbourne to the east (the first train ran in 1887), and Cockburn to the north-east, near the NSW border on the Broken Hill route. There were also 3200km of sealed roads.

Steam navigation commenced on the Murray River in 1853, and there were at least 100 boats engaged in the river trade by 1878.

Following the exploration feats of John MacDouall Stuart, SA gained control of the NT (previously part of NSW) and, in 1870, commenced work on an overland telegraph line to Darwin. This ambitious undertaking, which was completed in a mere two years, linked SA to the world telegraph network.

The drought of the early 1880s heralded a general recession that lasted until 1900. Public debt mounted, and in desperation the government became the first in Australia to introduce a tax on income. When this proved inadequate, the government initiated agricultural development schemes which offered new farmers blocks of land and government loans. These schemes resulted in significant irrigation projects along the Murray, and the draining of vast seasonal swamps in the South-East. The use of superphosphate fertiliser also meant that crops could be grown on previously exhausted soils.

A number of reforms were passed by the SA Parliament during this period. They included the establishment of Australia's first Juvenile Court in 1890 and the granting of free education in 1891. In 1895, SA became the first Australian colony to recognise women's right to vote in parliamentary elections, and the first place in the world to allow women to stand for parliament.

Early 20th Century

South Australia experienced slow but steady growth following amalgamation of colonies into the Commonwealth of Australia in 1901.

Manufacturing became increasingly important, particularly in the field of heavy engineering. The Port Pirie smelter, built to treat the lead-zinc ore of Broken Hill, was enlarged during WWI. It was soon producing 10% of the world's lead, as well as silver and zinc.

The war was a time of division in SA, with patriotic fervour on the one hand and shameful persecution of German immigrants on the other. Before 1914 the state had several German (or German-sounding) place-names, but in a fit of anti-German zeal these were either anglicised or replaced. Many were reinstated during the centennial celebrations in 1936, when the German settlers' huge contribution to SA's development was officially recognised.

The early 1920s brought brief prosperity before a four-year drought led into the Great Depression, which hit with a crunch

The Devastation of Aborigines

South Australia's Aborigines suffered the first ill-effects of European settlement long before the colony's establishment in 1836. Starting with smallpox soon after the arrival of the First Fleet in 1788, epidemics originating in Sydney swept westwards like bushfires along the Murray. In 1830, Sturt noticed great gaps in the age of the Aborigines he met, remarking how obvious it was that death was among them. Sealers based on Kangaroo Island had also been raiding the Encounter Bay area for women as early as 1803.

British colonies had a poor record of relations with indigenous people, who invariably suffered greatly as a result of settlement. The British Colonial Secretary had made it clear to SA's Board of Commissioners that this new colony was to be different – as in all other things, it would provide a model for others to follow. It was hoped that, in comparison to neighbouring colonies, 'the colonisation of South Australia [would extend] mercy to the native tribes'.

The commissioners appointed a 'Protectors of Aborigines' to ensure the welfare of Aboriginal people. (One such early protector was explorer Edward John Eyre.) They recognised that the indigenous inhabitants had rights over the land, which would only be occupied with their permission. Various other high-minded ideals were espoused by the commissioners, but in practice these were generally ignored.

Often violently, Aborigines objected to the takeover of their land. There were frequent bloody clashes in several areas, most notably around the Murray River and Eyre Peninsula. Although they landed some heavy blows, in the end their boomerangs and spears could not compete with bullets and poisoned flour. There are several recorded massacres of Aborigines. One infamous event occurred on the Birdsville Track, when a large group of men, women and children were shot in retaliation for the spearing of a bullock.

In the early 1840s, Governor Gawler opened ration distribution depots in an attempt to pacify Aboriginal people. He hoped that handouts of food would compensate for the loss of land and resources. Generally, the depots were at remote police stations, set up to protect settlers and overlanders from Aboriginal attack.

By the early 1860s the emphasis of most ration depots shifted from appeasement to providing succour for a people devastated by disease and deprivation. The Aboriginal population in settled areas declined dramatically, although in more remote parts it was probably still largely unaffected. Just 40 years after settlement it was estimated that the colony's Aboriginal population had fallen by 50%. By this time entire groups had been decimated, particularly in the areas closest to Adelaide.

While the north and north-east were eventually taken up by pastoralists, with the usual appalling consequences for Aboriginal people, the west and north-west were never permanently settled by Europeans. However, this did not necessarily mean escape from the 'benefits' of white civilisation. As recently as the 1950s, many SA Aborigines were forcibly relocated due to the atomic bomb tests at Maralinga, which caused great disruption and misery to many.

Denis O'Byrne

in 1929 and didn't really end until WWII. All the states suffered during this period, but SA suffered worst of all: in 1931 over 70,000 people out of a population of 575,000 were dependent on welfare. South Australians fled across the border in droves. Despite this, 24% of wage-earners were still out of work in 1933.

Australia's longest serving state premier, Tom Playford, took office in 1938 and presided over 26 years of state development. During WWII the first water pipeline was built from Morgan to Whyalla, ship building commenced at Whyalla, and the Leigh Creek coalfields were opened up for electricity production. In 1948 – the year that the 40-hour working week became a reality – work started on the Woomera rocket range north-west of Port Augusta.

Late 20th Century

Industrial development quickened during WWII and the momentum continued into the 1950s. Encouraged by a booming market and protective tariffs on imported goods, the number of factories increased dramatically. The state was now changing from a rural economy to a predominantly industrial one.

Under the shrewd guidance of Tom Playford, SA captured a relatively large share of the national growth in industry and overseas migration. There were so many new arrivals that in 1955 Adelaide gained the satellite city of Elizabeth, which mainly housed migrants from the UK.

Following WWII, a government scheme involving 'soldier settlers' – returned servicemen – was aimed at developing the infertile soils of higher rainfall areas. Previously these areas had been considered unsuitable for farming, but it was found that they could be turned into productive pasture with the addition of trace elements such as zinc and potassium. In this way a further 500,000 hectares were added to the state's agricultural land.

In 1965 the Playford government lost office to the Labor Party, ushering in an era of rapid change. One of the new government's first reforms was an act prohibiting racial discrimination, the first in Australia.

By this time the state's economy and population growth were stagnating, revealing the shortcomings of an economic base dependent on the manufacture of motor vehicles and household appliances.

Fuelled by overseas competition, the deepening industrial recession saw the last ship built at Whyalla roll down the slipway in 1978. Around this time, plans for a second satellite city, Monarto, were shelved.

Although the 1970s were a difficult time for SA, the Labor Government under controversial premier Don Dunstan could claim several important achievements, particularly in the arts. These included the creation of the SA Film Corporation (1972) and the State Opera of SA (1976), and the opening of the Adelaide Festival Theatre (1973).

Dunstan also presided over several major reforms, such as the Sexual Discrimination Act of 1975. Other reforms improved legislation dealing with women's issues, capital punishment (it was banned) and Aboriginal land rights.

Hope for an economic recovery came with the discovery of a huge deposit of uranium, copper, silver and gold at Roxby Downs in 1976, coupled with continued discoveries of oil and gas in the Cooper Basin throughout the 1970s. Employment growth through industrial development was a key goal of the Liberal government, which took over from Labor at the 1979 election.

The mining industry generally prospered through the 1980s and 1990s. However, older industries such as the manufacture of motor vehicles and household appliances, and steelmaking at Whyalla, fared poorly. By 1989 the rural sector too was in crisis, through a combination of drought, soaring interest rates and tumbling commodity prices.

Australia slipped into a general recession following a development and investment boom in the late 1980s. (As in the Great Depression of the 1930s, the effects were felt most in SA.) The state's economy has remained sluggish ever since, with high unemployment (particularly among youth) and low business confidence seemingly entrenched.

Aboriginal Land Rights

In 1966 the South Australian government made the first move of any state this century to give Aboriginal people title to their land. This involved the creation of the Aboriginal Lands Trust, in which was vested title to the missions and reserves still operating in SA. These lands are leased back to their Aboriginal occupants, who have repeated rights of renewal.

The Pitjantjatjara Land Rights Act came into effect in 1981, giving freehold title over a vast area in the far north-west to the Anungu Pitjantjatjaraku (Pitjantjatjara people). A further 76,000 sq km, which had been taken over by the federal government as part of the Maralinga project, was returned to its traditional owners in 1984.

Land held under Aboriginal freehold title cannot be sold or resumed. Entry by 'outsiders' is restricted – they need a permit from the appropriate council – and no development of any kind can take place without the permission of the traditional owners.

GEOGRAPHY

South Australia covers 984,400 sq km, or 12.8% of Australia. The fourth largest state or territory, it extends 1100km from WA to the Victoria, NSW and Queensland borders, and ranges between 630km and 1340km from the Southern Ocean to the NT.

The state's coastline stretches for 3700km and includes two major indentations: Gulf St Vincent and Spencer Gulf. It has around 100 islands, the largest by far being Kangaroo Island.

The topography of SA mainly consists of vast plains and low relief. More than 80% of the state is less than 300m above sea level and few points rise above 700m. The only hills of any significance are the Mt Lofty and Flinders ranges, which form a continuous spine stretching 800km northwards from the coast into the interior. The Musgrave Ranges in the far north-west include Mt Woodroffe (1435m), the state's highest point.

About 80% of SA is classed arid. Known as the Outback, this inland region is mainly covered by stunted saltbush and acacia or mallee scrub. There are extensive sandy and stony semi-deserts in the east and west; the Tirari, near Lake Eyre, is the closest thing to real desert in Australia. Huge, mainly dry salt pans, such as Lake Eyre and Lake Torrens, are a feature of the Outback's eastern half. Mining and low-intensity sheep and cattle grazing are the main economic activities.

The more temperate south is one of Australia's primary agricultural regions. However, the rainfall over most districts is low and generally unreliable, and if it wasn't for the liberal use of fertilisers the average farmer would be as poor as the soils. Faced with such meagre resources, SA's farmers have become as efficient as any in the world, although soil degradation is a major concern.

South Australia's main watercourse is the Murray River, which rises in the Australian Alps and ends near the sea at Lake Alexandrina, the state's largest permanent freshwater lake. Also important are the mainly dry Warburton River and Cooper Creek, which drain the mighty Lake Eyre Basin from Queensland. The Mt Lofty and Flinders ranges have many seasonal streams.

Extensive limestone formations underlie the Nullarbor Plain, the Eyre and Yorke peninsulas, the Murray Mallee and parts of the South-East. These are a major cause of soil infertility and the lack of watercourses in those areas. However, the use of superphosphate and trace elements has enabled all but the arid Nullarbor Plain to be developed for cereal crops.

Water Supply

South Australia's low rainfall and lack of permanent streams have created a huge challenge in developing the state. Many towns in the South-East and on the Eyre Peninsula rely on underground basins for survival. In some areas, these resources are being exploited beyond the recharge rate.

For the rest of the state, the solution to unreliable rainfall has been to supply communities, including Adelaide, with water piped over long distances. In fact, about 90% of the entire population is now either wholly or partly dependent on water from the Murray River.

GEOLOGY

Largely levelled by erosion and sedimentation, SA is made up of several ancient, stable blocks (or cratons) of igneous and metamorphic rocks separated by younger sedimentary basins. Rocks in the western part of the Gawler Craton, which comprises Eyre Peninsula and the Gawler Ranges, have been dated at 2700 million years old. These are the state's oldest, and probably formed part of the earth's first continental crust.

During the Cambrian period (545 to 500 million years ago), marine sediments accumulated in the basins that formed as the cratons separated. One such basin was a long trough known as the Adelaide Geosyncline. Its sediments, 24km thick, later folded and buckled during a period of strong earth movement. So were formed the Mt Lofty and Flinders ranges, now reduced by erosion to mere stumps.

Warm moist periods between 300 and 70 million years ago produced extensive forests in the state's north-east. Becoming deeply buried under more sediments, the trees turned into the thick coal seams which are now the source of oil and gas around Moomba. The marine sediments laid down during this period are a source of precious opal at Coober Pedy.

More recently, the sea invaded the Murray region, leaving the rich fossil deposits now exposed in cliffs along the Murray River. Lakebed deposits contain fossil remains of diprotodonts and other megafauna such as giant kangaroos – the precursors of today's marsupials.

Over the past two million years the sea level has risen and fallen many times, leaving parallel lines of coastal sand dunes now stranded well inland in the South-East. There have also been great fluctuations in climate, with periods of aridity much more extreme than today. The long parallel dunes of the Simpson and Great Victoria deserts were formed about 10,000 years ago in a time of peak aridity.

CLIMATE

South Australia has a Mediterranean climate of hot, dry summers and cool winters, with most rain falling between May and August – June is usually the wettest month. Although the winters are classed as 'mild', snow does fall from time to time along the higher points of the Mt Lofty and Flinders ranges.

Heat is the major climatic extreme, with daily maximums of around 35°C common in the Outback from late spring to early autumn (October to April). The highest temperature recorded so far is 50.7°C at Oodnadatta in January 1960; the lowest -8.2°C at Yongala, near Peterborough, in July 1976.

Over 80% of the state normally receives less than 250mm of rain annually, while nearly half has an annual evaporation rate exceeding 3000mm. This combination makes SA by far the driest Australian state. The only areas to exceed 750mm of rainfall are parts of Kangaroo Island, the Mt Lofty Ranges and the state's south-eastern corner. The wettest area is around Mt Lofty, just east of Adelaide, which receives an annual average of 1200mm.

Generally, the further north you go, the hotter and drier it gets. Australia's most arid region is in the north-east around Lake Eyre, where the average – and extremely erratic – annual rainfall is less than 150mm. This may not seem so bad until you compare it with the region's annual evaporation rate: a whopping 3500mm. Not surprisingly, light showers over the Outback often evaporate before they hit the ground.

ECOLOGY & ENVIRONMENT

When the first Europeans arrived in SA they found a people living more-or-less in harmony with their environment, using skills and knowledge developed over at least 45,000 years. In contrast, these new settlers had no understanding of the ecology of their

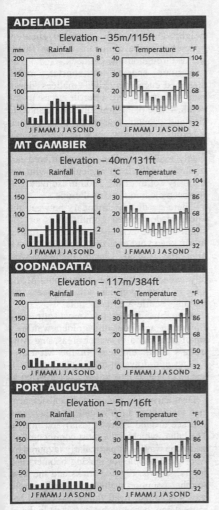

ADELAIDE
Elevation – 35m/115ft

MT GAMBIER
Elevation – 40m/131ft

OODNADATTA
Elevation – 117m/384ft

PORT AUGUSTA
Elevation – 5m/16ft

rainfall. Apart from the destruction of plantlife, huge quantities of topsoil were lost while the lessons of dryland farming were learned.

Public concern over this tremendous loss of biological diversity resulted in the declaration of the Native Vegetation Act 1983, which places strict controls on further clearances. Nevertheless, there is still constant pressure for the bush to be chopped down to allow for new developments such as vineyards.

Next came the changes wrought by the new grazing animals that settlers brought with them. While initial overstocking caused serious degradation of native pasture, the introduction of the European rabbit, which bred in countless millions after being released into the wild, resulted in massive and perhaps irreversible changes to the arid zone's original vegetation cover. It is hoped that the combined effects of the introduced myxomatosis and calici viruses will bring long-term control of these pests.

Australia has thousands of native plant and animal species which have evolved to survive in its unique physical environments, and SA has its fair share of both. However, the effects of habitat loss, predation and competition from introduced animals – particularly European foxes, domestic cats, goats, sheep and rabbits – has brought a shameful record of extinction. Since 1836 about 30% of SA's original land mammals have become extinct in the state, while others are now found only on off-shore islands. Although there have been successful reintroductions in small protected areas, large-scale recovery of threatened species is unlikely without the removal of foxes and feral cats.

Another key environmental concern is water supply – not surprising in such a dry state. The Murray is by far the most important source of water in SA, where most of the population relies on it to a greater or lesser extent. However, the river has been abused to the point where it is now dying and urgent action is needed to arrest the decline. Unfortunately, the management of the Murray-Darling system is in the hands of

adopted home, and probably had no inkling of the devastation their traditional farming practices and animals would cause.

First came the wholesale clearing of the bush to make way for wheat and grazing. These last 165 years have seen most of the native vegetation removed from land that receives 250mm or more of average annual

three state governments (NSW, Victoria and SA), as well as the federal government. Their past record of cooperation on matters affecting this vital waterway has been anything but brilliant.

While these are significant issues for SA, the state is a lot better off than many other industrialised parts of the world. Pollution of all kinds is relatively low, land-care programs are on the increase, and environmental awareness has risen dramatically. And because the state is so large and generally sparsely populated, vast areas are still in good condition.

See the Useful Organisations section in the Facts for the Visitor chapter for details of environmental groups.

FLORA

Over the ages SA's native vegetation has undergone massive change. Millions of years ago the state was covered by temperate rainforest. However, increasing aridity and bushfires brought about the present dominance of fire and drought-tolerant plants such as acacias, eucalypts and saltbush.

The arrival of Aboriginal people with their firestick technology helped to create the grasslands and open woodlands that so delighted the early explorers. Aboriginal practices would have benefited fire-tolerant species at the expense of others. However, Aboriginal effect on the environment was generally minor compared with the devastating impact of European-style land use.

Despite the changes wrought since white settlement, the native flora is still a magnificent feature of the landscape. Most obvious are the larger eucalypts – called 'gum trees' or just plain 'gums', after the resin that drips from wounds in their trunks – found in wetter areas. The state has about 60 species of eucalypt.

South Australia's most spectacular trees are the river red gums that grow along watercourses throughout the state. Also outstanding are the blue gums and candlebarks of the Mt Lofty Ranges and Lower South-East, and the sugar gums of Kangaroo Island and the southern Flinders Ranges. At their best, these species can exceed 30m in height. The coolibah – another eucalypt species – is the dominant tree on floodplains throughout the Outback.

Various species of shorter, multi-stemmed eucalypts called 'mallees' dominate the drier, more infertile areas in the south. These plants are superbly adapted to fire and drought; numerous buds in their tuberous roots allow quick recovery should disaster befall the surface growth. Unfortunately, mallee woodlands have suffered particularly badly from agriculture, with the majority south of the 200mm isohyet having been cleared for cereal crops.

There's a distinct boundary between the eucalypt-dominated communities of the south and the acacia communities further north; keep your eyes open and you'll see it along the Eyre and Lincoln highways west and south of Port Augusta. Acacias are usually called 'wattles' because plants of the species were popular with pioneers for making 'wattle-and-daub' huts.

Arguably, the state's most attractive flowering acacia is the golden wattle, a small tree found in wetter areas, and Australia's floral emblem. In the Mt Lofty Ranges and down in the South-East you'll see blackwood. This tall wattle (growing to 30m) is a prized furniture hardwood.

Distinctive and widespread Outback acacias include myall (the dark, gnarled trees you see around Port Augusta) and mulga. The latter, which is the most common of all arid-zone wattles, is particularly favoured by Aboriginal people for making boomerangs, spears, shields, digging sticks and the like. Another common wattle with hard, narrow leaves is called 'dead finish', so called because when these tough plants start to die in a drought you know the country's finished!

Shrubby saltbush forms major plant communities in the Outback, often in occurring with acacia. Although saltbush looks unpromising, it makes nutritious food for grazing animals such as kangaroos, sheep and cattle.

SA's mangrove forests, particularly along the shores of Gulf St Vincent and Spencer

Gulf, are also of interest. These are breeding areas for many waterbird species and marine creatures, including the King George whiting, SA's most popular table fish.

Last but by no means least are wildflowers, which range from delicate orchids to hardy paper daisies. The state's floral emblem is Sturt's desert pea, an annual ground creeper with large, vivid crimson blooms. In winter and early spring you often see great mats of these plants in the north.

Another famous wildflower is an introduced weed known as either Salvation Jane or Patterson's curse, depending on your point of view – apiarists love them, but they can be poisonous to stock. Their massed, rich-purple flowers are a stunning feature of the Mid-North and Flinders Ranges in early spring. Wild hops, another weed of the

Flinders, puts on a good springtime show with red, papery flowers.

Also magnificent are the heaths of coastal SA and the mallee belt. In winter and spring these normally drab areas are transformed by flowers of every hue. The same applies in the Outback after good autumn and winter rains. Here the sandy plains explode with colour as daisies and other annuals hurry to set seed before the soil dries out again.

The Australian Arid Lands Botanic Garden in Port Augusta is a good place to learn about arid-zone flora. The Adelaide Botanic Garden boasts a large collection of temperate-zone flora, including a mallee section, while the Wittunga Botanic Garden at Blackwood (a southern suburb of Adelaide) is also good for natives.

The Lungs of the Sea

Mangrove forests cluster around many sheltered bays and inlets along the South Australian coast between Port Adelaide and Ceduna. There is only one species, the grey mangrove, *Avicennia marina*, which is found in all mainland states and grows to 10m tall.

Mangroves grow only in the intertidal zone, where survival means coping with a harsh, constantly changing environment. The forest floor can be under 3m of water at high tide, then lie completely exposed as the water drains away.

The mud on the forest floor is so fine that oxygen cannot penetrate more than a millimetre or two below the surface. In response, mangroves have developed delicate aerial roots to enable them to breath – you'll see them sticking up like spikes from the mud. The roots also take in salt water. They filter out most of the salt, and any that remains is excreted from tiny glands on the underside of the leaves.

Sediments and vegetable material (such as leaves) fall off as the water slows down through the trees, creating rich organic deposits which are broken down by bacteria, crustaceans and other invertebrates. In turn, the waste products generated by these organisms are a major food source for plankton and small fish. Mangroves also attract insects, which are eaten by fish and birds. Apart from providing a nursery environment for many fish, such as the venerated King George whiting, mangroves are breeding sites for waterbirds.

Despite the fact that mangroves are unique and fill an important role in the natural environment, they have generally been used as sites for either rubbish dumps or for marinas and housing. A visit to the St Kilda Mangrove Trail (see the Mid-North chapter) or a guided canoe trip on the inlets around Port Adelaide (see the Outdoor Activities chapter) will convince you that mangroves are a lot more than just smelly, mosquito-infested places. An ecology that's often called 'the lungs of the sea' deserves to be treated with respect.

Denis O'Byrne

FAUNA

South Australia has a rich diversity of wildlife. All up, there are about 70 species of native land mammals (including 16 bats and two monotremes), 27 marine mammals, around 380 birds, 210 reptiles and 12 frogs. See the boxed text 'Marine Mammals of South Australia' in the Outdoor Activities chapter.

However, SA does not have a proud record in terms of wildlife management. Thanks largely to the impact of habitat degradation and introduced animals, at least 30 species of land mammals (including one bat) have become extinct since European settlement and a number of others are rare or endangered. Some species that were once found over vast areas of the state now survive only on islands. Almost all the marine mammals suffered greatly from overhunting during the 19th century, and many are still vulnerable. One bird – the dwarf emu of Kangaroo Island – has become extinct while several others are under threat.

Land Mammals

The state's native land mammals range in size from the red kangaroo, which stands up to 2m tall, to the silky mouse, which is about the same size as the common house mouse. They include koalas, platypuses, kangaroos, potoroos, bandicoots, water rats, marsupial moles, gliding possums, pygmy possums and various rats and mice.

South Australia has four species of kangaroo: the red kangaroo, western and eastern grey kangaroos, and the euro. The eastern grey is restricted to the eastern margin of the state, but the others are widely distributed and often common. Euros are generally found in dry, hilly country.

Kangaroos have actually benefited from European settlement due to improved pastures and watering points, and the reduction in hunting by Aboriginal people and dingoes. Good seasons lead to population explosions, which (to the outrage of many animal lovers) are reduced by culling under a quota system.

Rock-wallabies – smallish, agile relatives of the kangaroo – live in colonies in the rocky ranges. SA has two species, including the endangered yellow-footed rock-wallaby of the Flinders and Gawler ranges. See the boxed text 'Meet Petrogale Xanthopus' in the Flinders Ranges chapter.

When camping in sandy areas of the Outback, you'll often see tracks like those of tiny kangaroos around your swag in the morning. Most likely they will have been left by the spinifex hopping-mouse, which spends the daylight hours in deep burrows under vegetation. Similar tracks are left by Mitchell's hopping-mouse in southern mallee areas. Both species are common.

South Australia doesn't have many koalas, but you may see them in the Adelaide Hills, along the Murray River and on Kangaroo Island. They feed only on the leaves of certain species of eucalypt and are vulnerable to fox predation; they're also prone to eating themselves out of house and home if their numbers aren't controlled. Like most native mammals they're active mainly at night – koalas typically spend the daylight hours dozing way up in trees.

Wombats are much more common than koalas, to which they're related, but you're only likely to see them at night as they cross the roads. These slow, heavy marsupials (up to 30kg) are quite common along the Eyre Highway (Hwy 1) west of Ceduna.

Australia's two primitive monotremes (egg-laying mammals) are both found in SA. While the amazing duck-billed platypus is

The short-beaked echidna or spiny anteater

restricted to Kangaroo Island, where it was introduced, the short-beaked echidna (or spiny anteater) is found throughout the state. Feeding on ants and termites, the echidna is active on cool days in the temperate south.

Birds

Around 380 species of birds have been recorded in SA, including 35 migrants, eight introduced species, and a number of occasional visitors such as the albatross. They range in size from the tiny weebill (80mm long) to the flightless emu, which can look the average adult human in the eye.

The most numerous group is that of the wader with around 70 species, of which almost half are annual migrants from breeding grounds in the northern hemisphere. They range from tiny dotterels to cranes; many, particularly the migrants, are confined to the coast while others are found wherever there's surface water. Largest of the waders is the brolga, a crane with a wingspan up to 2m. You're most likely to see this bird stalking through the lignum on dried-up Outback floodplains.

There are 11 native ducks, including the endangered freckled duck, and a number of other waterbirds widespread through the state, such as terns and cormorants. Swans and pelicans are found in habitats ranging from Outback waterholes to coastal shallows.

The largest and most common bird family comprises the honeyeaters, with 30 species. You'll find them wherever there are insect-attracting flowering plants. Despite their common name they also eat insects, fruits and berries. Honeyeaters occupy every vegetation zone, with the singing and spiny-cheeked honeyeaters and the yellow-cheeked miner occurring throughout the state. Rarest of all is the endangered black-eared miner, which is restricted to mallee scrub on the Victorian border.

Many of SA's 25 species of parrots and nine species of cockatoos are very attractive. Several of these birds, including the glossy black cockatoo and orange-bellied parrot, have suffered dramatically from loss of habitat and are now endangered. You'll be famous if you can get a clear photograph of the night parrot. This secretive, nocturnal species lives in the spinifex grasslands of inland Australia and has been sighted only a few times this century.

Other species, such as the galah and little corella, have benefited from European farming practices. Great flocks of these two species of cockatoo are common in parts of the northern wheat belt.

Great flocks of bright yellow-and-green budgerigars are a magnificent feature of the Outback in good seasons. Also colourful are the fairy wrens (five species), chats (three species), robins (seven species) and finches (five species), each with representatives in most habitat types.

South Australia has 21 species of raptors (birds of prey), including peregrine falcons and six species of owls and nightjars. The largest is the wedge-tailed eagle, with a wingspan up to 3m. While you'll see falcons, kites, hawks and eagles in, or above, all habitats, the only owl you're likely to come in contact with is the boobook owl. Found in a wide range of habitats, its mournful 'boo-book' call is a common nightly sound throughout rural SA.

For more on birds, see Birdwatching in the Outdoor Activities chapter.

Reptiles

Of Australia's 750 known species of reptiles, 210 are found in SA. Surprisingly, the richest habitats in terms of species are the arid spinifex grasslands, particularly the Simpson and Great Victoria deserts.

Included in this number are four species of side-necked tortoises and three marine turtles. The side-necked tortoises are not true tortoises, which are land-dwelling – they are really freshwater turtles that are called tortoises to separate them from their saltwater cousins. Marine turtles that have strayed from northern breeding grounds are often sighted off the western and southern coasts of Eyre Peninsula.

Snakes All of SA's 42 species of snakes are protected, including the fierce snake (or inland taipan) of the far north-east. This large, aggressive species is the world's most venomous snake. Fortunately, it's quite rare.

There are several other dangerous snakes to stay away from, including the common death adder, the desert death adder, the common tiger snake and the black tiger snake. You'll know the death adder by its broad triangular head, short thick body and thin tail. The tiger snake grows to 1.5m and has broad crossbands, although these are not so obvious in the black variety, which is found on many islands.

Although a number of SA's snakes are dangerous to humans, many more are harmless. They include eight species of blind snake – they're mainly active at night, so are rarely seen – and four species of python, also mainly nocturnal. The largest of these generally slow-moving snakes is the carpet (or diamond) python, which grows to 3.5m.

Lizards The 161 species of lizards in SA include the pygmy blue-tongue, which was thought to be extinct until its recent rediscovery.

A couple of the strangest lizards are found in the arid north. These are the Lake Eyre dragon, which lives on the lake's dry salt crust, and the thorny devil, with its deceptively ferocious appearance. Both survive entirely on a diet of small black ants.

Largest of all is the perentie, which grows to over 2m. The perentie belongs to the goanna family, of which there are seven species in SA, and is easily identified by the regular pattern of large yellow spots on its back. Unlike other lizards, goannas have forked tongues.

Skinks and geckos make up the bulk of the lizard population, but as they're mainly very small and secretive, and often only active at night, you're unlikely to see them. Always check fallen branches for geckos – which may be hiding under bark or in hollows – before you throw them on the campfire. Shingle backs and blue tongues are the largest of the skinks; they're slow and sleepy, and will try to frighten you with gaping mouths if you get too close.

The most commonly seen lizards belong to the dragon family, of which SA has 63 species. They tend to hibernate in the coldest months, but as the weather starts to warm up you'll find them sunning themselves on the road or perched on rocks or posts. Generally they'll speed off when disturbed, although the larger ones might stand their ground – which results in many being squashed by speeding cars.

Amphibians

Australia's only amphibians are frogs. With 12 species, SA isn't particularly rich in frogs compared with other states, which isn't so surprising considering its dry climate. One of the best adapted is a unique water-holding frog. This species grows to 8cm in length and can live underground for years during drought, surviving on its last big drink until the next rains.

Introduced Feral Species

The dingo, or native dog, which arrived in northern Australia about 5000 years ago, has been linked with the extinction of a number of species on the mainland. More recently introduced species, such as rabbits, foxes and starlings, have become environmental as well as economic disasters. Fortunately, the introduction of the calici virus seems to be controlling rabbit populations in drier areas.

A number of the state's feral animal populations originated from livestock or pets that 'went bush'. Goats are a real problem in the Flinders Ranges, where thousands are shot or trapped each year. The camels that roam the far north are now being trapped and (ironically) sold back to Saudi Arabia. The major environmental problems that stem from these animals are soil degradation and changes in plant cover.

NATIONAL PARKS

South Australia has an impressive 314 conservation areas including national parks, conservation parks, recreation parks, game reserves, wilderness protection areas and regional reserves. In fact, about 210,000 sq km (21.3% of the state's land area) is under

The Dog Fence

Erected as a barrier against sheep-killing dingoes, the Dog Fence stretches for thousands of kilometres across south-eastern Australia, from the Nullarbor cliffs on the Great Australian Bight to Jimbour, in south-east Queensland. Originally a whopping 8614km long, it was shortened to around 5500km in 1980.

Made of wire-netting and reaching 1.8m high, the fence meanders for 2250km across SA – you pass through it on the Eyre Highway near Yalata, the Stuart Highway north of Coober Pedy and on the Oodnadatta and Birdsville tracks.

Maintenance is an ongoing headache. The job is shared by individual landholders and the state government, which spends $500,000 on upkeep each year. Parts of the fence are over 100 years old and in need of replacement, while even the newest sections are under constant assault from emus, kangaroos, livestock, floods and shifting sand.

Funding shortages have meant that the Dog Fence has been left to deteriorate in some areas, and dingo attacks on sheep inside the fence are on the increase. In 1995 a dingo was shot on a station near Port Augusta – about 300km inside the fence – but not before it had killed 100 sheep!

Denis O'Byrne

some form of official conservation management. All public land conservation areas in SA are under the control of the Department of Environment, Heritage & Aboriginal Affairs, with day-to-day management carried out by their National Parks & Wildlife Service (NPWS) SA division.

There is also the 20,000 sq km Great Australian Bight Marine Park, which includes a major breeding area of the southern right whale. This is more a multi-use area than a national park, however, as commercial activities such as fishing are allowed within its boundaries.

By far the largest category of land parks in terms of size are the seven regional reserves, which make up half the total area. These vast tracts of land provide a measure of protection for important habitats and natural features, while allowing other land uses such as mining and pastoralism to take place. They're restricted to the remote arid regions of the state.

There are 17 national parks covering a total of 42,263 sq km and ranging in size from 8.4 sq km (Belair National Park) to 13,492 sq km (Lake Eyre National Park). All the large national parks are in semi-desert areas, with the vast Lake Torrens and Lake Gairdner parks consisting of the beds of mainly dry saltpans. Similarly, about two-thirds of Lake Eyre National Park is saltpan. Inevitably, and mainly because there's not much left of it, the natural environment of major agricultural areas is poorly represented in national parks.

Many of the state's scenic and ecological highlights are protected in national parks. On Kangaroo Island, Flinders Chase National Park is best known for its coastal scenery and wildlife, including rare species of birds and mammals. The Flinders Ranges, Mt Remarkable and Gammon Ranges national parks in the Flinders Ranges have stunning scenery, great bushwalks and colonies of yellow-footed rock-wallabies. Canunda, Coffin

Bay, Innes and Lincoln are popular coastal parks; Nullarbor National Park, on the far-west coast, has massive cave systems; and Witjira in the far north has the fascinating Dalhousie Springs, a unique wetland habitat on the edge of the Simpson Desert.

The state's 10 game reserves cover 250 sq km and give some protection to native game species such as duck and quail. However, the safety factor disappears during annual open seasons, when licensed shooters are allowed in to hunt them.

Allan Fox's *Centenary Field Guide of Major Parks & Reserves of SA* gives descriptions and limited coverage of highlights and activities at 49 parks.

See under Useful Organisations in the Facts for the Visitor chapter for details of information outlets.

GOVERNMENT & POLITICS

South Australia is one of the six states and two territories that make up the Commonwealth of Australia.

The British monarch, who is also Australia's head of state, is represented in SA by a governor, who has a responsibility to maintain lawful government in the state. However, while governors retain important powers, they seldom become involved in political debate.

Australia's federal government, which is based on the British system, has a lower house (the House of Representatives) and an upper house of review (the Senate). South Australia contributes 12 senators and 12 members of parliament. By far the major players in both houses are the Liberal and Labor parties (this is also the case in state politics). Following the most recent federal election (1998) most of the SA members of both houses are from the Liberal Party. Voting is compulsory above 18 years of age in both federal and state elections.

The South Australian State Government consists of a House of Assembly (47 members) and a Legislative Council (22 members), with the leader of the majority party called Premier. It is Labor Party policy to abolish the Legislative Council.

Each parliament has a life of four years; the Liberal party won a narrow majority in the 1997 election, which was made more interesting than usual by the election of a 'No Pokies' Independent member – many South Australians are angered by the social problems caused by the proliferation of poker machines (pokies) in the state's pubs and clubs.

ECONOMY

South Australia's economy was based on copper, cereal crops and wool from the earliest days of settlement until after WWI. The latter two industries are still mainstays, but agriculture has now generally taken a back seat to manufacturing in terms of employment and income. Tourism is another major earner, with gross income exceeding that of mining.

In 1997-98 South Australian exports were worth $4,986 million, around 5% of the national figure; imports from overseas during the same period totalled $3,943 million. The major commodity groups exported were cereals and cereal preparations and metals and metal manufactures. Machinery and motor vehicle parts and accessories were by far the major imports.

Japan was SA's largest export market in 1995-96, accounting for 15% of all exports; all up, the countries of east Asia purchased 46%. Other key export markets were the European Union, the Middle East and New Zealand.

SA has still to recover from the national recession of the late 1980s and early 1990s. At the time of writing it had the highest unemployment rate of all the mainland states and territories (over 10% compared to 8% nationally), and youth unemployment was at a whopping 35% (25% nationally). Wool and grain prices remain depressed, but there are economic bright spots with the wine industry (everyone is drowning their sorrows), aquaculture and mining.

Tourism

Tourism is worth around $1900 million annually: in 1994-95 there were an estimated 858,000 visitors from interstate (52% from

Victoria) and 260,000 from overseas. Most international visitors came from the UK and Ireland (20%), USA and Asia (13% from each) and Germany (12.5%). The most popular destination by far with both domestic and overseas visitors was Adelaide; the South-East was second with interstaters, while the Barossa was runner-up with international visitors.

POPULATION & PEOPLE

The 1996 census revealed that SA's population was 1,427,936; in 1997 it was estimated to have grown to 1,479,800. One in five South Australians is aged under 15 years, and one in three is under 25 years.

Most South Australians (76%) were born in Australia. Of the remainder, 10.4% were born in the UK and Ireland, 2% in Italy, 1% in Greece and 1% in Germany. Nearly 2.5% of the population was Asian-born, with Vietnamese being the largest group (0.6%).

The 1996 census put the Aboriginal population at around 20,000, which is probably a little higher than it was at the time of European settlement. Most of the state's Aborigines (41%) live in Adelaide.

Population Distribution

Among Australian states and territories, SA has the highest concentration of its population living in the capital city. Only 17% of the state's population lives outside Adelaide.

The largest town outside Adelaide is Whyalla with 23,400 people, followed by Mt Gambier with 22,000. These are the only country centres with populations exceeding 15,000. Many smaller country towns are declining due to 'rationalisation' of services and a population shift, particularly of younger people to Adelaide and larger regional centres.

Only around 1% of all South Australians live in the dry Outback, which makes up around 80% of the state's land area. This amounts to a density of 0.02 persons per sq km. However, the spread is by no means even, as over 50% of the region's population lives in its four main towns: Coober Pedy, Leigh Creek, Roxby Downs and Woomera.

EDUCATION

Education is available to all South Australians, and school attendance is free and compulsory for those between the ages of six and 15 years. Primary and secondary education is available within state and private systems.

There are three SA universities, all in Adelaide: Flinders University, the University of South Australia, and the University of Adelaide, which was the first Australian university to admit women to degree courses. Each year around 50,000 students attend university in SA; 6.5% of the total population claims to hold a bachelor degree or higher.

ARTS

For a time SA called itself 'The Festival State', but 'State of the Arts' might have been more appropriate. The visual arts scene in SA includes a marvellous state gallery, while the performing arts boast an opera company, several good theatre companies, a dance company and a symphony orchestra.

Numerous museums throughout the state preserve examples of Aboriginal and European cultural heritage. Generally, the best in country areas are owned or managed by the National Trust.

Aboriginal Arts

The South Australian Museum in Adelaide has a comprehensive collection of Aboriginal art and cultural artefacts. Also in Adelaide, the Tandanya Centre has a gallery featuring exhibitions of Aboriginal art from around Australia.

Cultural sites featuring cave paintings and petroglyphs (rock carvings) are scattered through the northern Flinders Ranges, and several of them can be visited. Other well-known petroglyph sites are near Innamincka on Cooper Creek. In 1992 the world's oldest rock carvings (43,000 years) were found in the Olary region, 350km north of Adelaide.

Fine Arts

South Australia's first professional artists were the Chauncy sisters, Martha and Theresa, who arrived in the colony just six

Hans Heysen

Born in Hamburg, Germany, in 1877, Wilhelm Ernst Hans Heysen emigrated to Adelaide with his family at the age of seven. He started painting as a boy and sold his first watercolour, *The Wet Road*, at 16.

Recognising his talent, a group of Adelaide businessmen financed Heysen to study and paint in Europe between 1899 and 1903. He returned to Adelaide and became a private art teacher, winning the Wynne Prize in 1904 with *Mystic Morn*. It was the first of nine times he was to win this prestigious national landscape award.

Heysen's first major exhibition was held in 1908, and within 20 years he was extremely successful – sales of his work at a 1927 exhibition set an Australian record. A prolific artist, he had thousands of paintings and drawings to his credit over a career that spanned 73 years. His work hangs in all Australian state galleries, numerous provincial galleries and the British Museum.

Painting mainly in watercolours, Heysen focused on the majesty of the Australian gum tree and the rural landscape of the Mt Lofty and Flinders ranges. His paintings, for example *Grey Morning* and *Guardian of the Brachina Gorge*, skilfully highlight the interplay of light and nature, and reveal his great love of the Australian countryside. One of Heysen's favourite areas was the Adelaide Hills, where he lived for 50 years near the small German town of Hahndorf.

Heysen was knighted in 1950 and died in 1968.

Denis O'Byrne

NATIONAL GALLERY OF VICTORIA, FELTON BEQUEST, 1937

Guardian of the Brachina Gorge, 1937, watercolour, 48.2 x 62.4 cm

weeks after its proclamation. Each had trained as a miniature portraitist, with Martha painting in oil and watercolour and Theresa working in wax. As well as portraits, Martha also painted landscapes and flower studies. Both artists exhibited at the Royal Academy in London, then the most prestigious exhibition venue in the British empire. Despite this – and the fact that Martha was Australia's second professional female painter and Theresa its first female sculptor – they are still little-known in SA.

Women dominated SA's visual arts scene from the 1890s to the 1940s, when they were the most influential art teachers and the chief supporters of modernism. Significant painters during this period were Dorrit Black, Stella Bowen, the Hambidge sisters (Alice, Helen and Millicent), Nora Heysen and Margaret Preston. Heysen, a daughter of Hans Heysen, won the Archibald Prize, Australia's major award for portraiture, in 1938.

In contrast, the only really notable male painters of the period were Hans Heysen and Horace Trenerry. Heysen became SA's best-known artist and one of Australia's most famous landscape artists. Unlike many, he became a popular figure in his own lifetime; working in oil and watercolours, he captured the atmosphere and beauty of SA's rural landscapes very successfully.

There's a large collection of Heysen's work in the Art Gallery of SA, which purchased its first Heysen in 1904; it also has his last documented painting, executed in 1966, two years before his death. Established in 1880, the gallery contains a comprehensive collection of Australian, Asian and European art.

Architecture

Despite development, central Adelaide retains many fine stone buildings from the early days of settlement. The conservation of important heritage buildings became a major public issue after several historic landmarks were demolished in the 1970s. Today, many of the state's most significant heritage sites are protected by National Trust and by State Heritage legislation.

Adelaide has numerous gracious mansions and stately homes from the Victorian era, generally built for the colonial gentry who had profited from wool, copper or business. There is also an abundance of solid, 19th century middle-class villas and working-class cottages in the older suburbs. Most such buildings are in the city and nearby suburbs such as North Adelaide and Glen Osmond.

Many towns sprang from the copper and wheat booms of the 1840s to 1870s. Buoyed by wealth and optimism, their founders tended to build solidly and grandly in stone, particularly when it came to churches, hotels and public buildings. Since then, the lack of major development in such towns has generally preserved their historic streetscapes. You'll find some of the best examples at Burra, Kapunda, Mintaro, Moonta, Quorn and Robe.

Several country areas have architectural styles that reflect the culture of their first settlers. Fine examples of this are the distinctive Lutheran churches and German farmhouses of the Barossa Valley, the English country homes of the Adelaide Hills, the 'Englishness' of Mintaro, and the Cornish cottages and sombre Methodist chapels of the copper towns.

Many buildings (historic and otherwise) show clever adaptation to the local climate and, in many cases, the lack of readily available manufactured building materials. They include the miners' dugouts at Burra and Coober Pedy, the thatched farm sheds of the Mid-North and Barossa Valley, the pine-and-pug settlers' cottages in the Flinders Ranges, and the broad-verandahed homesteads throughout the pastoral districts.

National Trust The National Trust is dedicated to preserving historic buildings and artefacts as well as significant natural features in all parts of Australia. It manages around 140 sites in SA, most of which are open to the public. See the section on Useful Organisations in the Facts for the Visitor chapter.

Performing Arts

South Australia's focal point for performing arts is the Adelaide Festival Centre. It's the major venue for the biennial Adelaide Festival of Arts, regarded as the nation's foremost performing arts and cultural event. For more on this and other major Adelaide festivals, such as the Adelaide Fringe and Womadelaide, see Cultural Events in the Adelaide chapter.

The State Opera of SA was established in 1976 and is a major employer of local artists. It has premiered many major works in Australia, including Wagner's masterpiece *Der Ring des Nibelungen* (*The Ring Cycle*) in 1998, for which it received rave reviews.

Adelaide has a number of theatre companies, including the acclaimed State Theatre Company, which puts on major productions (see Entertainment in the Adelaide chapter). The Adelaide-based Australian Dance Theatre is one of the nation's most highly respected performing arts companies.

The SA Country Arts Trust has theatre complexes at Mt Gambier, Port Pirie, Renmark and Whyalla. As well as providing a touring program, it employs a number of arts development officers who support and promote cultural activities in country areas.

Music

Adelaide offers a wide variety of music. You can foot-tap to an Irish band in an Irish pub, gyrate to rock belted out by a pub band, or relax to the strains of the Adelaide Symphony Orchestra (ASO). There are also active jazz and folk scenes.

Some of the most enjoyable opportunities for listening to jazz and classical music are the wine festivals held annually in the Barossa and Clare valleys and at McLaren Vale (see Special Events in the Facts for the Visitor chapter).

The ASO holds around 100 concerts throughout the state each year, including the hugely popular 'Symphony under the Stars', held in Adelaide's Elder Park each February. Contact the ASO on ☎ 8343 4834 for details of forthcoming performances.

Rock Adelaide has plenty of rock venues where you can listen to anything from grunge to cover bands. Although things aren't so wonderful in the country, you can usually find a good band or two on a Friday and Saturday night in the larger towns.

Several Adelaide rock acts, such as Paul Kelly and Cold Chisel, have done well on the national and international stage.

Folk Lovers of folk music won't be disappointed as there are annual festivals and regular session venues throughout the settled areas. The major event is the Victor Harbor Folk Festival, held over the October long weekend (the first weekend of the month). Other significant events take place at Kapunda (the weekend before Easter), Carrick Hill in Adelaide (the Medieval Festival is held there in April) and Laura (also in April).

See Folk in the Entertainment section of the Adelaide chapter.

Literature

South Australia has produced a number of notable writers and poets. CJ Dennis (of *The Songs of a Sentimental Bloke* fame) and Adam Lindsay Gordon were famous colonial poets. John Bray was a more contemporary poet of note – the John Bray Award is the Adelaide Festival of Arts' poetry prize.

There are some excellent local writers, including novelists Peter Goldsworthy, Geraldine Halls, Barbara Hanrahan, Colin Thiele and Ben Winch and prize-winning poet Nan Whitcombe.

Goldsworthy's novels *Maestro* and *Honk if you're Jesus* have received critical acclaim. His most recent novel is *Kiss*, which followed the publication of *Wish*, a story of biologically engineered love involving a gorilla and a man.

Early feminist and colonial writer Catherine Helen Spence was a controversial figure when, 145 years ago, she wrote *Clara Morison*. This novel details the struggles of a young, educated Scottish woman who, after being jilted on arrival in SA in the 1850s, finds she must make a new life for herself among the working class. *Clara Morison* is considered a milestone in Australian literature.

Originally from Tumby Bay, popular travel writer and poet Kate Llewellyn has recently written *Floral Mother*, a collection of essays on nature, food and family.

Emerging young writer Ben Winch has set his *My Boyfriend's Father*, a rite of passage novel for the 1990s, in Adelaide. And novelist Garry Disher has charted one family's fortunes in the wheat and wool country of SA's Mid-North in his *The Sunken Road*.

Also worth reading is *Bringing the Water*, edited by Mary Costello and Barry Westburg, an anthology on the theme of clean water, which is an appropriate subject in such a dry state as SA. This collection of 35 stories from local writers was inspired by the fact that Port Adelaide was the only major port in Australia where ships refused to take on drinking water.

Geraldine Halls is a thriller writer of international fame, writing under the pen name Charlotte Jay. Halls' acclaimed and popular novel *This is my Friend's Chair* is a beautifully paced saga of the disintegration of an Adelaide family over 50 years from the 1920s.

The SA Writers' Centre (☎ 8223 7662, fax 8232 3994, sawriters@sawriters.on.net) at 187 Rundle St in Adelaide is an information and resource centre for creative writers. South Australia's major venue for public poetry readings is the Box Factory, 59 Regent St South, Adelaide. The Friendly Street Poets have meetings here on the first Tuesday of every month – contact the Writer's Centre for details.

Cinema

The SA Film Corporation was established in 1972 as a means of kick-starting a local film industry. It did this with commendable success, creating the possibility for acclaimed productions such as *Picnic at Hanging Rock*, *Sunday Too Far Away*, *Storm Boy* and *Breaker Morant* in the 1970s.

The corporation's key role these days is to encourage Australian and overseas producers to use the state as a base for low-budget features. Recent films made in SA and worthy of mention are Scott Hick's *Shine*, Bill Bennett's *Kiss or Kill* and Rolph de Heer's *The Quiet Room*.

RELIGION

By far the most common religion is Christianity, with 70% of the population claiming affiliation in the 1996 census – the number had dropped by 4% over the past five years. The largest denomination is Roman Catholic with 21% of the population, followed by Anglican (16%), Uniting Church (13%) and Lutheran (5%). Non-Christian religions count for 1.8% of the population, with almost half this number Buddhist.

About 22% of the population describe themselves as having no religion.

LANGUAGE

Visitors from abroad may find that Australian (that's 'strine') English is a strange collection of words and expressions, strung together at top speed. Some words have entirely different meanings here than in English-speaking countries north of the equator, while many commonly used words have been shortened almost beyond recognition. Others are derived from Aboriginal or foreign languages, from the slang used by early convict settlers or (shudder) from TV.

If you want to pass for a local, try speaking quickly and slightly nasally. When you've mastered that, shorten any word of more than two syllables and then add a vowel to the end of it, making anything you can into a diminutive – biscuits become 'bikkies', poker machines become 'pokies', and even the Hell's Angels are reduced to mere 'bikies'. Finally, if you want to get turfed out of the pikkies (the movies) or the spectator stands at the footy (football), pepper your speech with as many expletives as possible.

Lonely Planet publishes *Australian Phrasebook*, an introduction to both Australian English and Aboriginal languages.

Facts for the Visitor

HIGHLIGHTS

As you'd expect in a state as large and diverse as SA, the list of attractions is as long as your arm. Major ones include **Adelaide** (a relaxed, attractive city with a vibrant cultural scene), the **Barossa Valley** (for its outstanding wines and German heritage), the **South-East** (for more great wines, as well as wetlands, cave systems and beach resorts), the **Flinders Ranges** (which has superb bushwalking and dramatic landscapes) and the **Adelaide Hills** (with its beautiful wooded hills and historic villages).

Then there's the Cornish heritage of SA's historic copper-mining towns: **Burra, Kadina, Kapunda** and **Moonta**.

The only significant permanent waterway, the **Murray River**, has houseboating as well as water sports, paddle-wheeler cruises and the timeless atmosphere of a big river.

South Australia has many fine beaches and some spectacular coastal scenery, such as the cliffs of western **Eyre Peninsula** and southern **Yorke Peninsula**. Some of Australia's best surfing is found in these two areas. If you like fishing, there are countless places where there are far more fish than there are people trying to catch them, even in summer.

Kangaroo Island, with its seal colonies and koalas, has really caught on as an 'ecotourism' experience, as has whale-watching at places such as **Victor Harbor** and **Head of Bight**. There's also the opportunity to see a great white shark at close quarters off **Port Lincoln**.

In the vast **Outback** you can experience some of Australia's loneliest yet most compelling country along the Strzelecki, Oodnadatta and Birdsville tracks. The opal-mining town of **Coober Pedy**, where people not only work but live underground, is unique. **Andamooka**, another Outback opal town, is without doubt the closest thing in SA to frontiersville – it's like the moon with houses or, as the locals say, 'it's like Coober Pedy before it got civilised!'

SUGGESTED ITINERARIES

This is a toughie – let's face it, the perfect itinerary for a starry-eyed, ex-pat South Australian author might be sheer hell for others. Still, there are quite a few options, particularly if you have your own transport. The following suggestions assume that you want to explore things along the way, and want to feel more relaxed at the finish than you did at the start. Remember that SA is so big that you can't expect to see much in less than a fortnight.

One Week

In a week you could see many of the sights of Adelaide, and do a couple of day trips to the Barossa wineries and the Adelaide Hills. Many visitors also zoom down to Kangaroo Island for the day, but you may find that you really need a bit longer there. If you're in SA for the Adelaide Festival of Arts then that will probably chew up your entire week.

Two Weeks

With two weeks up your sleeve you could include a trip from Adelaide to the Barossa and Clare valleys, then on through Burra and up to Wilpena Pound in the Flinders Ranges. If you wanted to indulge in bushwalking and landscape photography you could easily spend five or six days in the Flinders Ranges alone.

Driving from Victoria to the Northern Territory (NT)? A fortnight would just about allow you to visit some of the South-East's main attractions (such as the Coonawarra wineries, the Naracoorte Caves and Robe), spend the best part of a week in and around Adelaide, then head north via the Barossa Valley and Wilpena Pound. You might even have time to 'do' the Oodnadatta Track.

One Month

A month would allow a good look at the Adelaide region (which includes the Barossa and the Adelaide Hills) as well as a reasonable amount of time for Kangaroo Island, the South-East, the Flinders Ranges and the Outback. If you want to work along the way, or see more of the state, you will obviously need more than a month.

PLANNING

When to Go

Any time is a good time to be in SA, but as you'd expect in a state this large, different parts of it are at their best at different times. Generally, spring and autumn give the greatest flexibility for a short visit as you can combine highlights of the whole state while avoiding extremes of weather.

Summer sees Crow-eaters (the local vernacular for South Australians) flock like migrating birds to the coast, where most days are warm enough for swimming and lazing around outdoors. In the north it's generally too hot to do anything much except slump under an air-conditioner with a cold drink.

In winter, when the south is often cold and wet, the Outback beckons with its mild to warm days and clear skies. It's cool – often freezing – at nights. This kills off the bushflies, which in the warmer months can be an absolute nightmare.

Late winter and spring usually bring out the magnificent wildflowers, which bloom all the way from the coastal heath up through the mallee and into the Flinders Ranges and Outback. Some years these can be worth a trip in themselves.

School Holidays The other key consideration when travelling in SA is school holidays. The main holiday period is from mid-December to late January, with fortnight holidays also occurring early to mid-April; late June to mid-July; and late September to mid-October. South Australian families take to the road (and air) en masse at these times. As a result, many places are booked out, prices rise and things become a little hectic, particularly over Christmas and Easter.

Maps

South Australia has a full coverage of touring maps. One of the best places to find them is the Royal Automobile Association (RAA) of South Australia's bookshop at 41 Hindmarsh Square in Adelaide (☎ 8202 4538). The RAA's own regional maps are generally the best available, and are free to members – each one includes maps of the main centres. The bookshop stocks Westprint's well-regarded maps of the Simpson Desert region, the Flinders Ranges and Yorke Peninsula.

Also excellent are Bicycle SA's cycle route maps, which are ideal for motoring as well. These are available from major cycle shops and Information SA (☎ 8204 1900), at 77 Grenfell St in Adelaide.

Touring maps published by the oil companies are available at most service stations.

You'll also find lavishly illustrated maps of regions such as the Adelaide Hills, Kangaroo Island, the Barossa and the Outback – these are ideal for laminating as mementos.

Universal Business Directories (UBD) and Gregory's street directories of Adelaide are invaluable if you're driving yourself around. Both cost around $28 and are available at various bookshops and newsagents. UBD also has a street directory which covers numerous country centres ($28).

The entire state has been topographically mapped at 1:250,000, and settled areas at 1:50,000 or 100,000 – the maps are published by the Australian Surveying & Land Information Group (AUSLIG). Two of the main outlets in Adelaide are run by the Department of Environment, Heritage & Aboriginal Affairs: Mapland (☎ 8226 4946) at 282 Richmond Rd, Netley; and the Land Information Centre (☎ 8226 3983), in the Colonel Light Centre, at 25 Pirie St. Both shops have an excellent range of topographic and special interest maps as well as guides for cyclists and bushwalkers. The department's Environment Shop (☎ 8204 1910) at 77 Grenfell St also sells topographic maps.

The Map Shop (☎ 8231 2033) at 16A Peel St, between Currie and Hindley Sts in the city, also has a comprehensive range. The more popular topographic sheets are generally available over the counter at shops specialising in bushwalking gear and outdoor equipment.

TOURIST OFFICES
Local Tourist Offices
The promotion of tourism in SA is overseen by the South Australian Tourism Commission (SATC). The main tourist information and booking office is SATC's Travel Centre at 1 King William St in Adelaide (☎ 8303 2033, 1300 366 770 toll free, fax 8303 2231, contact-us.visit-southaustralia@saugov.sa .gov.au). As well as having enough tourist and general information to bury you, it can book transport, tours and accommodation, and has a website at www.tourism.sa .gov.au.

A step down from SATC are local or regional tourist offices. All the larger towns have a tourist office of some kind, and in most cases these are a good source of information on the town and district. Such offices give you the benefit of local knowledge, which is something you don't really get from the SATC. Most small towns will have a place – often a pub, craft shop, service station or general store – where you can pick up brochures.

Interstate Tourist Offices
Contact details of the interstate SATC offices are:

Queensland
  (☎ 07-3229 8533, 1300 366 770)
  Level 1, 245 Albert St, Brisbane 4000
Western Australia
  (☎ 08-9481 1268, 1300 366 770)
  13/14 Mezzanine Floor, Wesley Centre, 93 William St, Perth 6000

Tourist Offices Abroad
Contact details for overseas SATC offices or representatives are:

Germany
  (☎ 89-2366 2137) Herzogspitalstrasse 5, D-80331 Munich
Japan
  (☎ 03-5214 0693) 28F The New Otani Garden Court, 4-1 Kioicho, Chiyoda-Ku, Tokyo 102

New Zealand
  (☎ 09-307 6600) 1st Floor, CML Building, 157 Queens St, Auckland
Singapore
  (☎ 333 1885) 153-B Rochor Rd, Bugis Village, Singapore 188428
UK
  (☎ 020-8944 5375) c/- Robert Hardless & Associates, Beaumont House, Lambton Rd, London SW20 0LW
USA
  (☎ 714-852 2270) c/- Australian Travel Headquarters Inc, Suite 215, 1600 Dove St, Newport Beach CA 92660

VISAS & DOCUMENTS
All visitors to Australia need a visa. Only New Zealand nationals are exempt, and even they receive a 'special category' visa on arrival.

Visa application forms are available from Australian diplomatic missions overseas, and you can apply by mail or in person. There are several types of visa, depending on the reason for your visit.

Visa regulations do change from time to time, so check the government website at www.immi.gov.au or talk to your travel agent or Australian diplomatic mission.

Tourist Visas
Tourist visas are issued by Australian diplomatic missions abroad and are valid for a stay of up to six months within a 12-month period. Each application is subject to a $50 processing fee.

Alternatively, you can get a free Electronic Travel Authority (ETA), valid for three months and available from travel agents abroad. These are usually obtained when you purchase your ticket.

When you apply for a visa or ETA, you need to present your passport and a passport photo, as well as sign an undertaking that you have an onward or return ticket and 'sufficient funds' – the latter is obviously open to interpretation.

Working Holiday Visas
Young visitors may be eligible for a Working Holiday Visa. To the Department of

Immigration and Multicultural Affairs, 'young' means between 18 and 25 (26 to 30 in special circumstances), and 'working holiday' means up to 12 months. However, the emphasis is supposed to be on casual employment rather than a full-time job, so you are only meant to work for a total of three months for any one employer. Residents of the UK, Canada, Ireland and the Netherlands can apply at any Australian diplomatic mission overseas, while all others must apply in their home country.

See the Work section later in this chapter for details on employment available in SA and where you'll find it.

Visa Extensions

The maximum stay in Australia is one year, including extensions.

Visa extensions are made through the Department of Immigration and Multicultural Affairs offices in Australia. The process takes some time, so it's best to apply a month before your visa expires. There is an application fee of $145, but beware – even if they turn down your application they can still keep your money.

To qualify for an extension you must have a ticket out of the country and sufficient funds to cover the period of extension – you may be asked to provide evidence of these funds. If you're aged 70 years or over you'll also need private medical insurance.

Other Documents

Your overseas driver's licence will be acceptable in SA, but an International Driving Permit is preferred. You'll need to organise this before leaving home.

For details on hostel cards, see the Youth Hostels and Backpacker Hostels entries later in this chapter.

EMBASSIES & CONSULATES
Australian Embassies

The Department of Foreign Affairs & Trade has a full listing of Australian diplomatic missions abroad on their website at www.dfat.gov.au. They include:

Canada
 (☎ 613-236 0841, fax 236 4376)
 Suite 710, 50 O'Connor St, Ottawa, Ontario K1P 6L2 (also in Toronto and Vancouver)
France
 (☎ 01-4059 3300)
 4 Rue Jean Rey, 75724 Paris Cedex 15, Paris
Germany
 (☎ 228-81 030, fax 810 3130)
 Godesberger Allee 103-107, 53175 Bonn (also in Frankfurt and Berlin)
Indonesia
 (☎ 021-522 7111, fax 522 7101)
 Jalan HR Rasuna Said Kav C 15-16, Jakarta Selatan 12940 (also in Bali)
Japan
 (☎ 03-5232 4111, fax 5232 4149)
 2-1-14 Mita, Minato-ku, Tokyo 108 (also in Nagoya, Osaka, Sapporo and Sendai)
Malaysia
 (☎ 03-242 3122, fax 241 5773)
 6 Jalan Yap Kwan Seng, Kuala Lumpur 50450 (also in Kuching and Penang)
Netherlands
 (☎ 070-310 8200, fax 310 7863)
 Carnegielaan 4, 2517 KH, The Hague
New Zealand
 (☎ 04-473 6411, fax 498 7135)
 72-78 Hobson St, Thorndon, Wellington (also in Auckland)
South Africa
 (☎ 012-342 3740, fax 342 8442)
 292 Orient St, Arcadia, Pretoria 0083 (also in Cape Town and Johannesburg)
Thailand
 (☎ 02-287 2680, fax 287 2029)
 37 South Sathorn Rd, Bangkok 10120
UK
 (☎ 020-7379 4334, fax 465 8217)
 Australia House, The Strand, London WC2B 4LA (also in Edinburgh and Manchester)
USA
 (☎ 202-797 3000, fax 797 3168)
 1601 Massachusetts Ave NW, Washington DC 20036 (also in Atlanta, Boston, Denver, Honolulu, Houston, Los Angeles, New York and San Francisco)

Foreign Embassies & Consulates

It's important to realise what your own embassy can and can't do to help you if you get into trouble. Remember, you are bound by the laws of the country you are in. In genuine emergencies you might get some assistance from your embassy, but only if other channels have been exhausted.

Some embassies used to keep letters for travellers or have a small reading room with home newspapers, but these days the mail holding service has usually been stopped and even newspapers tend to be out of date.

The principal diplomatic representations to Australia are in Canberra. The state capitals also have representatives of other countries, and you'll find them listed in the various *Yellow Pages* phone books under Consulates & Legations. Those in Adelaide include:

Germany
    Consulate:
    (☎ 8231 6320)
    23 Peel St, Adelaide
Indonesia
    Consul-General:
    (☎ 8217 8288)
    Level 1, 45 King William St, Adelaide
Italy
    Consulate:
    (☎ 8337 0777)
    398 Payneham Rd, Glynde
Japan
    Honorary Consul-General:
    (☎ 8381 6047)
    29 Winham Ave, Reynella
Netherlands
    Consulate:
    (☎ 8232 3855)
    99 Frome St, Adelaide
UK
    Consulate:
    (☎ 8212 7280)
    Level 22, 25 Grenfell Street, Adelaide

CUSTOMS

When entering Australia you can bring most articles in free of duty, provided that Customs is satisfied they are for personal use and that you'll be taking them with you when you leave. For each person over 17 there's also the usual duty-free quota of 1.125L of alcohol, 250 cigarettes and dutiable goods up to the value of A$400.

With regard to prohibited goods, there are two areas you need to pay particular attention to. Number one is, of course, dope. The Australian Customs Service has a positive mania about the stuff and can be extremely efficient when it comes to finding it. Unless you want to make first-hand investigations of conditions in Australian jails, don't bring any with you. Customs are particularly rigorous in their search if you are arriving from South-East Asia or the Indian subcontinent.

Number two is animal and/or plant quarantine. Australia has managed to escape many of the nasties prevalent in other parts of the world, so the authorities are naturally keen to prevent weeds, pests or diseases getting into the country. You will be asked to declare all goods of animal or vegetable origin – wooden spoons, straw hats, the lot – and to show them to an official. Obviously, any attempt to bring fresh food and live animals into the country will be frowned upon. (Even within Australia there are restrictions on taking fruit, vegetables, plant cuttings, cut flowers and so on between states.)

Weapons and firearms are either prohibited or else require a permit as well as safety testing. Other restricted goods include non-approved telecommunication devices and products (such as ivory) made from protected wildlife species.

MONEY
Currency

Australia's currency is the Australian dollar, which comprises 100 cents. There are coins for 5c, 10c, 20c, 50c, $1 and $2, and notes for $5, $10, $20, $50 and $100.

There are no notable restrictions on importing or exporting travellers cheques. However, cash amounts in excess of the equivalent of A$5000 (any currency) must be declared on arrival and departure.

Exchange Rates

In recent times the Australian dollar has fluctuated quite markedly against the US dollar, with lows around the 60c to 70c mark. Exchange rates at the time of this update were:

country	unit		dollar
Canada	C$1	=	A$1.02
European Union	€1	=	A$1.60
France	1FF	=	A$0.28

Germany	DM1	=	A$0.82
Hong Kong	HK$10	=	A$1.97
Japan	¥100	=	A$1.26
New Zealand	NZ$1	=	A$0.82
United Kingdom	UK£1	=	A$2.46
United States	US$1	=	A$1.53

Exchanging Money

Changing foreign currency or travellers cheques is no problem at most banks and, in Adelaide only, at licensed moneychangers such as American Express and Thomas Cook. You may be able to change foreign currency at your hotel or motel, although they'll usually give you less than what you'd receive at a bank.

Travellers Cheques There are a variety of ways to carry your money around. If your stay is limited, travellers cheques are the most straightforward; they generally enjoy a better exchange rate than foreign cash in Australia.

American Express, Thomas Cook and other well-known international brands of travellers cheques are widely used. A passport or driver's licence is usually adequate for identification.

Buying Australian-dollar travellers cheques is a recommended option. These can be exchanged at the bank teller's window without being converted from a foreign currency, thereby incurring commissions, fees and exchange rate fluctuations. Not only that, you may get caught short of cash outside banking hours; in country areas you'll find it much easier to change a travellers cheque in Australian dollars than one in an overseas currency.

Credit Cards Except in some remote areas, credit cards are widely accepted in SA and are a convenient alternative to carrying a wad of travellers cheques. The most common credit card is the purely Australian Bankcard system. Visa, MasterCard, Diners Club and American Express are also widely accepted.

Cash advances on credit cards are available over the bank counter and from many automatic teller machines (ATMs), depending on the card.

Local Bank Accounts If you're planning to stay longer than just a month or so, it's worth considering other ways of handling money that will give you more flexibility and are more economical. This applies equally to Australians travelling around the country.

Most travellers these days opt for an account that includes a cash card, which you can use to access your cash from ATMs found all over Australia. Westpac, ANZ, National and Commonwealth bank branches are found nationwide; in the larger country towns there is invariably at least one place where you can use your card.

ATM machines can be used day or night, and it is possible to use the machines of some other banks: for example, Westpac ATMs accept Commonwealth Bank cards and vice versa; National Bank ATMs accept ANZ cards and vice versa. There is a limit on how much you can withdraw from your account each day. This varies from bank to bank but is usually around $1000 per day.

Even in the Outback – although you'd be crazy to count on it – many businesses, such as service stations, supermarkets and motels, are linked into the EFTPOS system (Electronic Funds Transfer at Point of Sale). At places with this facility you can use your bank cash card to pay directly for services or purchases, and sometimes withdraw cash as well. Bank cash cards and credit cards can also be used to make local, national and international phone calls from special public telephones, found in many towns throughout the country.

Opening an Australian bank account is easy for overseas visitors – provided it's done within six weeks of arrival. Simply show your passport and away you go! After six weeks it's much more complicated. A points system operates and you need to score a minimum of 100 points before you can have the privilege of letting the bank take your money. A passport, driver's licence, birth certificate or other 'major' ID is worth at least 40 points; minor forms of

ID, such as credit cards, earn around 20 points. Just like a game show really!

A Commonwealth Bank savings account is useful if you're going to travel in the more sparsely settled areas. This is simply because in the bush, where banks are scarce and becoming scarcer, just about every post office has a Commonwealth Bank agency. However, the amount of cash you can withdraw at such places is often restricted, particularly in small remote centres.

Unfortunately, any interest earned on your holiday funds is regarded as income and will be taxed. To minimise the damage, ask the Australian Tax Office (ATO) to write a letter to your bank instructing them that any interest earned need only be taxed at the Non-Resident Withholding Tax System rate of 10%. Phone the ATO on ☎ 13 28 67 for more details.

Costs

Compared with the USA, Canada and European countries, SA is cheaper in some ways and more expensive in others. Manufactured goods tend to be more expensive: if they are imported they have all the additional costs of transport and duty, and if they're manufactured locally they suffer from the extra costs entailed in making things in comparatively small quantities. Thus you pay more for clothes, cars and other manufactured items.

On the other hand, food is generally high in quality and low in cost – surveys show Adelaide is consistently one of Australia's cheapest cities when it comes to food. Accommodation is also very reasonably priced. See the Accommodation section later in this chapter for types of accommodation available and the prices you can expect to pay.

The biggest cost in any extensive tour of SA will most likely be transport, simply because the state is so vast. If you're travelling with others, buying a second-hand car may be the most economical way to go if you want to see the lot. Provided you look after it – and don't pay too much in the first place – you should recover most of the purchase price when you sell it. See the Getting Around chapter for information on buying a car.

Tipping

It isn't customary to tip in SA. But if the service has been especially good and you want to tip, leave what you think is fair. Taxi drivers don't expect a tip, but of course they won't hurl it back at you either.

POST & COMMUNICATIONS
Postal Rates

Australia's postal service is relatively efficient and cheap. It costs 45c to send a standard letter or postcard within Australia.

For international post, aerogrammes cost 70c to any country; airmail letters/postcards cost 75/70c to New Zealand, 85/80c to Singapore and Malaysia, 95/90c to Hong Kong and India, $1.05/95c to the USA and Canada, and $1.20/1 to Europe and the UK; letters over 20gm cost more.

Sending Mail

Post offices are open from 9 am to 5 pm Monday to Friday. Outside these times you can often get stamps from newsagencies or, on Saturday morning, from Australia Post shops (mainly in Adelaide).

Receiving Mail

All post offices will hold mail for visitors. You can also have mail sent to you at American Express offices provided you have an Amex card or carry their travellers cheques.

Telephone

The Australian telecommunications industry has been deregulated and there are a number of providers offering various services. Telstra and Optus are the main players servicing private phones, while mobile and payphone markets have much stiffer competition.

Payphones & Phonecards There's a wide range of local and international phonecards. Lonely Planet's eKno Communication Card (see the insert at the back of this book) is aimed specifically at travellers and provides cheap international calls, a range of messaging services and free email – for local calls, you're usually better off with a local card. You can join online at www.ekno.lonelyplanet.com, or by phone from South Australia by dialling ☎ 1800 674 100. Once you have joined, to use eKno from Australia, dial ☎ 1800 11 44 78.

The cards issued by the various telecommunications companies can be used in any Telstra public phone that accepts cards – most do these days – or from most private phones by dialling a toll-free access number provided when you purchase your card.

Long-distance calls made from payphones are generally considerably more expensive than calls made from private phones. If you'll be using payphones a lot it will pay to look into the cards available from providers other than Telstra.

The important thing is to know how your calls are being charged, as charges vary from company to company. An explanatory booklet should be available from the card outlet – usually a newsagent.

Some public phones are set up to take credit cards only. While this is convenient, you need to keep an eye on the cost of the call. The minimum charge for a call on one of these phones is $1.60.

Local Calls Local calls from private phones/public phones cost 30/40c for an unlimited amount of time. Calls to mobile phones attract much higher rates.

Long Distance Calls & Area Codes It's possible to make long-distance calls – Subscriber Trunk Dialling (STD) – from virtually any public phone. These calls are cheaper in off-peak hours, particularly at nights and on weekends.

For the purpose of area (or STD) codes, Australia is divided into just four zones. All regular numbers (ie all but toll free, mobile or information service numbers) have an area code followed by an eight-digit number. All long-distance calls (ie over 50km) are charged at long-distance rates even if they are within the same zone.

The 02 code covers New South Wales (NSW) and Australian Capital Territory (ACT), 03 is for Tasmania and Victoria, 07 is for Queensland, and 08 is for SA, Western Australia (WA) and the NT. Calls within the same STD area can be dialled without using the area code.

International Calls You can also make International Subscriber Dialling (ISD) calls from most STD phones. Calls are generally cheaper if you use a provider other than Telstra. When making a call, the international dialling code will vary depending on which provider you are using.

International calls from Australia are among the cheapest you'll find anywhere, and there are often specials that bring the price down even further. Off-peak times vary depending on the destination – call ☎ 1222 for details.

Country Direct is a service that gives travellers in Australia direct access to operators in around 60 countries, for the purpose of making reverse-charge (collect) or credit card calls. For a list of countries hooked into this system, check the *White Pages* telephone book.

Toll-Free Calls Many businesses and some government departments operate a toll-free service – so provided you're ringing from outside the Adelaide metropolitan area, it's a free call. Toll-free numbers have the prefix 1800.

Other businesses, such as the airlines, have numbers beginning with 13 or 1300, and these are charged as local calls. These numbers may either be Australia-wide, or be applicable to a specific state or STD district only. Unfortunately, there's no way of telling without actually ringing the number.

Calls to these services still attract charges if you are calling from a mobile phone.

Mobile Phones Much of SA's settled areas has reasonable coverage from the digital mobile network, but as the towns thin out so does the service.

Phone numbers with the prefixes 014, 015, 018, 019 or 041 are mobile or car phones. The main mobile operators are Telstra, Optus and Vodafone.

Information Calls Numbers starting with 1900 are information services. These calls cost from 35c to $5 per minute (more from mobile and payphones).

Email & Internet Access

If you want to surf the net in SA, even if it's only to access your email, there are a number of service providers in Adelaide and regional areas. The major players include OzEmail (☎ 13 28 84) at www.ozemail .com.au (they have log-in numbers for Adelaide and Coober Pedy); and Telstra Big Pond (☎ 1800 805 874 toll free) at www.onaustralia.com.au (log-in numbers for Adelaide only).

Check the national magazine *Internet.Au* and local newspapers for other service providers.

CompuServe users who want to access the service in Adelaide should phone ☎ 1300 307 072 to get the local log-in numbers.

There are free internet-connected terminals in all public libraries in SA, but you usually have to book. To send and receive email you'll need an account with one of the free web-based email services, such as Hotmail or Rocket Mail. For more details on Net access see Information in the Adelaide chapter.

INTERNET RESOURCES

The world wide web is a rich resource for travellers. You can research your trip, hunt down bargain airfares, book hotels, check on weather conditions or chat with locals and other travellers about the best places to visit (or avoid).

There's no better place to start your Web explorations than the Lonely Planet website (www.lonelyplanet.com). Here you'll find succinct summaries on travelling to most places on earth, postcards from other travellers and the Thorn Tree bulletin board, where you can ask questions before you go or dispense advice when you get back. You can

also find travel news and updates to many of our most popular guidebooks, and the sub-WWWay section links you to the most useful travel resources elsewhere on the web.

As you would expect, the web has a number of sites relevant to SA. The major site for visitors is that of SATC at www.tourism .sa.gov.au. If this doesn't have what you're looking for, try www.saweb.com.au/saweb/directory/index.html – it's a search engine for SA sites.

The SA government's comprehensive site, www.sa.gov.au, has information on a wide range of topics, and gives access to many other sites including the SATC.

A number of useful organisations have websites and these are listed throughout the book. The way things are going, there'll be many more by the time you read this.

BOOKS

Adelaide has a large number of new and secondhand bookshops. Some of these are listed under Bookshops in the Adelaide chapter, otherwise look under Books in the *Yellow Pages*. Most general bookshops in the state have a section devoted to Australiana, with books on almost every subject you care to mention.

Lonely Planet

There is a section on SA in Lonely Planet's *Australia*. And Lonely Planet's *Outback Australia*, which includes remote tracks and highways in SA, has plenty of practical advice if you're thinking of getting off the beaten track.

Guidebooks

The RAA publishes the comprehensive regional guidebooks *Adelaide Region, Outback: South Australia & Central Australia, Mid North & Flinders Ranges* and *South East*.

The Royal Geographical Society of South Australia (RGSSA) publishes *Explore the Barossa* and *Explore the Flinders Ranges*, both of which are great value for anyone wanting a more in-depth look at these areas. At the time of writing a guide book for Kangaroo Island was also in the pipeline. It was expected to be available by late 1999.

History

Aboriginal History The award-winning *Triumph of the Nomads*, by Geoffrey Blainey, chronicles the life of Australia's original inhabitants, and convincingly demolishes the myth that the Aborigines were 'primitive' people trapped on a hostile continent. They were in fact extremely successful in adapting to and overcoming the difficulties presented by the climate and resources (or seeming lack of them) – the book's an excellent read.

Another very good book is Josephine Flood's *Archaeology of the Dreamtime*, which has quite a bit on SA.

For a sympathetic historical account of what has happened to the original Australians since European arrival, read *Aboriginal Australians* by Richard Broome. Mildred Kirk's *A Change of Ownership* covers similar ground, but does so more concisely, focussing on the land rights movement and its history.

More specific to SA, *Survival in Our Own Land*, edited by Christobel Mattingley and Ken Hampton, provides contemporary and historical accounts of life in SA by Nungas (South Australian Aborigines).

The book *Flinders Ranges Dreaming* by Dorothy Tunbridge is a collection of 50 Dreamtime stories from the Adnyamathanha of the northern Flinders Ranges. It has many maps and beautiful photographs and makes a great guide to important non-secret Aboriginal cultural sites in the region. The book was an initiative of young Adnyamathanha who were afraid of losing their heritage.

European History For a good introduction to the subject read *A Short History of Australia*, a most accessible and informative general history by the late Manning Clark, a highly regarded historian. *The Exploration of Australia*, by Michael Cannon, resembles a coffee-table book in size, presentation and price, but it's a fascinating reference about the gradual European exploration of the continent.

For serious students of SA history, the *Flinders History of SA*, in three hefty volumes, is extremely comprehensive and will take you from the genesis of the colony in London right up to the 1980s. Each volume covers a different aspect: social history, political history and economic history. Much more concise, and correspondingly cheaper, is *A History of SA: From colonial days to the present*, by RM Gibbs.

Alan Moorehead's *Cooper's Creek* is a classic account of the ill-fated Burke and Wills expedition, which dramatises the horrors and hardships faced by the early explorers. Charles Sturt, Edward John Eyre and John MacDouall Stuart were famous South Australian explorers who all kept detailed journals; these have been published and can be read at the State Library, if you're unable to find them elsewhere.

For something more light-hearted read *Maisie: Her life, her loves, her letters 1898-1902*, edited by Joan Willington. This collection of letters gives a fascinating view of the social life of colonial SA through the eyes of the enthusiastic young Maisie Smith.

NEWSPAPERS & MAGAZINES

Adelaide's single daily newspaper, the *Advertiser*, is published Monday to Saturday, while the *Sunday Mail* appears on Sunday. The free literary newspaper, *Adelaide Review*, appears monthly.

As well, there are around 30 suburban and country newspapers. Naturally, they focus on local issues, so are a good guide to what's going on in their particular area.

You can buy the major interstate newspapers and magazines at any good newsagent. The State Library on Adelaide's North Terrace has international newspapers in its reading area.

RADIO & TV

Radio and TV programming are published daily in the *Advertiser*.

SA has over 20 commercial and noncommercial amplitude-modulated (AM) radio services, with eight of these in Adelaide, and nearly 50 VHF-modulated (FM) services, of which 11 are in Adelaide. They include the Australian Broadcasting Corporation (ABC), which operates on both bands.

Services operating in the FM sub-band 87.5 to 88Hz provide information services such as tourist information, foreign language and religion programs. They are located at Glenelg (an Adelaide suburb), Hahndorf in the Adelaide Hills, Lyndoch in the Barossa Valley, and Bordertown in the South-East.

Sadly, there are no radio stations in the sparsely populated outback. If you've fitted a decent radio and a long-range aerial you should be able to pick up the ABC most of the way from Port Augusta to Alice Springs. If you haven't, buy a tape deck and tapes.

There are five TV stations in Adelaide, including the advertisement-free ABC (Channel 2). Affectionately known as 'Auntie', the ABC enjoys a good reputation for news, current affairs, drama and documentaries. SBS, the Special Broadcasting Service on Channel 0, shows foreign language news and movies, including alternative films.

Country SA receives five commercial TV services. These include Imparja, an Aboriginal-owned station operating out of Alice Springs, which has a 'footprint' covering much of rural South Australia. It broadcasts a variety of commercial and Aboriginal-oriented material.

VIDEO SYSTEMS
Australia uses the PAL system, so make sure that any prerecorded videos you buy are compatible with your system back home.

PHOTOGRAPHY
Film
Plenty of places offer one-hour processing for print film, and E6 processing is widely available – at least in Adelaide. You have to send your Kodachrome slide film to Melbourne for developing.

A roll of 36 exposure, 35mm format, amateur-grade Kodachrome 64 or Fujichrome 100 slide-film costs $26, including processing. A 36 exposure roll of 35mm format Kodak 100 print-film costs $10, with processing and printing an additional $15 or so.

Technical Tips
SA conditions present no special problems to photographers, provided you have a modicum of ability, and allow for the intensity of the light in the Outback. Best results in northern regions are obtained early in the morning and late in the afternoon, when the light (hence contrast) is much softer. As the sun gets higher, colours appear washed out and contrasts are much harsher. You must also allow for the intensity of reflected light when taking shots on the beach.

In the north, especially in summer, allow for temperature extremes and do your best to keep film as cool as possible, particularly after exposure; *never* leave your camera or film in the glovebox or on the dash when the vehicle's in the sun. The only other likely hazards are getting dust in the camera (keep it in a dustproof container) and running out of film.

Photographing People
As in any country, politeness goes a long way when taking photographs; always ask before taking pictures of people. Many Aboriginal people do not like to have their photographs taken, even from a distance.

TIME
Australia is divided into three time zones: Western Standard Time (WA only) is GMT/UTC plus eight hours, Central Standard Time (NT, SA) is plus 9½ hours, and Eastern Standard Time (Tasmania, Victoria, NSW, ACT, Queensland) is plus 10 hours. When it's noon in SA it's 10.30 am in the west and 12.30 pm in the east.

During summer things get slightly confusing as daylight saving (when clocks are put forward one hour) does not operate in WA, Queensland or the NT. In Tasmania it lasts for two months longer than in the other states.

In SA, daylight saving starts on the last Saturday of October and finishes the last Saturday of March.

ELECTRICITY
Voltage is 220-240V and the plugs three-pin, but not the same as British three-pin

plugs. Users of electric shavers or hair dryers should note that, apart from in fancy hotels, it's difficult to find converters to take either US flat two-pin plugs or the European round two-pin plugs. Adaptors for British plugs can be found in good hardware shops, chemists and travel agents.

WEIGHTS & MEASURES

Australia uses the metric system. Petrol and milk are sold by the litre, apples and potatoes by the kilogram, distance is measured by the metre or kilometre, and speed limits are in kilometres per hour (km/h).

For those who need help with the metric system there's a conversion table at the back of this book.

LAUNDRY

Most accommodation places in SA have laundry facilities. Otherwise there are self-service launderettes (usually open 12 hours daily) and dry cleaning outlets, with the larger country towns generally having at least one of each.

Most coin-operated washing machines will only take $1 and 20c coins. Expect to pay at least $2 for a 'normal' load of washing and $2 for the dryer.

It usually costs around $15 to dry clean three garments, provided none are pleated.

HEALTH

So long as you have not visited an 'infected' country in the 14 days prior to entering Australia (aircraft refuelling stops do not count) no vaccinations are required. Naturally, if you're going to be travelling around in places apart from Australia, appropriate immunisations are highly advisable.

The Traveller's Medical & Vaccination Centre (☎ 8212 7522, adel@tmvc.com.au) is at 29 Gilbert Place in Adelaide. It offers a pre and post-travel medical advisory service, and the doctors, several of whom specialise in tropical medicine, can help if you have a post-travel problem. It also has a general medical practitioner service, and a useful website (www.tmvc.com.au).

Medical care in SA is generally first-class and only moderately expensive. Health insurance cover is available, but there is usually a waiting period after you sign up before any claims can be made.

Visitors from the UK, New Zealand, Malta, Italy, Sweden and the Netherlands have reciprocal health rights in Australia and can register at any Medicare office. If you are eligible, you will be issued with a Medicare card and will be entitled to free or heavily subsidised medical treatment at public hospitals and from clinics that 'bulk bill' (ie the medical bill is sent direct to Medicare).

If you have an immediate and serious health problem, phone or visit the casualty section at the nearest public hospital; there are 81 hospitals (including 68 outside Adelaide) with a total of 5100 beds. Emergency visits to public hospitals are free for Medicare members; if you're not a member you'll be charged.

If you want to see a private doctor the consultation fee will be around $35, of which Medicare refunds $22. There are 42 private hospitals with a total 2100 beds.

Environmental Hazards

Heat Exhaustion Dehydration and heat-related illnesses are real dangers in warm weather, particularly if you're more accustomed to cool conditions. Take time to acclimatise, drink plenty of water (*not* alcohol or soft drinks, which increase dehydration) and take it easy – rest in the shade rather than run around in the sun.

Dehydration and salt deficiency can cause heat exhaustion. Salt deficiency is characterised by fatigue, lethargy, headaches, giddiness and muscle cramps; salt tablets may help, but adding extra salt to your food is better.

Sunburn Travellers from the northern hemisphere need to be aware of the intensity of the sun in SA, particularly in summer. The situation is even worse now that there's a hole in the protective ozone layer. Those ultraviolet rays can have you burnt to a crisp even on an overcast day; if in doubt wear protective lotion, a wide-brimmed hat and a long-sleeved shirt with a collar.

Calamine lotion or Stingose are good for mild sunburn. Protect your eyes with good quality sunglasses, particularly where there's a lot of glare – such as at the beach or in the Outback.

Infectious Diseases

Diarrhoea Simple things like a change of water, food or climate can all cause a mild bout of diarrhoea. A few rushed toilet trips with no other symptoms is not indicative of a major problem.

Dehydration is the main danger with any form of diarrhoea, particularly in children or the elderly as dehydration can occur quite quickly. *Fluid replacement* (at least equal to the volume being lost) is always the most important thing to remember. Weak black tea with a little sugar, soda water, or flat soft drinks diluted 50% with clean water are all good fluid replacements.

HIV & AIDS Infection with the human immunodeficiency virus (HIV) may lead to acquired immune deficiency syndrome (AIDS). Any exposure to blood, blood products or body fluids may put the individual at risk. The disease is often transmitted through sexual contact or dirty needles – vaccinations, acupuncture, tattooing and body piercing can be potentially as dangerous as intravenous drug use.

Fear of HIV infection should never preclude treatment for serious medical conditions.

For confidential advice and information on HIV/AIDS, contact the Aids Council of SA (☎ 8362 1611, 1800 888 559 toll free, mail@aidscouncil.org.au) between 9 am and 5.30 pm weekdays, or visit their website at www.aidscouncil.org.au. If you require urgent help with an AIDS-related illness outside these times, call Lifeline, the 24-hour counselling service (☎ 8212 3444).

Sexually Transmitted Diseases (STD) Gonorrhoea, herpes and syphilis are among these diseases; sores, blisters or rashes around the genitals, and discharges or pain when urinating are common symptoms. With some STDs, such as wart virus or chlamydia, symptoms may be less marked or not observed at all, especially in women. Syphilis symptoms eventually disappear completely but the disease continues and can cause severe problems in later years. While abstinence from sexual contact is the only 100% effective prevention, using condoms is also effective. The treatment of gonorrhoea and syphilis is with antibiotics. The different STDs each require specific antibiotics. Currently, there is no cure for herpes or AIDS.

Cuts, Bites & Stings

Bites & Stings Bee and wasp stings are usually painful rather than dangerous. However, in people who are allergic to them, severe breathing difficulties may occur and require urgent medical care. Calamine lotion or Stingose spray will give some relief and ice packs will reduce the pain and swelling.

Cuts & Scratches Wash well and treat any cut with an antiseptic such as povidone-iodine. Where possible avoid bandages and Band-Aids, which can keep wounds moist.

Snakes To minimise your chances of being bitten always wear boots, socks and long trousers when walking through undergrowth where snakes may be present. Don't put your hands into holes and crevices, and be careful when collecting firewood. Never attempt to pick up or kill a snake – that's when most people get bitten.

Snake bites do not cause instantaneous death and antivenins are available. Immediately wrap the bitten limb tightly, as you would for a sprained ankle, and then attach a splint to immobilise it. Keep the victim still and seek medical help – if possible with the dead snake for identification. Don't attempt to catch the snake if there is a possibility of being bitten again. Tourniquets and sucking out the poison are now comprehensively discredited.

Medical Kit Check List

It's a good idea to carry a basic medical kit, which would include:

- ☐ **Aspirin** or **paracetamol** (acetaminophen in the USA) – for pain or fever
- ☐ **Antihistamine** – for allergies, eg hay fever; to ease the itch from insect bites or stings; and to prevent motion sickness
- ☐ **Antibiotics** – consider including these if you're travelling well off the beaten track; see your doctor, as they must be prescribed, and carry the prescription with you
- ☐ **Loperamide** or **diphenoxylate** –'blockers' for diarrhoea; **prochlorperazine** or **metaclopramide** for nausea and vomiting
- ☐ **Rehydration mixture** – to prevent dehydration, eg due to severe diarrhoea; particularly important when travelling with children
- ☐ **Insect repellent, sunscreen, lip balm** and **eye drops**
- ☐ **Calamine lotion, sting relief spray** or **aloe vera** – to ease irritation from sunburn and insect bites or stings
- ☐ **Antiseptic** (such as povidone-iodine) – for cuts and grazes
- ☐ **Bandages, Band-Aids (plasters)** and other wound dressings
- ☐ **Water purification tablets** or **iodine**
- ☐ **Scissors, tweezers** and a **thermometer** (note that mercury thermometers are prohibited by airlines)

Insect-Borne Diseases SA's most significant insect-borne diseases are Ross River fever and Murray Valley encephalitis, both of which are carried by mosquitoes. Outbreaks are most likely to occur in January and February, but the chances of infection are slight. The best method of protecting yourself from mozzie bites is to wear light-coloured clothing, and smear (or spray) a repellent containing DEET on exposed skin.

WOMEN TRAVELLERS

South Australia is a reasonably safe place for women travellers. However, it's best to avoid walking alone late at night in any of the larger towns, especially near clubs and pubs. Sexual harassment is unfortunately still second nature to many Aussie males, particularly when they've had a few beers.

The Women's Information Service (☎ 8303 0590, fax 8303 0576, info@wif.sa.gov.au) in Station Arcade, 136 North Terrace, Adelaide, operates from 8 am to 6 pm on weekdays (9 am to 5 pm on Saturdays). It can give information, advice or referrals on just about anything of specific interest to women, including current issues, health, social venues, recreation and activities, and has a useful website at www.wis.sa.gov.au/. The service also offers free internet access for women.

For health matters, call the Women's Health Information & Counselling Line on ☎ 8267 5366, 1800 182 098 toll free (whs @peg.apc.org) between 9 am and 5 pm weekdays.

Check also Women's Organisations & Activities in the *Yellow Pages*.

MEN TRAVELLERS

The Men's Contact & Resource Centre (☎ 8212 0331, mcrc@camtech.net.au) is in the Torrens Building at 220 Victoria Square, Adelaide. Open from 9 am to 5 pm weekdays, it provides advice, information and referrals on a range of topics of interest to men, including health and current issues.

The Adelaide Men's Health Centre (☎ 8353 0765), at 314 Military Rd in Grange, provides confidential counselling as well as advice on and diagnosis of men's health matters.

GAY & LESBIAN TRAVELLERS

Attitudes in Adelaide towards homosexuality are fairly relaxed. For example, a recent survey on the question of same-sex marriages revealed overwhelming support among the general populace. However, as you'd probably expect, you have a much greater chance of meeting homophobes the further you travel into the country. Homosexual acts between consenting adults are legal in South Australia, and state legislation prohibits discrimination on the basis of sexual preference.

Gayline (☎ 8362 3223, 1800 182 233 toll free) in Adelaide operates between 7 and 10 pm daily (also 2 to 5 pm on weekends). It offers a counselling and referral service and can give information on social activities and other matters. It will also give you up-to-date information on gay-friendly doctors and other service providers. Visit the Gayline website at www.glcssa.org.au.

Publications

The fortnightly newspaper *Adelaide gt*, published by Adelaide Gay Times (☎ 8232 1544, fax 8232 1560, gt@adelaidegt.com.au) at 18 Freemasons Lane, is an excellent general reference for visiting gays and lesbians; apart from general articles, there's social news, reviews, venues, classifieds and community listings. Call them for details of outlets.

Also published by Adelaide Gay Times, the *Lesbian & Gay Adelaide Map*, which shows venues and services of interest in the city area.

Culture & Entertainment

Each year in Adelaide in late October-early November the SA Lesbian & Gay Cultural Festival brings three great weeks of performing arts, literary events, pool evenings, dance parties, cabaret and much more. Many international and interstate artists and performers are featured. For details contact ☎ 8231 8795.

See the Entertainment section in the Adelaide chapter for some of the city's more popular social venues.

Travel

The following Adelaide agencies specialise in gay and lesbian travel within SA and interstate: Parkside Travel (☎ 8274 1222, harveywrld@ezinet.com.au), at 70 Glen Osmond Rd, Parkside; and Sandford Travel (☎ 8267 3266, mlbyrnes@corpconn.com .au), at 139 Tynte St, North Adelaide.

SENIOR TRAVELLERS

Adelaide has several organisations that cater to the needs of older persons. Probably the best place to start your research is the Seniors Information Service (☎ 8232 1441, 1800 636 368 toll free, mmanning@ dove.mtx.au), at 45 Flinders St in Adelaide, or visit its website at www.seniors.asn.au. It can provide advice or referrals on a wide range of matters and issues affecting elderly travellers.

USEFUL ORGANISATIONS

South Australia has a swag of organisations formed for just about every conceivable purpose, and a handful of these are included here. You'll find further such groups listed under Organisations in the *Yellow Pages*.

National Parks Offices

The Environment Shop, (☎ 8204 1910, fax 8204 1919) at 77 Grenfell St in Adelaide, is the place to go for general information on parks and reserves throughout the state. It has a vast range of maps, national parks merchandise, brochures and publications.

Contact the appropriate National Parks and Wildlife Service (NPWS) regional office for anything relating to a particular park or group of parks. Regional office addresses are listed under Information at the start of the each regional chapter later in this book.

The NPWS publishes *Parks & Wildlife*, a quarterly newsletter with plenty of useful information. You can pick one up at the Environment Shop or NPWS offices throughout the state.

Park Passes If you're planning on visiting the state's conservation areas you should inquire about the various park passes on offer. These cover the cost of entry and camping at many of the most popular parks, and are valid for periods of four weeks to a year. The best value for short-term visitors is the Four Week Holiday Parks Pass, which costs $15 – though doesn't include Outback parks.

The Environment Shop has details on the passes and their retail outlets, and also sell them.

Access for Disabled Travellers

Many of South Australia's main tourist areas have wheelchair accessible features. Adelaide is regarded as Australia's most accessible city – it is compact with few gradients and has good crossovers at most intersections. There is plenty of accessible accommodation at the five-star end of the market: the Hilton has 25 rooms, the Hyatt 20 rooms and the Park Royal seven rooms. At Glenelg, the Stamford Plaza has nine rooms. Further information about accommodation is available from the Royal Automobile Association (☎ 8202 4500), 41 Hindmarsh Square, Adelaide.

Other information sources include: NICAN (☎ 02-6285 3713/TTY 1800 806 769 toll free, fax 02-6285 3714, email nican@spirit.com.au), PO Box 407, Curtin, ACT 2605, which has an Australia-wide directory providing information on accessible accommodation, sporting and recreational activities.

The Disability Information & Resource Centre (DIRC), 195 Gilles St in Adelaide (☎ (8223 7522/TTY 8223 7579, dirc@dircsa.org.au), has accessible toilet and shower facilities, and is the main information service in SA. Its staff can direct you to travel agencies experienced and knowledgeable about mobility restricted travel. DIRC also has an electronic bulletin board service called Common Ground (☎ 8223 2131, www.dircsa.org.au).

Easy Access Australia: A travel guide to Australia includes a chapter covering South Australia. It costs $24.85, including postage and handling, from PO Box 218 Kew 3101. DIRC has it in their library.

Accessible parking and toilets are available at Adelaide airport, but passengers board their flights via stairs from the tarmac. Both Ansett and Qantas board wheelchair passengers via a modified fork-lift arrangement that conveys them safely to the plane door.

From Melbourne you can take the V/Line train to Bendigo then change to an accessible V/Line bus for the journey to Adelaide. The *Indian Pacific* train runs from Sydney to Perth via Adelaide twice weekly with a wheelchair accessible carriage, but this is not suitable for all people. See the Train section in the Getting There & Away chapter.

The Adelaide City Council recognises disabled parking stickers issued in other states; there is an excellent supply of off-street car parking off North Terrace and Hindley St. The council's *City of Adelaide Access Map and Directory: a guide for people with a disability* is available from DIRC, SATC's Travel Centre at 1 King William St, and at the information booth in Rundle Mall.

Access Cabs (☎ 1300 360 940) provides wheelchair accessible taxis, while Avis and Hertz provide hand-controlled hire vehicles.

Bruce Cameron

Conservation Groups

The Conservation Council of SA (CCSA) (☎ 8223 5155, fax 8232 4872, general@ ccsa.asn.au) is at 120 Wakefield St in Adelaide. It's the major umbrella organisation for conservation groups in the state, with around 60 members. Major conservation issues in SA include water (such as overuse of ground-water resources and increasing salinity in the Murray River), clearance of native vegetation and the problems of land degradation. You can visit the CCSA website at www.ccsa.asn.au.

The Australian Conservation Foundation (☎ 8232 2566) and the Nature Conservation Society of SA (☎ 8223 6301) are in the same building.

Australian Trust for Conservation Volunteers (ATCV)

This nonpolitical, nonprofit group organises practical conservation projects (such as tree planting, walking track construction and flora and fauna surveys) for volunteers to take part in. Travellers are welcome. It's an excellent way to get involved with the conservation movement and, at the same time, visit some of the state's more interesting areas. Volunteers could find themselves working anywhere from the Nullarbor to Naracoorte, or Lake Eyre to Kangaroo Island.

ATCV projects are generally undertaken over a weekend or a week; all food, transport and accommodation is supplied in return for a small contribution (from $20 per day) to help cover costs. To find out more, contact the ATCV office at the State Tree Centre, Brookway Drive, Campbelltown, Adelaide 5000 (☎ 8207 8747, fax 8207 8755, atcvsa@camtech.net.au).

Willing Workers on Organic Farms (WWOOF)
WWOOF is well-established in Australia. The idea is that you do a few hours work each day on a farm in return for bed and board. All places have a minimum stay of two nights, but many will let you stay for months.

Becoming a WWOOFer is a great way to meet interesting people and to travel cheaply. There are about 60 WWOOF associates in SA, with most concerned to some extent with alternative lifestyles. You'll find them scattered as far afield as Kingscote on Kangaroo Island, Mannum on the Murray, Marree in the Outback, and Elliston on Eyre Peninsula.

To join, send $35/40 singles/couples (A$40/45 from overseas) with a photocopy of your passport data page to WWOOF, Buchan, Vic 3885. You can also phone or fax your credit card details to WWOOF on ☎ 03-5155 0218, fax 5155 0218, wwoof@net-tech.com.au. They'll send you a membership number and a booklet listing participating places all over Australia. The WWOOF website is at www.earthlink.com.au/wwoof.

National Trust & State Heritage
The National Trust's SA head office (☎ 8223 1655, fax 8232 2856) is at 452 Pulteney St, Adelaide. Annual membership costs $37/57 for individuals/families, along with an initial joining fee of $30. Membership entitles you to free entry to their properties, and a quarterly magazine.

The informative biannual *State Heritage Newsletter* is published by the State Heritage Branch of the Department of Environment, Heritage & Aboriginal Affairs. You can pick one up at the Environment Shop, 77 Grenfell St, Adelaide.

Other Information Centres
The Environment Shop has a swag of material on natural history, heritage, national parks and the environment generally. They also sell topographic maps.

Also at 77 Grenfell St, Information SA (☎ 8204 1900, fax 8204 1909) has material on natural history, outdoor activities, legislation and industries and environmental issues.

Both places are open weekdays from 9 am to 5 pm (from 9.30 am Wednesdays).

EMERGENCY
In the case of a life-threatening situation dial 000. This call is free from any phone and the operator will connect you with either the police, ambulance or fire brigade. To dial any of these services direct, check the inside front cover of any local telephone book.

Crisis Care (☎ 13 16 11, 008 131 611 toll free) offers an after-hours counselling and referral service for anyone experiencing a personal crisis, whether it be accommodation or a problem with your partner. The service operates weekdays from 4 pm to 9 am and 24 hours on weekends and public holidays.

For other crisis and personal counselling services (such as sexual assault, poisons information or alcohol and drug problems), check Community Help Reference near the front of the *White Pages* telephone directory.

DANGERS & ANNOYANCES
Animal Hazards
There are a few unique and sometimes dangerous creatures, although it's unlikely that you'll come across any of them – particularly

if you stick to the cities. Here's a run down just in case.

Snakes & Spiders The best-known danger in the bush, and the one that captures visitors' imaginations, is snakes. Although there are many venomous snakes there are few that are aggressive, and unless you have the misfortune to stand on one it's unlikely that you'll be bitten. Some, such as tiger snakes, will attack if alarmed; all will try to bite if they're provoked!

See the earlier section on Health for more details on snakes.

There are several dangerous spiders, with the main one being the female common redback spider. Be careful around buildings, where redbacks tend to congregate, and check outdoor furniture before using it. You should also look under the seat for spiders before sitting down in bush dunnies, particularly the long-drop variety. For redback bites apply ice and seek medical attention.

Insects For four to six months of the year – and longer in the hotter Outback areas – you'll have to cope with two banes of the Australian outdoors: flies and mosquitoes.

In Adelaide the flies are not too bad, despite what city folk might tell you. It's in the country that they start getting out of hand, and the further 'out' you get the worse the flies seem to be. In the north, where they can be particularly troublesome, they emerge with the warmer spring weather (late August) and last until winter. They love to crawl on your face and drink from your eyes (tears are a valuable source of protein), and in bad times they don't just come in twos and threes; they swarm!

If you're not used to flies (and who could be?) buy yourself a fly veil to cover your head before heading north – you can get them at the larger camping and outdoor shops in Adelaide. Failing that, you'll have to rely on either the 'Great Australian Wave' (ineffective and tiring) or repellents such as Aerogard and Rid.

Mossies too can be a problem in the warmer months, particularly near water

that's been laying about for a few days – it doesn't take long for them to breed. They can carry viruses such as the debilitating Ross River fever and the occasionally fatal Murray Valley encephalitis, so take precautions when in mosquito country. See the earlier Health section.

Bull-ants can give you a hard time in country areas. You'll know them by their aggressiveness and size (about 20mm), as well as by their bite – like a red-hot wire jabbed against the skin.

On the Road

Cows, kangaroos and other animals can be a real hazard on country roads, particularly in Outback areas where fences are few and far between. Animals lack road-sense, as do drivers who've been drinking alcohol. If you're going to get on the booze, give someone else the car keys.

See the Getting Around chapter for more on driving hazards.

Bushfires

Bushfires are an annual event in SA. Sometimes they're catastrophic, with many human deaths and the loss of millions of dollars worth of property and livestock. Don't be the mug who starts one! Always use the facilities provided – if there are any – and make sure your campfire is in an open space at least 4m from any flammable vegetation. Keep the fire small and provide a windbreak if necessary, and make sure it's out before you leave.

Campfires are banned in conservation areas during the Fire Danger Period (FDP), which varies from region to region but is usually from 1 November to 31 March (30 April in some places). There may be restrictions elsewhere during the FDP, so check with the Country Fire Service's 24-hour information hotline (☎ 1300 362 361) before you strike that match.

In hot, dry, windy weather, be extremely careful with any naked flame – no cigarette butts out of car windows, please. On a Total Fire Ban day (ring the hotline, listen to the radio or watch the billboards on country roads), it is forbidden to use even a camping stove in the open, let alone light a campfire. The locals will not be amused if they catch you breaking this particular law, which carries severe penalties, and they'll happily dob you in.

LEGAL MATTERS
If you have a legal problem of any kind you should start by contacting the Legal Services Commission (advisory service ☎ 1300 366 424) at 82 Wakefield St, Adelaide. They operate weekdays from 9 am to 5 pm and give free telephone and face-to-face advice on all legal matters, and will provide representation or referrals if warranted.

BUSINESS HOURS
Most shops open at 9 am and close at 5 or 5.30 pm weekdays, and either noon or 5 pm on Saturday. In most larger towns there is one late shopping night each week, when the doors stay open until 9 or 9.30 pm. In Adelaide, the larger stores are allowed to trade on Sundays in the central business district, but not out in the suburbs.

Of course there are many exceptions, and all sorts of places stay open late and all weekend – particularly milk bars, convenience stores, supermarkets and roadhouses.

Banks are generally open from 9.30 am to 4 pm Monday to Thursday, and until 5 pm on Friday. The notable exception to this is the Adelaide Bank, with most branches opening on Saturday morning.

Post offices are open between 9 am and 5 pm on weekdays (some open at 8.30 am and close at 5.30 pm), while Post Shops are also open on Saturday mornings.

PUBLIC HOLIDAYS & SPECIAL EVENTS
Public Holidays
The Christmas holiday season is part of the long summer school vacation. This period and Easter, are the times you are most likely to find long queues and that accommodation is booked out. There are three other shorter school holiday periods during the year (see When to Go earlier in this chapter).

On public holidays, particularly Christmas Day and Good Friday, you won't find very much open either in Adelaide or out in the country. The whole state all but shuts down on these two days.

Following is a list of public holidays in SA:

New Year's Day
 1 January
Australia Day
 26 January
Easter
 March/April – Good Friday, Easter Saturday to Monday
Anzac Day
 25 April
Adelaide Cup Day
 May – third Monday
Queen's Birthday
 June – second Monday
Labour Day
 October – first Monday
Proclamation Day
 December – last Tuesday
Christmas Day
 25 December
Boxing Day
 26 December

Special Events
The biennial three week Adelaide Festival of Arts is Australia's premier cultural celebration. See the Entertainment section in the Adelaide chapter for further details. Other notable events include music, food and wine festivals in the major wine-growing areas.

Migrants from many countries have added an international flavour to the SA cultural scene (eg the Kernewek Lowender – literally Cornish Festival – on Yorke Peninsula and the Oompah Fest in the Barossa). There are also typically Australian events – such as surf-lifesaving competitions during summer, and Outback race meetings, which draw together isolated town and station folk, and more than a few eccentric bush characters.

Each month there are many happenings in SA. SATC publishes a comprehensive annual calendar covering events throughout the state. Keith Martyn's *South Australian*

Almanac ($6) gives dates for a number of events not included in SATC's calendar, such as sheepdog trials, flower and garden shows, cat and dog shows, and country 'batchelor and spinster' (B&S) balls. Following is a brief overview of events.

January
Schutzenfest
This is a German festival held in Adelaide, with lots of feasting, music, folk dancing and fun.
Tunarama
Held in Port Lincoln, this festival celebrates the tuna industry.

February
Womadelaide
This 3 day world music and dance festival is held in Adelaide on odd-numbered years.
Compass Cup
Mt Compass on the Fleurieu Peninsula, hosts this event, at which you can watch cow-racing and cow turd throwing – dry ones, fortunately.
Oompah Fest
Held in Tanunda, this event celebrates German culture in the Barossa region.
Barossa Under the Stars
This is a weekend of live entertainment and night picnics, also held in the Barossa.

March
Adelaide Festival of Arts
The country's premier arts event, the Adelaide Festival of Arts is held in Adelaide on even-numbered years.
Adelaide Fringe
This event is held in conjunction with the arts festival, together presenting nearly three unforgettable weeks of music, theatre, opera, ballet and art exhibitions, as well as light relief and plenty of parties.
Australian Festival for Young People
Held in Adelaide and in country centres, the festival takes place in odd-numbered years.

April
Anzac Day
This national holiday commemorates the landing of Anzac troops at Gallipoli in 1915. Memorial marches by veterans of the various conflicts in which Australia has been involved are held all over the state on 25 April.
Celtic Folk Festival
Celebrating Celtic culture, this festival is held at Kapunda.

Barossa Vintage Festival
Held in odd-numbered years, the festival includes processions, maypole dancing, traditional dinners and much wine tasting.
Medieval Festival
Held at Carrick Hill in Adelaide, this celebration of Middle Ages culture includes jousting and other knightly activities, such as feasting

May
Kernewek Lowender
Held at Kadina, Moonta and Wallaroo, the festival celebrates the Cornish heritage of Yorke Peninsula's 'Copper Triangle'. There's plenty of Celtic fun and games, and you can try traditional Cornish pasties and beer.
Autumn Leaves Festival
This annual event is held in the Adelaide Hills.
Barossa Hot Air Balloon Regatta
Held in Nuriootpa, balloons fill the dawn and evening skies during the weekend-long regatta.
Clare Valley Gourmet Weekend
A festival of fine wine and food put on by local wineries and some of SA's top restaurants.

June
Country Music Festival & Awards
Held at Barmera, on the Murray, country music freaks will enjoy this festival.
Sea & Vines Festival
McLaren Vale, on the Fleurieu Peninsula, host this festival of seafood and fine wine.

July
Marananga Night of Music
This event is held in the Barossa each July.
Almond Blossom Festival
The centre of SA almond growing, Willunga celebrates its local industry.
Marree Australian Camel Cup
The Camel Cup is held at Marree, in the Outback, in odd-numbered years.

August
Barossa Classic Gourmet
A four day fest during which lovers of good food and wine may think they've found paradise.
Innamincka Picnic Races
This horse racing event takes place each August.
Apex Camel Cup
The cup takes place in Port Augusta annually.

September
CJ Dennis Festival
The festival is held annually in Auburn, birthplace of colonial author and poet CJ Dennis.

Royal Adelaide Show
This major agricultural show runs for seven days. There are also a number of country shows during the month, including Eudunda, Kimba, Orroroo and Wilmington.

October
Victor Harbor Folk Festival
Held annually in the Fleurieu Peninsula town.
Port Pirie Festival of Country Music
Held each October in Port Pirie.
Barossa International Music Festival
A popular festival that features jazz and classical music for over two weeks.
Oysterfest
This festival is held in Ceduna, on the state's west coast.
Continuous Picnic
Held around McLaren Vale, the picnic, as well as the Wine Bushing Festival, is a celebration of wine and food.
Glenelg Jazz Festival
Adelaide's beachside suburb celebrates jazz and food.

November
Clare Valley Spring Garden Festival
Private gardens around the valley are open to the public.
Christmas Pageant
Held annually in Adelaide this event is a fun time for kids, with a huge procession of floats featuring fairy tale characters and the like.

December
Carols by Candlelight
This event takes place in Adelaide's Elder Park.
Lobethal Christmas Lights
Lobethal, in the Adelaide Hills, hosts a spectacular display of decorative Christmas lights.

WORK
If you're in Australia on a 12 month Working Holiday Visa you can officially work for only three months for any one employer; working on a regular tourist visa is strictly *verboten*. Many travellers on tourist visas do find casual work in SA. However, the state has an unemployment rate hovering around 10% (much higher in many country centres), so it's becoming more difficult to find a job – legal or otherwise.

To receive wages legally in Australia you must be in possession of a Tax File Number (TFN), issued by the Australian Taxation Office (TFN inquiries ☎ 13 28 61). Forms are available from post offices. You'll need to show your passport, visa and one other ID document, such as a birth certificate or international driving permit.

With the demise of the Commonwealth Employment Service a number of private organisations now handle job placements in SA. Probably the largest is Employment National (☎ 13 34 44), which has country offices at Berri, Gawler, Port Pirie, Mt Gambier, Murray Bridge and Noarlunga – these all handle seasonal work. Employment National also has a number of offices in and around Adelaide

If you're after work you should also ask at hostels and pubs, and check the classified ads in the newspapers.

The main opportunities for casual work are in the fruit-growing and wine industries. But experience in tourism and hospitality helps in securing work in bars, restaurants, kitchens and other domestic areas.

Listed below are the main harvest times and crops in SA, and seasons and regions for other work.

Activity	Time	Region/s
Citrus picking	Jan-Dec	Riverland
Tourism	Jan-Feb	Coast
Hospitality	Jan-Feb	Coast
Fish processing	Jan-Sep	Port Lincoln, Ceduna
Grape picking	Jan-Apr	Riverland, Barossa, Clare, South-East
Peaches	Feb-Mar	Riverland
Apples/pears	Feb-Apr	Adelaide Hills
Vine pruning	Jun-Aug	Riverland, Barossa, Clare, South-East
Strawberries	Oct-Feb	Adelaide Hills
Stone fruits	Nov-Mar	Riverland

ACCOMMODATION
Unless otherwise stated, all rates given in this book are low season and for two people sharing.

South Australia has plenty of accommodation, particularly in Adelaide and popular holiday areas such as Yorke Peninsula and Kangaroo Island, and along the major highways. Apart from in remote areas, where you may have to rely on your own resources, you'll rarely have much trouble finding somewhere to lay your head – unless, of course, it's a peak holiday period and you haven't booked.

For the budget conscious there are youth hostels, backpacker hostels and caravan parks, while many hotels and holiday flats are also good value – the latter may not be so affordable in peak periods. There's a swag of motels right around the state, and B&Bs are common in some areas. However, neither of these are what you'd call cheap.

A typical town with 1000 people will have a basic motel and a hotel or two with rooms (shared facilities). There'll also be a caravan park, and perhaps a B&B or two. If the town is on a busy highway, or is a popular holiday destination, there will probably be a number of options.

The rates for four or five people in a room are always worth checking, as most hotels and motels have at least one 'family' room with five or six beds. On-site caravans and cabins have up to six beds and are very competitive for small groups.

There are a couple of free backpackers' newspapers and booklets available at hostels around the country, and these have fairly up-to-date listings of hostels.

For a more comprehensive reference, the RAA publishes the *Accommodation Guide* (members $5, nonmembers $10) which lists hotels, motels, guesthouses, B&Bs, holiday flats and farm stays around the country. They also put out *Tourist Park Accommodation* (members $4, nonmembers $8), which lists caravan parks, cabins and campgrounds. These references are updated every year so are fairly accurate.

Camping & Caravanning

South Australia has a large number of caravan parks and most times (apart from peak holiday periods) you'll find space available. If you want to get around on the cheap, an unpowered campsite usually costs around $9 to $12 (powered sites are a little more). Even better are the basic campgrounds you find in national parks; sites here are around $5 per vehicle.

Generally speaking, SA's caravan parks are well kept, conveniently located and excellent value. Most have on-site caravans, basic cabins with shared facilities and, to a lesser extent, cabins with en suite and cooking facilities. Although small, these cabins are generally less cramped than a caravan, and the price difference is not that great – typically around $28 for an on-site van and $35 for a basic cabin with cooking facilities; additional adults usually incur an extra fee of around $5.

In winter, if you're going to be using on-site vans and cabins on a regular basis, it's worth investing in a small heater of some sort as they're often unheated. As a rule you will have to provide your own sheets, blankets and (often) cooking utensils and so forth.

For many visitors, camping in the bush is one of the highlights of a visit to SA. In the Outback you won't even need a tent most of the time as it hardly ever rains. Swags are the way to go. A night spent around a campfire under the Southern Cross is unforgettable; the silence is immense, the stars magnificent.

Youth Hostels

The Youth Hostel Association (YHA) of Australia has 11 hostels scattered around the state. It belongs to the International Youth Hostel Federation (IYHF, also known as Hostelling International, HI), so if you're a member of the YHA in your own country, your membership entitles you to use South Australian hostels as well.

YHA hostels in SA provide basic accommodation, usually in small dormitories or bunk rooms. Except for a couple of small country hostels, all have cooking, toilet and bathroom facilities – these are very basic in some – and there's usually a communal area where you can sit and talk. Most have a maximum-stay period.

Charges in SA are rock bottom – between $8 and $14 a night, plus a $3 surcharge for nonmembers and a key deposit. Only the Adelaide hostel has a full-time manager.

To stay in these hostels you must have a regulation sheet sleeping bag or bed linen – for hygiene reasons a regular sleeping bag will not do. If you haven't got sheets they can be rented for a nominal sum at most hostels. YHA offices and some larger hostels sell the official YHA sheet bag.

The annually published *YHA Accommodation & Discount Guide*, available from all Australian and some overseas YHA offices, describes 130 YHA hostels around Australia. YHA members are eligible for discounts on around 800 products Australia-wide and these are listed in the guide.

The YHA office in Adelaide is at 38 Sturt St (☎ 8231 5583, fax 8231 4219, yhasa@ozemail.com.au). Here you'll find information on YHA hostels throughout the country, as well as a travel agency specialising in all aspects of budget travel. It is open between 9 am and 5 pm on weekdays. Take a look at the YHA's website at www.yha.org.au.

If you're not a member, think about joining. A senior membership costs $44 for the first year and $27 thereafter; it entitles you to discounts on such things as accommodation, travel insurance, bus passes and holiday packages. If you're an overseas resident joining in Australia, membership will cost $27.

Backpacker Hostels

In recent years the number of backpacker hostels has increased dramatically, particularly in Adelaide. The standard varies enormously: some are shabby and gloomy, with cramped facilities, while others are bright and cheerful. You'll find old houses and hotels – even a bakery and factory – that have been converted to backpacker hostels, while others have been purpose-built. Generally the standard is better in country areas, although the city hostels have tended to lift their game in recent times.

Hostel owners sometimes have backpackers running these places, in which case it's usually not too long before standards start to slip; the best places are invariably those where the owner is also manager. If you hear of any that promote themselves as 'party' hostels, don't go there if you want a quiet time.

The proliferation of city hostels has also brought about intense competition, hence the hostel staff touting for custom at Adelaide's central bus station. Many now have inducements, such as the first night's accommodation or breakfast free, and virtually all have courtesy transport.

Prices in the city start at around $11 – and you should remember that what you pay for is usually what you get. These days many hostels also have private single and double or twin rooms as well as bunk dorms.

One practice that many people find objectionable – in independent hostels only, since it never happens in YHAs – is the 'vetting' of Australians and sometimes New Zealanders, who may be asked to provide a passport or double ID which they may not carry. Most city hostels ask for some ID – usually a passport – but this can also be used as a way of keeping unwanted customers out.

If you're an Aussie and encounter this kind of reception, the best you can do is persuade the desk people that you're genuinely travelling the country, and aren't just looking for a cheap place to crash for a while. It may help if you produce a YHA or VIP card.

You can write to VIP Backpackers Resorts of Australia (☎ 07-3395 6111, fax 3395 6222, backpack@backpackers.com.au) at PO Box 600, Cannon Hill Qld 4170 to apply for membership. For $25 you'll receive a discount card (valid for 12 months) and a list of participating hostels – 134 in Australia and many more worldwide. Membership entitles you to a $1 discount on a night's accommodation, and 10% discounts on other services, such as bus passes and backpacker tours. You can also join at any participating hostel, Greyhound Pioneer bus terminals and the larger agencies dealing in backpacker travel.

YHA and VIP cards also come in handy at the few hotels and motels in the country that offer backpacker accommodation. In lieu of a passport, the managers will usually accept them as evidence that you really are a backpacker.

University Accommodation

Although it is students who get first option on these, nonstudents can also stay at a couple of Adelaide's university colleges during uni vacations. These places are reasonably cheap and comfortable and provide an opportunity for you to meet people. For details, see the Places to Stay section in the Adelaide chapter.

B&Bs

This is the fastest growing segment of the accommodation market, with new places opening all the time. Most B&Bs are 'self-catering' – that is, the breakfast ingredients are provided, and you cook them yourself. It's becoming increasingly difficult to find B&Bs under $80 for doubles anywhere near Adelaide.

The state network of B&Bs includes restored miners' cottages, converted stables, renovated guesthouses, upmarket country homes, shearers' quarters, romantic escapes and simple bedrooms in family homes. Some are listed in this book, otherwise check with local tourist offices.

SATC publishes a booklet detailing B&Bs around the state.

Hotels

Most of SA's numerous public hotels – even the smallest towns have one – are older places dating from at least early in the 20th century. A large proportion were built during the 1870s and 1880s, while some date back to the 1840s.

The older pubs tend to be very photogenic with great character; they're typically double storey, with solid stone walls and wide balconies with lots of iron lacework. Many were built during economic 'boom' times. As a result they're often among the largest and most extravagant buildings in town.

Many hotels have been tastefully renovated with the profits generated by poker machines; others are on the weary side, with sagging mattresses, smelly carpets and peeling wallpaper. In summer you should ask whether the rooms have ceiling fans or air-con (they can be a must in the hotter parts), and in winter ask whether there's wall heating or electric blankets. Otherwise check that there are enough woollen blankets. It's a good idea to request a room that's not above the bar or facing the street, particularly on Friday and Saturday nights.

If you don't mind the shared facilities, most hotels are great value. As well as atmosphere, you can usually get a plain but substantial meal for a good price, and there's usually a few local characters to meet in the bar. Rooms in the 'better' country pubs cost around $25/35 for singles/doubles including a light breakfast (more for rooms with en suites), but you can often find a single room for $20 or less.

Relatively few pubs have a separate reception area. What you do is march into the front bar or lounge and ask the bar staff if they have any rooms available.

Motels, Serviced Apartments & Holiday Flats

If you've got transport and want a more modern place with your own bathroom and other facilities, then you're moving into the motel bracket. There are stacks of motels in SA, but they're usually away from town centres unless a pub has decided to tack units on. With the motels, unlike hotels, singles are generally not much cheaper than doubles. If you're by yourself you'll seldom find a motel room for less than $40. In fact, finding anything much cheaper than $50/55 for singles/doubles is often a challenge, particularly in holiday towns.

Serviced apartments and holiday flats are much the same thing and bear some resemblance to motels. Basically, holiday flats are found in holiday areas, serviced apartments in Adelaide. A holiday flat is much like a motel room but usually has a kitchen.

Holiday flats are not serviced like motels – you don't get your bed made and the cups washed out. In some holiday flats you have to provide your own sheets and bedding, while others are fully equipped. Most motels in SA provide at least tea and coffee-making facilities and a small fridge; a holiday flat will have a stove, larger fridge, cooking utensils, crockery and so on.

The best way to find out about holiday flats in the country is to ring around the local real estate agents. To find an apartment or holiday flat in Adelaide, check at SATC or look in the *Yellow Pages* and the classified ads in the *Advertiser*.

Farm Stays

For something really different you can stay on a farm (known as 'stations' in the Outback) and get some first-hand experience of country living. With commodity prices the way they are, mountainous wool stockpiles and a general rural crisis, tourism offers the hope of at least some income for farmers.

Farm accommodation varies from renovated shearers' quarters to old homesteads to modern cabins. Often you'll eat with the owners, who may have activities arranged for you – or you may be left entirely to your own devices. You can usually stay in shearers' quarters for around $15 per person, although a minimum charge may apply.

SATC has a brochure listing a number of farm stays.

Houseboats

You can cruise the Murray River on a fully self-contained houseboat, with standards ranging from budget to luxury. On average, the weekly hire of a two-berth/four-berth houseboat will set you back around $485/540 in winter and $580/650 in peak periods.

The comprehensive booklet *SA Hire Houseboats*, put out by the Houseboat Hirers Association in Adelaide and available from SATC, has many listings and will give you the drum on what to expect. You can contact the association on ☎ 8395 0999, fax 8263 5373, hbc@kern.com.au,

or take a look at its website at www .southaustralia.com/houseboats.

Other Accommodation

There are plenty of places where you can camp for free, such as roadside rest areas where overnight camping is permitted. In the Outback there are tens of thousands of square kilometres where nobody is going to complain if you decide to put up a tent.

If you want to stay longer in Adelaide, the first place to look for a shared flat or a room is the classified ad section of the *Advertiser*.

FOOD

Tucker can be one of the real highlights of SA; Adelaide alone has around 700 restaurants, and even in the Outback you'll find eateries serving up a style of gourmet food that was unthinkable just a few years ago.

Immigration has resulted in a very exciting food scene in SA. The Greeks, Yugoslavs, Italians, Lebanese and many others who came to Australia from the late 1940s through to the 1960s brought with them, thank God, their food. More recent arrivals include the Vietnamese, who have added another facet to Adelaide's food scene.

Today you can have excellent Greek moussaka (and a bottle of retsina to wash it down), delicious Italian saltimbocca and pasta, or good, heavy German dumplings. You can perfume the air with garlic after stumbling out of a French bistro, or try all sorts of Middle Eastern and Arab treats. The Chinese have been sweet and souring since the gold-rush days, while more recently Indian, Thai and Malaysian restaurants have added their distinctive cuisines.

Australian Food

Although there is no real definition of what constitutes Australian cuisine, there is certainly some excellent local food to try. For a start there's the great Australian meat pie. Most small bakeries do a really good job on this classic dish, but the standard, factory-produced item tends to be an awful concoction of anonymous meat and dark gravy in a soggy pastry case. Avoid them! In Adelaide and a few country places you can really delve into local culture with a 'pie floater' (a meat pie with tomato sauce floating in thick, green pea soup). It sounds horrible and doesn't look so hot either, but tastes great.

The really good news about South Australian tucker is the fine ingredients. Nearly everything is grown or caught right here, so you're not eating food that's been shipped halfway around the world. Everybody knows about our wonderful steaks ('This is cattle country, so eat beef you bastards', declare the farmers' bumper stickers).

There's also a superb range of seafood: fish such as tommy-ruff, groper and the esteemed King George whiting, or succulent lobsters and home-grown oysters. Fish and chips is a popular take-away meal, although many cooks are heavy-handed with the salt and grease; if you don't want salt, say so.

Vegetarians get a fair go these days; there are some excellent vegetarian restaurants in Adelaide, while in the country you'll find that the better lunch shops usually have vegetarian dishes.

Places to Eat

If you want something familiar and utterly predictable you'll find McDonald's, KFC, Pizza Hut and all the other well-known names looking no different than they do anywhere else in the world. On the other hand, there are many fine restaurants offering most cuisines.

For a substantial lunch and dinner the best value meal is usually found in the pubs, particularly now that most have poker machines – there is often cut-throat competition to get customers through the door. Look for 'counter meals', so called because they used to be eaten at the counter in the front bar; they still are, but now you can get them in the lounge bars as well. Many pubs have fancy, almost restaurant-like dining rooms, where meals are a little more expensive than in the front bar – you pay more for the atmosphere, as the food comes out of the same kitchen.

Pub meals are usually simple (schnitzels, chicken and grills are perennial) but well-

prepared and substantial. You'll normally pay $6 to $10 for a hearty feed, although you can see them advertised for as little as $3 where competition is particularly fierce. If your conscience gets the better of you, you can always donate a few extra dollars through the pokies.

Counter meals are usually served as counter lunches or counter teas, the latter a hangover from the old northern English terminology where 'tea' meant the evening meal. In fact, Crow-eaters tend to refer to lunch as 'dinner' and dinner as 'tea'. One catch with pub meals is that they usually operate fairly strict hours; 'tea time' is typically just 6 to 7.30 or 8 pm.

Smoking Laws

In SA it's against the law to smoke in any enclosed public dining area, including hotel dining rooms – apparently you can smoke in bars provided meals aren't being consumed at that time. The law is strictly enforced in Adelaide and penalties are severe. If you're desperate you can nip outside and light up, although this may not be a pleasant option on a cold, wet, winter's night. To find out more – or complain or offer congratulations – ring ☎ 1300 363 703.

DRINKS
Beer

South Australians are rightly proud of their excellent beers; as enthusiasts will tell you, they make the stuff that comes out of Sydney and Melbourne taste like by-product. Mind you, any Australian beer tastes awful at room temperature on a warm day – drink it chilled. Beer is commonly called 'piss', and if you've had too much of it then you're 'pissed'.

Adelaide has two excellent large breweries: Coopers and SA Brewing. Coopers is the only Australian brewery still wholly owned by Australians; the Cooper family established the business in 1862 and has owned it ever since. It has a range of light and full-strength ales and beers for the connoisseur that have won many awards.

Coopers also produces an excellent stout; don't despair if you're desperate for a Guinness, as several pubs in Adelaide have it on tap. Some locals drink a mixture of stout and lemonade (called portagaff), or stout and beer (called black-and-tan).

A word of warning to visitors: local beer often has a higher alcohol content than British or American beers. Standard beers contain around 5% alcohol, while 'light' beers have between 2% and 3.5%.

And another warning: those who drive under the influence of alcohol and get caught lose their licence. The maximum permissible blood-alcohol level for drivers in SA is 0.05%.

All around Australia, the containers that beer comes in, and the receptacles you drink it from, are called by different names. In SA, you usually buy beer from the bottle shop in 'echoes' or 'stubbies' (375ml bottles); beer is served across the counter in glasses of various sizes – you ask for a 'butcher' (200ml glass), 'schooner' (285ml), 'pint' (425ml) or 'mug' (570ml). As well, you might be asked if you want

'super', 'heavy' or 'draught' (that's full-strength beer) or 'light' (low-alcohol beer).

Wine
If you don't fancy the local beer, try the wine. Overseas experts now realise just how good SA's wines can be, and exporting them has grown into a multimillion dollar industry. In fact, it's one of the few really bright lights in a generally gloomy economic climate. Furthermore, local wines are relatively cheap. You can still pick up a decent bottle of red or white from a liquor outlet for around $10, and if you aren't fussy you can do a fair bit better than that.

All over SA you'll find restaurants advertising that they're BYO. The initials stand for 'Bring Your Own' – it means that they're not licensed to serve alcohol, but you are permitted to bring your own with you. Most BYO restaurants charge a small 'corkage' fee if you do take your own.

An even more economical way of drinking wine is to do it free at the wineries; most have tasting rooms where you walk straight in and say what you'd like to try. However, the servings are generally tiny (particularly if it's a boutique winery) and it's expected that you will buy something if, for example, you ask to taste every chardonnay the vineyard has ever produced.

ENTERTAINMENT
Discos & Nightclubs
There's no shortage of these either, although they're confined to Adelaide and a handful of the larger towns. Clubs range from the exclusive 'members only' variety to barn-sized discos where anyone who wants to spend the money is welcomed with open arms. Admission charges for most range up to $10.

Some places have certain dress codes, which are generally left to the discretion of the people at the door – if they don't like the look of you, bad luck. The more upmarket nightclubs attract an older, more sophisticated and affluent crowd, so they tend to have stricter dress codes, smarter decor and higher prices.

Many city and suburban pubs have discos and/or live music. These are often great places for catching live bands, which can be either well-known names or up-and-coming performers trying to make a name for themselves. Most of Australia's popular bands started out on the pub circuit in one city or another.

Cinema
Adelaide has commercial cinema chains, such as Hoyts and Greater Union, and you'll find a cinema in most larger country towns. In Adelaide, the cinema centres have anything from two to 30 screens in the one complex. Admission to a new-release mainstream film usually costs around $12 ($8 for children under 15) – on 'specials' nights you can usually get in for around $7.

There are two or three drive-in cinemas out in Adelaide's suburbs, and a couple in the country as well.

Adelaide also has several art-house and independent cinemas. They offer films that are not generally made for mass consumption, as well as re-runs of classic and cult movies.

Gambling
South Australians love a bet, so much so that just about every decent-sized town boasts either a horse-racing track, a Totalisator Agency Board (TAB) betting office or a licensed bookmaker. In fact, Adelaide must be one of the few cities in the world to have a public holiday for horse racing (Adelaide Cup Day). As well, the whole state more-or-less grinds to a standstill while the Melbourne Cup is being run.

Legal on and off-course betting is available for horse racing, harness racing (the trots), greyhound racing, foot racing and various sporting events. Gambling in the country is usually centred around the pubs; PubTabs (pubs acting as TAB betting offices) have big-screen Sky-TV, which allows you to drown your sorrows while watching your cash go down the drain.

Adelaide has a large casino, and poker machines are just about everywhere in pubs

and clubs throughout the state. As well, there are always lotteries and 'instant money games' on the go – you can buy tickets at most newsagents as well as many shops and hotels.

SPECTATOR SPORTS
There are many sports to watch other than those listed below, such as surfing, netball, rugby (both codes), judo, athletics and hockey. If you have a special interest in any sport, contact the organising body and they'll tell you all you want to know – there's a long list of them under Organisations – Sporting in the *Yellow Pages*.

Australian Rules Football
The most popular spectator sport by far is Australian rules football, which is played from April to October.

A fast, tactical and physical game featuring spectacular high-marking and bone-crushing tackles, Aussie rules is unique – only Gaelic football is anything like it. Although there are some enthusiastic punch-ups on the field, the crowds, in contrast, are noisy but law-abiding (a nice surprise for visiting British soccer fans).

SA is a stronghold of Aussie rules, with two local teams – the Adelaide Crows and Port Adelaide – in the national Australian Football League (the AFL). To the huge delight of Crow-eaters everywhere, the Crows defeated Victorian teams to win the AFL premierships in 1997 and 1998.

Soccer
Soccer is very much a poor cousin: it's widely played on an amateur basis but the national league is only semiprofessional and attracts only a relatively small following. However, it's slowly gaining in popularity. At the local level there are teams representing a range of ethnic origins.

Cricket
During the other (non-football) half of the year there is cricket and tennis. Both interstate and international cricket games are played on the Adelaide Oval – see Botanic

Gardens & Other Parks in the Adelaide chapter.

Tennis
Tennis is very popular; most towns have courts and there are active clubs all over the place. Every summer the Memorial Drive Tennis Club in Adelaide hosts the SA Men's Open and the SA Country Carnival.

Basketball
Basketball is growing in popularity, particularly since SA has both a men's team and a women's team in the national league (the NBL). The importation of US talent has done wonders for the game locally; both teams were national champions in 1998.

Cycling
The inaugural six day Tour Down Under, an international teams race in the style of the Tour de France, was held in Adelaide and country areas in January 1999. It was such an overwhelming success that the organisers plan to make it an annual event.

SHOPPING
There are lots of things *not* to buy – like plastic boomerangs, Mary MacKillop dolls and all the other terrible things that fill the tackier souvenir shops. Most of these 'goods' come from Taiwan or Korea anyway! Before buying an Australian souvenir, turn it over to check that it was actually made here.

Aboriginal Art
Top of the list for any real Australian purchase would have to be Aboriginal art.

In recent decades, and partly in response to tourism, Aboriginal art has flourished and the media for recording traditions and stories has changed. Many paintings are now done in acrylic on canvas or linen, and other items produced for sale are traditional wooden tools and weapons, carved wooden animals, woven baskets and necklaces. Didgeridoos (tubular wooden wind instruments from 1 to 2m long) come from the Top End of the NT, but you can find them for sale at many places around SA.

The prices being asked for the best paintings – which are mainly from the NT and form part of the international art market – are way out of reach for the average traveller. However, there are plenty of cheaper but still excellent mementos such as prints, small carvings and beautiful screen-printed T-shirts produced by Aboriginal craft co-operatives – there are copies, so it's worth shopping around and paying a few dollars more for the real thing.

One of the best places in the state to buy Aboriginal arts and crafts is Tandanya, in Adelaide. You'll find local outlets in a few remote places such as Coober Pedy, Marree and Yalata.

Australiana
The term 'Australiana' is a euphemism for souvenirs – the things visitors typically buy as gifts for all the folk back home. They are supposedly representative of Australia and its culture, although many are extremely dubious.

The seeds of many SA native plants are for sale, but check that you'll be allowed to take them home. Sturt's desert pea (the state's floral emblem) makes a great souvenir in the garden – provided you live somewhere hot and dry.

Another favourite is bush tucker, such as quandong jam and canned witchetty grubs. Some places are even experimenting with putting emu and kangaroo into tins.

Opals
The opal is Australia's national gemstone, and opal jewellery is a popular souvenir. Most of the state's production comes from Coober Pedy, and this is a good place to buy – though it's reported that you can get better deals in Andamooka, which doesn't have so many tourists. Don't despair if you're not going to visit either place, as there are several good outlets in Adelaide.

When selecting an opal it's very much a case of beauty being in the eye of the beholder. A flawless opal with brilliant colour in an interesting pattern may be out of your price range, but if you shop around you should be able to pick up something that's affordable as well as appealing. Always ask the shop assistant for advice and get them to explain anything you're not sure of. A reputable shop will give you a written guarantee on more expensive purchases.

Finally, overseas visitors don't have to pay the 30% sales tax on opal. If anyone is offering discounts of, say, 50%, it's a good sign that their prices are way too high.

See the boxed text 'Colour in Opal' in the Outback chapter for more on opal.

Outdoor Activities

With its dry temperate climate, 3700km coastline, rugged hills and wide open spaces, SA is a great place to indulge in outdoor activities. If you want to do things like horse or camel riding, abseiling, caving, bushwalking, cycle touring, surfing, fishing, scuba diving, canoeing, windsurfing and skydiving, there are many opportunities available.

The Office of Recreation & Sport (☎ 8416 6677, fax 8416 6724, leak.bronte@ saugov.sa.gov.au), at 27 Valetta Rd in Keswick, Adelaide, has an extensive recreation directory. The website is at www .recsport.sa.gov.au.

There's also State Association House (☎ 8410 1052, fax 8211 7115), at 1 Sturt St in the centre of Adelaide. It houses a number of sporting and outdoor organisations, including Bicycle SA, Bushwalking Leadership SA and Canoe SA Education, and is the primary contact point for other such organisations.

Other places to check are the South Australia Tourism Commission (SATC), the *Yellow Pages* telephone book, and the outdoors shops on Rundle St, in Adelaide.

Bushwalking

In SA, tramping, trekking and hiking are called bushwalking. Throughout the state there are well over 3000km of designated walking trails, of which the Heysen Trail is the longest and best known. As well there are 4WD tracks to walk on, and plenty of places with no tracks at all apart from cattle, sheep and kangaroo pads. You don't have to be an expert, or incredibly fit, as there are a swag of opportunities for the inexperienced bushwalker or for those with only moderate fitness.

Note that many trails, particularly in forested areas, are closed during the Fire Danger Period or on Total Fire Ban days.

Information

Every conservation area in SA has an office where you can seek information on walks. The rangers or foresters will be able to advise you on what's available – telephone numbers are listed under Information in the relevant regional chapters.

The following organisations can also help:

Federation of SA Walking Clubs (☎ 8410 1470), State Association House, 1 Sturt St, Adelaide
Bushwalking Leadership SA (☎ 8410 1414), State Association House, 1 Sturt St, Adelaide
Friends of the Heysen Trail & Other Walking Trails (☎ 8212 6299, fax 8211 8041), 10 Pitt St, Adelaide

Books & Brochures Most of the following guides should be used in conjunction with a large-scale topographical map. As you can imagine, Lonely Planet's *Bushwalking in Australia*, which includes the Mt Remarkable and Wilpena Pound areas, has relatively good maps.

Regional guides include the excellent *Explore the Barossa* and *Explore the Flinders Ranges*, both by the Royal Geographic Society of SA (RGSSA), which describe a number of bushwalks in those areas. Adrian Heard's *Walking Guide to the North Flinders Ranges* and the Conservation Council of SA's *Flinders Ranges Walks* are useful but not extensive in their coverage.

For the Adelaide area there's *50 Real Bushwalks Around Adelaide* by George Driscoll, *Walks with Nature (20 Nature Walks in the Mount Lofty Ranges)* by the Nature Conservation Society of SA, and *20 Bushwalks in the Adelaide Hills* by Thelma Anderson.

Books specifically on the Heysen Trail are *The Heysen Trail: Encounter Bay to the Barossa Valley* and *The Heysen Trail: Parachilna to Hawker*, both edited by Terry Lavender and others.

Information SA and the Environment Shop, both at 77 Grenfell St in the city, have a large selection of publications describing walks throughout the state. The Royal Automobile Association (RAA) at 41 Hindmarsh Square also has bushwalking guidebooks.

Maps With the exception of the northern Flinders Ranges, the more popular bushwalking areas have been mapped at 1:50,000 or 1:100,000. Although the maps are generally very good, remember that they were all out of date before they were printed! This means you should never take them too literally when it comes to water supplies in remote areas – that permanent waterhole may have silted up, or the tank rusted away.

Flinders Camping, the Scout Outdoor Centre and Paddy Pallin – all outdoors shops on Rundle St in Adelaide – as well as the Environment Shop and Friends of the Heysen Trail, sell maps and guides to the Heysen Trail, and have a range of free brochures. See the Planning section in the Facts for the Visitor chapter for details of major map outlets.

Outside Adelaide, ask at National Parks & Wildlife Service (NPWS) offices: if they don't sell maps they should know who does, although it may be a bit late if you haven't organised yourself by then.

Volunteer Programs
Friends of the Heysen Trail have a program if you want to spend some time doing volunteer work, such as walking track maintenance and development.

Guided Walks
A number of operators in and around Adelaide offer guided bushwalks. They include:

Women of the Wilderness (☎ 8227 0155, ywca@ dove.net.au), at the YWCA, 17 Hutt St, runs outdoor courses and activities for women, such as bushwalking, canoeing and surfing.
Ecotrek (☎ 8383 7198, ecotrek@ozemail .com.au), at Dashwood Gully Rd, Kangarilla, has been around a long time, offering walks into the northern Flinders Ranges, Kangaroo Island and other areas.

The Scout Outdoor Centre (☎ 8223 5544, snowgum@eastend.com.au), at 192 Rundle St, leads day and weekend walks, mainly close to Adelaide.
Friends of the Heysen Trail (☎ 8212 6299, fax 8211 8041), at 10 Pitt St, Adelaide, do guided walks on alternate Sundays.
Nature Trek (☎ 8387 3588, naturetrek@ dove.net.au), at Vaucluse Drive, Happy Valley, takes day walks in the Adelaide Hills and Deep Creek Conservation Park (near Victor Harbor). It also does longer trips further afield, including walks in the Flinders Ranges.

Local operators on Kangaroo Island and in the South-East also offer guided walks (see Organised Tours in the chapters on these regions).

Preparation
If you want to go on longer walks by yourself in SA you'll often have to rely on your own resources. Many areas are sparsely populated and the lack of facilities away from settled areas makes preparation the key to an enjoyable walk.

Winter is the best time for walking in the north, although you can never count on the weather being fine; a few years back it snowed on St Mary Peak, and maximums of around 10°C with light rain and a bitter wind are sometimes experienced. In the south, autumn and spring are more popular because weather conditions are usually less extreme.

Don't forget that spring is very changeable, particularly in the south; the day can start off sunny, but end with rain and frigid blasts from the South Pole. Summer is generally too hot for either safe or enjoyable walking in most parts of SA.

Always carry windproof clothing in the cooler months, as many southern ridges are very exposed and often the vegetation is no higher than your ankles. In fact, hypothermia (overcooling of the body) can be a real health risk during winter, particularly if you're poorly prepared and happen to get lost.

Finally, always ask a local expert for advice on safety and preparation, and heed their recommendations.

Bushwalking Safety

Bushwalking safety is basically commonsense and includes the following rules:

- Know what to expect and don't do the walk if you think it might be outside your limitations; always get expert advice if you're not sure.
- *Always* let someone responsible know your plans (times, route and so on); this should be a person (your mother, for example) who's sure to raise the alarm if you don't show up on time. Never simply drive off after your walk without telling the person looking out for you that you've returned.
- Walk with at least one other person, preferably two. It's nice to have company, and if there's a problem someone can go for help.
- To be on the safe side, carry extra water in army canteens (not flimsy plastic bottles) even on short walks. Allow four litres per person per day in warm weather.
- To avoid dehydration, drink constantly in warm weather. Soft drinks may taste good, but they won't quench your thirst and are potentially dangerous because they contribute to water loss from the body. Have a couple of big drinks before setting out, then have more at regular intervals – don't wait until you start feeling thirsty.
- Always cover up against the sun. Wear a wide-brimmed hat and loose-fitting, close-weave cotton clothing that gives maximum skin protection; smear 15+ broad-spectrum sunscreen on exposed skin. The more comfortable you are, the less fluids you'll lose through sweating, and the less likely you'll be to suffer heat exhaustion or worse. This is not to say you can't enjoy bushwalking in summer; you can, but you have to be sensible. Confine your walking to early in the morning and late in the day, when it's relatively cool, and rest up in the swimming pool (or shade) while it's hot.
- Wear long trousers and closed footwear in warm weather – poisonous snakes are common in some places.
- Be prepared for unseasonable cold weather.
- Never light wood fires in the open during the fire danger period; if you light one at other times (assuming you're allowed to) keep it small to conserve firewood for others. Make sure it's dead when you've finished with it.
- *Never* wander away from tracks or other obvious features unless you know you can find your way back. If you find yourself geographically challenged (ie lost), don't panic. If you can't retrace your steps, sit quietly and wait for someone to come – which will happen when you're reported missing. It may help if you're carrying a mirror so you can signal any aerial searchers.
- Finally, carry a first-aid kit and know how to use it.

Denis O'Byrne

THE HEYSEN TRAIL

Completed in 1992, the 1200km Heysen Trail starts at Cape Jervis, south of Adelaide, winds along the ridgetops of the Mt Lofty and Flinders ranges finishing in Parachilna Gorge north of Wilpena Pound. It was named after the famous SA landscape artist Hans Heysen (see the boxed text on Heysen in the Facts about South Australia chapter).

The trail features some of the state's major scenic and historical highlights, and traverses two of its finest conservation areas: the Mt Remarkable and Flinders Ranges national parks.

From Cape Jervis the trail heads east along the coast, where you'll pass lookout points for seasonal sightings of southern right whales. The trail then winds north through the often steep and forested Mt Lofty Ranges. In the Barossa Valley you can relax at a winery or two before setting off for the old copper-heritage towns of Kapunda and Burra. Next you'll come to rugged Mt Remarkable and Mt Brown, with the ramparts of Wilpena Pound in sight. You will pass through the pound en route to beautiful Aroona Valley, after which you're only a day or two from a celebratory beer in the Blinman or Parachilna pubs.

Although the Heysen Trail is designed as a long-distance route, the many access points along the way make it ideal for half and full day walks. You'll find details of transport services in later chapters.

The trail varies from narrow pads to formed roads and, for the most part, is clearly marked with orange direction arrows and red markers. Apart from a handful of very steep or rough areas the going is seldom difficult for fit and experienced walkers.

Due to fire restrictions, the trail is generally closed each year from November to April inclusive.

As much of the trail crosses private property, the following 'country code' has been devised to keep walkers on-side with the landholders (obviously this code applies to all other walks, too):

- Leave gates as you find them (either shut or open).
- Do not pollute or otherwise abuse water supplies; bury toilet waste at least 50m from watercourses.
- Do not disturb livestock or set up camp near stock-watering points – keep dogs on leads at all times.
- Protect fences by climbing the stiles provided.
- Take your rubbish home or dispose of it at an authorised dumping place.
- Observe fire restrictions.
- Regularly check your clothing for the seeds of noxious plants; if you find any, put them in a plastic bag and hand them in to a NPWS or district council office.
- Stay on the track when crossing private property.

There are quite a few places to stay along the trail, including campgrounds, YHA hostels, huts and shearers' quarters, although they become fewer north of Quorn. Most of the pubs and caravan parks en route will be covered later in the book. While there are plenty of bush campsites, a permit is required to camp in conservation areas and in some state forests. You must have the landholder's permission to camp on private property.

Each of the trail's 15 sections is described by its own foldout map-guide ($6.50), which includes an excellent 1:50,000 topographic strip map. However, most of the information is repetitive and deficient in terms of providing distances and walking conditions. You can purchase these maps in advance of your visit by writing to the Office for Recreation & Sport (☎ 8416 6677, fax 8416 6724, leak.bronte@saugov.sa.gov.au) at PO Box 219, Brooklyn Park, 5032.

The various sections have been summarised to give a rough idea of what to expect; all distances are an indication only.

Cape Jervis to Newland Hill (60km)

Starting at Cape Jervis, the trail follows the rugged coastline eastwards around to Newland Head, at about 50km, where it turns inland.

Although conditions are often far from easy, there are some rewarding highlights, including superb coastal views, sandy beaches and beautiful forest. A spectacular waterfall on Deep Creek, in Deep Creek Conservation Park, runs all year round, and is the only reliable water in this section of the trail. There's also a good chance of seeing southern right whales in winter and early spring.

Newland Hill is beside a sealed road about 6km south-west of Victor Harbor.

Conditions There are many tough stretches of dense forest, spiky scrub, long

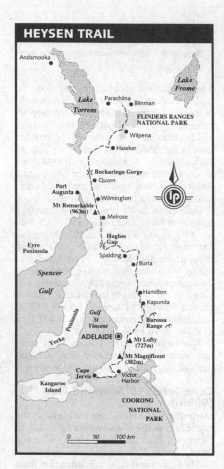

HEYSEN TRAIL

Andamooka
Lake Frome
Lake Torrens
Parachilna • Blinman
FLINDERS RANGES NATIONAL PARK
• Wilpena
• Hawker
) Buckaringa Gorge
• Quorn
Port Augusta •
• Wilmington
Mt Remarkable (963m) •
• Melrose
Eyre Peninsula
Hughes Gap
Spalding •
• Burra
Spencer
Gulf
• Hamilton
• Kapunda
Gulf St Vincent
Barossa Range
ADELAIDE ◎
Mt Lofty (727m)
Yorke Peninsula
Mt Magnificent (382m)
Cape Jervis
Victor Harbor
Kangaroo Island
COORONG NATIONAL PARK

0   50   100 km

Getting There & Away A daily bus service runs from Adelaide to Cape Jervis ($14). Good roads lead in to Deep Creek Conservation Park and Waitpinga Beach, and you can get a taxi from Victor Harbor to Newland Hill. Otherwise, access points are limited.

Newland Hill to Mt Magnificent (65km)

This section meanders through a mix of native forest and farmland, with stunning views from high points such as Mt Cone and Mt Magnificent. Near the former (a bald and barren place) you'll get a panoramic view that includes the Bluff at Victor Harbor and Mt Lofty near Adelaide. En route you'll pass through the little towns of Inman Valley and Mt Compass.

Mt Magnificent is 25km north north-east of Victor Harbor.

Conditions The whole of this section is hilly, with parts of it being particularly steep and rugged. There are several wet creek crossings in spring – and don't try to cross the Finniss River if it's in flood. Windproof clothing is a must as many ridgetops are exposed.

Places to Stay & Eat There are plenty of places to stay in Victor Harbor, and Inman Valley has a *hostel* (☎ 8558 8376).

You can also camp in the Finniss, Myponga and Yulte conservation parks. Contact the NPWS office in Victor Harbor (☎ 8552 3677) for details.

Meals and supplies are available in Victor Harbor, Inman Valley and Mt Compass.

Getting There & Away There are a number of access points where roads cross the trail. Daily buses travel from Adelaide to Victor Harbor ($12) where you can get a taxi to Newland Hill ($10) and Inman Valley ($15).

Mt Magnificent to Mt Lofty (50km)

There's plenty of variety on this section of the trail, which crosses an attractive, hilly

steep slopes and soft beaches; you need to be fit, experienced, well-equipped and have tough clothing (including gardening gloves) that will protect you against thorns.

Places to Stay & Eat There's accommodation in Cape Jervis, and basic *campgrounds* in the Deep Creek and Newland Head conservation parks.

You can buy meals and supplies in Cape Jervis and Victor Harbor.

mosaic of farmland, native bush, pine forest and the townships of Mylor, Bridgewater and Piccadilly.

Past Piccadilly is the 97 hectare Mt Lofty Botanic Gardens, from where you'll make the final ascent to Mt Lofty. From there it's a short downhill walk to the Cleland Conservation Park.

Other highlights along the trail include the abandoned Echunga goldfield (near Mylor), the old Bridgewater Mill (now an upmarket winery restaurant) and Engelbrook (a National Trust property near Bridgewater).

Mt Lofty is 10km south-east of the city centre.

Conditions The walk is hilly throughout, but not particularly arduous except in the steeper areas between Mt Magnificent and Kuitpo. Parts of the Kuitpo Forest are boggy when wet, and crossing the Onkaparinga River near Mylor when it's in flood is definitely not recommended.

Places to Stay & Eat You'll find *YHA hostels* scattered along the trail at Kuitpo, Mylor and Mt Lofty. As well, there are very basic campgrounds in the Kuitpo Forest – a rough hut at the *Rocky Creek Hut Campground* is handy if it's raining.

You can purchase meals and supplies in Mylor, Bridgewater and Picadilly.

Getting There & Away There are numerous access points where the trail crosses sealed and unsealed roads.

Public buses run daily from Adelaide to the Cleland Conservation Park and Aldgate ($2.80).

Mt Lofty to the Barossa Range (80km)

This section often follows the high ridgetops through native bush, pine forest and farmland close to Adelaide. The trail passes through the little townships of Norton Summit and Cudlee Creek, and short detours can be made to Gumeracha and Kersbrook. The section finishes in beautiful hills on the edge of the Barossa Valley.

Conditions The Mt Lofty Ranges are extremely steep at first, giving plenty of excuses to stop and admire the views. These ranges are magnificent, particularly around Montacute Heights. A couple of detours near Norton Summit take you to the National Trust property of Marble Hill and down to the waterfalls in Morialta Conservation Park (best in winter and early spring).

There's some very steep, hard going between Mt Lofty and the Warren Conservation Park; the slopes are particularly difficult around Montacute Heights and the Montacute Conservation Park, so don't attempt this part unless you're really fit.

Past Warren Conservation Park the going is much easier, apart from some testing little climbs such as Mt Crawford.

Places to Stay & Eat There are *YHA hostels* at Mt Lofty and near Norton Summit and Kersbrook. You can camp in the *Mount Crawford Forest*, and there's the *Cudlee Creek Caravan Park* (☎ 8389 2270).

You can buy meals and supplies in Norton Summit, Cudlee Creek, Gumeracha and Kersbrook.

Getting There & Away There are numerous access points off sealed and unsealed roads, including Gorge and Main North-East Rds between Adelaide and Birdwood.

Daily buses run from Adelaide to the Cleland Conservation Park near Mt Lofty ($2.80).

Barossa Range to Hamilton (85km)

After crossing the Barossa Range, with its magnificent gums and the Kaiser Stuhl Conservation Park, the trail leads into wine country at Tanunda in the Barossa Valley. From here it wends its way through farmland and vineyards, bypassing Nuriootpa before leaving the valley past Greenock. Short detours will take you to some good wineries along the way.

Basically, you follow fences from Greenock to tiny Hamilton, about 15km north-west of Kapunda. The country is mainly open, rolling farmland, and there are some great rural views – Mt Belvidere, near Greenock, is well worth the climb.

Conditions There are steep slopes in the Barossa Range, but nothing too daunting if you survived the previous section of the trail. Past the ranges the country is undulating and open; make sure to take windproof clothing.

Places to Stay & Eat There are numerous places to stay and eat in Tanunda, Nuriootpa and, to a much lesser extent, Kapunda. Nuriootpa has an excellent backpacker *hostel* (☎ *8562 2260*) – it's on Nuraip Rd, 3.5km walk from the trail.

You can stop for supplies and meals in Greenock.

Getting There & Away Access points are limited in the Barossa Range, but from Tanunda on you can join the trail at numerous road crossings. There's a daily bus to the Barossa from Adelaide ($10.50), and a daily bus (weekdays only) to Kapunda from Adelaide ($10.50) and Gawler ($6).

Hamilton to Logans Gap (75km)

From Hamilton the trail follows a timbered ridge before climbing Peters Hill, which gives a great view of the saw-toothed Tothill Range. Cross the intervening farmland, then follow the range for the final 43km to Logans Gap. Tothill Range is very scenic in places and has plenty of trees and wildlife, and a number of ruined farmhouses along its foot. As the crow flies, Logans Gap is 16km south of Burra.

Conditions Apart from some steep rugged sections, the going is fairly easy.

Places to Stay The entire section is on private property, with no facilities for walkers apart from a basic *hut* with bunks and drinking water just north of Peters Hill.

Getting There & Away There are a number of access points from minor roads in the area, including access to Logans Gap.

Logans Gap to Newickie Creek (55km)

This section of the trail encompasses hilly, mainly open country, with many fine views. The sense of open space is amazing as you follow the ridgetop that leads into historic Burra.

Past Burra, which is about 23km from Logans Gap, the trail enters a wide belt of jumbled, rounded hills – they're scenic, if barren, and there's very little water for the next 20km or so. In dramatic contrast, the final stretch is well-watered and has plenty of attractive bushland.

Newickie Creek is about 23km north-east of Burra.

Conditions There are many steep slopes in this section, including some long ones. The going varies from easy to moderately difficult, and the track is quite stony in parts. The ford over Burra Creek, in the hills south-east of Burra, requires care if it's been raining.

Places to Stay & Eat There are plenty of beds and several eateries in Burra.

Getting There & Away Daily bus services from Adelaide pass through Burra ($17). Otherwise, access points are limited to a few minor road crossings.

Newickie Creek to Spalding (85km)

This area is sparsely populated. Apart from a few scattered farms the only two townships are Hallett and Spalding. You can expect to find a varied landscape along this section, with rugged hills and gorges in the east and more gentle topography in the west. There are fantastic sweeping panoramas from the higher points – arguably the best view is from Mt Bryan (936m), the highest peak in the Mt Lofty Ranges. Other highlights include Tourillie Gorge (once the wagon road between Hallett and the Murray Plains) and abundant wildlife, particularly near the abandoned settlement of Mt Bryan East.

Conditions There are a couple of ranges with steep rugged slopes in the 40km section between Newickie Creek and Hallett, but other than that the going is generally easy. A lack of trees on most higher points means little protection from bitter winter winds.

Places to Stay & Eat There are a couple of basic places to stay between Hallett and Spalding, and the latter has a pub and campground.

Meals and supplies are available in both Hallett and Spalding.

Getting There & Away There are buses daily from Adelaide that pass through Hallett ($18.60), and three days a week through Spalding ($18.60). The only access points between Newickie Creek and Hallett are a couple of minor roads near Mt Bryan East. Between there and Spalding the trail crosses a network of minor roads.

Spalding to Hughes Gap (85km)
The trail crosses the sparsely populated hills of the northern Mt Lofty Ranges, then enters the Flinders Ranges at Crystal Brook; Hughes Gap is about 10km further on. There's some beautiful walking en route, particularly along Never Never Creek (between Bundaleer Reservoir and the Bundaleer Forest) and Crystal Brook, where the river red gums are superb. Great views are common; the best are from high points in the Campbell Range and the hills east of Crystal Brook.

Conditions There are some long steep sections, but the generally the walk is very easy. The crossing over Rocky River is a wet one (don't attempt it in a flood), and there's always boggy ground just past Bowman Park.

Places to Stay & Eat There are *pubs* with rooms and meals at Spalding, Georgetown and Crystal Brook, and *caravan parks* at Spalding, Crystal Brook and Bowman Park. You can also stay at *Bowman Park (☎ 8636*

2116) near Crystal Brook, and 11km east of Georgetown at *Wirrilla Homestead (☎ 8842 3762)*.

Check with the forester at the Wirrabara Forest (☎ 8668 4163) before camping in the Bundaleer Forest Reserve.

Getting There & Away There is a bus service that runs three days a week from Adelaide to Spalding ($18.60), and daily to Crystal Brook ($24). Other than this access points are extremely limited, but they include the Bundaleer Reservoir and Bundaleer Forest, both off the main road between Spalding and Jamestown.

Hughes Gap to Melrose (75km)
The trail leaves Crystal Brook just past Hughes Gap and climbs onto the main spine of the southern Flinders Ranges. For most of the next 35km, the trail follows fire tracks along the remote timbered ridgetop, from where there's a detour to the Wirrabara Forest headquarters. The ridge varies from 350 to 700m in height, and almost all the way along there are marvellous views over Spencer Gulf to the west. You are likely to see euros, and there is plenty of birdlife.

In the northern half the trail descends the range and crosses rolling farmland with big gums to picturesque Melrose, under Mt Remarkable. It passes within 1km of Murray Town, a tiny village with a good pub.

Conditions Apart from some rough and steep sections the going is mostly easy.

Places to Stay & Eat In the Wirrabara Forest there's a *YHA hostel* and a basic *campground*. Otherwise there's a *caravan park* and two hotels in Melrose.

You can buy meals and supplies in Wirrabara, Murray Town and Melrose.

Getting There & Away In the southern half of this section, access points are limited to Hughes Gap (reached from Crystal Brook township) and the Wirrabara Forest. For the final 20km the trail is within a kilometre of Main North Rd.

Melrose to Woolshed Flat (70km)

This spectacular section takes you to Woolshed Flat, in Pichi Richi Pass about 16km south of Quorn. Its numerous highlights include wildlife, views, magnificent gums and a strong sense of solitude; the pubs in Melrose and Wilmington are pretty good too.

You'll start by toiling up through the trees from Melrose to the summit of Mt Remarkable, in Mt Remarkable National Park. From here the trail slowly descends along steep, rugged ridges to Wilmington, near the halfway point. Along this section you can visit the old Spring Creek copper mine and detour to Alligator Gorge in the national park.

From Wilmington you'll walk up the Port Augusta road to Horrocks Memorial, after which are 30km of rough, timbered ridges to Woolshed Flat. There are plenty of outstanding views, particularly from Mt Brown and the hilltops just east of the memorial.

Conditions Fitness and solid preparation are essential for the entire section, which is remote and often steep and rocky. Wear boots suitable for boulder-hopping along creeks, and tough clothes for protection against dense scrub.

Places to Stay & Eat There are *caravan parks* and *pubs* in Melrose and Wilmington, plus basic bush *campgrounds* in the national park and at Woolshed Flat.

Getting There & Away The main access points are at Melrose, Wilmington and Woolshed Flat. A bus from Adelaide via Port Augusta goes through Woolshed Flat ($38.40 from Adelaide, $6.40 from Port Augusta) three days a week, en route to Quorn and Wilpena.

Woolshed Flat to Buckaringa Gorge (65km)

There are plenty of attractions in this generally rugged, remote section of the trail, which passes through Quorn and Dutchmans Stern Conservation Park, including spectacular scenery, sweeping panoramas and a chance to see the rare yellow-footed rock-wallaby.

From Woolshed Flat you can follow the main road to Quorn or take the 9km longer route via the steep and scrubby Emeroo Range – it's tough going but the views are worth it.

From Quorn you'll be faced with 40km of mainly hard, isolated country with excellent views, attractive gums and rock formations to admire along the way. Dutchmans Stern has great scenery and plenty of wildlife, and you can literally see to the edge of the world from Mt Arden, near the northern end. En route you'll pass one of Edward John Eyre's 1839 camps.

Buckaringa Gorge is about 27km north of Quorn.

Conditions You shouldn't attempt this section unless you know what you are doing. There's limited water on the trail and there are many difficult sections.

Places to Stay & Eat There's plenty of accommodation in Quorn, including an excellent *hostel* (☎ 8648 6655). You can also stay in the *homestead* at Dutchmans Stern (☎ 8648 5300).

Getting There & Away A bus runs three days a week from Port Augusta to Quorn. Access points on this section are limited and include Woolshed Flat, Quorn, Dutchmans Stern and Buckaringa Gorge.

Buckaringa Gorge to Hawker (62km)

Although rugged in parts, the country over much of this section is more subdued and open than before, and there are even a few isolated homesteads en route.

Near its northern end the trail climbs Jarvis Hill, from where you can see the distant purple wall of Wilpena Pound. This section of the trail ends just past the ruins of Old Wonoka, about 7km north-west of Hawker on the Leigh Creek road.

Conditions The going varies from easy to difficult throughout, with careful navigation required in the rougher areas.

Places to Stay & Eat Hawker has plenty of accommodation and several eateries.

Getting There & Away There's a bus service three days a week from Port Augusta to Hawker ($17), which continues on to Wilpena. The limited access points include Buckaringa Gorge, Simmonston and Old Wonoka.

Hawker to Wilpena (50km)

There are some stunning scenic highlights on this section, which takes you through semiarid station country dominated by the spectacular Elder Range and Wilpena Pound's south wall. As well as the Elder Range, towering 700m above the trail as you skirt its rugged eastern flank, there's abundant wildlife, beautiful gum-lined creeks and native pine forest to enjoy.

About 9km before the resort at Wilpena, you'll cross the Wilpena Pound Range at Bridle Gap, from where the view is magnificent, and enter the pound. The range marks the southern boundary of the Flinders Ranges National Park.

Conditions The remoteness and often tough conditions make this section one for the experienced, well-prepared walker. Water supplies are extremely limited.

Places to Stay & Eat *Mt Little Homestead* (☎ 8648 4206), 16km from Hawker, has a range of accommodation styles including a good bush campground right on the trail. The *Wilpena Pound Resort* (☎ 8648 0004) has a motel, campground and store.

Getting There & Away The main access points are at Hawker and Wilpena, and on the Moralana Scenic Drive between the Wilpena and Leigh Creek roads. A bus service travels from Port Augusta to Hawker and Wilpena three days a week.

Wilpena to Parachilna Gorge (65km)

This section features the dramatic landscapes for which the Flinders Ranges are famous; it also features historic ruins and abundant wildlife.

Leaving Wilpena you'll head north-west along the foot of the towering Wilpena Range, then north along scenic valleys in the ABC Range before leaving the national park at the old Aroona homestead, about 46km from Wilpena. From here the trail follows a deep, narrow valley between the ABC and Heysen ranges leading to beautiful Parachilna Gorge.

The trail's northern end is on the main road between Blinman (15km) and Parachilna (17km). Both these places have good pubs where you can down a celebratory drink or two.

Conditions The trail crosses extremely rugged country, but for the most part isn't as difficult as you might think. Even so, you'll have to be experienced, fit and well prepared to do the entire section. There's good potential for short walks at the various access points.

Places to Stay & Eat Meals and beds are available at Wilpena, Blinman, Parachilna and the *Angorichina Tourist Village* (☎ 8648 4842), which is a short walk from the end of the trail. Otherwise there are a couple of basic *campgrounds* in the national park.

Getting There & Away There's a bus service that operates three days a week from Port Augusta to Wilpena. Other than at the section ends, access points are limited to a handful of spots in the national park.

OTHER WALKS

There are networks of tracks in the Flinders Ranges and Mt Remarkable national parks, and in the Arkaroola Wildlife Sanctuary. The Gammon Ranges National Park has stacks of potential for walkers who don't need a track to follow.

In the Mid-North, the 26km Riesling Trail follows a dismantled railway through the Clare Valley between Auburn and Clare, with excellent wineries along the way.

The Barossa, too, has good walks, even though it is relatively closely settled. You can wander (or wobble!) between wineries and historic Lutheran churches, or explore the timbered hills all around. The Para Wirra Recreation Park and Kaiser Stuhl Conservation Park, both in the Barossa Range, are worth visiting for their walks, native bushland and wildlife.

You'll find plenty of opportunity for walking in the conservation parks and state forests in the Mt Lofty Ranges near Adelaide. Belair National Park, Morialta Conservation Park and Cleland Conservation Park, all on Adelaide's outskirts, have some excellent walks.

Further south, on Fleurieu Peninsula, Deep Creek Conservation Park near Cape Jervis is very scenic, but walking conditions can present a challenge.

On Kangaroo Island, Flinders Chase National Park and Cape Gantheaume Conservation Park are also good; the two day coastal walk around Cape Gantheaume to Seal Bay is for experienced walkers only.

In the lower South-East, the Coorong and Canunda national parks have plenty of walks, including huge dunes and long, empty beaches. Ngarkat Conservation Park in the upper South-East has magnificent wildflowers in late winter and early spring, as do other areas in the mallee belt. There are several mallee parks on Eyre Peninsula.

Although many visitors feel a little awed by – and uncomfortable in – the Outback's vast and unpopulated spaces, there are countless good walks in its various environments. Cooper Creek in the Innamincka Regional Reserve is outstanding, as is Lake Eyre when there's water in it.

Cycle Touring

There are some great cycling areas in SA and touring cyclists are a reasonably common sight. Cycling through the Outback wouldn't be everyone's cup of tea – it's often very monotonous, as is the Murray Mallee. However, regions like the Fleurieu Peninsula, Mt Lofty Ranges, Barossa Valley and Flinders Ranges offer plenty of variety, as well as challenges if you want them.

In Adelaide there's a good network of cycle routes, and free maps are available from most specialist bike shops. One worthwhile route follows the path through the River Torrens Linear Park, taking you about 40km along the River Torrens from the sea into the foothills of the Mt Lofty Ranges.

Several places in Adelaide and Glenelg rent well-maintained bikes (see the Getting Around sections in the Adelaide chapter), and you can also rent them at various places in the country.

Information

Bicycle SA (☎ 8410 1406, fax 8410 1455, office@bikesa.asn.au), at State Association House, is the state's umbrella organisation for touring cyclists. It can provide advice on such matters as touring routes, conditions, preparation and suppliers, and is a good source of pamphlets, guides and maps. It has a useful reference library, and the website is at www.bikesa.asn.au. Visitors are welcome to join in the association's various activities, which include supported rides, camping weekends and guided tours; ask for a calendar.

Maps As well as the Australian Surveying & Land Information Group's (AUSLIG) maps, the Office of Recreation & Sport has a series of folding map-guides ($7.30) which cover the most popular cycling areas in country SA. These are very informative, and the map, which may highlight several worthwhile routes, is a useful 1:250,000 or larger. (Use them in conjunction with an RAA touring map so you can see where you are in relation to nearby towns.) They are available from Bicycle SA, map shops (see Maps in the Facts for the Visitor chapter) or any good touring-cycle shop.

THE MAWSON TRAIL

Like bushwalkers, cyclists have their own SA long-distance challenge: the 800km Mawson Trail from the Festival Centre, in the heart of Adelaide, to Blinman in the northern Flinders Ranges.

The trail is named after Sir Douglas Mawson, a great Australian explorer and geologist who, like Sir Hans Heysen, found inspiration in the Flinders Ranges (see the boxed text 'Sir Douglas Mawson' in the Flinders Ranges chapter). The trail makes use of a series of mainly dirt roads and 4WD tracks that takes cyclists into the scenic back country away from main roads. Much of it is remote from people and facilities, and there's quite a bit of difficult cycling – all of which make it an unforgettable experience. It has been marked throughout at intersections and at 1km intervals.

Obviously your bike and associated equipment (like panniers and pumps) will need to be in tip-top condition for the Mawson Trail, particularly its more rugged sections. If you're not sure, have it checked by an expert and then go for a fully laden test ride *before* you leave home. John Harland's *The Australian Bicycle Book: Maintenance & Road Skills* is recommended as a general reference.

For convenience, the trail is broken into five sections, each with its own brochure complete with excellent strip maps ($10). However, they're reductions of 1:50,000 topographical maps, so you'll need a low-power magnifying glass to read them comfortably.

Apart from the section north of Wilmington, where you should allow for a bush camp or two, the Mawson Trail can be planned as a series of day rides between towns. You'll find details on accommodation and bus services in later chapters.

Adelaide to Marrabel (170km)

Starting at the Festival Centre, you'll pass through the suburbs along the River Torrens Linear Park cycle path to Athelstone, on Gorge Rd. From here you'll head north – with several steep climbs en route – through

the scenic Adelaide Hills via Lobethal and Birdwood to the Barossa Valley wineries. The trail continues to the copper heritage town of Kapunda; this section ends near Marrabel, about 23km further on.

Marrabel to Spalding (220km)

The trail passes through the bald hills around Burra en route to Spalding, doing a major switch back along the way. Apart from these towns there's not much sign of civilisation apart from scattered farmhouses; between Burra and Spalding you pass close to tiny Hallett, which has a pub and store. There are challenging hills almost all the way along this section.

Spalding to Wilmington (170km)

You'll cycle through the townships of Spalding, Laura, Melrose and Wilmington, and pass close to Gladstone, Jamestown and Wirrabara. The country is mainly rolling farmland, but near Wirrabura you'll push (or stagger!) up onto the southern Flinders Ranges in the Wirrabara Forest. This is a great, if testing, introduction to the stunning views you'll find further north.

Wilmington to Hawker (140km)

This section is extremely scenic, particularly between Wilmington and Quorn where you pass Mt Brown – your leg muscles will be screaming if you try to do this bit in one go. Between Quorn and Hawker are more testing climbs separated by plains and gum-lined creeks, with marvellous landscapes all around. Along the way you'll pass picturesque Warren Gorge, where there's a basic camping area.

Hawker to Blinman (100km)

The route will take you via Wonoka and the Moralana Scenic Drive to Rawnsley Park, then on to the Wilpena Pound Resort. From here it mainly follows vehicle tracks through the Flinders Ranges National Park, rejoining the main road about 20km before Blinman, where there's a good pub. The scenery on this section is terrific, and you should see plenty of wildlife. There are a few ups and downs, but conditions are generally easy to moderate. There are several places at which to stay.

GUIDED TOURS

If you get tired of talking to sheep, it might be a good idea to include a tour or two in your itinerary. Bicycle SA (☎ 8410 1406) has a program of activities throughout the year, including half to nine-day tours, camping weekends and endurance rides of 200 to 1200km.

Ecotrek (☎ 8383 7198, ecotrek@ozemail .com.au) has extended cycling tours in the Flinders Ranges and on Kangaroo Island. It also runs weekend winery tours in the Barossa and Clare valleys, the Coonawarra and McLaren Vale.

Rolling On Cycle Tours (☎ 8358 2401, mobile 0419 843 069, rolling@dove.net.au) offers a variety of rides, including extended trips into the Flinders Ranges and on the Mawson Trail, and day and weekend rides near Adelaide.

For more details on cycling see the Bicycle section in the Getting Around chapter.

Other Land Activities

ROCK CLIMBING

Popular rock-climbing areas near Adelaide are the Morialta Conservation Park and Onkaparinga Gorge in the Onkaparinga River Recreation Park. Both have cliffs 10 to 15m high, with routes suitable for beginner and advanced grades.

At Moonarie, on the south-eastern side of Wilpena Pound in the Flinders Ranges National Park, cliffs to 120m offer plenty of scope for skilled climbers.

There are several pocket-size guides to climbing in SA: Nick Nagle's *A Rock Climber's Guide to the Flinders Ranges* describes 400 routes, and his *Rock Climbs in the Adelaide Hills* has details on a large number of mainly short climbs; *Moonarie: A*

Rockclimber's Guide, edited by Tony Barker, describes numerous climbs in that area.

Paddy Pallin (☎ 8232 3155) and the Scout Outdoor Centre (☎ 8223 5544), both on Rundle St, Adelaide, specialise in rock climbing and can give you information about the local scene. Both run courses in outdoor adventure skills.

Rock Solid Adventure (☎ 8322 8975, rocksolid@picknowl.com.au) runs courses in abseiling and rock climbing near Adelaide, and can take experienced climbers further afield to the Flinders Ranges.

CAVING

South Australia has extensive cave systems in the South-East, and in the far west under the Nullarbor Plain. However, the majority of these are off-limits to casual cavers. You can visit 'show' caves on guided tours at Tantanoola and Naracoorte, both near Mt Gambier in the South-East, and at Kelly Hill on Kangaroo Island; Naracoorte and Kelly Hill also offer adventure caving. For details see the regional chapters.

The only way for most people to see the Nullarbor caves, which are all in the Nullarbor National Park and adjoining Nullarbor Regional Reserve, is with an accredited tour company. Contact the NPWS office at Ceduna for details of current operators – there were none at the time of this update.

BIRDWATCHING

South Australia has many different habitats, ranging from wetlands to arid gibber plains and from eucalypt forests to mulga scrub and saltbush plains. If you visit the right places you can expect to see many of the 380 species that have been recorded throughout the state.

Generally, the most species are found where there's a diversity of habitats in close proximity. Parts of the Flinders Ranges, such as the Mt Remarkable, Flinders Ranges and Gammon Ranges national parks, have large trees, dense scrub, massive rocky outcrops, open grassy areas, reedbeds and waterholes virtually side by side. Many coastal areas, such as St Kilda and the Coorong, have shallows backed by scrub or mangroves. The Murray River has billabongs, lakes, grassy flats, large trees and extensive cane-grass thickets.

The best areas for seeing parrots and cockatoos are along the Murray and in timbered areas of the South-East and the southern Mt Lofty Ranges.

In the arid Outback, any isolated source of permanent water, whether it be a tank or a waterhole, becomes a focus for birds which must drink regularly to survive. Prime spots include Cooper Creek, near Innamincka, and Purnie Bore, in Witjira National Park. Flocks of cockatoos and pigeons come in to drink at such places, which also provide stepping stones for migratory waterbirds on their long journeys across Australia. The inland salt lakes are mainly dry, but when they fill after rare floods they can become major nesting areas.

Although much of South Australia below the 200mm isohyet has been cleared for agriculture, there are still large areas of native bush in conservation parks in the Murraylands, the upper South-East and Eyre Peninsula. These areas are fantastic for honeyeaters and insect-eaters when the mallee gums and banksia are in flower (July to October is the best period). Here you'll also find the elusive mallee fowl, which incubates its eggs in a huge pile of rotting vegetation.

On Kangaroo Island, where 243 bird species have been recorded, the native vegetation has suffered rather less from agriculture. You may see several species considered uncommon on the mainland, including the glossy black cockatoo and the Cape Barren goose. The island's northern coastal shallows are excellent places to observe waterbirds such as gulls, ducks, pelicans, swans and waders. Elsewhere, you might spot an osprey or white-bellied sea-eagle patrolling the coastal cliffs.

The South-East has major wetlands at the Coorong and Bool Lagoon, where waterbirds reign supreme. The Coorong is noted for its large flocks of ducks and pelicans, while Bool Lagoon has a huge ibis rookery.

Little penguins on parade

Other good spots to see nesting waders and other waterbirds are the mangrove swamps around both gulfs.

There are penguin-watching tours on Kangaroo Island and Granite Island (off Victor Harbor). The little (or fairy) penguin is the only species to breed on the Australian mainland and nearby islands. Several islands off the far west coast are breeding grounds for millions of short-tailed shearwaters.

There are several reference books on Australian birds. A good one is Graham Pizzey's *A Field Guide to the Birds of Australia*.

FOSSICKING

In SA, fossicking is officially defined as 'the gathering of minerals for recreation, providing this is done without disturbing the land or water by machinery or explosives'. There's reasonable fossicking potential in SA, with precious and semiprecious gemstones occurring in a number of areas. At present the only gems being mined commercially are jade, near Cowell on Eyre Peninsula, and opal, at Andamooka, Coober Pedy and Mintabie. Gold and copper were mined at many places in the past. The Mt Lofty Ranges (including the Adelaide Hills) and an arc of country between Burra and Olary have a number of old goldfields.

Diamonds, emeralds, sapphires and rubies have been found, but not in commercial quantities. In terms of numbers of minerals, the most interesting places to look are in the far northern Flinders Ranges, the eastern Flinders Ranges between the Barrier Highway and Lake Frome, and the Middleback Ranges on Eyre Peninsula.

The minimum equipment required for fossicking is sharp eyes and a basic knowledge of where to look. Most fair dinkum fossickers will also have at least a geological pick, a couple of small sieves and a small shovel. Because water is usually in short supply, a drum for washing sieved material may also be required.

You don't need a permit to fossick, but you must have the landholder's permission. The only exception to this rule is a declared fossicking area, which you'll find on the three major opal fields and the old gold diggings at Jupiter Creek and Chapel Hill (both near Echunga in the Adelaide Hills) and at Watts Gully (in the Mt Crawford Forest, also in the Adelaide Hills).

The best place to start is the Department of Primary Industries & Resources (☎ 8463 3000) at 101 Grenfell St, Adelaide. The department has a series of useful brochures on fossicking, and others on self-guided tours of historic mines. You can also get geological maps here.

HORSE & CAMEL RIDING

There are plenty of chances to see the countryside on a horse, but rather less on a camel. You can do rides lasting from 30 minutes to seven days, but most trail-ride operators will only take you out for a day at the most.

The Flinders Ranges is one of the most popular regions: horse rides are offered at a number of places including Balcanoona, Burra, Quorn and Rawnsley Park. At Balcanoona you can learn about the country from local Aboriginal guides. Camel treks through station country are on offer at Blinman.

You can also take a camel trek along the Murray River or the coast of Yorke Peninsula; alternatively, take a camel out for dinner at a McLaren Vale winery.

There are many more options for horse rides throughout the state. This book mentions a number of them under Organised Tours in the regional chapters, and you should also check with SATC and local tourist offices.

Water Activities

CANOEING & KAYAKING

Canoeing opportunities are generally limited to the Murray River and its associated lakes and wetlands. However, the fact that the Murray winds through SA for 650km helps make canoeing a major form of recreation.

Other minor areas of interest include the mangrove inlets between Port Adelaide and St Kilda (these are good for dolphins and birdlife), the Onkaparinga River south of Adelaide and, although most of it is in Victoria, the Glenelg River in the state's far south-eastern corner.

For an adventure, there's nothing like a trip along Cooper Creek when it comes down in flood through the dry Outback. However, this is only for experts – the main danger is getting lost when the creek spreads out over a vast floodplain covered in coolibahs.

While the Murray lacks white-water excitement, there's plenty of wildlife, good fishing, magnificent river scenery and quiet places to camp. For most of the year conditions are suitable for beginners in the company of a skilled guide or instructor. Novices should stay on dry land during periods of maximum flow, which usually occur in November and December. At such times you have to be extremely careful of trees and snags, as in a strong current you can easily end up capsizing and becoming trapped under the canoe. Weirs must be avoided at all times because of their potentially lethal backpull.

You may be tempted to canoe across Lake Alexandrina. Don't do it! Being shallow, the lake becomes extremely choppy in windy conditions. If the wind comes up you may find it difficult to make it back to shore, in which case you'll be at extreme risk of fatal hypothermia (not to mention drowning).

Many of the codes and safety rules for bushwalking apply to canoeing. Others are:

- Be skilled in handling capsizes and rescue situations, and know resuscitation procedures.
- Know how to treat hypothermia.
- Avoid weirs and snags.
- Don't drink river water without first boiling it, and don't pollute it more than it already is.
- Pack belongings in waterproof containers (an obvious one, but you'd be amazed how many don't).
- Kayakers must be able to do the Eskimo roll.

Sea kayaking is a growing sport in SA, and there are some good spots in which to do it. These include the Rapid Bay area, south of Adelaide, the northern coast of Kangaroo Island, Boston Bay at Port Lincoln, the bays of Spencer Gulf and Gulf St Vincent, and the islands off Victor Harbor.

Information

The first stop for information on canoeing and kayaking is Canoe SA Education (☎ 8410 0700, fax 8410 1288, pcarter@ acslink.net.au), at State Association House. Although the emphasis is on education, it can provide advice on route options and tour operators.

Hire & Tours

Hire canoes and/or kayaks are available on a daily, weekly or longer basis from Adelaide, and from several places along the Murray.

Guided canoe tours operate on such waterways as the Murray River, the Port Adelaide mangrove inlets, the Coorong and the Cooper Creek system. You can also do kayak trips of up to a day along the coast between Second Valley and Cape Jervis. The following operators in and around Adelaide do canoe and/or kayak tours:

Canoeing

Ecotrek (☎ 8383 7198, ecotrek@ozemail .com.au), at Dashwood Gully Rd, Kangarilla, offers two day trips on the Murray and longer on Cooper Creek and the Coongie Lakes.

Scout Outdoor Centre (☎ 8223 5544), at 192 Rundle St, Adelaide, offers occasional trips to the Murray River and Port Adelaide mangrove inlets.

Mangrove Fun Paddles (☎ 8449 7252), at 40 Exmouth St, Clanville, has day trips to the mangrove inlets.

Rock Solid Adventure (☎ 8322 8975, rocksolid@ picknowl.com.au), in Happy Valley, has overnight trips to the Coorong and Murray River.

Sea Kayaking

Blue Water Sea Kayaking (☎ 8558 2657), at the Wirrina Cove Paradise Resort, near Normanville on the Fleurieu Peninsula, offers day trips along the coast south of Adelaide.

Blue Water Glenelg (☎ 8295 8812), at 7 Hastings St, Glenelg South, offers short trips off Glenelg.

Scout Outdoor Centre (☎ 8223 5544) does occasional trips near Adelaide.

SWIMMING & SURFING

There are fine swimming beaches right along the South Australian coast, with the safest generally being on Gulf St Vincent and Spencer Gulf. You have to be very wary of rips and undertows anywhere that's exposed to the Southern Ocean and Investigator Strait, which separates Kangaroo Island from the mainland.

Adelaide has a number of good beaches. Further south there are several with reasonable surf in the right conditions – Seaford and Southport have reliable, if small, waves. Skinny dipping is permitted at Maslins Beach South, 40km from the city.

You'll find potential surf spots in any area exposed to the Southern Ocean's rolling swells. The closest surf to Adelaide of any real consequence is near Victor Harbor at Waitpinga Beach, Middleton and Port Elliot. Kangaroo Island's southern coast also has some worthwhile spots – Pennington Bay is the most consistent. Pondalowie, on the 'foot' of Yorke Peninsula, has the state's most reliable strong breaks, although when conditions are right there are more powerful ones nearby. Other notable surfing spots are scattered between Port Lincoln, at the southern tip of Eyre Peninsula, and famous Cactus Beach in the far west.

Riding the big one at Cactus Beach

Surfing SA (☎ 8327 2802) can provide general advice to visiting surfies. They also produce *The Surfer's Handbook*, a guide to beaches of the south coast and lower Gulf St Vincent – it's available from most surf shops in this area.

Ring ☎ 1900 931 543 or 8272 6954 for surf reports along the coast between Adelaide and Goolwa.

WINDSURFING

There's endless potential for windsurfing (also known as wave sailing, sailboarding and boardsailing) along the coast and on many lakes.

Adelaide beaches present conditions as extreme as anywhere, and in summer there are strong sea breezes – ideal for slalom surfers. The windiest beaches (from north to south) are Semaphore, Henley Beach, North Glenelg, Somerton and Seacliff. Each has its own set of hazards, so check with locals

before plunging in. Sellicks Beach, 50km or so south of the city, is another good spot in the right conditions.

The state's most popular place for both advanced and novice windsurfers is Goolwa, on the Fleurieu Peninsula, where you get a range of conditions in a reasonably small area. Other hot spots include Barmera (Lake Bonney), Beachport (Lake George), Meningie (Lake Albert) and Milang (Lake Alexandrina). Kingston SE, Port Lincoln and the beaches around Yorke Peninsula are good coastal spots.

If you're interested in entering competitions, get hold of a copy of *Boardsailing News* from any windsurfing shop. Glascraft Marine (Sailboards) (☎ 8223 3055), at 243 Pirie St in Adelaide, is a good source of general information on what's happening around the state.

SCUBA DIVING

There are plenty of good dive spots along the coast, including jetties, wrecks, drop-offs, caves, reefs and sponge beds.

While shore-diving off Adelaide's metropolitan beaches is limited, there are numerous worthwhile spots for boat divers. These include the 40m sunken dredge *South Australian*, which lies at 20m about 6km off Glenelg. Built in Holland in 1911, it was sunk in 1985 to form a sunken reef and is now home for a staggering variety of marine life. It's regarded by many as the best of Adelaide's dive sites.

At Port Noarlunga, 18km south of Adelaide, you can shore dive or snorkel in the Marine Reserve – accessible from the end of the jetty – or boat dive to the HA *Lumb*, a sunken fishing vessel. The reef has a signposted underwater trail suitable for snorkellers. Port Noarlunga is the state's most popular diving area thanks to its accessibility.

Further south, the reefs off Snapper Point (42km) and Aldinga (43km) are still good for fish and other creatures despite the effects of stormwater run-off from nearby housing developments. You can snorkel off the shore at Snapper Point, but the Aldinga

Reef, with its drop-off (to 22m) and swim throughs, is more suited to boat diving.

The Rapid Bay jetty, 88km from Adelaide, has a wonderful abundance of marine life. Unfortunately, the jetty is very long and the best diving is (you guessed it) off the end – but everyone says the walk is worth it. Take a rope for hauling your gear out of the water at low tide.

Further afield, Yorke Peninsula has great potential under almost any wind conditions – if one side is too rough, the other will usually be diveable. Attractions here include several jetty dives (fish, starfish, colourful sponges, nudibranches and soft corals), the wrecks around Wardang Island and Edithburgh, and spectacular underwater topography off the south coast.

Other good areas are the reefs off Robe and nearby Cape Jaffa in the South-East, the marine life at Point Sir Isaac near Port Lincoln, and the reefs, wrecks and drop-offs around Kangaroo Island. At Dangerous Reef, off Port Lincoln, you can watch white pointer sharks from the safety of a suspended cage (see the Port Lincoln section in the Eyre Peninsula & West Coast chapter).

Although out of date, Peter Christopher's slim but informative *Divers' Guide to South Australia* covers numerous sites around the state. The *Australian Divers' Guide*, by Peter Stone, has a section on SA. As well, the Adelaide Skin Diving Centre, at 7 Compton St, Adelaide, publishes a leaflet describing 75 dive sites in SA.

Dive charter operators in and around Adelaide include:

Adelaide
Adelaide Skin Diving Centre (☎ 8231 6144) goes to sites off Adelaide and Kangaroo Island.
Glenelg Scuba Diving Centre (☎ 8294 7744) goes to sites off Adelaide and the near coast, and publishes a program of dives in its monthly newsletter.
Super Elliotts Dive Centre (☎ 8264 9811) offers mainly weekend dives off Adelaide, leaving from Glenelg on Saturday and O'Sullivans Beach on Sunday.

Fleurieu Peninsula
Victor Harbor Boat Charters (☎ 8552 3142, 0414

527 475) offers dives on the south coast near Victor Harbor.

Kangaroo Island
Adventureland Diving (☎ 8553 1284) is based in Penneshaw and mainly dives at the island's eastern end.
Kangaroo Island Diving Safaris (☎ 8559 3225) specialises in the island's northern coast.

CAVE DIVING

There's world-class cave diving around Mt Gambier, in the South-East, where you'll find dozens of sites including huge caverns and deep sink holes. The area holds excellent potential for suitably trained divers, and the formations and water clarity are said to be legendary.

As a result of several tragedies in the early 1970s, however, the only chance you have of getting permission to scuba dive in most of these caves is to join the Cave Divers Association of Australia (CDAA) and be trained to their requirements. Information on the different memberships can be obtained by writing to CDAA at PO Box 290, North Adelaide, 5006.

With a permit from the NPWS office (☎ 8735 1111) in Mt Gambier, you can dive and snorkel in crystal-clear water at the Piccaninnie Ponds and Ewens Ponds conservation parks south of the town. Only certified divers will be granted permission to scuba dive.

FISHING

There are fantastic opportunities for fishing in many parts of SA. Apart from the coast, where conditions range from pounding surf to millpond calm, there's the Murray River and numerous lakes and freshwater streams. You can even catch fish in many Outback waterholes.

Surf beaches are good for large species such as Australian salmon (actually a perch), mulloway and shark, and smaller ones like tommy-ruff (usually known as tommies), trevally, bream, tailor and flathead. Popular spots include the ocean beaches between Port Lincoln and Ceduna on the west coast, Browns Beach on the southern tip of Yorke

Marine Mammals of South Australia

One of the great thrills of any visit to SA is observing marine mammals at close quarters. The state's waters are home to 25 species of cetaceans (dolphins and whales), almost a third of all those on the globe. As well, one species of fur seal and one of sea lion live in permanent colonies along the coast. Other seals, such as the leopard seal, are occasional visitors from Antarctic waters.

Whaling and sealing were SA's first industries. Seals were killed for their skins on Kangaroo Island from 1803, while the first two whaling stations were established in 1837 at Victor Harbor. Other stations were established at Port Lincoln and sites further west near Smoky Bay and Ceduna. The industry was based on the southern right whale, called 'right' by whalers because it had large quantities of valuable oil and baleen, and because it was easy to kill. The southern right existed in large numbers, but over-exploitation soon reduced the population to uneconomic levels. All whaling operations in the state had ceased by the early 1870s.

The southern right whale comes close to shore on its annual breeding migration, and so is often seen from clifftops and other vantage points. The state's two dolphin species are also a common sight, but the remaining 22 species of cetaceans are rarely seen – even from boats as they all live out near the edge of the continental shelf. They include the blue whale, fin whale, sperm whale, humpback whale and killer whale. Every year there are several strandings along the coast, usually of one to three animals at a time.

Southern Right Whale

Once numbering an estimated 100,000 worldwide, only a few hundred southern right whales (*Eubalaena australis*) remained by 1935, when they became fully protected. For decades the whales were rarely sighted along the SA coast and the outlook was gloomy. Now the population appears to be recovering and they're returning to breed each year in increasing numbers. Today there are an estimated 1500 to 3000 southern right whales worldwide, with about 500 living in the Southern Ocean off Australia.

Every year between June and October, over 100 mostly adult whales are seen on their annual breeding migration to warmer waters along the South Australian coast. At least half make for the head of the Great Australian Bight, where around 20 calves are born along a 20km stretch of coastline. This nursery area is included in a new marine park – the Great Australian Bight Marine Park (see the Head of Bight section in the Eyre Peninsula chapter).

Southern right whales sieve their food through fine bones known as baleen, hence their classification. They can easily be identified by the large white lumps (or callosity) on the head and because they have no dorsal fin. Adults reach 18m in length, 4m in diameter, and weigh up to 90 tonnes. Calves are around 5m long at birth. The peak of the southern right whale season along the coast is August and September.

Peninsula, Waitpinga Beach near Victor Harbor, Pennington Bay on Kangaroo Island, and the Ninety Mile Beach near Kingston.

Generally the best sea fishing is from a boat, particularly where the sea floor shelves gently away as it does in the gulfs.

Fortunately, SA has plenty of jetties (about 80 of them) that allow you to fish in deeper water. There are some beauties on Yorke Peninsula and Eyre Peninsula, where large cargo vessels come in to load wheat; Port Giles, Wallaroo and Ceduna have outstand-

Marine Mammals of South Australia

Bottlenose Dolphin
This dark-grey species is found right along the coast. *Tursiops truncatus* normally grows to 3m and has a relatively short beak compared to its cousin, the common dolphin. Bottlenose dolphins are extremely powerful swimmers and will sometimes leap several metres out of the water. They'll also act cooperatively in such matters as rounding up a school of fish and taking turns to feed. Several bottlenose dolphins live in the Port River near Adelaide.

Common Dolphin
These, the most common of dolphins (hence the name), are found throughout the world. In SA *Delphinus delphis* grows to 2m and is often seen playing in the waves – they will surf with humans if given half a chance. You'll recognise them by their relatively long beak and the yellow-and-black pattern along their sides. Like the bottlenose dolphin its favourite foods include squid.

False Killer Whale
Growing to 6m, the black to dark-grey *Pseudorca crassidens* has been recorded numerous times along the SA coast. They're difficult to tell apart from pilot whales, which are also often reported. Both are the same colour and have protruding foreheads, or melons, used in echolocation.

New Zealand Fur Seal
Once slaughtered in their thousands for their luxuriant skins, fur seals (*Arctocephalus forsteri*) are now thriving around New Zealand, parts of southern Australia and on sub-Antarctic islands. They're usually seen basking on rocks, particularly on Kangaroo Island where there are several colonies. Males grow to 2.5m, females to 1.5m; they have grey-brown fur and a more pointed nose than the Australian sea lion.

Australian Sea Lion
This is the only pinniped (seal) endemic to Australia. Sea lions (*Neophoca cinerea*) are about the same size as the New Zealand fur seal, but you can easily identify the males by their black to dark-brown back and sides, and white crown and nape; the females are silvery grey above and cream below. Both sexes are extremely territorial during the variable breeding season.

The total population of Australian sea lions is around 12,000, making it one of the rarest seal species. The largest populations are on the Pages Islands east of Kangaroo Island (2250), Dangerous Reef off Port Lincoln (1000) and Seal Bay on Kangaroo Island (500). Other colonies are found along the west coast of SA and on islands off the Western Australia coast as far around as Geraldton.

Denis O'Byrne

ing deep-water jetties where you can catch a wide range of species.

Many jetties are also good for catching squid and blue-swimmer crabs. The latter can be caught in shallow sheltered water in the northern coastal areas of the two gulfs and in suitable habitats along the west coast.

Rock fishing yields species such as sweep, groper, snapper, salmon trout and trevally; you can also catch salmon and mulloway where the rocks are exposed to the Southern Ocean. However, you've got to watch out for the huge killer waves (known as 'king waves') that occasionally roll in from the ocean. Rock fishing is one of the most dangerous recreational sports, and there are several drownings every year thanks to king waves and recklessness. It's smart to wear lightweight clothing and a buoyancy vest if you're fishing close to the water, particularly where the rocks are exposed to swells.

As well as from deteriorating water quality and the interference of its natural flow, the poor old Murray River has suffered through the introduction of European carp. These things have had a devastating effect on native aquatic species through both competition and their feeding habits, which muddy the water. Catch as many carp as you like, then chop them up and feed the pelicans – it's illegal to throw them back alive.

The most popular eating fish in SA is the succulent King George whiting – they even taste wonderful after being frozen. You can catch them right along the coast, but the best spots are in sheltered waters with sandy bottoms. Most whiting are caught in the gulfs, Investigator Strait and bays along the west coast.

Any town where tourists go to fish will have a place – either a gear shop, service station or seafood wholesaler – where you can buy bait and at least basic equipment.

Information

Where to Fish in South Australia by SA Fishing Tackle Agencies mentions a large number of spots and has 88 maps. David Capel's *Diary of Fishing & Boating for SA* is less detailed, but worth having.

To find the current hot spots, check Saturday's *Advertiser* and the *Sunday Mail*. Alternatively, tackle shops can give you pointers for their particular area.

Regulations

Fishing restrictions in SA include bag limits, legal sizes, seasonal closures, restricted areas and protected species. To find out about restrictions, read the *South Australian Recreational Fishing Guide*, a free booklet put out by the Department of Primary Industries & Resources. It's available at most specialty tackle shops.

And no, you don't need a licence to fish in SA, provided you're a recreational angler using a hook and line.

Charters

There are a number of fishing charter operators around the coast, and this book mentions some of them. Costs typically start at $45 per person for a half day trip including bait and tackle, but not meals; invariably, minimum numbers apply.

Provided you have a South Australian or interstate boat licence, you can hire dinghies with outboards at several places.

MARINE MAMMAL WATCHING

For nature enthusiasts, the icon of South Australia's 27 species of marine mammals is the southern right whale, which is often seen along the ocean coast during its annual breeding migration. Unlike the state's other whales, it often comes to within a few hundred metres of shore. Hot spots for whale watching include Victor Harbor, the south coast of Kangaroo Island, Port Lincoln, Elliston and, the hottest and most reliable of them all, Head of Bight on the far west coast.

The best place to watch for southern right whales is from a high vantage point through low to medium-power binoculars. The glossy black animals have bus-like dimensions, and when feeling frisky they can put on spectacular displays of breaching (leaping out of the water), tail-splashing, courting and mating. Watching these magnificent creatures in action is an unforgettable experience.

The only other cetaceans you're likely to see are common and bottlenose dolphins. These playful animals often frolic among surfers at places such as Middleton (near Victor Harbor) and Blackfellows (near Elliston). Dolphins are a common sight in the mangrove inlets near Adelaide.

New Zealand fur seals and Australian sea lions breed on a number of islands, including Kangaroo Island. You'll also find sea lion colonies on the mainland at Cape Labbatt (near Streaky Bay) and along the mighty Nullarbor Cliffs. The easiest way to tell the two species apart is that sea lions prefer sandy beaches, while fur seals like rocky platforms. Kangaroo Island is the best place to see them.

Information

The SA Whale Centre in Victor Harbor operates the Whale Information Network from its interpretive centre on Railway Terrace. To report a sighting, call the centre on ☎ 8552 5644; for current information on the whereabouts of whales, call ☎ 1900 931 223. Otherwise, write to PO Box 950, Victor Harbor, 5211, or email the centre at whale@ webmedia.com.au, and it will send the very informative *SA Whale Watching Information Booklet* ($4 including postage). The website is at www.webmedia.com.au/whales/.

Essential reading for whale lovers is *The Australian Guide to Whale Watching*, by Tina Dalton and Ross Isaacs. It includes information on identification, behaviour, biology and conservation, as well as on popular whale-watching spots.

Another good publication is the SA Museum's *A Guide to Whales & Whale Watching in SA*, a much slimmer volume but with plenty of good information and illustrations.

Organised Tours

Whale-watching tours to Head of Bight are offered by Whales & Wildlife Eco Tours (☎ 8379 0203), which combines aerial survey work and clifftop observations as part of an ongoing scientific research project.

See the Organised Tours section at the start of the Eyre Peninsula chapter for details of other operators offering whale watching.

NPWS rangers will take you to visit the sea lion colony at Seal Bay, on Kangaroo Island.

Aerial Activities

SCENIC FLIGHTS

A number of operators around the state offer scenic flights in helicopters and light planes, usually from the local aerodrome or private landing areas. Arguably, the most spectacular area to see from the air is the Flinders Ranges, where you fly over bold bluffs and stark ridges with views to huge saltpans and vast, arid plains on either side. In the warmer months the ranges are at their best for colour and contrast, as well as smooth flying, in the early morning and late afternoon.

Also spectacular is the coastline, particularly the more rugged areas fronting the Southern Ocean. You can admire soaring cliffs west of Investigator Strait, and between June and October there's a good chance of seeing southern right whales.

Any flight over the Outback is fascinating simply because of the vastness of unbelievably empty space. Actually it's not always that empty, it just seems like it! Depending where you are, you fly over scattered homesteads, station bores, salt lakes, gum creeks, desert sand ridges and endless gibber plains. You might even see ringers (Australian cowboys) on horses or motorbikes pushing a mob of sheep or cattle along. Lake Eyre is impressive enough when dry, and definitely shouldn't be missed when there's plenty of water in it.

A word of warning here! Don't go flying over the Outback or the Flinders Ranges in the middle of a hot day, particularly if you're prone to airsickness. The bumpy conditions may cause nausea.

Most scenic flight operators are mentioned in this book under Organised Tours at the start of each regional chapter. Otherwise check with SATC and local tourist offices.

BALLOONING

There's nothing quite like drifting silently over the countryside in a hot-air balloon, but the sport hasn't taken off at all in SA. In fact, you can only do it in the Barossa

Valley (see the section on Organised Tours in that chapter).

SKYDIVING

The state's only skydiving clubs are SA Skydiving (☎ 8272 7888), at Murray Bridge, the SA Sport Parachute Club (☎ 8351 9339), at Lower Light on Port Wakefield Rd (about 45 minutes drive north of Adelaide), and Sky Dive Adelaide (☎ 8371 2766), at Strathalbyn. All are professional training organisations, so if you've never tried the adrenaline rush of skydiving, now's your chance.

First timers must do about 10 hours of theory and practice before launching themselves into space – with instructors, of course. The all-inclusive cost for training

and a first jump is around $350 (video $60 extra).

For licensed skydivers it's $25 a jump.

HANG GLIDING

Popular spots for hill jumps near Adelaide are Seaford, Maslins Beach, Normanville, Cape Jervis and Victor Harbor around the Fleurieu Peninsula coast, and the Barunga Ranges in the Mid-North region.

The Hang Gliding Association of SA, at the State Association House, 1 Sturt St, Adelaide, can be contacted on ☎ 8410 1391. The association controls all hang gliding and paragliding operations throughout the state, and it can advise you on the opportunities available.

Getting There & Away

AIR – INTERNATIONAL
The Adelaide airport has domestic and international terminals 7km west of the city centre. See Getting Around in the Adelaide chapter for details on getting to and from the airport.

There are plenty of travel agents in Adelaide. Probably the best for discounted fares are Flight Centre (☎ 8231 0044) at 136 North Terrace, STA Travel (☎ 8223 2426) at 235 Rundle St, and the YHA travel office (☎ 8231 5583) at 38 Sturt St. Flight Centre and STA have several offices around town.

International airlines currently flying into Adelaide are:

Cathay Pacific
  (☎ 13 17 47) 45 Grenfell St
Garuda Indonesia
  (☎ 1300 365 330) 76 Waymouth St
Malaysia Airlines
  (☎ 13 26 27) Riverside Plaza, 144 North Terrace
Qantas Airways
  (☎ 13 12 11) 144 North Terrace
Singapore Airlines
  (☎ 13 10 11) booking inquiries
  (☎ 8238 2747) 50 King William St

Round-the-World Tickets
Round-the-World (RTW) tickets are very popular and many of these will take you through Australia. The airline RTW tickets are often real bargains. Since Australia is pretty much at the other side of the world from Europe and North America, it can be no more expensive, or even cheaper, to keep going in the same direction right round the world rather than U-turning to return.

The official airline RTW tickets are usually put together by a combination of two airlines, who permit you to fly anywhere you want on their route systems so long as you do not backtrack. Other restrictions are that you (usually) must book the first sector in advance and cancellation penalties then apply. There may be restrictions on how many stops are permitted, and usually the tickets are valid from 90 days up to a year. A typical price for a South Pacific RTW ticket is around US$2000.

An alternative type of RTW ticket is one put together by a travel agent using a combination of discounted tickets from a number of airlines. A UK agent like Trailfinders can put together interesting London-to-London RTW combinations that include Australia for £800 to £1200.

Circle Pacific Tickets
Circle Pacific fares are a similar idea to RTW tickets and use a combination of airlines to circle the Pacific, combining Australia, New Zealand, North America and Asia. As with RTW tickets there are advance purchase restrictions and limits to how many stopovers you can make. Typically, fares range between US$1900 and US$2200. A possible Circle Pacific route is Los Angeles-Honolulu-Auckland-Sydney-Melbourne-Singapore-Bangkok-Hong Kong-Tokyo-Los Angeles.

The UK
The cheapest tickets in London are from the numerous 'bucket shops' (discount ticket agencies), which advertise in magazines and papers like *Time Out*, *LAM* and *TNT*. Pick up one or more of these publications and ring round a few bucket shops to find the best deal. *Time Out* gives useful advice on precautions to take, as not all bucket shops are honest.

The cheapest London to Adelaide (not direct) bucket shop fares are about £385 one way or £638 return. Such prices are usually only available if you depart London in the low season – March to June. In September and mid-December fares go up by about 30%, while the rest of the year they're somewhere in between.

Many cheap tickets allow stopovers on the way to or from Australia. Rules vary, but recently most return tickets have allowed you to stay away for any period between 14 days and one year, with stopovers permitted anywhere along your route. Typically, with heavily discounted tickets the less you pay the less you get. Direct flights, leaving at convenient times and flying with popular airlines, are obviously going to be more expensive.

Departing Adelaide in the UK low season you can expect to pay around A$925/1399 one way/return for a normal excursion to London, with stops in Asia en route. Again, fares increase by up to 30% in the European summer and at Christmas.

North America

There are a variety of connections across the Pacific from Los Angeles, San Francisco and Vancouver to Australia, including direct flights, flights via New Zealand, island-hopping routes and more circuitous Pacific rim routes via Asia. Qantas, Air New Zealand and United Airlines all fly USA-Australia; Qantas, Air New Zealand and Canadian Airlines International fly Canada-Australia. An interesting option from the east coast is to fly with Japan Airlines via Japan.

To find good fares to Australia check the travel ads in the Sunday travel sections of papers such as the *Los Angeles Times*, *San Francisco Examiner*, *New York Times* or the *Globe & Mail*. You can usually get a return ticket from the west coast for US$1150, or US$1550 from the east coast.

At peak seasons – particularly the Australian summer/Christmas – seats will be harder to obtain and the fare will rise considerably. In the USA good agents for discounted tickets are the two student travel operators, Council Travel and STA Travel, both of which have lots of offices around the country. Canadian west coast fares out of Vancouver will be similar to those from the US west coast. From Toronto fares are around C$2230 return.

If Pacific island-hopping is your aim, check out the airlines of Pacific Island nations, some of which have good deals on indirect routings. Qantas can give you Fiji or Tahiti along the way, while Air New Zealand can offer both destinations and the Cook Islands as well. See the Circle Pacific section for more details.

Sample low season one-way/return fares available from Adelaide to North America include New York A$1149/1749, San Francisco A$1550/2180 and Vancouver $1560/2190.

New Zealand

Air New Zealand, Ansett and Qantas operate a network of trans-Tasman flights, linking Auckland, Wellington and Christchurch with most major Australian gateway cities. From Adelaide to either Auckland or Wellington you're looking at around A$572/747 one way/return during the NZ low season.

Asia

Ticket discounting is widespread in Asia, particularly in Singapore, Hong Kong, Bangkok and Penang. There are a lot of fly-by-nights in the Asian ticketing scene, so a little care is required. Invariably, flights between many Asian centres and Adelaide are notoriously heavily booked, particularly by university students at the start and finish of the main semester breaks. Flights to or from Bangkok and Singapore are often part of the longer Europe-Australia route, so are often full. Plan ahead.

Typical fares from Adelaide to Singapore are A$855/1160 one way/return. In Asia you can pick up some interesting tickets that include Australia on the way across the Pacific. Qantas and Air New Zealand offer discounted trans-Pacific tickets.

From Adelaide, return excursion fares to Kuala Lumpur and Bangkok are A$1210 and A$1270, respectively.

Lonely Planet's *South-East Asia on a Shoestring* gives further information on travel between Australia and Asia.

Africa

There are a number of direct flights each week between Africa and Australia, but only between Perth and Harare (Zimbabwe) or Johannesburg (South Africa). Qantas,

South African Airways and Air Zimbabwe all fly this route.

Other airlines that connect southern Africa and Australia include Malaysia Airlines (via Kuala Lumpur), Air Mauritius (via Mauritius) and Singapore Airlines (via Singapore).

From eastern Africa the options are to fly via Mauritius or the Indian subcontinent and on to South-East Asia, and from there connect to Australia.

South America

Two routes operate between South America and Australia. The Chile connection involves Lan Chile's Santiago-Easter Island-Tahiti service, from where you can fly Qantas or another airline to Australia. Alternatively, Aerolineas Argentinas flies from Buenos Aires to Auckland and Sydney.

Leaving Australia

There is a $30 departure tax when leaving Australia. This is incorporated into the price of your air ticket, so you don't have to pay it separately.

Warning

The information in this chapter is vulnerable to change – prices for international travel are volatile, routes are introduced and cancelled, schedules change, rules are amended and special deals come and go.

Airlines and governments seem to take a perverse pleasure in making price structures and regulations as complicated as possible. Check directly with the airline or travel agent to make sure you understand how a fare (and the ticket you may buy) works.

In addition, the travel industry is highly competitive and there are many lurks and perks. The upshot of this is that you should get quotes and advice from as many airlines and travel agents as possible before you part with your hard-earned cash.

Details given in this chapter should be regarded only as pointers and cannot be any substitute for your own careful, up-to-date research.

AIR – DOMESTIC

Adelaide is a long way from other capitals (the closest, Melbourne, is 729km by the shortest road route), so if your time is limited you may have to think about flying.

The key domestic carriers within Australia are Qantas and Ansett, both of whom offer daily flights to the various state capitals, with connections to many of the larger country centres. Kendell Airlines (an Ansett subsidiary) and Airlink (Qantas) have flights into SA from regional centres such as Kalgoorlie and Broken Hill. The lack of competition means relatively high prices, although discounting is a regular feature of the domestic flights scene.

Random Discounting

One of the key features of Australia's deregulated air travel industry is random discounting. As the airlines try harder to fill planes, they often offer substantial discounts on selected routes. Although this applies mainly to the heavy volume routes, mainly between state capitals, it's not always the case.

To make the most of the discounted fares, you'll need to keep in touch with what's currently on offer. There are usually conditions attached to cheap fares, such as booking seven, 14 or 21 days in advance, and flying on weekends only or between certain dates. Also the number of seats available is usually fairly limited.

On virtually every route covered by Qantas or Ansett the full economy fare will not be the cheapest way to go. Because the situation is so fluid, the special fares will more than likely have changed by the time you read this. For that reason we list the full one-way economy fares throughout the book, although you can safely assume that there will be a cheaper fare available.

Discounts tend to be greater for return rather than one-way travel.

If you're planning a return trip and have 21 days up your sleeve, you can save over 50% of the full fare by travelling Apex. You have to book and pay for your ticket 21 days in advance and must stay away at least one Saturday night. Flight details can be changed at any time, but must be consistent with the 21 day booking period. The tickets are nonrefundable. If you book 14 days in advance the saving is 45% to 50%, while seven-day advance bookings save you 35% to 40%. Advance-purchase savings on one-way travel are much more modest.

University or other higher education students under the age of 26 can get a 25% discount off the full economy fare. An airline tertiary concession card (available from the airlines) is required for Australian students, while overseas students can use their International Student Identity Card. The advantage of this option over Apex is its flexibility, and the fact that you can get a refund.

All nonresident international travellers can get up to a 40% discount on internal Qantas flights and 25% on Ansett flights simply by presenting their international ticket when booking. It seems there is no limit to the number of domestic flights you can take, and it doesn't matter which airline you fly into Australia with. However, you may have to show your passport and ticket out of Australia at the point of sale. The discount applies only to the full economy fare, so in many cases it will be cheaper to take advantage of other discounts offered.

Another thing to keep your eyes open for is special deals at certain times of the year. For example, when the Grand Prix is on in Melbourne in March extra flights are put on. Planes travelling in the opposite direction will be nearly empty, so special fares are offered to people exiting Melbourne at that time.

Air Passes

Qantas offers two air passes. The **Australia Boomerang Pass** can only be purchased overseas and in conjunction with your international ticket. It involves purchasing coupons for either short-haul flights (for example, Hobart to Melbourne) at $220 one way, or for long-haul sectors (such as just about anywhere to Alice Springs) for $275. You must purchase a minimum of four coupons before you arrive in Australia, and once here you can buy up to six more. You

can change the date and time of your ticket at no charge, but if you change the route there's a reissue fee of $50.

The Qantas **Backpackers Pass** can only be purchased in Australia, and that's provided you can produce identification such as a membership card of the YHA, VIP Backpackers Resorts, Independent Backpackers or another acceptable organisation. You must purchase a minimum of three sectors (such as Adelaide-Melbourne, Sydney-Brisbane and Darwin-Perth), and spend a minimum of two nights at each stop. The discount is quite substantial; for example Adelaide to Sydney with the pass is $170 one way, as against the full economy fare of $391.

Ansett's **Kangaroo Airpass** gives you two options: 6000km with two or three stopovers for $949 and 10,000km with three to seven stopovers for $1499. A number of restrictions apply to these tickets, although they can be a good deal if you want to see a lot of country in a short period of time. Fortunately, you don't need to start and finish at the same place.

Restrictions include a minimum (10 nights) and a maximum (45 nights) travel time. One of the stops must be at a non-capital city destination and be for at least four nights, and you can only stay at each destination once. All sectors must be booked when you purchase the ticket, although these can be changed without penalty unless the ticket needs rewriting, in which case there's a $50 charge. Refunds are available in full before travel commences, but not at all once you start using the ticket.

On a 6000km air pass you could, for example, fly Sydney-Alice Springs-Cairns-Brisbane-Sydney. That will give you three stops with two of them in non-capital cities. The full economy fare for that circuit would be $1825, while discounted fares are $1105/963 for seven/14 days advance purchase.

Economy Fares

From Adelaide, typical one-way economy fares are: Alice Springs $414, Brisbane $551, Darwin $675, Hobart $392, Melbourne $272, Perth $582 and Sydney $391. To make a reservation, contact Ansett on ☎ 13 13 00, or book online at www.ansett. com.au; for Qantas call ☎ 13 13 13, or make online bookings at www.qantas.com.au. Both airlines have travel centres around Adelaide.

Kendell Airlines (Ansett ☎ 13 13 00) flies direct from Adelaide to Broken Hill ($174). Airlink (Qantas ☎ 13 13 13) flies to Alice Springs ($414), Canberra ($337) and Kalgoorlie ($495).

Note that some airports charge special taxes which are payable separate to your ticket. For example, Sydney has a 'noise tax' of $3.40 which must be paid on arrival.

LAND
Bus

Bus travel is generally the cheapest way of getting from A to B, other than hitching of course, and there are some good deals available. Many travellers prefer to see SA by bus because it's one of the best ways to come to grips with the state's size – also the bus companies have far more comprehensive route networks than the railway system.

There is only one truly national bus company – Greyhound Pioneer Australia (☎ 13 20 30, express@greyhound.com.au), which has services between Adelaide and all major mainland cities.

McCafferty's (☎ 13 14 99, infomcc@ mccaffertys.com.au) is the second largest, with services around Australia except for Western Australia (WA) and the long haul between Perth and Port Augusta – here you can take the *Indian Pacific* train using a McCafferty's bus pass. Both Greyhound and McCafferty's buses have air-conditioning, toilets and videos, and smoking is forbidden.

Both operators are forever changing their fares, but the following will give you an idea. From Adelaide they charge $45 to Melbourne (11 hours), $96 to Sydney (22 hours) via Broken Hill or Renmark, $199 to Perth (34 hours), and $135 to Alice Springs (20 hours). Each company offers a 10% discount to backpackers.

Buses depart from Adelaide's central bus station at 101-111 Franklin St, where both companies have their offices.

Another option is Firefly Express (☎ 8231 1488, 1800 631 164 toll free), which runs a service to Melbourne daily at 8.30 pm for $45 and on to Sydney for $85 ex-Adelaide. It leaves from 110 Franklin St, opposite the central bus station.

As well, the Victorian government's V/Line service (Adelaide ☎ 8231 7620, 1800 817 037 toll free) runs daily to Melbourne for $49 ex-Adelaide. The bus drops passengers at Bendigo in Victoria, from where they catch the train to Melbourne. V/Line leaves from the central bus station at 8.30 am, and arrives in Melbourne 12 hours later.

Both Greyhound Pioneer and McCafferty's have a variety of passes available, so it's a matter of deciding which suits your needs best.

Greyhound Pioneer Bus Passes The **Aussie Kilometre Pass** gives you a specified amount of travel, the shortest being 2000km ($185) going up in increments of 1000km to a maximum of 20,000km ($1400). As an example, if you purchase a 4000km pass ($325) you could travel from Sydney to Cairns, with a detour to Yeppoon en route, and still have 500km to play with. These passes are valid for 12 months from the first day of travel; you can travel in any direction, stop wherever you like, and visit any destination as many times as you want.

The **Unlimited Travel Pass** gives you a set number of days bus travel within a specified period, the shortest is seven days travel in 30 days ($499), the longest 21 days in 60 days ($982). The advantages of these passes are that you can travel one route as many times as you like, and have unlimited km.

The **Explorer Pass** gives you six or 12 months to cover a set route. You haven't got the go-anywhere flexibility of the unlimited travel bus pass but if you can find a set route which suits you – and there are 38 to choose from – then it generally works out cheaper than the Unlimited Travel Pass. For passes that follow a circular route, you can start anywhere along the loop, and finish at the same spot. The main limitation is that, while you can travel in whichever direction you like, you can't backtrack, except on 'dead-end' short sectors such as Darwin to Kakadu, and Townsville to Cairns.

One set-route pass is **Aussie Highlights**, which allows you to loop around the eastern half of Australia from Sydney taking in Melbourne, Adelaide, Coober Pedy, Uluru (Ayers Rock), Alice Springs, Darwin (and Kakadu), Cairns, Townsville, the Whitsundays, Brisbane and Surfers Paradise for $920.

Another is the **Best of the Outback** from Adelaide to Darwin via Alice Springs for $440. Some Explorer Passes include sightseeing tours. For example, the Best of the Outback includes two tours at Uluru.

There's even an **All Australia Pass** which takes you right around the country, including up or down through the centre, for $1550.

McCafferty's Passes With the **Australian Roamer Pass** you purchase a set number of kilometres (minimum 2000km) and can then travel wherever you like on the McCafferty's network, including across to Perth on the *Indian Pacific*. You can travel in whatever direction you like, get on and off wherever you like, and stay as long as you like at any stop. These passes cost around 7c/km, are valid for 12 months from the first date of travel, and availability is restricted.

McCafferty's has several set-route passes that include SA. These are valid for between three and 12 months and have much the same advantages and disadvantages as Greyhound Pioneer's Explorer Passes.

One such pass is the **Coast & Centre Pass**, which loops from Cairns via Sydney, Melbourne, Adelaide, Uluru, Alice Springs and Tennant Creek for $660. The **Best of the East & Centre** ($820) is the same but with the addition of travel to Darwin and Kakadu. Both passes are valid for 12 months, and offer sightseeing as an optional extra.

Also with a sightseeing option, the **Territory Adventurer** ($390) goes from Sydney to Darwin via Melbourne, Adelaide and Alice Springs, with detours to Uluru, Kings Canyon and Kakadu.

Other Bus Options Several smaller companies offer flexible transport options into SA. These trips, which are generally aimed at budget travellers, are a combination of straightforward bus travel and an organised tour. The buses are generally smaller and not necessarily as comfortable as those of the big bus companies, but it's a much more interesting way to travel.

There are a number of companies that include Adelaide in their itineraries.

Oz Experience (☎ 02-9368 1766, 1300 300 028 toll free, enquiries@ozex.com.au) is basically a transport network for backpackers and like-minded travellers. They offer frequent services in a big loop around the eastern half of Australia including Darwin, Adelaide and the east coast. The website for Oz Experience is www.ozexperience.com.

There are various route options with visits to most major destinations, as well as off-the-beaten-track detours to cattle stations and national parks. Oz Experience has 18 passes, which are valid for six or 12 months and range from $35 to $1275 depending on distance. All passes entitle you to get on and off the bus whenever and wherever you like. The drivers act as guides, providing commentaries and advice; they can also pre-book your hostels, stop at supermarkets so you can do your shopping, and arrange discounts on most tours and activities along the way.

The Wayward Bus (☎ 1800 882 823 toll free) enjoys a very good reputation. Three times weekly it travels from Adelaide to Melbourne via the Coorong and Great Ocean Road (three days, $170); three times weekly from Adelaide to Sydney via the Riverland, Griffith and Bathurst (minimum four days, $190); weekly to Alice Springs via the Clare Valley, Flinders Ranges, Oodnadatta Track, Coober Pedy and Uluru; and to Kings Canyon (eight days, $640).

Unlike the Oz Experience runs, these trips include sight-seeing and may also include meals and accommodation. Check

before booking. Visit the website at www
.waywardbus.com.au.

Groovy Grape (☎ 8395 4422, 1800 661
177 toll free) is a relatively new company
offering seven-day camping trips from Adelaide to Alice Springs. It follows much the
same route as the Wayward Bus, but takes
smaller groups. Its price of $590 includes all
meals, campground charges and national
park entry fees. Take a look at the Groovy
Grape website at www.groovygrape.com.au.

Heading Bush 4WD Adventures (☎ 1800
639 933 toll free, headbush@dove.net.au)
does a 10 day 4WD expedition from Adelaide to Alice Springs, visiting such places
as the Flinders Ranges, William Creek,
Coober Pedy, the Painted Desert, Dalhousie
Springs (except summer) and Uluru. The
tour takes a maximum of 10 passengers,
costs $750 all-inclusive and will suit those
who want to rough it.

Heading Bush returns to Adelaide from
Alice Springs every Friday, taking 2 days
($79 per person) for the return journey; you
can jump on regardless of whether or not
you did the main tour.

Nullarbor Traveller (☎ 8364 0407, 1800
816 858 toll free, nullarbor@kem.com.au)
offers relaxed camping and hostelling trips
between Adelaide and Perth. It has two
tours – seven days ($529) and nine days
($699) – and these can include bushwalk-
ing, surfing, whale watching, and swimming with sea lions and dolphins. Its prices
include all accommodation and national
park entry fees, and almost all meals.

Train
Train services into SA are provided by
Great Southern Railway (inquiries and
bookings ☎ 13 21 47). It runs direct services
from Adelaide to Melbourne (on the *Over-
land*), Alice Springs (on the *Ghan*), and
Perth and Sydney (on the *Indian Pacific*),
and has connections to Brisbane and Cairns.
All interstate train services departing
Adelaide leave from the interstate terminal

on Railway Terrace, Keswick, just south-
west of Adelaide city centre.

Discounted fares are available, but, like
the airlines, these aren't advertised – you
have to ask.

The *Overland* goes to Melbourne nightly,
except Wednesday and Sunday. The trip
takes about 13½ hours and costs $58 in econ-
omy, $116 in 1st class and $182 with sleeper.

The fastest service between Sydney and
Adelaide is Speedlink – you travel from
Sydney to Albury on the XPT train, and
from Albury to Adelaide on a V/Line bus.
The travel time is just under 20 hours, and
an economy/1st-class seat is $103/156.

Alternatively, the *Indian Pacific* has a
twice weekly service to Sydney via Broken
Hill. This takes around 25 hours and costs
$152/303/456 for an economy seat/economy
sleeper (no meals)/1st-class sleeper (meals).

The *Indian Pacific* also runs twice
weekly between Adelaide and Perth, taking
37 hours. Fares are $248/520/805 for an
economy seat/economy sleeper (no meals)/
1st-class sleeper (meals).

Between Adelaide and Alice Springs the
Ghan runs weekly from November through
April, and twice weekly for the rest of the
year. The trip takes 20 hours and costs
$170/351/539 for an economy seat/economy
sleeper (no meals)/1st-class sleeper (meals).

Rail Passes There are two national rail
passes allowing unlimited economy-class
rail travel across the country; a surcharge is
payable for sleeping berths on the *Ghan* and
the *Indian Pacific*. Both passes are only
available to holders of overseas passports.

The **Austrail Pass** costs $545 for 14 days
travel, $705 for 21 days and $850 for 30 days.

The **Austrail Flexipass** differs in that it
allows a set number of travelling days
within a six-month period. It costs $450 for
eight days of travel, $650 for 15 days, $915
for 22 days and $1175 for 29 days. The
eight-day pass cannot be used between Adelaide and Perth or Alice Springs.

Getting Around

AIR

Kendell Airlines (☎ 13 13 00) is the main regional operator, with flights from Adelaide to Ceduna, Coober Pedy, Kangaroo Island, Mt Gambier, Port Lincoln and Woomera.

A number of smaller airlines fly to country destinations. See the Getting There & Away sections later in regional chapters.

BUS & TRAIN

Country services within SA are provided by a number of mainly small bus companies of which Premier Stateliner Coach Service (☎ 8415 5555, premstat@premierstateliner .com.au) is by far the largest. It runs mostly daily buses from Adelaide to such far-flung places as Ceduna, Clare, Mt Gambier, Port Augusta, Port Lincoln, Renmark, Victor Harbor and Wilpena Pound. For details on other services see the Getting There & Away sections in regional chapters.

All intrastate bus services depart from Adelaide's central bus station (☎ 8415 5533) at 101-111 Franklin St, where Premier Stateliner has its office. *The StateGuide* is a comprehensive guide to SA's country bus services, and is available here and from other outlets around town, including SATC.

Other than Adelaide suburban trains and a handful of tourist trains, there are no intrastate train services in SA. You can, however, get on and off the interstate trains as they travel through the state.

The following table gives bus fares from Adelaide and Port Augusta to various SA destinations, current at the time of writing.

destination	Adelaide (A$)	Port Augusta (A$)
Victor Harbor	12	–
Robe	30.50	–
Mt Gambier	39	–
Murray Bridge	11	–
Bordertown	29	–
Pinnaroo	33	–
Renmark	28	–
Tanunda	10.50	–
Clare	17	–
Burra	17	–
Peterborough	24	–
Port Augusta	29	–
Kadina	15.50	–
Edithburgh	25	–
Wilpena Pound	52	25.50
Roxby Downs	63	36
Coober Pedy	76	62
Cowell	48	19
Port Lincoln	58	41
Wudinna	58	36
Ceduna	68	54

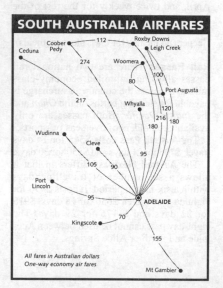

SOUTH AUSTRALIA AIRFARES

- Coober Pedy — 112 — Roxby Downs
- Ceduna
- Leigh Creek
- 274 — Woomera
- 80
- 100
- Port Augusta
- 217 — Whyalla
- 120
- 216
- 180
- 180
- Wudinna
- Cleve
- 95
- 105 — 90
- Port Lincoln
- 95 — ADELAIDE
- 70
- Kingscote
- 155
- Mt Gambier

All fares in Australian dollars
One-way economy air fares

CAR

Many towns have bus services only two or three days a week, and much of the state has no public transport at all. For this reason the car is the accepted means of getting from A to B.

Road Rules

Driving in SA holds few real surprises. Australians drive on the left-hand side of the road, and there are a few local variations on road rules as applied elsewhere in the West. The main one is the 'give way to the right' rule – if an intersection is unmarked (unusual), you *must* give way to vehicles entering the intersection from your right.

The speed limit in built-up areas is usually 60 km/h, while on the open highway it's 110 km/h. Traffic police have speed radar cameras and are very fond of using them in hidden locations – in the Outback they often use aircraft to detect speedsters.

Oncoming drivers who flash their lights may be giving you a friendly indication of a speed camera ahead; they may also be telling you that you've left your headlights on, or they may just be flashing a greeting. The right thing to do is flash back – and slow down if you're speeding.

All new cars in Australia have seat belts back and front; if your seat has a belt you're required to wear it. You'll be fined if you don't. Small children must be belted into an approved safety seat.

Although overseas licences are acceptable in SA, an International Driving Permit is preferred.

On the Road

Road Conditions South Australia has few multi-lane highways; there simply is not enough traffic and the distances are too great to justify them. Generally, the state's main roads are bitumen-surfaced and two lane. However, you don't have to go very far off the beaten track to find yourself on dirt roads; in the Outback, most of the beaten tracks are dirt!

Drink Driving Driving under the influence of alcohol causes many road deaths, especially in country areas. Serious attempts have been made in recent years to reduce the road toll, and random breath testing stations are not uncommon. If you're caught with a blood-alcohol level of more than 0.05% then be prepared for a hefty fine and the loss of your licence.

Fuel Diesel, super and unleaded petrol are available from most service stations sporting the well-known international brand names (diesel isn't sold everywhere, and auto-gas is less widely available). Prices vary from place to place and from price war to price war, but in and around Adelaide all fuels are generally in the 65c to 75c a litre range (unleaded petrol is cheapest). In the Outback the price of fuel soars to $1 per litre; distances between fill-ups can be 200km or more even on main roads, so check your car's consumption and carry spare fuel for emergencies.

Signposting Signposting on the main country roads is generally OK, but around Adelaide and other large towns it can be less so. In fact, you can spend a lot of time trying to find street name signs and, as for finding your way out of the city, the best thing to do is buy a street directory and try to remain calm.

Animals Cows, horses, sheep and kangaroos are common hazards in many country areas, particularly in the Outback where land tends to be unfenced – even if there are fences, kangaroos easily leap over or crawl underneath them. Often the only green grass in sight is along road edges, so grazing animals tend to congregate there. Wedge-tailed eagles may fly up directly in front of you from where they've been feasting on road kills.

None of these animals has any road-sense whatsoever, so be careful; a collision is likely to kill or injure the animal (you may have to put it out of its misery) and could seriously damage your vehicle.

Being nocturnal, kangaroos are most active from dusk to dawn, but you also see them out and about on overcast days. They usually travel in family groups, so if you see one hopping across the road in front of you, slow right down – mum and the kids are probably just behind. Many Australians avoid travelling in country areas at night because of the hazard posed by animals. If you must travel at night, keep the speed down.

Finally, if a 'roo or cow appears out of the darkness in front of you, hit the brakes, dip your lights (so you won't continue to dazzle it, making it even more confused) and sound the horn. Only take more extreme evasive action if it is safe to do so. Many people have died in accidents caused by the driver swerving to miss an animal – it's better to damage the car than kill yourself and others with you.

Outback Travel The Outback offers some great touring experiences on remote dirt roads and tracks. In fact the Stuart Highway and the main roads to Lyndhurst, Roxby Downs and Wilpena Pound are the only bitumen roads in the entire Outback and northern Flinders Ranges. All other routes are dirt or gravel surfaced; their condition varies depending on factors such as when it last rained and when the last grader went through.

It's common sense to make sure your vehicle is in first-class mechanical shape before attempting any remote roads or tracks. Garages (and fuel supplies) are few and far between in these places; if you break down and become stranded in some small town waiting for parts, the experience could wreck your holiday budget. The SA Royal Automobile Association (RAA) can advise on the essential spares and tools to carry. Always pack extra water for the radiator – you may need it if you blow a hose, and it's best not to use up your drinking ration.

Most vehicle accidents on Outback roads are due to speed and inexperience. But try to avoid the temptation to get the driving over with as quickly as possible. Common hazards on dirt roads include loose surfaces, bends, blind crests, cattle grids, potholes and gutters; never drive through a dust cloud thrown up by another vehicle unless you can see what's coming.

Many unsealed roads are closed by heavy rain; some can become impassable for weeks if there's been extensive flooding. If the weather looks like closing in, either get out fast or find somewhere high and dry to camp for a few days. Hopefully you'll have packed enough supplies for such emergencies.

Finally, if you do run into trouble in the back of beyond, stay with your car. It's easier to spot a car than a human being from the air, and you won't be able to carry your jerry cans of drinking water very far anyway.

For recorded information on road conditions in the Outback and Flinders Ranges phone ☎ 1300 361 033. Otherwise, contact police or roadhouses/hotels for local updates.

For the full story on safe Outback travel, get hold of Lonely Planet's *Outback Australia*.

Car Rental

Adelaide has plenty of car-rental companies, but outlets are more scarce in country areas apart from the larger towns. Competition among city outlets is pretty fierce, so rates tend to be variable and lots of special deals pop up and disappear again. For a group, car hire can be reasonably economical. And there are many places – such as the Flinders Ranges – where, if you haven't got your own transport, the only realistic options are to take a tour or hire a vehicle.

The main companies are Avis, Budget, Hertz and Thrifty, though Adelaide also has a large number of local firms. Generally, but by no means always, the big operators will have higher rates than the local firms, but they also have a number of advantages. First of all they're at Adelaide airport and in most of SA's larger country towns. If you want to pick up or leave a car at the airport, then they're the best companies to deal with. However, you should keep in mind that many country outlets only have one or two cars, so always book ahead.

Their second advantage is one-way rental – pick up a car in Adelaide and leave it in Sydney or Port Lincoln, for example. However, a variety of restrictions apply: usually it's a minimum-hire period rather than repositioning charges, and only certain cars may be eligible for one-way journeys. Check the small print on one-way charges before deciding on one company over another.

The major companies offer a choice of deals, either unlimited kilometres or a flat charge plus so many cents per kilometre. On straightforward off-the-card city rentals they're all pretty much the same price. It's on special deals, odd rentals or longer periods that you find the differences. Weekend specials – usually three days for the price of two – are usually good value. If you just need a car for three days around Adelaide make it the weekend rather than midweek. Budget offers 'stand-by' rates, and you may see other special deals available.

Daily rates are typically about $50 for a small car (Holden Barina, Ford Festiva, Daihatsu Charade, Suzuki Swift), about $75 for a medium car (Mitsubishi Magna, Toyota Camry, Nissan Pulsar) and about $100 a day for a big car (Holden Commodore, Ford Falcon), all including basic insurance. Most firms require drivers to be at least 23 years old.

If you want a car for a week, a month, or longer, you will be offered lower rates.

Don't forget the 'rent-a-wreck' companies. They specialise in renting older cars and have a variety of rates, typically around $25 a day. If you just want to travel around the city, or not too far out, they are worth considering.

One thing to be aware of when renting a car is that if you travel on dirt roads you may not be covered by insurance. If there is no cover and you have an accident, you'll be liable for all the costs involved. This applies to all companies, although they don't always point this out – read the fine print and make sure you understand the conditions before renting.

4WD Rental Having a 4WD will enable you to get right off the beaten track into wilderness and Outback areas where you'll experience some wonderful things beyond the reach of most travellers. Several companies in Adelaide rent 4WDs; Hertz and Avis offer one-way rentals between Adelaide and the NT.

Renting a 4WD vehicle is within the budget range if a few people get together. Caudell's (☎ 8410 5552) is one of the few companies that hires out small vehicles, such as a Toyota Rav4 (around $100 per day). Most companies provide larger vehicles, such as Toyota Landcruisers and Nissans; typically around $140 a day, including basic insurance and 200km free.

As always, check the insurance conditions, especially the excess, as they can be onerous. Even in a 4WD the insurance cover of most companies does not cover damage caused when travelling 'off-road', which basically means anything that is not a maintained bitumen or dirt road.

Britz Camper Vans (☎ 1800 331 454 toll free) and Caudell's (☎ 8410 5552) hire fully equipped 4WD vehicles fitted out as campervans – just the thing if you're going to 'do' the Outback and the Flinders Ranges. They start at around $140 per day for unlimited kilometres, plus collision damage waiver ($20 per day). Caudell's are associated with Thrifty, and Britz have offices in all the mainland capitals, as well as in Cairns and Alice Springs, so one-way rentals are possible.

Buying a Car
Reliability is all-important if you're buying a second-hand vehicle. Mechanical breakdowns in the Outback can be very inconvenient, not to mention dangerous.

Shopping around for a used car involves much the same cautions as anywhere in the Western world but with a few local variations. First of all, you'll probably get any car cheaper by buying privately rather than through a car dealer – some of whom are less than honest.

Having said that, we've had some very good reports concerning Boomerang Cars, 579 Grand Junction Rd, Gepps Cross, Adelaide. They specialise in buying and selling cars for backpackers. You can contact Nick Adams, the owner, on ☎ 0414 882 559, boomerangcars@senet.com.au, or take a look at his website (www.senet.com.au/~boomcars).

Buying from a dealer has the advantage of a guarantee, provided the car is less than 15 years old, has less than 200,000km on the clock and costs over $3000. Mind you, a guarantee isn't going to be much use if you're buying a car in Adelaide one week and setting off for Perth the next. In SA there are no compulsory safety checks prior to the registration of a vehicle in a new name.

One certainty is that the further you get from civilisation, the better it is to be in a Holden or a Ford. When your fancy Japanese car expires on the Birdsville Track it's likely to be a one or two week wait for the new part. On the other hand, if your old Holden goes bang there's probably another old Holden sitting at the nearest roadhouse or garage with just the part you're looking for. Every scrapyard in SA is full of Holdens.

Note that in SA third-party personal injury insurance is included in the vehicle registration cost. This ensures that every vehicle (as long as it's registered) carries at least minimum insurance. You'd be wise to extend that to at least third-party property insurance as well, however, as minor collisions with Rolls Royces or Mercs can be disastrously expensive.

Finally, make use of the RAA. They can advise members on local regulations, give general guidelines about buying a car, and, for a fee of around $95 for an on-site mechanical inspection, will check over a used car before you agree to purchase it. They also offer car insurance.

You can pick up the *Guide to Buying a Used Car*, by the Office of Consumer & Business Affairs, free from the RAA bookshop.

Royal Automobile Association

The RAA provides a range of travel literature, excellent maps, detailed accommodation guides and vehicle inspection and emergency breakdown services. Its headquarters, including bookshop and information centre, is at 41 Hindmarsh Square in Adelaide (☎ 8202 4500, fax 8202 4520) and the website address is www.raa.net.

The RAA has reciprocal arrangements with other state automobile associations and with similar organisations overseas. So, if you're a member of the NRMA in New South Wales (NSW), the AAA in the USA or the RAC or AA in the UK, you can enjoy all the benefits of RAA membership.

The little yellow RAA sign you see on vehicle workshops as you're travelling around means the establishment is an authorised agent and provider of services to members. It's also a good guarantee that you won't be ripped off by an unscrupulous mechanic.

MOTORCYCLE

Motorcycles are a popular way of getting around. The climate is just about ideal for biking much of the year, and the many small trails from the road into the bush often lead to perfect spots to spend the night in the world's largest campground.

The state's long, open roads are made for large-capacity machines above 750cc, which Crow-eating bikers prefer once they outgrow their 250cc learner restrictions. But that doesn't stop enterprising individuals – many of them Japanese – from tackling the length and breadth of the continent on 250cc trail bikes. Doing it on a small bike is not impossible, just tedious at times.

Buying a Motorcycle

The *Advertiser* has an extensive classified advertisement section where $4000 or so should get something that will take you around the country, provided you know a bit about bikes. However, then comes the hassle of selling it when you've finished with it.

An easier option is a buy-back arrangement with a large motorcycle dealer in Adelaide (look in the *Yellow Pages* under Motor Cycles and/or Accessories). You'll find some that are keen to do business: basic negotiating skills allied with a wad of cash (say, $6000 for a trail bike and $8000 for a road bike) should secure an excellent second-hand bike with a written guarantee that they'll buy it back in good condition minus around $2000 after your trip.

You'll also need a rider's licence, helmet and basic spare parts (motorcycle repair shops and parts are like hen's teeth in most country areas in SA and interstate). A fuel range of 350km will cover fuel stops up the centre and on Hwy 1 around the continent.

Another thing, beware of dehydration in the dry, hot air – force yourself to drink plenty of water, even if you don't feel thirsty. In the Outback, where it can be a long way between drinks, you'll need to carry at least four litres per day in warm weather.

For general tips on road safety see the Car section earlier this chapter.

BICYCLE

Whether you're hiring a bike to ride around the city or wearing out your chain-wheels on a Mt Gambier to Marla marathon, you'll find that SA is a great place for cycling. There are some excellent bike tracks in Adelaide, and in the country you'll find thousands of kilometres of roads carrying so little traffic that the biggest hassle is waving back to the drivers. The state's major cycling route, the Mawson Trail, will take you 800km from Adelaide to Blinman, mainly on back roads. Especially appealing is the fact that in most areas – with the Mawson Trail a notable exception – you'll ride a long way between hills of any consequence.

Bicycle helmets are compulsory in Australia. It's best to make yourself as visible as possible to other road-users by wearing light-coloured and (at night) reflective gear.

If you're coming specifically to cycle, it makes sense to bring your own bike – check with your airline for costs and for the degree of dismantling/packing required. Alternatively, Adelaide has many good cycling shops where you can buy one, and there are a few bike-hire places offering long-term rental. Otherwise check the *Advertiser* newspaper for second-hand bikes.

While you can load your bike onto a bus to skip the boring bits, the bus companies require you to dismantle your bike, and some don't guarantee that it will travel on the same bus as you. And Adelaide metropolitan buses do not carry bikes at all.

In SA, the most popular bike for serious touring cyclists is a mountain bike, followed by a wide-tyred touring bike. These give the flexibility to ride on dirt roads and tracks, which are usually bad news for narrow-tyred racers. Be warned that cycling on walking tracks in national parks and other conservation areas is strictly *verboten*, although the policy is under review. In the meantime, you can only use public roads and designated cycle paths in these areas.

Until you get fit you should be careful to eat well – remember that exercise is an appetite suppressant. It's surprisingly easy to become so depleted of energy that you end up camping under a gum tree just 10km short of a shower and a steak. No matter how fit you are, water is vital. Dehydration is no joke and can be life-threatening.

It often gets very hot in summer, and you should take things slowly until you're used to the heat. South Australian heat is usually dry, so cycling in 35°C-plus temperatures isn't too bad if you wear a hat and plenty of sunscreen, and drink *lots* of water. Be aware of the blistering 'northerlies' that make north-bound cycling a nightmare in summer. In April, when the clear autumn weather begins, the South-East Trades prevail, and you can have (theoretically at least) tailwinds all the way to Darwin.

Always check with locals if you're heading into remote areas, and notify a responsible person (like your mother) if you're about to do something particularly adventurous. That said, you can't rely too much on local knowledge of road conditions because most people have never ridden a heavily laden touring bike; what they think of as a great road may be pedal-deep in bull dust, while cyclists have happily ridden along roads that were officially flooded.

For more details refer to the Cycle Touring section in the Outdoor Activities chapter.

HITCHING

Hitching is never entirely safe in any country; travellers who decide to hitch should understand that they are taking a small but potentially serious risk. Before making a decision, talk to local people about the dangers. Then, if you decide to go ahead, let someone who cares about you know the details of your proposed trip. The advice that follows should help to make your journey as safe as possible.

First is safety: more than two people hitching together will make things difficult, and solo hitching is unwise for men as well as women. Two women hitching together may be vulnerable, and two men hitching together can expect long waits. The best option is for a woman and a man to hitch together.

Second is position: look for a place where vehicles will be going slowly and can stop easily. A junction or freeway slip-road is a good place if there's stopping room. The ideal location is on the outskirts of a town – hitching from way out in the country can be as hopeless as from the centre of a city.

Third is appearance: the ideal look for hitching is a sort of genteel poverty – threadbare but clean. Don't carry too much gear; if it looks like it's going to take half an hour to pack your bags aboard you'll be left on the roadside. Likewise if you look like you haven't washed for a week.

Finally, know when to say 'no'. Saying no to a car-load of drunks is pretty obvious, but you should also be prepared to abandon a ride if you begin to feel uneasy for any reason. Don't sit there hoping for the best; make an excuse and get out at the first opportunity.

It can be time-saving to refuse a short ride that might take you from a good hitching point to a lousy one. Wait for the right ride to come along. On a long haul, it's pointless to start walking as it's unlikely to increase the chance of your getting a lift.

Of course people do get stuck in outlandish places, but that is the name of the game. In remote areas it's unwise to get dropped off at lonely turn-offs far from water.

If you're visiting from abroad, a nice prominent flag on your pack will help, and a sign announcing your destination can also be useful. Uni and hostel notice boards are good places to look for hitching partners. The main law against hitching is 'thou shalt

not stand in the road' – so when you see the law coming, step back.

Just as hitchers should be wary when accepting lifts, drivers who pick up fellow travellers to share the costs should also be aware of the possible risks involved.

BOAT

The only passenger services in SA are the ferries that operate between Cape Jervis and Kangaroo Island. See Getting There & Away in the Kangaroo Island chapter.

ORGANISED TOURS

Taking an organised tour is a useful way to get around if you don't have your own transport, have only limited time or would like the commentary. South Australia has a large number of tour operators specialising in all sorts of activities. See the sections on Organised Tours in regional chapters, and the earlier Outdoor Activities chapter.

If you're a backpacker, some companies combine a tour with getting from A to B – see the Bus section in the Getting There & Away chapter for details. Otherwise there are plenty of conventional tours. Adventure Tours & Holidays in the *Yellow Pages* gives a good cross-section of what's available.

For budget tours in luxury coaches, Premier Stateliner (☎ 8415 5555) and Adelaide Sightseeing (☎ 8231 4144) mainly go to areas near Adelaide. Intrepid (☎ 1300 360 667) and Wallaby Tracks (☎ 1800 639 933) are among many smaller operators running 4WD tours. If you're into eco-tourism, several companies in Adelaide, such as Ecotrek (☎ 8383 7188), have a variety of experiences to offer. Desert Tracks (☎ 02-6680 8566), Fray Cultural Tours (☎ 8648 4182) and Gecko Tours (☎ 8339 3800) specialise in Aboriginal culture and heritage.

Adelaide has many travel agents. Good for bargain hunters are STA Travel (☎ 8223 2426) at 235 Rundle St and the Youth Hostel Association (YHA) travel office (☎ 8231 5583) at 38 Sturt St. Most backpacker hostels have travel agencies or booking offices that specialise in the cheaper end of the market.

Adelaide

- **pop 1,070,000**

Adelaide is a solid and gracious city; when the early colonists built they generally used stone and plenty of style. Although sterile office towers now dominate the central business district, there are still many fine public and commercial buildings and stately homes dating from the Victorian era.

The solidity goes further than architecture, however. Despite the liberalism of the Don Dunstan years (Dunstan was a flamboyant former premier), Adelaide has not lost its conservatism: it's still an 'old money' place.

Adelaide is dignified and calm in a way no other Australian capital city can match. It also enjoys a superb setting. The city centre is surrounded by parklands and gardens, while the metropolitan area is bounded by the picturesque Adelaide Hills on one side and the sandy swimming beaches of Gulf St Vincent on the other.

Adelaide once had a reputation for wowserism, and is still referred to rather patronisingly as 'the city of churches'. It's true there are plenty of churches, including magnificent cathedrals. However, these are far outnumbered by pubs, nightclubs and licensed restaurants, and the arts and cultural scene is second to none in Australia.

Adelaide is also an exceptionally easy place to get away from. The mighty Murray River, the historic towns and gardens of the Adelaide Hills, and the wineries of the Barossa Valley and McLaren Vale are all less than an hour's drive from the city centre. Even closer are some wonderful bushwalks in the conservation areas that fringe the metropolitan area.

History

At the time of European settlement, the area that is now Adelaide was occupied by the Kaurna people, a peaceful group numbering around 300. Their territory extended south towards Cape Jervis and north towards Port Wakefield, and they had close ties with the

HIGHLIGHTS

- Enjoy some of the many performances of music, dance and drama at the biennial Adelaide Festival of Arts
- Slurp down a pie floater, bought from a street cart
- Take the vintage tram to Glenelg and laze on the magnificent white sandy beach – or go sailboarding
- Admire the many gardens and gracious Victorian buildings in and around the city centre
- Explore the rainforest and other displays in the Adelaide Botanic Garden
- Indulge yourself at one of Adelaide's many excellent restaurants – from Russian to Australian bush tucker, and everything between

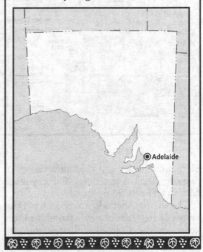

Narungga of Yorke Peninsula. Little is known of their social life. However, they were skilled at working with skins and fibres.

ADELAIDE

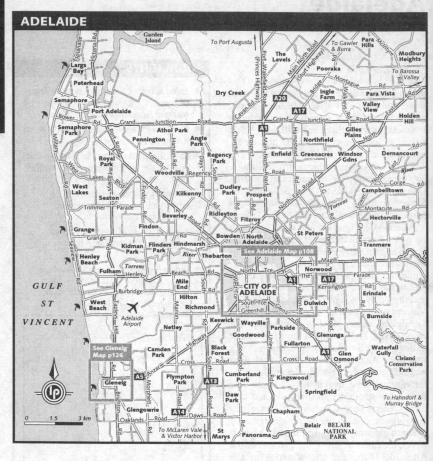

ADELAIDE

Skins were tanned and used for a variety of purposes, such as waterbags, and they made baskets and nets from reeds.

The site for Adelaide was chosen in December 1836 by the colony's far-sighted surveyor-general, Colonel William Light, who created its remarkable design. The land Light chose was well-drained, had fertile soil and straddled the Torrens River, which guaranteed a ready water supply. However, the fact that it was 10km from the coast caused anxiety to some, including Governor Hindmarsh, who tried to have it moved. Hindmarsh named the new capital after the wife of the British monarch, William IV.

Adelaide's European population was 6557 in 1840 and 14,577 in 1851. By the early 1840s it had about 30 satellite villages, including the German settlements of Hahndorf, Klemzig and Lobethal. The capital's growth since then has reflected the state's cycle of boom and bust. A building boom in the 1870s and 1880s coincided with the wheat boom, and was responsible for much of today's fine architectural heritage. Rapid expansion also took place during WWI, the 1920s and the post-WWII years.

More recently, as the suburbs race towards Maslins Beach in the south and Gawler in the north, Adelaide has become a linear city squeezed between the Mt Lofty Ranges and the sea. Nearby towns such as Victor Harbor, Gawler and several Adelaide Hills centres are becoming dormitory suburbs for city workers. Fortunately, town-planning restrictions prevent the rural Barossa Valley, Adelaide Hills and Southern Vales from being gobbled up by housing developments.

Orientation

The city centre is laid out in a grid pattern bounded by broad terraces, with several park-like squares. The main street is King William St, which has Victoria Square at the city's geographical centre; most cross streets change their name at King William St. Walk north up King William St and you'll come to the South Australian Tourism Commission (SATC) on the corner of North Terrace.

Rundle Mall is colourful, with flower and fruit stalls; it's usually a hive of activity (except most Sundays and public holidays) and most of the big department stores are here. Busy arcades and food halls link the mall with North Terrace to the north and Grenfell St to the south. The Royal Automobile Association (RAA), the Environment Shop and Information SA are on Grenfell St.

Cross King William St at Rundle Mall and you'll be on Hindley St, which has a number of good restaurants, glitzy bars and nightclubs. These days, however, much of Hindley St looks decidedly weary, with empty shops and a general air of seediness. Rundle St (the eastern extension of Rundle Mall) has become Adelaide's cosmopolitan heart. Here you'll find several good pubs and bars, and some of the city's best in alfresco dining, camping and outdoor gear, and boutiques.

North of Hindley and Rundle Sts, North Terrace is one of SA's heritage jewels: a 1.6km grand boulevard lined on the north side with a string of magnificent public

buildings. They include the Art Gallery of SA, the State Library of SA, museums and universities to the east of King William St, and Old Parliament House and the suburban train station to the west. SATC is on the corner of North Terrace and King William St.

Continue across North Terrace and you'll be on King William Rd. Keep heading north and you'll pass the Festival Centre on your left, before arriving at the Torrens River. From here you can either walk east through parklands to the zoo and Botanic Garden, or continue straight ahead into North Adelaide.

Information

Tourist Offices SATC's travel centre is at 1 King William St (☎ 8303 2033). It opens from 8.45 am to 5 pm on weekdays and 9 am to 2 pm on weekends and public holidays. It has a large selection of tourist and general information, and will also make bookings for you – but only over the telephone or internet.

Community Information Local radio station SA-FM has a 'community switchboard' that provides current information on everything from forthcoming concerts, art shows and festivals to fire ban days, surf conditions and beach reports. You can phone the switchboard on ☎ 8271 1277 between 9 am and 5 pm daily.

The Disability Information & Resource Centre is at 195 Gilles St (☎ 8223 7522). It opens from 9 am to 5 pm Monday to Friday.

Details of other information services can be found in the Facts for the Visitor chapter.

Arts & Culture Information Arts SA (☎ 8207 7100, fax 8207 7159, artsa@sa .gov.au) is a useful source of information on cultural attractions, venues, performing arts, festivals and special events in Adelaide. It puts out an arts directory and a comprehensive and informative brochure, which is also available from SATC.

Money Exchange Adelaide's out-of-hours alternatives for changing foreign currency include the American Express office on the 5th floor at 13 Grenfell St, and the 'General Office' on the 5th floor of the Myer department store on Rundle Mall. The latter has the best hours; it opens at 9 am from Monday to Saturday, and closes at 5.30 pm from Monday to Thursday, 9 pm on Friday and 5 pm on Saturday – on Sunday it opens from 11 am to 5 pm.

Post & Communications The main post office is in the city centre at 141 King William St. It opens for business from 8 am to 6 pm weekdays and 8.30 am to noon Saturday; the poste restante, on the ground floor (off King William St), is open from 7 am to 5.30 pm weekdays and 9 am to 1 pm Sunday. The post office also has public telephones (coin and card), a fax service, a philatelic section and an Australiana gift shop.

Email & Internet Access Adelaide has a couple of internet cafes, and no doubt there will be more by the time you read this. The Ngapartji Multimedia Centre (☎ 8232 0839) at 211 Rundle St has 20 terminals, facilities for scanning, word processing and printing, and a free email service. Internet access costs $5/10 for 30/60 minutes.

The Norwood Oz Net Cafe (☎ 8363 7733) at 160A Magill Rd, Norwood, has 10 terminals, facilities for scanning and printing, and great coffee. They charge $4/6 for 30/60 minutes.

During the academic year the State Library of SA has 10 internet-connected terminals for public use, but there is a lot of competition for them. More terminals are made available in December and January, when things are relatively quiet. Phone ☎ 8207 7248 for internet bookings.

A growing number of hostels have coin-operated internet terminals.

Bookshops Adelaide has numerous new, second-hand and antiquarian bookshops. You'll find them listed in the *Yellow Pages* telephone book.

The RAA has a travellers' bookshop with a good selection of publications including

travel within and outside the state, bushwalking, natural and social history, and Aboriginal culture. The larger general bookshops include Mary Martin's, at 249 Rundle St East, Dymocks, at 136 Rundle Mall, and Angus & Robertson, next door at No 138. Dymocks has a particularly large travel section.

Smaller, more specialised outlets include the Europa Bookshop at 238 Rundle St East, which has a good selection of foreign-language novels, travel books and maps. Imprints Booksellers, at 80 Hindley St, has quality literature, biographies and a gay and lesbian section.

Murphy Sisters Bookshop, at 240 the Parade, Norwood, specialises in feminist and lesbian works, and also has an excellent section on Aboriginal studies. They have another shop at Semaphore: Sisters by the Sea, Shop 1, 14 Semaphore Rd.

The Conservation Council of SA, at 120 Wakefield St, has a very good selection of books on conservation and environmental issues, as well as a decent reference library.

For cheap second-hand books, try the Orange Lane market (see the Markets section for details).

Dangers & Annoyances You'll hardly ever meet a beggar in Adelaide but, like most places in the world, if you go looking for trouble you'll find it, particularly at night. Prime spots to avoid are the side streets off Hindley St and in the vicinity of the casino and the suburban train station. Don't go wandering at night through the parklands along the Torrens River.

Always try to park your car in a well-lit area. If you must park in a dark spot, remove the rotor button or use an anti-theft device. *Never* leave valuables or important documents like your passport in the car. A camera or bag left in full view on the seat is an invitation for some idiot to relieve you of it.

The city centre is the favourite hunting ground for car thieves, and people who steal from cars. The worst areas are North Terrace, Rundle Mall, the Adelaide Parklands, the casino and Hindley St.

Museums

On North Terrace, the **South Australian Museum** is an Adelaide landmark with huge whale skeletons in the front window. Although primarily a natural history museum, it has a superb display featuring the Ngarrindjeri people of the Coorong and lower Murray. Included in the display is the story of 'Dreamtime' spirit ancestor Ngurunderi, and how the Murray was created. There's also a pleasant coffee shop, and many surprises in the adjoining souvenir shop. The museum opens between 10 am and 5 pm daily, and admission is free.

The excellent **Migration Museum**, at 82 Kintore Ave next to the State Library, is dedicated to the migrants who have come from all over the world to make SA their home. Many fascinating displays explain how the state's rich multicultural society has evolved. It opens weekdays from 10 am to 5 pm, and weekends and public holidays from 1 to 5 pm. Admission is by donation.

The free **Museum of Classical Archaeology** on the first floor of the Mitchell Building (in the University of Adelaide grounds on North Terrace) has a small but representative collection of antiquities dating from the third millennium BC (Egypt and Mesopotamia) to the European Middle Ages. It opens from noon to 3 pm during semester.

On the corner of King William and Flinders Sts, in the Old Treasury Building, there's the **Museum of Exploration, Surveying & Land Heritage**. For $3, which includes coffee, you can make an interesting two-hour tour of this grand old building (it dates from 1839), taking in the museum, Cabinet Room and underground tunnels. It opens weekdays only from 10 am to 3 pm.

The **Maritime Museum**, at 126 Lipson St in Port Adelaide, has several vintage ships including the *Nelcebee*, the third-oldest ship on Lloyd's shipping register. There's also a historic lighthouse and a computer register of early migrants. The museum opens daily from 10 am to 5 pm and admission costs $8.50. West-bound bus No 151 or 153 will get you there from North Terrace, or you can take the train.

Next door is the **Port Dock Station Museum**, which features a huge collection of railway memorabilia. It opens daily from 10 am to 5 pm and entry is $7. Between September and April they run steam trains to Semaphore from noon on Sundays (and daily during school holidays).

The **Investigator Science & Technology Museum**, at the Wayville Showgrounds off Goodwood Rd, takes an entertaining look at science. It usually opens daily between 10 am and 5 pm, but may be closed while exhibitions are being changed (check by phoning ☎ 8410 1115); admission costs $7.50. To get there, take bus No 212, 214, 216, 296 or 297 from King William St.

Also interesting is the **Old Adelaide Gaol** on Gaol Rd, Thebarton, which opened in 1841 and closed in 1988. Its features include the hanging tower, where 45 people were executed, and various gaol artefacts. You can do self-guided tours between 11 am and 4 pm on weekdays ($5), and guided tours between 11 am and 3.30 pm on Sundays ($6).

Aboriginal Cultural Centre

Tandanya, at 253 Grenfell St, is an Aboriginal cultural institute containing galleries, arts and crafts workshops, performance spaces, a cafe and a good gift shop. Phone ☎ 8224 3200 to find out what's on. The centre opens daily from 10 am to 5 pm, and admission is $4.

State Library of SA

As well as an extensive selection of books and other printed material, the State Library on North Terrace has changing exhibitions and displays, including memorabilia of local hero and cricket star Sir Donald Bradman. Open daily, the Bradman collection is housed next door in the Institute Building; admission is $3.

The library's newspaper reading room has publications from around the world – these come by surface mail, so don't expect yesterday's (or even last week's) editions. They also provide free internet access. However, for most of the year demand is high, so make bookings on ☎ 8207 7248.

ADELAIDE

CENTRAL ADELAIDE

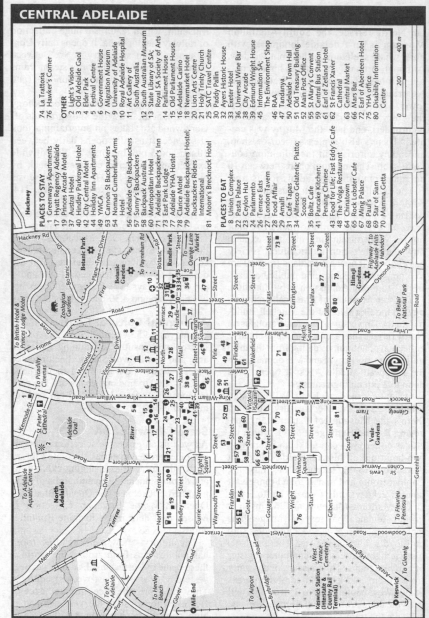

PLACES TO STAY
1 Greenways Apartments
17 Hyatt Regency Adelaide
19 Princes Arcade Motel
37 Austral Hotel
40 Hindley Parkroyal Hotel
42 City Central Motel
44 Holiday Inn Apartments
49 YMCA
53 Cannon St Backpackers
54 Nomad Cumberland Arms Hotel
56 Adelaide City Backpackers
57 Sunny's Backpackers
58 Backpack Australia
60 Metropolitan Hotel
71 Adelaide Backpacker's Inn
73 East Park Lodge
77 Adelaide YHA Hostel
78 Clarice Motel
79 Adelaide Backpackers Hostel; Rucksackers International
81 Moore's Brecknock Hotel

PLACES TO EAT
8 Union Complex
22 Pasta Palace
23 Ceylon Hut
24 Parlamento
26 Terrace Eats
27 London Tavern
28 Food Affair
29 Amalfi
31 Cafe Tapas
34 Alfresco Gelateria; Piatto; Scoozi
35 Boltz Cafe
41 Pancake Kitchen; Penang Chinese
43 Food for Life; Fast Eddy's Cafe
48 The Volga Restaurant
65 Chinatown
66 Rock Lobster Cafe
67 Ming Palace
68 Pauli's
69 Star of Siam
70 Mamma Getta

74 La Trattoria
76 Hawker's Corner

OTHER
2 Light's Vision
3 Old Adelaide Gaol
4 Elder Park
5 Festival Centre
6 Government House
7 Migration Museum
9 University of Adelaide
10 Royal Adelaide Hospital
11 Art Gallery of South Australia
12 South Australian Museum; State Library of SA; Royal SA Society of Arts
13 Parliament House
14 Old Parliament House
15 Adelaide Casino
16 Newmarket Hotel
20 Lion Arts Centre
21 Holy Trinity Church
25 SATC Travel Centre
30 Paddy Pallin
32 Ayers Historic House
33 Exeter Hotel
36 Universal Wine Bar
38 City Arcade
39 Edmund Wright House
45 Information SA; The Environment Shop
46 RAA
47 Tandanya
50 Adelaide Town Hall
51 Old Treasury Building
52 Main Post Office
55 St Mary's Convent
59 Central Bus Station
61 Earl of Zetland Hotel
62 St Francis Xavier Cathedral
63 Central Market
64 Mars Bar
72 Earl of Aberdeen Hotel
75 YHA office
80 Disability Information Centre

The library opens from 9.30 am to 8 pm weekdays (5 pm Thursday) and noon to 5 pm weekends, but is closed on public holidays.

Art Galleries

Next to the museum of SA on North Terrace, the free **Art Gallery of SA** houses the world's largest display of Australian art, with works by many well-known artists such as Dorrit Black, Russell Drysdale, Hans Heysen, Tom Roberts and Clifford Possum Tjapaltjarri; and particularly notable is the collection of colonial art. The free audio-tour of the Australian collection is very instructive.

Works by overseas masters include a 375-year-old painting of a seated couple by Sir Anthony Van Dyck, and a significant collection of 20 bronze sculptures by Auguste Rodin (see the boxed text). There's also a wonderful display of South-East Asian ceramics and a good art bookshop.

The gallery opens daily from 10 am to 5 pm, with tours at 11 am and 2 pm (3 pm weekends). Activities, such as the free Tuesday lunchtime talks, and highlights are publicised in the *Art Gallery of South Australia News*. The gallery also presents the **Adelaide Biennial of Australian Art**, which coincides with the Adelaide Festival of Arts, celebrates contemporary forms of Australian visual arts.

The **Royal South Australian Society of Arts**, in the Institute Building on the corner of North Terrace and Kintore Ave, next to the State Library, has major exhibitions. It opens weekdays from 11 am to 5 pm and

The Six Million Dollar Man

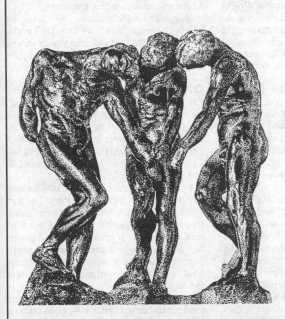

The Three Shades (1880) is one of 20 bronze sculptures by master French sculptor Auguste Rodin acquired in March 1996 by the Art Gallery of South Australia.

Coming from the private gallery of New South Wales collector Mr William Bowman, the gallery's acquisition is the largest public collection of Rodin works in the southern hemisphere.

The Rodin coup, which cost $6 million, together with the $26 million renovation of the art gallery, is part of the South Australian government's cultural tourism push.

Paris-born Rodin (1840-1917) is considered by many to be the world's best-known and most important sculptor after the great Michelangelo.

weekends from 2 to 5 pm, and admission is free.

Other galleries include the **Union Gallery** on level 6, Union House, at the Adelaide University (open weekdays from 10 am to 5 pm) and the **Art Space Gallery** in the Festival Centre (open the same hours as well as Saturday afternoon).

Grand City Buildings

Ayers Historic House Museum is at 288 North Terrace, close to the city centre. This elegant bluestone mansion was originally constructed in 1846 for Sir Henry Ayers (seven times SA's premier, and after whom Ayers Rock (Uluru) in the NT was named), with additions over the next 30 years. It opens from Tuesday to Friday between 10 am and 4 pm and on weekends and public holidays between 1 and 4 pm. Admission is $5 and guided tours are available (bookings ☎ 8223 1234).

At 59 King William St, **Edmund Wright House**, built in 1876, was originally constructed in an elaborate Renaissance style with intricate decoration for the Bank of SA. The historic foyer and reception area are open daily from 9 am to 4.30 pm and admission is free.

The imposing **Adelaide Town Hall**, built between 1863 and 1866 in 16th century Renaissance style, looks out on to King William St between Flinders and Pirie Sts. The faces of Queen Victoria and Prince Albert are carved into the facade. There are free one-hour tours on Tuesday, Wednesday and Thursday, but you'll need to book (☎ 8203 7563).

Opposite the Town Hall, the **Main Post Office** was commenced in 1867 and altered in 1891. Both these wonderful buildings were designed by architect Edmund Wright, who would turn in his grave if he could see the glass-fronted office blocks that crowd around today. Then again, maybe he'd love them!

On North Terrace, **Government House** was built between 1838 and 1840, with further additions in 1855. You can tour the gardens in autumn and spring (contact SATC on ☎ 8303 2033 for details).

Just across King William Rd, **Parliament House** has an elegant facade featuring 10 marble Corinthian columns. It was built in two stages: the west wing was completed in 1889 and the east wing in 1939. When Parliament isn't sitting there are free tours on weekdays at 10 am and 2 pm (inquiries ☎ 8237 9100); when it is, you're allowed inside at 2 pm to watch the action.

Built in 1838, Holy Trinity Church, also on North Terrace, was the first Anglican church in the state. Other impressive early churches are St Francis Xavier Cathedral on Wakefield St (1856) and St Peter's Cathedral on Pennington Terrace, North Adelaide (1869-76).

St Francis Xavier Cathedral is beside Victoria Square, where you'll find a number of other important early buildings: the **Magistrate's Court** (1847-50); the **Supreme Court** (1869); and the **Old Treasury Building** (1839), where you can take tours (see the Museums section earlier for details).

Adelaide's Architecture & Arts, by Michael Queale and Nicolette Di Lernia, describes walks that will take you to around 320 sites, including many examples of public art.

Other Historic Buildings

On Jetty St, Grange (west of the city centre), is **Sturt's Cottage**, home of the famous early Australian explorer. It is open Friday to Sunday and public holidays from 1 to 5 pm (4 pm in winter); admission is $2.50. Take bus No 130 or 137 from Grenfell St and get off at stop 29A.

North-west of the city, **Fort Glanville** is at 359 Military Rd, Semaphore Park. The fort was built in 1878, when Australia was going through a Russophobic phase as a result of the Crimean War. It opens from 1 to 5 pm on the third Sunday of each month between September and May, when local enthusiasts hold a full-dress military re-enactment ($3.50).

In Springfield (7km south-east of the city) magnificent **Carrick Hill**, at 46 Carrick Hill Drive, is built in the style of an Elizabethan manor house. Its 40 hectares of bushland, lawns and manicured English-style gardens are the venue for the **Medieval Festival**, held in April. Carrick Hill opens Wednesday to Sunday and public holidays from 10 am to 5 pm; the $8 admission includes guided tours at 11.30 am and 2.30 pm. Catch bus No 171 from King William St and get off at stop 16.

Festival Centre
The Adelaide Festival Centre is on King William Rd close to the Torrens River. Looking vaguely like a squared-off version of the Sydney Opera House, it performs a similar function with its variety of auditoriums and theatres. However, it provides a venue for a much greater range of entertainment.

While the centre is visually uninspiring – let's face it, it's damned ugly – it does have a marvellous riverside setting; you can picnic on the grass in front of the theatre, and there are several places to eat. Pedal boats and bicycles can be hired nearby.

Light's Vision
On Montefiore Hill, north of the city centre across the Torrens River, stands the statue of Colonel William Light, Adelaide's founder. Light is said to have stood at this point and mapped out his visionary plan for Adelaide city. In the afternoon there's a nice view of the city's gleaming office towers rising above the trees, with the Adelaide Hills making a scenic backdrop.

Botanic Garden & Other Parks
The city and North Adelaide are surrounded by attractive parkland, gardens and large trees. They're separated by the Torrens River, which is itself bordered by public gardens and lawn. Native waterbirds such as swans and pelicans are often seen here looking for a free feed.

At the eastern end of North Terrace, the splendid 20 hectare **Adelaide Botanic Garden** is only a short stroll from the city centre. Its highlights include a unique prefabricated palm house (1877), the **Museum of Economic Botany** (check out its stencilled ceiling), and the wonderful 1988

DENIS O'BYRNE

Colonel William Light surveys his empire

Bicentennial Conservatory (it recreates a tropical rainforest environment). A comprehensive **wine museum** is to be opened in late 1999 or early 2000.

The gardens are open weekdays from 8 am to sunset, and on weekends and public holidays from 9 am to sunset. Free 1½ hour guided tours leave from the kiosk every Tuesday, Friday and Sunday at 10.30 am. The Bicentennial Conservatory opens between 10 am and 4 pm daily (5 pm during daylight saving), and admission is $3.

Rymill Park in the East Parkland has a boating lake and a 600m jogging track. The South Parkland contains **Veale Gardens**, with streams and flower beds. To the west are a number of sporting grounds, while the **North Parkland** borders the Torrens River and surrounds North Adelaide.

The restful **Himeji Gardens** on South Terrace blends two styles of Japanese garden: *senzui* (lake and mountain) and *kare senzui* (dry garden). Adelaide and Himeji are sister cities. Details of guided tours are available from the ranger on ☎ 8203 7483.

Adelaide Walking Tour

There are several good walks in and around the city centre. This tour, of about 4km, takes you on a loop starting at the intersection of King William Rd and North Terrace. It includes evocative reminders of Adelaide's more halcyon past, as well as attractive parks and gardens; most of the places mentioned are covered elsewhere in the chapter in greater detail. Allow a day for more than just a quick look.

The **South African War Memorial** is right on the corner of North Terrace and King William Rd, outside the wrought-iron gates of **Government House** (1838). Heading east from here you'll soon pass **London Tavern** (on your right). This is a great spot for a cool drink at the end of the tour.

On the corner of Kintore Ave is the **National War Memorial**. The **Institute Building** (1836) on the opposite corner is the terrace's oldest building – it houses major art exhibitions and the **Sir Donald Bradman collection** of cricketing memorabilia. It's a few steps from here to the **State Library** and a few more to the **Migration Museum**, on Kintore Ave.

Continuing along North Terrace, the **SA Museum** has many fine natural history exhibits; if you're tired already there's a very pleasant coffee shop here. Next door is the **Art Gallery of SA** with its marvellous collections, particularly of Australian work.

Keep walking east and you'll pass the imposing facade of the **University of Adelaide**. Founded in 1874, it was the first in Australia to admit women to degree courses. The much smaller **University of South Australia** is next door on the corner of leafy Frome Rd. If you want, you can shorten the tour by turning left (north) on Frome Rd to the **Zoological Gardens**.

A little farther, and on the right, is **Ayers Historic House** (1846). Continuing on you pass the classic **Botanic Hotel** on the corner with East Terrace – there are some good cafes between here and **Rundle St**, which is full of eateries at this eastern end.

The entrance to the wonderful **Botanic Garden** is on North Terrace directly opposite the Botanic Hotel. From here, a network of pathways criss-cross the 20 hectare gardens, leading to highlights such as a **rainforest conservatory** and a historic **palm house**.

Head north through the gardens to **Plane Tree Drive**, then turn left. Leave the road at the elbow bend and continue straight ahead (west) to Frome Rd. Turn right and the zoo entrance is just in front by the Torrens River.

From the zoo, pleasant walks meander through the parkland and gardens that line both banks of the Torrens as far as King William Rd. Having reached this busy thoroughfare, turn left (south) and follow it past the **Festival Centre** to North Terrace and the end of this tour.

Denis O'Byrne

Walks & Rides An extensive network of walking and cycle paths runs through Adelaide's parklands, including a sealed route that takes you from the coast to the Adelaide Hills along the **Torrens River Linear Park** and **O-Bahn Busway**.

Parkland guides for walkers and cyclists are available from Information SA (☎ 8204 1900) at 77 Grenfell St.

The Adelaide Oval

The Adelaide Oval, hallowed site of interstate and international cricket matches, is in the North Parklands on the Torrens' north bank. Established in the 1870s – it hosted its first test match in 1884 – it's an attractively open ground with a marvellous atmosphere. It also has the oldest scoreboard (1911) still in use for test matches in Australia. When there are no games on you can take **tours** of the complex, which includes a cricket museum (contact the curator on ☎ 8300 3853). Among other things, the museum features one of Joel Garner's one-day outfits and a 1949 portrait of Sir Donald Bradman.

Adelaide Zoo
On Frome Rd, the zoo exhibits around 1500 exotic and native mammals, birds and reptiles, and also has a children's zoo. Its South-East Asian rainforest exhibit is a major drawcard. The zoo opens daily (including Christmas Day) from 9.30 am to 5 pm, and entry is $10.

For a different way of getting there, take a cruise on the *Popeye* ($5), which departs daily (weather permitting) every 20 minutes from Elder Park in front of the Festival Centre. You can also catch bus No 272 or 273 from Currie St, or walk there from Elder Park or the Adelaide Botanic Garden.

Markets
Close to the centre of town, the busy **Central Market** (☎ 8203 7345), off Victoria Square between Grote and Gouger Sts, is a great place for self-catering travellers. It sells a vast range of fresh produce, and you'll be buying direct from the producer, so things are generally quite a bit cheaper than in the shops.

The market opens Tuesday (7 am to 5.30 pm), Thursday (9 am to 5.30 pm), Friday (7 am to 9 pm) and Saturday (7 am to 3 pm). You can pick up some real bargains just after lunch on Saturday, when unsold produce is disposed of at giveaway prices – mainly because it's no longer fresh. Tours are available (see Organised Tours later in this chapter).

The **Orange Lane Market**, off Norwood Parade in Norwood, will appeal to alternative lifestylers; it's the place to go for Indian fabrics, second-hand clothing, massage, tarot readings, palmistry, remedies, bric-a-brac and junk. It is open on weekends and public holidays from 10 am to 6 pm. A few steps away on the Parade are several coffee shops and cafes.

Haigh's Chocolates
Haigh's are generally considered to make Australia's finest chocolates at their factory at 154 Greenhill Rd, Parkside (☎ 8271 3770). The visitor centre is open weekdays from 8.30 am to 5.30 pm and Saturday from 9.30 am to 4.45 pm; free tours run at 2.30 pm daily except Sunday. You can watch truffles being hand-dipped in chocolate (bliss!) and taste their many mouth-watering products.

To get there from the city, take bus No 190, 191, 191B or 192 from King William St. Get off at stop 1 on Unley Rd just over Greenhill Rd.

Mother Mary MacKillop Sites
Mary MacKillop, who is to be canonised as Australia's first saint, lived in Adelaide for 16 years, and there are a number of sites associated with her. They include **St Mary's Convent** at 253 Franklin St, Adelaide, where she was excommunicated, and **St Ignatius Church** on Queen St, Norwood, where she assisted at mass during her excommunication period.

Another site is **St Joseph's Convent** at 286 Portrush Rd, Kensington, where you'll find the **Mary MacKillop Centre** (☎ 8364 5311). The centre has displays of historic photos and various artefacts, as well as a leaflet describing eight significant pilgrimage sites. It opens weekdays except Wednesday from 10 am to 4 pm and Sunday from 1 to 4 pm.

Ice Skating
Adelaide's ice-skating rink (☎ 8352 7977), at 23 East Terrace in Thebarton, is open daily. There are two ice rinks and a 150m-long slope surfaced with artificial snow, where you can ski, toboggan and snowboard. Take bus No 151 or 153 from North Terrace and get off at stop 2.

Swimming Centres
Aquatic centres with 25m or 50m pools are scattered around the suburbs; you'll find them listed under 'Swimming Pools' in the *Yellow Pages*. Closest to the city is the Adelaide Aquatic Centre (☎ 8344 4411) on

Jeffcott Rd in North Adelaide. It has swimming and diving pools, as well as a gym and other facilities.

Adelaide Beaches

There are a number of good beaches stretching from Maslins Beach in the far south to Grange in the north; beaches beyond Grange often have too much seaweed for real enjoyment. SATC has a self-drive touring guide to the Adelaide coast.

Maslins Beach South, about 40km south from the city centre, is Adelaide's only nudist beach. It's backed by colourful cliffs, and to get to the sand you have to walk down a steep path from the Tuitt Rd carpark.

Heading north, **Seaford** and adjoining **Moana** have a small beach that's popular with novice surfers. You can drive onto the sand from the beach ramp at Moana.

Christies Beach is much larger and has a jetty and reef popular with scuba divers. For a generally quieter time you can visit nearby **O'Sullivans Beach**, where there's a concrete ramp leading off Galloway Rd.

The first of the 'old-time' metropolitan beaches is **Seacliff**, about 16km from the city centre. This beach – which includes **Brighton** – is very popular for swimming, windsurfing and sailing. There's a clifftop monument to the Aboriginal Dreamtime ancestor Tjilbruke at Kingston Park, just south of Seacliff.

Glenelg has a magnificent white sandy beach, the most popular in Adelaide. Nearby Jetty Rd is lined with cafes and restaurants, and the popular front bar of the Stamford Grand Hotel is right by the waterfront. This is an easy beach to get to from the city; simply catch the tram in Victoria Square and get off outside the Stamford Grand.

There's another lovely stretch of sand at nearby West Beach, the closest beach (10km) to the city. Continuing north there are more good beaches and eateries at Henley Beach and **Grange**. The last remnant of Adelaide's original dune system is at West Lakes. The beach here isn't wonderful, but you can swim and windsurf in the nearby lake; if it's

been raining heavily, give the lake a couple of days to rid itself of rubbish.

North from here are the last of Adelaide's metropolitan beaches, **Semaphore** and **Largs Bay**. The water at both is shallow, making them good for swimming when there's no weed about. Semaphore is another popular windsurfing spot.

Organised Tours

The many tours in and around Adelaide include gardens, birdwatching, historic buildings, art galleries and the usual sightseeing tours by various means of transport. Some have already been mentioned in earlier sections of this chapter.

For $23 you can get a day pass on the Adelaide Explorer (☎ 8364 1933), a road-registered tram replica that does a continuous circuit of a number of attractions, including Glenelg and the Botanic Garden. The tour takes 2¾ hours and you can get on and off en route; daily departures from 38 King William St are at 9 and 10.20 am, and 12.15, 1.35 and 3 pm.

Funky Earth (☎ 8353 8240, mobile 0414 835 382) has a range of day trips from Adelaide for $35, including wine tasting and bushwalking – they promise loads of laughs. Its afternoon 'hike & bike' tour around Adelaide and the hills costs $25.

The University of Adelaide conducts guided birdwatching walks along the Torrens and in the parkland. The tours take 1½ to two hours, cost $15 and operate daily except public holidays. Call ☎ 8303 5594 for further details.

Among its gastronomic adventures, Adelaide Top Food & Wine Tours (☎ 018 842 242) does a 90 minute discovery of the Central Market for $22 – you'll meet the stallholders and taste samples of their fare. Tours run on all market days.

Premier Stateliner (tour bookings ☎ 8415 5566) has $25 half-day tours, which include the city sights, Hahndorf in the Adelaide Hills, Mt Lofty and the Cleland Wildlife Park. Adelaide Sightseeing (☎ 8231 4144) and Festival Tours (☎ 8374 1270) do much the same tours for much the same prices.

Busway (☎ 8262 6900) is a smaller company with several tours including Hahndorf, Cleland and Adelaide.

Shaun's Bound-Away Tours (☎ 8371 3147) offers a day tour to the Adelaide Hills and Fleurieu Peninsula for $39, not including lunch; among other highlights you'll visit Hahndorf and a McLaren Vale winery.

Another company is Bee-init Tours (☎ 8332 1401). Its excursions include a three hour 'city and hills' tour for $27.

There are several Harley-Davidson tour operators. Two who have been around a while are Aces High (☎ 8212 7800) and Adelaide Harley Tours (☎ 8276 5456). Both charge around $60 for the first hour and $40 for the second.

See Organised Tours in regional chapters for details of tours outside Adelaide.

Boat Cruises The MV *Foxy Lady* (☎ 8341 1194, mobile 0418 817 837) offers cruises on the Port River from Fishermans Wharf at Port Adelaide. Scheduled public cruises operate on Sunday, public holidays and school holidays (Wednesday to Saturday).

Also at Port Adelaide, Falie Charters (☎ 8341 2004) has day cruises from $80 and twilight cruises from $69 on Gulf St Vincent in the tall ship *Falie*. Twilight cruises only operate during the daylight saving period.

Special Events

One of the nation's premier cultural events, the Adelaide Festival of Arts takes place in February and/or March of even-numbered years. Accommodation fills up and things generally go a little crazy as a vast horde of culture vultures descends on the city for 17 days of drama, dance, music and visual arts. Each festival features exclusive Australian and international performances, plus a number of world premieres. A highlight of the 2000 Festival will be the Peter Greenaway-Louis Andriessen opera collaboration, Writing to Vermeer. Contact the Festival Centre (☎ 8216 4444, fax 8216 4455, ausfest@ adelaide.on.net) for further details.

Writers' Week, which forms part of the Festival, is one of only three or four top international literary festivals; a number of international and Australian writers of note are invited for a week of panels, readings and meet-the-author sessions.

Held at the same time as the Adelaide Festival of Arts, the Adelaide Fringe celebrates innovation in the arts. Once a relatively minor event compared with the Festival of Arts, the Fringe is now just as big and possibly even more popular. In 1998, 335 companies from 14 countries performed and exhibited their work to an attendance of over 857,000. Contact the Fringe on ☎ 8231 7760, fax 8231 5080, buzz@adelaidefringe.com.au, or take a look at its website at www.adelaidefringe .com.au.

The Womadelaide world music festival (inquiries ☎ 8271 1488, fax 8271 9905, apadmin@artsprojects.com.au) is held over three days and nights in February of odd-numbered years. This hugely successful event, which takes place outdoors in Botanic Park, features music and dance by artists from around the globe. Past artists have included Afro-Celt Sound System, Peter Gabriel, Shiela Chandra and Youssou N'dour.

There's also the Australian Festival for Young People, a major international event taking place in March of odd-numbered years. It presents a broad program including theatre, dance, visual arts and writing, and is aimed at audiences aged from three to 26 years. For details contact ☎ 8267 5766, fax 8239 5038, afyp@adelaide.on.net.

The annual Glendi Festival, also held in March, features the traditional customs of Greece. It's said to be one of the largest ethnic cultural festivals in the southern hemisphere.

Places to Stay

Prices for many caravan parks, motels and some hotels rise between Christmas and the end of January, when accommodation is extremely scarce. Some places also put their prices up on weekends and during school holiday periods. All prices given here are off-peak.

Places to Stay – Budget

Camping There are quite a few caravan parks around Adelaide. The following are within 10km of the city centre – check the tourist office for others. All prices given are for two people.

Adelaide Caravan Park (☎ 8363 1566, 8 Bruton St) in Hackney, 2km north-east of the city centre, has campsites starting at $20, on-site vans at $38 and cabins at $58. *Windsor Gardens Caravan Park* (☎ 8261 1091, 78 Windsor Grove) in Windsor Gardens, 7km north-east of the city centre, has campsites starting at $10 and cabins for $35 ($50 for three or four adults).

West Beach Caravan Park (☎ 8356 7654, Military Rd) in West Beach, 8km west of the city centre, has campsites starting at $14, on-site vans at $38 and cabins at $53. This park is close to the beach and only a couple of kilometres from Glenelg. *Marine Land Holiday Village* (☎ 8353 2655) also on Military Rd, West Beach, has basic cabins for $49, self-contained cabins for $59, two-bedroom holiday units for $75 and two-bedroom villas for $95. There are no campsites.

Colleges At the University of Adelaide on North Terrace, *St Ann's College* (☎ 8267 1478) operates as a hostel from the first week in December through to the end of January; beds are $16, or $20 with bed linen. At other colleges, accommodation usually includes meals so is much more expensive.

Hostels There are a number of backpacker hostels, with the standard varying from excellent to very ordinary. Generally speaking, however, Adelaide's hostels have lifted their game in recent times.

Because competition is fierce, all sorts of freebies (tours, breakfasts, apple pie and so forth) are offered to tempt you through the door, particularly in the winter off-season. Almost all hostels have licensed travel agencies or booking offices on the premises, and most have internet access for sending and receiving email.

As well, most hostels offer a free pick-up and drop-off service for the airport, central bus station and train station. Several hostels are within easy walking distance of the central bus station.

When you leave the bus station, turn left onto Franklin St and on the next corner you'll find *Sunny's Backpackers Hostel* (☎ 8231 2430, 1800 631 391 toll free, 139 Franklin St). Off-street parking is available and there's a travel agency (open at 6 am). Dorm beds start at $13 and twins and doubles are $15 per person. This is a quiet place; if you want to rage the *Hampshire Hotel*, a good backpacker place, is nearby in Grote St.

Opposite the bus station is the large (150 beds) and somewhat cavernous *Cannon St Backpackers* (☎ 8410 1218, 1800 069 731 toll free, cannonst@senet.com.au, 110 Franklin St). It isn't what you'd call intimate, but it is gaily painted, friendly and has good facilities – these include cheap meals, a bar (not a public one), secure under cover parking, a smoking room, bicycle hire and a travel agency. Dorm beds start at $11 and singles/doubles are $28/34.

Backpack Australia (☎ 8231 0639, 1800 804 133 toll free, bpa_adelaide@hotmail .com, 128 Grote St) is opposite the Central Market. They own the nearby Hampshire Hotel, which is a popular party place – if you're not a party animal you should stay in the hostel, not the hotel. Other facilities include cheap meals, a tiny camping space on the roof of the hostel, and a travel agency. Dorm beds start at $11, single rooms are $17 and twins and doubles are $26.

The comfortable old pub *Cumberland Arms Hotel* (☎ 8231 3577, 1800 355 599 toll free, 205 Waymouth St) has a variety of accommodation options; an 11 bed dorm is $11 per person, and twin and double rooms are $16 per person. There is no kitchen, but you can get cheap meals in the public bar.

Adelaide City Backpackers (☎ 8212 2668, 239 Franklin St) is in a lovely old two storey house. Its dorms are reasonably spacious, if gloomy, with dorm beds starting at $13, and private rooms at $18/35; all rooms have ceiling fans and heating. There's also a pleasant bar (parties are not encouraged) and cheap meals.

Most of the other hostels are clustered in the south-eastern corner of the city centre. You can get there on bus No 191 or 192 from Pulteney St or take any bus going to the South Terrace area (Nos 171 and 172 to Hutt St; 201 to 203 to the corner of King William St and South Terrace). Otherwise, it's not that far to walk.

The *Adelaide YHA Hostel* (☎ 8223 6007, adelyha@chariot.net, 290 Gilles St) has the best standard of any of the city hostels. Its facilities include a travel agency, limited off-street parking and mountain-bike hire; however, the reception is closed between 11.30 am and 4 pm daily. Beds in dorms and twin rooms cost $14 for members (bed linen extra).

Nearby is the *Adelaide Backpackers Hostel* (☎ 8223 5680, 1800 677 351 toll free, 263 Gilles St). Dorm beds cost from $14 and double rooms are $32; some bedrooms have ceiling fans and others air-con, and most are heated in winter. They also have mountain bikes for hire, and can book tours for you.

Next door, *Rucksackers Riders International* (☎ 8232 0823, 257 Gilles St) is popular with motorbike and bicycle travellers, particularly Japanese – Margaret, the owner, has a reputation for being extremely helpful. This lovely 110-year-old bluestone villa is clean and comfortable, and its rooms are heated day and night in winter. Dorm beds cost $12, while twin rooms start at $14 per person.

The *Adelaide Backpacker's Inn* (☎ 8223 6635, 1800 247 725 toll free, abackinn@tne .com.au, 112 Carrington St) is two streets closer to the city centre. This is an ex-pub with dorm beds from $14. The annexe across the road at 109 is more upmarket, with a much better kitchen and small, but reasonably comfortable, twins and doubles for $20 per person. It also has a travel agency and limited off-street parking.

Close to the attractive East Parklands, the triple storey, red brick *East Park Lodge*

(☎ 8223 1228, 1800 643 606 toll free, eastpark@dove.net.au, 341 Angas St) was built 90 years ago as a Salvation Army hostel for young country ladies. It's large and labyrinthine, but owners Dave and Kathy have done a lot of work to brighten it up. The facilities are good (they include a travel agency, mountain-bike hire and a small, in-ground swimming pool), and it enjoys the nicest location of any of the city's hostels. Dorm beds start at $14 and private rooms are $25/35 for singles/doubles, and there are ceiling fans in most bedrooms.

The centrally located *YMCA* (☎ 8223 1611, adelaidey@ymcasthaust.asn.au, 76 Flinders St) takes guests of either sex and has a very good standard. There's an excellent kitchen as well as gyms and squash courts, which you can book in at any time. Dorm beds cost $15 and singles/twins are $25/35, with a 10% discount for members.

Hotels The following provide basic pub-style accommodation with shared facilities.

The *Metropolitan Hotel* (☎ 8231 5471, 46 Grote St) is oppisite the Central Market and next to Her Majesty's Theatre. It charges $20 per person.

At 205 Rundle St, the *Austral Hotel* (☎ 8223 4660) charges $25/35 for singles/doubles. There's a trendy bar downstairs, and it's just a few steps to several good restaurants, cafes and bars.

Moore's Brecknock Hotel (☎ 8231 5467, 401 King William St) has singles/doubles for $30/50, including a light breakfast. This is a popular Irish pub, with Irish folk groups performing on Friday nights.

Places to Stay – Mid-Range

The *City Central Motel* (☎ 8231 4049, 23 Hindley St) has small but comfortable units for $52/59 singles/doubles. Off-street parking can be arranged (from $5 for 24 hours).

A little farther from the action, the *Princes Arcade Motel* (☎ 8231 9524, 262-66 Hindley St) has units from $45/50 for singles/doubles. Off-street parking is available.

The *Clarice Motel* (☎ 8223 3560, 220 Hutt St) has basic twin rooms with shared facilities for $28/45, and motel units for $49/59/69. All tariffs include a light breakfast, and off-street parking is available.

Festival Lodge (☎ *8212 7877, 140 North Terrace*) is opposite the casino and has rooms from $69/80. There's no on-site parking, but the motel negotiates reduced rates with a nearby carpark (from $5 for 24 hours).

In North Adelaide, the friendly **Princes Lodge Motel** (☎ *8267 5566, 73 Lefevre Terrace*) is a grand old town house with loads of character – it's set in a row of impressive homes opposite a park. Its rooms start at $30/58, including a light breakfast. The motel is within walking distance of the city, and handy to the restaurants and cafes on O'Connell and Melbourne Sts.

Although there are motels all over Adelaide, it's worth noting that there's a 'motel alley' along Glen Osmond Rd, which leads into the city centre from the south-east. This route is very busy, so some places are a bit noisy – keep this in mind when booking in.

Powell's Court (☎ *8271 7033, 2 Glen Osmond Rd*), 2km south-east of the city centre, has one-bedroom units for $52/58/68/78 and two-bedroom units for $5 per person extra. There's also a three-bedroom unit that sleeps up to nine; it is $120 for the first six, and $5 per person thereafter. All units have kitchens.

Alessandro Maandini's *Ryokan* (☎ *8370 3507, maandini@adam.com.au, 16 Brightview Ave)* in Blackwood, a southern hills suburb, is a contemporary Japanese-style house with a wonderful calm atmosphere. It's hardly a budget place, but Alessandro, an entertaining fellow, is an experienced backpacker who enjoys having like-minded people around. If there's a spare bed he may be prepared to give you a good deal – you can only ring and ask!

Apartments There are numerous holiday apartments in and around Adelaide; you'll find them listed under Apartments & Flats and Apartments – Serviced in the *Yellow Pages.*

Close to the inner city is *Greenways Apartments* (☎ *8267 5903, bpsgways @camtech .net.au, 45 King William Rd)* in North Adelaide. They have basic but comfortable one, two and three-bedroom apartments. A one-bedroom unit costs $77 for two people per night up to three nights ($73 after three nights, $70 after seven nights).

Apartments on the Park (☎ *8223 0500, 1800 882 774 toll free, reservations@majesticapartments.com.au, 274 South Terrace)* is a more upmarket place. It has a pleasant setting on the edge of the city across from the South Parklands, diagonally opposite the Himeji Gardens. Studio apartments are $99 (singles and doubles) and two-bedroom apartments are $120 (singles and twins).

The *Tynte Street Apartments* (☎ *8223 0582, 1800 882 774 toll free, reservations@ majesticapartments.com.au, 82 Tynte St)* in North Adelaide are comfortable, and priced at $105 for a studio apartment. It's a short walk from here to the cafes and restaurants on O'Connell St.

Places to Stay – Top End

The following are right in the city centre. Most offer package deals on weekends, when room prices are generally a fair bit cheaper than during the week.

Grosvenor Vista Hotel (☎ *8407 8888, 1800 888 222 toll free, 125 North Terrace)* has standard rooms that start at $85/105, executive suites at $180. Standard rooms start at $125 at the *Stamford Plaza Hotel* (☎ *8461 1111, 1800 500 175 toll free, 150 North Terrace)* and a suite at $255. There are panoramic views from above the 5th floor; rooms with a park view start at $155. Also on North Terrace, the *Hyatt Regency Adelaide* (☎ *8231 1234, 13 12 34, North Terrace)* has standard rooms starting at $240 and suites at $390.

The *Hilton International Adelaide Hotel* (☎ *8217 2000, fom_adelaide@hilton.com, 233 Victoria Square)* has standard rooms starting at $135, with suites at $380, while the *Hindley Parkroyal Hotel* (☎ *8231 5552, 65 Hindley St)* prices start at $150 for a standard room and $190 for a suite.

Holiday Inn Apartments (☎ *8231 8333, 1800 882 601 toll free, adelaide@holidayinn .com.au, 255 Hindley St)* has one and two-bedroom suites for $180 and $240 respectively. Secure under cover parking is available.

Places to Eat
Adelaide supposedly has more restaurants – there's around 700 in total – per head of population than any other city in Australia, and its huge variety of cuisine makes dining here a culinary adventure. Licensing laws are liberal in SA, so a high proportion of restaurants are licensed.

The *Advertiser* newspaper normally publishes a useful reference to the constantly changing food scene. Check their front counter at 121 King William St, or the larger newsagencies.

Adelaide is very well supplied with hotels offering counter meals, particularly at lunchtime. Just look for those tell-tale black-boards standing outside. You won't have to search for long to find one with substantial meals under $5, particularly now that most hotels have poker machines. Many places offer meals at ridiculous prices just to get people through the door.

Rundle St The eastern end of Rundle St (off Rundle Mall) is Adelaide's Bohemian quarter, with shops specialising in Art Deco artefacts and alternative clothing, and a swag of restaurants and cafes.

Terrace Eats is a large, casual dining area in the basement of the Myer Centre, between Rundle Mall and North Terrace. Its numerous eateries include Asian, English, Italian and Mexican. From here there's access through to the evocative *London Tavern*, at the North Terrace end, which does pub-style meals.

Amalfi (29 Frome St), just off Rundle St, has Italian cuisine and a great menu. It's often difficult to get in, but hang around as it's worth the wait.

Cafe Tapas (242 Rundle St) is a Spanish bar and restaurant. Imagine tucking into treats such as 'kid goat braised in Moroccan spices with an apricot and walnut infused

couscous'. Alternatively, you can enjoy the delicious snacks they bring to your table.

For something spicier, *Taj Tandoor* at No 253 is one of Adelaide's best Indian restaurants. Main courses start at around $10.

Just up the street is 'little Italy'. The *Alfresco Gelateria* at No 260 is a good place for gelati, cappuccino and a variety of sweets. *Scoozi*, at No 272, is a huge, cosmopolitan cafe noted for its wood-oven pizzas. In between is *Piatto*, with more pasta and pizza. The tables on the sidewalk outside these places are popular on balmy nights.

At No 286 is *Boltz Cafe*, another indoors and alfresco place. It specialises in modern Australian fare with Asian and Mediterranean influences. Their upstairs bar has stand-up comics on Thursday nights.

Hindley St Adelaide's original 'sin strip', this street has gone to seed in recent years. Nevertheless, there are still many good eateries to be found among the glittery bars and discos.

On Gilbert Place, which dog-legs between Hindley St and King William St, the *Pancake Kitchen* is open 24 hours a day and has main-course specials from $8. Next door, the *Penang Chinese Restaurant* is open Monday to Saturday from 11 am until 10 pm. Mains are a little cheaper here.

Cafe Boulevard (15 Hindley St) is a pleasant coffee lounge with hot meals for under $9 and cheap and delicious sweets on display.

Ceylon Hut (27 Bank St), just off Hindley St, has tasty curries starting at $12.

Abdul and Jamil's *Quiet Waters*, downstairs at No 75, is a friendly Lebanese coffee lounge serving predominantly vegetarian dishes. Take-aways are available, and if you want to eat in it's BYO. There's a belly dancer on Wednesday nights.

Across the street at No 76, *Fast Eddy's Cafe* is open 24 hours and does a range of meals and snacks. It's licensed, so if you've been up all night you can enjoy a beer with your burger for breakfast.

Upstairs at No 79, *Food for Life*, a Hare Krishna restaurant, has a good vegetarian smorgasbord for $5, including dessert. It opens for lunch from noon to 3 pm Monday to Friday.

Pasta Palace at No 90 is another institution, with mains from $9. They specialise in Italian cuisine (what else?) and claim their food is 'justa like mamma used to make'.

North Terrace *Parlamento*, at No 140 on the corner with Bank St, has chef's specials for under $10. It's one of the city's best pasta places and has a great atmosphere.

At No 150, *Pasta Hound* in the Fox & Hounds Pub (part of the Stamford Plaza Hotel) is similarly priced. The pub has live jazz Monday through to Thursday from 7 pm.

Food Affair at the Gallerie Shopping Centre, which runs from North Terrace through to Gawler Place, and John Martins on Rundle Mall, has numerous international eateries.

Gouger St This is another street of restaurants, with many local institutions.

The *Central Market* between Gouger and Grote Sts near Victoria Square is good value for all types of food, fruit, vegetables and bread. Tacked on at the market's western end is *Chinatown*, which has a large collection of mainly Asian-style eateries; one group of kitchens shares a busy communal eating area, providing a cheap and popular option.

At No 55, the very popular *Mamma Getta Restaurant* is an authentic Italian place with most dishes around $8.

Just down the street, *Star of Siam* at No 67 serves delicious Thai food.

Paul's, at 79, is one of the best fish & chip places in town. Across the road at No 76 is *Stanley's*, also specialising in seafood. The *Rock Lobster Cafe*, at 108, is even better – it's a more upmarket place and well worth the splurge.

Ming Palace is an unpretentious Chinese restaurant at No 201. It's renowned for its Peking duck.

Around Town *Goodies Grub* at 108 Franklin St is directly opposite the central bus station. It opens from 7 am to 5.30 pm Monday to Friday and 7 am to 1 pm Satur-

day for eat-in and take-away meals. Cooked breakfasts cost around $4.

The trendy *Equinox Bistro* at Adelaide University is in the Union Complex above the Cloisters off Victoria Drive, close to the city. It opens weekdays from 10 am to 10 pm (8 pm in university holiday periods), and has main courses from $5. *Union Cafeteria* on the ground floor is even cheaper.

Also good value is *Hawker's Corner*, on the corner of West Terrace and Wright St. It opens daily, except Monday, for lunch and dinner and is popular with overseas students. In fact, there's a student hostel on the premises.

The Volga Restaurant, upstairs at 116 Flinders St, is Adelaide's only Russian restaurant. It's a friendly place, with Roma (gypsy) violinists on Friday and Saturday nights, and beluga caviar for those with expensive palates.

At 346 King William St, *La Trattoria* is an Adelaide institution for pizza and pasta. Mains start at $10, and there are cheaper lunch specials.

The *Festival Bistro*, in the Festival Centre on King William Rd, overlooks the Torrens River. It has sandwiches and snacks, and is open late into the evening. (It's closed on Sunday unless there's a performance.)

Pie Floaters

If you're after a new experience in late-night eating, look for the pie carts that appear every night on city streets from 6 pm till the early hours; they're an institution. The carts sell 'pie floaters', a chunky meat pie doused in tomato sauce and floating in thick pea soup. Judging by the number of people tucking in with obvious enjoyment, the floaters don't taste as bad as they look. You'll find pie carts near the train station and on the corner by the main post office. If you can't face a pie floater, they sell more conventional pies as well as tea and coffee.

Denis O'Byrne

North Adelaide There are a number of good restaurants and cafes on O'Connell St in North Adelaide. The ***Royal Oak Hotel*** at No 115 is an old stone pub that has been done up in a lively, quirky style and which offers interesting food (mains around $12). It has live jazz on Wednesday and Sunday nights.

At No 101 the ***Oxford*** is a stylish renovated pub that's won heaps of awards for the inventive modern food served in its restaurant. It's a bit pricey with mains around $16 to $20, but still it's a must for foodies.

Cafe Paesano, on the corner of O'Connell and Tynte Sts, is an Italian place with large pasta dishes from $10. It's chaotic, but light and airy, and there's alfresco dining on the pavement.

Also popular is ***Scuzzi***, another Italian cafe across the road. It's a little more expensive and generally attracts an older clientele.

Himeji, at No 61, is an authentic Japanese restaurant with one of the best sushi bars in town. It's rather expensive, but the experience is said to be worth it.

At No 43, the ***Blue & White Cafe*** is an Adelaide institution for take-aways – the taxi drivers eat here, so you know it's good. It opens at 11.30 am daily and closes at 2.30 am Sunday to Thursday and 4.30 am other nights.

A few steps towards the city from the Blue & White Cafe is ***Rakuba Restaurant***. It is pretty basic, but it's Adelaide's only authentic African restaurant. It's open daily for lunch and dinner.

Amarin Thai *(106 Tynte St)* serves excellent Thai food in attractive surroundings, and is very popular with locals. It's open for dinner daily from 6 pm and is licensed.

There's a string of cafes and restaurants along Melbourne St, a main thoroughfare into the city. You might find the traffic noise a bit much during peak periods, but there's no denying the quality and variety of the eateries on offer.

The ***Lion Hotel***, an old favourite at No 161, on the corner of Jerningham St, is a good place to start – or finish. It has a pleasant beer-garden, a couple of good bars and an upmarket restaurant.

Diagonally opposite is ***Cafe Flash***, a very busy eatery with a strong Italian influence. And opposite Cafe Flash is ***Bacalls*** at No 149. It's known for its grills and New Orleans Creole Cajun dishes. Once you've checked these there are many more continuing along the street.

The ***British Hotel*** *(58 Finniss St)* has been beautifully restored and boasts a great atmosphere. It also has an attractive beer garden where you can grill your own steak at the barbecue. Large meals are around $14 to $15 ($2 to $3 less if you cook your own).

Entertainment

Bookings for music and the performing arts at the various Adelaide venues can be made through BASS (Best Available Seating Service) on ☎ 13 12 46. There are numerous BASS outlets around town, including one at the Festival Centre (open from 9 am to 6 pm Monday to Saturday). Look in the *White Pages* telephone book for more.

SATC and BASS outlets have a lot of information on what's happening on the cultural scene generally. Also check the *Advertiser* and the free newspapers *Arts Monthly* and *Adelaide Review* – the latter has theatre and gallery reviews.

Major concert venues include ***Elder Hall*** in the University of Adelaide. It's considered one of Australia's finest concert halls, and has free performances every Friday from 1 to 2 pm during the academic year. The Bach Festival is held here annually in October. On Port Rd in Hindmarsh, the multi-purpose ***Adelaide Entertainment Centre*** hosts everything from ballet to opera to rock 'n roll concerts.

Cinema Adelaide has a number of multiscreen cinema complexes – Greater Union's ***Megaplex Marion***, in the huge Westfield ShoppingTown Marion at Oaklands Park, has 30 screens. A couple of drive-in theatres are still going out in the suburbs. Check the entertainment pages in the *Advertiser* for what's on around town.

The *IMAX Theatre* (☎ *8227 0075, 272 Rundle St)* has SA's largest screen (350 sq m). It shows a variety of 2D and 3D films daily, with admission around $13 for 2D and $14 for 3D.

Palace East End Cinemas (☎ *8232 3434, 274 Rundle St)* is Adelaide's key venue for alternative film. It opens daily and shows Australian, foreign language, classic and art-house films on its four screens. Monday is cheap night ($7). They host the Young Film Makers Awards, held in December. Also worth checking is the *Nova Cinema* (☎ *8223 6333)*, just down the street at No 251.

The *Mercury Cinema* (☎ *8410 1934)* in the Lion Arts Centre publishes a quarterly calendar detailing its films and festivals. Other cinemas screening alternative film are the wonderful old *Piccadilly Cinema* (☎ *8267 1500, 181 O'Connell St)* in North Adelaide, *Trak Cinemas (8332 8020, 375 Greenhill Road)* and the *Capri Theatre* (☎ *8272 1177, 141 Goodwood Rd)* in Goodwood.

Theatre Adelaide has an active and varied performing arts scene. For comprehensive information on what's happening, check SATC, the *Adelaide Review* or ring TheatreSA (☎ 8443 6200), for events by the smaller theatre companies, or Arts Around Adelaide (☎ 8232 8177) for events mainly by the larger companies.

The *Adelaide Festival Centre* is at the hub of performing arts in SA. Based here is the State Theatre Company, who present the state's major drama productions.

Other popular venues are *Her Majesty's Theatre* (☎ *8212 8600, 58 Grote St)*, the *Lion Theatre & Bar* (☎ *8212 9200)* in the Lion Arts Centre, and *Theatre 62* (☎ *8234 0838)*, at 145 Burbridge Rd in Hilton.

Apart from the major companies, there are a number of smaller ones whose productions are worth considering. These include *Junction Theatre* (☎ *8443 6200)*, on the corner of South Rd and George St in Thebarton. It presents all new local and interstate material and is a good place to see the work of upcoming playwrights.

Vitalstatistix (☎ *8447 6211, 11 Nile St)* in Port Adelaide specialises in feminist works. In fact they're the major national production house for women's theatre.

At the Lion Arts Centre, *Doppio Parallelo* (☎ *8231 0070)* produces works with multicultural themes.

For youth theatre, check what's happening with *Patch Theatre* and *Urban Myth*. The *Restless Dance Company* (☎ *8212 8495, 240 Franklin St)* specialises in youth dance theatre, and runs an extensive program of workshops.

Rock There's the usual pub rock circuit, and only a sample is listed here. To find out who's playing around town either check *The Guide* in Thursday's *Advertiser* newspaper, or phone the radio station SA-FM (☎ 8272 1990) for a recorded run-down.

As well, the free music paper *Rip it Up* is worth checking for its listings. You'll find it at most music shops, hotels, cafes and night spots around town.

In North Adelaide, and handy to the restaurants, the *Oxford Hotel (101 O'Connell St)* has a DJ on Friday nights and live bands most other nights. It's 'in' with the yuppie set.

The *Earl of Aberdeen*, on Carrington St at Hurtle Square, is a very nice, very trendy place with lots of timber, and it usually has a rock band on Friday and Saturday nights. It's handy to the backpacker hostels southeast of the city centre.

On Rundle St, the *Austral Hotel* and *Exeter Hotel* at Nos 205 and 246 respectively, often have bands and DJs. They're popular with business folk and office workers during the day (both pubs have interesting lunchtime menus), while at night they're university student hang-outs. Try them if you're looking for a place to go for a drink before heading out to dinner.

Also good for a pre-dinner drink is the *Universal Wine Bar (285 Rundle St)*. It's got a pleasant atmosphere, with lots of iron filigree and doors that fold back on summer nights so you can catch the breeze.

Most popular of Adelaide's clubs is *Heaven Nightclub*, in the very grand old

Newmarket Hotel on the corner of West and North Terraces. It has DJs playing Wednesday to Saturday nights. In the same building is *Joplins Nightclub*, which is more appealing to the older set with live bands nightly.

Heaven's major competitor is *The Planet* (*77 Pirie St*), which also opens Wednesday to Saturday nights.

The *UniBar* (☎ 8303 5856), in the Union Complex at the University of Adelaide, often features big-name and up-coming rock bands during lunchtime, afternoons and evenings – usually on Fridays. The bar is also a venue for social, cultural and avant-garde performances and activities; there's always something interesting taking place, and visitors are welcome. The complex is off Victoria Drive and above the Cloisters.

There are free concerts at the *Adelaide Festival Centre* on Saturday evenings during January, and Sunday afternoons during February and March and June through to August (inquiries ☎ 8216 8600).

Jazz The Adelaide jazz scene has something happening most weeks. Find out by ringing the Jazz Hot Line on ☎ 8303 3755 or getting hold of the free street newspaper *Adelaide Jazz News*, available at universities, clubs and music shops. The *Adelaide Review* also has a section on jazz.

There are a number of regular venues, with the *Governor Hindmarsh Hotel* (☎ 8340 0744, 59 Port Rd) in Hindmarsh offering contemporary jazz on Sunday evenings. The Jazz Coordinator (☎ 8303 4339) – the major jazz promoter in SA – holds two or three concerts here each month.

In the city centre, the Fox & Hounds Pub in the *Stamford Plaza Hotel (150 North Terrace)* has live bands on Sunday to Thursday nights.

Folk Adelaide has numerous folk clubs and bands of various persuasions. Regular venues include the *Governor Hindmarsh Hotel* (see Jazz) for bluegrass and folk, and the *Kings Head Hotel (353 King William St)*.

If you'd like to hear original music, the Songwriters, Composers and Lyricists

Association (SCALA) performs on Wednesday night at *The Office*, a club at 110 Pirie St. Adelaide's major venue for world music is *Nexus* (☎ 8212 4276) in the Lion Arts Centre.

For information on folk events throughout the state, contact the Folk Federation of SA (☎ 8340 1069) – they're located in the Governor Hindmarsh Hotel. Alternatively, get hold of the federation's monthly newspaper *Infolkus*, available from selected outlets around Adelaide.

Gay & Lesbian Places There are a number of places around town and out in the suburbs. You'll find them advertised in *Adelaide gt*; see Gay & Lesbian Travellers in the Facts for the Visitor chapter.

Venues include the very popular *Mars Bar*, a dance club for the younger set at 120 Gouger St. It opens nightly from 10 pm until late. *Beans Bar*, another dance club at 258 Hindley St, is also open nightly – Fridays from 5 to 9 pm is 'women only'.

The *Edinburgh Castle Hotel (233 Currie St)* has DJs on Friday and Saturday nights. You can get good counter meals here.

Pubs Several pubs brewed their own beer until fairly recently, but it seems the only survivor is the *Port Dock Brewery Hotel (10 Todd St)* in Port Adelaide. It produces four distinctive beers – the process is overseen by a German brew specialist – and an alcoholic lemonade.

The bar at the *Earl of Zetland Hotel (57 Flinders St)* near the YMCA claims to have the world's largest collection of malt whiskies, with over 275 varieties available by the nip.

Gambling The *Adelaide Casino* (☎ 8218 4100) is housed in the impressive old train station on North Terrace – the magnificent foyer is its most outstanding feature. Apart from a wide range of gambling facilities (including a two-up game, of course) there are three bars and two restaurants; informed sources reckon that the best odds are offered by craps and baccarat. It opens daily from 10 am to 4 am (6 am from Friday to Sunday and on public holidays). Smart casual dress is required.

Most of the pubs around town have poker machines.

Things to Buy

There's great shopping in Adelaide, with Rundle Mall at the heart of the action. The Myer Centre has 150 speciality shops as well as the huge Myer department store on five levels. Off the mall are several arcades and side-streets crammed with interesting shops selling all manner of wares.

Out at Oaklands Park, a south-western suburb, the huge Westfield ShoppingTown Marion is SA's largest shopping complex.

For clothing there's a swag of places. Rundle St is recommended for retro clothes and boutiques, while the Orange Lane Market is worth checking for second-hand and alternative clothing (see the earlier Markets section). There are good bargains in designer label seconds on Glen Osmond Rd in Parkside; several shops on King William Rd in Hyde Park and Unley Rd in Unley feature name and up-coming Australian designer labels.

T-Shirt City at 72 Hindley St lets you design your own travel record of Australia, SA and the world – a fun way to show where you've been and get a great souvenir. A T-shirt takes about 20 minutes to print and costs $25.

Unley Road in Unley also has some wonderful antique shops. You can combine antique shopping with a visit to the Adelaide Hills, where there are some good shops in Nairne and Strathalbyn.

Tandanya, the Aboriginal cultural institute at 253 Grenfell St, includes a crafts and souvenir shop.

A range of high-quality craftwork is produced and sold at the Jam Factory Craft & Design Centre, in the Lion Arts Centre on the corner of Morphett St and North Terrace. They also have a shop at 74 Gawler Place, in the city centre.

If you're after bushwalking, climbing and outdoor gear, there are several shops conveniently grouped on Rundle St: Flinders Camping at No 187, the Scout Outdoor Centre at No 192, Mountain Designs at No 203, the Annapurna Outdoor Shop at No 210, and Paddy Pallin at No 228.

Getting There & Away

All international and interstate flights to and from Adelaide go via Adelaide airport, and interstate train services leave from the Keswick terminal. The bus terminal for Greyhound Pioneer, McCafferty's, Premier Stateliner and minor regional bus lines is at 101-111 Franklin St; the Firefly Express is opposite at 110 Franklin Street.

For details of travel to and from Adelaide see the Getting There & Away chapter.

Getting Around

To/From the Airport Adelaide's fairly modern international and domestic airport is a convenient 7km west of the city centre. An airport bus service (☎ 8381 5311) operates between city hotels and some hostels at least half-hourly from around 7 am to 9.30 pm on weekdays and hourly on weekends and public holidays for $6.

The trip from Victoria Square to the domestic terminal takes about 30 minutes – a little less to the international terminal. Let the driver know if you're catching a flight on one of the smaller regional airlines, as the drop-off point is different.

A taxi from the city centre to the airport costs about $15. Alternatively, you can travel to the airport entrance on bus No 276 or 278 leaving from opposite Harris Scarfe's in Grenfell St and stop V1 in Currie St.

Budget, Hertz, Avis and Thrifty have desks at the airport.

Most of the hostels will pick you up and drop you off if you're staying with them.

To/From the Train Station The airport to city bus service calls in to the interstate train station at Keswick on its regular run. It costs $3 from the station to the city centre.

Public Transport Adelaide has an extensive integrated transport system operated by

TransAdelaide (TA) (☎ 8210 1000). The TA Information Bureau, where you can get timetables and free brochures and guides on services, is on the corner of King William and Currie Sts.

The system covers metropolitan buses and trains, as well as the vintage tram service to Glenelg. Tickets purchased on board buses are $2.80 before 9 am, after 3 pm and on weekends, and $1.60 between 9 am and 3 pm weekdays. They are valid for two hours from the commencement of the first journey. Train tickets can be purchased from vending machines on board trains, or at staffed train stations.

The best deal is the day-trip ticket, which permits unlimited travel for the whole day and costs $5.40. They can be purchased on buses, trams and at staffed train stations, and from any deli or newsagent displaying a Metro sticker.

There are two free Bee Line bus services. No 99B runs in a loop from the Glenelg tram terminus at Victoria Square, down King William St and round the corner to the train station. It leaves the square every five to eight minutes on weekdays from 7.47 am to 6 pm and every 15 minutes to 9.20 pm on Friday, and from 8.37 am to 5.37 pm on Saturday.

No 99C runs around the margins of the city centre from the train station, passing the Central Market en route. It leaves the station every 15 minutes on weekdays between 7.54 am and 6.09 pm (9.09 pm Friday) and every 30 minutes on Saturday between 8.39 am and 5.09 pm.

See Glenelg's Getting There & Away section for details of Adelaide's vintage tram service.

Taxi Adelaide has around 1000 licensed taxis. You can either order a taxi by phone, flag one down or find a rank. Friday and Saturday nights are particularly busy, so if you want to book a cab do it early.

Car & Motorbike Rental The *Yellow Pages* lists over 20 vehicle rental companies in Adelaide, including all the major national companies. Those with cheaper rates include

Access Rent-a-Car (☎ 8223 7466), Action Rent-a-Car (☎ 8352 7044), Airport Rent-a-Car (☎ 8443 8855; 1800 631 637 toll free), Delta (☎ 13 13 90), Rent-a-Bug (☎ 8234 0911) and Smile Rent-a-Car (☎ 8234 0655). Access and Smile allow their cars to be taken over to Kangaroo Island.

Show & Go (☎ 8376 0333), at 236 Brighton Rd, Somerton Park, has motor scooters for $59 per day and motorcycles from 250cc ($69) to 1000cc ($89). You need a car driver's licence to rent a scooter, while a full motorcycle licence is required for the bikes – a motorcycle learner's licence is acceptable for scooters and 250cc bikes.

Bicycle Adelaide is a relatively cyclist-friendly city, with good cycling tracks through the parks and cycle lanes on some main city roads. However, you can't take your bike on trams or buses (you can on trains).

Linear Park Mountain Bike Hire (☎ 0411 596 065) is at Elder Park near the Popeye Landing, just below the Festival Theatre. It's right on the Linear Park Bike & Walking Track, which wends its way mainly along the Torrens River from the beach to the foot of the Adelaide Hills. Bicycles are $8 per hour, $20 per day, and from $80 per week – groups of four or more get a 25% discount.

Flinders Outdoor Leisure (☎ 8359 3344), at 235 Pirie St, rents mountain bikes from $15 per day or $70 for a week.

Adelaide Bike Hire (☎ 8293 2313, mobile 0416 072 905), at 42 Gertrude St in Glandore, charges $20 for four hours and $30 for the first day. It supplies train timetables and maps if you want to tour the Barossa and other areas accessible by train. It delivers and collects cycles for free anywhere within 15km of the main post office.

Around Adelaide

GLENELG

The first South Australian governor, Captain John Hindmarsh, landed on the beach here on 28 December 1836 and later that day proclaimed SA a province. Glenelg quickly became a busy seaport and a favoured spot for wealthy squatters, who built their grand townhouses near the beach.

Often referred to simply as 'The Bay', Glenelg was one of the first of Adelaide's seaside resorts. It remains a very popular destination for day trippers and holiday makers, and makes a relaxed contrast to the city.

The Glenelg Tourist Information Centre (☎ 8294 5833), by the beach next to the Town Hall on Moseley Square, opens from 9 am to 5 pm daily. There's a travel agency on the premises, and a good seafood restaurant upstairs.

Things to See & Do

Glenelg is at its best in warm weather, when you can dine alfresco, laze on the lawns and beach in front of Moseley Square or go for a swim. In summer, there's daily entertainment on the foreshore, including bands, folk dancing and singing. Many shops on Jetty Rd – the main shopping precinct – are open daily.

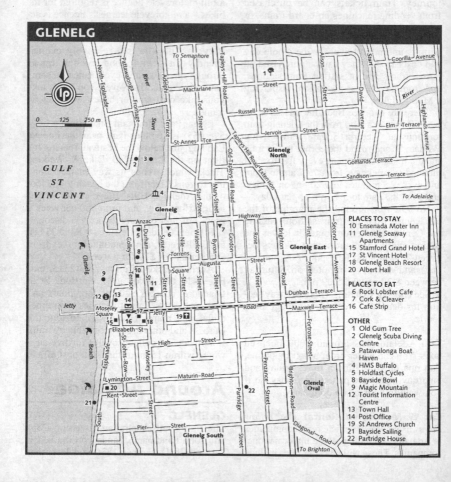

GLENELG

PLACES TO STAY
10 Ensenada Moter Inn
11 Glenelg Seaway Apartments
15 Stamford Grand Hotel
17 St Vincent Hotel
18 Glenelg Beach Resort
20 Albert Hall

PLACES TO EAT
6 Rock Lobster Cafe
7 Cork & Cleaver
16 Cafe Strip

OTHER
1 Old Gum Tree
2 Glenelg Scuba Diving Centre
3 Patawalonga Boat Haven
4 HMS Buffalo
5 Holdfast Cycles
8 Bayside Bowl
9 Magic Mountain
12 Tourist Information Centre
13 Town Hall
14 Post Office
19 St Andrews Church
21 Bayside Sailing
22 Partridge House

The bluestone **Town Hall** on Moseley Square, the Gothic-style **St Andrews Church** on Jetty Rd and numerous fine Victorian mansions and stately homes are imposing reminders of Glenelg's prosperous past. The Tudor-style **Partridge House**, at 38 Partridge St, is owned by the town council. It's not a museum, unfortunately, but you can enjoy the grounds and admire the architecture.

Maps which will guide you to these and other historic places on walks around Glenelg are available from the tourist office. On the foreshore near the Town Hall is **Magic Mountain**, an amusement parlour with a water-slide, bumper boats, arcade games and other activities. It opens daily in summer and most days at other times.

The Patawalonga Boat Haven has Glenelg's premier attraction: a splendid replica of **HMS Buffalo**, one of the ships that brought the original settlers out from England. On board is an interesting little museum, which opens from noon to 5 pm daily.

About 15 minutes walk away, the **Old Gum Tree,** on McFarlane St, was the spot chosen by Governor Hindmarsh to read the proclamation that established the colony. Each year, on Proclamation Day, there's a full-costume re-enactment on the site.

Beach Gear & Water Sports Glenelg's 215m jetty is a popular fishing spot where you can usually catch tommy-ruff, whiting and garfish.

Next door to the tourist information office, Beach Hire (☎ 8294 1477) has deckchairs, umbrellas, jet skis and body boards. It is open from September to April only, and opening times vary – but if it's sunny, it'll be open.

Bayside Sailing rents out catamarans, windsurfers and jet skis on the beach, a short walk south of the jetty. It's there most days between November and February, and at other times when the weather is suitable.

Glenelg Scuba Diving Centre (☎ 8294 7744), on Patawalonga Frontage, hires snorkelling and scuba gear and also does dive charters.

Places to Stay

There's a swag of places to stay in Glenelg. Many are covered in the accommodation directory *Seaside Holidays – Glenelg,* available from SATC and the Glenelg Tourist Information Centre. The following places are close to the action in Jetty Rd

Hostels The *Glenelg Beach Resort* (☎ 8376 0007, 1800 066 422 toll free, 7 Moseley St) is in a grand old apartment building around the corner from the tram terminus. It has comfortable beds (not bunks) from $13 in dorms and $22/32 for singles/doubles in private rooms with fridges. The kitchen is pokey, but there's a cheap licensed cafe on the premises. This is a good place for entertainment, with its public bar, live bands, stand-up comics, karaoke and games area. There is a book exchange across the road.

Albert Hall (☎ 8376 0488, 1800 060 488 toll free, fax 8294 1966, 16 South Esplanade) is a grand old Victorian house in a great location by the beach. It has an impressive exterior but some of its rooms are less so. We have had good reports of its front rooms – those on the first floor have balconies and sea views. Dorm beds cost $14 and beds in private rooms start at $18. There's a travel agency and free videos four nights a week.

Hotels & Motels Close to the tram stop, the *St Vincent Hotel* (☎ 8294 4377, 28 Jetty Rd) has standard rooms from $33/55 and rooms with private bathroom from $45/65, including a light breakfast.

Somewhat more luxurious is the *Ensenada Motor Inn* (☎ 8294 5822, 13 Colley Terrace), which has standard rooms for $83/87 and executive suites for $90/94.

At the top of the comfort scale, the towering *Stamford Grand Hotel* (☎ 8376 1222) on Moseley Square overlooks Gulf St Vincent from opposite the tram stop. Rooms with ocean views start at $200.

Holiday Flats & Serviced Apartments There are many holiday flats and serviced apartments in Glenelg; most quote weekly rather than daily rates.

The *Glenelg Seaway Apartments (☎ 8295 8503, 18 Durham St)* is about a one minute walk from the tram stop. It has backpacker rooms with a shared kitchen for $15 per person, and self-contained apartments costing $50 off-peak ($60 peak) for doubles. This place is good value and Vladimir, the owner, is very friendly and helpful. Off-street parking is available.

Places to Eat

Glenelg has a swag of eateries of all styles and ethnic origins. In sunny weather the alfresco cafes at the beach end of Jetty Rd are extremely popular – if you can't get a seat, the benches under the date palms in Moseley Square are nice spots to enjoy a takeaway meal.

Eateries in the Stamford Grand Hotel range from inexpensive cafes to silver service in the *Calypso* restaurant. The front bar, which looks onto the foreshore, is also popular on warm days.

Cafe Zest (shop 4, 47 Jetty Rd) is a funky little cafe and gallery with a laidback at-

mosphere and great food. There's all-day breakfast, light lunches from around $6, yummy cakes and desserts and good coffee.

Goodies & Grains (55 Jetty Rd) is a wholefoods store that also serves light lunches and healthy snacks. Vegan wraps are $2.50, salads from $3.50 and juices and smoothies around $3.

On the 12th floor of the Atlantic Tower Motel Inn, at 760 Anzac Highway, the revolving *Rock Lobster Cafe* offers stunning panoramic views. About 300m north across the park, the *Buffalo* has a superb atmosphere – this is one of Adelaide's finest seafood places.

Good places for steak meals include the upmarket *Cork & Cleaver (712 Anzac Hwy)* and the *Hog's Breath Cafe*, upstairs at 36 Jetty Rd, next to the St Vincent Hotel.

Lungomare (☎ 8376 1255, 1 Colley Terrace) is a stylish Italian cafe and bar overlooking Moseley Square. It has pasta and pizza from around $9, and focaccia from $6.50.

Entertainment

The Cinema Centre (☎ 8294 3366, 119 Jetty Rd) shows a good range of mainly mainstream films, and offers movie-and-meal deals with local restaurants from around $20.

Getting There & Around

The best way to get from the city to the heart of Glenelg is by TransAdelaide's vintage tram service. Trams leave Victoria Square every 15 minutes from 5.57 am weekdays, 7.32 am Saturdays and 8.50 am Sundays, and arrive at Moseley Square about 25 minutes later. The last tram leaves Glenelg at 11.20 pm daily.

Alternatively, you can take bus Nos 263, 266, 275 and 278 from the city to the last stop on Anzac Hwy, about five minutes walk from Jetty Rd.

Holdfast Cycles (☎ 8294 4537), at 768 Anzac Hwy, hires out well-maintained mountain bikes for $5 per hour or $20 per day. It is open weekdays from 9 am to 5.30 pm and Saturday 10 am to 3 pm.

DENIS O'BYRNE

The famous Glenelg Tram

he western grey, at home on Kangaroo Island

Cape Barren goose at Kangaroo Island

JOHN ARMSTRONG

SIMON ROWE

Pelicans frequent the coasts and the wetlands.

RICHARD I'ANSON

C GROENHOUT

:urt's Desert Pea: South Australia's floral emblem

Wildflowers bloom from July through November.

RICHARD I'ANSON

Australian sea lions at play in Seal Bay

DENIS O'BYRNE

Adelaide's skyline reflected in the glassy waters of the Torrens River

Moonlit skydiving, Adelaide

Queen Victoria Fountain, Adelaide

Catching the Glenelg tram

The site of Captain John Hindmarsh's landing in 1836, Glenelg is now Adelaide's most popular beach.

Adelaide Hills

Only 30 minutes drive from the city centre, the scenic Adelaide Hills, which form part of the Mt Lofty Ranges, encompass the region bordered by the towns of Clarendon and Strathalbyn to the south, Mt Barker and Nairne to the east, and Mt Pleasant to the north.

Not surprisingly, the hills are a popular day trip destination from Adelaide. Apart from the beauty of the landscape, there are numerous attractions such as conservation parks, botanic gardens, wineries and historic villages. There are also plenty of bushwalking options: the region is crisscrossed by hundreds of kilometres of trails, including the Heysen Trail (see the Outdoor Activities chapter).

European History

German settlers escaping religious persecution were on the scene early, establishing Hahndorf in 1839 and several other villages, including Lobethal, Grunthal (now Verdun) and Blumberg (now Birdwood), within a decade. Mixed in with these are typically British places such as Strathalbyn (established by the Scots), Stirling (by the English) and Callington (by the Cornish).

Copper and gold were mined at several locations from the 1840s, with the major goldfields being at Echunga and Woodside. The colony's first highway, from Adelaide to Mt Barker, opened in 1845. And by the 1850s, Adelaide's colonial gentry were beginning to build grand summer houses, many with stunning gardens, at higher places like Crafers and Stirling.

The Adelaide Hills are a lush contrast to the rest of the state owing to their relatively high rainfall. Huge eucalypts are a magnificent feature of the landscape, which varies from high steep ridges to gentle hills and valleys. Many buildings of the initial boom period, from 1837 to the 1860s, have survived, giving the hills a distinctive European heritage. In autumn this is reinforced

HIGHLIGHTS

- Browse through the antique shops of Strathalbyn, a classified 'heritage town'
- Discover the unique heritage of Hahndorf, Australia's oldest German settlement
- Enjoy the autumn colours of towns near Stirling
- Experience nature at one of the conservation areas near Adelaide
- Sample some first-rate wines in Australia's oldest wine-producing region
- Take a relaxing stroll (or a testing hike) on one of the many walking trails that criss-cross the hills

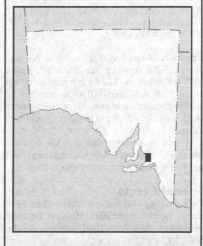

by the glorious colours of introduced deciduous trees, particularly in the wetter central area around Mt Lofty.

129

Hahndorf, these days, is very touristy, and many – no doubt shackled by day trip itineraries – only go there and to the more popular parks, such as Belair and Cleland. This is a pity as there are many more interesting places to visit once you leave the main tourist routes. Most visitors come to Hahndorf on weekends, so many places, particularly restaurants, are closed from Monday to Wednesday or Thursday.

Information

Tourist Offices The Adelaide Hills Visitor Centre is in Hahndorf, at 41 Main St (☎ 8388 1185, 1800 353 323 toll free, fax 8388 1319). It is open daily from 9 am to 5 pm. There's another tourist office at Mt Lofty summit.

National Parks Belair National Park (☎ 8278 5477, fax 8278 8587, PO Box 2, Belair 5052) is responsible for parks in the southern Mt Lofty Ranges.

Parks in the central and northern ranges are managed from the National Parks & Wildlife Service (NPWS) office at 115 Maryvale Rd, Athelstone 5076 (☎ 8336 0901, fax 8336 0900).

Books & Maps Royal Automobile Association's (RAA) travel guide *Adelaide Region* ($15 for members, $30 for nonmembers) includes the Adelaide Hills. A number of walking guides are also mentioned under Bushwalking in the Outdoor Activities chapter.

If you're driving, the RAA's *Central North* and *Central South* touring maps will get you around without too much fuss.

Special Events

Held annually on the last weekend in February, the Adelaide Hills Harvest Festival celebrates the agricultural produce of the hills, including its wines.

The Autumn Leaves Festival is held in Aldgate in May of even-numbered years.

Organised Tours

A number of Adelaide operators offer half and full-day sightseeing tours to the Adelaide Hills, and these are covered in the Organised Tours section of the Adelaide chapter. Generally you can expect to pay from $25 for a half-day tour and from $35 for a full day.

Gecko Tours (☎ 8339 3800) has an interesting day tour ($95) that will take you exploring the Aboriginal heritage of the Eden Valley area, with some wine tasting thrown in.

There are trail rides available at Woodside, for which you'll find details in the later section on this town.

Accommodation

There are cheap places to stay in the hills, but not very many of them. They include the YHA's five 'limited access' hostels for members at Para Wirra, Norton Summit, Mt Lofty, Mylor and Kuitpo. These are all on the Heysen Trail and cost between $8 and $12 per night, plus a key deposit of $20. You must book in advance and obtain a key from the YHA office (☎ 8231 5583) at 38 Sturt St in Adelaide.

There are numerous B&Bs, ranging from boutique to homely. They're generally pricey, being popular with escapists from Adelaide, but you'll find a few for around $80 – rates are invariably more expensive on weekends. The tourist office in Hahndorf (☎ 8388 1185, 1800 353 323 toll free) has details of many of them, and can arrange bookings.

Otherwise there are a handful of caravan parks, and a few pubs and motels.

Getting There & Around

Bus Several bus lines have services into the Adelaide Hills from the city and outlying regional centres, but most only nibble at the edges. The main exception is Hills Transit (☎ 8339 1191), which has mostly daily services to towns along its routes from Mt Barker to Adelaide, Lobethal and Strathalbyn. Its Mt Barker-Adelaide service visits Hahndorf, Bridgewater, Aldgate, Stirling and Crafers, while the Lobethal service also calls in at Hahndorf.

TransAdelaide (☎ 8210 1000) buses service the area between Summertown, Crafers and Aldgate.

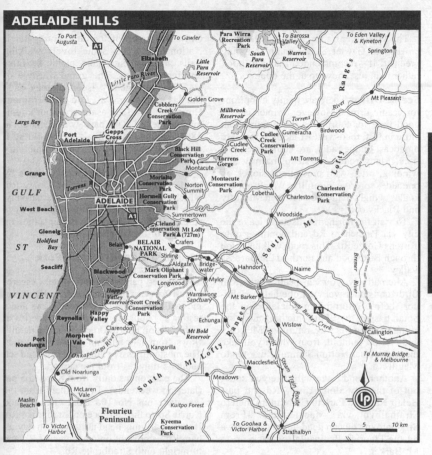

ADELAIDE HILLS

ADELAIDE HILLS

In the south, Premier Stateliner (☎ 8415 5563) does a return trip each weekday through Clarendon and Meadows on its run between Adelaide and Victor Harbor.

On weekdays, ABM Coachlines (☎ 8347 3336) runs through Birdwood and Mt Pleasant on its Adelaide to Mannum run.

Taxi Car hire and/or taxi services are provided by Hilltop Taxis & Hire Cars (☎ 8388 2211), which is based at Stirling; Mt Barker & Hills Taxi Service (☎ 8391 1888), at Mt

Barker; and Tony's Hills Hire Car Service (☎ 8388 5988) based at Mylor.

Train SteamRanger (☎ 8391 1223) runs two tourist trains from Mt Barker, which operate most Sundays between the end of May and the end of November. The trains operate on alternate Sundays; the *Highlander* goes to Strathalbyn ($18 return), alternating with the *Southern Encounter*, which goes to Victor Harbor ($35 return) via Strathalbyn, Goolwa and Port Elliot –

you can get on and off at any of these places.

The Mt Barker train station is at the eastern end of Gawler St, the main shopping precinct. It's recommended that you book rather than just show up at the door.

Scenic Drives There are plenty of options for scenic drives. However, winter isn't a good time for touring as the weather can close in fast; road-weather alerts, which are broadcast on the radio, are common at this time. Many roads are steep, narrow and winding, often with precipitous slopes on one side, so drive carefully. Watch out for koalas at night in the area between Mt Lofty and Blackwood.

To visit the northern hills area, leave the city via Payneham Rd and continue onto Torrens Gorge Rd. This route will take you through Birdwood and north to the Barossa Valley.

Alternatively, you can head south from Birdwood and travel via Lobethal to Hahndorf before returning to Adelaide on the South Eastern Fwy. For something more exciting than the freeway, return via Mt Lofty and Norton Summit, from where you take the spectacular Norton Summit Rd down to Magill Rd.

Another good route will take you south out of the city along Unley Rd and past Belair National Park to Clarendon, then to Strathalbyn via Macclesfield. From Strathalbyn you can head down to Goolwa on the Fleurieu Peninsula, or back up to Mt Barker.

NATIONAL PARKS & GARDENS

The NPWS has a brochure that lists numerous conservation parks in the Adelaide Hills, with several on the edge of the suburbs. All may be closed on total fire ban days.

You can also visit several botanic gardens in the area; inquire at the Adelaide Botanic Garden (☎ 8228 2311), which also has brochures. A number of outstanding private gardens in the central hills area participate in the seasonal 'Open Garden Scheme'. The tourist office in Handorf has a list of these.

Belair National Park (840 hectares)

Only 9km south of the city centre, Belair National Park has some lovely walking trails, an ornamental lake, picnic facilities and tennis courts. The grand lifestyle of SA's colonial gentry is on display each Sunday afternoon at **Old Government House**, built in 1859 as the governor's summer residence. The park was declared in 1891, making it Australia's second oldest. It opens daily from 8 am to sunset and entry costs $5 per car.

You can get to Belair from Adelaide by heading south from the city on Unley Rd, which becomes Belair Rd. Alternatively, take bus No 195 from King William St to stop 27, or take the train to Belair station on the edge of the park.

Morialta Conservation Park (532 hectares)

This rugged park is on the western escarpment 10km east of the city centre. It has picnic facilities, some spectacular views and a testing 2½ hour return walk past a series of **waterfalls** on Fourth Creek, which generally flows from late autumn to early summer. The most impressive falls are the second set, about 45 minutes from the carpark.

The park opens daily from 8 am to 5 pm (later on weekends). To get there from the city, take bus No 105 from Grenfell and Currie Sts to the entrance on Stradbroke Rd. If you're driving, head north-east on Payneham Rd, veer right onto Montacute Rd and turn right onto Stradbroke Rd.

Cleland Conservation Park (993 hectares)

This steep park, only 7.5km south-east of the city centre, stretches from the western foothills up to Mt Lofty. It has many excellent bushwalks through its tall eucalypt forest and moist gullies, as well as picnic areas and a decent restaurant at **Waterfall Gully**.

The park's major attraction is the 35 hectare **Cleland Wildlife Park**, which has numerous species of Australian fauna. It is open from 9.30 am to 5 pm daily and admission is

$7.50; between 2 and 4 pm daily you can have your photograph taken while cuddling a koala ($8). Guided night walks leave at 7 pm from 1 May to 30 October and at 8 pm for the rest of the year (starting at $11.50).

To got to the wildlife park from Adelaide take bus No 822 from outside Harris Scarfe on Grenfell St; on weekends you need to get off at Crafers, from where you can call a taxi. Otherwise you can take a day tour from the city.

A short detour south along Summit Rd from the turn-off to the wildlife park takes you to **Mt Lofty summit**, 727m above sea level (it's a 30 minute walk from the wildlife park). The lookout has a restaurant, as well as impressive views over the city, particularly so at night. Nearby are the substantial remains of **St Michael's Monastery**, destroyed in the 1983 bushfires.

Other Parks
Other good parks for bushwalking and wildlife are: **Charleston Conservation Park** (63 hectares), 8km east of Lobethal; **Black Hill Conservation Park** (701 hectares), 10km north-east of the city centre; **Kenneth Stirling Conservation Park** (253 hectares), 5km west of Oakbank; **Mark Oliphant Conservation Park** (145 hectares), 4km south of Stirling; and **Scott Creek Conservation Park** (900 hectares), between Mylor and Clarendon.

Mt Lofty Botanic Garden
From Mt Lofty, continue south for about 1.5km to the large and scenic Mt Lofty Botanic Garden, which has main entrances off Summit and Piccadilly Rds. Here you'll find stunning views, nature trails, a lake system, exotic temperate plants and native stringybark forest. It has spectacular seasonal displays of camellia, magnolia and rhododendron.

The garden is open weekdays from 8.30 am to 4 pm, and weekends from 10 am to 5 pm. Admission is free.

Wittunga Botanic Garden
On Shepherds Hill Rd in Blackwood, a southern suburb of Adelaide, this garden has fine displays of Australian and South African plants, as well as different habitats such as lakes and a sandplain garden. It is open weekdays from 8 am to 4 pm and weekends from 10 am to 5 pm. You can get there on an No 728 or 729 bus from Flinders St in the city.

Beechwood Heritage Garden
This marvellous garden is on Snows Rd in Stirling. Surrounding one of the early summer residences of Adelaide's colonial gentry, it features the state's oldest conservatory, an old-fashioned rose garden, a Victorian rock garden and beautiful rhododendron hybrids. Beechwood is open for a limited season in spring and autumn only.

National Trust Reserves
The National Trust (☎ 8223 1655) has a number of small nature reserves in the Adelaide Hills, several of which are dedicated to preserving rare remnants of native forest.

WINERIES
The Adelaide Hills wine region stretches for about 70km through the southern Mt Lofty Ranges from Williamstown in the north to Mt Compass in the south.

Although it's relatively unknown today, the hills had a thriving wine industry between 1840 and 1900. In fact, the Echunga hock, sent to Queen Victoria in 1845, was the first wine ever exported from Australia. What killed it off was fashion; most Australians drank beer, and those who drank wine preferred big reds – as did the imbibers overseas.

The industry was reborn in the early 1980s following the growth in popularity of table and sparkling wines. Now there are about 30 local wineries including the well known labels **Petaluma** and **Bridgewater Mill**, which you can taste at the historic flour mill (1860) in Bridgewater. The mill has a huge waterwheel, and there's a very popular upmarket restaurant on the premises.

Local wine makers have produced a brochure with a map, which you can get from the South Australian Tourism Commission (SATC) and local tourist offices.

STIRLING AREA

The pretty little townships of **Aldgate**, **Crafers**, **Piccadilly** and **Stirling** are noted for their autumn colour, thanks to extensive plantations of exotic deciduous trees.

You'll find some glorious old English-style gardens in all four towns – most notable are those of **Stangate House** at Aldgate and **Beechwood** at Stirling, as well as **Mt Lofty Botanic Garden**, near tiny Piccadilly. See the earlier National Parks & Gardens section for details of Beechwood Heritage Garden and the Mt Lofty Botanic Garden.

There are **historic walks** you can take through Aldgate, Crafers and Stirling, which were established around 1840. Crafers has a huge **oak tree** that is said to have been planted in 1838.

Places to Stay & Eat

The famous *Eagle on the Hill Hotel* (☎ *8339 2211, Mt Barker Rd*) is about 3km west of Crafers. It burned down in the 1983 bushfires, but has since been resurrected and offers self-contained rooms for $70 for singles and doubles, including a continental breakfast. The pub has a good bistro with great night views of the city lights.

Overlooking the Mt Lofty Botanic Garden from its eyrie at 74 Summit Rd, Crafers, the baronial *Mt Lofty House* (☎ *8339 6777)* was built as a family home in the 1850s. It now offers rooms and meals for equally impressive prices: starting at $198 B&B for doubles (dinner and B&B packages start at $295).

There are some good, reasonably priced eateries in Aldgate and Stirling. In Aldgate, the *Aldgate Pump Hotel* and the *Cafe Foljambes*, both on Strathalbyn Rd (the main street), are popular.

In Stirling, the *Organic Market Cafe (5 Druids Ave)* specialises in vegetarian food and has great coffee.

Getting There & Away

The region is serviced by Hills Transit buses. See Getting There & Around at the start of the chapter.

If you've cycled up Mt Barker Rd from Adelaide, you'll have to get off at the Crafers exit – before Mt Barker Rd turns into the South Eastern Fwy. The western extension of the freeway to Adelaide was due to open in late 1999; it may change the situation.

MYLOR

- **pop 100**

The main attraction in Mylor is **Warrawong Sanctuary** (☎ 8370 9422), about 3km from town. Covering 14 hectares, it was a tree-less dairy farm in 1969. The bush has since been re-established and 15 native mammal species, several of them endangered, live behind a vermin-proof fence. There are guided bushwalks ($15) at dawn, 2 pm and sunset; the 2 pm walks operate on weekends only, and the dawn tour is generally the best one for wildlife watching.

To reach the sanctuary from Adelaide, turn off the freeway at Stirling and follow the signs from the Stirling roundabout. The entrance is on Stock Rd, 300m from Longwood Rd, or 2.7km from Strathalbyn Rd if you're coming from Mylor.

The highlight of the sanctury's restaurant is the huge windows, which give you a close-up view of the many native birds that congregate for a feed right outside. Most obvious are the rainbow lorikeets; they're beautiful, but their screeching and squabbling are unbelievable.

For $99 you can spend the night in a luxury tent, complete with reverse-cycle air-conditioning. The price includes dinner, guided sunset and dawn walks, and breakfast. Bookings are essential for all walks and accommodation.

HAHNDORF

- **pop 1660**

The oldest surviving German settlement in Australia, Hahndorf was established in 1839 by about 50 Lutheran families who emigrated to Adelaide on the *Zebra*. They named their new home in honour of the ship's captain, Hahn, who helped them obtain land on arrival; *dorf* is German for 'village'.

ADELAIDE HILLS

The town was placed under martial law during WWI; its Lutheran school was closed and, in 1917, its name was changed to Ambleside. It was again named Hahndorf in 1935. Hahndorf still has an honorary Burgermeister, who acts as the town's goodwill ambassador.

The Adelaide Hills Visitor Centre (☎ 8388 1185, 1800 353 323 toll free, fax 8388 1319), at 41 Main St, opens daily from 9 am to 5 pm.

Things to See & Do

Hahndorf's commercial heart is on Main St between English St and Hereford Ave. The pavements are lined with more art galleries, craft and gift shops, and eateries than you can poke a stick at – the pace is often frenetic on weekends and during holiday periods, when visitors from the city descend in droves.

Despite this, a strong sense of history pervades the town. On Main St are numerous old buildings that show distinctive German architecture. They include the first **butcher's shop** (1839), **Thiele Cottage** (1842), the former **Australian Arms Hotel** (1854) and the still-licensed **German Arms Hotel** (1862). Most form part of a heritage walk, which can be made with the assistance of a brochure available from the tourist office.

The old Australian Arms Hotel, at 46 Main St, now houses a **leathersmith** and bush gallery. This is one of the best shops in town.

At 68 Main St, the **Hahndorf Academy** was established in 1857. It houses an art gallery, craft shop and museum, which has several original sketches by Sir Hans Heysen – see the boxed text on Heysen in the Facts about South Australia chapter. It is open weekdays and Saturday from 10 am to 5 pm and Sunday from 12 to 5 pm, and admission is $2.

There are a number of original Heysen works in the late artist's former studio and house, **The Cedars**. Tours are conducted daily, except Saturday, at 11 am and 1 and 3 pm for $4 (studio only) and $7 (house and studio). The Cedars is on Heysen Rd about 4km from the centre of town.

The **Antique Clock Museum** at 91 Main St has a fine collection of some 650 timepieces dating from 1680. The museum has what's claimed to be the largest cuckoo clock in the southern hemisphere. Admission is $5.

Also worth visiting is **German Model Train Land**, in the historic butcher's shop at 47 Main St. It presents a fascinating world of model trains – there are hundreds of replicas – complete with button-faced people and a handmade miniature working carousel. Admission is $6, or $14 per family.

Places to Stay & Eat

The friendly McMullen family has emergency accommodation for a maximum of three backpackers at their home at 54 English St (☎ 8388 7079). They charge $20 per person, including linen and breakfast (second night $15).

On the Adelaide side of town, the *Hahndorf Resort (☎ 8388 7921, 145A Main St)* is about 1.5km from the town centre. It has campsites starting at $11, cabins with kitchens starting at $46, motel units at $79/89/104 for a single/double/triple and chalets at $89/105/120.

There are also several motels, most of which offer various accommodation options. *Hahndorf Inn Motor Lodge (☎ 8388 1000, 35 Main St)* has rooms starting at $75/79 for single/double; *Old Mill Motel (☎ 8388 7888, 98 Main St)* has units for $85; *The Stables (☎ 8388 7988, 74 Main St)*

German Arms Hotel, Hahndorf

offers accommodation for $120; and *Zorro Hacienda* (☎ *8388 1309, 60 Main St)* has motel units starting at $85 and holiday apartments at $130 for doubles.

Main St has numerous eateries, and several feature German food. Locals recommend *Karl's German Coffee House Restaurant* at 17 Main St for authentic German cuisine. Also worth trying are the *German Arms Hotel*, at 69 Main St, and the *German Cake Shop*, at 2 Pine St.

The *Beerenberg Strawberry Farm*, at the east end of Main St, allows you to pick your own strawberries between October and May. Their popular Beerenberg-brand preserves are available all year round.

Getting There & Away
Hills Transit runs several buses daily from the central bus station in Adelaide ($4.50).

NAIRNE
* **pop 2000**
If you find Hahndorf a little too commercialised, the quiet charm of Nairne will appeal. Only 10 minutes down the South Eastern Fwy and the old Princes Hwy from its busy neighbour, Nairne was founded by a Scottish sheep farmer in 1839. It was originally a wheat-growing centre – SA's first flour mill was built nearby on the Woodside road in 1841 – and grew rapidly after the railway arrived in 1883.

As with neighbouring **Littlehampton** and Mt Barker, the near surrounds of Nairne's historic centre are being gobbled up by brick-and-tile suburbs as city workers build their dream homes on 800 sq metre allotments.

The town tourist office is downstairs in the Albert Mill, on Junction St. It opens between 11 am and 5.30 pm Thursday to Sunday.

Things to See & Do
Many stone buildings remain from Nairne's formative years, and you can explore them with a **self-guided walk**. Pick up *Nairne: An Historic Walking Tour* from the tourist office. It lists 28 sites including the classic **District Hotel** (1850), and several cottages from the early 1850s.

The **Albert Mill** was built as a steam-driven flour mill in 1857 and was used for this purpose until 1906. Today it has a good craft and antique shop upstairs and a restaurant downstairs. From here it's a short walk to another good antique shop at **Upstairs Downstairs**, on Main Rd.

The summit of **Mt Barker**, about 4km from town, offers a superb panorama to the west and down towards Lake Alexandrina in the south-east. To get to the summit, turn off Main Rd opposite Chapman's smallgoods factory and follow the signs to the communications towers – it's a five minute walk from here to the lookout. The hill was named after the explorer Captain Collett Barker, killed by Aborigines at the Murray Mouth in 1831.

Continue west along the Murray Bridge road from Nairne and you'll pass through the tiny township of **Kanmantoo** (15km from Nairne) before coming to **Callington**, a farther 5km on. Having been bypassed by the freeway, this quietly decaying little town – established by Cornish miners in 1850 – has loads of character. If you're an artist or photographer, don't miss it!

Places to Eat
Both pubs in Nairne offer counter meals, and for something more stylish there's the *Albert Mill*. It has a beautiful atmosphere – all wood and huge beams – and does reasonably priced lunches and dinners from Wednesday to Sunday and public holidays.

On Main Rd, the tiny *Nairne Bakery* has delicious products, all baked on the premises.

Getting There & Away
The Murray Bridge Passenger Service (☎ 8532 2633) can drop you off at Nairne on weekdays ($11) coming from Murray Bridge. Hills Transit's bus service calls in several times each weekday, leaving from the central bus station in Adelaide ($5).

MT BARKER
* **pop 6200**
The largest town in the Adelaide Hills, and only 25 minutes from Adelaide along the South Eastern Fwy, Mt Barker is a fast-

growing commercial centre. It was the first town established in the hills, founded in 1839 by the pastoralist Duncan McFarlane.

There's a tourist office in the district council office (☎ 8391 1633) at 23 Mann St, which opens from 9 am to 5 pm weekdays.

Things to See & Do
While Mt Barker isn't a tourist town, the **tourist trains** that run from there to Strathalbyn and Victor Harbor have increased interest on weekends. See the Getting There & Away section at the start of this chapter.

The tourist office has brochures covering **walks** in and around town. One such brochure details 11 rural walks from three to 9.5km, while another will take you to 37 sites in the town area.

The town's oldest buildings are **Dunn's Steam Flour Mill** and the **Miller's Cottage**, both built in 1844. The former, one of the first flour mills in SA, operated until 1894. It's now used as a coffee shop and B&B.

Places to Stay & Eat
The attractive *Mt Barker Caravan Park (☎ 8391 0384, 40 Cameron Rd)* has tent/caravan sites for $9/13 and on-site vans starting at $25 ($20 for subsequent nights). Self-contained cabins cost $45.

At the friendly *Hotel Barker (☎ 8391 1003, 22 Gawler St)* standard pub rooms start at $25/40 for singles/doubles. The publican's name is Brew – don't bother, he's heard all the jokes!

Otherwise, try *The Flour Mill (☎ 8398 2232, 14 Cameron Rd)*, which has heritage-style B&B rooms on the first floor of the old mill. Downstairs is a wonderfully cosy coffee shop – you can get lunch there on Sunday.

In the town centre, locals recommend *Millies Bakery (5 Gawler St)* for light lunches and *Giovanni Bistro (15 Morphett St)* for pizza and pasta. The *Littlehampton Chinese Restaurant*, 3km away at Little-hampton, also has a good reputation.

MT BARKER TO STRATHALBYN
If you're in a hurry you can drive straight to Strathalbyn via **Wistow**. But it's far more

interesting to go via **Echunga**, **Meadows** and **Macclesfield**. The buses servicing these towns are listed in the Getting There & Around section at the start of this chapter.

At Echunga (population 450) there's the **Jupiter Creek Gold Field**, about 5km out of town on the Meadows road. Gold was discovered in 1852 and the field was worked at various times until 1930. To explore the overgrown diggings there are walking trails, interpretive signs and the brochure *Gold at Jupiter Creek*.

Meadows and Macclesfield are both quiet, pretty little places with some interesting heritage buildings. The willows by the **Angas River** at Macclesfield are said to have grown from cuttings brought from near Napoleon's grave. There are magnificent views from the Macclesfield-Strathalbyn road as it winds down to the foothills.

Meadows is handy to the 3600 hectare **Kuitpo Forest**, where there are walking tracks, picnic areas and pleasant bush camp-sites – the camping season is from 1 April to 30 November. For camping permits and a brochure, call in to the forest headquarters (☎ 8388 3267) on the Willunga road.

All three towns have take-away outlets and pubs where you can buy meals; Meadows has a great bakery. The 1841 Tudor-style *Three Brothers Arms* in Macclesfield has a wonderful ambience with meals to match.

STRATHALBYN
- pop 2600

On the Angas River, this picturesque town was established in 1839 by Scottish immigrants. Much of its historic centre has been preserved – Strathalbyn is a classified 'heritage town' – and as a result there are some wonderful old streetscapes and impressive buildings. These include **St Andrew's Church**, which is unusually large and decorative for a country town.

The tourist office (☎/fax 8536 3212), in the train station on South Terrace, is open daily from 9.30 am to 4 pm.

A walking tour pamphlet ($2) lists historic buildings and other sites of interest in the township. The old courthouse and police

ADELAIDE HILLS

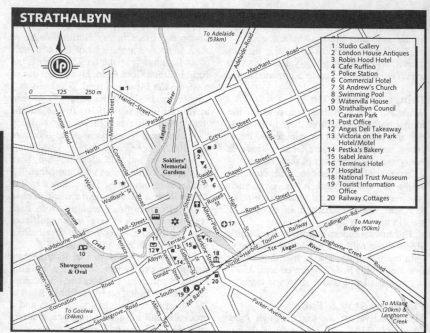

STRATHALBYN

To Adelaide
(53km)

0   125   250 m

Soldiers'
Memorial
Gardens

Showground
& Oval

To Goolwa
(34km)

To Murray
Bridge (50km)

To Milang
(20km) &
Langhorne
Creek

1 Studio Gallery
2 London House Antiques
3 Robin Hood Hotel
4 Cafe Ruffino
5 Police Station
6 Commercial Hotel
7 St Andrew's Church
8 Swimming Pool
9 Watervilla House
10 Strathalbyn Council
   Caravan Park
11 Post Office
12 Angas Deli Takeaway
13 Victoria on the Park
   Hotel/Motel
14 Pestka's Bakery
15 Isabel Jeans
16 Terminus Hotel
17 Hospital
18 National Trust Museum
19 Tourist Information
   Office
20 Railway Cottages

station is now a National Trust **museum**, with historic displays about the town and its Celtic heritage. It is open from 2 to 5 pm weekends and school and public holidays, and admission is $2.

Strathalbyn is well known for its **antique shops**. Probably the best if you're on a budget is Isabel Jeans on Rankine St, a good place for bric-a-brac. You could easily spend a couple of hours browsing in the antique shops and arts and crafts galleries clustered on High St; London House Antiques is one such long-established shop.

Strathalbyn is about 12 minutes drive from the wineries at **Langhorne Creek** (see the Fleurieu Peninsula chapter).

Places to Stay & Eat

The modest **Strathalbyn Council Caravan Park** (☎ 8536 3681), in the showgrounds off Coronation Rd, has campsites for $10 and a

couple of on-site vans from $22. Apart from this there is no cheap accommodation.

The **Robin Hood Hotel** (☎ 8536 2608, 18 High St) charges $30/45 for singles/doubles, but the rooms are very basic. The tariff does, however, include a light breakfast.

The much more upmarket **Victoria on the Park Hotel/Motel** (☎ 8536 2202, 16 Albyn Terrace) has motel units from $58/65 for a single/double.

There are several good B&Bs here. They include the cosy, self-contained **Railway Cottages** (☎ 015 601 692, Parker Ave), which cost $95/110 with breakfast provisions.

The grand 1840s residence **Watervilla House** (☎ 8536 4099, 2 Mill St) charges $95/110, and you'll be suitably impressed by its high ceilings and Victorian decor. For something more intimate, try the **Studio Gallery** (☎ 8536 3069, 17 Harriet St) which charges $60/90 – most days you can watch artist Helen Stacey at work. Both are traditional B&B.

The four hotels all sell meals. *Victoria on the Park Hotel/Motel* has a decent bistro and also does counter meals. *Cafe Ruffino*, on High St among the antique shops, specialises in pasta and pizza, with a large serve of pasta costing $6.

Getting There & Away

Hills Transit has two bus services each weekday from Adelaide ($6) and one each weekday from Mt Barker ($3.50).

The *Highlander* tourist train runs from Mt Barker on alternate Sundays between the end of May and the end of November, spending about 2½ hours in town. On other Sundays you can get on and off the *Southern Encounter*. See the Getting There & Around section at the start of this chapter.

CLARENDON
• pop 300

Pretty Clarendon grew up in a scenic valley at a major crossing point on the Onkaparinga River. Originally called Toondilla, after the Aboriginal name for a nearby ceremonial ground, it was renamed after the Earl of Clarendon in 1846.

There are numerous historic buildings, including the **Royal Oak Hotel** (1844). Dominating the town is the **Old Clarendon Winery Complex** – part of the original Clarendon Vineyard Estate, established with vines brought from Spain in the late 1840s. Today it has cellar-door sales and tastings, as well as craft shops and a restaurant.

A weekday bus between Adelaide and Victor Harbor stops at Clarendon (see Getting There & Around at the start of this chapter).

Places to Stay & Eat

The *Old Clarendon Winery Complex* (☎ 8383 6166) has comfortable rooms with views over the township, from $80/85/105 for singles/doubles/triples, including a light breakfast. Their weekend package includes a large cooked breakfast with champagne.

The *Royal Oak Hotel* (☎ 8383 6113) offers counter lunches and refurbished rooms

with private facilities for $65 singles and doubles. The rooms can be a little noisy up to midnight on Friday and Saturday.

Down by the river, the *Stone Cottage Restaurant* is said to be excellent, but it's only open for lunch and dinner from Wednesday to Sunday. For bookings phone ☎ 8383 6038.

The tiny *Clarendon Bakery* makes delicious pastries, bread and cakes.

NORTON SUMMIT AREA

Perched on the edge of the western scarp, the pretty township of **Norton Summit** (population 250) was the birthplace of Sir Thomas Playford, SA's longest serving state premier.

The post office has a small **museum** (open weekdays 9 am to 2 pm) featuring displays on **Marble Hill**, the state governor's former summer residence, about 6km away off the Lobethal road. The mansion was destroyed in the 1955 bushfires, but still makes an impressive sight in its hilltop setting. Between 11 am and 5 pm on Sundays you can explore the ruins and enjoy bushwalks and superb views for $2.

At Norton Summit you're within easy striking distance of Adelaide's main apple, pear, cherry and salad-vegetable growing area, which is around **Ashton**, **Summertown** and **Basket Range**. There are also several vineyards and wineries.

Places to Stay & Eat

The *Scenic Hotel* in the centre of Norton Summit has a lovely cosy restaurant. In warm weather it's nice to eat on the back verandah and enjoy the views over Adelaide.

The friendly *Fuzzies Farm* (☎ 8390 1111, Colonial Drive) is about a kilometre from Norton Summit and 15km east of the city. Set in a scenic valley next to Morialta Conservation Park, it offers an opportunity to learn practical skills in a farm environment. You can join in a wide variety of activities such as animal care, organic gardening, building construction and wood crafts.

Like the setting, their cafe and self-contained bushland cabins are great. The daily rate for helpers is $10 including city transfers, a bed, all meals and laundry. Stays of at least a week are preferred and bookings are essential. Budget package tours are also available.

There are a number of 'pick your own' farms and roadside stalls selling fruit and salad vegetables in the agricultural area.

LOBETHAL AREA
Lobethal
* pop 1500

Established by Lutheran settlers in 1842, attractive Lobethal has many interesting old buildings including **German-style cottages** and houses from the 1840s. Brochures that will guide you on a walking tour of them are available from the town's tourist office (☎ 8389 6996), at the intersection of the main roads to Woodside, Adelaide and Mt Torrens. It is open daily between 10 am and 4 pm.

Motorbike enthusiasts may be interested in the crowded **Motor Cycle & Heritage Museum**, at 1 Lenswood Rd, a few steps from the tourist office. It is open daily from 10 am to 5 pm, and entry is $3.50.

Lobethal's major event is the **Christmas Lights** during December. The whole town is ablaze with decorative lighting, and things can go a little crazy as sightseers from the city swarm in to admire the many displays.

Other attractions include **Bushland Park**, a 60 hectare council reserve with a picnic area, reservoirs, nice views and bushwalks about 600m out on the Gumeracha road. Kids will love **Fairyland Village**, which features life-size German fairy tales, tame deer and native animals.

Hills Transit buses run to Lobethal, calling in to Woodside and Oakbank (see Getting There & Around at the start of this chapter).

Woodside
* pop 1300

At the Lobethal end of town is **Melba's Chocolate Factory**, where chocoholics can watch their favourite sweet being prepared in a converted cheese factory. There's a large variety of confectionery for sale, most of which is made on the premises. As well, various craftspeople have their workshops and sales areas here. The complex opens weekdays from 10 am to 4 pm, and weekends and public holidays from noon to 5 pm.

Almost next door, the **Woodside Horse & Trail Riding Centre** (☎ 8389 7794) has escorted rides lasting from one hour ($20) to a full day ($66); half and full-day rides include a barbecue lunch and drinks. They also offer weekend packages at scenic Formby Bay, on the rugged south-west coast of Yorke Peninsula, to the west of Adelaide.

Oakbank
* pop 340

Each year at Easter, this small village is swamped by visitors who've come to enjoy the hugely popular **Oakbank Easter Racing Carnival**. It's said to be the greatest picnic race meeting in the world. If horse racing, dust and crowds have appeal, you'll love it.

Oakbank has several good craft shops including the **Oakbank Weaver** in the old Dorset Brewery, at 9 Elizabeth St. You can visit this and 39 other historic sites with the guidance of a walking brochure available from local shops.

BIRDWOOD AREA
Gumeracha
* pop 400

From Adelaide you can drive up through the scenic **Torrens River Gorge** to Gumeracha, 7km before Birdwood. Here you find **Chain of Ponds Wines**, which has won several awards for its whites – they're about 1km before town, and are open daily for tastings.

On the Birdwood side of town is **The Toy Factory**, with its giant rocking horse. The horse fortunately doesn't rock, but if you want to buy the kids some wooden toys this is a good spot to do so.

Birdwood
* pop 580

Originally called Blumberg ('the hill of flowers'), this pretty town was founded by German settlers in 1848. During WWI it was renamed after the commander of the Australian forces, Field Marshall Lord Birdwood.

In the 1850s Birdwood was a busy gold-mining and agricultural centre, and its old flour mill (1852) is an impressive reminder of those times. The town has a number of buildings classified by the National Trust, including several German-style cottages.

These days the flour mill forms part of the excellent **National Motor Museum**, which traces a century of motoring history in Australia. The complex houses a collection of around 300 trucks, buses, cars and motorbikes, from vintage to modern day. It opens daily from 9 am to 5 pm; admission is $8.50.

Birdwood Cottage, next door to the Birdwood Mill, is a long-established craft shop with beautiful pottery and ceramics.

Held each year in November, the **Rock 'n' Roll Rendezvous** is a good one for ageing rockers, and features cars of the era.

Between Birdwood and Williamstown, the 12,000 hectare **Mt Crawford Forest** has native forest and plantations of eucalypt and *Pinus radiata*. Here there are several picnic areas, bush campsites and bushwalks – the Heysen Trail passes through the forest. You can get camping permits and a brochure from the forest headquarters (☎ 8524 6004, 018 807 824 toll free), 13km from Birdwood on the Williamstown road.

ABM Coachlines runs from Adelaide to Birdwood on weekdays and cost $7.50.

Places to Stay & Eat

There are several B&Bs. *Birdwood B&B Cottages* (☎ 8568 5444, 38 Olivedale Rd) has a good reputation. They have three romantic cottages (two with spas) that start at $80 for doubles.

Also worth mentioning is *Blumberg Mews* (☎ 8568 5551, 7 Cromer Rd), where you can stay in a tastefully renovated 1870s stone barn. Rooms cost $95/65/110 for a single/twin share/double.

The *Blumberg Tavern* on the main street near the Birdwood Mill does lunches and dinners daily.

At Mt Pleasant, 10km beyond Birdwood towards Springton, there's the basic *Talunga Caravan Park* (☎ 8569 3048), which has tent and caravan sites. Alternatively, the *Talunga Hotel/Motel* (☎ 8568

2015) has motel-style units. You can get meals here and at the *Totness Inn Hotel*.

EDEN VALLEY

This scenic area, which lies between the Adelaide Hills and the Barossa Valley, is noted for its massive gum trees and high-altitude riesling wines. Coming from Adelaide, the valley starts between Mt Pleasant and Springton and includes the attractive hamlets of Springton, Eden Valley and Kyneton.

Johann Menge named it the Rhine Valley in 1838, recognising its potential for producing fine wines. He knew what he was on about, as you'll discover when you visit winery cellars such as **Grand Cru** (near Springton), **Mountadam** (near Eden Valley) and **Henschke** (near Kyneton).

Springton
- **pop 240**

The main attraction in this lovely old place is the **Herbig Tree**, a gnarled river red gum on the Mt Pleasant side of town. Friedrich and Caroline Herbig used its hollow trunk as a home for two years in the late 1850s before moving to a new pug-and-pine cottage. The first two of their 16 children were born here.

It's definitely worth stopping to browse in the **Springton Gallery**, which has a range of quality arts and crafts. It is open Friday to Monday between 11 am and 5 pm.

About 3km before Springton is the **Merindah Mohair Farm**, where you can buy knitted and woven wool products.

The *Springton Loft* (☎ 8568 2001), a renovated hay loft behind the Springton Gallery, is one of several local B&Bs. It charges $100 for couples including a cooked breakfast.

Next door, the Craneford Cellars, *Cafe C* has an interesting menu with light lunches from $12 and main courses from $15. It enjoys a good reputation, but is only open on Friday night and weekends.

Other places serving meals in the valley include the *pubs* in Springton and Eden Valley, and the *Eden Valley Winery* in Eden Valley.

The basic *Eden Valley Caravan Park* (☎ 8564 1107), 500m from Eden Valley on the Springton road, has tent and caravan sites.

Fleurieu Peninsula

The rolling Fleurieu Peninsula, south of Adelaide, is bounded by the Adelaide Hills to the north, Lake Alexandrina to the east and, to the west and south, the coastline from Hallett Cove (on Gulf St Vincent) around to the mouth of the Murray River. The peninsula has many attractions and, because most of it is within an hour's drive of Adelaide, it's popular with day-trippers.

Much of the coastline is extremely scenic. In the south are booming surf and rugged cliffs, while Gulf St Vincent has quieter beaches. There are several coastal resort towns, all of which tend to overflow during the summer school holidays. A few small conservation parks provide some good opportunities for camping and bushwalking, with the Heysen Trail meandering through en route to the Adelaide Hills.

On a more relaxed note, you can explore historic villages such as Old Noarlunga, Yankalilla and Willunga, and taste fine wines around McLaren Vale and Langhorne Creek.

History

The peninsula was named in 1802 by the French explorer Nicholas Baudin after Napoleon's minister for the navy. Baudin met up with Matthew Flinders at Encounter Bay where, 35 years later, two whaling stations were established.

The Foundation Inn was built at Encounter Bay in 1838 and quickly became a rendezvous for desperadoes, such as the escaped convicts from Tasmania who lived in the central ranges. However, by the middle of the next decade there were settlements all along the Adelaide road, and things were quieter.

By then the Aborigines were in serious decline. Today, just about all that remains of their culture, apart from canoe trees and museum exhibits, are musical place-names such as Yankalilla, Noarlunga, Carrickalinga, Tunkalilla and Willunga.

- Ride a booming breaker at one of the southern surfing spots
- Enjoy superb views from Mt Magnificent on the Heysen Trail
- Go whale-watching on The Bluff near Victor Harbor
- Escape the heat of summer at a picturesque coastal resort
- Spend a day or three sampling the fine wines produced by the many wineries

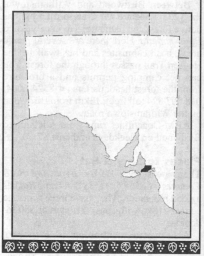

Agricultural development of the peninsula was rapid. Goolwa was a busy river port by the 1850s, when other ports were springing up around the coast. Flour mills were built at places such as Yilki (on Encounter Bay), Second Valley and Normanville, although these were soon suffering as soils became exhausted through overcropping.

FLEURIEU PENINSULA

Grand summer retreats began to appear at Port Elliot and Victor Harbor from the 1850s.

Information

Tourist Offices The region's main information outlets are in Goolwa, McLaren Vale and Victor Harbor. See the sections on these towns for details.

National Parks For information on conservation areas in the peninsula's southern half contact the National Parks and Wildlife Service (NPWS) office at 57 Ocean St in Victor Harbor (☎ 8552 3677, fax 8552 3950). Alternatively, write to them at PO Box 721, Victor Harbor 5211.

Parks in the north are administered from the Belair National Park (☎ 8278 5477, fax 8278 8587, PO Box 2, Belair 5052).

Books & Maps The Royal Automobile Association's (RAA) informative travel guide *Adelaide Region* (members $15, non-members $30) includes the Fleurieu Peninsula. Its *Central South* road map provides good coverage of the area; also worthwhile is the Office of Recreation & Sport's cycle-touring map.

Organised Tours

Bus Tours Several operators, including Premier Stateliner and Adelaide Sightseeing, offer day tours from Adelaide.

We've had good reports about Bee-init Tours (☎ 8332 1401), which has a 'penguin and wine' tour for $44 – visit three McLaren Vale wineries before continuing on for an evening penguin walk at Victor Harbor. The price includes the penguin walk but not meals.

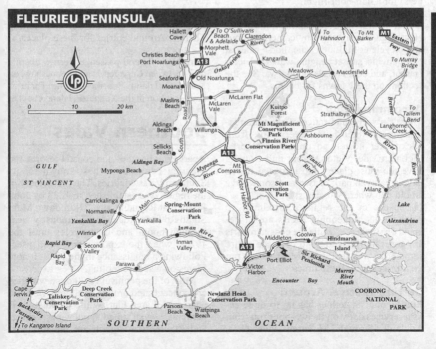

FLEURIEU PENINSULA

Also good is Shaun's Bound-Away Tours (☎ 8371 3147), which visits Victor Harbor and a McLaren Vale winery as part of a day tour from Adelaide. You can get off at Victor Harbor and take the shuttle to Cape Jervis, or do a Coorong cruise from Goolwa.

Ecotrek (☎ 8383 7198) does weekend cycling tours around the McLaren Vale wineries.

Gecko Tours (☎ 8339 3800) has a day tour ($95) that takes you on an exploration of the region's Aboriginal heritage. You visit an 8400-year-old campsite, canoe trees, cave paintings and coastal middens, and learn about local Dreamtime ancestors.

Scenic Flights You can do these from Aldinga (South Coast Air Centre, ☎ 8556 5404), Goolwa (Air Goolwa, ☎ 8555 4075) and Cape Jervis (Kangaroo Island Scenic Flights, ☎ 8598 0004). Prices vary, but you start at $45 per seat (minimum two passengers) for a half-hour flight.

Other Tours There are walking tours at Old Noarlunga, winery tours by camel, minibus and bicycle at McLaren Vale, horse rides at Normanville, sunset penguin walks at Victor Harbor, and boat cruises at Goolwa. See the sections on these towns for details.

Accommodation

There's a very good range of accommodation on the Fleurieu – everything from backpacker hostels to upmarket resorts. McLaren Vale, Victor Harbor and Goolwa have the most places; most coastal towns have a caravan park or two and some have an old pub where you can stay.

Because of the region's proximity to Adelaide its burgeoning B&Bs are in demand on weekends, while the coastal resorts are generally booked solid over the entire summer as well as Easter. Most places put their prices up at these times.

Getting There & Around

Bus Premier Stateliner has up to three return services daily on its two-hour run from Adelaide through McLaren Vale ($5), Willunga ($5.50), Port Elliot ($12) and Goolwa ($12) to Victor Harbor ($12).

Adelaide Sightseeing (☎ 8231 4144) has a return service once daily from Adelaide through Yankalilla ($12) to Cape Jervis ($14).

Transit Regency Coaches (☎ 8381 5311) has several departures each weekday from the Noarlunga Centre train station to McLaren Vale, Willunga and Aldinga.

A casual shuttle service operates from Victor Harbor to Cape Jervis. See the Getting There & Away entry for Victor Harbor.

Train SteamRanger's tourist train runs from Mt Barker to Victor Harbor via Goolwa. See the Getting There & Around section at the start of the Adelaide Hills chapter.

The little Cockle Train runs between Victor Harbor and Goolwa. See the Victor Harbor section.

There are suburban trains several times daily from Adelaide to Noarlunga Centre.

Bicycle You can hire bicycles in McLaren Vale and Victor Harbor. See the Getting There & Around entries for these places.

Ferry Vehicle and passenger ferries operate daily between Cape Jervis and Penneshaw, on Kangaroo Island. See the Getting There & Away section in the Kangaroo Island chapter.

Southern Vales

Apart from beaches and coastal resorts, the Fleurieu Peninsula is best known for its Southern Vales wineries. The first winery in the region was established in 1838 by John Reynell at Reynella, just 21km down Main South Rd from Adelaide. The industry went through boom and bust cycles until the 1920s, when the export market collapsed. Following a renaissance in the 1960s it now seems on a secure footing.

Most of the peninsula's 70 or so wineries are concentrated around McLaren Vale and nearby McLaren Flat. While this district is particularly well suited to red wines – shiraz and cabernet sauvignon are the foremost varieties – a trend towards white wine consumption in the 1970s prompted growers to diversify.

These days the old villages of Reynella, Morphett Vale and Old Noarlunga are outer suburbs of Adelaide. However, their historic precincts are largely intact and include numerous interesting buildings. Morphett Vale has **St Mary's** (1846), the state's first Roman Catholic church. Some wineries still survive near Reynella, including **Hardys**, one of the largest in the district.

The 1587 hectare **Onkaparinga River Recreation Park** extends down the river from near Clarendon to the sea. There are good walks through the gorge (you need to be fit), and you can canoe year round between Old Noarlunga and the sea – the return paddle is a leisurely day outing.

MCLAREN VALE
* **pop 2000**

Only 37km from Adelaide and just off busy Main South Rd, this picturesque town is the district's tourist centre. Most of the 45 wineries with cellar door sales are within a few minutes drive of town.

Information

The McLaren Vale & Fleurieu Visitor Centre (☎ 8323 9944, fax 8323 9949, rhand@ mclarenvale.aust.com) is on Main Rd at the northern end of McLaren Vale. It opens daily from 10 am to 5 pm.

Wineries

Most local wineries are open daily for tastings, and you can get times and a map from the tourist centre. Each winery has its own appeal, but it's not always the house product – it may be a superb setting or a particularly interesting cellar. Following are some suggestions.

Chapel Hill, Chapel Hill Rd, McLaren Vale south, has a magnificent hill-top location with views over Gulf St Vincent. This is a small vineyard producing sophisticated whites and reds.

d'Arenberg, Osborne Rd, McLaren Vale, has produced consistently good wines since 1928.

There's a fine view of the valley from its restaurant.

Kay Brothers, Kay Rd, McLaren Vale, has a beautiful rural view overlooking its vineyard.

Maxwell, Field St, McLaren Vale, specialises in mead, a great drop made from fermented honey. They do good table wines too!

Noon's, Rifle Range Rd, McLaren Vale south, specialises in full-bodied reds. This winery is in a pleasant rural setting beside a small creek, and has barbecue facilities.

Seaview, Chaffeys Rd, McLaren Vale, is a large and historic winery with a great atmosphere. It's worth visiting just to see the wonderful old Vat Gallery.

Woodstock, Douglas Gully Rd, McLaren Flat, is in a tranquil garden setting. It's well known for its tawny port and botrytis sweet wines.

A walking/bicycle track follows the old railway line from McLaren Vale to Willunga, 6km south. A number of wineries are within easy walking distance of the town centre.

Special Events

Best known is the Wine Bushing Festival, which takes place annually over a week in late October and/or early November. It's a busy time of wine tastings and tours, and the whole thing is topped by a grand feast.

The Sea and the Vines Festival is a celebration of wine and seafood over the June long weekend. During the Continuous 'Picnic, which takes place on the Labour Day long weekend in October, there's a free bus service that wanders from winery to winery picking up and dropping off imbibers.

Organised Tours

A great way to visit a few wineries is on a camel. The Bush Safari Co (previously the Outback Camel Co; ☎ 8543 2280) has several options, including a one day trek for $85, but not in winter. The tourist office has details of other camel rides in the area.

Sea & Vine Tours (☎ 8384 5151) has minibus tours that visit four wineries for $45 ex-Adelaide, including lunch. It also has a private hire car that will take you around for $75 per person, including lunch (minimum two passengers).

For the history buff, Heritage Research & Walks (☎ 8384 7918) of Port Noarlunga offers guided walks around Reynella, Morphett Vale, Port Noarlunga and Old Noarlunga. These take 1½ to two hours and cost $9; times are flexible.

Ecotrek (☎ 8383 7198) has scheduled weekend cycling tours.

Places to Stay
The *McLaren Vale Lakeside Caravan Park* *(☎ 8323 9255)* off Field St is in a pretty rural setting by a creek. It has tent/caravan sites from $13/15, on-site vans from $32 and self-contained cabins from $48.

Also with an attractive setting, the up-market *McLarens on the Lake (☎ 8323 8911, Kangarilla Rd)* charges $90/110/130 for singles/doubles/triples. We've heard that it can be noisy if there's a convention on.

Alternatively, the *McLaren Vale Motel* *(☎ 8323 8265, Caffrey St)*, at the northern end of town, has spacious units from $68/78/90.

There are numerous B&Bs starting at around $75 for doubles; the tourist office has details and can arrange bookings. They include *Southern Vales B&B (☎ 8323 8144, 13 Chalk Hill Rd)*, which is pleasant without being ostentatious and has a colonial authors' theme. Tariffs start at $85 for doubles, and you eat with the owners.

Places to Eat
There are several good restaurants in McLaren Vale. *Magnum's* in the Hotel McLaren serves pub food, while *The Barn* and *Marienberg Limeburners* have more upmarket dining. All are on Main Rd.

Best of all is the historic *Salopian Inn*, just out of town on Willunga Rd; it has a fascinating menu – imagine seared soy-basted squid, or roasted Tilbaroo calves' kidneys. Main courses start at $20 and

The striated winery landscape of McLaren Vale

you'll need to book (☎ 8323 8769) as it's small and popular.

You can eat at several wineries. *Haselgrove Wines*, on the corner of Kangarilla and Foggo Rds, is open for lunch from Wednesday to Sunday, with mains around $18. 'Picker's platters' feature at the *Wirilda Creek Winery (McMurtrie Rd)* and the *Woodstock (Douglas Gully Rd)*.

Fortunately for those on a strict budget there are several inexpensive eateries and take-aways in town, including a good bakery.

Getting There & Around
Bus & Train See the Getting There & Around section at the start of this chapter.

Bicycle Cyclomobile Bicycle Hire (☎ 8326 3427, 0417 838 545) has well-maintained mountain bikes from $15 for a half-day. It provides maps and route information, and can deliver within the McLaren Vale area.

WILLUNGA
- **pop 1200**

First established as a staging post on the Encounter Bay road, Willunga really took off in 1840 when the mining of high-quality slate commenced nearby. The slate was carted to Port Willunga and exported all around Australia. Today, this quiet, pretty little town is an almond growing centre – it hosts the Almond Blossom Festival in July.

The lack of development in Willunga since its boom years has preserved numerous heritage buildings dating from the 1850s. You can visit them with the booklet *Willunga Walks* ($4), which is widely available around town.

On High St, the old Court House and Police Station (1855) is now a small **National Trust museum**. It opens on weekends and public holidays from 1 to 5 pm and Tuesday from 10 am to 4 pm ($2).

Rose lovers will enjoy **Ross Roses**, just beyond the overpass on St Andrews Terrace. It's open daily, although the display garden has only a few flowers in winter.

Willunga is central to the **Kuitpo Forest** to the north-east (see the Mt Barker to Strathalbyn section in the Adelaide Hills chapter) and small conservation parks to the south-east. These include the 90 hectare **Mt Magnificent Conservation Park**, 13km from Willunga. The park is an access point for the Heysen Trail, and there are outstanding views from the summit of Mt Magnificent, which can be reached by a steep 150m walking track off a dirt road from Mt Compass (see below). You'll also find beautiful native forest and plenty of wildlife. From here it's about an hour's walk down to the 103 hectare **Finniss River Conservation Park**.

On Victor Harbor Rd, 9km south of Willunga, tiny **Mt Compass** is best known for the annual Compass Cup, a fun day of cow racing and other activities in February. About 8km west of Mt Compass on Cleland Gully Rd is the **Tooperang Trout Farm**, where even the most incompetent angler should be able to catch a fish. If you've never tried smoked trout this is the place to start. It opens between 10 am and 5 pm from Thursday to Sunday.

Places to Stay
The *Willunga Hotel (☎ 8556 2135, High St)* has basic singles/doubles for $20/35.

There are several good B&Bs in town and you can book through the tourist office in McLaren Vale. For heritage accommodation try the two-storey 1850s *Willunga House (☎ 8556 2467, St Peters Terrace)*. Rooms here are $110/130 and it has a great reputation.

Off St Johns Terrace about 2km from town, *Almond Views (☎ 8556 2625)* has a self-contained guest wing with B&B for $85/90. This is a relaxing place in a pleasant rural setting.

Emu Retreat (☎ 8556 2467) off Hahn Rd is a small, alternative lifestyle farm about halfway between Willunga and Aldinga Beach. It has bunk beds in a dorm for $20 and twin/double rooms for $40 per person, including a substantial breakfast. Stephan, the owner, hires out kayaks and mountain bikes, and can arrange a variety of outdoor activities including surfing and rock climbing.

FLEURIEU PENINSULA

About 3km south-east of Mt Compass, *Compass Country Cabins* (☎ 8556 8425) has comfortable, fully self-contained units from $70 for doubles. They're on Cleland Gully Rd, 1.5km east of Main South Rd.

Places to Eat
Willunga has several restaurants, cafes and other eateries, but there isn't the same variety (or prices) as in McLaren Vale.

The best of the three pubs in terms of atmosphere is the *Willunga Hotel*, which has daily counter meals and a good dining room.

Gulf St Vincent Coast

Popular swimming beaches line the coast from Adelaide to Sellicks Beach, 50km from the city; conditions are generally quiet unless there's a strong westerly blowing. Beyond Sellicks the coast is rocky virtually all the way to Cape Jervis, although there's a good stretch of sand at Carrickalinga and Normanville. The suburbs have gobbled up all the old coastal resorts as far south as Maslins Beach.

NORTHERN BEACHES
The first swimming beach on Gulf St Vincent south of Adelaide is **O'Sullivans Beach**, about 35 minutes drive from the city centre. From here a string of sandy beaches stretches south for 13km past the outer suburbs of **Christies Beach**, **Seaford** and **Moana** to **Maslins Beach South**, where you can legally go skinny dipping. For further details on these places see Adelaide Beaches in the Adelaide chapter.

Outposts of suburbia have developed south of Maslins Beach around the old coastal resorts of **Port Willunga** and **Aldinga Beach**. Both have potential for skin-diving. A lovely white ribbon of sand stretches the entire 6km from Aldinga Beach to **Sellicks Beach**, a popular sailboarding spot.

Places to Stay
Between Christies Beach and Maslins Beach are the *Christies Beach Tourist Park* (☎ 8326 0311, Sydney Crescent), the *Moana Beach Tourist Park* (☎ 8327 0677, 44 Nashwauk Crescent) and *Beach Woods Eco Tourist Park* (☎8556 6113, 2 Tuart Rd). All are close to the beach and have tent and caravan sites and cabins.

South of Maslins Beach you can stay at the *Port Willunga Caravan Park* (☎ 8556 5430), the *Aldinga Bay Holiday Village* (☎ 8556 5019, Esplanade), and the *Aldinga Caravan & Holiday Park* (☎ 8556 3444, Cox Rd).

SOUTHERN TOWNS
Past Sellicks Beach Main South Rd to Cape Jervis leaves the coast and passes through some beautiful rural scenery to Yankalilla. It returns to the sea at nearby Normanville, then it's back into scenic hill country to Cape Jervis. From here you can look across Backstairs Passage to Kangaroo Island, 13km away.

Yankalilla
• pop 550
This pretty valley town is at the junction of the Cape Jervis road and the 32km scenic drive via **Inman Valley** to Victor Harbor. If you're heading to Victor Harbor and you're interested in geology, check out the 250-million-year-old gouge marks left by a glacier at **Glacier Rock**, 20km from Yankalilla. The site is in the creek behind the restaurant.

Yankalilla has gained recent fame thanks to the image of Jesus and the Virgin Mary which has mysteriously appeared on a wall of the **Anglican church**. Cynics may tell you it's just salt damp.

The small house at 48 Main St (the road to Victor Harbor), was the first country **school** established by the Sisters of St Joseph, the teaching order founded by Mary MacKillop and Julian Tenison Woods. See the boxed text 'Champion of the Poor' in the South-East chapter.

Places to Stay At the picturesque hamlet of Inman Valley, 13km from Yankalilla en route to Victor Harbor, *The Old School House* hostel (☎ 8558 8376) charges $12 for its bunk beds (minimum charge $30 per room). This is a good friendly place. Inman Valley is an access point for the Heysen Trail, and maps are available at the hostel. Sadly, there is no public transport through Inman Valley, but you can take a taxi ride from Victor Harbor for around $25.

Normanville & Carrickalinga

Just to the west of Yankalilla, these twin coastal resorts are 3km apart and have the only decent stretch of sand between Sellicks Beach and Cape Jervis. They're both good swimming beaches.

High Country Trails (☎ 8558 2507) at Normanville has a range of short and full day **trail rides** costing from $20 for an hour to $85 for a day, including lunch. Its 'pub ride' along the beach for lunch at the Normanville Hotel is popular.

There are several guided activities at the **Wirrina Cove Paradise Resort** (☎ 8598 4001), 12km south of Normanville. They include sea kayaking ($50, three hours), horse riding ($45, three hours), scuba diving, deep sea fishing ($80, half day) and nature walks ($12, two hours).

Places to Stay & Eat The *Normanville Beach Caravan Park* (☎ 8558 2038, *Jetty Rd)*, right on the beachfront, has tent/caravan sites for $13/15, self-contained cabins from $55 and cottages from $80.

About 2km towards Cape Jervis, the *Beachside Caravan Park* (☎ 8558 2458, *Cape Jervis Rd)* has tent and caravan sites, basic cabins ($36) and en suite cabins ($46). The cabins have excellent shade, but the campsites are exposed.

Wirrina Cove Paradise Resort (☎ 8598 4001, 1800 083 111 toll free, bookings@ wirrina.in/sa.com.au) has a range of up-market options starting at $150 for a one-bedroom apartment. The package deals are worth investigating.

The well-shaded *Second Valley Caravan Park* (☎ 8598 4054, *2 Park Ave)* is by the sea 16km from Normanville and 21km from

Cape Jervis. Its prices are the cheapest on the coast – tent/caravan sites for $12/14, onsite vans for $28 and basic cabins for $38.

Historic *Leonards Mill* (☎ 8598 4184, *Cape Jervis Rd)* has more upmarket accommodation ($75/85 for singles/doubles) as well as a decent restaurant. It's popular with city folk on Saturday nights.

There are several other places to eat in the area. Locals recommend the *Normanville Hotel* for consistently good meals, and the *beach kiosk* by the Normanville jetty for fish and chips.

Cape Jervis
* **pop 100**

At the end of Main South Rd, 107km from Adelaide, this little fishing and holiday centre has the terminal for ferry services to Kangaroo Island. It's also the starting point for the Heysen Trail (see the Outdoor Activities chapter).

If it's a hot day, and you've arrived early for the ferry, there's a good **swimming beach** 2km by road to the north of the ferry terminal.

From Cape Jervis you can visit the 4180 hectare **Deep Creek Conservation Park** (☎ 8598 0263) for spectacular coastal views, good fishing, bush camping and some testing bushwalks.

A short detour from the Adelaide road leads you to the 210 hectare **Talisker Conservation Park**. It has attractive bush, views to Kangaroo Island and the interesting remains of a historic (1862) silver-lead mine.

Cape Jervis Charter Services (☎ 8598 0222) takes parties of up to seven people on **fishing trips** for snapper and whiting. It also offers dive charters.

Kangaroo Island Scenic Flights (☎ 8598 0004) does **flights** from Cape Jervis over the Fleurieu Peninsula and Kangaroo Island. One-way trips across to the island can also be arranged.

Places to Stay On the main road about 3.5km before the ferry terminal, the *Old Cape Jervis Homestead* (☎ 8598 0233) has a range of options, all in 1840s buildings with log

FLEURIEU PENINSULA

fires on cold nights. For $20 you can stay in the shearers' quarters, with use of a kitchen, while a self-contained cottage costs $80 for doubles. Otherwise there's traditional B&B in the homestead for $95 for doubles.

In the centre of town and about 1.5km from the ferry terminal, the *Cape Jervis Tavern* (☎ *8598 0276, Main Rd)* has motel units for $50/55 singles/doubles. It serves counter meals.

About 800m from the ferry terminal, *Island View Units (☎ 8598 0123)* has a couple of pleasant, motel-style units for $70 for doubles, including a light breakfast.

Deep Creek Conservation Park has five basic but attractive bush camping areas ($5 per car). Within the park are two cottages ($60 for doubles) and a homestead ($100 for doubles); ring ☎ 8598 4169 for information and bookings.

Surf Coast

Some of SA's most popular resort towns and surfing beaches are on the peninsula's south coast. Port Elliot has the most powerful waves, with swells often holding at 3m; other good breaks for experienced riders are at Waitpinga Beach and Parsons Beach west of Victor Harbor. The best months for surfing are March to June inclusive, when northerly winds prevail.

VICTOR HARBOR
• pop 8650

The main town on the peninsula, and 84km south of Adelaide, Victor Harbor has so many retired residents that irreverent types refer to it as 'God's Waiting Room'. It looks out onto Encounter Bay where Flinders and Baudin had their historic meeting in 1802. There's a memorial to the event up on the steep headland known as **The Bluff**, about 4km south of town.

Victor Harbor was founded as a sealing and whaling centre. The first whaling station was established in 1837 at **Rosetta Harbor** (below The Bluff), with another following soon after on **Granite Island**. The

unrestrained slaughter of southern right whales, on which the industry was based, eventually made operations unfeasible, and they ceased in 1864.

Information

The tourist office (☎ 8552 5738, fax 8552 5476) is by the mainland end of the causeway to Granite Island. It opens daily from 10 am to 4 pm (9 am to 5 pm in summer).

Surf Power (☎ 8552 5466) at 15 Albert Place can give advice on local surfing conditions and locations.

Things to See & Do

Victor Harbor has several historic buildings, and the tourist office has a pamphlet detailing a self-guided walk. They include **St Augustine's Church of England** (1869) on Burke St, the **Telegraph Station** (1869) on Coral St and the **Fountain Inn** (1838) at Yilki, on the road to The Bluff.

The **Old Customs House & Station Master's Residence** (1866), on Flinders Parade opposite the causeway, is now a **National Trust museum**. It adjoins the **Encounter Coast Discovery Centre**, where interesting displays explore local history from pre-European times to around 1900. The centre and museum are open daily ($4) from 10 am to 4.30 pm (shorter hours in winter).

The old Telegraph Station houses an **art gallery** where you can often see exhibitions by well-known Australian artists. It opens from Monday to Saturday from 10 am to 4 pm (1 to 4 pm Sunday).

Victor Harbor is protected from the angry Southern Ocean by **Granite Island**, now being developed (many would say ruined) as a major tourist drawcard. The 26 hectare island is connected to the mainland by a causeway; you can ride out there on a double-decker **tram** pulled by Clydesdale draught horses for $4 return. There are good views across the bay from the top of the hill.

Granite Island is a rookery for penguins. The **Penguin Interpretive Centre** (☎ 8552 7555) on the island has excellent audiovisual displays and guided tours can be arranged. It operates one-hour **guided**

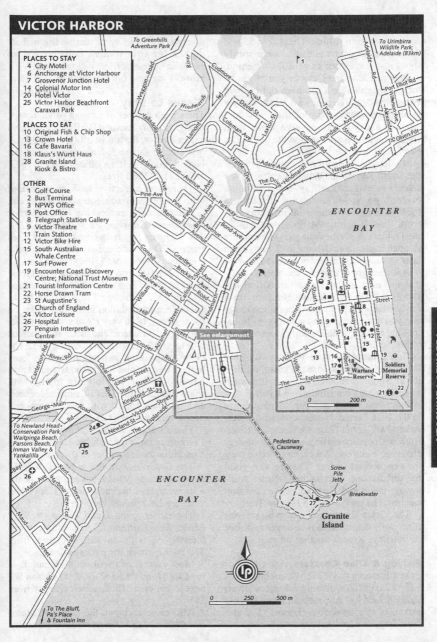

VICTOR HARBOR

PLACES TO STAY
4 City Motel
6 Anchorage at Victor Harbour
7 Grosvenor Junction Hotel
14 Colonial Motor Inn
20 Hotel Victor
25 Victor Harbor Beachfront
   Caravan Park

PLACES TO EAT
10 Original Fish & Chip Shop
13 Crown Hotel
16 Cafe Bavaria
18 Klaus's Wurst Haus
28 Granite Island
   Kiosk & Bistro

OTHER
1 Golf Course
2 Bus Terminal
3 NPWS Office
5 Post Office
8 Telegraph Station Gallery
9 Victor Theatre
11 Train Station
12 Victor Bike Hire
15 South Australian
   Whale Centre
17 Surf Power
19 Encounter Coast Discovery
   Centre; National Trust Museum
21 Tourist Information Centre
22 Horse Drawn Tram
23 St Augustine's
   Church of England
24 Victor Leisure
26 Hospital
27 Penguin Interpretive
   Centre

FLEURIEU PENINSULA

walks every evening to watch the penguins come home from fishing. These cost $5 and leave from the centre at dusk – wear sturdy shoes and leave your camera flash behind.

Between June and October you might be lucky enough to see a **southern right whale** swimming near the causeway. Victor Harbor is on the migratory path of these splendid animals and you can observe them from several lookout points around the bay – The Bluff is a good one.

If you want to learn more about whales, the **South Australian Whale Centre**, at the causeway end of Railway Terrace, is the place to go. It has interesting displays, a theatrette, and a 'whale information network' (see Watching Marine Mammals in the Outdoor Activities chapter). The centre is open daily from 10 am to 5 pm (often later in summer) and entry costs $6.

Another good spot to see native Australian fauna is the 16 hectare **Urimbirra Wildlife Park**, on Adelaide Rd 5km from town. Many of the displays are open range and you can easily spend a couple of hours looking around. It opens daily from 9 am to 6 pm ($6.50).

Greenhills Adventure Park on Waggon Rd is an ideal spot to lose the kids for a day. It's also good for adults, with activities such as canoeing on the Hindmarsh River.

Waitpinga Beach and Parsons Beach are in the 1036 hectare **Newland Head Conservation Park**, about 12km south-west of town. Both are popular surfing spots, but strong, changeable currents make them suitable only for experienced surfers. They're also good for **surf fishing**, with salmon, mullet, mulloway, tailor and flathead being common catches. The park is on the Heysen Trail.

The **Victor Theatre**, on Ocean St, screens films daily during school holidays and four or five days a week at other times.

Fishing & Dive Charters Victor Harbor Boat Charters (☎ 8552 3142, mobile 0414 527 475) offers fishing charters from $65/100 half/full day, including bait (tackle extra). It also does dive charters ($30 per dive, no gear supplied).

Victor Harbor's major attraction for divers is its diversity of marine life including sea lions (in winter), dolphins and an endemic species of leafy sea dragon. Visibility is variable but averages around 15m.

Places to Stay

There are a number of caravan parks, hotels, motels, holiday flats and B&Bs in and around Victor Harbor; the tourist office and the RAA office at 66 Ocean St have details. You can book through the RAA office (☎ 8552 1033, 1800 241 033 toll free).

There's an attractive *bush campground* near Waitpinga Beach. Sites cost $5 per car.

Travellers recommend the *Victor Harbor Beachfront Caravan Park* (☎ 8552 1111, 114 Victoria St). It has tent/caravan sites from $12/14, basic cabins from $40, self-contained cabins from $50 and villas for $60.

The heritage listed *Anchorage at Victor Harbor* (☎ 8552 5970, victor@anchorage .mtx.net, 21 Flinders Parade) has backpacker accommodation in historic villas on the seafront. It's a very clean and tidy place, with good kitchens and beds in spacious two to eight-bunk dorms costing $15. The German-speaking owners can arrange tours to the Coorong and Kangaroo Island. It also has simple but comfortable rooms with share facilities for $35/50 singles/doubles, and luxurious rooms with spa, balcony and ocean view for $90/125.

There's another *hostel* at Inman Valley, 19km from town towards Yankalilla (see the Yankalilla section earlier in this chapter).

The *Grosvenor Junction Hotel* (☎ 8552 1011, 40 Ocean St) also has a good standard – its renovated bedrooms cost $25/49 and there are backpacker beds for $20.

The rather grand *Hotel Victor* (☎ 8552 1288, The Esplanade) has singles/doubles/triples with en suite costing from $70/80/90; check the package deals.

Most central of the town's 11 motels is the *City Motel* (☎ 8552 2455, 51 Ocean St), next to the post office, which charges from $55/65.

Also close to town, the *Colonial Motor Inn* (☎ 8552 1822, 2 Victoria St) has standard units from $65/75 and units with kitchenette from $70/80.

Out under The Bluff, the upmarket **Whalers Inn Resort** (*☎ 8552 4400, whalers .inn@senet.com.au, Franklin Parade*) has a restaurant, cocktail bar and apartments with bay views for $148 for doubles. They also have package deals.

Places to Eat

There are plenty of take-aways, cafes and restaurants in Victor Harbor, but not too many are noted for excellence. If you're buying a take-away meal and it's a sunny day, eat it among the large Norfolk Island pines on the grassy foreshore.

The **Original Fish & Chip Shop** in the town centre on Ocean St is popular, but the best of all the local seafood take-aways is **Pa's Place**, on Franklin Parade next to the Yilki Store out towards The Bluff. Both also have sit-down meals.

Locals recommend the **Grosvenor Junction Hotel** as being good value for pub meals (from $7), but for more formal dining the **Hotel Victor** is best. The **Crown Hotel** has a bistro and counter meals.

For a different eating experience, **Klaus's Wurst Haus**, run by the ebullient Klaus himself, claims to sell the best German hot dogs in Australia. You'll find his tiny van, on weekends only, in the small park at the causeway end of Railway Terrace.

Across at the **Cafe Bavaria (11 Albert Place)**, you can get delicious German-style pastries and cakes as well as light lunches. This would have to be the nicest small eatery in town.

Also worth mentioning is the licensed **Anchorage Cafe**, in the Anchorage at Victor Harbor. Its bar is made from a 9m-long river boat, and the room is heated by the boiler from a pilot boat. You can dine alfresco in sunny weather.

Getting There & Away

Premier Stateliner has three bus services daily (less on weekends) from Adelaide for $12.

Smart Car (*☎ 8554 3788*) offers a casual shuttle service from Victor Harbor to connect with the Kangaroo Island ferry at Cape Jervis. One-way tickets cost from $15.

SteamRanger's tourist train *The Southern Encounter* does a return trip ($35) from Mt Barker on alternate Sundays from June to November inclusive, spending about three hours in town. See the Getting There & Around section at the start of the Adelaide Hills chapter.

Every Sunday, and more frequently during school holidays and Easter, the little Cockle Train travels the scenic Encounter Coast between Goolwa and Victor Harbor. The return fare is $15 and tickets can be purchased at the train stations in Victor Harbor, Port Elliott and Goolwa.

A cycle path follows the coast from The Bluff north-east to Middleton, and there are plans to extend it to the Murray Mouth.

Getting Around

The Victor Harbor Taxi Service (*☎ 8552 2622*) operates 24 hours. Approximate fares to outlying areas from the centre of town are: Port Elliot $10, Goolwa $20 and Inman Valley $25.

Motor scooters can be hired for $25 per hour from Victor Leisure (*☎ 8552 5772*), in the Shell service station at 105 Victoria St. You can negotiate a day rate in quiet times.

Victor Bike Hire (*☎ 8552 4458*) at 12 Flinders Parade has mountain bikes and tandems for $8 an hour and $30 a day.

PORT ELLIOT
• **pop 1200**

On Encounter Bay just 8km east of Victor Harbor, Port Elliot was established in 1854 as the seaport for Goolwa. It soon became a popular place for Adelaideans to escape the summer heat.

The town has many old buildings and several great beaches, and even in peak periods is a quiet contrast to the bustle of Victor Harbor. You can explore its interesting heritage on a **self-guided walk** – the historical centre in the old train station has a brochure.

Picturesque **Horseshoe Bay** has a sheltered swimming beach and a pleasant clifftop walk; **Commodore Point** at the eastern end is a good surf spot for experienced surfers, but there are better ones at nearby **Boomer Beach** and **Knights Beach**. The Southern Surf Shop, a few doors west of the Royal Family Hotel, has surfing gear for hire and can give advice on prevailing conditions.

Freemasons Nob, above the western end of Horseshoe Bay, is a good lookout point for whale watching between June and October.

The **Cockle Train** passes through town on its run between Victor Harbor and Goolwa (see the earlier Victor Harbor section for details).

Places to Stay & Eat
Port Elliot Caravan & Tourist Park (☎ 8554 2134) on Horseshoe Bay has tent/caravan sites from $13/15, self-contained cabins from $48, and cottages from $63.

At 32 North Terrace (the main road to Goolwa) the *Royal Family Hotel (☎ 8554 2219)* has basic pub rooms for $25/35 singles/doubles; counter meals start at $7.

Built in 1880, *The Strand Inn (☎ 8554 2067, 7 The Strand)* has motel-style units from $70/75.

Thomas Henry B&B (☎ 8554 3388, 8 Charteris St) is a lovely old guesthouse with spacious rooms (shared facilities) costing $70/80 including a large cooked breakfast. In warm weather you can eat outside under the grape vines – the guesthouse also does lunch and dinner. The *Hotel Elliot (35 The Strand)* also serves meals.

Locals recommend the *Flying Fish Cafe*, on the foreshore at Horseshoe Bay, for a seafood experience.

MIDDLETON
* pop 400

The main attraction at this pleasant little holiday spot is **Middleton Beach**, a good place for novice surfers.

Big Surf Australia (☎ 8554 2399), on Goolwa Rd near the Strathalbyn turn-off, has up-to-date advice on local conditions. It also hires out surfboards and wet suits, and can arrange surfing lessons.

The *Middleton Caravan Park (☎ 8554 2383, 21 Goolwa Rd)* is a short walk from the beach. It has powered sites from $14, on-site vans from $32 and cabins with kitchens from $34.

Alternatively, the grand turn-of-the-century guesthouse *Mindacowie (☎ 8554 3243, 48 Goolwa Rd)*, at the Port Elliott side of town, does B&B from $145. Across the road, the *Middleton Tavern* does good meals.

GOOLWA
* pop 3000

On Lake Alexandrina near the mouth of the Murray River, Goolwa became Australia's most productive river port after Echuca, in Victoria. As large sea-going vessels were unable to get through the sandbars at the Murray Mouth, the state's first railway line was built in 1854 to nearby Port Elliot, which became Goolwa's sea port. In the 1880s a new railway linking Adelaide and Melbourne via Murray Bridge spelt the end for Goolwa as a major port.

Information
The tourist office (☎ 8555 3488, fax 8555 3810), open from 9 am to 5 pm daily, is in the modernist **Signal Point River Murray Interpretive Centre** near the main wharf. The centre has displays on river ecology and various aspects of river life both past and present ($5).

Things to See & Do
Goolwa has a number of **heritage buildings** dating from the 1850s and 60s and you can visit them on a self-guided walking tour – the tourist office has a brochure. They include the **Goolwa Hotel** (1853), the **Corio Hotel** (1857), and the former **Customs House** (1859).

The National Trust **museum** on Porter St opens between 2 and 5 pm daily (closed Monday and Friday except public holidays). It's worth a visit for its displays on early settlement and farming ($2).

For something different, the **Goolwa Maritime Gallery** ($3), on the waterfront a short walk upstream from the main wharf, is an interesting complex which includes an art gallery in a WWII barge, and a riverboat museum in an 1882 stone building – you can buy many of the memorabilia on display.

Goolwa is a very popular centre for **water sports** such as windsurfing and sailing. You can hire jet skis, catamarans and sailboards on the waterfront between the wharf and the barrage.

The **Sir Richard Peninsula**, which separates the sea from Goolwa Channel (part of the lower Murray River) has a long stretch of firm sandy beach leading from Goolwa to the river mouth. You can drive along it (4WD only) and enjoy good fishing and surfing en route – the trip takes about 20 minutes one way. The beach continues all the way to Kingston from the opposite side of the mouth, but unfortunately there's no way across in a vehicle.

A vehicle ferry near the main wharf links Goolwa with nearby **Hindmarsh Island**, where there's a marina and tourist accommodation.

Milang (population 350), on Lake Alexandrina about 33km from Goolwa, also has an interesting history. It was established in 1853 as a river port, with bullock wagons carrying goods overland to and from Adelaide. In its heyday Milang handled more than half the total Murray River exports from SA. It's a sleepy little place these days, but comes alive in late January when the Freshwater Yachting Classic is held between here and Goolwa.

Further south, tiny Clayton is noted for **yabby fishing**. It's also a popular spot for water-skiing and sailing.

Special Events
Held over three days in March of odd-numbered years, the Wooden Boat Festival recalls the days when Goolwa was one of the Murray's major boat-building centres. It features numerous restored wooden boats, boat building demonstrations and a paddleboat race.

The Goolwa Cocklefest, held on a weekend in November, celebrates the humble cockle (a kind of clam). Events include cockle-eating competitions and surf boat races.

River Cruises
Between them, the MV *Aroona* and PS *Mundoo* – a replica paddle-wheeler – offer a variety of cruises, including the Murray Mouth and (provided the channel is deep enough) the Coorong. Both do lunch cruises for around $20; a pelican-feeding cruise on the *Aroona* costs $12.

Much more personalised – and more humorous – is a trip with the hearty Coorong Pirate (☎ 018 812 000), a large ocker gentleman who runs fun trips ($6) on the hour between 10 am and 3 pm (school holidays and weekends, October to April only). The kids should enjoy this one.

The MV *Wetlands Explorer* and MV *The Spirit of the Coorong* do longer cruises into the Coorong. Both give an informative commentary.

Places to Stay – Budget
The basic *Goolwa Camping & Tourist Park* (☎ 8555 2144, 40 Kessell Rd) is about 15 minutes walk from the town centre. It has tent/caravan sites (from $10/14), on-site vans (from $25) and self-contained cabins with cooking facilities (from $45).

On Noble Ave beside the Murray, about 4km from town, the more upmarket *Goolwa Caravan Park* (☎ 8555 2737) has tent and caravan sites, on-site vans and self-contained cabins. There are canoes and bicycles for hire, and boat access to the river.

The *Hindmarsh Island Caravan Park* (☎ 8555 2234, Madsen St) is about 100m from the river and has tent and caravan sites and two-bedroom cabins. There's also a bottle shop and scooter hire.

About 2km from the town centre and 500m from the beach, *Graham's Castle* (☎ 8555 2182, Bradford Rd) has basic twin rooms ($15 per person) and kitchen facilities. They'll pick you up from the town centre if you give them a ring.

Now decommissioned, the PS *Murray River Queen* (☎ 8555 1733, mrqueen @olis .net.au) is permanently moored at the town wharf as a floating motel. It has bunk beds for $15 in what was previously the crew's quarters, and there's a kitchen (no stove) you can use. There are also twin rooms with en suite from $40/46 for singles/doubles.

Right in the centre of town, the **Corio Hotel** (☎ *8555 1136, Railway Terrace)* has pub rooms for $25 per person, including a light breakfast.

Places to Stay – Mid-Range

The **Goolwa Central Motel** (☎ *8555 1155, bruceone@dove.net.au, 30 Cadell St)*, in the centre of town, has 'standard' units from $75/80 and spa units for $120.

The **Goolwa South Lakes Motel** (☎ *8555 2194, Barrage Rd)* charges from $54/59 – all units have a kitchenette.

The **Goolwa Riverport Motel** (☎ *8555 5033, Noble Ave)*, 4km from town, charges from $55/65. All units open onto a pleasant lawn area at the rear.

There are several cottages and B&B places. Close to the town centre, **Goolwa Cottage** (☎ *8555 1021, 3 Hays St)*, charges $50/70 including a light breakfast.

On Hindmarsh Island, **Narnu Farm** (☎ *8555 2002)* has rustic cottages with air-con and pot-belly stoves from $70 singles and doubles. This is a pioneer-style farm where many things are done the old fashioned way. Guests are encouraged to take part in farm activities, such as feeding the animals and hand-milking the cows.

Places to Eat

There are several eateries in the centre of town, including two 1850s hotels.

The **Goolwa Hotel** *7 Caddell St* has the figurehead from the *Mozambique*, wrecked at the Murray mouth in 1864, on its roof. The tables and chairs in its dining room were also salvaged from the wreck – some of the chair backs show the marks where sailors and passengers held them in their teeth while running races up and down the deck. Talk about being desperate for entertainment!

The nearby **Corio Hotel** also does meals, and is the more upmarket of the two. Another good place to eat is the Irish pub in the

Goolwa Central Motel (see the previous Places to Stay – Mid-Range entry).

Off the Strathalbyn road 10km from town, the **Currency Creek Winery** serves lunch and dinner daily, but bookings are essential (☎ 8555 4013). This family winery has won numerous awards, particularly for its whites. It opens daily for wine tastings and also has motel-style accommodation.

Getting There & Around

Premier Stateliner has three services daily (less on weekends) from Adelaide for $12.

See the earlier Victor Harbor section for details of steam trains which pass through Goolwa – the train station is next to Signal Point and the wharf.

The Goolwa Taxi Service (☎ 8552 8222) charges around $40 to Strathalbyn and $15 to Port Elliot.

Marine Charters (☎ 8555 3206), at the marina on Hindmarsh Island, offers a variety of dinghies, yachts and cruisers for hire.

LANGHORNE CREEK WINERIES

Established in 1850, the hamlet of Langhorne Creek, 16km east of Strathalbyn, is one of Australia's oldest wine growing regions. After a long period of stagnation, things started to happen in the late 1980s. There are now several wineries producing shiraz, cabernet sauvignon and chardonnay varieties, and at least four have tastings.

Worth visiting is **Bleasdale's**, the district's first winery, about 2km from Langhorne Creek on the Wellington road. Apart from its large range of wines, the main attraction is its historic cellars, which are classified by the National Trust. The old lever press, made from red gum, is awesome.

There's also the little **Lake Breeze Winery**, which has produced some prize-winning reds. It's in magnificent red gum country by the Bremer River, off Step Rd about 3km south of the township. You may notice Aboriginal canoe trees in this area – the most recent dates from the 1930s.

Kangaroo Island

A deeply dissected plateau nearly 150km long, up to 55km wide and reaching 307m at its highest point, Kangaroo Island is Australia's third-largest island (after Tasmania, and Melville Island near Darwin). It was cut off from the mainland by rising sea levels about 9500 years ago; Investigator Strait, the intervening stretch of water, is 13km across at its narrowest point.

Greater awareness of the island's scenic coastline, conservation areas, plentiful native wildlife and genuinely friendly residents has brought increasing numbers of visitors. It is linked to the mainland by airline and ferry services, and there are many organised tours on offer.

History

The island was uninhabited in 1802, when Matthew Flinders made the first recorded visit. To the Aborigines of the Encounter Bay area it was Karta, 'the island of the dead'. Only in 1903 was evidence found of previous Aboriginal habitation, and early stone implements have since been discovered scattered across the entire island. Archaeologists are uncertain what caused the demise of those early inhabitants, but it's thought they disappeared about 2250 years ago. Charcoal deposits indicate a dramatic decrease in the frequency of bushfires on the island around that time.

The first thorough coastal survey was carried out by the French explorer Nicholas Baudin on two visits in 1802 and 1803 – this explains the numerous French place names. The island itself was named by Matthew Flinders. He and his crew landed at Kangaroo Head, near Penneshaw, where they slaughtered a number of the marsupials and enjoyed a welcome feast of fresh meat.

European settlement took place soon after when a motley collection of whalers, sealers, escaped convicts and ship deserters began to make their homes on the island. They brought Aboriginal women from Tasmania

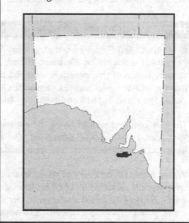

with them, and abducted others from tribes on the mainland. Before long, Kangaroo Island had a reputation as one of the most lawless and vicious places in the British empire. The worst scoundrels were rounded up in 1827, and thereafter a rough sort of respectability was achieved.

South Australia's first official settlement was established on Kangaroo Island at Reeves Point (near Kingscote) in July 1836.

It struggled on for two years, but the lack of fresh water was a major handicap and most of the colonists moved to Adelaide. Those who were left embarked on a semi-subsistence lifestyle which typified the island until the 1940s.

Since then, the application of superphosphate and trace elements has made the mineral-deficient soils suitable for large-scale farming. As a result, most of the native vegetation has been cleared for cereal crops and grazing, and Kangaroo Island has become one of the state's most productive agricultural districts.

Climate

Kangaroo Island's small size and the surrounding ocean have given it a milder climate than most other parts of the state –

winter frosts and summer days above 35°C are rare. On average, daily sunshine varies from 8½ hours in summer to four hours in winter.

Flora

Kangaroo Island was originally covered by mallee and tea-tree scrub, with large trees generally confined to the wetter western end. Although most of the island is farmed, there's quite a bit of native bush remaining in road reserves and conservation areas. From July through to November it's obvious why Kangaroo Island is referred to as a wildflower garden.

One of the island's most common eucalypts – the narrow-leafed mallee – is an excellent source of eucalyptus oil, and it once supported a thriving industry. Distilleries

Henry Wallen

One of SA's first European settlers, Henry Wallen, left the brig *Sophia* in 1820 and took up permanent residence on Kangaroo Island. At that time the island was inhabited by an unsavoury bunch of ship deserters, escaped convicts and other desperados. There were also a number of Aboriginal women, whom the men kept in virtual slavery. A Captain Sutherland visited the island in 1819 and described the men as little better than pirates:

They are complete savages, living in bark huts ... not cultivating anything, but living entirely on kangaroos, emus and small porcupines, and getting spirits and tobacco in barter ... They dress in kangaroo skins without linen, and wear sandals made of seal skins. They smell like foxes.

Wallen proved to be a man of strong character and a good leader. When the worst scoundrels were forcibly removed in 1827 he soon dominated the community, becoming its unofficial governor. He established a successful farm at Cygnet River and lived in a comfortable home made from wattle-and-daub. In 1834 he was reported to have seven men and five women all living peacefully as his subjects. Unfortunately for Wallen, however, this idyllic situation was not to last much longer.

In 1836 the South Australia Company's ship *Duke of York* arrived off Reeves Point with the first colonists. Wallen was on the beach to meet them, and after an altercation with the company's manager, Samuel Stephens, he agreed to give up his governorship in favour of Stephens. Then Stephens visited Wallen's farm, to which of course Wallen had no legal title. When Stephens saw what had been achieved he was so impressed that he took the farm as well.

Wallen received virtually no compensation for the loss of all his property and eventually moved to the mainland. He died penniless and alone in Adelaide and was buried in the Kingscote cemetery.

Denis O'Byrne

KANGAROO ISLAND

KANGAROO ISLAND

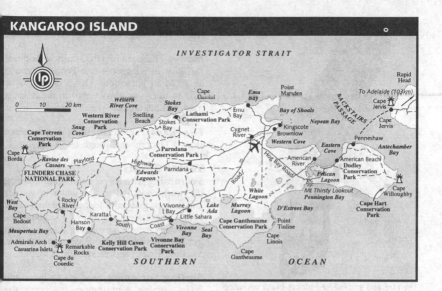

still operate on the island, and you can visit one on a guided tour.

Fauna

Dingoes, foxes and rabbits are absent, so wildlife tends to be more of a feature here than on the mainland. Grey kangaroos, wallabies, bandicoots and possums are fairly common, as you'll be able to tell from the number of road kills. Fortunately, live animals abound in wilderness areas, particularly the Rocky River area of Flinders Chase. Tammar wallabies are a serious pest to many farmers and thousands are shot each year.

Koalas and the platypus were introduced to Flinders Chase many years ago when it was feared they might become extinct on the mainland. Ironically, koala numbers on the island have increased to the point where they are at risk of starvation, and many are now being relocated to the mainland. Echidnas are native to the island, but, like the platypus, they are shy and rarely seen. Around the southern coast are colonies of New Zealand fur seals and Australian sea

lions, and dolphins and southern right whales are often seen offshore.

Of the 243 bird species recorded, several are either rare or endangered on the mainland. One species – the dwarf emu – has become extinct on the island since European settlement, and there are fears the glossy black cockatoo may soon join it. Only a few hundred of these large, noisy birds are left due to the widespread destruction of coastal she-oak woodlands both here and on the mainland (she-oak seeds are their exclusive diet).

Information

Tourist Offices The Kangaroo Island Gateway Visitor Information Centre (☎ 8553 1185, fax 8553 1255, tourki@ozemail .com.au) is on the Kingscote road just outside Penneshaw. It is open weekdays from 9 am to 5 pm, weekends and public holidays from 10 am to 4 pm, and has a useful website at www.tourkangarooisland.com.au.

National Parks The main National Parks & Wildlife Service (NPWS) office is at 37 Dauncey St in Kingscote (☎ 8553 2381, fax

The rare and endangered glossy black cockatoo

8553 2531). You can write to them at PO Box 39, Kingscote 5223.

The **Island Parks Pass** covers NPWS entry fees for all conservation areas. It covers all ranger-guided tours except the penguin walks. Passes are available from NPWS offices on the island and the tourist office at Penneshaw ($20).

Books & Maps The Royal Society of SA's *Natural History of Kangaroo Island* gives comprehensive coverage of the island's natural history, although to the layperson much of it will be scientific mumbo jumbo.

A much easier read is *Kangaroo Island Shipwrecks*, by Gifford Chapman, which gives accounts of 48 wrecks around the coast.

The Royal Automobile Association (RAA) does a small touring map of the island, while Tourism KI puts out a useful souvenir map with plenty of information and good artwork.

Email & Internet Access Ellson's Seaview Guesthouse in Kingscote has an internet cafe where you can send and receive email. The charge is $6/11 for 30/60 minutes.

Money There are EFTPOS cash-withdrawal facilities in Kingscote and Penneshaw, and an ATM in Kingscote. Don't expect to be able to use your plastic card in the island's more remote areas.

Fire Bans Fire restrictions are in place from 1 December through to 30 April.

Water Sports
Swimming The safest swimming is along the north coast, where the water is warmer and the rips generally less savage than in the south. There are a number of good beaches, but access can be a problem; those you can get to include Emu Bay, Stokes Bay, Snelling Beach and Western River Cove.

Surfing For surfing you go to the south coast, where Pennington Bay has the strongest, most reliable waves. Vivonne Bay and Hanson Bay in the south-west can also be good, but you need to be careful of rips – Hanson Bay is only for experienced surfers. A popular break near Point Tinline in D'Estrees Bay is called 'the Sewer'.

Scuba Diving There's a huge variety of marine creatures and plant life around the coast, including soft and hard corals such as you might expect to see on the Great Barrier Reef. There are something like 230 species of fish here, including colourful blue groper and blue devil fish. A number of the island's 60 known shipwrecks have been located and these make interesting, but not spectacular, dive sites.

The best diving is off the east and north coasts, which are well sheltered and hence the water is clearer: visibility is 10 to 20m on average. The east coast has sheer drop-offs covered in invertebrates and corals – some of the caves have rare black tree corals; waters of the north coast are shallower and have numerous rocky reefs, with drop-offs and chasms. You can expect to meet seals, sea lions or dolphins on most dives.

KANGAROO ISLAND

The Adelaide Hills viewed from Mt Torrens

Downtown Adelaide from up high

Adelaide's Festival Centre on the Torrens River

The brilliant colour of roses in Willunga, the town that hosts the Almond Blossom Festival

The weather-sculpted Remarkable Rocks at Kirkpatrick Point, Kangaroo Island

Directions are a rare find on Kangaroo Island.

No long drives for posties on Kangaroo Island

On a warm day, you might find 200 or more of the eponymous inhabitants of Seal Bay.

A Watery Grave

Since 1847, when the cutter *William* went down in Hog Bay, the rugged storm-swept coast of Kangaroo Island has claimed around 60 ships and dozens of lives. The shipwrecks range in size from the eight-tonne oyster cutter *Atlanta* (1860) to the 5865-tonne Japanese steamer *Portland Maru* (1935).

The hazards of navigating between the island and the mainland were recognised early. Lighthouses were built at Cape Willoughby (1852) and Cape Borda (1858), but it wasn't until a string of disasters occurred on the wild west coast that a lighthouse was constructed on Cape du Couedic in 1906.

News of Kangaroo Island's worst shipwreck was first heard on 19 May 1877, when three ragged, foot-sore seamen appeared out of the bush at the Cape Borda lighthouse. They were the sole survivors of the 39 passengers and crew of the wooden brigantine *Emily Smith*, which had been wrecked on rocks in heavy seas near Cape du Couedic five days earlier. Although five people had made it to shore, two – a male passenger and a female crew member – soon became exhausted and were left behind. Their skeletal remains were eventually found near West Bay.

In 1899, the three-masted iron barque *Loch Sloy* ran onto rocks close to the wreck of the *Emily Smith*. Only four of the 35 people on board managed to get through the breakers to shore, where an exhausted passenger was left while the others sought help. Fifteen days later, one of the survivors stumbled into the isolated Rocky River homestead and raised the alarm. A search party found his two companions almost dead two days later; the passenger left on the beach had already died and was buried on the clifftop.

Yet another tragedy involved the iron barque *Loch Vennachar*, last sighted 250km west of Kangaroo Island on 6 September 1905 while en route from London to Port Adelaide. Although reported overdue, it wasn't until wreckage from the ship began turning up along the island's south coast that its fate was confirmed. A single body was washed up on the beach at West Bay, but no trace of the other 26 people on board was ever found. In fact, the wreck's whereabouts remained a mystery until 1976 when it was discovered by a diver. It appeared that the ship had sailed straight into the cliffs at Point Vennachar, near West Bay.

Denis O'Byrne

Fishing There's plenty of good fishing around the island, which has jetties at Kingscote, Penneshaw, Emu Bay and Vivonne Bay. Emu Bay is a poor spot, but the others – particularly Kingscote – can be good. Common catches are garfish, tommy-ruff and squid, while the Kingscote jetty also has gummy shark and snook.

Rock fishing right around the coast can yield trevally and sweep, but you have to watch out for 'king waves', particularly on the south coast.

Good surf beaches that you can get to easily are Pennington Bay, the mouth of South

West River at Hanson Bay, and West Bay in Flinders Chase. Salmon, flathead, tommies and whiting are common catches here.

In March and April, most beaches yield good catches of mullet. The best places for King George whiting are the southern end of D'Estrees Bay, near Point Tinline, and King George Beach, between Snelling Beach and Stokes Bay on the north coast.

Organised Tours

Ranger-Guided Tours The NPWS operates guided tours and walks at the sea lion colony at Seal Bay, the show cave at Kelly

Hill Caves, the historic lighthouses at Cape Borda and Cape Willoughby, and the penguin rookeries at Kingscote and Penneshaw.

Details about these tours are under the Things to See & Do headings later in this chapter. Various other ranger-guided activities, such as birdwatching and nocturnal walks, may be on offer during school holidays at various parks; check with NPWS offices for details.

Package Tours The ferry operator (Kangaroo Island Sealink) and various local tour operators offer packages ex-Adelaide; competition is fierce, so if you shop around you should pick up a good deal. Most of the hostels in Adelaide sell packages to the island.

If you're short on time Sealink (☎ 31 31 01), the Penneshaw Youth Hostel, and Kangaroo Island Ferry Connections (☎ 8553 1233, 1800 018 484 toll free, kifc@kin .on.net) have day tours from Adelaide from around $150, including a visit to Seal Bay. Their options include the bus trip to Cape Jervis and the ferry across to Penneshaw, and return.

For budget travellers wanting to stay longer, Daniel's Tours (☎ 1800 454 454 toll free, dannyki@hotmail.com), Kangaroo Island Ferry Connections and the Penneshaw Youth Hostel have two-day packages ex-Adelaide from around $200. Kangaroo Island Air & Sea Adventures (☎ 8231 1744) at 101 Franklin St, Adelaide, also has a good range.

Some packages offer a free half day in Penneshaw. While this may sound appealing, keep in mind that you may not find much to do there.

Bus Day Tours Tours for backpackers and other budget travellers are run by Kangaroo Island Ferry Connections, the Penneshaw Youth Hostel and Sealink. They charge between $70 and $85 for a day tour that includes lunch and a visit to Seal Bay and Flinders Chase.

If money is no object, several operators specialise in luxury 4WD tours for small groups. Expect to pay upwards of $160 a day per person, inclusive of lunch and entry

fees, and they'll tailor the tour to suit your requirements. The tourist office has details.

Walking Tours You can do a 1½ hour creekside nature walk ($7) near Stokes Bay with Kate Stanton (☎ 8559 2251). The walk features native flora and fauna.

At the island's western end, the beautiful De Mole River can be explored on a one hour guided walk, which costs $5. To book ring ☎ 8559 3254.

NPWS rangers sometimes offer guided bushwalks during peak holiday periods.

Horse Rides Yarraman Ridge Trail Rides (☎ 8559 4296) at Vivonne Bay has beach and bushland rides lasting one to three hours, and you can combine your ride with a spot of kayaking on the Harriet River. It also has a stone cottage in which you can stay.

Felstead Farm Trail Rides (☎ 8553 9009) takes rides along bush tracks and the shore of Nepean Bay, about 16km from Kingscote.

Fishing Charters & Safaris Several operators can take you fishing from Kingscote, Emu Bay and American River; the tourist office has details. The usual charge is around $45 for four hours fishing and upwards of $80 for a day trip, although these rates depend on numbers.

Kangaroo Island Sports Fishing Safaris (☎ 8553 2325) offers tailor-made one to four-day safaris with shore and/or boat fishing. It operates from the Kingscote Caravan Park.

Yacht Charters Kangaroo Island Sailing (☎ 8553 2111, harris@kin.on.net), at the Kingscote jetty, offers skippered yacht charters and cruises along the northern coast and across to the Althorpe Islands and Gulf St Vincent. Half-day cruises on Nepean Bay cost around $50, full-day cruises around $80 (minimum of four passengers).

Scuba Diving Tours The island's two operators cater for new and experienced divers, and offer courses leading to internationally recognised dive certificates.

Adventureland Diving operates from the Penneshaw Youth Hostel (☎ 8553 1284). It runs one-day ($150) to five-day ($690) diving packages, which include accommodation, meals and equipment. They also offer abseiling, canoeing and rock climbing for beginners, as well as dive charters.

Near Western River Conservation Park, on North Coast Rd, about 75km from Kingscote, Kangaroo Island Diving Safaris (☎ 8559 3225, kids@kin.on.net) has one-day ($150) to five-day ($650) dive tours, not including accommodation. You can dive with fur seals and see 30cm-long leafy sea-dragons.

Other Tours Among other things, you can visit a sheep dairy and cheese factory (their products are delicious), a honey farm and a eucalyptus-oil distillery. Most people will find the distillery tour, at Emu Ridge between American River and Kingscote, particularly interesting. The Penneshaw tourist office can provide details of these places.

Scenic Flights Kangaroo Island Wilderness Flights (☎ 8559 4254) does scenic flights from Parndana, or you can depart from somewhere more convenient if you prefer. Half-hour flights cost $55 per seat and hour flights $100, with a minimum of two passengers.

Kangaroo Island Scenic Flights (☎ 8598 0004) departs from Cape Jervis. See the section on that town in the Fleurieu Peninsula chapter.

Accommodation

As in other popular coastal holiday areas, rates for most places – particularly flats – rise during the summer school holidays and Easter.

There's a good range of accommodation in Kingscote and Penneshaw, including caravan parks, hostels, hotels, motels and guesthouses. American River has a couple of motels and several flats.

A growing number of homes offer B&B; the Penneshaw tourist office has details of most and handles bookings. Ferry Island Connections also has a number of listings.

Holiday flats and cottages seem to be almost everywhere, with the cheapest around $55 a night for two people; once again, the main booking agents are Kangaroo Island Ferry Connections and the Penneshaw tourist office.

The NPWS has a number of remote historic cottages for rent. These range from basic huts (starting at $10 per person) to the lightkeepers' cottages at Cape Willoughby, Cape Borda and Cape du Couedic (starting at $30 per person). Contact the NPWS office at Flinders Chase (☎ 8559 7235) for details and bookings.

Getting There & Away

Air Several small airlines service Kingscote from Adelaide at least three times daily. The standard one-way fare with Emu Air (☎ 8234 3711, 1800 182 353 toll free) is $70; with Kendell Airlines (bookings ☎ 13 13 00) it is $82; and with Southern Sky (☎ 1800 643 300 toll free) $72. Other fares, such as 14-day advance purchase fares, are also available.

Kendell has the largest planes (19 seaters), while the others offer a courtesy shuttle bus from the airport to Kingscote.

Ferry Departing from Cape Jervis, Kangaroo Island Sealink (☎ 13 13 01, kiexpert@ sealink.com.au) operates two vehicle ferries, which run all year except Christmas Day, taking about 45 minutes to Penneshaw. There are at least a couple of sailings each day, with up to 10 in December and January. Return fares are $60 for passengers, $10 for bicycles, $40 for motorcycles and $130 for cars.

Ask when booking about contingency arrangements (and who pays for them) should rough conditions leave you stranded on Kangaroo Island. Having said that, cancellations are very rare as Backstairs Passage is sheltered from the ocean.

Sealink has a bus service from Adelaide's central bus station to connect with ferry departures ($14). Bookings are essential.

Getting Around

It's important to realise that Kangaroo Island is a big place, and that there is no public transport. Unless you're taking a tour, the only feasible way to get around is to bring or hire your own transport.

Kingscote and Penneshaw are linked by a good bitumen road that continues past Parndana to the western end of the island. Another sealed road goes from Kingscote to Seal Bay and beyond – this should reach Flinders Chase in the not-too-distant future.

Otherwise the island's roads are unsealed, often rough and have a terrible reputation for accidents. The danger lies in their loose surface of pea gravel and the inexperience of most visiting motorists; they drive too fast and come to grief, usually by overturning or 'going bush' on corners.

To/From the Airport A bus runs from the Kangaroo Island airport to Kingscote for $10. The airport is 14km from the town centre.

To/From the Ferry Landings The Sealink Shuttle (☎ 13 13 01), which connects with most ferries, links Penneshaw with Kingscote ($11) and American River ($6.50). You'll have to book.

Car Rental There are three car-hire companies, all based in Kingscote: Budget (☎ 8553 3133); Hertz/Kangaroo Island Rental Cars (☎ 8553 2390, 1800 088 296 toll free); and Koala Car Rentals (☎ 8553 2399).

Very few of Adelaide's car-rental outlets will allow their vehicles to be taken across to Kangaroo Island. The only ones we're aware of are Access Rent-a-Car (☎ 8223 7466), Smile Rent-a-Car (☎ 8234 0655) and Thrifty Car Rental (☎ 8211 8788). While there is no island surcharge, you may have to pay additional insurance.

Motorcycle Rental The Country Cottage Shop (☎ 8553 2148), at 6 Centenary Ave in Kingscote, has 50cc scooters for $30/45 per half/full day. You can't take them on dirt roads.

Bicycle Hire Bernard O'Connor (☎ 8553 0169, mobile 015 721 676) in Brownlow, near Kingscote, hires out well-maintained

mountain bikes and panniers by the day or week. He'll deliver bikes to any specified location on the island, and can arrange group tours and/or vehicle support. He charges $20 per day up to four days and $15 per day over four days.

Walks The NPWS publishes a leaflet that briefly describes 12 walks from 1km to 18km. Rangers can provide details on more serious treks around the coast.

Boat Hire American River Rendezvous (☎ 8553 7150) has dinghies with outboard motors, but you need a licence; the half-day rate is $45. You can hire similar craft at Emu Bay (☎ 8553 5247) for much the same price.

PENNESHAW
* **pop 300**

Looking across Backstairs Passage to the Fleurieu Peninsula, Penneshaw is the arrival point for ferries from Cape Jervis. It's a quiet resort town nestling under scenic hills, with several points of minor interest.

Information
Tourist Offices The island's main information outlet is just outside town on the road to Kingscote. See under Information at the start of this chapter.

Money Sharpys Store has an ANZ agency, Servwel has the Bank SA agency, and the post office is an agent for the Commonwealth Bank. All have EFTPOS cash-withdrawal facilities.

Things to See & Do
Right by the vehicle ferry terminal is **Hog Bay**, with its beautiful sandy beach. The small white dome at the far end protects a replica of **Frenchman's Rock**, a boulder carved by a member of Baudin's expedition.

In the evenings, NPWS officers take visitors on walks to view the **little penguins** that nest along the shore near town – you'll generally see more penguins here than at Kingscote. Tours ($5) depart from the 'Penguin Rookery' on the foreshore next to the ferry terminal at 7.30 and 8.30 pm (8.30 and 9.30 during daylight saving). Take sturdy shoes and leave your camera flash behind.

Penneshaw Maritime & Folk Museum has some interesting memorabilia, including artefacts from local shipwrecks. It is open Monday, Wednesday and Saturday from 10 am to noon and 3 to 5 pm, and admission is $2.

The 1852 **Cape Willoughby Lighthouse**, 28km south-east of town, is the state's oldest lighthouse. Ranger-guided tours of around 45 minutes ($5) operate between 10 am and 2 pm daily (later between September and April).

About 24km out towards Kingscote you come to **Mt Thisby**. Used by Flinders as a lookout while mapping the coast, this large sandhill offers panoramic views north towards American River and south over **Pennington Bay**, one of the island's best surfing and surf-fishing spots. A steep staircase leads up to the summit, where there's a table you can collapse on for heart massage.

Places to Stay – Budget
Caravan Parks & Hostels Down by Hog Bay is the pleasant, if cramped, *Penneshaw Caravan Park* (☎ 8553 1075, Talinga Terrace). It has shady tent/caravan sites for $12/15 and on-site vans starting at $25.

Alternatively there's the *Penneshaw Youth Hostel* (☎ 8553 1284, 1800 686 620 toll free, adv.host@kin.on.net, North Terrace), where beds are $14 in dorm rooms and $16 in twin rooms. It's basic but clean, and there's a budget cafe out the front. The owners run diving tours and have bicycles for hire.

The *YHA Penguin Walk Hostel* (☎ 8553 1233, 1800 018 484 toll free, kife@kin on.net), operated by Kangaroo Island Ferry Connections, is by the ferry landing. Beds in spacious dorms (each with its own kitchen and bathroom) cost $14 for members, and it also has twin rooms with shared bathroom and kitchen facilities for $18 per person ($25 with private bathroom).

Hotels At the top of North Terrace, the *Penneshaw Hotel* (☎ 8553 1042) has twin rooms for $30.

Places to Stay – Mid-Range
The *Sorrento Resort Motel* (☎ 8553 1028, North Terrace) has very comfortable rooms starting at $59/78 for singles/doubles. It also has chalets for $73 for doubles and cottages for $86; there's an overnight surcharge of $25 and $35 respectively.

The most gracious B&B in town, if not on the entire island, would have to be the *Seaview Lodge* (☎ 8553 1132, lodge@kin .on.net), at the Kingscote end of town. Built as a farm homestead in 1860, it was first used as a guesthouse in 1890 and has now been beautifully restored. Rates start at $74 twin-share with shared facilities; rooms with a queen-size bed and private facilities start at $108.

Places to Stay – Out of Town
The tourist office issues camping permits ($3.50) for bush sites at *Chapmans River* (on Antechamber Bay), *Browns Beach* (12km from town on the Kingscote road) and *American River*; outside business hours you can get them from Sharpys Store. Some of the sites are quite attractive, but facilities are rudimentary.

At Cape Willoughby, *Seymour and Thomas Cottages* (the old lighthouse keeper's quarters) cost $30 per person with a minimum charge of $60. See under Accommodation at the start of this chapter.

Places to Eat
The *Old Post Office Restaurant (North Terrace)* has a very good reputation. It is open for dinner from Thursday to Monday and main courses start at $9; there's often live entertainment, usually provided by the musical chef.

You can also get meals at the *pub* and *Sorrento Resort Motel*, and there are takeaways available in town.

AMERICAN RIVER
• **pop 300**
On the coast between Kingscote and Penneshaw, this attractive holiday settlement takes its name from the American sealers who built a trading schooner there in 1804.

The town is on a small peninsula and shelters a calm inner bay named **Pelican Lagoon** by Flinders. Perhaps 'Swan Lagoon' might have been a better name!

At 4.30 pm daily you can watch or take part in **pelican feeding** down on the wharf. You'll get a free bucket of fish, and the pelicans provide the feeding frenzy. At night you'll often see **wallabies** hopping around in the town area.

Places to Stay & Eat

A pleasant restaurant with a lovely view over Eastern Cove is the highlight of *Matthew Flinders Terraces (☎ 8553 7100, Bayview Rd)*. The well-appointed motel units, perched on a steep hillside with gardens and native trees, start at $86/98/113 for singles/doubles/triples.

The sprawling *Linnetts Island Club (☎ 8553 7053, The Esplanade)* appears to have grown like Topsy, with each addition a different style. It has a bistro and a wide range of accommodation options from tent sites at $15 and very basic twin rooms at $20 per person to luxurious, rammed-earth suites at $150.

There are several holiday units in town, including the *Casuarina Holiday Units (☎ 8553 7020)* next to the post office. Here you'll find basic self-contained units starting at $50 for doubles and $10 for extra adults.

KINGSCOTE

- **pop 1440**

Kingscote, the main town on the island, dates from 1836 when it became the first official colonial settlement in South Australia. It's a quiet, attractive town with a great seaside atmosphere, and it makes a good base from which to explore the island.

Information

The main local outlet for tourist information is in the Kingscote Gift Shop, on the corner of Dauncey and Commercial Sts.

There are branches of the ANZ and Bank SA, and these are side-by-side on Dauncey St. Bank SA has an ATM, and EFTPOS cash-withdrawal facilities are available at several places. There's an agency for the Commonwealth Bank at the post office.

The district council office on Dauncey St issues camping permits for Western River Cove in the island's north-west.

Things to See & Do

The site of the first settlement is at **Reeves Point Historic Site**, within walking distance of the town centre. It's very picturesque with lawns and shady trees, but there's not much left apart from the cemetery, a well and a few bits and pieces. The point itself has shallows and sandbars, making it a good spot to observe waterbirds.

Hope Cottage overlooks Reeves Point from the top of the hill on Centenary Ave. Built in 1857, it's now a National Trust museum furnished in period style. In the grounds are a reconstructed lighthouse and a eucalyptus-oil distillery. It is open from 2 to 4 pm daily, and admission is $3.

Kingscote doesn't have a good swimming beach so most locals head out to **Emu Bay**, 18km north-west of town. The tidal **swimming pool** about 500m south of the jetty is the best place in town to swim.

At 4 pm daily (5 pm during daylight saving) there's **bird feeding** at the wharf near the town centre. Around 40 of those majestic (if somewhat comical) beaked battleships, pelicans, as well as a Pacific gull or two, usually turn up for the free tucker. A 'donation' of $2 is requested.

Each evening at 7.30 and 8.30 pm (8.30 and 9.30 pm during daylight saving) NPWS officers take visitors on **Discovering Penguins** walks for $5. These start at the reception area of the Ozone Hotel or Kingscote Terrace; wear sturdy footwear and leave your camera flash behind.

The Gallery on Murray St has an excellent selection of local arts and crafts. It is open daily between 10 am and 5 pm. On the wharf, and open at the same times, **Jenny Clapson's Gallery** has some beautiful work.

Places to Stay – Budget

Caravan Parks On the Esplanade, a short walk from the town centre, the modest

Kingscote Caravan Park (☎ 8553 2325) has tent/caravan sites starting at $12/16, on-site vans at $30, self-contained cabins with kitchens at $45 and holiday flats at $55 – the rates for the cabins and flats are for up to four adults. Ask here about fishing charters.

About 3km south-west of town at Brownlow, the *Nepean Bay Tourist Park* (☎ 8553 2394, First St) has tent/caravan sites starting at $11/14, on-site vans at $28, cabins with cooking facilities at $33 and holiday units at $50.

Hostels The *Kangaroo Island Central Backpackers Hostel* (☎ 8553 2787, 19 Murray St) has dorm beds for $14, twin and double rooms for $37, and a family room, sleeping four people, for $65. While the place is well-maintained, its kitchen is miniscule and the dorms are crowded.

Places to Stay – Mid-Range

Hotels In the centre of town, the attractive *Queenscliffe Family Hotel* (☎ 8553 2254, 57 Dauncey St) has rooms (some with

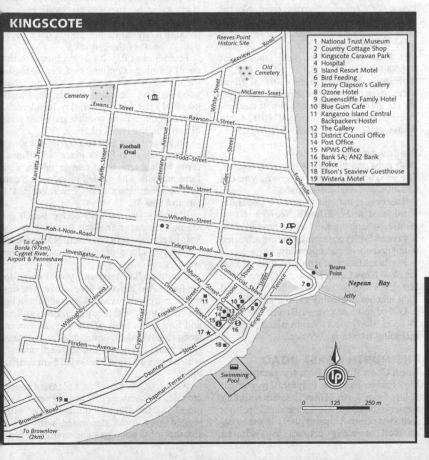

KINGSCOTE

1 National Trust Museum
2 Country Cottage Shop
3 Kingscote Caravan Park
4 Hospital
5 Island Resort Motel
6 Bird Feeding
7 Jenny Clapson's Gallery
8 Ozone Hotel
9 Queenscliffe Family Hotel
10 Blue Gum Cafe
11 Kangaroo Island Central
   Backpackers Hostel
12 The Gallery
13 District Council Office
14 Post Office
15 NPWS Office
16 Bank SA; ANZ Bank
17 Police
18 Ellson's Seaview Guesthouse
19 Wisteria Motel

0   125   250 m

KANGAROO ISLAND

four-poster beds) from $40/50 for singles/doubles. On the downside, the rooms over the bar can be noisy, particularly on Friday and Saturday nights.

Down on the foreshore by the jetty, the more upmarket *Ozone Hotel (☎ 8553 2011, 1800 083 133 toll free, general@ozonehotel .com, Kingscote Terrace)* has singles and doubles starting at $80 ($100 with great sea views). The hotel's family rooms sleep four and cost $110.

Motels & Guesthouses *Ellson's Seaview Guest House (☎ 8553 2030, ellsons@ kin.on.net, Chapman Terrace)* overlooks the tidal swimming pool. This charming, old-style guesthouse has comfortable rooms with shared facilities for $35/44/51 singles/doubles/triples. Its motel units cost $74/88/96.

Wisteria Motel (☎ 8553 2707, wisteria @kin.on.net, Brownlow Road) overlooks the sea about 1km south of town. It has luxurious standard units for $98/110/124 and deluxe units with spa for $127/146/165.

Places to Eat

Both pubs and the motels have restaurants. The pubs have $6 nights, otherwise you can usually get a feed for around $9.

The best restaurant in town is generally considered to be *Ellson's Seaview Guest House*, where mains start at around $13. It's noted for its ornamental ceilings, varied menu and air of quiet gentility.

For breakfast you won't be able to beat the *Blue Gum Cafe*, next to the Queenscliffe Hotel. It's also popular for coffee, cakes and light lunches, including vegetarian fare.

Out of town at Cygnet River, *The Cafe* (☎ 8553 9187) specialises in island produce including free-range chooks.

THE NORTH COAST ROAD

North Coast Rd runs from Kingscote along the coast to meet the Playford Hwy about 85km from town. There's some stunning scenery (beaches, cliffs, bushland, rolling farmland) en route, particularly in the west, as well as along detours to sheltered beaches. Apart from small shops at Emu Bay and Stokes Bay there are no facilities along this road.

Things to See & Do

The bitumen stops at **Emu Bay**, 18km from town. This is one of the island's best swimming beaches: a beautiful sweep of sand about 5km long. It's very popular in summer and is one of the few beaches onto which you can drive a car.

About 36km further west is **Stokes Bay**, which has a penguin rookery and a large rock pool suitable for swimming. The beach is attractive, but there's a dangerous rip outside the pool. To get there you'll walk through a natural tunnel among huge boulders just east of the carpark.

From Stokes Bay it's 22km inland to the small farming community of **Parndana**, in the centre of the island. The township has good services including a hotel, supermarket, fuel sales and a seven-day launderette. There's quite a good **wildlife park** just west of town on the Playford Hwy.

En route from Stokes Bay to Parndana you can call in to **Paul's Place**, an off-beat farm with many hand-reared native and farm animals. The guided tours, which can be good fun, operate between noon and 4 pm and cost $6.

Probably the most attractive beach on the north coast is **Snelling Beach**. It looks absolutely magnificent from North Coast Rd as you climb onto the plateau to the west.

Continue 7km west and you'll come to the turn-off to **Western River Cove**. The detour is extremely scenic as it winds about on the ridge tops, with big gums, deep gullies and fine views most of the way. However, steep slopes make it unsuitable for caravans – the same applies to the southern access, which turns off North Coast Rd 6km further on.

Western River Cove has a pleasant **beach** crowded by sombre cliffs at either end. The mouth of the river is quite pretty, with jagged grey rocks decorated with vivid splashes of green algae and orange lichen.

About 3km west as the crow flies, but 26km by road, is the 2400 hectare **Western River Conservation Park**. Its major scenic highlight (in winter and early spring) is a picturesque waterfall that tumbles into a deep, dark gully. Don't try to get to the bottom of the hill in a conventional vehicle if the track is anything but dry.

Places to Stay & Eat

The *Emu Bay Caravan Park (Kingscote Caravan Park ☎ 8553 2325)* is close to the beach. It has tent/caravan sites for $8/10 and self-contained cabins for $65 for up to four people. There are no showers for campers, although these facilities are planned. There's a reasonable take-away nearby.

The *Rock Pool Cafe (☎ 8559 2277)* at Stokes Bay has a small grassed area where you can camp for $3 per person (powered sites $5). There's rainwater for drinking, but no showers. The cafe sells interesting meals served alfresco, and basic provisions.

Although uninspiring in itself, the *camping area* at Western River Cove is only a short walk from a nice beach. It has toilets and a picnic shelter, but no showers. Permits, $3.50 per site, are available from the council office in Kingscote.

THE SOUTH COAST ROAD

South Coast Rd turns off the Kingscote to Penneshaw road about 15km from Kingscote and terminates at West Bay, in Flinders Chase National Park, 105km further on. En route there are detours to attractions such as Seal Bay and Kelly Hill Caves (there are ranger-guided tours at both places). Apart from the coast and the wildflowers in spring, the scenery along the road itself is nothing startling until you get to the tall timber at Kelly Hill Caves.

Kangaroo Island's south coast, is exposed to the Southern Ocean, and a vivid contrast to the sheltered north. Given any sort of blow from the south the shore is awash with booming breakers and great clouds of spray. It's easy to see why some of the island's worst shipwrecks occurred here.

Things to See & Do

The turn-off to the 21,300 hectare **Cape Gantheaume Conservation Park** is 24km from Kingscote, then it's a rough 16km to the ranger's office (☎ 8553 8233) at **Murray Lagoon**. This is the island's largest wetland and you'll usually see hundreds of swans, ducks, waders and other waterbirds. Ospreys and sea eagles nest along the coastal cliffs of Cape Gantheaume.

From the ranger's office it's 23km to **Point Tinline**, a good surfing and surf-fishing spot on **D'Estrees Bay**. If you're feeling fit you can walk around the coast to Seal Bay, seeing spectacular cliffs and colonies of New Zealand fur seals and Australian sea lions en route. It's mostly an easy and enjoyable walk, but it takes two days and there's no drinking water; check with the ranger at Murray Lagoon before setting out.

Seal Bay, with its large colony of Australian sea lions, is one of the island's major tourist attractions. Ranger-guided tours ($7.50) leave from the information centre between 9 am and 4.15 pm daily (7 pm during the summer school holidays).

About 500 sea lions live here, but you won't see that many. If it's cold, there may only be four or five on the beach – the rest will be sheltering up in the sandhills. On a warm day there might be 200 or more basking along the water's edge. Although you'll get close-up photos, don't expect exciting action unless it's the breeding season. Most times the animals lay about having the occasional scratch but otherwise showing no interest in anyone or anything.

The information centre has some interesting displays, including a disturbing one on the effects of plastic rubbish on sea birds and mammals. Nearby is a **lookout** offering a fine view along the beach.

Back on South Coast Rd, the next turnoff on your left (just before the Eleanor River, about 7km from the Seal Bay road) will take you to **Little Sahara**, a vast expanse of huge white sandhills rising above the surrounding mallee scrub.

Further west, **Vivonne Bay** has a beautiful sweeping beach, and the sea looks most inviting on a hot day. However, there are some fierce undertows, so get local advice before plunging in. This is another good surfing spot, with some of the strongest waves on the coast.

Getting close to Flinders Chase is the 7400 hectare **Kelly Hill Caves Conservation Park** (☎ 8559 7231), where the main attraction is a series of limestone caves. Apparently, these were 'discovered' in the 1880s by a horse named Kelly, which fell into them through a hole.

Guided tours of the show cave ($5) leave on the hour between 10 am and 3.30 pm daily (4.30 pm during the summer school holidays); adventure caving in small groups is available by prior arrangement. There's a pleasant picnic area among tall gums and some interesting short walks. The 9km walk from the cave to the mouth of South West River at Hanson Bay takes you through mallee scrub and past freshwater wetlands, with fine coastal views at the end.

Places to Stay & Eat
Kaiwarra Cottage near the Seal Bay turn-off is a good spot for light meals and Devonshire teas.

The *Vivonne Bay Store* does the usual take-aways, and you can buy fresh and cooked lobster (called crayfish here) during the season. The crayfish sandwiches are very tasty.

There are *bush camping areas* at Murray Lagoon and Point Tinline, in Cape Gantheaume Conservation Park, for which permits cost $5 per car.

The small *Vivonne Bay Camping Ground* (☎ 8559 4287) is pleasantly situated in bushland off the road to the jetty. It has toilets but no showers.

Further on towards Rocky River, *Attarak Farm* (☎ 8559 7202, vborg@kin.on.net) is a very friendly place offering traditional B&B in the family home for $35/60 singles/doubles. You can wander around the farm on foot, or go on horse rides and nocturnal wildlife tours – and I hear that the musical evenings around the piano are 'a rollicking good time'. The farmhouse is off

Mt Taylor Rd about 5km from South Coast Rd (18km from the Playford Hwy).

FLINDERS CHASE NATIONAL PARK
Occupying the western end of the island, 73,800 hectare Flinders Chase is one of South Australia's most significant national parks. Much of the park is mallee scrub, but there are some beautiful, tall sugar-gum forests, particularly around Rocky River and the Ravine des Casoars, 5km south of Cape Borda. There's wild, often spectacular, scenery right around the coast, which you can reach in several places from roads and walking tracks. A map is available from the park headquarters.

Information
The park headquarters (☎ 8559 7235) at Rocky River – over the hill past the information centre – is open from 9 am to 5 pm in summer (10 am in winter).

Things to See & Do
Once a farm, **Rocky River** is an excellent spot to see wildlife. As I drove up a koala, pursued by a small excited boy, galloped across the road and scrambled up a gum tree. It sat there and stared down as if wondering what all the fuss was about, while its pursuer danced and squealed below.

Kangaroos at Rocky River have become so brazen that they'll badger you for food and won't take no for an answer. This is amusing at first, but not for long. Fortunately, the picnic and barbecue areas are fenced off to protect visitors from their unwelcome demands.

From Rocky River a road leads south to wild and remote **Cape du Couedic**, where there are dramatic cliffs and a lighthouse that was built in 1906. A pathway leads down to **Admirals Arch**, a spectacular archway formed by pounding seas; the raised walkway passes through a colony of New Zealand fur seals.

At Kirkpatrick Point, a couple of kilometres east of Cape du Couedic, the **Remarkable Rocks** are a cluster of huge, weather-sculpted

Sculpted by time and weather – the Remarkable Rocks

granite boulders perched on a dome that swoops 75m down to the sea. En route you pass **Weirs Cove**, where a flying fox once brought supplies up the cliffs from the small landing far below.

Another road will take you from Rocky River to picturesque **West Bay**, a good surf-fishing spot. Behind the beach, a wooden cross marks the grave of an unknown sailor from the windjammer *Loch Vennachar*, lost nearby with all hands in 1905.

This road passes the starting points of three short walking tracks that lead down to the sea: the longest, and arguably the most interesting, is the 6km return walk to **Break-neck River**. It features beautiful gums, chuckling tea-coloured water and spectacular coastal scenery.

To get to **Cape Borda**, which features a lighthouse (1858) atop soaring cliffs, you'll have to go the long way around via the West End Hwy. There are guided tours of the lighthouse between 11 am and 3.15 pm (11 am to 2 pm in winter and 10 am to 4 pm during the summer school holidays) costing $5.

Nearby, at **Harvey's Return**, a poignant cemetery speaks volumes about the reality of isolation in the early days. It's a long scramble down to the stony beach, which has unusual striped rocks and the remains of a haulage way. This is where supplies for the lighthouse staff were landed. You have to wonder how they managed to get the cargo out of the boat without losing half of it, not to mention the work involved in getting it up the hill.

From Harvey's Return you can drive to **Ravine des Casoars** (literally 'Ravine of the Cassowaries', referring to the now-extinct dwarf emus seen here by Baudin's expedition). There's a beautiful walk down to the coast, with tall gums beside a gurgling stream. It's a great spot for birdwatching and listening to the sounds of nature.

KANGAROO ISLAND

Places to Stay & Eat

In Flinders Chase you can camp at *Rocky River* for $12 per car and in other designated areas for $5 per car. Don't leave any food exposed in your tent, even if you've closed it up: kangaroos and possums will rip their way in and cause a lot of damage. Keep all food secured in your car if you have one.

There are limited hot showers in the park, but facilities are better at the friendly *Western KI Caravan Park* (☎ 8559 7201), on a farm beside South Coast Rd, a few minutes drive east of Rocky River. It has tent/caravan sites for $10/15, on-site vans for $35 and a double-decker bus for $45. There are plenty of wild koalas here as well.

The NPWS has *huts and cottages* for hire at Rocky River, Cape du Couedic and Cape Borda. Huts start at $10 per person, while the better appointed cottages start at $20 (minimum numbers apply). See Places to Stay at the start of this chapter.

Just outside the park boundary on South Coast Rd, *Tandanya* has an upmarket restaurant (open daily for lunch), and also does take-aways. It sells petrol and a limited line in groceries.

On West End Hwy about 10 minutes drive from Rocky River, *Flinders Chase Farm* (☎ 8559 7223) has bunk beds in a self-contained farmhouse for $15 per person. Alternatively, you can stay in a basic but comfortable timber 'love shack' for $50.

Murray River

Australia's greatest river rises in the Australian Alps and for most of its length forms the boundary between NSW and Victoria. It meanders for 650km through SA, first heading west to Morgan then turning south for the coast, which it meets at Lake Alexandrina. For virtually its entire course through the state it forms a wide valley often lined with high yellow cliffs. In this semiarid landscape the cool ribbon of water and lush vegetation is a welcome contrast to the mallee scrub and wheat paddocks on either side.

Thanks to irrigation and a dry sunny climate, the Murray is a major agricultural producer; there's dairying at Murray Bridge, vegetable-growing at Mannum, and an extremely productive fruit and wine area between Morgan and Renmark. It's also a holiday playground for South Australians, particularly the area closest to Adelaide. Water sports (such as canoeing and waterskiing), camping and fishing are popular activities, as is houseboating.

The Murray is lined almost throughout with huge river red gums, while its backwaters are important habitats for waterbirds and aquatic creatures. Although the thousands of trees killed by stream regulation are a depressing sight, the timeless mystique of this big river still makes it one of the greatest places in Australia to spend a holiday.

European History
In 1838, only eight years after Charles Sturt's epic journey to the mouth, Joseph Hawdon brought the first herd of cattle to SA from the eastern colonies. He travelled along the Murray from the Goulburn River to Adelaide, so pioneering one of the first of Australia's major overland stock routes. On more than one occasion he was confronted by armed Aborigines in groups up to 100 strong: 'The men stood threatening us with their spears, and motioning us to go away. Not being in a humour to hold conversation with them we passed on ...'

HIGHLIGHTS

- Cruise the mighty Murray in a paddle-wheeler or canoe its quiet backwaters
- Go fishing and catch as many European carp as you like
- Camp on the river bank among majestic river red gums
- Get to know a numbat at Swan Reach's Yookamurra Sanctuary

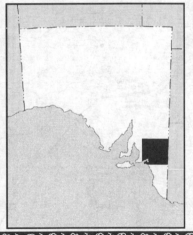

A flood of cattle followed in Hawdon's footsteps, and soon open warfare existed between the drovers and the Aborigines. Hostilities peaked in 1841, when police parties were sent to the Murray to 'restore order'. A detachment of the 96th Regiment was stationed 5km south of Blanchetown at Moorundie, established by the explorer Edward John Eyre in 1841. This was the first European settlement on the Murray. Within a decade virtually the entire river frontage in SA was part of vast grazing properties.

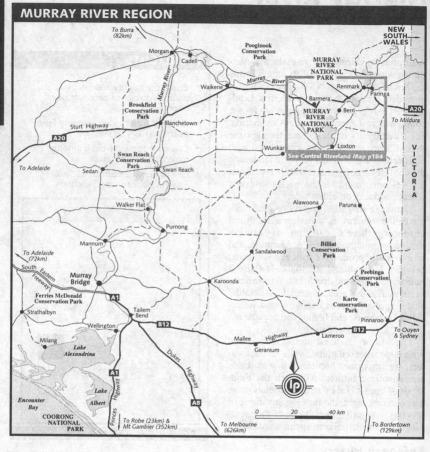

MURRAY RIVER REGION

The first paddle-wheelers appeared on the scene soon after. In 1853 William Randell in the *Mary Ann*, and Francis Cadell in the *Lady Augusta*, steamed from the lower reaches all the way into NSW. Their journeys proved that the Murray was a viable transport route, so stimulating the development of a massive river trade that stretched from Goolwa (the 'New Orleans of Australia') into NSW along the Murrumbidgee and Darling rivers. Busy ports sprang up, with dozens of paddle-wheelers and barges queuing to off-load their cargoes of wool, wheat, timber and other goods.

Railways sounded the death knell for the river trade, but in the 1890s, when it was already in decline, another industry appeared to take its place. In 1887, the Canadian brothers George and William Chaffey established an irrigation colony at Renmark that proved a huge success. Within a few years a thriving export trade had developed in oranges and dried fruits, particularly sultanas and currants. More irrigation schemes followed, as well as

The Dying Murray

Depending on rainfall in SA, the Murray River provides between 40% and 90% of Adelaide's water supply. The Murray is also vital to the economic health of south-eastern Australia. Water taken from the river irrigates crops worth $3 billion annually in SA, Victoria and NSW, and supplies many towns and urban centres. Yet the river is beset by a multitude of inter-related problems, the environmental and economic impact of which are only beginning to be understood.

Three major problems include: insufficient river flow; excessive nutrients in the water (particularly phosphates); and increasing salinity, both in sections of the river itself and on the land that it drains. These problems and others are all inter-related in a complex web that is partially natural and partially a result of rural and urban human activity.

The river is being overused to the extent that, based on current trends, average use will equal average river flow by 2020. Predictions are that the Murray in SA will soon be experiencing drought-like flows in six out of 10 years, which is already the case in some of the Murray's tributaries, and that the mouth will dry up in three of every four years.

In the last decade blooms of noxious blue-green algae caused partially by reduced flow leading to increased pollution from nutrients, increased temperatures and reduced turbidity, attracted much publicity and concern. The nutrients come from farm run-off and from the effluent that's pumped into the river system from towns along the river.

Reduced river flow has also had catastrophic consequences for other aspects of the environment. Over the past century the flood-plain wetlands have declined by 70%, with a subsequent reduction in animal life. One species to suffer is the giant Murray cod, one of the world's largest freshwater fish and a prime table fish, which must swim onto the flood plains to breed. The annual SA catch of Murray cod declined from 100,000kg in the 1950s to 10,000kg in the 1980s. The introduced European carp doesn't need the flood-plains to breed and now accounts for over 80% of all fish in the river.

The past removal of deep-rooted native plants and over irrigation have raised water tables bringing salts to the surface causing salinity. Salinity and raised water tables are beginning to threaten urban centres, as well as rendering sterile large swathes of formerly productive land. Problems for urban centres are made worse by domestic overwatering and inadequate drainage of buildings and other sealed surfaces such as roads and carparks.

Management to prevent further deterioration of the river system is complicated by the size of the catchment area (over a million square kilometres) and the fact that it straddles several government jurisdictions. In an effort to reverse the damage and sustainably manage this major resource the federal government and the state governments of SA, Victoria, NSW, the Australian Capital Territory and Queensland have jointly formed the Murray-Darling Basin Commission, which is responsible for implementing a wide range of strategies to regulate water flow, reduce pollution and reverse salination. Unfortunately, examples of governments working cooperatively on matters related to the Murray are rare. Many cynics in SA suspect that nothing much will happen in the short term.

Denis O'Byrne

swamp reclamation to allow dairying along the lower Murray flats.

Both navigators and irrigators experienced problems with the river's variable

flow; there were floods in some years and no flow at all in others. In 1914, under the River Murray Agreement with NSW, Victoria and the Commonwealth, SA commenced work on a series of locks and weirs along the river to regulate its flow and maintain a constant water level. Dams were constructed closer to the Murray's source to allow controlled release of water during times of low rainfall.

These works have made the Murray lands one of Australia's, if not the world's, most productive irrigation areas. It's certainly a river of life for South Australians, most of whom rely wholly or partly on it either for their livelihood or their domestic water supplies. However, there's an unfortunate tendency to take it for granted. As a result, deteriorating water quality has become a major conservation issue.

Information

Tourist Offices The major tourist offices are at Barmera, Berri, Loxton, Murray Bridge and Renmark. Others are at Mannum and Waikerie. See the sections on these towns for details.

National Parks All conservation areas along the river and in the Murray Mallee are administered by the National Parks and Wildlife Service (NPWS) office (☎ 8595 2111, fax 8595 2110) at 28 Vaughan Terrace in Berri. You can write to it at PO Box 231, Berri SA 5343.

Books & Maps The *Murray River Pilot*, by R & M Baker and W Reschke is an interesting book with useful maps for those on the water. If you're keen on history, the Department of Environment, Heritage & Aboriginal Affairs has the excellent *River Boat Trail – South Australia*. It takes you on a tour of relics associated with shipping on the Murray.

The Royal Automobile Association of South Australia's (RAA's) touring map *Riverland & Central Murray* is the best one for the river between Mannum and Renmark, and includes the northern Murray Mallee. The river's lower reaches, including Lake Alexandrina, are covered by its *Central South* touring map; its *Upper South-East* map includes the southern Murray Mallee.

The Office of Recreation & Sport has a series of five canoeing guides to the Murray and associated wetlands – they're out of print, but you may be lucky enough to find a set. One map covers the section between Morgan and Swan Reach, while the remainder cover most of the river between Overland Corner and the Victorian border. Also useful are its cycle-touring maps, which cover the lower Murray and Riverland.

Fishing

This is a popular activity along the Murray, where there are several species on offer. Minimum legal lengths and bag limits apply to golden perch (or callop), catfish, Murray cod and silver perch, all of which are natives. However, you can haul in as many introduced European perch (or redfin) and European carp as you like. Yabbies (freshwater crayfish) can be caught in summer and at times of high river flow; backwaters are the best places and stale mutton makes excellent bait.

For general information, mud maps and equipment try Hook, Line & Sinker at 17 William St in Berri; it opens seven days a week. Remember that fishing on the Murray is subject to various rules and regulations – most tackle shops can tell you about these.

Organised Tours

One of the highlights of any trip to the Murray is a cruise on an old paddle-wheeler. Several of these shallow-draught vessels have been restored and you can relive the past on cruises that last from a few hours to several days. They include the huge sternwheeler PS *River Murray Princess*, which regularly makes its stately passage up and down the river from Mannum. Other paddle-wheelers are based at Morgan, Murray Bridge and Renmark.

Premier Stateliner (☎ 8415 5566) offers a day tour from Adelaide that includes a one hour cruise on the PS *Proud Mary*, and a pub lunch at Mannum ($63). For something more personalised, Shaun's Bound-Away Tours (☎ 8371 3147) does an 11 hour tour ($74) that includes six hours on a houseboat, as well as bushwalking and a barbecue lunch.

There are a number of local tours on offer. You'll find camel treks and river rafting near Morgan, eco-tours at Swan Reach, Morgan and Renmark, and boat cruises on boats other than paddle-wheelers at Murray Bridge, Mannum, Berri and Renmark. Check the sections on these towns for details.

Accommodation

The Murray is a popular holiday destination, so there's plenty of accommodation. Even small towns have at least one caravan park and a hotel or motel. In addition, there's a backpacker hostel in Berri, and you'll also find backpacker beds in Loxton, Mannum and Murray Bridge.

Houseboats can be hired in most centres. However, they're very popular from October to April inclusive, when it's wise to book well ahead. Prices vary hugely, but in peak times you can expect to pay from around $25 per person per night depending upon such factors as size of boat and duration of hire. Costs are invariably much lower in winter.

The Houseboat Hirers Association (see Accommodation in the Facts for the Visitor chapter) has an information and booking service with access to over 100 houseboats. For others check with SATC and local tourist offices.

Getting There & Away

Bus Premier Stateliner (☎ 8415 5555) has daily services from Adelaide through Blanchetown to Waikerie, Barmera, Berri, Loxton and Renmark, while other country services go to Mannum and Murray Bridge. See the sections on these towns for details.

Greyhound Pioneer and McCafferty's run daily through the Riverland en route to Sydney. Coming from Adelaide, however, you can't get off until you're past Renmark.

Apart from Premier Stateliner's daily run through Blanchetown there is no public transport to the towns between Mannum and Waikerie.

MURRAY BRIDGE
- pop 13,500

South Australia's largest river town is only 82km from Adelaide and connected to it by the South Eastern Freeway. It was named for its original bridge, which was built in 1879 and was the first to span the Murray. To the detriment of Goolwa and Mannum, the town became a major port after the railway from Adelaide arrived in 1884.

While the river trade is a thing of the past, the town is still an important agricultural and tourism centre. Dairying is a major industry, with cows being grazed on irrigated pastures sown on reclaimed swamp right along the river. Milk factories at Murray Bridge and nearby Jervois process 85% of SA's dairy products. It is also an important vegetable-growing centre.

Information

The Murray Bridge Information Centre (☎ 8532 6660, fax 8532 5288) is at 3 South Terrace. On weekdays it opens from 8.30 am to 4 pm and on weekends it opens from 10 am to 4 pm on Saturday and to 2 pm on Sunday and public holidays.

Things to See & Do

The tourist office has details of self-guided walks and drives you can do in the area. Attractions include the **Anglican Cathedral**, on Mannum Rd, which was built in 1887 and is Australia's smallest. The **Round House** (1873) in Railway Reserve was built to accommodate the engineer responsible for constructing the original bridge.

The **Captain's Cottage Museum**, at 12 Thomas St, has some interesting exhibits on the town's early farming and riverboat days. It opens on weekends only between 10 am and 4 pm ($3).

Dundee's Wildlife Park is 4km out of town on Jervois Rd, just beyond the freeway. Its tropical hothouse contains juvenile saltwater and freshwater crocodiles (feeding at 2 pm daily), native birds (including many gorgeous parrots) in walk-through aviaries, a children's zoo and various native mammals. The doors are open daily from 10 am to 5 pm ($7).

Also good for kids is **Puzzle Park**, right next door, which has among its attractions a maze, minigolf and paddle-boats. It opens the same hours.

Cameo Cinema at 2 First St in town shows films every evening except Monday. The **Murray Bridge Drive-in Cinema** on Swanport Rd is also open most evenings.

Canoes can be hired from the Riverscape Cafe-Restaurant, at Sturt Reserve, for $6 per hour or $20 per day.

River Cruises

The MV *Barrangul* and PS *Captain Proud*, both of which have a restaurant on board, operate irregular full-day and short cruises – check at the tourist office for times. Both vessels offer two-hour lunch cruises that cost around $20.

The PS *Proud Mary* departs from Murray Bridge on two and five-night cruises. Contact Proud Australia Holidays (☎ 8231 9472) in Adelaide.

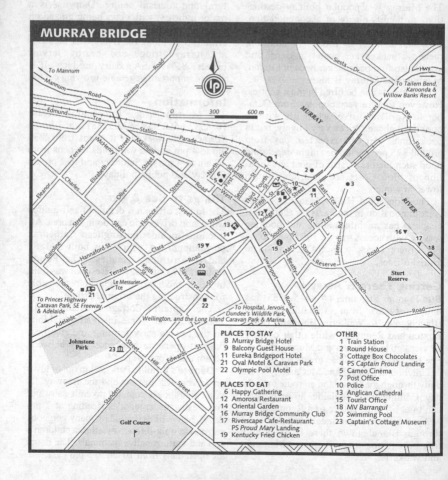

MURRAY BRIDGE

PLACES TO STAY	OTHER
8 Murray Bridge Hotel	1 Train Station
9 Balcony Guest House	2 Round House
11 Eureka Bridgeport Hotel	3 Cottage Box Chocolates
21 Oval Motel & Caravan Park	4 PS *Captain Proud* Landing
22 Olympic Pool Motel	5 Cameo Cinema
	7 Post Office
PLACES TO EAT	10 Police
6 Happy Gathering	13 Anglican Cathedral
12 Amorosa Restaurant	15 Tourist Office
14 Oriental Garden	18 MV *Barrangul*
16 Murray Bridge Community Club	20 Swimming Pool
17 Riverscape Cafe-Restaurant;	23 Captain's Cottage Museum
PS *Proud Mary* Landing	
19 Kentucky Fried Chicken	

Places to Stay – Budget

The *Long Island Caravan Park & Marina* (☎ 8532 6900), on Roper Rd off Swanport Rd and about 4km from the town centre, has caravan sites from $14, on-site vans for $30 and cabins from $35.

A little farther from town, but upstream and on the eastern bank, the friendly *Avoca Dell Caravan Park* (☎ 8532 2095) is next to the river on Murray Drive. It has tent/caravan sites for $12/14 and self-contained cabins for $38.

At the Adelaide end of town, the *Princes Highway Caravan Park* (☎ 8532 2860) has campsites, caravan sites, on-site vans and self-contained cabins.

About 16km upstream from town (off the road to Karoonda), the *Willow Banks Resort* (☎ 8535 4203) has campsites and cabins, as well as jet ski and ski boat hire.

The *Murray Bridge Hotel* (☎ 8532 2024, 20 Sixth St) charges $22/34 for singles/doubles in its standard pub rooms, while the *Eureka Bridgeport Hotel* (☎ 8532 2002, 2 Bridge St) charges $25 per person. Both also have rooms with private bathrooms.

The *Balcony Guest House* (☎ 8531 1411, 6 Sixth St) is a friendly place with several options, including backpacker beds for $18 and B&B for $25/55 singles/doubles.

Places to Stay – Mid-Range

The *Balcony Guest House* also has a room with a spectacular, antique four-poster bed and private bathroom for $55/70. This price includes a light breakfast.

There are several motels around town and all are at least reasonable.

Motel Greenacres (☎ 8532 1090, Princes Hwy) is 5km east of the town centre and has singles and doubles from $50.

Murray Bridge Motor Inn (☎ 8532 1144, 212 Adelaide Rd) is 3km west of the town centre and charges from $45/55.

Oval Motel (☎ 8532 2388, 4 Le Messurier St) is 1km south-west of the town centre and charges from $53/59.

Olympic Pool Motel (☎ 8532 2359, 1800 088 322 toll free, 34 Standen St) is 1km west of the town centre and charges $45/53.

The tourist office has details of the several B&Bs around here.

For a dash of romance, *Treetops Cottage* (☎ 8532 6483, 117 Murray Drive) is a one-bedroom retreat overlooking a wetland with lots of birds. There's no phone, but there is a canoe and a complimentary book of original poems. Accommodation for two people for two nights costs $200; this place is not suitable for children.

Places to Eat

The leaflet *Eating Out in Murray Bridge* lists over 40 eateries ranging from fast food outlets, such as *KFC*, to fine dining at the *Amorosa Restaurant (55 Bridge St)*. The latter offers international cuisine, with Italian the speciality; it offers lunch most days and dinners daily except Monday.

The town's two *pubs* have the usual good-value counter meals, as does the *Murray Bridge Community Club* down by the river at Sturt Reserve.

Alternatively, the *Happy Gathering* Chinese restaurant, on the corner of First and Seventh Sts, and the *Oriental Garden (18 Adelaide Rd)* offer large serves for reasonable prices.

It's a fair way out, but the *Italian Club (Lincoln Rd)* serves dinners from Thursday to Sunday. Thursday is pasta night – all you can eat for $8.

There's also the *Riverscape Cafe-Restaurant*, at the Proud Mary landing in Sturt Reserve. It's a pleasant place to sit with coffee or a meal and watch the river go by.

Getting There & Away

Bus seats to Adelaide cost $11 with the Murray Bridge Passenger Service (☎ 8532 6660); they leave four times a day from outside the tourist office, where tickets can be purchased. If you're travelling from Adelaide, bookings should be made with Premier Stateliner.

Tickets from Murray Bridge to Mt Gambier with Premier Stateliner cost $39. If you're heading to Melbourne, Greyhound Pioneer and McCafferty's both charge $45.

Great Southern Railway's *Overland* train passes through Murray Bridge every evening (except Wednesday and Saturday) en route from Adelaide to Melbourne, departing Adelaide at 7.15 pm. The economy fare is $58 – the same as the Adelaide to Melbourne fare.

Getting Around

Murray Bridge Taxis (☎ 8531 0555) operates 24 hours a day and charges around $35 to Mannum and Wellington, and $25 to Old Tailem Town at Tailem Bend. It also has hire cars.

The Riverside Bus Service (☎ 8532 1081) operates a regular town service with buses running weekdays only between 8 am and 5.45 pm. The tourist office has route maps and timetables.

AROUND MURRAY BRIDGE

On 1000 hectares 20km west of town, the **Monarto Zoological Park** has Australian and international exhibits, including rare species and herds of grassland animals such as zebras and giraffes. The park opens daily between 9 am and 5 pm; entry costs $10 and includes a bus tour through the Asian and African habitat areas (departing daily 10.30 am to 3.30 pm).

About 14km south of the zoo, the 845 hectare **Ferries-McDonald Conservation Park** preserves a rare remnant of the mallee that covered this area prior to the arrival of wheat farmers last century. There are some interesting walks, plenty of grey kangaroos and good birdwatching. If you're very lucky you'll see a mallee fowl.

TAILEM BEND

• **pop 1600**

The main attraction in this otherwise uninspiring railway town is **Old Tailem Town**, the fascinating re-creation of an 1880s pioneer settlement complete with period furnishings. Its dusty collection of over 70 buildings (most have been brought from other places) includes a cow-dung house, and a fisherman's hut made from flattened tar drums. It opens from 10 am to 5 pm daily ($10).

Down by the river and off the highway 6km north-west of town, the attractive *Westbrook Park River Resort* (☎ 8572 3794) has

tent/caravan sites for $12/14, on-site vans from $25 and two-storey cabins from $45.

WELLINGTON

• **pop 200**

This sprawling hamlet is on the river 33km from Murray Bridge, 12km from Tailem Bend and 11km from Lake Alexandrina. First settled in the 1840s, it was the main river crossing on the overland route to Victoria. Today there's a **ferry** across the river on the road from Tailem Bend, and only one of its four original pubs is still trading.

Built in 1864, the old courthouse now houses an interesting **National Trust museum** – complete with original courthouse furnishings – as well as a cafe/licensed restaurant.

The basic but attractive *Wellington Caravan Park* (☎ 8572 7302) across from the hotel has tent and caravan sites and cabins.

Between the pub and the ferry landing, the *Old Wellington Court House* (☎ 8572 7330) has heritage bedrooms where you can treat yourself to B&B for $90 for doubles; it also offers packages.

The *Wellington Hotel* sells counter meals and boasts a nice view of the river from its shaded front lawns. This is a great place to relax with a cold drink on a hot day.

MANNUM

• **pop 2030**

A thriving port until Murray Bridge took all its trade, picturesque Mannum has many relics of its early boom times.

Things to See & Do

The boiler from the original *Mary Ann*, is now in **Mary Ann Park** down by the river. The famous paddle-wheeler commenced its historic journey nearby in 1853.

A leaflet details three scenic and historical **walks** you can do around town. The attractions listed include the 1898 paddle-wheeler *Marion*, now moored as a **floating museum** ($2.50). It's alongside the tourist office (☎ 8569 1303) off Randell St near the ferry landing. Both are open weekdays from 9 am to 4 pm and weekends from 11 am to 3 pm.

Mannum Old Wares, in the old butter factory at 40 Randell St, is well worth a visit for its large selection of bric-a-brac and collectables.

You can observe numerous waterbirds in the **bird sanctuary**, which starts at the Mannum Caravan Park and runs for several kilometres along the Purnong road. Pelicans are a feature; the roosts in the water beside the caravan park are a good spot to see these ungainly birds, especially late in the afternoon. Otherwise, go down to Mary Ann Park and start eating lunch – at least one pelican should soon appear and stand eyeing you expectantly.

The **Cascade Waterfalls**, 9km from town off the main road to Murray Bridge, are worth a visit for their picturesque and rugged scenery. Although the falls only flow during winter, the beautiful river red gums in the creek downstream of the gorge can be enjoyed at any time.

There's a ferry crossing at **Purnong**, 33km north of Mannum. You can hire canoes and kayaks for extended periods at the Ferryman's Cottage (☎ 8570 4323); rates are negotiable.

Mannum Canoe Hire (☎ 8569 1768, 018 105 125) rents out canoes and dinghies by the hour, day or week; it will organise drop-offs and pickups if you want.

Organised Tours

The grand paddle-wheeler *Murray River Princess* offers two, three and five-night cruises from Mannum. Contact Captain Cook Cruises (☎ 8569 2511, 1800 804 843 toll free, captcookcrus@captcookcrus .com.au) for dates and prices – its two-night cruises start at around $350 per person twin-share.

The MV *Lady Mannum* does short cruises; you can check the times with Lady Mannum Cruises (☎ 8569 1438), in Randell St. Alternatively, the MV *Dragon Fly* (☎ 8569 2631) will take small groups on a half hour cruise for $6 per person.

The PS *Marion* has been recommissioned and also does short trips; ask at the tourist office for a schedule.

Mannum Canoe Hire (☎ 8569 1768, 018 105 125) runs weekend trips on which you canoe during the day and retreat to the comfort of a houseboat at night. These operate in winter only.

They may not sound too inviting, but Scruffs Tours (☎ 8569 1554) are actually very good. These are tag-along tours (you follow the tour guide's vehicle in your own car) and they'll take you to plenty of interesting places you otherwise won't find in the Mannum area.

Places to Stay

The *Mannum Caravan Park* (☎ 8569 1402, mannpark@lm.net.au), at the town side of the ferry crossing, is a pleasant spot to stay. It has tent/caravan sites from $11/14 and cabins with private facilities from $45. It also has backpacker accommodation in the old pumphouse, with bunk beds in small dorms costing $13; only international travellers are accepted. This place is very clean and has a good kitchen.

Alternatively, you can *camp* for free across the river near the ferry and use the caravan park's shower facilities for $2.50. (Note that shower facilities are only available to campers between noon and 6 pm.)

The *Mannum Motel* (☎ 8569 1808, 76 Cliff St), above the ferry landing, has comfortable units from $55/65/75 for singles/doubles/triples, and well-appointed holiday apartments for $75 for doubles (extra adults are charged $10).

There are several B&Bs in town; the tourist office has details. One is *Randell House* (☎/fax 8569 2747, or mobile 0418 854 774, 88 Cliff St), the historic two storey home of Captain Randell of *Mary Anne* fame. Built in 1869, the house and its furnishings epitomise gracious living. You can stay there for from $85 a double.

Mannaroo Farm (☎ 8569 1646) has an excellent reputation. It offers B&B for $60/90 a single/double and full board for $90 per person, including farm tours, boating and fishing. The farm is 11km from Mannum on East Front Rd, which goes to Purnong along the eastern bank.

MURRAY RIVER

Places to Eat
Best value in town are the regular specials put on by the *Pretoria Hotel* and the *Mannum Club* (meals on Tuesday to Saturday only), both on Randell St. Otherwise the *Mannum Motel* has a good á la carte restaurant.

There's a choice of take-aways, bakeries and coffee shops. Locals recommend *The Bakershop* on Randell St for delicious home-baked products; they positively rave about the quality of meat and service at their local *butcher shop*.

Getting There & Around
ABM Coachlines (☎ 8347 3336) has a daily service on weekdays from Adelaide ($11.50).

Mannum Taxis (☎ 018 834 861) runs weekdays (6 am to 6 pm) and Saturday morning, charging around $35 to Murray Bridge.

SWAN REACH
• pop 230

This sleepy old town has picturesque river scenery thanks to the high yellow cliffs that line the eastern bank.

Things to See & Do
The Swan Reach Hotel (1905) is perched on the clifftop above the ferry landing and commands a great view: it's surprising that someone hasn't knocked it down and built a flash resort in its place!

Despite the town's name there aren't many swans around, but pelicans are common.

Vermin-proof fencing encloses over 1000 hectares of virgin mallee at the Yookamurra Sanctuary (☎ 8562 5011), 17km to the north-west. Following the removal of foxes, cats and rabbits, several locally extinct mammals, such as the numbat, were introduced and are now breeding. See the following Places to Stay section for more details.

Between Swan Reach and Sedan, to the west, the 2017 hectare Swan Reach Conservation Park has diverse vegetation and plenty of wildlife, including southern hairy-nosed wombats, emus and kangaroos. About 15km south-west (more by road) there are magnificent red gums along the Marne River in the 105 hectare Marne Valley

Conservation Park. This is a great spot for picnics and walks.

Just downstream from Swan Reach, the Murray makes a tight meander known as Big Bend; the lookout beside the road to Walker Flat, 9km from town, gives a dramatic view of sweeping curves and towering ochre-coloured cliffs. This is one of the best vantage points for photography along the river.

Organised Tours
River Murray Educational Nature Tours (☎ 018 085 184) has a range of interesting options including wetland tours in a flat-bottom boat, nocturnal kangaroo and wombat walks, and fishing trips. They also have camping and caravan accommodation.

You can also visit an Aboriginal heritage site with Aboriginal rangers (☎ 8569 2569).

Places to Stay & Eat
The renovated *Swan Reach Hotel* (☎ 8570 2003) has daily counter and dining-room meals. Basic twin rooms are $35/40 single/twin and double rooms $55, including a light breakfast. Its dining room has views of the Murray through its picture windows.

The *Punyelroo Caravan Park* (☎ 8570 2021) is about 8km downstream from town. It has caravan sites, on-site vans and cabins; there's plenty of lawn, but not much shade.

Yookmurra Sanctuary (☎ 8562 5011) has campsites, cabin-style accommodation, meals, habitat walks and wildlife walks. A one-night package costs from $40; bookings are essential, and it's best to organise things at least two days in advance.

SA's fauna emblem, the hairy-nosed wombat

The Riverland

The section between Blanchetown and Renmark is usually known as the Riverland. It has the Murray's only national park (Murray River National Park, between Loxton and Renmark) and the flourishing fruit-growing and wine-making centres of Waikerie, Barmera, Loxton, Berri and Renmark.

BLANCHETOWN
- **pop 250**

The historic pub (1856) in Blanchetown is a reminder of the days when this was a stagecoach stopover on 'the Sydney road'.

Lock 1 is the start of the system of locks and weirs that keeps the river at a fairly constant level between Blanchetown and Wentworth, in NSW. Completed in 1922, it's a good spot to observe pelicans; there's a licensed floating restaurant nearby.

Brookfield Conservation Park (5500 hectares) is about 9km west of town on the Sturt Hwy. The park was originally purchased by the Chicago Zoological Society as a wombat reserve, and it still supports research into the animal's needs. A 10km 'nature drive' takes you through the haunts of southern hairy-nosed wombats, emus and kangaroos, and there's some good bushwalking.

Places to Stay

In town, the **Riverside Caravan Park** (☎ 8540 5070, Sanders St) has tent/caravan sites for $11/14, a range of cabin styles from $36 and a pontoon to fish from. This place is small and friendly, although the cabins are crowded together.

About 5km from town and off the main road to Morgan, the much larger if more basic **Blanchetown Caravan Park** (☎ 8540 5073) is also by the river. It has tent/caravan sites for $10/14, basic cabins for $25, and self-contained cabins with air-conditioning and kitchens for $47.

Splendid upmarket accommodation is available at **Portee Station** (☎ 8540 5211, portee@riverland.net.au), 10km south of Blanchetown. First settled in 1841, this working sheep property covers about 250 sq km and has 12 km of river frontage. Guests stay in a magnificent 1870s colonial-style homestead, with lawn sweeping down to the water's edge in front and a good restaurant out the back. It offers single/double B&B for $130/160 and full board for $310/390; tours include boat trips, a 4WD station tour in a converted rocket launcher, and a Barossa Valley winery tour.

MORGAN
- **pop 1350**

Established in 1878, when a railway was built from Adelaide to tap the river trade, the Morgan of the 1880s was one of the busiest river ports in Australia. Its wharves towered 12m high and stretched 170m along the bank, and gangs of 40 wharfies worked continuous shifts to unload the cargoes of the barges and paddle-wheelers that queued alongside.

Not much happens in Morgan these days. In fact, the town's commercial life had quietened down so much by 1969 that the railway was closed.

The main tourist office is in the Shell service station on Fourth St (☎ 8540 2205).

Things to See & Do

A leaflet details a **historical walk** which includes the PS *Mayflower*. Built in 1884, it's the oldest operating paddle-wheeler in SA. Also worth seeing are the old **customs house** (1879) and the **Post Office Row** streetscape (1889) on Railway Terrace.

The **Port of Morgan Historic Museum** in the old train station, next to the wharf, has interesting exhibits on the paddle-wheeler days. It opens on weekends from 2 pm to 4 pm.

Also worth visiting is the large museum (inquiries ☎ 8540 3237) at historic **Norwest Bend** homestead, 8km from town on the Renmark road. The museum reflects the days when Nor-west Bend covered 5000 sq km, and was an important settlement on the Murray.

Carmine's Antiques, in Post Office Row, is reputedly one of the best shops on the river for antiques, bric-a-brac and collectables.

MURRAY RIVER

CENTRAL RIVERLAND

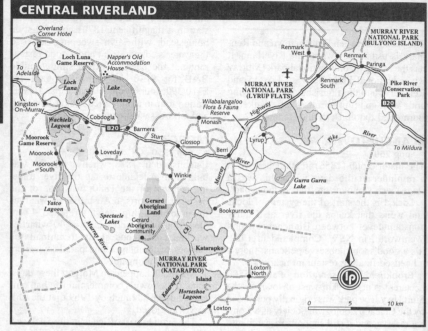

About 2km south of town, and on the western side of the river, **fossil quarries** yield fossilised sea shells, sharks' teeth and, apparently, the odd fish.

A **ferry** crosses the Murray on the Waikerie road just outside Morgan, and there's another at Cadell.

Organised Tours
The Bush Safari Co (☎ 8543 2280, good fellow@riverland.net.au) has **camel treks** along the river and through semi-arid station country from its base 20km east of Morgan. Rides range from 1½ hours ($25) to three days ($485). It also offers **river rafting**, birdwatching and 4WD tours, as well as an eight day camel/boat/4WD combination.

Morgan Eco Experiences (☎ 8540 4035, atriplex@riverland.net.au) offers **guided walks,** with a biological emphasis, to river

wetlands, red gum forests and mallee bushland. Prices start at $10 per person.

Places to Stay & Eat
Next to the ferry, the large *Morgan Riverside Caravan Park* (☎ 8540 2207) has tent/caravan sites from $10/14, on-site vans for $27 and cabins from $35. It hires canoes for $6 per hour or $20 per day.

The *Commercial Hotel* (☎ 8540 2107, Railway Terrace) has basic rooms with airconditioning for $15 per person. Across the road, the *Terminus Hotel/Motel* (☎ 8540 2006) also charges $15, but there's no airconditioning; its motel units cost $40/45 a single/double. Both pubs have good counter and dining room meals.

If you're in town on Friday or Saturday night you might be better off booking into the *Colonial Motel* (☎ 8540 2277, Federal St) off the road to Burra. It charges $50/60/70 for singles/doubles/triples and is a lot quieter than the pubs.

There are good bush campsites with no facilities among beautiful big red gums in the *Morgan Conservation Park*, across the river from town. To get there, turn left about 500m from the ferry landing.

You'll find more bush sites among huge gums beside the water at *Hogwash Bend*, 8km past Cadell on the road to Waikerie. This area is not recommended on weekends, when the local yobboes often descend in force.

WAIKERIE
* **pop 1800**

It's thought that the town takes its name from a local Aboriginal word for 'anything that flies', after the teeming birdlife on the nearby lagoons and river. Appropriately (with a name like that) it's one of Australia's major centres for gliding, but is better known for its oranges. There are several thousand hectares of irrigated orange orchards, with the fruit being packed and processed at a large factory in town.

The main tourist office is in **The Orange Tree** (☎ 8541 2332), on the Sturt Hwy on the Barmera side of town – look for the large, green fibreglass sphere with red spots. Open daily on weekdays from 9 am to 5.30 pm, and weekends from 10 am to 4 pm, it sells a comprehensive range of local fruit and nut products.

Things to See & Do
There's a bird hide beside **Hart Lagoon**, just out of town on the road to Cadell.

The Waikerie International Soaring Centre (☎ 8541 2644), on the Sturt Hwy on the Barmera side of town, has glider **joy flights** costing $50 for 20 minutes.

On the northern side of the river 12km from town, the 2850 hectare **Pooginook Conservation Park** consists of rolling sand ridges covered in mallee. Early spring is the best time to visit for wildflowers and birdlife.

Places to Stay & Eat
Bush camping is available in the *Pooginook Conservation Park* (see previous section).

Down by the river on the Cadell side of town, the *Waikerie Caravan Park* (☎ 8541 2651, Ramco Rd)* has tent/caravan sites for $10/14, air-conditioned cabins for $30 and cottages for $50.

The *Waikerie Hotel/Motel* (☎ 8541 2999, McCoy St)* has pub rooms with private bathrooms and air-conditioning for $35/45 a single/double and motel rooms for $40/50, as well as counter meals and a bistro. Noise can be a problem in the pub section on Friday and Saturday nights.

On the Sturt Hwy on the eastern outskirts of town, the well-appointed *Kirriemuir Motel & Cabins* (☎ 8541 2488)* has a range of styles of motel unit from $50/65, and self-contained cabins for $45/50.

Bush camping with basic facilities (hot water but no power) is available at *Eremophila Park* (☎ 8589 3023)*, a private nature park with plenty of birdlife, including mallee fowl, off the Sturt Hwy 20km east of town. Campsites in mallee woodland cost $4 per person and there's a basic hut sleeping six for $40 – extra people are charged $5. For directions, call in and see the friendly owner, Stella Mack, at the homestead 3km from the main road.

The *Waikerie Club (Crush Terrace)* is good for meals. It serves evening meals on Wednesday, Friday and Saturday nights, with specials from $5.

Getting There & Away
Premier Stateliner stops at Waikerie daily from Adelaide ($22.50).

BARMERA
* **pop 4500**

On the shores of Lake Bonney, a large body of freshwater that fills from the Murray via Chambers Creek, Barmera was an important resting point on the overland stock route from NSW to SA. The name is a corruption of Barmeedji, the name of the Aboriginal group that lived in this area at the time of white settlement.

The town is another irrigation centre, with its large lake being a popular holiday attraction.

Information

The tourist office (☎ 8588 2289, fax 8588 2777, brmtrvl@sa.ozland.net.au) is in the Barmera Travel Centre, at the top of Barwell Ave (the main street) next to the roundabout. It opens weekdays from 9 am to 5.30 pm, and Saturday until noon.

Things to See & Do

Lake Bonney is very popular for swimming and water sports, and even has a nudist beach – at **Pelican Point**, on the lake's western shore. The lake is ringed by large dead red gums, whose stark branches are often festooned with cormorants.

On Dean Drive, the **Lake Bonney Aquatic Centre** hires windsurfers, pedaloes, canoes and catamarans. It opens between September and May, but only on weekends and during school holidays.

About 9km from town on the Morgan road, the stone ruins of **Napper's Accommodation House**, built in 1850 at the mouth of Chambers Creek, are a reminder of the droving era.

So too is the evocative **Overland Corner Hotel**, 11km farther out, which is still trading. The pub takes its name from a bend in the Murray River where drovers and travellers once camped. Built in 1859, it's now owned by the National Trust – the trust has a brochure detailing the fascinating geology of the cliffs at nearby **Herons Bend**. There's an interesting 8km self-guided **nature trail** down to the river from the pub, and you can pick up a leaflet at the bar.

The **Cobdogla Irrigation Museum**, at nearby Cobdogla, features steam engines including the Humphrey Pump, an awesome affair that's fired up only a few times each year (check with Barmera Travel Centre for details). The museum opens each Sunday and on long weekends.

On the Sturt Hwy on the Waikerie side of town, the friendly **Bonneyview Winery** has tastings daily. It's one of the Riverland's few small wineries.

There's a game reserve at **Moorook** (on the road to Loxton) and another at **Loch Luna** across the river from the small irrigation

centre of **Kingston-on-Murray**. Both reserves have nature trails and are good spots for birdwatching and canoeing; the Kingston-on-Murray Caravan Park hires canoes for $25 per day, and you can paddle across to the reserve.

Organised Tours

Riverland Safaris (☎ 8588 2869) offers various **guided tours** including winery visits (from $10) and fishing and yabbying trips (from $12).

Places to Stay – In Town

On Lakeside Drive within walking distance of town, the popular *Lake Bonney Holiday Park* (☎ 8588 2234) has tent/caravan sites from $12/15, air-conditioned cabins from $25 and cottages from $45.

The *Lake Resort Motel* (☎ 8588 2555), also on Lakeside Drive, charges $60/65 a single/double for its units.

The *Barmera Hotel/Motel* (☎ 8588 2111, Barwell Ave) has basic rooms for $30 a double, self-contained hotel rooms with air-conditioning for $38 a double, and motel units for $45/50.

The town's most exclusive accommodation is at the *Barmera Country Club* (☎ 8588 2888, Hawdon St), which has 'standard' rooms for $82/86 and spa rooms for $98 a single or double.

Places to Stay – Out of Town

The *Greenwood Park Caravan Park* (☎ 8588 7070) on Lake Bonney is small, quiet, remote (5km from Barmera) and an ideal place for birdwatchers. It has campsites by the water for $9, powered sites for $12 and air-conditioned cabins for $33.

Also on Lake Bonney, the *Pelican Point Nudist Resort* (☎ 8588 7366) is beside the nudist beach and off the Morgan road. It has tent/caravan sites for $15/18, on-site vans for $33 (linen included), a camper's kitchen and a sauna.

You'll also find attractive caravan parks at *Cobdogla* (☎ 8588 7164) and beside the water at Kingston-on-Murray (☎ 8583 0209). The *Motel Kingston Bridge* (☎ 8583

0206), on the Barmera side of Kingston-on-Murray, boasts nice views over the river.

At Moorook the ***Moorook B&B*** *(☎ 8583 9355)* has rooms starting at $25/40 for singles/doubles. Alternatively, you can pitch your tent on the riverfront just across from the Moorook General Store for $3; the area has good shade and lawn areas, but little in the way of facilities (there are no showers).

There's no shortage of good bush campsites ($5 per car per night) in the ***Moorook and Loch Luna game reserves***. You'll need to talk to staff at the NPWS office in Berri about permits.

The ***Overland Corner Hotel*** *(☎ 8588 7021)* has two small double rooms for $35/50, including breakfast.

Places to Eat

The best-value meals in town are served at the ***Barmera Hotel/Motel***, the ***Barmera Monash Football Club*** on the lake front, and the ***Cobdogla Club*** (Thursday to Sunday nights only). All have specials priced from $6.

The ***Pagoda Chinese Restaurant*** *(Barwell Ave)* is consistently good and reasonably priced, while for more elegant dining there's the ***Barmera Country Club***.

There are several take-aways and cafes in town. ***Barmera Bakery*** *(Barwell Ave)* enjoys a good reputation, as does the ***Moonlite Cafe*** *(Bice St)*.

For atmosphere and fine food ***Bonneyview Winery*** has a lot going for it. You can get a delicious ploughman's lunch or something fancier, and the wines are reasonably priced.

The ***Overland Corner Hotel*** sells hearty home-cooked meals in the tiny front bar. It also has a dining room, but you have to book.

Getting There & Around

Premier Stateliner buses departing from Adelaide ($28) call in daily, stopping at the tourist office.

Barmera Taxi Service (☎ 8588 2869, 0409 839 387) operates 24 hours a day. It costs about $20 to Berri and $35 to Renmark.

LOXTON
* **pop 3320**

From Berri the Murray makes a large loop south of the Sturt Hwy, with Loxton at the base of the loop. The town was established in 1907, although settlers (mainly of German descent) had been successfully growing wheat in the area for 10 years prior to that. Today it's an important service centre for surrounding farms and irrigation areas.

Information

The tourist office (☎ 8584 7919, fax 8584 6225) is in the Loxton Tourism & Art Centre at the roundabout on Bookpurnong Terrace, in the centre of town. It opens weekdays from 9 am to 5 pm, Saturday from 9.30 am to 12.30 pm, and Sunday and public holidays from 1 to 4 pm. There's a small art gallery and arts and crafts shop on the premises.

Things to See & Do

The **Katarapko** section of the Murray River National Park occupies much of the area within the loop; there's great canoeing in the backwaters here, as well as walks along the timbered banks. The park is on the opposite side of the river to Loxton, but you can easily canoe across from town – there is no vehicle access from this side.

Canoes can be hired from Riverland Canoeing; see the following Getting There & Around section.

If you're not a canoeist, the main attraction here is the **Loxton Historical Village**, which has over 40 buildings furnished from days gone by. Structures on display include a pine-and-pug settler's hut, a pine slab shearing shed and a barn and stable built of mallee roots. It opens on weekdays from 10 am to 4 pm and on weekends to 5 pm, and admission is $5.

The tourist office has a leaflet describing a **heritage walk**, which takes you on an exploration of Loxton's historic places. The office has details of tours in the area.

Down by the caravan park is a large gum tree with markers showing **flood levels** and dates. With the notable exception of the mighty 1956 flood at 5m – the highest since white settlement – most are around the 1m mark.

The **Australian Vintage winery** on Bookpurnong Rd (the road to Berri) is open daily except Sunday from 10 am to 5 pm for tastings and cellar-door sales.

Visitors come from far and wide to admire the **Christmas lights** during December, when over 350 homes put on decorative displays.

Riverland Canoeing Adventures (☎ 8584 1494 after hours) on Alamein Ave, off the road to Berri, rents single kayaks for $15 per day and double kayaks and canoes for $25. Concession rates apply after five days. Transport (allow 50 c/km for drop-off and pick-up), touring maps and camping equipment can be arranged for an extra fee.

Places to Stay & Eat
Right on the Murray and with many beautiful red gums, the *Loxton Riverfront Caravan Park (☎ 8584 7862)* is 2km from town. It has backpacker beds for $12 (no linen supplied, minimum four people) as well as tent/caravan sites for $11/15, on-site vans with air-conditioning for $25 and air-conditioned cabins from $32. You can hire a canoe for $25 per day.

The *Loxton Hotel/Motel (☎ 8584 7266, East Terrace)* has basic pub rooms for $20/25 a single/double (air-conditioning and private bathroom $41/46) and motel units from $57/62.

The hotel has a very good bistro plus counter meals, and you can get a hearty feed for a reasonable price at the *Loxton Community Club (Bookpurnong Terrace)*. Otherwise there are coffee shops, take-aways and bakeries.

You can camp on *Katarapko Island* for $5 per car per night; contact the NPWS office in Berri for permits.

Getting There & Around
Premier Stateliner buses call in daily except Saturday from Adelaide ($28), stopping at the tourist office.

Loxton Taxis (☎ 0418 839 289) offers 24-hour-a-day service around Loxton and farther afield; approximate fares from Loxton are

$40 to Renmark, $40 to Barmera and $25 to Berri.

BERRI
- **pop 7100**

Proclaimed in 1911, Berri was another irrigation town (along with Waikerie, Barmera and Loxton) established after the success of Renmark. Today it's a major wine-making, fruit-growing and processing centre.

At one time a refuelling stop for the wood-burning paddle-wheelers, the town takes its name from the Aboriginal *berri berri*, meaning 'big bend in the river'.

Information
The tourist office (☎ 8582 1655, fax 8582 3201) is in the Berri Tourist & Travel Centre at 24 Vaughan Terrace. It opens weekdays from 9 am to 5 pm (Saturday to 11.30 am).

Things to See & Do
There are several wineries in the area. **Berri Estates** at Glossop, 13km west of Berri, is the largest winery and distillery complex in Australia. It's open for tastings and cellar-door sales Monday to Saturday between 9 am and 5 pm. On Nixon Rd at Monash, about 7km north-west of town, **Norman Wines** is open for tastings and sales on weekdays only from 9 am to 4.30 pm.

Berrivale Orchards, on the Sturt Hwy towards Renmark, has an educational video on the Riverland, and there are factory-direct sales.

The **Berri Arts Centre** at 23 Wilson St houses local and touring exhibitions of fine arts and crafts. It opens weekdays from 9.30 am to 4.30 pm.

On Riverside Drive, between the Berri Resort Hotel and the caravan park, is a **monument** to Jimmy James, a famous Aboriginal tracker. In 30 years service with the police, he contributed to the arrest of around 40 criminals and the rescue of 10 lost people.

Managed by the National Trust, **Wilabalangaloo** on the way to Renmark is a 100 hectare flora and fauna reserve with river views, walking trails, a tiny historic paddle-wheeler (now grounded) and an interesting museum. It opens Thursday to Monday from 10 am to 4 pm and daily during school holidays ($4).

Canoes can be hired for $25 per day from Lyons Motors (☎ 8582 1449), near the water on Riverview Drive. They're available by the hour, day or week.

Places to Stay – In Town
The *Berri Riverside Caravan Park* (☎ *8582 3723, Riverview Drive*) has tent/caravan sites from $11/16, on-site vans from $30 and cabins from $38. It also has air-conditioned backpacker accommodation – twin and double rooms cost $20, including use of a camper's kitchen. The operators can help you obtain seasonal work.

Berri Backpackers (☎ *8582 3144, Sturt Hwy*), at the Barmera end of town, is one of the best-equipped hostels you'll find anywhere – but it's only for international visitors. Guests have free use of its pool, sauna, games room, volleyball court, bicycles and canoes; the manager has excellent contacts if you want seasonal work in local orchards and vineyards. Dorm beds are $15 ($90 per week) with a VIP card.

The only budget motel accommodation in town is the modest *Berri Bridge Motel* (☎ *8582 1011*), on the Sturt Hwy in town. Units here cost $45/60 a single/double.

At the *Berri Resort Hotel* (☎ *8582 1411, 1800 088 226 toll free, bjah@murray .net.au*), which overlooks the river on Riverview Drive, self-contained single/double pub rooms are priced from $48/53, while motel units are priced from $82/88.

Alternatively, the *Big River Motor Inn* (☎ *8582 2688, Sturt Hwy*) on the Renmark side of town has units from $80/88. Guests have a golf course right outside their door.

Places to Stay – Out of Town
About 300m from Wilabalangaloo, friendly *Riverbush* (☎ *8582 3455, 1800 088 191 toll free*) has very well-appointed eight-berth cottages costing $130 a double for two nights ($280 for eight people for two nights). It has river access, and fishing gear and bait are available.

You can camp on *Katarapko Island* for $5 per car per night; contact the NPWS office for a permit.

Places to Eat
The *Berri Resort Hotel* has counter meals, a bistro, restaurant, a coffee lounge and one of the best gaming rooms in country Australia.

The *Berri Club* across the road from Berri Backpackers has great-value meals from Thursday to Sunday nights; it's open every night for drinks, which you'll find are cheaper here than in town. Not quite in the same league, but still good value, are the specials at the *Big River Tavern (Shiell Rd)*.

Berri's finest dining is found in the *Big River Motor Inn*.

Getting There & Around
Premier Stateliner calls in daily from Adelaide ($28).

The Avis agent is Berri Decorative & Building Supplies (☎ 8582 3784) – its drop-off and pickup point is the Caltex Service Station on the Sturt Hwy in town.

RENMARK
• pop 8320
Information
The tourist office (☎/fax 8586 6704) is in the Renmark Paringa Tourist Centre on Murray Ave, beside the river. It opens from 9 am to 5 pm on weekdays, to 4 pm on Saturday and from noon to 4 pm on Sunday and public holidays. Attached is an interpretive centre that includes the recommissioned 1911 paddle-wheeler *Industry* (admission $2).

Things to See & Do
Olivewood Homestead is on the corner of Renmark Ave and 21st St. A Canadian-style log cabin with wide Australian verandahs, it was designed by Charles Chaffey who lived in it while administering the Renmark estates. It has an interesting museum – check out the mountain lion trap, which was brought here to catch dingoes – and

beautiful gardens where you can enjoy lunches and teas. It opens daily from 10 am to 4 pm, except Tuesday, when it opens at 2 pm, and Wednesday, when it's closed ($4).

A must for rose lovers, **Ruston's Rose Gardens** has 50,000 roses (4000 varieties) on 10 hectares about 5km from town – turn off Renmark Ave at the Renmano Winery and follow the signs. As well as its colourful blooms and delicate scents, the gardens offers pleasant walks among shady groves of introduced trees. It's open daily from 1 September to 30 June from 9 am to 6 pm ($3).

Goat Island, also known as Paringa Paddock, is on the Sturt Hwy between the Paringa Bridge and Renmark. There are walking tracks among the gums, where you may see koalas – although they're more likely to be found near the caravan park on the other side of the road.

Upstream from Renmark, the huge **Chowilla Regional Reserve** is great for bush camping, canoeing and bushwalking. Access is along the north bank from Renmark.

Angoves winery, on Bookmark Rd, and **Renmano Wines**, on Renmark Ave, have cellar-door sales and tastings on weekdays between 9 am and 5 pm; Renmano is also open on Saturday between 9 am and 4 pm.

The **Chaffey Theatre**, on 18th St, has films or live theatre most weeks, usually on Friday and Saturday nights.

Organised Tours

Bush & Backwaters 4WD Tours (☎ 8586 5344, bbwaters@riverland.net.au) runs half-day ($50) and day ($90) trips to conservation areas, wineries, orchards and historic sites around Renmark. It also runs guided walks and will take you out in a dinghy for fishing, birdwatching and other activities.

Renmark River Cruises (☎ 8595 1862) has day and night cruises from $16 (for two hours) on the MV *River Rambler*, departing from the town wharf. It also offers backwater dinghy trips (four passengers maximum).

The historic PS *Industry* runs occasional cruises; the tourist office can give times.

Berri Air Tours (☎ 8582 2799) offers scenic flights from the Renmark airport.

Both caravan parks hire canoes. Alternatively, Rivermate (☎ 8586 6928) has outboard-powered aluminium dinghies, with a minimum hire time of half a day.

Places to Stay & Eat

Idyllically situated on the river 1km east of town, the **Renmark Riverfront Caravan Park** (☎ 8586 6315) has campsites from $5, on-site vans for $27, cabins with en suite facilities for $48 and villas from $65. Canoe hire starts at $5 per hour.

Farther along the Murray River beside the Paringa Bridge, the **Riverbend Caravan Park** (☎ 8595 5131) has campsites starting at $10, on-site vans at $26, en suite cabins $36. It also has canoe hire starting at $5 per hour.

The **Renmark Hotel/Motel** (☎ 8586 6755, Murray Ave) has hotel rooms for $40/50 a single/double and motel units from $65/75 plus $10 for each extra person; it's 100 years old, but doesn't look its age. You can get good meals in the front bar, bistro and dining room.

The tourist office has details of the town's five other motels, all of which are on the highway.

Settlers Retreat (☎ 8595 5400 business hours) is a tastefully furnished three-bedroom house among vineyards by the river in Renmark West. It charges $65 for two people per night, with a minimum stay of two nights.

Camping in the **Chowilla Regional Reserve** costs $5 per car per night; contact the NPWS office in Berri.

There are several restaurants and takeaways in town. For value it's hard to beat the **Renmark Club**, across from the Renmark Hotel, which has huge specials on Tuesday and Thursday nights.

Getting There & Around

Premier Stateliner calls in daily from Adelaide ($28), stopping on Renmark Ave a block from the central business district.

Greyhound Pioneer and McCafferty's travel daily through Renmark on their Adelaide to Sydney run. Both charge $79 from Sydney to Renmark.

Renmark Taxis (☎ 014 951 155) operates a 24-hour-a-day service, charging about $25 to Berri and $50 to Loxton.

PARINGA
* pop 1000

Just 4km from Renmark and 19km from the Victorian border, Paringa is the last town in SA.

There's a magnificent view over the river and its high ochre-coloured cliffs from the lookout tower on **Headings Cliffs**. To get there, head north of town for 12km and turn onto Murtho Rd. Afternoon is the best time for photos of the cliffs.

It's worth stopping at **Cammies Country Living** on the Sturt Hwy in central Paringa to browse among bric-a-brac and collectables.

You can swim at the **Lock 5 Sandbar**. However, there have been numerous drownings here because of deep holes, so if you're not a strong swimmer it's smart to wear a lifejacket – or stay out of the water. To get here, turn off the Sturt Hwy between Paringa and the Paringa Bridge, near Renmark, and drive past **Lock 5**, which is open to the public. En route to the river you pass a **houseboat marina**; several operators are based here, making it a good spot to hire a houseboat.

Places to stay are limited. The *Paringa Caravan Park* (☎ 8595 5178) and the *Paringa Hotel/Motel* (☎ 8595 5005) are both in the centre of town – the motel is one of SA's cheapest, with units for $32/38/50 a single/double/triple and a salad bar in the dining room.

We have received very good reports about *Mundic Grove Cottages* (☎ 8595 5116), which charges from $50 for doubles, and *Wilkadene Cottage* (☎ 8595 8037), from $90. Both are in rural settings near the river.

MURRAY RIVER NATIONAL PARK

The park is broken into three sections: **Katarapko** (8905 hectares) between Loxton and Berri; **Lyrup Flats** (2000 hectares) on the southern side of Renmark; and **Bulyong Island** (2380 hectares). All are popular spots for bush camping, fishing, canoeing and birdwatching. Locals descend on the river in droves over Easter – obviously a good time to avoid the place.

Lyrup Flats is one of the most devastated areas on the Murray, with many trees killed by high water levels and salt intrusion. It looks like a bomb has hit the place, but all is not lost. The salty pools are ideal habitats for brine shrimp, a rich food for ducks and other waterbirds, while the dead trees provide nesting sites.

You can get to Katarapko and Lyrup Flats by road off the Sturt Hwy and to Bulyong Island from Renmark North. Alternatively, it's easy to canoe across to both these areas from the opposite bank.

For park information contact the NPWS office in Berri.

DANGGALIE CONSERVATION PARK

This 253,230 hectare park is 90km north of Renmark and, together with the Murray River National Park and other parks and reserves in the area, forms part of the enormous **Bookmark Biosphere Reserve**. The park, an amalgamation of four sheep stations, is dominated by mallee and black oak woodlands.

Things to do include nature drives (there's a 100km 4WD route), walks, wildlife watching and beautiful wildflowers in spring. There is no food or fuel in this remote area, and water is extremely limited. In other words, BYO everything.

Bush camping is permitted and you can stay in the *old shearer's quarters* – contact the ranger at Canopus on ☎ 8595 8010 or the NPWS office in Berri.

Murray Mallee

Forming part of the Murraylands region, the Murray Mallee is bordered by the Murray River to the north and west, the Victorian border to the east, and the Mallee Hwy to the south. To the first settlers, this rolling sea of mallee scrub was considered 'unfit for any purpose', and drovers took pains to avoid its waterless sandhills. Eventually shallow ground water was found, enabling wells and soaks to be dug. From the 1860s most of the region was taken up for low-intensity grazing.

By the early 1900s, improved wheat varieties and more efficient farming methods had made the Mallee an attractive proposition. Huge areas were cleared for cropping, particularly after 1906 when a railway was opened between Tailem Bend and Pinnaroo. More railways were constructed and 36 townships were surveyed, but the realities of drought and poor soils eventually brought decline.

These days the Mallee is still an important wheat-growing area. However, the farms are much larger and the population much smaller than in those early boom years. Many of the early townships no longer exist, and there are numerous abandoned homes and empty schools throughout the region. Only the towns of **Lameroo** (population 560) and **Pinnaroo** (population 650) on the Mallee Hwy have retained any significance as service centres.

MALLEE HIGHWAY

You'd take the Mallee Hwy, which runs east from Tailem Bend to Pinnaroo, if you were in a hurry to get from Adelaide to north-western Victoria or Sydney. This good sealed road passes through several small towns, all with basic facilities.

Apart from a couple of major conservation parks, which require long detours, there's not much to see along the way. In Pinnaroo, the **Printers Museum** will appeal if there's ink in your veins. Off the road to Loxton, about 30km from Pinnaroo, the fascinating **Gum Family Collection** (☎ 8577 5322) comprises 80 antique stationary engines and other memorabilia. It's definitely worth a visit, but

at the time of writing they were proposing to move it into town, so check first.

The 59,148 hectare **Billiatt Conservation Park** is 37km north of Lameroo, or 54km south of Loxton via Alawoona. An undulating sea of mallee and sand dunes, the park is home to rare western whipbirds and red-lored whistlers – mallee fowls also live here. The only access is off the unsealed road from Lameroo to Alawoona, which runs through the centre of the park. There are no facilities or drinking water.

South of the Mallee Hwy and adjoining the Victorian border is the huge **Ngarkat Conservation Park**, which you can reach from Lameroo, Pinnaroo and towns on the Dukes Hwy. For details see the South-East chapter.

Places to Stay

At Lameroo there is the *Lameroo Community Hotel/Motel* (☎ 8576 3006, Railway Terrace North), which has single/double units for $43/53.

Pinnaroo has the *Pinnaroo Motel* (☎ 8577 8261, Mallee Hwy), with units for $44/54, and the friendly *Golden Grain Hotel* (☎ 8577 8009, 9 Railway Terrace), with basic pub rooms for $15/25. The *Pinnaroo Caravan Park* (☎ 8577 8224, Mallee Hwy) has tent and caravan sites and basic cabins.

Meranwyney Host Farm (☎ 8576 5215), 17km south of the Mallee Hwy (turn off at Wilkawatt), is near the north-west corner of Ngarkat Conservation Park. It offers full board for $90 per person including farm tours, visits to heritage sites, bushwalks and other activities.

Getting There & Away

The Murray Bridge Passenger Service (☎ 8532 6660) runs from Adelaide to Pinnaroo ($33) on weekdays.

The life-saving lighthouse of Cape du Couedic

RICHARD I'ANSON

Cottages at Cape du Couedic, Kangaroo Island

RICHARD I'ANSON

Heaven, where the Rocky River meets the sea

DENIS O'EYRNE

Crayfishing jetty, Vivonne Bay, Kangaroo Island

SIMON ROWE

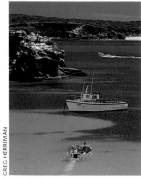
Cruising on jade at Nora Creina

In the Barossa Valley, grape vines grow amid German heritage.

Houseboats and holiday homes nestle along the shores of the idyllic Murray River.

Shell middens are markers of Aboriginal heritage at Beachport.

Lobsters grow BIG in Kingston.

The South-East

Bordered by the Murray Mallee to the north, Victoria to the east and the Southern Ocean to the west and south, the South-East (SE) is one of SA's most diverse and productive agricultural regions. Kingston is the dividing point between the drier Upper SE, north of the town, and the more lush Lower SE, to the south.

Although it makes up only 3.5% of the state's area, the SE accounts for nearly 20% of its farm output; softwood timber, beef cattle, sheep for wool and meat, cereals, hay, vegetables and grapes are all important contributors to the local economy. Australia's largest concentration of *Pinus radiata* (Monterey pine) plantations is in the Lower SE. All its ports have rock lobster fishing fleets, with the state's largest at Port MacDonnell; Crow-eaters generally refer to rock lobsters as 'crayfish' or simply 'crays'.

There are a number of extinct volcanic vents around Mt Gambier and Millicent (see the boxed text 'The Earth Trembled'). Otherwise the region is mostly flat to undulating; in the south, vast swampy areas lie between ancient coastal sand dunes which now form low ranges running parallel to the coast. Many swamps have been drained since 1863 and this has created rich agricultural land.

The SE has a number of attractions apart from its long coastline of surf beaches, sheltered bays and rugged cliffs. These include wineries and Mother Mary MacKillop sites around Penola, waterbirds at the Coorong and Bool Lagoon, and significant limestone caves near Millicent and Naracoorte. There are also the historic ports of Robe, Beachport and Port MacDonnell, whose brief boom times left many interesting buildings for today's heritage hunters to admire.

Information

Tourist Offices The major tourist office for the Lower SE is in Mt Gambier, and there are smaller outlets in Meningie, Millicent,

HIGHLIGHTS

- Marvel at the prolific birdlife of the Coorong and Bool Lagoon
- Wander through normally sleepy Robe and photograph its many historic sites – or enjoy a freshly cooked crayfish
- Explore some of the South-East's 16 extinct volcanoes and the impossibly blue Blue Lake
- See how 250,000 bats get along in the Bat Cave near Naracoorte
- Plumb the depths of the Cathedral at Piccaninnie Ponds, one of the world's best freshwater dives
- Meander through the renowned Coonawarra wineries and sample a classic red – or three
- Experience the solitude of the vast Ngarkat Conservation Park, where a sea of mallee extends to the horizon

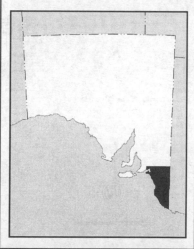

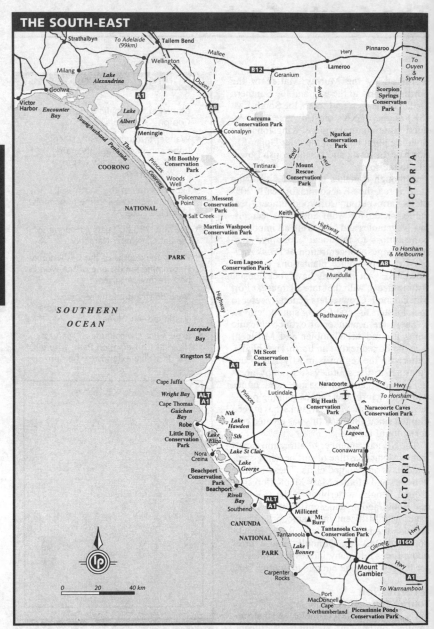

THE SOUTH-EAST

THE SOUTH-EAST

Strathalbyn   To Adelaide (99km)   Tailem Bend   Mallee   Pinnaroo   Hwy   To Ouyen & Sydney

Milang   Wellington   B12   Geranium   Lameroo

Goolwa   Lake Alexandrina

Victor Harbor   Encounter Bay   A1   Lake Albert   Scorpion Springs Conservation Park

Meningie   Carcuma Conservation Park   Coonalpyn   Ngarkat Conservation Park

COORONG   Mt Boothby Conservation Park   Tintinara   Mount Rescue Conservation Park

Woods Well   Dukes   Princes   Coorong

NATIONAL   Policemans Point   Messent Conservation Park   Keith   Highway

Salt Creek   Martins Washpool Conservation Park   Bordertown   A8

PARK   Gum Lagoon Conservation Park   Mundulla   To Horsham & Melbourne

SOUTHERN OCEAN   Padthaway

Lacepede Bay   Highway

Kingston SE   A1   Mt Scott Conservation Park

Cape Jaffa   Naracoorte   Wimmera   Hwy

Wright Bay   ALT A1   Princes   Lucindale   Big Heath Conservation Park   To Horsham

Cape Thomas   Naracoorte Caves Conservation Park

Guichen Bay   Nth Lake Hawdon

Robe   Bool Lagoon

Little Dip Conservation Park   Lake Eliza   Sth   Lake St Clair   Coonawarra

Nora Creina   Lake George   Penola

Beachport Conservation Park   Rivoli Bay

Beachport   ALT A1   VICTORIA

Southend   Millicent   Mt Burr

CANUNDA   Tantanoola Caves Conservation Park

NATIONAL   Tantanoola   Glenelg   B160

PARK   Lake Bonney   Hwy

Carpenter Rocks   Mount Gambier   A1   To Warrnambool

0   20   40 km

Port MacDonnell   Cape Northumberland   Piccaninnie Ponds Conservation Park

Naracoorte, Penola and Robe. See the sections on those towns for details.

National Parks The National Parks and Wildlife Service (NPWS) regional office (☎ 8735 1177, fax 8735 1110) for the SE is at 11 Helen St, Mt Gambier. The postal address is PO Box 1046, Mt Gambier SA 5290.

Parks between Meningie and the Dukes Hwy, including the Coorong National Park, are managed by the NPWS office at 32-34 Princes Hwy, Meningie (☎ 8575 1200, fax 8575 1496).

Check the NPWS's free newspaper *The Tattler* for details of what's happening in coastal parks between the mouth of the Murray and the Victorian border. It's widely available at information outlets and NPWS offices along the coast.

Books & Maps The Royal Automobile Association of South Australia (RAA) publishes *South East*, a comprehensive travel guide to the region ($4 to members, $8 to nonmembers). Also useful is the Royal Society of SA's *Natural History of the South-East*.

The RAA has the best touring maps: there's one each for the Upper SE and Lower SE. The Office of Recreation & Sport's cycling map covers most of the Lower SE.

Organised Tours

Coorong Nature Tours (☎ 8574 0037, 015 714 793) of Meningie offers a range of tours to conservation areas all over the SE. These include three-day trips to the Lower SE ($490), two days in the Upper SE ($350), tag-along tours, overnight bushwalks and special trips for birdwatchers and nature-study enthusiasts.

See the South Australian Tourism Commission (SATC) and the Mt Gambier tourist office about other tours in the area. Several companies visit the Coorong from Goolwa and Adelaide.

Accommodation

There are plenty of places to stay in the Lower SE, particularly at Mt Gambier,

Naracoorte, Penola and Robe. In this region, backpacker places, caravan parks, hotels, motels, guesthouses and B&Bs are all well represented. A 'vacancy' sign is a rare species anywhere along the coast between the end of November and the end of March, when prices generally go up.

Most of the accommodation in the Upper SE is along the Mallee and Dukes Hwys into Victoria.

Getting There & Around

Air Kendell Airlines and O'Connor Air Services fly daily from Mt Gambier to Adelaide and Melbourne. See Mt Gambier's Getting There & Away section.

Bus Premier Stateliner (Adelaide ☎ 8415 5555, Mt Gambier ☎ 8642 5055) runs daily except Saturday from Adelaide's central bus station to Mt Gambier. You can travel either along the coast via the Coorong, Robe and Beachport, or go inland via Bordertown and Penola. See the sections on these towns.

A V/Line bus and train service runs between Mt Gambier and Melbourne. See Mt Gambier's Getting There & Away section.

Train A tourist railcar runs between Mt Gambier and Penola on Sunday, departing from the Mt Gambier train station at 10 am and returning at 4 pm; it spends three hours in Penola, which is plenty of time for you to have a quick look around. A return ticket costs $15 and you can book at the tourist office in Mt Gambier.

Princes Highway

From Murray Bridge the Princes Hwy (Hwy 1) follows the coast southwards to Kingston, where it veers inland to Millicent and Mt Gambier and travels on to Portland in Victoria. A more interesting route from Kingston is to take Alternative Hwy 1. It continues along the coast through the picturesque fishing and holiday ports of Robe and Beachport before rejoining Hwy 1 at Millicent.

MENINGIE
- pop 800

On Lake Albert, a large arm of Lake Alexandrina, Meningie was established as a minor port in 1866. It's a popular windsurfing spot, which isn't surprising, as the wind here always seems to be blowing.

The main tourist office is the Melaleuca Centre, a craft shop on the Princes Hwy.

Things to See & Do
Messent Conservation Park, covering 12,250 hectares, has plenty of wildlife and diverse vegetation, including large pink gums and spectacular wildflowers in spring. It has good bushwalking, and you can camp, but vehicle access within the park is 4WD only. The park is 6km from **Salt Creek** on the Coorong.

En route to Messent you pass the 1880 hectare **Martins Washpool Conservation Park** (4WD access only), which has winter wetlands surrounded by vegetated dunes.

The mallee habitats in 4050 hectare **Mt Boothby Conservation Park** also feature walks and wildlife; the fact that Mt Boothby is only 129m high gives you some idea of how flat it is around here. This park is 40km east of Meningie and is best reached from Woods Well on the Coorong, or from the Dukes Hwy to the north.

Places to Stay
The *Lake Albert Caravan Park* (☎ 8575 1411) has lots of shade and lawn beside the lake about 1km out on the Narrung road. It has tent/caravan sites from $12/15, on-site vans from $25 and cabins from $35.

The 1860s *Meningie Hotel* (☎ 8575 1007, 62 Princes Hwy) which has pub-style rooms from $25/40 for singles/doubles. Alternatively, the *Lake Albert Motel* (☎ 8575 1077, 38 Princes Hwy) charges $54/60.

We've had excellent reports about historic *Polltalloch Station* (☎ 8574 0088), on the shore of Lake Alexandrina about 30km by road north of Meningie. Its charming 1840s cottages have from two to four bedrooms and singles and doubles cost from $72 (extra people $15). Activities on offer include canoeing, birdwatching, walks and tours.

THE COORONG
A wetland of international significance, the Coorong is a slender saltwater lagoon that curves along the coast for about 145km from the mouth of the Murray River. The Coorong's main attraction is the 46,750 hectare **Coorong National Park**. The park also includes the Younghusband Peninsula, a narrow line of massive white dunes that separates the Coorong from the sea.

In 1836 the rich resources of the Coorong supported a large population of Ngarrindjeri Aborigines, but by 1860 their numbers had dwindled alarmingly. Today many of their descendants still live in the district, and stone fish traps and middens remain as evidence of a vanished way of life. You can learn more about the Ngarrindjeri at their cultural centre at **Camp Coorong**, 10km south of Meningie and off the Princes Hwy. It's run by the Ngarrindjeri Lands & Progress Association.

The Coorong is home to huge numbers of **waterbirds**, particularly waders, ducks, swans and pelicans – there's a major pelican rookery in the lagoon. The film *Storm Boy*, based on the novel by Colin Thiele, about a young boy's friendship with a pelican, was shot here. Among the best places to watch birds are the freshwater soaks on the coastal side of the lagoon. There's plenty of other wildlife here, including kangaroos and wombats, so be careful driving at night.

There is road access across the Coorong at Tea Tree Crossing (summer only) near Salt Creek, and the 42-Mile Crossing farther south. With a 4WD you can continue on from both crossings to **Ninety Mile Beach**, a popular surf-fishing spot (mulloway, flathead, salmon and shark).

The endangered **hooded plover** breeds on the beach, so if you're going to drive along it make sure to keep below the high-water mark. To protect the plovers' nests, the beach is closed north of Tea Tree Crossing between 24 October and 24 December every year.

At Salt Creek there's a full-scale **replica** of the rig used to drill SA's first oil exploration hole, in 1866. This was brought about

y the discovery of a rubbery substance
alled coorongite, which was thought to
ave originated from oil seepages. It turned
ut to be a hydrocarbon produced by vast
lgal blooms in the lagoon.

Organised Tours

Coorong Nature Tours (☎ 8574 0037, 015
14 793) has a very good reputation. It of-
ers half-day (from $60 ex-Meningie) and
lay (from $110) 4WD tours of the Coorong,
vith pick-ups in Adelaide by arrangement. It
lso offers 4WD tag-along tours to the ocean
each, as well as a range of bushwalking
rips including drop-off and pickup options.

Between them, the tourist office in
Goolwa and the NPWS office in Meningie
an give you the names of other companies
hat take tours to the Coorong.

Places to Stay

Coorong National Park has a number of
ush campsites, most with no facilities. Per-
nits cost $5 per car per night, and you can
urchase one from various outlets including
oth roadhouses at Salt Creek, the NPWS
ffice in Meningie, and the Big Lobster in
Kingston. The 42-Mile Crossing camp-
round has long-drop dunnies, drinking
vater and good shelter. It's a 20 minute
valk over the sandhills to the ocean beach.

Camp Coorong (☎ 8575 1557) has self-
contained units and a bunkhouse, but you
have to book; rates available on application.

The Coorong Hotel/Motel (☎ 8575
7061) at Policeman's Point, 51km south-
east of Meningie, offers comfortable rooms
for $44/49 a single/double.

Six kilometres past Policeman's Point, the
Gemini Downs Holiday Village (☎ 8575
7013) at Gemini Downs homestead has
tent/caravan sites from $10/11, cabins from
$35 and two-bedroom units from $40. It also
has canoes for hire.

The Shell Roadhouse (☎ 8575 7021) at
Salt Creek has basic units (with kitchen facilities) sleeping six for $25 per unit. These
are quite clean and comfortable, so represent excellent value – which is why they're
popular with holidaying anglers.

KINGSTON SE
- pop 1400

Established in the mid-1850s as the port for
the Upper SE, this small fishing and holiday
town is near the southern end of the
Coorong.

Things to See & Do

Kingston is a centre for cray fishing, and the
annual Lobsterfest is held in the second
week of January.

The pelican, renowned for its beak which can hold more than its belly can

The Australian obsession with gigantic fauna and flora is apparent in **Larry the Big Lobster**, which looms over the highway on the Adelaide approach to town. Larry fronts a tourist office and cafe.

Registered by the National Trust, the **Cape Jaffa Lighthouse** was originally placed at nearby Cape Jaffa in 1869, but is now next to the Kingston Caravan Park. You get a nice view from the top – except for the town's water tank it's the highest point for quite a distance. Ask at the caravan park about opening times.

From Kingston, conventional vehicles can drive 16km north along **Ninety Mile Beach** to an access point at **The Granites** carpark. With 4WD you can – depending on the tide and sea conditions – continue to the mouth of the Murray. Late in January each year the Lions Club holds a hugely popular **surf fishing competition** on this beach; prizes total $10,000 and there are usually around 1200 entrants.

From Kingston it's about 20km to **Cape Jaffa**, a small fishing village with good swimming and fishing off a long white beach. If you've got your own scuba gear you can dive on **Margaret Brock Reef**, which has caves and deep holes. This is a marine sanctuary so you should see plenty of crays and other marine life. The caravan park can refill your tanks.

You can taste and purchase local wines from 10 am to 4 pm daily at **Cape Jaffa Wines**, near Cape Jaffa, and **Mt Benson Vineyards**, about 30km from Kingston off Alternative Hwy 1. This district has seen great interest from wine makers in recent times, with large areas being planted to vines.

Places to Stay & Eat

The small and homely *Backpackers Hostel* (*☎ 8767 2107, 21 Holland St)* has bunks in small dorms for $12, including use of the kitchen. There's a seven day laundrette across the road.

Near the waterfront, the friendly *Kingston Caravan Park (☎ 8767 2050, Marine Parade)* has tent/caravan sites from $10/13, on-site vans from $26 and cabins from $30.

Out at Cape Jaffa, and also close to th beach, the *Cape Jaffa Caravan Par* *(☎ 8768 5056)* charges similar prices.

Standard single/double pub rooms are available at the *Crown Inn Hotel (☎ 876 2005, Agnes St)* for $16/28 and at the *Roya Mail Hotel (☎ 8767 2002, Hansen St)* fo $20/30. Alternatively, there are severa motels.

In the cray season (October to April), yo can buy cooked cray, fresh fish and fish an chips daily from *Lacapede Seafoods*, on Ma rine Parade by the jetty. *Zadow's*, also on Ma rine Parade, sells cooked crays and fresh fish

Getting There & Away

Premier Stateliner goes daily except Satur day to Adelaide ($30.50) and Mt Gambie ($20.50). The booking office is at the Bi Lobster.

ROBE

- **pop 750**

A small fishing port and holiday town es tablished in 1845, this was once the thir most important port in SA. It was the mai terminal for wool from the region until i trade was diverted through Port MacDonne and Kingston in the 1860s.

Robe made a fortune in the late 1850s a a result of the Victorian gold rush. The Vic torian government had placed a substantia entry tax on Chinese gold miners, and man avoided it by landing at Robe, or ports far ther west, and walking overland to the gold fields; 10,000 arrived in 1857 alone However, the flood stopped as quickly as i started when the SA government slapped it own tax on the Chinese. The Chinamen' Wells in the region (there's one on th Coorong) are a reminder of that time.

Robe is an extremely popular summer hol iday destination. To the delight of local busi nesses, and the despair of anyone wantin quiet and solitude, the population leaps fro 750 to around 9000 the day after Christmas

Information

The tourist office (☎ 8768 2465) is in th public library at the intersection of Smilli and Victoria Sts. There's an interesting display of old photographs here. The library opens weekdays from 10 am to 5 pm and Saturday from 10 am to 12.30 pm.

Outside these times the Robe Gallery on Victoria St is a helpful alternative.

Things to See & Do

There are numerous heritage-listed buildings dating from the late 1840s to 1870s, and you can find them with the leaflet *Robe Walking Tours*. They include the **Customs House** (1863), on Royal Circus, which is now a nautical museum. Nearby is a **memorial** to the 16,500 Chinese diggers who landed at the port from 1856 to 1858.

Wilsons of Robe is an excellent arts and crafts shop on Victoria St. Across the road, the **Focus on Nature** gallery has many beautiful works by local photographer Jill Murch.

The town has a sandy **swimming beach** enclosed by a reef. **Long Beach**, 2km north off the Kingston road, is good for surfing and windsurfing; Steve's Place, on Victoria St, hires out boogy boards.

Little Dip Conservation Park (2000 hectares) runs along the coast for about 13km south of town. It features a variety of habitats including wetlands and dunes, and the popular fishing spots of **Bishops Pate**, **Long Gully** and **Little Dip** – accessible off the corrugated Nora Creina road.

The **Narraburra Woolshed**, 14km from town on the Millicent road, has demonstrations of working sheep dogs, shearing, wool classing and baling (inquiries ☎ 8768 2083). If you've never seen a shearing shed in action, this is the place to start.

You can do unforgettable **scenic flights** with Captain Boggles in a Tiger Moth (☎ 8768 2989, or mobile 018 505 616). Flights start at $40 and operate daily, weather permitting. The air strip is 5km out on the Millicent road.

Places to Stay

There are numerous accommodation options in Robe, including caravan parks, hotels, motels, flats, cottages and B&Bs.

There are several bush campsites in *Little Dip Conservation Park* (see the previous section); for permits and information contact the ranger in Robe (☎ 8768 2543).

Real estate agents Weston, Raine & Horne (☎ 8768 2028) have a booklet detailing around 50 places for rent. Weekly rentals range from $420 to $1200 during the high season.

Places to Stay – Budget

Friendly *Bushland Cabins* (☎ 8768 2386) is about 1.5km from town and off the Nora Creina road. It has a self-contained backpacker cabin ($13 per person), bush campsites ($11), basic self-contained cabins ($36), and plenty of wildlife, including echidnas and possums. The complex is in eucalypt woodland adjoining Little Dip Conservation Park and pretty Lake Fellmongery.

On the Robe side of Lake Fellmongery, the *Lakeside Tourist Park* (☎ 8768 2193) has a nice setting with good shade. Tent/caravan sites cost from $13/15, on-site vans from $34 and self-contained cabins from $45; the cabins sleep up to 10, plus $5 for each extra adult.

THE SOUTH-EAST

A sheep dog in action

Otherwise there's the much more formal **Long Beach Tourist & Caravan Park** (☎ *8768 2237*), about 3km from town near Long Beach, and the **Sea-Vu Caravan Park** (☎ *8768 2273, 1 Squire Drive)* in town. Both have tent and caravan sites, on-site vans and self-contained cabins.

Places to Stay – Mid-Range
The historic **Caledonian Inn** (☎ *8768 2029, Victoria St)* has basic heritage rooms with shared facilities for $30/50 for singles/doubles, and motel-style units a stone's throw from the beach for $80/100.

Overlooking Guichen Bay from Mundy Terrace, the **Robe Hotel** (☎ *8768 2077)* has pub-style rooms from $35/50 and rooms with private facilities from $50/70; some of the latter have private balconies with sea views.

The cheapest of Robe's six motels is the **Guichen Bay Motel** (☎ *8768 2001, Victoria St)* at the entrance to town. It has basic units from $50/60.

There are also a number of historic buildings you can stay in, several of which offer B&B, including out at Lake Fellmongery, the grand 1880s **Lakeside Country House** (☎ *8768 2042)*, which has a good reputation. It does B&B in huge bedrooms for $105 for doubles with shared facilities ($125 with private bathroom).

Grey Masts Guesthouse (☎ *8768 2203, 1 Smillie St)* has heritage-style B&B with shared facilities for $95. There's a very good restaurant attached.

Also well regarded is **Wilsons at Robe** (☎ *8768 2459, Victoria St)*. Its charming 1850s cottage costs from $105 for doubles, including breakfast provisions.

Others worth checking are the 1840s **Robe House** (☎ *8768 2270)*, the 1850s **Campbell Cottages** (☎ *8768 2236)* and the 1850s **Criterion Cottage** (☎ 8768 2137).

Places to Eat
The best value meals in town are the winter specials at the **Caledonian Inn** (which has a great old-world atmosphere and a very cosy bar) and the counter meals at the **Robe Hotel**.

Locals recommend the **Wild Mulberry Cafe** *(Robe St)* for delicious lunches (though it's also open for breakfasts and dinners), while the **Imaj Cafe**, across from Wilsons at Robe, does good take-aways. During the cray season (October to April) you can get cooked crays, fresh fish, and fish and chips at **Stanke's Seafoods**, at the fisherman's wharf at Lake Butler.

Getting There & Away
Premier Stateliner runs daily except Saturday from Adelaide ($34.50) and Mt Gambier ($16.40).

BEACHPORT
- **pop 440**

If you have a yen for peace and solitude you will love this quiet little seaside town with its aquamarine bay and historic buildings. The **Old Wool & Grain Store Museum** ($2) is housed in a National Trust building next to Bompa's, on Railway Terrace. There is also an interesting **Aboriginal Artefacts Museum** ($2) in the former primary school on McCourt St. If you want to see either building, ask at the district council office for keys.

There's good surfing at the local **surf beach**, and windsurfing is popular at **Lake George**, 5km north of the township. The hypersaline **Pool of Salome** is a pretty swimming lake among vegetated dunes on the outskirts of town.

The town **jetty**, 800m long, occasionally provides memorable fishing (whiting, school shark, mullet, squid and many more). Lake George mullet are considered excellent tucker.

Penguin Island, a rookery for little penguins, is in Rivoli Bay about 200m offshore. Each summer the parent birds take their young on swimming lessons between the island and the groyne opposite the Beachport Caravan Park.

The 700 hectare **Beachport Conservation Park** is sandwiched between the coast and Lake George 2km north of town. Its attractions include Aboriginal shell middens, sheltered coves and bush camping; the anger (☎ 8735 6053) at Southend can provide permits and details.

The little fishing town of **Southend** (population 300) is at the southern end of Rivoli Day, 22km from Beachport. It has a quiet swimming beach, a small caravan park and **Canunda National Park** on its doorstep (see the later section on Canunda National Park).

On the Robe road, the impressive **Woakwine Cutting** through the Woakwine Range illustrates the lengths to which a determined farmer will go to drain a swamp.

Places to Stay & Eat

You can camp in the *Beachport Conservation Park*, 2km north of town; ring the ranger for details *(☎ 8735 6053)*.

The *Beachport Caravan Park (☎ 8735 3128, Beach Rd)* is rather ordinary but has a great location near the surf beach. Much more attractive is the *Southern Ocean Tourist Park (☎ 8735 8153, Somerville St)*, which has tent/caravan sites for $12/14 and self-contained cabins from $45. There is also a *caravan park (☎ 8735 6035)* at Southend, 22km south.

Right on the beach near the jetty, *Beachport Backpackers (☎ 8735 8197)* is in the historic harbourmaster's house. It's a friendly place with a cosy log fire in winter and a spacious kitchen. Dorm beds cost $15, and there are mountain bikes, surfboards and fishing gear for guests' use.

The *Beachport Motor Inn (☎ 8735 8070)*, on the corner of Railway Terrace and Lanky St, has units from $50/55 a single/double.

Bompa's (☎ 8735 8333), on Railway Terrace near the jetty, has spacious, comfortable bedrooms costing from $55 with shared facilities and $85 with private facilities, including a light breakfast. It also has a licensed restaurant and bistro.

During the cray season (October to April) you can get cooked crays, fresh fish, and fish and chips at *Stanke's Seafoods*, at the jetty.

Getting There & Away

Premier Stateliner runs daily except Saturday from Adelaide ($36.50) and Mt Gambier ($11).

MILLICENT
• pop 5120

Finding they were virtually cut off by seasonal swamps for much of the year, Millicent's first settlers threatened to secede from the colony unless something was done to improve communications. Out of this protest came the SE's first drainage scheme, in 1863. More followed soon after, creating some of the region's richest agricultural land.

At the Mt Gambier end of George St, the tourist office (☎/fax 8733 3205) is open daily from 9.30 am to 4.30 pm. It has a good **craft shop** and an excellent National Trust **museum** ($4) with many interesting exhibits on the district's early years. Enthusiasts should allow at least an hour to have a look through the complex.

The **Millicent Gallery** in the civic centre on George St hosts some excellent travelling exhibitions.

Places to Stay & Eat

About 2km from the post office, the pleasant *Lakeside Caravan Park (☎ 8733 3947, 12 Park Terrace)* is beside a small swimming lake. It has tent/caravan sites for $9/15, on-site vans for $25 and basic cabins from $35.

In the centre of town, the *Somerset Hotel/Motel (☎ 8733 2888, 2 George St)* has self-contained single/double pub rooms for $35/45 and motel units for $45/60. Alternatively, the *Diplomat Motel (☎ 8733 2211, 51 Mt Gambier Rd)* charges $50/60.

There are three hotels on George St and all have *counter meals*; there's the usual cut-throat competition because of pokies.

Getting There & Away

Premier Stateliner runs daily except Saturday from Adelaide ($36.50) and Mt Gambier ($8).

CANUNDA NATIONAL PARK

Covering 9300 hectares, and only 13km west of town, this is Millicent's main tourist attraction. The elongated park has a number of attractions including giant shifting sand dunes, rugged coastal scenery, wombats, walks and 4WD tracks. In summer you can drive along the beach and through the dunes all the way from Southend to **Carpenter Rocks**, a boat haven with a *caravan park* (☎ 8738 0035).

Cullens Bay Blowhole near Southend is spectacular in the right conditions; nearby there's a great view along the coast from **Boozy Gully Lookout**. It was off the coast near here that the 1056-tonne, three-masted barque *Geltwood* was wrecked in 1876 with the loss of all 31 people aboard. Now a declared historic site, the wreck makes a spectacular dive but is generally inaccessible because of the ocean swells.

There are *bush campsites* in the park near Southend; you can get permits and park brochures from the ranger's office (☎ 8735 6053) near the jetty.

TANTANOOLA

In tiny Tantanoola, a *Pinus radiata* centre 15km south-east of Millicent, the stuffed 'Tantanoola Tiger' is on display at the Tantanoola Tiger Hotel. This beast, actually an Assyrian wolf, was shot in 1895 after creating havoc among local sheep flocks. It was presumed to have escaped from a shipwreck, although why a ship would have a wolf on board isn't clear!

Formed as coastal caves in dolomite, and part of a 2000 hectare conservation park, the decorative **Tantanoola Caves** are on the Princes Hwy another 6km to the south-east. The tourist office (☎ 8734 4153) runs tours ($6) of the show cave daily every hour from 9.15 am to 4 pm (more frequently over Easter and the summer school holidays). It's the only cave in SA with wheelchair access.

MT GAMBIER
- **pop 22,000**

Built on the lower slopes of the extinct volcano from which it takes its name, Mt Gambier, 486km from Adelaide, is the region's major town and commercial centre. It was one of the earliest parts of SA to be settled. Stephen Henty, the first squatter in the M

The tracings of journeys through Canunda National Park

Gambier district, built his home on the mount in 1839. However, a settlement was not established until 15 years later.

The volcano itself is a striking feature, rising 152m above the plain. It was named Gambier's Mountain by Lieutenant James Grant, commander of the tiny brig HMS *Lady Nelson*, who saw it while sailing along the coast en route to Sydney from England in 1800.

Information

The impressive Lady Nelson Visitor Information & Discovery Centre (☎ 8724 9750, 800 087 187 toll free, fax 8723 2833, theladynelson@mountgambiertourism.com .au), on Jubilee Hwy East, is open daily from 9 am to 5 pm.

Allow at least an hour to look through the centre ($6), which features a replica of the *Lady Nelson*, complete with sound effects and taped commentary. It also has superb natural history displays, including a walk-through cave and a swamp habitat. An audio-visual display acknowledges the work of Christina Smith, who attempted to mediate between the settlers and local Aborigines.

Things to See & Do

The **Old Courthouse Museum** at 42A Bay Rd next to the police station is open between 11 am and 3 pm ($3) daily except Saturday. Built in 1865, it still has the original courtroom furniture.

For culture vultures, the free **Riddoch Art Gallery** on Commercial St East is one of SA's best regional galleries. It opens daily, except Monday, from 10 am (noon Sunday) to 4 pm (2 pm on Saturday and 3 pm on Sunday). Next door, **Studio One** has some fine work by local artists.

Mt Gambier has three volcanic craters, two of which are filled with water; the beautiful **Blue Lake** is the best known and most spectacular, although from about March to November the water is more grey than blue.

Blue Lake averages 77m in depth and there's a 5km scenic drive around it. The lakes are a popular recreation spot and have been developed with boardwalks (over **Valley Lake**), a fauna park, picnic areas, lookouts

The Earth Trembled

The South-East's 16 extinct volcanoes are found in two distinct groups: one at Mt Gambier and the other at Mt Burr, about 40km north-west. The largest is Mt Burr itself, which rises 240m above sea level and 158m above the plain.

Mt Burr has 15 major eruption centres. Its volcanic structures were formed by varying styles of activity, from fissure flows to explosions, between 20,000 and two million years ago. The ejected material was deposited on limestone then covered with beach sand up to 50m thick.

The much smaller Mt Gambier group comprises Mt Gambier, with three volcanic centres, and Mt Schank, with one. These were formed by violent explosions caused by ground water mixing with molten rock at depth; the Mt Schank event occurred around 7000 years ago and the Mt Gambier event 3000 years later. Mt Gambier is one of the youngest volcanic features on the Australian mainland.

There is no doubt that the Aborigines saw all these events. The Booandik people had a legend of the giant *Craitbul*, who dug ovens at Mt Muirhead (near Mt Burr) and Mt Gambier; at the latter, the water kept rising to put his fire out.

Since European settlement several earth tremors have shown that the region is still unstable. Two of the state's most powerful earthquakes rocked Kingston in 1897 and Robe in 1948.

Denis O'Byrne

and walking trails. Leg of Mutton Lake dried up when the water table dropped; its bed is now covered in trees.

The Mt Gambier district is well known for its numerous caves. One that you can visit easily is the **Umpherston Cave**, which is on Jubilee Hwy East. It has been attractively landscaped with terraced gardens,

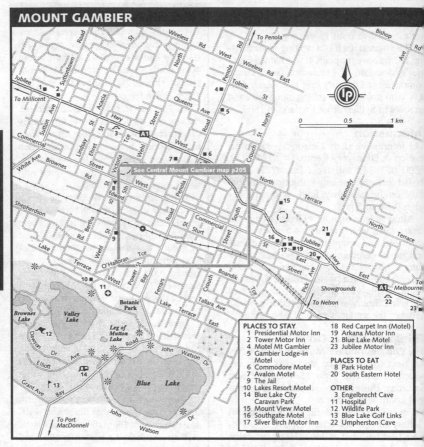

MOUNT GAMBIER

PLACES TO STAY
1 Presidential Motor Inn
2 Tower Motor Inn
4 Motel Mt Gambier
5 Gambier Lodge-in Motel
6 Commodore Motel
7 Avalon Motel
9 The Jail
10 Lakes Resort Motel
14 Blue Lake City Caravan Park
15 Mount View Motel
16 Southgate Motel
17 Silver Birch Motor Inn
18 Red Carpet Inn (Motel)
19 Arkana Motor Inn
21 Blue Lake Motel
23 Jubilee Motor Inn

PLACES TO EAT
8 Park Hotel
20 South Eastern Hotel

OTHER
3 Engelbrecht Cave
11 Hospital
12 Wildlife Park
13 Blue Lake Golf Links
22 Umpherston Cave

See Central Mount Gambier map p205

THE SOUTH-EAST

and floodlights enable you to watch the possums feeding at night.

Engelbrecht Cave, on Jubilee Hwy West, is popular with cave divers. You can also take a guided tour of this cave ($4); check with the tourist office for times.

At **Glencoe**, 23km north-west of town, the 36 stand Glencoe Woolshed (1863) is a reminder of the region's early pastoral wealth. It is now owned by the National Trust and is open daily (collect a key from the general store).

Organised Tours

Lake City Tours (☎ 8723 2991) visits local attractions on its half/full-day tours for $27/55. Lake City Taxis (☎ 8723 0000) also does town tours, while other operators can take you to Glenelg National Park (in Victoria), Cape Northumberland, a local timber mill and the Coonawarra wineries.

Places to Stay

Mt Gambier has numerous caravan parks, hotels, motels and B&Bs. A complete list o

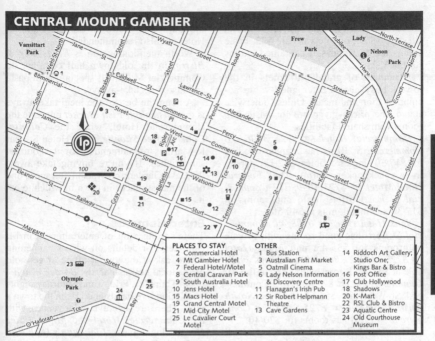

CENTRAL MOUNT GAMBIER

PLACES TO STAY
2 Commercial Hotel
4 Mt Gambier Hotel
7 Federal Hotel/Motel
8 Central Caravan Park
9 South Australia Hotel
10 Jens Hotel
15 Macs Hotel
19 Grand Central Motel
21 Mid City Motel
25 Le Cavalier Court Motel

OTHER
1 Bus Station
3 Australian Fish Market
5 Oatmill Cinema
6 Lady Nelson Information & Discovery Centre
11 Flanagan's Irish Pub
12 Sir Robert Helpmann Theatre
13 Cave Gardens
14 Riddoch Art Gallery; Studio One; Kings Bar & Bistro
16 Post Office
17 Club Hollywood
18 Shadows
20 K-Mart
22 RSL Club & Bistro
23 Aquatic Centre
24 Old Courthouse Museum

THE SOUTH-EAST

places to stay is available from the tourist office.

All prisoners have left *The Jail* (☎ 8723 0032, 1800 626 844 toll free, turnkey@seal .net.au, Langlois Drive), which is located off Margaret St. This place has been redeveloped as a backpacker hostel. Dorms beds start at $15 and there are twin beds in the old cells for $16 per person. This place was being converted at the time of the update, so we haven't yet had a chance to check it out.

There are six caravan parks within 5km of the post office.

The Blue Lake City Caravan Park (☎ 8725 9856, Bay Rd), near the lakes 2km south of town, has tent/caravan sites starting at $11/14 and on-site vans at $28. There are also self-contained cabins at this park that start at $51 and holiday units starting at $55.

Central Caravan Park (☎ 8725 4427, 6 Krummel St), 600m east of the post office has tent/caravan sites for $9/12, on-site vans from $25, basic cabins from $28, and self-contained cabins $38.

Three and a half kilometres east of town is *Jubilee Holiday Park* (☎ 8723 2469, Jubilee Hwy East), with powered sites with private facilities from $14, basic cabins from $29 and self-contained cabins from $45.

Tent/caravan sites are $13/16 at *Kalganyi Caravan Park* (☎ 8723 0220, Penola Rd), 3km north of town; on-site vans are $30, basic cabins start at $35, self-contained cabins at $46, and units at $55.

Pine Country Caravan Park (☎ 8725 1899, Bay Rd), 4km to the south has tent/caravan sites for $8/12, powered sites with private facilities for $15, and self contained cabins from $31.

At *Willow Vale Caravan Park* (☎ *8725 3631, Princes Hwy)*, 5km east; tent/caravan sites are $8/10, on-site vans are $23, basic cabins are $23 and self-contained cabins start at $32.

A number of grand old hotels in the town's busy centre offer good-value accommodation and meals. Unless otherwise stated, the prices given are for basic pub rooms with shared facilities.

Commercial Hotel (☎ *8725 3006, 76 Commercial St West)* has standard rooms for $17/30 singles/doubles; $12 per person in a backpacker dorm. The *Federal Hotel/Motel* (☎ *8723 1099, 112 Commercial St East)* offers basic pub rooms at $17/30 and motel units at $40/50.

Jens Hotel (☎ *8725 0188, 40 Commercial St East)* has good rooms with private bathrooms for $35/45, and *Macs Hotel* (☎ *8725 2402, 21 Bay Rd)* has rooms available at $22/33. Rooms with a spa at the *Mt Gambier Hotel* (☎ 8725 0611, 2 Commercial St West) are $55/65; and the *South Australia Hotel* (☎ *8725 2404, 78 Commercial St East)* has rooms for $20/30.

The *Blue Lake Motel* (☎ *8725 5211, 1 Kennedy Ave)*, just off the highway and about 2km from the town centre, has cramped twin rooms for $12 per person, which includes the use of a small kitchen. Its standard units cost from $38/45 for singles/doubles.

The *Mount View Motel* (☎ *8725 8478, 14 Davison St)* charges $33 for singles and $38/40 doubles/twins for its standard units; those with kitchens are $3 more. Few of the other 18 motels in town come anywhere near this price.

Places to Eat

The tourist office has a brochure listing over 30 eateries, not including take-aways.

Other than the pubs, locals reckon the best value in town is the *Barn Steakhouse*, about 2km out of town on Nelson Rd, which serves huge meals. Generous helpings and several cuisines are a feature of *Charlie's Family Diner*, in the Western Tavern on Jubilee Hwy West.

The *RSL Club & Bistro (16 Sturt St)* and the *Cafe Bar* bistro in the Mt Gambier Hotel are also recommended.

Worth mentioning too is *Kings Bar & Bistro*, in the old town hall complex on Commercial St East. It specialises in pasta and also does take-aways.

Among the best of the local take-aways is the *Australian Fish Market* opposite the Commercial Hotel, while the *Colonial Court Coffee Shoppe*, at 10 Helen St near K-Mart, is recommended for its gourmet sandwiches. If you're buying take-away, the Cave Gardens on Watson Terrace is one of the nicest places in town in which to eat it.

Entertainment

There's quite a bit of entertainment in Mt Gambier. For details on what's happening where, ask at the tourist office or get hold of the local newspaper, the *Border Watch*.

On Thursday, Friday and Saturday nights you'll find live bands and DJs in the town's pubs. There are several regular venues, with the *Commercial Hotel* and *Mt Gambier Hotel* being popular. *Flanagan's Irish Pub (6 Ferris St)* has karaoke on Friday nights and live Irish bands or cover bands on Saturday night.

As well, there are two nightclubs in the city centre: *Club Hollywood*, in the Ripley Arcade off Commercial St West, and *Shadows (Bay Rd)*.

The *Oatmill Cinema (Percy St)* has three screens and shows films daily.

Finally, the excellent *Sir Robert Helpmann Theatre* is in the Civic Centre on Watson Terrace. It's the South-East's major entertainment venue and has something on every week whether it be live theatre, variety concerts, music, ballet or movies.

Getting There & Away

Air Kendell Airlines (Ansett ☎ 13 13 00) and O'Connor Air Services (Qantas ☎ 13 13 13) have daily flights to Adelaide and Melbourne for around $155 to either city. Departures from Mt Gambier are subject to a $5 tax.

Bus Mt Gambier's bus station is the Shell Blue Lake service station (☎ 8725 5037) at 100 Commercial St West.

Premier Stateliner buses depart daily, except Saturday, to/from Adelaide for $39. See the Getting There & Away section at the start of this chapter.

Victoria's V/Line bus and train service (☎ 1800 817 037 toll free) runs to/from Melbourne on weekdays for $48 – you take the bus from Mt Gambier to Ballarat, where you hop onto the train to Melbourne.

Train See the Getting There & Around section at the start of this chapter for details of the tourist railcar from Mt Gambier to Penola.

Getting Around
From the city centre, Lake City Taxis (☎ 8723 0000) charges around $6 to the Blue Lake and $15 to the airport.

The local hire car agents are Budget (☎ 13 27 27), Hertz (☎ 8723 0870) and Thrifty (☎ 8723 2488).

PORT MACDONNELL
• pop 680
Only 28km south of Mt Gambier, this quiet fishing and holiday village has the state's largest cray fishing fleet. It was once a busy port, hence the surprisingly large and handsome **customs house** (1863).

Twenty-five ships have been wrecked along the coast near here since 1844. You can see artefacts from some of them at the **Maritime Museum**, open Wednesday, Sunday and public holidays from 12.30 to 4.30 pm; admission costs $2.50.

About 2km north-west of town, the flamboyant colonial poet Adam Lindsay Gordon's little cottage home **Dingley Dell** (1860) is now a museum (admission $5). It contains some of his works and belongings, which you can view Friday to Wednesday between 10 am and 4 pm (Thursday to 2 pm).

There's a footpath to the top of **Mt Schank**, an extinct volcano on the Mt Gambier road 13km north of Port MacDonnell. **Little Blue Lake**, about 3km west of Mt

Schank, is a popular swimming place – it's icy cold even on the hottest day. Nearby is the **Mt Schank Fish Farm**, where you can catch your own rainbow trout.

On the coast adjacent to the Victorian border, the 660 hectare **Piccaninnie Ponds Conservation Park** has walks, camping and reputedly the world's best freshwater dive feature: **the Cathedral**, a large underwater cavern with 40m visibility. The water is so clear that flowering plants grow 6m down. Permits from the NPWS office in Mt Gambier are required before you dive or snorkel either here or farther west at tiny **Ewen Ponds Conservation Park** – you can book by phone.

Places to Stay & Eat
You can camp at *Piccaninnie Ponds* (see the previous entry).

The *Port MacDonnell Harbour View Caravan Park (☎ 8738 2085, 59 Sea Parade)* has powered sites, on-site vans and self-contained cabins.

Starks Bakery in the *Malibu Cafe* has fresh-baked goodies daily, including the ultimate in Australian cuisine: crayfish pies. Sadly, they're only available during the open season.

Eastern Wine District

Consisting of a vast system of swamps, most of which have been drained, the redgum country between Mt Gambier and Bordertown has some of the richest fodder-growing land and sheep and cattle grazing in SA. There's also a fast-growing wine industry centred on Coonawarra and Padthaway. Other points of interest in the area include historic Penola, Bool Lagoon and the Naracoorte Caves.

PENOLA
• pop 1200
A quiet little town, Penola has won fame recently for its association with the Sisters of St Joseph of the Sacred Heart – this was

THE SOUTH-EAST

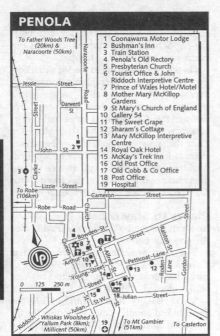

PENOLA

To Father Woods Tree (20km) & Naracoorte (50km)

Jessie Street
Naracoorte Road
Darwent St
Jessie Street
Street
John St
Clarke
Lizzie Street
To Robe (106km)
Robe Road
Cameron Street
Church Street
Ralston St
Street
Bowden St
Queen
Arthur
Young Street
Street
Alfred St
Petticoat Lane
Roden Lane
Gordon St
St
Julian
0   125   250 m
St E
St W
Julian Street
Whiskas Woolshed & Yallum Park (8km); Millicent (50km)
Riddoch
To Mt Gambier (51km)
To Casterton

1 Coonawarra Motor Lodge
2 Bushman's Inn
3 Train Station
4 Penola's Old Rectory
5 Presbyterian Church
6 Tourist Office & John Riddoch Interpretive Centre
7 Prince of Wales Hotel/Motel
8 Mother Mary McKillop Gardens
9 St Mary's Church of England
10 Gallery 54
11 The Sweet Grape
12 Sharam's Cottage
13 Mary McKillop Interpretive Centre
14 Royal Oak Hotel
15 McKay's Trek Inn
16 Old Post Office
17 Old Cobb & Co Office
18 Post Office
19 Hospital

co-founded in 1866 by Mary MacKillop, who is to be canonised as Australia's first saint. There's a MacKillop Park, a MacKillop School, a MacKillop Tourist Drive and many tacky MacKillop souvenirs on sale. The town has been named as a significant MacKillop pilgrimage site, and there seems a real danger that they'll overdo it.

The tourist office (☎ 8737 2855, fax 8737 2206), on Arthur St, opens on weekdays from 9 am to 5 pm, and on weekends and public holidays from noon to 4 pm. It's in the same building as the **John Riddoch Interpretive Centre**, which has displays about the district's history. Geologists will be interested in the large hydrocarbons display (the district is an important producer of natural gas).

Things to See & Do
The tourist office has a leaflet describing a **heritage walk** that takes in Penola's many in-

teresting old buildings. A number of these are classified by the National Trust, including the 1850s **post office** and the 1857 **Cobb & Co office** (now housing a BYO restaurant).

The **Mary MacKillop Interpretive Centre**, open from 10 am to 4 pm daily ($3), is on the corner of Petticoat Lane and Church St. It includes the **Woods-MacKillop Schoolhouse**, which was founded by Mary MacKillop and Father Julian Tenison Woods in 1867. This was the first school in Australia to accept students from lower socio-economic backgrounds.

You'll love **Petticoat Lane** and its quaint old slab cottages, several of which are open to the public, including Sharam's Cottage (1850), the first dwelling in Penola. Watch out the lintel doesn't take your head off as you walk in!

On Arthur St, the magnificent little **St Mary's Church of England** (1873) was designed by an accountant. Who said accountants have no soul?

In dramatic contrast to the cottages is the opulent two storey mansion **Yallum Park** (1880), built in the Italianate style by the district's first pastoralist, John Riddoch. The house, which is in original condition right down to the William Morris wallpaper, is a showpiece of how the wealthier Victorian-era squattocracy lived. It's on the Millicent road about 8km from town; Mrs Clifford, the friendly owner, will take you on a guided tour for $3 (bookings ☎ 8737 2435).

Gallery 54 on the corner of Church and Arthru Sts is a good arts and crafts shop featuring the work of local artists.

About 20km north of Penola on the Naracoorte road is **Father Woods Tree**. This huge, rather sick-looking red gum was used as an outdoor church by Father Julian Woods, who held services here for the first settlers.

Places to Stay & Eat
For something a bit different you can stay at *Whiskas Woolshed* (☎ 8737 2428, 0418 854 505), on a farm 12km south-west of town off the Millicent road. Rooms in the old iron shearing shed sleep up to nine, with beds for $7 (linen extra); each bedroom has

Champion of the Poor

Mary MacKillop (or McKillop) was born of Scottish immigrant parents in Fitzroy, Melbourne in 1842 and became a school teacher at the age of 21. Three years later she moved to Penola in SA to take charge of a Catholic school that had been taken over by the Jesuit priest Father Julian Tenison Woods. At that time the district had many poor and struggling families whose children were denied an education. Mary and Father Woods agreed that all children, regardless of their parents' social or financial position, should have the right to attend school. So they established Australia's first 'free' school, where fees were paid only by those who could afford to pay.

The new school was opened in 1866, Jointly founded by herself and Father Woods, the Order of the Sisters of St Joseph of the Sacred Heart was the first Australian order of nuns whose primary purpose was to educate and care for the poor.

Mary took her vows in Adelaide on 25 August 1867. A year later, there were 30 sisters in SA running eight Josephite schools, an orphanage and a home for 'fallen' women. The following year they opened their first school in Queensland. These remarkable achievements were testament to the vision and determination of the order's co-founders.

Unfortunately, however, Mary's single-mindedness soon brought her into conflict with SA's Catholic religious hierarchy. Several previous allies turned against her, and there were a number of complaints that the sisters were incompetent. It didn't help that one of her worst enemies was the Bishop of Adelaide's most influential advisor.

Finally, in September 1871, the attacks culminated in Mary's excommunication and the virtual disbandment of the Josephites. Cleared of any wrongdoing by a Commission of Inquiry, she was reinstated two years later by Pope Pius IX, who gave his approval of the Josephites.

Despite this happy outcome Mary continued to find powerful enemies among the colonial clergy, but at the same time had many influential friends both there and in the wider community. This was partly due to the egalitarian spirit she imparted to the Order – every person should be respected and valued as an individual regardless of colour, creed or social status.

By 1890 the Josephites had established schools or charitable homes in most Australian colonies and New Zealand (NZ), and Mary's health was beginning to suffer from years of overwork and worry. In 1891 she almost died from a severe case of bronchitis. More bouts of ill-health followed until, while in NZ in 1902, she suffered a disabling stroke. She died in Sydney in 1909, aged 67 years.

By the time of Mary's death the Order had founded 117 schools and 11 charitable homes, mainly in Australia and NZ. Today many of these institutions are still operating, while around

1300 Josephite sisters continue the Order's work of providing education and social services to anyone in need.

The case for Mary to be declared 'blessed' (or beatified) was first made in 1925, but it was not until 1973 that her cause was formally introduced by the Vatican. Her beatification was finally approved by Pope John Paul II in 1993 – this being the first of two stages on the path to sainthood. It is a fitting tribute to an outstanding Australian.

Australia's first free school

Denis O'Byrne

THE SOUTH-EAST

oil heating (you'll need it on cold nights), and there's a good kitchen and laundry. This place is pretty basic, but Andy, the genial owner, is a real character.

In Penola itself, *McKay's Trek Inn* (☎ *8737 2250, 1800 626 844 toll free, trekin@penola.mtx.net.au, Riddoch St)* offers a good standard. Dorm beds cost $16, including linen and a light breakfast; there's a kitchen but no laundry on the premises – the owners run the laundrette just down the road. Mountain bikes are available free to guests.

At the Millicent end of town, the *Penola Caravan Park* (☎ *8737 2381)* has powered sites and cabins. It's popular with seasonal workers, so always ring first.

The refurbished *Royal Oak Hotel* (☎ *8737 2322, Church St)* has pleasant pub-style rooms with TV and washbasin for $25/45/65 for singles/twins/doubles – the doubles have four-poster beds and most have direct access to a huge balcony.

Just down the road at the *Prince of Wales Hotel/Motel* (☎ *8737 2402)*, basic motel units cost $42/50 for singles/doubles.

The *Coonawarra Motor Lodge* (☎ *8737 2364, 114 Church St)* has comfortable units from $67/75, and there's a solar-heated swimming pool on the premises. You'll find a good restaurant right next door in the historic *Bushman's Inn*.

Alternatively, over 20 mainly historic cottages in and around town offer accommodation, with prices starting at $70 for twin share – the tourist office has details. The town's only traditional B&B is *Penola's Old Rectory* (☎ *8737 2684, 5 Bowden St)*. Built in 1885, its three spacious bedrooms with antique furnishings cost $85 for doubles including a hearty cooked breakfast.

Both the *pubs* do good meals. Otherwise, try the *Sweet Grape*, a cosy cafe in the commercial centre on Church St that is recommended for teas and light lunches.

Getting There & Away
Premier Stateliner buses depart Penola daily except Saturday for Adelaide ($37) and Mt Gambier ($8).

A tourist train operates on Sundays from Mt Gambier. See the Getting There & Around section at the start of this chapter.

COONAWARRA WINERIES
The compact (24 sq km) wine-producing area of Coonawarra, which is renowned for its reds, starts at Penola's northern outskirts and straddles the road to Naracoorte for the next 14km. The first vines were planted in 1891, and now the district attracts wine lovers from all over Australia.

Wynn's Estate is the best-known winery, but there are over 20 others offering cellar-door sales, mostly on a daily basis; the tourist office has a leaflet giving times. If you can't try them all, at least check out the following – they're listed in order starting at Penola:

Hollick Wines is a very friendly place where you can taste good, reasonably priced reds and whites in a historic miner's cottage.

Balnaves of Coonawarra has a friendly, if pretentious, tasting area with a small art gallery and trout pond. Balnaves produces some of the best reds and whites in the district; its cabernet sauvignon is worth trying but we found it difficult to get past the chardonnay.

Leconfield Coonawarra is noted for its big reds.

Katnook Estate has a good variety of styles and prices. Its Riddoch wines are reasonably cheap, while those under the Katnook brand are more expensive but delicious.

Wynns Coonawarra Estate is at Coonawarra township, 9km from Penola. As the district's first winery, it's worth visiting just to see the historic stone complex (1891) and the large wooden kegs in its cellar.

Redman Winery produces classic Coonawarra reds at reasonable prices.

Places to Stay & Eat
The *Chardonnay Lodge Motel* (☎ *8736 3309)*, 8km from Penola, has spacious units for $105 for doubles, and a good restaurant. Otherwise you can stay at numerous cottages in the area; contact the Penola tourist office for details.

Nibs, in Coonawarra, is a pleasant cook-it-yourself bistro grill with a salad bar where you can fill up for as little as $6.

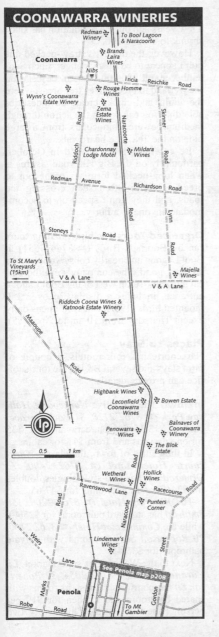

COONAWARRA WINERIES

Redman Winery
To Bool Lagoon & Naracoorte
Brands Laira Wines
Coonawarra
Nibs
Iricia
Reschke Road
Rouge Homme Wines
Wynn's Coonawarra Estate Winery
Zema Estate Wines
Skinner Road
Naracoorte Road
Riddoch Road
Chardonnay Lodge Motel
Mildara Wines
Redman Avenue
Richardson Road
Lynn Road
Stoneys Road
To St Mary's Vineyards (15km)
V & A Lane
Majella Wines
V & A Lane
Riddoch Coona Wines & Katnook Estate Winery
Maroupe Road
Highbank Wines
Leconfield Coonawarra Wines
Bowen Estate
Penowarra Wines
Balnaves of Coonawarra Winery
The Blok Estate
0   0.5   1 km
Wetheral Wines
Hollick Wines
Ravenswood Lane
Racecourse Road
Naracoorte Road
Punters Corner
Lindeman's Wines
Weirs
Street
Lane
See Penola map p208
Marks
Penola
Gordon
Robe Road
To Mt Gambier

THE SOUTH-EAST

NARACOORTE
- pop 4710

Established by Scottish settlers in 1845, this attractive town is the service centre for a rich grazing and agricultural district. Naracoorte is a corruption of the Aboriginal name for a waterhole in the area.

The tourist office (☎ 8762 1518) is at the **Sheep's Back Museum** on MacDonnell St (the Bordertown road). Open daily from 10 am to 4 pm, the museum ($5) is housed in a three storey flour mill (1870) and has interesting displays on the wool industry.

It has a brochure describing a **self-guided historical walk** to 20 sites of interest.

On Jenkins Terrace, the **Naracoorte Museum & Snake Pit** ($8) is worth a visit for its rather higgledy-piggledy collection of everything from fossils to cameras to venomous reptiles. It closes from 25 July to the end of August, but otherwise is open daily from 10 am to 5 pm (2 to 5 pm Sunday). There are daily feeding demonstrations in the snake pit from October to April.

At **Padthaway**, 47km north of town on the Keith road, the **Padthaway Estate winery** has tastings in an old stone shearing shed. The original 1847 settler's cottage is next door.

The nearby **Padthaway Conservation Park** (1000 hectares) is set on a former coastal sand dune.

Naracoorte Caves

The 600 hectare **Naracoorte Caves Conservation Park** (☎ 8762 2340) is 12km southeast of town and off the Penola road. Its limestone caves featured in David Attenborough's *Life on Earth* series, and have earned World Heritage listing thanks to the significance of the Pleistocene mammal fossil deposits in **Victoria Fossil Cave**. Species found include a marsupial lion and a giant koala.

There are four show caves: **Alexandra Cave** (the main attraction), **Blanche Cave**, Victoria Fossil Cave and **Wet Cave**. Wet Cave can be seen without a guide. Tours of the others run daily from 9.30 am to 3.30 pm.

Bat Cave, from which around 250,000 common bent-wing bats make a spectacular departure on summer evenings, isn't open to the public because of its importance as a maternity cave – it's the only one for this species in the SE. Instead, infra-red TV cameras allow you to view the cavern and the fascinating goings-on inside it.

As well as caves the park has attractive bushland, so between caving trips you can go birdwatching and walking. There's also a good cafe and the excellent **Wonambi Fossil Centre**, which has a self-guided tour. The latter, which houses a re-creation of the rainforest environment that covered this area 200,000 years ago, features life-size reconstructions of some of the animals whose bones are found in Victoria Fossil Cave. These are computer controlled and are said to be very life-like. The cost of these tours, including Bat Cave and the Wonambi Fossil Centre, is calculated using a sliding scale: one tour costs $8, two cost $14 and so on.

Yulgibar Wood Gallery, opposite the park's main entrance, is worth a visit for its fine woodcrafts.

Organised Tours Adventure tours of the undeveloped caves are run by the rangers and cost $20 per person for novices (minimum of three) and $180 per party for advanced grades (minimum of three, maximum of six). Overalls and knee-pads can be hired for $5; otherwise wear sneakers or sandshoes and old clothes.

Alternatively, Rock Solid Adventure (☎ 8322 8975, rocksolid@picknowl.com.au) has weekend adventure **caving trips** for $195 per person ex-Adelaide (minimum of six passengers).

Bool Lagoon

There are around 155 bird species, including 79 waterbirds, at the 3100 hectare **Bool Lagoon Game Reserve**, 24km south of Naracoorte. With adjoining **Hacks Lagoon Conservation Park** (2000 hectares), this is one of the SE's best wetland habitats. The chain of shallow freshwater lagoons stretches 14km and covers 3000 hectares.

A diminishing number of brolgas, once widespread in the region, spend the summer

at Bool Lagoon; there were several hundred a few years ago but the population has since shrunk to around 100.

However, the district's straw-necked ibis don't appear to be in any danger. Each September about 200,000 of them descend on the wetland to breed in tea tree areas, where the adults and chicks create an indescribable din. You can watch the action through medium-powered binoculars from a large hide on the Tea Tree boardwalk.

Be careful driving around in October, particularly on the Big Hill road, as this is when long-necked tortoises come out to breed. They're often seen crossing the roads, and they don't speed up to accommodate anyone in a hurry.

Organised Tours The birdwatching tours run by Bourne's Birds (☎ 8764 7551) at Bool Lagoon and nearby conservation parks are very good. The company's ornithological museum, 10km west of the Bool Lagoon entrance, includes a display of over 350 mounted birds (199 species). It opens daily except Thursday from 10 am to 5 pm ($5).

Places to Stay

Naracoorte has four motels, a couple of farm stays and several B&Bs; the tourist office can provide details.

In Town The attractive *Naracoorte Holiday Park (☎ 8762 2128, 81 Park Terrace)* charges $13/15 for tent/caravan sites, $35 for on-site vans and from $41 for cabins.

In the centre of town, the classic *Naracoorte Hotel/Motel (☎ 8762 2400, 73 Ormerod St)*, has pub-style singles/doubles for $24/43 and motel units for $47/65.

The *Kincraig Hotel (☎ 8762 2200, 158 Smith St)* has standard pub rooms for $25/40, while the *Commercial Hotel (☎ 8762 2100, 20 Robertson St)* has rooms with private bathroom for $35/45.

Next to the Woolworths supermarket, *La Eurana House (☎ 8762 2054, 32 Robertson St)* has comfortable upstairs rooms with shared bathroom and kitchen for $19 per person (linen $5 extra). This lovely two storey home was built as a convent in 1903 – no, Mary MacKillop didn't stay here, but one of her relatives did!

Worth mentioning is historic **Dartmoor Homestead** (☎ 8762 0487, dartmoor@rbm .com.au, 30 McLay St), which offers guesthouse-style accommodation in large, tastefully furnished bedrooms. It does traditional B&B for $95/125 with shared facilities ($115/145 with private bathroom). You can also stay in an 1840s settler's cottage.

Out of Town At *Naracoorte Caves*, a pleasant but basic camping area has campsites for $12 per vehicle. You can light a fire here (except during the Fire Danger Period), but you need to bring your own wood.

Bool Lagoon has two grassy camping areas with shade near the park office. Sites cost $12 per vehicle including the park entry fee ($5). Wood fires are not permitted at any time.

Alternatively, you can stay at friendly *Tintagel* (☎ 8764 7491), a traditional B&B on the Penola road 1km south of the Bool Lagoon turn-off – it's about 8.5km from Bool Lagoon. The house is in a large remnant patch of native bush, with several species of native mammals and good birdwatching. It charges $50/75/100 for singles/doubles/triples including a three-course cooked breakfast.

Next door to the *Padthaway Estate* winery (47km north at Padthaway) is an 1882 chateau-style homestead (☎ 8765 5039), where B&B plus a silver-service dinner costs $150 per person.

Places to Eat

Locals recommend the food at the three *pubs*. Alternatively, *Caffe Nostro (31 Robinson St)* has a good reputation; obviously, it specialises in Italian.

Getting There & Around

Premier Stateliner runs daily except Saturday from Adelaide ($36) and Mt Gambier ($13.50).

Naracoorte Taxi (☎ 8762 4111) offers a range of tours to the surrounding district and provides a normal taxi service.

Dukes Highway

The busy Dukes Hwy, from Tailem Bend through Bordertown, provides the most direct route between Adelaide and Melbourne (729km). Most of the country it passes through is scenically uninteresting, but you can take some worthwhile detours along the way to conservation areas and wineries.

The highway generally follows a **gold escort route** that was blazed through the waterless mallee from Wellington, on the lower Murray, to the Bendigo diggings in central Victoria in 1852. Concerned at how the Victorian gold rush was draining its finances, the SA government established a monthly gold escort as part of a short-lived scheme to make Adelaide a financial centre for the goldfields.

Thanks to its mineral-deficient soils, much of the Upper SE was once known as the **Ninety Mile Desert** – a good place to avoid. Development of the district was mainly confined to low-intensity grazing until after WWII, when improved farming practices, including the use of superphosphate and trace elements, brought closer settlement. These days, the 'desert' is a productive mixed farming area.

There are several service towns with good facilities along the highway: Coonalpyn (64km from Tailem Bend), Tintinara (90km), Keith (128km) and Bordertown (177km).

TINTINARA

- **pop 320**

The name of this small railway town is said to come from *tin-tin-yara*, supposedly the Aboriginal name for the stars of Orion's Belt. Tintinara is an access point for **Mt Boothby Conservation Park**, 22km to the west, as is the tiny township of **Coonalpyn** west towards Tailem Bend.

Places to Stay

Historic *Tintinara Homestead* (☎ 8757 2146) has bush camping and shearer's quarters where you can stay. The 930 hectare

THE SOUTH-EAST

property is 6km west of town towards Mt Boothby.

In town, the **Tintinara Motel** (*☎ 8757 2095, 19 Becker Terrace*) has campsites, on-site vans without air-conditioning, and self-contained cabins with air-conditioning. Alternatively, the **Tintinara Hotel** (*☎ 8757 2008, 41 Becker Terrace*) has basic pub rooms.

Near Coonalpyn, **Bayree Farm** (*☎ 8571 1054*) offers B&B in a cottage and self-contained train carriage for $120; the price includes bushwalks (in 400 hectares of mallee bushland) and farm activities. The farm is about 50 minute's drive from the Coorong.

NGARKAT CONSERVATION PARK

A vast sea of mallee and jumbled sandhills, the 262,700 hectare Ngarkat group of conservation parks is 19km east of Tintinara. It's a magnet for 4WD enthusiasts looking for a big place to drive around in. In the west, a network of 4WD tracks between Tintinara and Lameroo takes you for 81km via **Gosse Hill** and **Mt Rescue**. In the east, you can leave the Pinnaroo road at **Pertendi Bore**, 85km north of Bordertown, and detour to Pinnaroo on the 4WD track via **Pine Hut Soak** in the park's north-east.

Other attractions here include solitude, wildflowers (the banksias are stunning in

early spring), walks, relics of the pastoral era and birdwatching (particularly when the mallee and banksia are in flower).

Places to Stay

There are several **bush camping areas**, some of which are at soakages where emus and kangaroos come to drink.

For camping permits and park information contact the ranger at Tintinara on ☎ 8562 3412.

KEITH
* pop 1180

Another access point for the Ngarkat Conservation Park, Keith is at the highway's junction with the Naracoorte road. You can detour to the Padthaway Estate winery, 63km south of Keith towards Naracoorte, then head north-east to Bordertown. Eleven kilometres from Keith, the 93 hectare **Mt Monster Conservation Park** is a prime birdwatching spot in a sea of lucerne paddocks and scattered red gums.

Places to Stay

The **Keith Caravan Park** (*☎ 8755 1851, Naracoorte Rd*) has campsites, on-site vans and basic air-conditioned cabins. Alternatively, there are cottages and powered sites at **Desert Park Farm Stay** (*☎ 8756 7042*), off the highway and 14km east of town.

The **Keith Hotel/Motel** (*☎ 8755 1122, Makin St*) has self-contained pub rooms with air-conditioning ($43/50 single/double) and motel units ($49/57). The **Keith Motor Inn** (*☎ 8755 1500, Dukes Hwy*) charges $60/66 for its units.

BORDERTOWN
* pop 2300

The last (or first) town in SA is at the junction of the highway and the main road from Mt Gambier to the Riverland. Bordertown is the main service centre for the Upper South East.

The main tourist office is in the Tatiara District Council office (*☎ 8752 1044*) at 43 Woolshed St. It opens from 8.30 am to 5 pm weekdays.

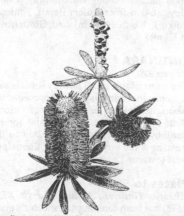

The flowers and seed cone of a coastal banksia

Things to See & Do

Former Australian prime minister RJ (Bob) Hawke was born in Bordertown; there's a bust of Bob outside the town hall, and photos and other memorabilia of him in **Hawke House Museum**, on the corner of Farquhar and Binnie Sts.

On the right as you leave town for Victoria is a **wildlife park** with various Australian species, including rare white kangaroos, lazing behind a fence.

Somewhat more inspiring is historic **Clayton Farm**, 3km south of town on the Kingston SE road. Classified by the National Trust, it has many old-style farming exhibits in and around its original 1870s outbuildings. It opens daily except Saturday from 1 to 5 pm ($4).

Places to Stay & Eat

The **Bordertown Caravan Park** (☎ 8752 1752) has tent/caravan sites for $12/14, on-site vans from $25 and cabins from $45. While it's right on the busy Dukes Hwy, the entrance is off Penny Terrace near the town centre.

On East Terrace, the grand old **Bordertown Hotel** (☎ 8752 1016) has comfortable air-conditioned singles/doubles for $30/50. Its counter meals are considered the best in town.

Bordertown has several transit-style motels. By far the cheapest of these is the **Parklands Motel** (☎ 8752 1622, 105 Park Terrace), where basic units cost $35/45.

Built in 1859, the **Woolshed Inn** (Woolshed St) also does good meals. Most of the town's roadhouses sell fast food.

Barossa Valley

Only 65km from Adelaide, the Barossa Valley is renowned for its excellent wines and German heritage. Colonel William Light named the range on the valley's eastern side the 'Barrosa' after a Peninsula War battle-site in Spain (Barrosa is close to where Spanish sherry comes from). However, a later misspelling changed it to Barossa.

Running north-east for about 25km from Lyndoch to Stockwell, and up to 11km wide, the valley was colonised in 1842 by 25 German families who established the settlement of Bethany. The following year more families settled at Langmeil (now Tanunda).

Small groups continued to arrive over the next 20 years, creating a Lutheran heartland where German traditions persisted well into this century. The signs of this are everywhere. The valley is dotted with the steeples of distinctive little churches, while German-style farmhouses and cottages are common. Other legacies of the early settlers include brass bands and singing societies (*Liedertafel*).

As is so often the case, you must get off the main roads to begin to appreciate the Barossa Valley's true character. Take the scenic drive between Angaston and Tanunda, the palm-fringed road to Seppeltsfield and Marananga, and wander through sleepy Bethany, and you'll see what I mean.

Although the Barossa is promoted as a day-trip destination from Adelaide, you could easily spend several days enjoying the many attractions on offer.

Information

Information Office The very efficient and helpful Barossa Wine & Visitor Centre (☎ 8563 0600, 1800 812 662 toll free, fax 8563 0616, bwta@dove.net.au) is at 66-68 Murray St, Tanunda. It opens weekdays from 9 am to 5 pm and weekends and public holidays from 10 am to 4 pm, or you can check out its website at barossa.mtx.net. The complex includes a wine interpretation

HIGHLIGHTS

- Hop on a bicycle and discover vine-lined back roads, historic Lutheran churches and old German farmhouses

- Look down from the basket of a hot-air balloon over Australia's most famous wine region

- Learn how to nose a pinot noir, swirl a shiraz and savour a semillon at the Barossa wineries

- Eat Bavarian brezel, pastries baked in a wood-fired oven and quaff quan-dong mead

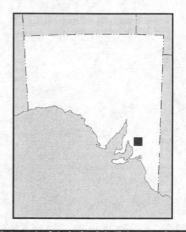

centre (admission $2) designed to educate visitors about wine making.

Books & Maps *Explore the Barossa*, by the Royal Geographical Society of Australia (SA), is an excellent guidebook. It has a swag of general information, including natural and social history, and descriptions of town and country walks and drives. Also

BAROSSA VALLEY WINERIES

1 Wolf Blass	12 Saltram Wine Estate	22 Old Barn Wines	32 Orlando
2 The Willows Vineyard	13 Yalumba	23 Basedow Wines	33 Liebichwein
3 Elderton Wines	14 Tarchalice Winery	24 Barossa Wine &	34 Miranda Wines
4 Penfolds; Tarac	15 Hardy's Siegersdorf	Visitor Centre	35 Jenke Vineyard Cellars
5 Branson Wines	16 Chateau Dorrien	25 Turkey Flat Vineyards	36 Charles Cimicky Wines
6 Greenock Creek Cellars	17 Stanley Brothers	26 Bethany Wines	37 Chateau Tanunda
7 Seppelts	18 Richmond Grove Barossa	27 Krondorf	38 Kies Family Wines
8 Gnadenfrei Estate;	Winery	28 Charles Melton Wines	39 Kellermeister Wines
Viking Wines	19 Peter Lehmann	29 Rockford Wines	40 Barossa Settlers
9 Heritage Wines	20 Langmeil Winery	30 St Hallett Wines	41 Twin Valley Estate
10 Kaesler Estate	21 Veritas	31 Grant Burge Wines	42 Mountadam Winery
11 Barossa Cottage Wines			

BAROSSA VALLEY

good is the Royal Automobile Association of South Australia's (RAA's) *Adelaide Region* guide, which includes the Barossa ($15 members, $30 nonmembers).

Barossa Journeys: Into a Valley of Tradition, by Noris Ioannou, is required reading for the cultural tourist.

The tourist office has free road maps that show most the wineries. The RAA's *Central North* map includes the Barossa and access routes from Adelaide, but its scale is too small to be useful around the valley. A much better one is the Office of Recreation & Sport's cycle-touring map *Barossa Valley* – it encompasses the valley and extends as far as Springton, Gawler and Kapunda.

The Department of Environment, Heritage & Aboriginal Affairs has a colourful souvenir map with plenty of illustrations and information.

Wineries

Johann Gramp planted the valley's first grapes on his property at Jacob Creek in 1847, and produced the first wine three years later. However, the industry saw only slow growth until the 1890s, when phylloxera disease devastated vineyards in the eastern colonies. As a result, plantings in the Barossa increased dramatically; it became Australia's major wine producer after tariffs were removed following Federation in 1901.

Today, local wineries, with their many varieties of reds and whites produced from pure Barossa fruit, dominate Australian wine shows. The valley is best known for shiraz, with riesling the most important of its whites. There are over 50 wineries ranging from boutiques to huge complexes, the latter mostly owned by multinationals. Almost all are open to the public for free wine tastings; the visitor centre has a brochure giving locations and opening hours.

Following are some well-known (and some not so well-known) wineries:

Basedow Wines, in Murray St, Tanunda, is within walking distance of the town centre. The wine tasting area, which is in a real cellar lined with barrels, has a great atmosphere.

Bethany Wines, Bethany Rd, Bethany, is a small family-operated winery in a scenic location. Its white port is highly recommended.

Branson Wines, Seppeltsfield Rd near Greenock, is one of the valley's newest small wineries. It's already earning a fine reputation for its semillons and full-bodied reds.

Chateau Dorrien, on the highway between Tanunda and Nuriootpa, has tastings of wine and mead – its quandong liqueur mead is a knockout. A series of colourful murals painted on wine vats tells the story of the Barossa.

Chateau Yaldara, Lyndoch, was established in 1947 in the ruins of an older winery and flour mill. It has a notable antique collection that can be seen on conducted tours ($4).

Kellermeister, near Lyndoch, has a good range of wines that can only be bought at the cellar door. One worth tasting is its chocolate port.

Orlando, Rowland Flat, between Lyndoch and Tanunda, was established in 1847 and is one of the valley's oldest wineries. This is the place to try the famous Jacob's Creek label.

Peter Lehmann Wines, Para Rd, Tanunda is a large, family-owned winery set by the Para River. You can buy a bottle at the cellar door and enjoy it on a picnic in the grounds.

Rockford Wines, Krondorf Rd near Tanunda, is another small, family-owned winery noted for its full-bodied wines. Its intimate tasting room is in a historic stable.

Saltram Wine Estate, Angaston, is another old winery. Established in 1859, it's set in beautiful gardens.

Seppelts, at Seppeltsfield, was founded in 1852. Its old bluestone buildings are surrounded by gardens and date palms, and there's a Grecian mausoleum on the road in. This extensive complex includes a picnic area with gas barbecues. Tours cost $4.

Yalumba, Angaston, dates from 1849 and is Australia's largest family-owned wine company – in the Barossa it's the only major winery still in family ownership. The old winery is topped by a clocktower and surrounded by gardens.

Few wineries have restaurants, mainly because there are too many others in opposition, but those that do are all of a high standard. They include *Kaesler Estate* (near Nuriootpa), *Chateau Yaldara* (Lyndoch), *Saltram* (Angaston) and *Gnadenfrei* (Marananga). Also check out *Chateau Dorrien*, between Tanunda and Nuriootpa,

Wine Tasting

There are a few terms and practices in wine tasting that are worth knowing if you don't want to act like a complete ignoramus. For starters, perhaps the most important principle is be true to your own impressions. Trust yourself; you at least know whether you like it or not.

Whether seriously appraising or simply tasting a wine, consider these three elements: colour and appearance, nose, and palate.

Colour & Appearance Use a clean, clear glass in good light and examine the wine's colour and appearance by holding it against a white background.

White wines vary in colour from water white to intense gold depending on age, grape variety and wine making techniques. It should not be brown. A red wine will generally progress from crimson through brick red to tawny as it ages. In all but aged wines and especially with white wines, the colour should be brilliant and clear with no deposit.

Nose When nosing a wine, preferably use a glass with a tapered mouth. This assists in concentrating the volatile aromas rising from the wine. Your nose is a particularly potent sensory organ – accordingly it is essential to remember that we smell much of what we would describe as 'tastes'. Characteristics such as 'berries', 'spicy' or 'wood' are not tasted in the mouth, but registered through the nose. (You only have to hold your nose to prove it, or remember how things have no taste when you have a cold.) The wine's nose should have several pleasant smells and be free of any obvious rank odours.

Palate Your tongue and mouth can basically only detect four taste sensations. These are salt, sweetness, bitterness and acid, and they are apparent on different areas of the tongue. Your palate is used to qualify the expectations of the wine's colour and nose. When ideally 'savouring' a wine in your mouth, consider the wine's balance. The amount of fruit must be in balance with the acids and tannins.

Persistence of flavour is a major virtue of any wine. The longer it lasts, the greater the pleasure. A very easy test of how 'good' a wine is is its persistence of flavour.

One important lesson: a wine that is not good to begin with will not 'come good in a couple of years'. Good wine gets better. Poor wine gets worse.

Finally, if you want to purchase a bottle of wine to accompany your meal, it is usually best to select one that matches the cuisine. For example a fresh, herbaceous sauvignon blanc or semillon with warm salads, more robust white wines such as wood-aged chardonnay with pasta, lighter red styles such as pinot noir with rich chicken dishes, rich opulent reds such as shiraz and cabernet sauvignon with hearty roasts and barbecued foods. Desserts are complemented by luscious botrytised rieslings and semillons.

Adam Marks

BAROSSA VALLEY

which, at the time of writing, was planning to reopen its bistro.

The Vines New vines are planted in September and October and take four to five years to reach maturity (their useful life is usually around 40 years). The vines are pruned back heavily during the winter months (July to August), then grow fruit over the summer for harvesting from March to early May.

Special Events

There's at least one festival or some other event on every month except December.

The colourful Barossa Vintage Festival – one of SA's big events – takes place over seven days starting on Easter Monday in odd-numbered years. It features processions, music (including brass bands), tug-of-war contests between the wineries, maypole dancing, traditional dinners and, of course, a lot of wine tasting.

The format of the Barossa Classic Gourmet, held over five days in August or September, was being changed at the time of this update – while the previous format had proved popular, drunks were too much of a handful. Check with the South Australian Tourism Commission (SATC) or the Barossa Wine & Visitor Centre.

The Barossa International Music Festival in October is two weeks of picnics, wine, theatre and big-name bands playing jazz, rock and classical music. Barossa Under the Stars, held in January or February, features night picnics and top entertainment.

Other events worthy of note include the German Oompah Fest in February and the Barossa Hot Air Balloon Regatta in May.

Organised Tours

The major operators offering day tours from Adelaide are Premier Stateliner (☎ 8415 5566), Festival Tours (☎ 8374 1270) and Adelaide Sightseeing (☎ 8231 4144). Smaller operators include Prime Mini Tours (☎ 8293 4900), Groovy Grape (☎ 8395 4422) and Busway (☎ 8262 6900). Busway visits four/six wineries for $35/45.

A handful of local operators offer tours of the Barossa. Valley Tours (☎ 8563 3587) charges from $37 for the day, including visits to several wineries and a two-course winery lunch. If cost is no object, Fruits of Inheritance (☎ 8563 3483, fruit@dove .net.au) is excellent value from $150 per person; its friendly, down-to-earth, tailormade tours can include private wine tastings, bushwalks and church tours conducted by Lutheran pastors.

Ecotrek (☎ 8383 7198) and Rolling On (☎ 8358 2401) have cycling tours around the wineries on weekends.

A one hour, hot-air balloon flight with Balloon Adventures (☎ 8389 3195) costs $210, including a champagne picnic breakfast.

Sadly, health and safety regulations have killed off the winery tours that were once so popular. While Seppeltsfield and Chateau Yaldara have tours, these have a heritage bias and are not of working wineries.

Accommodation

The Barossa Valley has plenty of accommodation, including YHA and backpacker hostels, several caravan parks, hotels, generally pricey motels, and a large and growing number of B&Bs. The latter are mainly over $100 for doubles (you cook your own breakfast at most places), and prices tend to soar at weekends and during festivals. Barossa B&B Booking Service (☎ 8524 4873, 1800 244 873, bookings@dove.net .au) lists a number of properties.

If accommodation in the valley is booked out, you may be able to find something at Gawler or Kapunda. Both towns are only a short drive from the action.

Getting There & Away

There are several routes from Adelaide to the valley. The most direct is via Main North Rd through Elizabeth and Gawler, but if you're in no hurry, try the more interesting and picturesque routes through the Torrens Gorge and Williamstown, or via Birdwood and Springton. The latter takes you past several wineries in the Eden Valley – see the Adelaide Hills chapter for details.

If you're coming from the east and want to tour the wineries before hitting Adelaide, the scenic drive from Mannum via Springton and Eden Valley to Angaston is recommended.

Bus The Barossa Adelaide Passenger Service (☎ 8564 3022) runs from Adelaide via Williamstown and Gawler. It has three services daily on weekdays (fewer on weekends and most public holidays), and visits Lyndoch ($8), Tanunda ($10.50), Nuriootpa ($11) and Angaston ($12).

Train The *Bluebird* railcar leaves the Adelaide suburban train station for Tanunda on Tuesday, Thursday and Sunday mornings and costs $55 return ($40 one way). It spends about five hours in Tanunda before making the return journey.

Getting Around
Taxi & Car Rental The Barossa Taxi Service (☎ 8563 3600, 019 697 490) has a 24-hour-a-day service throughout the valley. From Tanunda it costs around $15 to Angaston and $10 to Nuriootpa.

Alternatively, you can rent a sedan from the Caltex service station (☎ 8563 2677), on Murray St in Tanunda, for $65 per day for up to 150km.

Bicycles You can rent a bike from the Bunkhaus Travellers Hostel in Nuriootpa, the Zinfandel Tea Rooms and the Tanunda Caravan & Tourist Park in Tanunda, and the Barossa Caravan Park in Lyndoch.

There's plenty of potential for cyclists, with many interesting routes and gradients varying from easy to challenging. A cycle path runs between Nuriootpa and Tanunda, passing the Bunkhaus Travellers Hostel en route.

LYNDOCH
• pop 960
Coming up from Adelaide via Gawler, you arrive in the Barossa Valley at Lyndoch, at the foot of the scenic Barossa Range.

Off Yettie Rd, about 7km south-east of Lyndoch, the Barossa Reservoir has the famous **Whispering Wall**. The acoustics of this massive curved structure are such that you can stand at one end and listen to a normal conversation taking place at the other, 150m away.

Places to Stay & Eat
Barossa Caravan Park (☎ 8524 4262), 2km out on the Barossa Valley Hwy to Gawler, has tent/caravan sites from $10/15, on-site vans from $25 and self-contained cabins from $45. It hires out well-maintained mountain bikes for $10 per day.

On the edge of Sandy Creek Conservation Park, about 3.5km south of town on the Cockatoo Valley road, *The Vale* YHA hostel is a restored stone farmhouse with views of vineyards and bush. Beds are $9 for members and you obtain a key from YHA in Adelaide.

The *Chateau Yaldara Motor Inn* (☎ 8524 4268, Barossa Valley Hwy), on the Gawler side of Lyndoch, has well-appointed units from $75/83.

On the Barossa Valley Hwy in town, the wonderful *Lyndoch Bakery & Restaurant* is one of the valley's three German-style bakeries (the others are at Greenock and Tanunda). The nearby *Lyndoch Hotel* has good-value counter meals.

TANUNDA
• pop 3100
In the centre of the Barossa, this is the most Germanic of the valley's towns and the acknowledged tourist centre. Many of its highlights are on Murray St, the main road through town.

Things to See & Do
Tanunda has numerous historic buildings including the early cottages around Goat Square, on John St. This was the *ziegenmarkt*, a meeting and market place laid out in 1842 as the original centre of Tanunda.

There are some interesting Lutheran churches. The **Tabor Church** in Murray St dates from 1849. In Jane Place, the 1868 **St John's Church** has life-size wooden statues of Christ, Moses, and the apostles Peter,

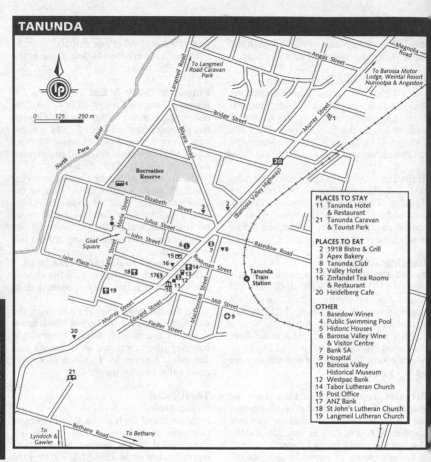

TANUNDA

0   125   250 m

To Langmeil
Road Caravan
Park

To Barossa Motor
Lodge, Weintal Resort
Nuriootpa & Angaston

Magnolia
Road

Angas Street

Langmeil Road

Bridge Street

Bilyara Road

Murray Street

(Barossa Valley Highway)

North Para River

Recreation
Reserve

Elizabeth   Street

Julius Street

Maria Street

John Street

Goat
Square

Maria Street

Jane Place

Bushman Street

Basedow Road

Tanunda
Train
Station

Murray Street

Edward Street

Fiedler Street

MacDonnell Street

Mill Street

To
Lyndoch &
Gawler

Bethany Road

To Bethany

PLACES TO STAY
11 Tanunda Hotel
     & Restaurant
21 Tanunda Caravan
     & Tourist Park

PLACES TO EAT
2 1918 Bistro & Grill
3 Apex Bakery
8 Tanunda Club
13 Valley Hotel
16 Zinfandel Tea Rooms
     & Restaurant
20 Heidelberg Cafe

OTHER
1 Basedow Wines
4 Public Swimming Pool
5 Historic Houses
6 Barossa Valley Wine
     & Visitor Centre
7 Bank SA
9 Hospital
10 Barossa Valley
     Historical Museum
12 Westpac Bank
14 Tabor Lutheran Church
15 Post Office
17 ANZ Bank
18 St John's Lutheran Church
19 Langmeil Lutheran Church

Paul and John; these were donated in 1892. The **Langmeil Lutheran Church**, in Maria St, is associated with Pastor Kavel, who arrived in SA in 1838 and was its first Lutheran minister.

At 47 Murray St the **Barossa Valley Historical Museum**, in the old telegraph station (1866), has exhibits on the valley's early days. These include a 'church room' with a beautiful marble altar from the Immanuel Lutheran Church at Bower. It opens daily from 11 am to 5 pm (Sunday 1 to 5 pm).

Brauer Biotherapies, at 1 Para Rd, produces homeopathic medicines and remedies for local consumption and export throughout the world. Free tours (30 to 45 minutes) are conducted throughout the day on weekdays (☎ 8563 2932).

On the Barossa Valley Hwy about halfway between Tanunda and Nuriootpa, the excellent **Kev Rohrlach Technology & Heritage Centre** ($8, see the Barossa Valley Map) features an amazing collection of everything from postcards and aerospace ckets to steam engines. It opens from 11 am to 4 pm daily (10 am to 5 pm on Sunday and public holidays); allow at least an hour to do it justice.

Three kilometres out on the Gomersal Road, trained sheepdogs go through their paces at **Breezy Gully farm** at 2 pm on Monday, Wednesday and Saturday. Admission costs $6 and is well worth it.

For children, **Storybook Cottage**, off the highway towards Lyndoch, has hands-on models and a rabbit warren where they can play at being Peter the Rabbit. **Kiddy Park**, on the corner of Menge Rd and Magnolia Rd, has a minizoo, train rides, a playground and other amusements – it only opens on weekends and public and school holidays.

Murray St has several good **antique shops** and **arts & crafts** outlets.

From Tanunda, take the scenic route to Angaston through Bethany and via **Mengler Hill**. It runs through beautiful rural country featuring huge gums; the view over the valley from Mengler Hill is superb if you can ignore the unfortunate 'sculpture park' in the foreground. If you're cycling, travel in the opposite direction.

En route, the 390 hectare **Kaiser Stuhl Conservation Park** has walking tracks and attractive bush on top of the Barossa Range. The turn-off is about 1km towards Angaston from Mengler Hill, and the tiny carpark is 1km farther on.

Places to Stay

Tanunda The *Tanunda Caravan & Tourist Park* (☎ 8563 2784, Barossa Valley Way) is an attractive place 1km out of town towards Lyndoch. It has tent/caravan sites for $11/14, on-site vans from $27, basic cabins for $35 and self-contained cabins for $45. You can rent well-maintained bicycles for $12 per day.

Alternatively, if you're camping, you can try the much more basic *Langmeil Road Caravan Park* (☎ 8563 0095, 70 Langmeil Rd). It's by the pretty North Para River about 1km from the town centre, and has powered and unpowered sites.

The *Tanunda Hotel* (☎ 8563 2030, 51 Murray St) has singles/doubles with private

bathroom for $54/60 (it charges $44/50 without).

Towards Nuriootpa, the *Barossa Motor Lodge* (☎ 8563 2988, 182 Murray St) charges $79/87. The *Barossa Weintal Resort* (☎ 1800 648 269) is 400m farther on and charges from $85/95/115.

Halfway between Tanunda and Nuriootpa, the *Barossa Junction Motel* (☎ 8563 3400) has a train theme; its units, which are in converted carriages, cost from $69/79/95 a single/double/triple.

Seppeltsfield About 1km from the Seppelts winery, *Seppeltsfield Holiday Cabins* (☎ 8562 8240, Seppeltsfield Rd) has self-contained cabins with wood fires and air-con from $60 (a single or double) for one night and $55 a night for two nights. Deluxe cabins with spas and saunas cost from $99.

Right at Seppeltsfield, *The Lodge Country House* (☎ 8562 8277, thelodge@dove.net.au) is a licensed guesthouse with luxury accommodation. B&B for couples is $255, with a silver-service dinner $100 extra (alcohol not included).

Places to Eat

Connoisseurs of country bakeries should head straight to the *Apex Bakery (Elizabeth St)*. This traditional bakery with a German bias produces a variety of breads, pastries and cakes in a wood-fired oven.

There are plenty of good places to eat on Murray St. Two German institutions are the *Heidelberg Cafe* at No 8 and the *Zinfandel Tea Rooms & Restaurant* at No 58. The former is open for lunch and dinner, while the latter does breakfast and lunch. Both are reasonably priced.

Counter meals are offered by the *Tanunda Hotel* at No 51 and *The Valley Hotel* at No 73, while the *1918 Bistro & Grill*, at No 94, has a trendy atmosphere and prices to match – the sound of mobile phones can be a turn off at lunchtime.

The *Tanunda Club (45 MacDonnell St)* sells good hearty meals from around $6. It opens for lunch and dinner seven days a week.

BAROSSA VALLEY

Finally there's the *Siegersdorf Wine Co & Restaurant (Barossa Valley Way)*, about halfway between Tanunda and Nuriootpa. This place does three-course lunches for $10 and dinners for $12; this is cheaper than most pubs, and the food is better. It has open fires in winter, and in warm weather you can eat al fresco on the lawns.

NURIOOTPA
* pop 3500

At the northern end of the valley, Nuriootpa is the commercial centre of the Barossa Valley. There are pleasant picnic areas along the **Para River**, which winds through town.

Luhrs Cottage is a delightful little dwelling in the hamlet of **Lights Pass**, about 3km east of Nuriootpa. Built in 1846 of mud and straw, it's now a museum (open weekdays from 9.30 am to 3.30 pm and weekends from 10 am to 4 pm). There's a school museum and ancient farm implements out the back.

The **Barossa Quilt Centre**, on the Angaston road, is the place to go if you're into quilting.

Places to Stay & Eat
The attractive *Barossa Valley Tourist Park (☎ 8562 1404, barpark@dove.net.au, Penrice Rd)* has tent/caravan sites for $12/15, basic cabins for $30 and self-contained cabins from $40.

Just off the Sturt Hwy 1.5km north of town, the basic (and shabby) *Barossa Gateway Motel & Hostel (☎ 8562 1033, Kalimna Rd)* has a lodge section with kitchen where beds in twin rooms with private facilities cost $10 per person ($14 if you want a room to yourself). Otherwise there are motel units for $36 a single or double. This place is chock-a-block with workers when grape picking and vine pruning are in full swing.

Much nicer is the *Bunkhaus Travellers Hostel (☎ 8562 2260, Nuraip Rd)*, set on a vineyard 1km from town on the highway to Tanunda (look for the keg on the corner). This is a very pleasant and welcoming place with dorm beds for $12, plus a comfortable cottage where a double bed costs from $36.

Mountain bikes can be hired for $8 per day, and Jan Matthew, the proprietor, will help you plan an outing.

Another friendly, good-value place in this area is *Karawatha Guesthouse (☎ 8562 1746)*, about halfway between Nuriootpa and Greenock. It's clean and comfortable, with rooms with private bathroom costing from $45/70 for B&B – you eat with the very down-to-earth owners. They will also make you up a lunchtime picnic hamper if you want.

Back in town, the *Vine Inn Hotel/Motel (☎ 8562 2133, 14 Murray St)* has executive-style units for $80/95/110 a single/double/triple. The *Top of the Valley Motel (☎ 8562 2111, 49 Murray St)* charges $58/63/73.

On the outskirts of town towards Tanunda, the *Kaesler Estate Restaurant* has great food that you can eat outside in a lovely garden setting. Mains cost from around $16.

The *Angus Park Hotel* and the *Vine Inn* are best for meals if you're on a budget; otherwise there are several eateries on the main street.

ANGASTON
* pop 2000

On the eastern side of the Barossa Valley, this picturesque town was named after George Fife Angas, one of the area's pioneers. Unlike its two neighbours it has managed to retain a strong rural flavour.

About 7km from town towards Springton, the magnificent **Collingrove Homestead** shows how the other half once lived. Built by George Angas' son, John, in 1856, it's now owned by the National Trust and is furnished with the family's original antiques. The homestead and gardens are open weekdays from 1 to 4.30 pm and weekends and festival days from 11 am to 4.30 pm. Admission is $4.

Bethany Arts & Crafts, in the old police station on the corner of Fife and Washington Sts, is one of the best of its genre in the valley, if not country SA. It often holds exhibitions.

Postcard scenes along Main North Road near Laura, once home to poet CJ Dennis

Auburn's streets recall the 1870s, when it was an important commercial hub in the Clare Valley.

DENIS O'BYRNE

Kanyaka Homestead, near Hawker, saw better days when the region grew the colony's finest wheat

RICHARD I'ANSON

The long and winding yellow dirt road through Bunyeroo Valley, Flinders Ranges National Park

This Lutheran church is a fine example of the German influence on local architecture

At 3 Murray St, the **Angas Park Fruit Company** has a promotion centre where you can purchase an amazing variety of dried and glacé fruits, nuts, chocolates and other confectionery. The products aren't necessarily cheaper than in the shops, but they are fresher.

Places to Stay & Eat

Angaston is normally much quieter than Tanunda, so in busy times check here for accommodation before going farther afield.

The *Barossa Valley Hotel (☎ 8564 2014, 41 Murray St)* and the *Angaston Hotel (☎ 8564 2428, 59 Murray St)* both have basic pub rooms and charge $20/$25 per person with breakfast.

Two kilometres out of town, the friendly *Vineyards Motel (☎ 8564 2404, Stockwell Rd)* has standard units starting at $49/55 for a single/double and deluxe units at $55/65; its family rooms sleep four and cost $80.

Across the road, *Vintners Restaurant* serves elegant meals, with mains for around $17. It opens daily for lunch and every day but Sunday for dinner.

For something cheaper in the food line, *Roaring Fordies (Murray St)* is a bakery, cafe and licensed steakhouse where mains cost from $9. It's very popular with locals, as is the *Alphorn Swiss Restaurant* across the street.

The *Saltram Bistro*, at Saltram's winery, does lunch daily with mains from $9.

If you really want to pamper yourself, the acclaimed *Collingrove Homestead (☎ 8564 2061)* has B&B accommodation in antique-furnished rooms in the old servants' quarters for $160 a double.

OTHER BAROSSA TOWNS
Bethany
- pop 70

The site of the first German settlement in the Barossa, this sleepy hamlet is about 5km from Tanunda on Bethany Rd. You can stroll along the tree-lined avenue admiring its historic dwellings, which include the tiny **Landhaus**. Built of stone, mud and straw in the 1840s, it is now a licensed restaurant seating 12 diners; the first resident was a shepherd and, judging by the height of the lintels, not a very tall one.

Also worth a visit is the little **cemetery**, which has headstones in Gothic script dating from the 1860s. The depressing number of children's graves illustrates the hardships faced by the early settlers.

Stockwell
- pop 400

This quiet English-like village is at the northern end of the valley about 9km from Nuriootpa. It has many old stone buildings, including **St Thomas Lutheran Church**. On a cold, wet day, the Stockwell Hotel is the cosiest pub in the valley.

Williamstown
* pop 850

In the Barossa Range 8km south of Lyndoch, picturesque Williamstown is on an alternative scenic drive between Adelaide and the Barossa Valley.

The 1410 hectare **Para Wirra Recreation Park**, which has good walking trails, views, picnic areas and tennis courts, is 5km east of town. At the park's northern end, the **Barossa Gold Field** was the scene of a frantic rush in the late 1860s when 4000 diggers descended on the scene. The frenzy soon fizzled out, although gold continued to be mined into the 1930s. There's a walking trail around the diggings.

Three kilometres south-east of Williamstown, the hilly 191 hectare **Hale Conservation Park** is good for walks and birdwatching. You can walk from here to the nearby **Warren Conservation Park** (363 hectares), which is traversed by the **Heysen Trail**.

Places to Stay In Williamstown you can stay at *Queen Victoria Jubilee Park (☎ 8524 6363, Springton Rd)*, a small caravan park with tent/caravan sites for $10/13, on-site vans for $28 and self-contained cabins for $45.

About 5km north of Kersbrook (20km south of Lyndoch), on the road from Torrens Gorge to Williamstown, the *Kersbrook YHA Hostel* has beds costing $9 for members. It's in the grounds of a National Trust property called **Roachdale**, which has an interesting nature walk through a rare patch of pristine native forest. Contact YHA in Adelaide (☎ 8231 5583) for bookings and a key.

Gawler
* pop 14,000

On Main North Rd, 43km from Adelaide and 33km south-west of Nuriootpa, this fast-growing dormitory and service centre was the second country town established in SA. There are a number of **heritage sites**, including some 1840s cottages, and you can visit them using the brochure *Gawler Walking Tours*.

The tourist office (☎ 8522 6814, fax 8522 6817, visitor.centre@gawler.sa.gov.au) is at 2 Lyndoch Rd. It opens daily at 8.30 am, closing at 5.30 pm, or you can check out its website at www.gawler.sa.gov.au.

Gawler is a jumping-off point for the Barossa Valley and may have accommodation available when the valley is full. The town has three caravan parks, of which the *Gawler Caravan Park (☎ 8522 3805, Main North Rd)* is recommended. The *South End Hotel (☎ 8522 1065, 23 Murray St)* has basic pub rooms for $25/35; otherwise there's a motel and several B&Bs.

The Mid-North

Stretching from the Barossa Valley in the south to Port Pirie and Jamestown in the north, the Mid-North is a region of rolling hills and plains almost entirely covered by a patchwork of farms. To the west it butts onto Yorke Peninsula, while to the east of Burra and Eudunda it fades into the more arid Murraylands. There are some beautiful timbered areas in the hills, but often the landscape is entirely treeless. Much of the Mid-North was open grassland at the time of European settlement, and farmers and miners created more.

Tourism, an important (if localised) industry, is centred on the region's old copper-mining towns and Clare Valley wineries. There are also many wonderful colonial buildings at places like Auburn, Bungaree and Mintaro. Apart from that, the region has numerous small, friendly towns that don't appear to have changed much since their heyday of last century.

European History
The explorer Edward John Eyre crossed the northern part of the region in 1839 and found rich grazing land. His glowing reports attracted squatters, and by the mid-1840s almost the entire Mid-North was taken up by huge runs. One of the first people on the scene was George Hawker, who established Bungaree Station in 1841 with 2000 ewes. By the early 1850s the station covered nearly 700 sq km and had a flock of 100,000 sheep.

The second major development was the discovery of rich copper lodes at Kapunda (1842) and Burra (1845). Miners and their families – mostly Cornish but also Welsh and German – flocked to the area in their thousands. It was Australia's first mining rush and put the infant colony of SA on its feet.

Railways followed the miners, and by the 1860s the great runs were being broken up into farms. The resulting wheat boom brought a wave of prosperity and many

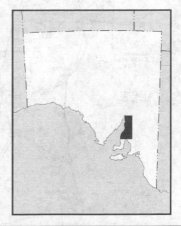

towns were established. Today the Mid-North is the heartland of SA agriculture, with wool, beef and grain being its major products.

Information
Tourist Offices The main tourist offices are at Burra, Clare and Port Pirie; see the sections on these towns for details.

THE MID-NORTH

227

THE MID-NORTH

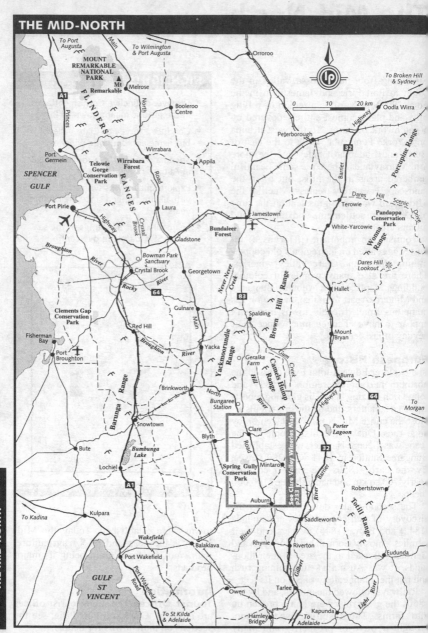

SA's tourism authorities have decided to lump together the Mid-North and Yorke Peninsula and market them as 'Classic Country'. This is the name to look for in promotional material.

Books & Maps The Royal Automobile Association of South Australia (RAA) has a comprehensive travel guide called *Flinders Ranges & Mid North* ($15 members, $30 nonmembers).

In addition, its road map of the Mid-North is by far the best available. The Office of Recreation & Sport's larger-scale cycle touring map *Lower Mid-North* covers the area from Riverton to Clare and Burra.

Organised Tours

There are several tour operators in and around Burra, and the Burra tourist office runs tours throughout the Mid-North. Otherwise there is very little on offer – Festival Tours (☎ 8374 1270, 1800 634 724 toll free) does a weekly day tour from Adelaide to the Clare Valley for $54.

Accommodation

Burra, the Clare Valley and Port Pirie have plenty of accommodation, including B&Bs. Elsewhere, most of the larger towns have a caravan park and a pub or two, and there are motels along Highway 1. There's backpacker-style accommodation in or near Clare, Crystal Brook and Port Pirie.

Getting There & Away

Bute Buses' Mid-North Passenger Service (☎ 8826 2346) has the most comprehensive service. Departing from Adelaide, it visits the Clare Valley, Jamestown and Peterborough daily except Monday and Saturday, Burra and Orroroo on Wednesday and Friday, and Gladstone on Tuesday and Thursday.

Premier Stateliner (☎ 8415 5555) runs four times a day from Adelaide to Port Augusta, calling in to towns along Hwy 1.

Greyhound Pioneer's daily service from Adelaide to Sydney runs up the Barrier Hwy.

See the sections on Kapunda and Port Wakefield for details of services to those towns.

Highway 1

Hwy 1 is by far the best bet if you're in a hurry to get to the north. However, there's always the risk of being stuck behind a road train past Lochiel, where single-trailer semis pick up an extra trailer for the long haul to Darwin or Perth.

ST KILDA

Just 30 minutes from Adelaide, this seaside hamlet has the excellent **St Kilda Mangrove Trail** and interpretive centre (☎ 8280 8172, ecoart@camtech.net.au), which highlight the ecology of SA's mangrove forests. Great flocks of waders (mainly spoonbills) descend on the mangroves to breed in early summer – you can view the goings-on from hides along the 1.7km boardwalk. In late summer and March the birds leave and the mosquitoes take over.

The centre opens daily from 10 am to 3 pm (5 pm on weekends) and admission is $6; guided walks are conducted on weekends and public and school holidays.

PORT WAKEFIELD
* **pop 500**

It's a mistake to judge Port Wakefield by the plethora of ugly roadhouses, motels and fast-food joints out on Hwy 1. Only 100km from Adelaide, this sleepy historic town was established in 1850 as the port for the Burra mine. The boom times for Port Wakefield ended when the mine closed in 1877.

A self-guided **heritage walk** will take you to 34 sites. These include the diminutive **Bubners Inn**, once a stop on the stagecoach run from Adelaide to Wallaroo. There is also a group of classic 1860s **cottages**, and a police station and courthouse (1858).

Balaklava (pop 1300) is about 25km east of Port Wakefield on the Auburn road and also has many fine old buildings. There are two National Trust **museums** as well as the

THE MID-NORTH

Courthouse Gallery, which receives some excellent travelling exhibitions.

Places to Stay

Port Wakefield The *Port Wakefield Caravan Park (☎ 8867 1151, Wakefield St)* is shaded and pleasant despite being on the edge of the mangroves. It has powered and unpowered sites, on-site vans and cabins.

Alternatively, the *Port Wakefield Hotel (☎ 8867 1016, Burra St)* has basic pub rooms for $20 per person.

Balaklava The basic *Balaklava Caravan Park (☎ 8862 1261, Short Terrace)* has powered sites for $9.

Otherwise you can stay at the grand 1870s *Royal Hotel (☎ 8862 1607, 9 Edith Terrace)* – it has comfortable rooms with shared facilities for $25/45 a single/double, including a light breakfast. The much more basic *Terminus Hotel (☎ 8862 1006, Railway Terrace)* charges $14 per person.

Getting There & Away

The Yorke Peninsula Passenger Service (☎ 1800 625 099 toll free) visits daily on its run from Adelaide to Ardrossan and beyond ($12).

REDHILL
- pop 200

This quiet little place is on Hwy 1 about 75km north of Port Wakefield. Its main claim to fame is up in the local rubbish dump, where a **geological monument** is reputed to mark the southern end (geologically speaking) of the Flinders Ranges.

Redhill Relics in the main street is worth a browse for its bric-a-brac and collectables.

The friendly 1870s *Eureka Hotel (☎ 8636 7120, Bowman St)* has comfortable beds in basic pub rooms for $15, and does counter meals daily.

CRYSTAL BROOK
- pop 2000

In 1839 the explorer Edward John Eyre stopped for a drink at a gurgling stream, and was so impressed by the clarity of the water

that he gave it this lovely name. Maybe the water isn't so clean today, but many of the huge river red gums that Eyre saw along the creek are still there.

The National Trust's two-storey **Old Bakehouse Museum** ($2) on Brandis St has displays on local history and the household effects of various pioneers; it's open from 2 to 4 pm on Sunday and public holidays.

The site of one of the district's earliest homesteads, **Bowman Park**, is in a beautiful valley 5km north-east of town. It's a popular recreation area and an access point for the Heysen Trail.

Places to Stay

Near town on the Port Pirie road, the basic *Crystal Brook Caravan Park (☎ 8636 2640)* has ancient gum trees and good shade. Alternatively, the *Crystal Brook Hotel (☎ 8636 2023, Railway Terrace)* has pub rooms for $20/35 a single/double.

At *Bowman Park (☎ 8636 2116)* you can camp among huge gums at a bush camping area for $3 per person. There's also a dormitory with kitchen ($7 per person), a B&B ($35 per couple) and a licensed restaurant.

Getting There & Away

Premier Stateliner calls in daily en route from Adelaide to Port Augusta ($24).

PORT PIRIE
- pop 15,100

Port Pirie, 231km north of Adelaide, is an industrial centre with a huge silver, lead and zinc smelter which processes ore from Broken Hill. Established on mudflats as an unofficial loading point for nearby sheep stations in 1847, it became a focus for new railways that tapped its hinterland in the 1870s. The settlement really took off when the first smelting works started up in 1888.

Unfortunately, your first impression of Port Pirie isn't likely to be a favourable one. Driving into town from Hwy 1, the skyline is an unsightly jumble of power pylons, belching chimneys and banks of huge grain silos. Over everything towers the 205m 'Big Stack' – a brick chimney.

THE MID-NORTH

Information

The tourist office (☎ 8633 0439, 1800 000
24 toll free, fax 8632 1136, fretwell@
l,com.au) is in the Tourism & Arts Centre
on Mary Ellie St, opposite the silos. It opens
weekdays from 9 am to 5 pm, Saturday 9
am to 4 pm, and Sunday and public holidays
0 am to 3 pm.

Things to See & Do

The **Art Centre**, open the same hours as the
ourist office, receives some excellent touring
exhibitions. Ask to see its exquisite silver tree
ern.

You can take a 45 to 60-minute **self-
guided walk** of interesting sites in and
around the town centre with the brochure
National Trust Walking Tour.

In the town centre on Ellen St, the Na-
ional Trust **museum complex** ($2) features
liprotodont bones, a marine exhibition, old
hopfronts and a steam shunting engine. It
ncludes Port Pirie's first train station, with
ts ornate Victorian facade, together with
he old customs house and police station. It
pens Monday to Saturday from 10 am to 4
m and Sunday 1 to 4 pm.

Places to Stay

Caravan Parks Most highly recommended
f the town's four caravan parks is the *Port
Pirie Caravan Park (☎ 8632 4275, Beach
Rd)*. It has tent/caravan sites for $8/13, on-
ite vans for $25 and cabins from $42.

Hotels & Motels Beds are $15 in the
*Central Hotel (☎ 8632 1031, 30 Alexander
St)*, while the *Newcastle Hotel (☎ 8632
365, 18 Main Rd)* has air-conditioned
ooms for $25/40 a single/double including
light breakfast.

At the more upmarket *International
Hotel/Motel (☎ 8632 2422, 40 Ellen St)*
otel rooms with TV and private bathroom
re $22/35, while motel units are $45/55.

The cheapest of the town's seven motels is
he centrally located *Abaccy Motel (☎ 8632
701, 46 Florence St)*, which charges $45/
5/60 a single/double/triple. The tourist of-
ice has full details of other motels.

Places to Eat

Locals recommend *Harvey's Restaurant
(105 Gertrude St)* for fine dining. Otherwise
the *John Pirie Motel*, on Main Rd outside
town, and the *Flinders Ranges Motor Inn
(151 Main Rd)* have decent restaurants.

Annie's Coffee Shop (15 Jubilee Place)
and *Cafe Florence (Norman St)* are popular for light meals.

A *pie cart* parks near the museum from 10
pm on Thursday, Friday and Saturday nights.

Getting There & Around

Premier Stateliner calls in four times a day on
its run between Adelaide and Port Augusta
($23). The bus station is next to the tourist
office.

The Port Pirie Taxi Service (☎ 8633 1888)
operates 24 hours a day.

Main North Road

At Tarlee, on the Barrier Hwy 89km from
Adelaide, you continue heading north for
6km then veer left on Main North Rd to
Clare and Gladstone. If you're making for
the Flinders Ranges you can easily cut
across to Burra on the Barrier Hwy, then
head back to Main North Rd and continue
on through Gladstone to Melrose.

The Clare Valley, which starts at Auburn
(30km from Tarlee), is described later in
this chapter.

GLADSTONE
• **pop 1000**

Once an important railway junction, Gladstone prospered because it had three railway
gauges meeting at a single siding. The resulting chaos was great for employment, as ongoing freight had to be transferred from one
train to another before it could go any farther.

With the demise of SA's country railways, Gladstone now relies almost entirely
on farming: its grain silos, which hold a
total 82,800 tonnes, make up the state's
largest inland grain storage facility.

The impressive 125-cell **Gladstone Gaol**
was built in 1881 and closed in 1975. It's

THE MID-NORTH

well worth visiting simply to roam its eerie, echoing halls, and to wonder what it must have been like to be incarcerated there. It opens daily from 9 am to 5 pm ($3).

Places to Stay
The small and basic **Gladstone Caravan Park** (☎ 8662 2036), off Main North Rd at the Laura end of town, has plenty of trees but no lawn. Its tent/caravan sites cost $8/12 and the town swimming pool is right next door.

Alternatively, air-conditioned pub-style rooms with colour TV cost $20/35 a single/double at the **Commercial Hotel** (☎ 8662 2148, 2 Gladstone St).

JAMESTOWN
* **pop 1300**
This prosperous service town has one of the widest main streets (about 60m) in SA. Like its neighbours, Jamestown was established during the wheat boom of the 1870s, and there are a number of attractive stone buildings dating from those heady days. These include the town's four pubs and its courthouse; I assume the former provided customers for the latter.

The caravan park is the best source of tourist information in town. It'll give you a brochure that describes a self-guided **walking tour** around a number of sites. These include a National Trust **museum** in the old railway station. It has a variety of exhibits and opens Monday to Saturday from 10 am to 4 pm and Sunday 2 to 4 pm ($2).

Ten kilometres out on the Spalding road is the headquarters of **Bundaleer Forest**. Turn west to a pleasant bush picnic area, from where you can do scenic walks of up to 5km.

Places to Stay & Eat
At the southern end of town, the **Jamestown Country Retreat Caravan Park** (☎ 8664 0077, Bute St) has tent/caravan sites for $10/12, on-site vans for $25 a single or double, and self-contained air-conditioned cabins for $45/50/55. The town swimming pool is next door.

Right in the town centre, the **Belalie Hotel/Motel** (☎ 8664 1065, 36 Ayre St) has

air-conditioned pub rooms for $20 per person and basic motel units for $40/50.

Across the street, the **Commercial Hotel** (☎ 8664 1013, 35 Ayre St) has air-conditioned rooms for $25/40 with shared facilities and $30/45 with private facilities, including a light breakfast.

Jamestown Hotel (☎ 8664 1387, 79 Ayre St) has basic rooms (no air-conditioning) for $25/40 including a light breakfast.

The **Railway Hotel/Motel** (☎ 8664 1035, 32 Alexandra Ave) charges $45/55 for its motel units.

Bundaleer Cottage (☎ 8842 3196) is a charmingly rustic place offering seclusion in the Bundaleer Forest. It has two bedrooms, an open fireplace in the lounge, and beautiful views from the verandah; this will cost you $110 for doubles and $25 for extra adults, including breakfast provisions. You can go horse-riding in the forest by prior arrangement.

LAURA
* **pop 800**
This pleasant little town is the craft centre of the Mid-North, as witnessed by the antique shops and arts & crafts galleries in its broad main street. They include **Possum Park Crafts**, in the old Laura Standard office – a good place for local information.

Laura dines out on the fact that CJ Dennis lived here for a time during his early years; he had his first poem published by the Laura Standard when he was in his late teens. A 4m-high copper **statue** of Dennis sits in front of Dick Biles Gallery, on Main North Rd.

The **Laura Folk Fair** is a fun time of buskers, dancing, music, craft stalls and so on held on the first or second weekend in April (it doesn't clash with Easter).

Places to Stay
There's plenty of shade and space at the basic **Laura Caravan Park** (☎ 8663 2292, Main North Rd), which has tent/caravan sites for $8/10.

Otherwise, **North Laura Hotel** (☎ 8663 2421, Main North Rd), at the northern end of town, has small twin rooms (no air-conditioning) for $20/30 a single/double. A cooked breakfast here costs $6.

There are also a couple of B&Bs in town.

Clare Valley

The Clare Valley, which stretches 30km from Auburn in the south to beyond Clare in the north, is the state's second most important grape-growing area. It's also very scenic thanks to its hilly topography and mosaic of small villages, vineyards, farmland and native bush, including big gum trees. Amongst its major attractions are numerous historic buildings dating from the 1840s, particularly around Auburn, Mintaro (a declared heritage town), Watervale and Clare.

Information

The Clare Valley Visitor Information Centre (☎ 8842 2131, fax 8842 1117) is in the Clare town hall. See the Clare section for further details.

Wineries

The first winery in the Clare Valley was established by Jesuit priests at their **Sevenhill College** in 1851. They wanted to produce altar wine for their Catholic brethren in the colony and overseas, and did so with great success. In fact, a Jesuit brother still oversees the making of altar wine there.

Today the valley – which has over 30 wineries – is noted for its rieslings, but it also produces other good whites as well as reds, particularly shiraz. There are some big-name wineries here, such as Leasingham and Taylors, and several good boutique wineries. The tourist office has details of all wineries, including opening hours for tastings.

The following shouldn't be missed:

Crabtree of Watervale, near Watervale, is a boutique winery that does a very nice shiraz-cabernet.

Jim Barry Wines is just north of Clare. Although the tasting area is rather ordinary, the staff are friendly and its shiraz is very popular.

Knappstein Wines, in an old brewery and soft-drink factory in central Clare, has a very pleasant if cavernous tasting area. Try its hand-picked riesling.

Leasingham Wines, on the southern outskirts of Clare, produces the award-winning Classic Clare range of wines, featuring cabernet and shiraz. The winery is in an old jam factory.

Mt Horrocks Wines, in the historic Auburn train station, has a very nice cordon cut riesling made from grapes from the Watervale area.

Paulett Wines, between Penwortham and Mintaro, is perched high on the ridge that divides the Clare and Polish Hill River valleys. There's a magnificent view over the latter from its verandah; its sparkling riesling isn't a bad drop, either.

Quelltaler Estate, near Watervale, has a large winery complex that includes an interesting little museum of early wine-making equipment.

Sevenhill Cellars, just east of Sevenhill township, has several marvellous old stone buildings, including a church, set in attractive grounds. Its fortified verdelho (a Portuguese-style white port) is excellent. There are no tastings on Sunday, of course.

Skillogalee Wines, between Penwortham and Sevenhill, has a delightful tasting room in a historic cottage. It's noted for its shiraz, and also makes a decent port.

Lunches are served at several wineries, including: *Eldredge Wines* (Sevenhill, Friday to Monday), *Kilikanoon* (Penwortham, Thursday to Sunday), *Mt Horrocks Wines* (Auburn, weekends and public holidays), *Reilly's Wines* (Mintaro, daily), *Skillogalee Wines* (Penwortham, daily).

Organised Tours

The Clare Valley Taxi Service (☎ 8842 3372, or mobile 018 847 000) offers personalised winery tours from $30 per hour (one to four passengers).

Special Events

The major cultural event is the Clare Valley Gourmet Weekend, a festival of fine wine, food and music put on by local wineries over the Adelaide Cup weekend in May. It's like an all-day progressive lunch! Several venues put on good live music ranging from jazz to classical.

There's also the Romeria del Rocio Spanish Festival, held over four days in April.

THE MID-NORTH

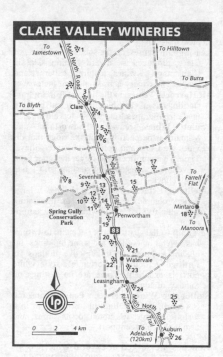

CLARE VALLEY WINERIES

1 Emerald Estate Wines
2 Jim Barry Wines
3 Knappstein Wines
4 Leasingham Wines
5 Wendouree Cellars
6 Tim Adams Wines
7 Sevenhill Cellars
8 Eldredge Wines
9 Stringy Brae Wines
10 Jeanneret Wines
11 Mitchell Winery; Kilikanoon Winery
12 Skillogalee Wines; Waninga Wines
13 Waninga Wines
14 Pearson Wines
15 Paulett Wines
16 The Wilson Vineyard
17 Pikes Wines
18 Mintaro Cellars; Reilly's Wines
19 Penwortham Wines
20 Olssen Wines
21 Quelltaler Estate
22 Crabtree Of Watervale; Stephen John Wines
23 Clos Clare
24 Tim Grant Wines
25 Taylors Wines
26 Grosset Wines; Mt Horrocks Wines

The main feature (apart from fiestas and flamenco dancing) is a pilgrimage behind a statue of the Virgin Mary, carried in an open carriage from Clare to Sevenhill. Spanish people from all over Australia attend.

The Clare Valley Spring Garden Festival takes up a weekend in early November. It features visits to several of the valley's magnificent private gardens.

Accommodation
There's a good choice of places to stay and the Clare tourist office can provide details. Included are two caravan parks, 14 hotels and motels, and around 50 B&Bs ranging from mansions to cottages. Only a small selection is mentioned in this chapter.

Getting There & Around
Bute Buses' Mid-North Passenger Service (☎ 8862 2346) travels daily except Saturday

and Monday from Adelaide to Auburn ($13), Clare ($17) and towns in between.

The Clare Valley Taxi Service (☎ 8842 3372, 018 847 000) operates throughout the valley. It costs around $12 to get from Clare to the Sevenhill Cellars winery, and $30 from Clare to Auburn.

You can wander on foot or by bicycle past some of the valley's finest wineries on the **Riesling Trail**, which follows the old railway alignment from Auburn to Clare. Clare Valley Cycle Hire (☎ 8842 2782), at 32 Victoria Rd in Clare, has well-maintained mountain bikes for $15/20 per half/full day.

AUBURN
• pop 330
There are many beautiful heritage buildings in this historic township, 24km south of Clare. It was established in 1849 and in its infancy serviced the bullockies and South

THE MID-NORTH

American muleteers whose wagons – up to 100 a day – trundled to and fro between the Burra copper mines and Port Wakefield.

Auburn grew to become an important commercial centre in the 1870s, when it boasted a flour mill, gas works and two breweries. Sadly, there are no beers brewed here today, but the Clare Valley's largest winery, **Taylor's Wines**, is nearby.

You can get **local information** from the post office on St Vincent St on week days, and on weekends and public holidays from Petherick's Antiques, which you'll find across from the Rising Sun Hotel on Main North Road.

Twenty-four of Auburn's historic places, including the birthplace of famous colonial poet CJ Dennis, are featured on a 3km **heritage walk** described in the leaflet *Walk with History at Auburn*. Some of SA's finest stonework can be seen here, particularly in the buildings grouped near the intersection of Main North Rd and St Vincent Street.

Places to Stay & Eat
The *Rising Sun Hotel* (☎ 8849 2015, *Main North Rd)* once won the 'best small hotel in Australia' award. You'll see why as soon as you enter! The dining room is charming and the food excellent – as is the wine cellar – yet meals are reasonably priced (main courses are from $10). Its elegant bedrooms have ensuites and cost $40/65 a single/double.

Next door, the historic *Rising Sun Mews* (same phone number) has heritage-style rooms with private facilities for $60/80, including a decent breakfast.

Next door again, and with wonderful heritage-style rooms, the more personalised *Tatehams* (☎ 8849 2030, tatehams@capri .net.au) does B&B for $100/140. Its gourmet restaurant produces superb meals (the cuisine is European with Asian influences); imagine tucking into Tian of Hoisin marinated lamb loin, or Tandoori-style barramundi, followed by a white chocolate basket filled with black pepper ice cream and strawberries (or mango sauce). Drool!

If you don't want to splurge, the closest thing to budget accommodation here is the modest *Auburn Motel* (☎ 8849 2125, *Main North Rd)*, at the Tarlee end of town. It has a decent restaurant and motel units from $35/40/50/58 for one/two/three/four people.

LEASINGHAM TO SEVENHILL
Like Auburn, Leasingham and Watervale grew from camping places along the Burra to Port Wakefield road; turn off at Leasingham if you're going to Mintaro.

Watervale, 8km north of Auburn, has several heritage-listed buildings, including the impressive **Stanley Grammar School**. You can explore them with the aid of a historic walks brochure.

The main concentration of wineries is between Penwortham (12km north of Auburn) and Clare. Penwortham was laid out by pastoralist John Horrocks in 1840, making it the first town in SA north of Gawler. Horrocks lies in the local cemetery; he died in 1846, aged 28 years, after accidentally shooting himself during an expedition in the north.

The main attraction at Sevenhill, 15km north of Auburn, is the winery established by the Jesuits in 1851 – they arrived here from Vienna in 1848, naming the site after the seven hills of Rome. Of interest are its stone buildings, which include **St Aloysius Church** (1875).

About 3km south-west of Sevenhill, the 400 hectare **Spring Gully Conservation Park** features blue gum forest and SA's only stand of red stringybarks. There are 18m-high cascades here in winter, as well as kangaroos, birdlife (50 species) and 4WD and walking tracks. You can get a brochure from the Clare tourist office.

Places to Stay
Leasingham Village Cabins & Caravan Park (☎ 8843 0136), at the intersection of Main North Rd with the road to Mintaro, has comfortable, self-contained cabins (some with kitchen facilities) from $50 a single or double. Dinner, B&B packages are available. Otherwise you can camp in an unpowered/powered site for $5/12.

In Watervale, the *Watervale Hotel* (☎ 8843 0109, *Main North Rd)* has a couple of nice

THE MID-NORTH

rooms for $35/45 a single/double. Locals recommend its counter meals.

Bryvon Homestay (☎ 8843 4331), on a hilltop off Horrocks Rd near Penwortham, has B&B for $85 a couple. It boasts lovely views of the surrounding countryside and is within walking distance (if you're fit!) of Spring Gully Conservation Park.

Just north of Sevenhill, *Miss Nobel's B&B* (☎ 8843 4326, Quarry Rd) is a delightful historic cottage in a rural setting. It has country walks, open fires and farm-style breakfasts for $90 a single or double; the cottage sleeps seven, and extra people are charged $15 each.

MINTARO
* pop 80

Off the main tourist route and 19km southeast of Clare, this historic village was established in 1848. Its main industry is slate mining; Mintaro slate is used internationally in the manufacture of billiard tables. Like a little piece of England plonked down in the Australian countryside, Mintaro is so well preserved that the whole town is a declared heritage site. Call in to the tourist office at Clare or Auburn for a historic walk brochure.

Among Mintaro's more interesting relics is the **Magpie & Stump Hotel** (1851), which has tourist information.

There's also **Martindale Hall**, a spectacular 1880 Georgian mansion with period furnishings, a magnificent blackwood staircase and Italian marble fireplaces. Its grandeur makes a totally unexpected sight amongst the gum trees – even the imposing coachhouse near the entrance doesn't prepare you for it. The mansion, which is 3km from town, opens daily from 11 am to 4 pm except weekends, when it opens at noon; admission is $5.

Places to Stay & Eat
In and around town are a number of old houses and cottages offering B&B.

If you've saved up you can pamper yourself at *Martindale Hall* (☎ 8843 9088, marthall@capri.net.au), which charges from $65 per person for B&B, and from

$120 for dinner and B&B – dinner is served formally by a butler and maid. They make up sumptuous picnic hampers for $20 per person, but require 24 hours notice.

The *Magpie & Stump Hotel* has counter lunches and teas daily, while nearby *Reilly's Wines* does lunches. For dinner, try the *Mintaro Mews* – it opens daily except Wednesday, and you can also stay there (B&B costs $120 for doubles; ☎ 8843 9001).

CLARE
* pop 2600

This attractive and prosperous town, 135km from Adelaide, was settled in 1842 and named after County Clare in Ireland. Although tourism is a growth industry, so far the town has managed to avoid many of the trappings characteristic of the Barossa Valley.

Information
Open daily from 9 am to 5 pm (10 am to 4 pm Sunday and public holidays), the Clare Valley Visitor Information Centre (☎ 8842 2131, fax 8842 1117) is in the Clare town hall on Main St. It's very friendly and efficient, and has an excellent stock of leaflets and brochures.

Things to See & Do
Clare has a number of heritage-listed buildings, many of which are covered by the brochure *Clare Historic Walk*. They include **St Michael's Church** (1849), the valley's first substantial building.

The former police station and courthouse (1850) is now a National Trust **museum** featuring displays of Victorian clothing, furniture and household effects. It opens weekends and public and school holidays from 10 am to noon and 2 to 4 pm ($2).

Also of interest is the splendid **Wolta Wolta Homestead** (1864), home to four generations of the Hope family. However, it only opens on Sunday (and then not always) from 10 am to 1 pm.

Just outside the northern end of the valley, and 12km from Clare, the once vast **Bungaree Station** has shrivelled to a mere 2200 hectares. At one time the homestead was like a small town, with its own council chambers, police station and Anglican church (still in use). If you're staying there (see Places to Stay) you can do a self-conducted cassette tour of the old buildings.

Geralka Farm, 25km north of Clare on the Spalding road, also caters for visitors. It features the fascinating Wheal Sarah mine, and you can take wagon rides and guided walks. The farm closes during February, but otherwise opens on weekends and public and mid-year school holidays; admission is $8.

Arts & Crafts
The **Corella Hill Studio** at Watervale features the distinctive work of well-known local artist Murray Edwards. The mud-brick gallery is on a ridge with fine views.

At Blyth, a small township 11km west of Clare, is the **Medika Gallery** of artist Ian Roberts. Ian is noted for his beautiful watercolours of birds and plants. The gallery, in the photogenic 1886 **St Petrie Kirche Lutheran Church**, opens weekdays from 10 am to 5 pm and weekends 2 to 5 pm.

Places to Stay
Caravan Parks & Cabins The very friendly and attractive *Clare Caravan Park* (☎ 8842 2724, Main North Rd) is 4km south of the town centre. It has tent sites for $11 ($8 if you're travelling solo), powered sites for $15, on-site vans for $30, basic cabins for $40 and self-contained cabins from $46.

Clare Valley Cabins (☎ 8842 1155) is in a peaceful bush setting with lots of birds about 6km north-east of town. The cabins, which sleep up to six, have fans and pot-belly stoves and cost from $54 for singles and doubles.

At *Geralka Farm* (☎ 8845 8081), on the Spalding road, you can camp on an unpowered/powered site for $11/14 or stay in on-site vans from $28. There's also a fully self-contained unit for $55.

Bungaree Station (☎ 8842 2677) has accommodation in the shearers' quarters for $15 per person. Heritage cottages sleep from two to eight for $40 per person for B&B.

Hotels & Motels On Main St, the *Taminga Hotel* (☎ 8842 2808) has singles/doubles for $20/32, while the *Clare Hotel* (☎ 8842 2816) has basic pub rooms for $17 per person ($45/50 a single/double with private bathroom).

Bentleys Hotel/Motel (☎ 8842 1700, 191 Main North Rd) has a range of accommodation. Standard pub rooms are $35 a double, air-conditioned rooms with private facilities are $45, and motel units are $55. A separate (and very basic) backpacker section has bunk beds for $10 – there's no kitchen, but you can get cheap meals in the bar.

The more luxurious *Clare Central Motel* (☎ 8842 2277, 325 Main North Rd) charges $78/88 including a light breakfast. Alternatively, the *Clare Country Club Motel* (☎ 8842 1060, White Hut Rd), about 1km north of town, charges from $89/98.

The *Clare Valley Motel* (☎ 8842 2799, Main North Rd), 2km south of town, looks expensive but its 'budget' units are reasonably priced at $55/60.

B&Bs There are many B&Bs in and around Clare. Recommended as being excellent value is *Green Gables* (☎ 8842 2576, 24 Mill St), a grand stone house set in a beautiful garden a short walk from Main St. It has luxurious rooms for $65 per person, including a large breakfast that you eat with the friendly owners.

Six kilometres north of town, *Wuthering Heights* (☎ 8842 3196) gets rave reviews for its three secluded cottages on 30 hectares of trees and farmland. All have a wonderful rustic charm, with fires in winter and coolers in summer. Prices start at $80 for couples ($20 for extra adults) including full breakfast provisions.

Places to Eat
All the hotels and motels have meals. The bistro at *Bentleys Hotel/Motel* is very light and airy, and represents the best dining on the hotel scene.

On Main St, *Chaff Mill Country Kitchen* has a lovely atmosphere and is noted for its country-style meals. Steaks are a speciality.

The *Mehfil Restaurant* at the Clare Valley Motel specialises in northern Indian cuisine – it's hot! Meals are reasonably priced for the standard, with mains around $11.

Barrier Highway

Running mainly through open sheep and wheat country, the Barrier Hwy is the most direct route from Adelaide to Burra, the old copper-mining town. You can go this way to the Flinders Ranges by turning off at Terowie, or continue north-east from Terowie to Sydney via Broken Hill.

KAPUNDA
* **pop 2000**

Kapunda, which is just outside the Barossa Valley, is on the most direct route from Nuriootpa to the Barrier Hwy. It's an extremely friendly place, and a quiet contrast to the busy tourist areas of the Barossa.

A rich copper deposit was found here in 1842. Cornish miners were soon hard at work, and Kapunda became the first mining town in Australia. At its peak, in 1861, it had 11 hotels and was the colony's major commercial centre outside Adelaide. Large-scale operations ceased in 1878 and the mines closed altogether in 1912. Thanks to the lack of development since then, many of the solid stone buildings erected during the boom years have survived intact.

The Kapunda Tourist Information Centre (☎ 8566 2902) is at 76 Main St. It opens weekdays from 9 am to 5 pm, Saturday and public holidays from 10 am to 1 pm, and Sunday from noon to 3 pm.

Things to See & Do

At the main entrance of town is an 8m-high bronze statue of '**Map Kernow**' (the 'Son of Cornwall' in old Cornish). The town's Cornish heritage is celebrated by the annual Celtic Folk Festival, held over three days on the weekend before Easter. It features traditional Celtic music, singing and dancing.

Out at the old mine site there is a **lookout** with views over the open cuts and stone chimneys. A 1.5km walking trail has information signs to guide you through the area.

Many of Kapunda's fine old buildings can be viewed on a 10km **heritage trail** around the streets and mine site, and on a much shorter walk through the town centre. Both are described in the booklet *Discovering Historic Kapunda*, available at the tourist office.

Learn more about the boom times at **Bagot's Fortune**, a mining interpretive centre on Hill St in the middle of town. There's a half-hour video of the town and its history, as well as displays on mining. It opens on weekends and public holidays from 1 to 4 pm ($2).

Two doors down the street, the heritage-listed Baptist Church (1866) houses the **Kapunda Historical Museum**. It has a fascinating collection of memorabilia, and is considered one of the best museums in country SA; it opens daily from 1 to 4 pm ($3).

The **Kapunda Gallery** on the corner of Hill and Main Sts is a good place to see the work of local artists and craftspeople. It also hosts regular touring exhibitions.

Off the Eudunda road, **Anlaby Station** once covered 650 sq km and employed a team of 14 gardeners to keep the homestead grounds in order. Those days are long gone (the property now covers about 110 hectares) but many of the original features remain. You can admire the stately homestead and its grounds – which include a coachhouse containing a collection of 40 horse-drawn coaches – on weekends and public holidays between 10 am and 4 pm ($10).

Places to Stay & Eat

Plenty of trees and birdlife are features of the *Dutton Park Caravan Park* (☎ 8566 2094, Baker St). It has tent/caravan sites for $11/13, and fully self-contained cabins for $40.

There are two classic 1849 hotels where you can stay; both offer basic pub-style rooms. The *Sir John Franklin Hotel* (☎ 8566 3233, Main St) charges from $25/45 a single/double. Diagonally opposite, the *North Kapunda Hotel* (☎ 8566 2205) charges $10 per person – how long this will last is anyone's guess! Both offer good, cheap counter meals.

Alternatively, there are several B&Bs in and around town. They include ***Bergnor's Vault*** *(☎ 8566 3355, bergnor@bigpond .com.au, 45 Main St)*, in the old Bank of Adelaide building. It charges $60 for couples and the price includes a hearty breakfast, which you eat with the very friendly owners. There's a pleasant coffee lounge and bookshop on the premises, and you can access the internet for a small fee.

Fresh Fields *(Main St)* has a cosy atmosphere, friendly service and good-value meals – lunches average $5.

Out of town, ***Anlaby Station*** *(☎ 8566 2465)* offers upmarket B&B from $60 per person in its historic buildings.

Getting There & Away

The Barossa Adelaide Passenger Service (☎ 8564 3022) has two buses a day on weekdays to Kapunda from Gawler ($6) and Adelaide ($10.50).

TARLEE
- **pop 100**

Halfway between the Barossa and Clare valleys is Tarlee, whose main attraction is **Tarlee Antiques**. It's one of the best antique shops in SA and has seven rooms crammed with a fascinating selection of antiques, collectables and bric-a-brac.

The shop has a cosy, licensed ***restaurant*** with an open fire and delicious lunches and dinners. Out the back is a pine-log ***motel*** *(☎ 8528 5328)* with comfortable, well-appointed rooms for $55/65.

RIVERTON
- **pop 750**

Originally a camping place for the wagon teams carting copper ore from Burra to Port Adelaide in the 1840s, Riverton was the scene of a dramatic shoot-out in 1921. It happened at the train station, when a crazed passenger on the Broken Hill Express fired numerous shots into the crowded dining room. Several people were wounded and Broken Hill MP Percy Brookfield was killed trying to disarm the gunman. Apparently you can still see one of the bullet holes in the wall.

Scholz Park Museum, in the main street, has an 1870s cottage, coach-building shop and blacksmiths shop, furnished and equipped as they would originally have been. Check with the council office (☎ 8847 2305) on Masters St about opening times.

Eighteen kilometres farther north, at **Saddleworth**, there's a folk museum with an extensive collection of memorabilia. It opens Sunday from 2 to 5 pm.

Places to Stay

In Riverton you can stay at the little ***Riverton Caravan Park*** *(☎ 8847 2419, Torrens Rd)*, which has powered and unpowered sites. Also on Torrens Rd, the ***Hotel Central*** *(☎ 8847 2314)* and ***Riverton Hotel*** *(☎ 8847 2303)* have basic pub rooms for around $25/40 a single/double.

Saddleworth has basic camping at the town oval. There's also the ***Hotel Saddleworth*** *(☎ 8847 4013, 3 Belvidere Rd)*, where pub rooms cost $29/45 with a hearty cooked breakfast.

BURRA
- **pop 1200**

Only 42km north-east of Clare, this pretty little town is literally bursting at the seams with sites dating from the 1840s to 1870s. The district, Burra Burra, takes its name from the Hindi word for 'great' by one account, and from the Aboriginal name of the creek by another.

Thomas Pickett, a shepherd, discovered copper at Burra in 1845. The deposit proved to be phenomenally rich, and by 1850 it was supporting the largest metalliferous mine in Australia. In 1851 Burra had a population of 5000, which made it Australia's seventh largest town at that time. By then Pickett had met a terrible fate; he'd fallen into his lonely campfire while drunk and burned to death.

Burra originally consisted of several villages. The mining company had set up Kooringa (now the township's central part), but most people preferred to live outside company control. As a result, the Cornish (who were the most numerous) established Redruth, the Scots Aberdeen, the Welsh

THE MID-NORTH

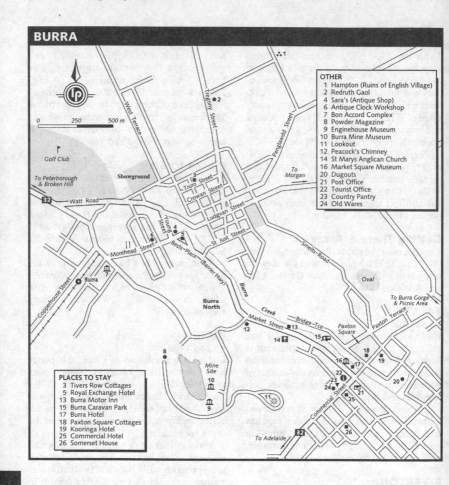

BURRA

OTHER
1 Hampton (Ruins of English Village)
2 Redruth Gaol
4 Sara's (Antique Shop)
6 Antique Clock Workshop
7 Bon Accord Complex
8 Powder Magazine
9 Enginehouse Museum
10 Burra Mine Museum
11 Lookout
12 Peacock's Chimney
14 St Marys Anglican Church
16 Market Square Museum
20 Dugouts
21 Post Office
22 Tourist Office
23 Country Pantry
24 Old Wares

PLACES TO STAY
3 Tivers Row Cottages
5 Royal Exchange Hotel
13 Burra Motor Inn
15 Burra Caravan Park
17 Burra Hotel
18 Paxton Square Cottages
19 Kooringa Hotel
25 Commercial Hotel
26 Somerset House

(who ran the smelter) Llwchwr, and the English Hampton.

By 1860 the mine was producing 5% of the world's copper; over 1000 men and boys, most of them Cornish, were employed there at that time. It closed 17 years later, mainly because of flooding problems and falling ore grades, but reopened for 10 years from 1971.

Information

The helpful and efficient Burra Visitor Centre (☎ 8892 2154, fax 8892 2555, bvc@

capri.net.au,), on Market Square, is open daily from 9 am to 5 pm. Check out its website at www.weblogic.com.au/burra.

The Burra Visitor Centre stocks the *Discovering Historic Burra* booklet, which describes around 60 heritage sites. You can see them all by doing an 11km heritage trail (either drive or walk) and a short walking tour around Market Square.

The booklet forms part of the **Burra Passport**, which gives access to eight National Trust sites and the town's main museums. It

THE MID-NORTH

costs $10 per person if you just want to visit the eight sites ($18 including the museums).

Things to See & Do

Burra has many evocative relics of the mining days. Most are made of stone and include tall chimneys, enginehouses, classic hotels, massive churches and tiny cottages. You'll also notice the lack of trees on the grassy hills around town. Their original light cover of she-oaks and gums was stripped to feed the smelter furnaces.

Right in Burra's commercial centre, the **Market Square Museum** (admission $4) is across from the tourist office; it features a shop, post office and house as they might have looked during the period between 1880 and 1930. Opening hours are Friday, weekends and public holidays from 1 to 3 pm.

In Burra's early days about 1800 people lived in **dugouts** along the creek, but a flood in 1851 drove most of them out. Since then floods have destroyed all but two dugouts.

The 33 attached cottages at **Paxton Square** were built for Cornish miners in the 1850s as an alternative to the dugouts. One of them, **Malowen Lowarth**, has been furnished in 1850s style, and provides a fascinating glimpse of how a mine manager (or mine captain) lived at the time. It opens on Saturday from 1 to 3 pm and Sunday and public holidays from 10.30 am to 12.30 pm ($3). The other cottages are available for accommodation (see Places to Stay).

Another good place to see attached Cornish cottages is on Truro St in old Aberdeen (now North Burra).

Other substantial relics include **Redruth Gaol** (1856), which featured in the film *Breaker Morant*, **St Mary's Anglican Church** (1849), and **Peacocks Chimney**. The latter provided updraught for the boilers at a now-demolished enginehouse.

The open-air **Burra Mine Museum** has numerous sites including tall stone chimneys, a powder magazine, ore-dressing floors and a deep open-cut mine – there are lookouts and excellent information signs with historic photos. Included is **Morphetts Enginehouse Museum** ($4), a three storey building that features a model of the mine workings. The enginehouse opens on weekdays from 11 am to 1 pm, but you can wander elsewhere around the mine site at any time.

The **Bon Accord Mine** was a Scottish enterprise that ended in failure; instead of rich copper ore, the miners discovered plentiful underground water. Not to be deterred, the canny Scots sold their lease to the town, and the mine shaft supplied Burra's water until the 1960s. Now a mining interpretive centre, the old surface buildings are open daily from 12.30 to 2.30 pm ($4).

Organised Tours

Minibus heritage tours leave the tourist office on demand for $20; the tours take two hours and visit eight major sites. The tourist office also runs day and half-day tours from Burra to destinations throughout the Mid-North, including the Clare Valley wineries ($28). You can also do **4WD tours** through rugged station country.

Mongolata Gold Mine Tours (bookings ☎ 8892 2233) has an interesting 1½ hour tour of its working **gold mine** 23km east of town. You can pick up a mudmap from its shop at 20A Commercial St (next to the Commercial Hotel).

Mongolata also has an informative 1½ hour guided **walking tour** of heritage sites in and around the town centre for $6. This is a great way to explore the early social scene of Burra. Its 1½ hour 'tombstones by torchlight' tour through Burra cemetery starts around 7 pm (5 pm in winter) and costs $6 – bring your own torch.

Three kilometres from town off the Morgan road, Burra Trail Rides (☎ 8892 2627), on Basin Farm, offers escorted **horse rides** through the scenic Burra Hills. These range from one hour ($15) to all day ($60 including a picnic lunch), and the company also has two to three-day sheep **droving trips** for $90 per day. The latter are a great experience.

Places to Stay

Caravan Parks The *Burra Caravan Park* (☎ *8892 2442, Bridge Terrace*) is by peaceful Burra Creek, near the centre of town. It's basic but pleasant, and has good shade; tent/caravan sites are $10/13 and there are on-site vans without air-conditioning for $30.

Hotels & Motels There are four historic hotels offering much the same standard of pub-style accommodation, and one motel.

Burra Hotel (☎ *8892 2389, 5 Market Square*) has rooms with ceiling fans for $30/50 a single/double, including a cooked breakfast. The *Commercial Hotel* (☎ *8892 2010, 22 Commercial St*) offers rooms for $25/40 with a light breakfast. The *Kooringa Hotel* (☎ *8892 2013, Kitchen St*) similarly includes a light breakfast in its $35/50 charge. At the time of writing this edition, the *Royal Exchange Hotel* (☎ *8892 2392, 1 Bests Place, North Burra*) was refurbishing its rooms; however, these go for $20/35 for a single/double.

The *Burra Motor Inn* (☎ *8892 2777, Market St*), is somewhat more luxurious than the pubs; it has large rooms overlooking the creek for $54/64/74 a single/double/triple.

Cottages There are also a number of historic cottages and houses where you can stay. Most are described in a brochure you can get from the tourist office, which can arrange bookings.

Paxton Square Cottages (☎ *8892 2622*) reflect the lifestyles of early Burra. They're basic, but fully self-contained, and cost from $25/35 ($30/40 if you need sheets); breakfast, which is extra, is served in the old Methodist chapel.

Tivers Row (☎ *8892 2461, Truro St*) in North Burra is a charming example of attached Cornish cottages. They're very homely – each has comfortable older-style furnishings (not antiques), an open fire in winter, and a private garden – and cost from $90 for couples including breakfast provisions.

Forming part of the Bon Accord complex, *Bon Accord Cottage* (☎ *8892 2116*), which is owned by the National Trust, was the mine manager's residence. It accommodates up to eight people in four bedrooms,

charging $105 for the first two people and $25 for extra adults, including breakfast provisions.

Somerset House (☎ *8892 2198, 14 Kangaroo St*) is a welcoming place within easy walking distance of the town centre. It's the only fully hosted B&B in Burra and is a fine example of country hospitality. Staying here will cost you $50/80 a single/double.

Places to Eat
The hotels sell counter meals from around the $5 mark, with the *Kooringa* and *Burra* having the most imaginative menus.

The *Country Pantry (Commercial St)* near the tourist office, is good for light lunches.

Shopping
Burra has several antique and bric-a-brac shops. If you're keen on clocks, the **Antique Clock Workshop** on Morehead St is excellent. Also worth visiting are **Old Wares**, on Commercial St, and **Sara's**, on Young St in North Burra.

Getting There & Away
Greyhound Pioneer's daily service from Adelaide to Sydney via Broken Hill can drop you off in Burra ($20).

Bute Buses' Mid-North Passenger Service (☎ 8826 2346) calls into Burra ($17) on Wednesday and Friday en route from Adelaide to Orroroo.

HALLETT
* **pop 100**

Noted for fine Merino wool, Hallett is at the start of the 91km **Dares Hill Scenic Drive**, which takes you the roundabout way to Terowie. You can get a route map and notes from Hallett Country Corner, a friendly craftshop on the Barrier Hwy in town.

The unsealed road takes you via several abandoned settlements including **Mt Bryan East**, an accommodation point on the Heysen Trail. There's good variety in the landscapes along the way, including a panoramic outlook towards the Murray River from **Dares Hill**, 27km from Hallett. About 43km farther on, in the Wonna

Range, the 1056 hectare **Pandappa Conservation Park** has attractive hill scenery and plenty of wildlife, including euros and red and grey kangaroos.

Tooralie Homestead is a sheep grazing property in scenic hilly country 11km east of Hallet. The friendly owners offer various activities on their 2000ha farm, including bushwalks on the Heysen Trail, mountain biking on the Mawson Trail, birdwatching, horse and pony riding, and 4WD tours.

Places to Stay
Tooralie Homestead (☎ 8894 2067) offers B&B from $40 per person (it offers an impressive cook-out breakfast in fine weather), while full board costs from $72 per person.

The *Wildongoleechie Hotel (☎ 8894 2014)* in Hallett has basic rooms, as does the interesting old *Whyte-Yarcowie Hotel (☎ 8659 1131)*, 21km farther north on the highway in tiny Whyte-Yarcowie.

TEROWIE
- **pop 200**

Almost but not quite a ghost town, Terowie is definitely worth the short detour off the Barrier Hwy. The town was originally linked by broad-gauge railway to Adelaide and narrow-gauge to Peterborough. Because goods had to be transferred between carriages from one line to the other, the sprawling railway yards – they stretched for 3km – provided hundreds of jobs. At its

peak, during WWII, the population exceeded 2000 people.

But in 1969, when the broad-gauge line was extended to Peterborough, the death knell sounded for Terowie as a major centre. Today, this gutsy town is worth a visit as much for its lingering air of a bygone age as for its wonderful, though sadly deteriorating, historic streetscapes. If you're a photographer or artist, and keen on old buildings, you'll easily spend an enjoyable day capturing its character.

Places to Stay
The *Terowie Hotel (☎ 8659 1012, Main St)* has basic rooms for $20/35, including breakfast. There's also the *Old Terowie Hospital (☎ 8659 1061, Mitchell St)*, where B&B is $20 per person.

TEROWIE TO BROKEN HILL
From Terowie you can either head northwest to Peterborough (24km) and Orroroo (61km), or north-east along the sealed Barrier Hwy to Broken Hill (296km).

The Barrier Hwy passes through semiarid station country, with small service centres at **Oodla Wirra** (35km), **Yunta** (97km), **Mannahill** (137km), **Olary** (178km) and **Cockburn** (246km and right on the border). Each has a pub and fuel sales.

Oodla Wirra has a fruit-fly check point for travellers coming from NSW. You'll have to stop and declare all fresh fruit and vegetables.

THE MID-NORTH

Yorke Peninsula

Explorer Matthew Flinders described Yorke Peninsula as an 'ill-shaped leg', with its heel in Gulf St Vincent, the sole of its foot in Investigator Strait and its knee in Spencer Gulf. The peninsula is mainly flat to undulating and there are no watercourses to speak of, but much of its coastline is very attractive – you can fish, dive or swim almost all the way around it. In the south are the spectacular Innes National Park and some of SA's best surfing and fishing. At the northern end, Wallaroo, Moonta and Kadina preserve a rich copper-mining heritage from the 19th century. Almost all the native bush has been cleared for farming.

European History

White settlement on Yorke Peninsula began in 1846 when a sheep station was established at Stansbury, on the east coast. Others soon followed, but those first settlers had a hard time of it: the Aborigines were hostile, the thick mallee scrub made poor pasture and there was little fresh water.

The peninsula was looking distinctly unpromising until major copper deposits were discovered at Kadina and Moonta around 1860. Worked mainly by Cornish miners, the largest mines remained open until the early 1920s and made a massive contribution to the state economy.

By 1880 most of the big stations had been subdivided into farms, and scrub rollers pulled by horses were busily flattening the mallee. Soon wheat was being exported to England in windjammers (large, square-rigged sailing ships), the last of which departed from Port Victoria in 1949.

Today, thanks largely to the application of superphosphate and a relatively cool, moist climate, the peninsula is the nation's richest barley-growing district. Most of the harvest is exported through the shipping terminals at Ardrossan, Port Giles and Wallaroo.

HIGHLIGHTS

- Discover the copper-mining heritage of Moonta, Kadina and Wallaroo
- Catch the waves at Pondalowie and other surf beaches around Innes National Park
- Feast, folk dance, drink lots of Cornish beer and chase sprites at the Kernewek Lowender Festival
- Scuba dive among the shipwrecks around Wardang Island
- Survey Australia's richest barley belt from a gypsy wagon pulled by Clydesdales

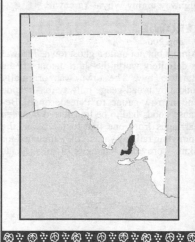

Information

Tourist Office In their infinite wisdom, SA's tourism authorities have decided to lump the Mid-North and Yorke Peninsula together and market them as 'Classic Country'. This is the name to look for in promotional material.

The main tourist office for Yorke Peninsula is in Moonta. See the section on that town for details.

National Parks Conservation areas in the region are managed by the National Parks and Wildlife Service (NPWS) rangers based at Innes National Park (☎ 8854 4040, fax 8854 4072). You can write to them at Innes National Park, CMB Stenhouse Bay 5577.

Maps The Royal Automobile Association of South Australia (RAA) has a good road map. Also useful is the Office of Recreation & Sport's cycle touring map. Westprint puts out a very informative map.

Activities

There are diving and/or fishing charters at Edithburgh, Foul Bay, Port Broughton, Port Hughes, Port Victoria and Wallaroo. Expect to pay at least $80 for a day's fishing.

You can take camel treks at Corny Point, yacht cruises at Wallaroo, and a variety of other tours in the Copper Triangle. See the sections on these places for details.

Fishing Several towns have good fishing jetties. The best is the deep-water jetty at Port Giles, where you can catch a variety of species including snapper, salmon, squid, garfish and tommies. Wallaroo offers a similar variety.

Garfish, squid and tommies are the main catches at most other jetties, the best of which are at Ardrossan, Edithburgh, Moonta Bay, Port Hughes, Port Victoria and Port Vincent. Unfortunately, you need a boat at most places to get among the King George whiting.

Blue-swimmer crabs are plentiful in the open season (September to April) at beaches and jetties north of Port Vincent and Port Victoria. Shallow mud flats are the best places; you can often catch a feed simply by wading around at night with a dab net and torch.

Accommodation

There are numerous caravan parks, hotels, motels and holiday flats throughout the peninsula, particularly near the sea. However,

the coast is an extremely popular destination during Easter and the October and January school holiday periods. As a result, coastal caravan parks and any form of self-contained accommodation are usually booked out at these times, when many places put their prices up.

There's bunkhouse accommodation at Innes National Park and Port Vincent, and bush campsites in the national park. Bush camping is also permitted at a number of other places on the 'foot'. Contact council offices for details of where you can camp on public land outside conservation areas.

For something entirely different, you can hire a horse-drawn gypsy caravan in Brentwood, near Minlaton.

Getting There & Away

Premier Stateliner (☎ 8415 5555) has daily buses from Adelaide to Port Broughton

($21) and the Copper Triangle – see that section for details.

The Yorke Peninsula Passenger Service (☎ 1800 625 099) runs daily to Yorketown, alternating between the east coast and down the centre. Fares from Adelaide are $18.50 to Ardrossan and Port Victoria, $24 to Port Vincent, and $25 to Edithburgh, Warooka and Yorketown.

There is no public transport beyond Edithburgh and Warooka.

East Coast

The sealed road from the top of Gulf St Vincent down to Stenhouse Bay near Cape Spencer is generally within a kilometre or two of the sea. En route, tracks and roads lead in to sandy beaches and secluded coves. Small fishing and holiday towns dot the coast.

PORT WAKEFIELD TO ARDROSSAN

Turning off Highway 1 (Hwy 1) just north of Port Wakefield, you soon pass the 1960 hectare **Clinton Conservation Park**. The park, which has tidal shallows and mangroves, is noted for its migratory wading birds and breeding colonies of cormorants.

Price is a small salt-mining centre 18km farther on. The basic but friendly *Price Progress Association Caravan Park (☎ 8837 6311)* has tent/caravan sites for $9/10 and onsite vans with air-conditioning for $30.

Between Price and Ardrossan, dirt roads turn off to **Macs Beach** and **Tiddy Widdy Beach**. Both are good crabbing spots.

ARDROSSAN
• pop 1000

This attractive grain-exporting port is dominated by its huge silos. Ardrossan is a far cry from the town it was in the early 1870s, when it was called Clay Gully and its residents lived in dugouts. You get a nice view of the town from the **lookout** at BHP's dolomite mine on the Port Vincent road.

Ardrossan was the birthplace of the famous **'stump-jump' plough**. This ingenious invention, developed at nearby Arthurton, could jump over the mallee stumps and rocks that made land development a nightmare for SA's early grain farmers.

The **National Trust museum** on Fifth St features agricultural history including, of course, the stump-jump plough. It opens Sunday and public holidays between 2.30 and 4 pm.

The wreck of the barque *Zanoni*, which sank during a storm in 1867, is a popular local **dive site**. It lies in 20m of water about 16km south-east of town, but to dive on it you need permission from the Department of Environment, Heritage & Aboriginal Affairs in Adelaide. A number of relics are displayed in the museum.

Places to Stay
Almost on the waterfront, and with plenty of shady gums, the *Ardrossan Caravan Park (☎ 8837 3262, Park Terrace)* has tent/caravan sites for $11/12 and air-conditioned cabins from $32.

High View Holiday Village (☎ 8837 3399) is off the Port Wakefield road on the northern side of town. This more upmarket place has powered sites with private facilities for $14 and self-contained cabins from $40.

The *Ardrossan Hotel (☎ 8837 3008)*, on the corner of First and Fifth Sts in the town centre, has motel units for $40/50 a single/double.

ARDROSSAN TO EDITHBURGH
South of Ardrossan the main road passes the tiny coastal resort of **Pine Point**, where there's a basic caravan park *(☎ 8838 2239)*. From here you can drive to **Black Point**, where there is bush camping. Along the way you pass a long, sandy beach and numerous ugly holiday shacks on the shore of Port Alfred.

Farther south is **Port Julia**, another holiday spot with a good beach. It's reputed to be one of the peninsula's best crabbing spots.

Port Vincent
* pop 500

This quiet, picturesque resort town is set on a sweeping bay with a safe swimming beach. It has many old stone buildings, an interesting 2km nature trail along the coast and reasonable fishing off the jetty.

The *Tuckerway Youth Hostel (☎ 8853 7285, 14 Lime Kiln Rd)* is opposite the water tower at the entrance to town on the Ardrossan road. A well-run place with good facilities, it has bunk beds in dorms and twin rooms ($10) as well as grassy campsites ($5 per person) and powered sites ($7 per person). It's a five minute walk to the beach.

Both the town's caravan parks are on the waterfront. The *Port Vincent Foreshore Caravan Park (☎ 8853 7073, Marine Parade)* has powered sites and on-site vans. *Port Vincent Seaside Flats & Caravan Park (☎ 8853 7011, Minlacowie Rd)* has campsites and self-contained cabins (from $35).

On the corner of Marine Parade and Main St, the *Hotel Ventnor (☎ 8853 7036)* charges $40 a double in basic pub rooms.

The *Grainstore (☎ 8853 7398, 5 Main St)* has tastefully furnished rooms in a heritage-listed building. It charges from $100 a double, including a cooked breakfast; this place is also recommended for light lunches.

Port Vincent has several holiday flats. Locals recommend *Port Vincent Holiday Cabins (☎ 8853 7411, 12 Main St)* in the town centre, which has comfortable units costing from $60 a double.

The main agent for holiday homes in the area is LJ Hooker (☎ 8853 7018).

Stansbury
* pop 500

This was the site of the Oyster Bay homestead, the first White settlement on Yorke Peninsula. Proclaimed in 1873, Stansbury was originally called Oyster Bay after the molluscs that were harvested here until the 1880s.

There are jetties and swimming beaches here and farther south at Wool Bay.

In the early days many farmers eked out a living by burning limestone to extract lime for use in cement manufacture. A large lime kiln built into the cliff at Wool Bay is a relic of those times; from the lookout here is a nice view along colourful coastal cliffs to the huge grain silos at Port Giles.

Places to Stay The *Stansbury Foreshore Caravan Park (☎ 8852 4171)* has plenty of lawn and trees and is handy to town. It charges from $12 for powered sites and from $48 for self-contained cabins.

The *Dalrymple Hotel (☎ 8852 4188, Anzac Parade)*, also on the waterfront, has basic rooms facing the sea breeze for $25 per person, including a cooked breakfast. There's also the *Stansbury Holiday Motel (☎ 8852 4455)*, just outside town on Adelaide Rd. It has ocean views and comfortable units with cooking facilities from $61/71 a single/double.

A more basic, but very clean and friendly option is *Oyster Court (☎ 8852 4136)*, on the corner of South and West Terraces. Its motel rooms cost $40/50 a single/double, while its holiday units are good value at $40/50 a double/family.

Coobowie
* pop 200

There's a safe swimming beach here, and some interesting old buildings left over from busier times when it was a shipping centre. Nearby Salt Creek inlet is a good spot for birdwatching.

The pleasant *Coobowie Caravan Park (☎ 8852 8132)* has tent/caravan sites from $10/11, on-site vans from $25 and cabins from $25.

EDITHBURGH
* pop 500

Once a thriving port exporting salt, grains and wool, this attractive service town has a great seaside atmosphere and many lovely old buildings.

The museum on Edith St near the jetty has a fascinating collection of memorabilia, including displays on local shipwrecks. Featured is a large, red 1942 fire engine – the sort that small boys once dreamed of driving. It opens on Sunday, and public and school holidays, from 2 to 4 pm ($2).

From the clifftop above the town jetty there's a view across to **Troubridge Island**, about 6km off shore. The island is a conservation park and has important rookeries of little penguins, black-faced shags and crested terns. Guided tours are available, and you can stay there.

There's good **scuba diving** on wrecks and reefs near Edithburgh, with visibility usually from 5m to 8m. Its reefs have soft corals, fish, drop-offs and caves. The most popular wreck dive is the 3600 tonne cargo steamer *Clan Ranald*. It went down in 1909 with the loss of 40 lives and lies in 23m about a kilometre off **Troubridge Point**. The drowned seamen are buried in a mass grave in the town cemetery.

There are some pleasant nature walks in the pretty 17 hectare **Edithburgh Flora Park** and along the coast from Edithburgh to **Sultana Point** (4km) and **Coobowie** (6km).

Diving & Fishing Charters

Troubridge Island Charters (☎ 8852 6290) does diving and fishing trips for two to five people. Fishing costs $80 a day per person, while diving trips to the *Clan Ranald* are $40 per person; a one tank dive on a reef costs from $25.

There's also Edithburgh Charter (☎ 8852 6288). Its 9m powered catamaran takes up to eight people – a full day charter costs $650 not including lunch.

Organised Tours

Troubridge Island Charters has an interesting two hour tour out to Troubridge Island for $20. Here you'll see the cast-iron **lighthouse** (1856) and keepers' cottages, all of which were prefabricated in England, and learn about local shipwrecks.

Places to Stay & Eat

The *Edithburgh Caravan Park (☎ 8852 6056)* is right on the waterfront on O'Halloran Parade. It has tent/caravan sites from $10/12, on-site vans from $28 and self-contained cabins from $40.

There are two pubs, both on the corner of Edith and Blanche Sts. The classiest is the grand old Edithburgh Hotel, with the *Edithburgh Seaside Motel (☎ 8852 6172)* attached – it charges $50/55/67 a single/double/triple for its units.

Diagonally opposite, the more basic *Troubridge Hotel/Motel (☎ 8852 6013)* has pub rooms for $18/30 a single/double and motel units for $40/48.

Edithburgh House (☎ 8852 6373, Edith St) has very nice, old-style guesthouse accommodation for $80 per person for dinner and B&B. Its *Rose Cottage* sleeps four for $65.

The *Ocean View Holiday Units (☎ 8852 6029, O'Halloran Parade)* has basic but clean two-bedroom flats sleeping up to six from $35 per unit. They were about to be renovated at the time of writing.

Just along the road, the more up-market *Anchorage Motel & Holiday Units (☎ 8352 6262)* charges from $45/55 in the holiday flats/motel units – these prices are for doubles.

You can stay in the historic lighthouse keeper's cottages on *Troubridge Island*, where a minimum stay of two nights costs from $200 for two people to $500 for 10, including transfers. For information and bookings contact Troubridge Island Charters.

Both pubs serve large, inexpensive meals. For the town's best wining and dining, visit *Faversham's Restaurant* in Edithburgh House.

EDITHBURGH TO MARION BAY

As an alternative to the main road through Yorketown and Warooka, you can drive to Marion Bay via the 82km unsealed coast road from Edithburgh. A tall lighthouse and rugged cliffs mark **Troubridge Point**, 18km from Edithburgh. This is a good spot for whale watching between June and October.

Fifty kilometres farther on, **Hillocks Drive** (☎ 8854 4002) is a large farm with basic visitor facilities and a 7km coastal frontage. The friendly Butler family offer wonderful coastal scenery, safe swimming beaches, surfing, salmon fishing and bushwalks;

wildflowers are a feature from July to November. Bush camping is $5 per car and old on-site vans are $22 to $25; you pay extra for showers, and there's a $3 entry fee for day visitors. Every year the farm closes on 18 June for two months.

Five kilometres past Hillocks Drive, **Mehan Hill Lookout** affords a fine view across Investigator Strait to Kangaroo Island. To the east are dramatic cliffs, while westwards a long, white surf beach stretches all the way to Marion Bay.

Yorketown
- **pop 750**

Established in 1872, Yorketown is the region's business and administrative centre. There are some interesting old buildings here, including two classic 1870s pubs – you can visit the various sites on a self-guided walk. The town is a good base for fishing trips to various spots on the 'foot'.

About 200 small **salt lakes** in the immediate area once supported a thriving salt-mining industry.

The district council office on Edithburgh Rd has a good range of brochures on the southern Yorke Peninsula.

Places to Stay The pretty little *Yorketown Caravan Park (☎ 8852 1563, Memorial Drive)* is very good value – its tent/caravan sites cost $5/10, its on-site vans $25 – you can rent a TV for $3.

In the centre of town, the modest but friendly *Yorke Hotel (☎ 8852 1221, 1 Warooka Rd)* has basic rooms for $20 including a light breakfast.

Both pubs have counter meals daily. *Thorpy's Pizza*, nearby on Minlaton Rd, is a good spot for breakfast.

Warooka
- **pop 250**

This pleasant little town has some nice old buildings including the original police station (1879), which now houses a **folk museum**. Its elevated position – a rarity on Yorke Peninsula – affords good views of the surrounding farmland. The down side is the weather; Warooka is a local Aboriginal word meaning 'windy hill'.

About 36km from town on the Marion Bay road is the entrance to the 4000 hectare **Warrenben Conservation Park**. There's bush camping here and plenty of good birdwatching in the mallee.

The *Warooka Hotel/Motel (☎ 8854 5001, Main St)* has motel units for $40/50/60 a single/double/triple.

Marion Bay
- **pop 20**

Originally the port for nearby gypsum mines, Marion Bay was almost abandoned when the present shipping facility was developed at Stenhouse Bay. These days, however, its one of the fastest growing resort centres on Yorke Peninsula.

The Marion Bay Store (☎ 8854 4008) is a good spot to get information on fishing, diving and surfing in the area. It also sells provisions, take-aways and ice, fills scuba tanks and can arrange boat hire.

Foul Bay Fishing Charters (☎ 8854 6503) specialises in whiting and snapper, charging from $80 for a full day's fishing.

The friendly *Marion Bay Caravan Park (☎ 8854 4094)* has tent/caravan sites for $10/12, on-site vans from $25 and self-contained cabins from $45 – all vans and cabins have air-conditioning. To get there from the store, head towards Innes National Park; it's just a short walk from the beach.

Opposite the store, the *Marion Bay Seaside Apartments (☎ 8339 1909, 8854 4066)* has elevated units sleeping five from $60. There are several other holiday places in town and the store can provide contact details.

INNES NATIONAL PARK

At the south-western tip of Yorke Peninsula, the popular 9140 hectare Innes National Park comprises mainly coastal heath and rolling mallee country bounded by a spectacular coastline. Some roads within the park are unsealed and can be rough – there are plenty of blind corners and inexperienced drivers, so be careful.

High and dry: the mallee fowl's nest can measure up to 5m high x 10m wide

Information

Entry permits cost $5 per car and you pay at the entry station (☎ 8854 4040) at Stenhouse Bay; it has useful brochures on heritage sites, walks, fishing and surfing. Otherwise try the Stenhouse Bay Trading Post across the road, which also sells fishing tackle, bait, ice and take-aways.

Things to See & Do

There's plenty of **wildlife** including the endangered mallee fowl – the park is one of its last refuges on the peninsula. While you're unlikely to meet a mallee fowl, you should see plenty of other birds, including emus. Western grey kangaroos are fairly common.

The coastline boasts impressive grey-and-orange limestone cliffs, particularly at **Cape Spencer**, **The Gap** and **West Cape**. There's a beautiful view from Cape Spencer across to the rugged **Althorpe Islands** and beyond to Kangaroo Island.

Just past The Gap you can look down on **Ethel Beach**, where waves crash in over the rusting remnants of the Norwegian barque *Ethel*. Amazingly, only one person was drowned when it blew ashore in 1904.

Apparently people actually **surf** off Ethel Beach, but you'd have to know what you were doing. Fortunately there are plenty of other surfing breaks, of which **Pondalowie Bay** is the most popular and consistent. It's suitable for beginners, but not so **Chinamans Hat**. This has the park's most powerful break

and is definitely only for experienced surfers; national competitions are sometimes held here.

There's also good **fishing**. Among the most popular spots are **Browns Beach** (salmon), the southern end of Pondalowie Bay (garfish, King George whiting, flathead, squid and salmon, among others), **West Cape** (sweep, tommy-ruff, salmon) and **Stenhouse Bay** (tommies and King George whiting).

The park includes the abandoned gypsum-mining settlement of **Inneston**. Established in 1913 and closed in 1930, it housed 130 people and even had its own plaster factory. A signposted walk (allow one hour) takes you around the old stone buildings and ruins.

Wildflowers are a highlight from July to November, when the normally drab heath and mallee communities burst into colourful blooms.

Places to Stay & Eat

There are a number of sheltered *bush campsites* close to nice beaches. The surfers' camp at Pondalowie Bay is the best appointed – it has solar-heated showers, but don't expect hot water in winter. Permits cost between $5 and $15 per car depending on the location of the camp site and its facilities. Drinking water is limited (bring your own in summer), and you can purchase firewood at the store outside the fire danger period.

Alternatively, you can stay in rudimentary but comfortable houses at *Inneston* (from $50 to $60, minimum two nights) or a shepherd's hut at *Shell Beach* ($22 for four persons). Contact the park office for details.

Beds cost $15 in a self-contained bunkhouse at *Stenhouse Bay* (store ☎ 8854 4066).

The *Stenhouse Bay Trading Post* has a general store and adjoining tavern which sell meals (dine in and take-away), liquor and basic provisions.

West Coast

The west coast is more sparsely settled than the east, with fewer and smaller towns. Unlike the east it tends to miss out on the sea breezes in summer (these prevail from the south-east), so as a result is generally hotter. There are plenty of good fishing and surfing beaches in the south-west.

MARION BAY TO POINT TURTON

Heading north from Marion Bay, a dirt road with many loose corners runs through mallee and farmland to meet the bitumen near **Corny Point** after 42km. Rough tracks en route lead off to remote surfing, fishing and bush camping spots along the wild stretch of coast between Innes National Park and the Corny Point lighthouse.

One of the strongest surfing breaks is at **Trespassers** on Formby Bay, the turn-off to which is 17km from Marion Bay. A lookout on the clifftop affords you a nice view of the bay's white, sandy beach, which is backed by large dunes.

Farther north, **Daly Heads** has the area's largest surfable waves (up to 4m high). There's easy access to the surf beach from **Dust Hole**, just south of Daly Heads – look southwards over Formby Bay for one of the best coastal views in SA.

There are more views, although not such spectacular ones, at rugged Corny Point in the north-western corner of the 'foot'. You can visit this area on a **camel ride** with

Coastline Camel Safaris (☎ 8855 3400), based near the Corny Point store. It operates from November to February inclusive and charges around $20 per person per hour.

The coast road from Corny Point to the tiny resort of **Point Turton**, on the peninsula's 'instep' about 30km eastwards, passes a number of quiet beaches. En route there's the 490 hectare **Leven Beach Conservation Park**, which conserves dunes and native bush.

Places to Stay & Eat

As shown on the RAA touring map, a string of bush camping areas runs along the coast between Formby Bay and Point Turton. All are managed by the Yorketown council office (☎ 8852 1433), whose workers come around to collect fees ($5 per site) and dispense local knowledge and rubbish bags.

The most popular areas are *Gleesons Landing* in the west and *Burners Beach* in the north. Both are very basic, but have good shelter and are sufficiently large that you can usually find a spot to yourself.

There are *caravan parks* at Corny Point (☎ 8855 3368) and Point Turton (☎ 8854 5222). Both these areas have general stores where you can get provisions and take-away meals.

POINT TURTON TO PORT VICTORIA

Dirt roads and tracks take you along the coast from Point Turton to Port Victoria, with more remote **fishing spots** and small resorts en route. Alternatively, you can take the sealed road through Minlaton in the centre of the peninsula.

An old grain port, tiny **Port Rickaby** has the nicest beach and the best swimming on this stretch of coast; there's also a basic caravan park (☎ 8853 1177) with powered sites and on-site vans. The 22km coastal track from here to Port Victoria is suitable only for 4WD.

Minlaton
- **pop 750**

This attractive service town, which describes itself as the 'barley capital of the world', makes an ideal base for exploring the central peninsula. There's a tourist office at the Harvest Corner tea rooms, on the corner of Main and Fifth Sts.

On Main St is a **memorial** to local pioneer aviator and WWI ace Captain Harry Butler. Open daily, it contains the Bristol fighter he flew in France during the war. The town also has a National Trust **museum** (open every morning except Sunday and Monday) and two good **art galleries**.

You can stay at the quiet and leafy **Minlaton Caravan Park** (☎ 8853 2345, Maitland Rd), which has powered and unpowered sites, air-conditioned vans and air-conditioned cabins. Alternatively, the **Hotel Minlaton** (☎ 8853 2014, 26 Main St) has motel units for $40/50 a single/double.

Gypsy Waggons (☎ 8853 4201) near Brentwood, 13 km south of Minlaton, has horse-drawn caravans carrying up to five adults. The owners, who provide back-up, have established an interesting route including campsites along tracks and quiet back roads in the Hardwicke Bay area. You can hire the vans for three to seven nights, and the minimum rate is $470.

PORT VICTORIA
- pop 500

At one time this was the state's fourth largest export shipping terminal, with windjammers calling in as late as 1949 to load wheat bound for England. Nowadays, however, Port Victoria slumbers undisturbed except for the annual summer onslaught of holidaymakers.

At the jetty there's a small but interesting **nautical museum** with displays featuring the windjammer era. Ask at the kiosk for a key.

There are two fine swimming beaches south of town at **Rifle Butts Beach** and **Second Beach**.

Port Victoria has good scuba diving potential. You can dive with sea lions around **White Rock** and the **Goose Islands**, and there are a number of shipwrecks dating from 1871 in the shallow waters off **Wardang Island**. These are described in the booklet *Wardang Island Maritime Heritage Trail*.

Wardang Island Charters (☎ 8834 2235) offers **fishing and diving charters** for $100 per person per day, lunch not included.

Places to Stay & Eat
Above the jetty, the basic but clean and friendly *Port Victoria Progress Association Caravan Park* (☎ 8834 2001) has tent/caravan sites for $9/11 and on-site vans for $30. If you get tired of fishing you can hire a TV for $3 a day.

Right next door is the much larger and better appointed **Gulfhaven Caravan Park** (☎ 8834 2012). It has tent/caravan sites from $10/12 and self-contained cabins from $38.

At the *Port Victoria Hotel/Motel* (☎ 8834 2069), on Main St near the jetty, motel units sleep up to seven for $40/55/65 a single/double/triple.

Bay View Holiday Flats (☎ 8834 2082, 29 Davis Terrace) has spacious family units with air-conditioning starting at $35 for two adults and two children. It's a short walk from here to the jetty.

If the fish aren't biting you can get *fresh seafood* daily at the two local fisheries, both in the centre of town.

MAITLAND
- pop 1100

Established in 1872, attractive Maitland is the commercial centre for this part of the peninsula.

The National Trust **museum** in the old state school on Gardiner Terrace has displays on local Aborigines and early German settlers. It opens Sunday and public and school holidays from 2 to 4 pm.

Places to Stay & Eat
You'll find a free *camping area* with toilets beside the Maitland sportsground at the northern end of town.

Alternatively, the *Hotel Maitland* (☎ 8832 2431, Robert St) has a good restaurant and basic pub rooms (no fans or air-conditioning) for $25/40.

Eothen Farm Stay (☎ 8836 3210) is 13km from town off the Balgowan road. Its farmhouse sleeps eight people and costs are on a sliding scale from $76 a single/double for one night. The price includes guided tours of the property, which has about 120 hectares of native bush.

PORT BROUGHTON
• **pop 1400**

North of the Copper Triangle, this quiet holiday and fishing town is home to a large prawn fleet. **Fishing charters** are usually available – check at the BP Roadhouse, on Day St. The best swimming in town is off the jetty.

The popular *Port Broughton Caravan Park* (☎ 8635 2188), on the foreshore south of the jetty, has tent/caravan sites for $13/15, on-site vans for $26 and cabins with air-conditioning from $31.

Otherwise there's the classic old *Hotel Broughton* (☎ 8635 2004, Bay St), which overlooks the water. It serves counter meals daily, and has basic pub rooms with comfortable beds and fans or air-conditioning for $30/40 a single/double.

The *Sunnyside Hotel/Motel* (☎ 8635 2100) farther up the street has units for $45/50/55 a single/double/triple.

The Copper Triangle

In 1859 a shepherd working on Wallaroo Station found traces of copper in the bush. The station owner staked a claim and brought four Cornish miners down from Burra to sink a trial shaft. They hit a mother lode of copper, and so began nearly two decades of Croesus-like prosperity that saved SA from bankruptcy.

The Wallaroo mine was in full swing a year later when news came of another strike only 16km away. From this came the even richer Moonta mine. Cornish miners and their families flocked to the area, and the towns of Kadina and Moonta sprang up to service the mines. The Cornish influence was so strong that even today the area is referred to as 'Little Cornwall'.

In 1861 a port and a copper smelter were developed at nearby Wallaroo, which joined with Kadina and Moonta to form the so called 'Copper Triangle'. By 1875 the district had a population of 20,000, about 60% of whom lived in and around Moonta. However, the lack of clean drinking water was a huge health problem. Hundreds of children died in the typhoid epidemics that raged unabated until 1890, when a safe water supply was developed.

Falling copper prices, dwindling ore reserves and industrial problems saw the mines close in 1923. By this time the underground workings extended for 150km and had produced 334,000 tonnes of copper.

Sixty years of prosperity gave the Copper Triangle many fine public and commercial buildings, churches and homes. A large number have survived thanks to the lack of development since then, and this is a major drawcard for today's visitors.

Special Events
Held on odd-numbered years over several days, usually in May, the Kernewek Lowender Festival is a celebration of the Copper Triangle's Cornish heritage. The festivities are held in all three towns and include Celtic games, a Cornish fair, feasting, folk dancing and town walks. Meanwhile, the tables groan under the weight of traditional Cornish pasties and beer.

You might even meet a piskey – a mischievous sprite that superstitious Cornish people believe brings good luck. If no piskeys come your way, it's probably a sign that you haven't had sufficient beer.

Getting There & Away
Premier Stateliner (☎ 8415 5555) has four buses a day from Adelaide, charging $15.50 to the three copper towns. You can also get there from Port Augusta with the same carrier by changing buses at Port Wakefield.

Getting Around
Copper Triangle Cabs (☎ 8821 3444) of Kadina provides a 24-hour taxi service. It charges around $22 from Wallaroo to

Moonta, $20 from Kadina to Moonta, and $14 from Kadina to Wallaroo.

A tourist train consisting of a 1960s diesel locomotive and three 100-year-old carriages runs between Wallaroo and Kadina on the second Sunday of every month and also over Easter and Kernewek Lowender. Return tickets cost $8 and you can book by phoning ☎ 8823 3308.

MOONTA
- pop 2300

In 1861, an illiterate alcoholic shepherd, Patrick Ryan, found copper at the entrance to a wombat burrow. So began the richest mine that SA has ever seen. Not that this did Paddy much good; he'd drunk himself to death within a year of his great discovery.

Numerous mines were developed around Paddy's find, but by far the most successful was the Moonta Mine. By 1870, when over 5000 people depended on it for their livelihood, it was producing over 20,000 tonnes of dressed ore annually. Although profits declined after the 1870s, the Moonta Mine was so rich that large-scale operations continued for another 40 years.

In the boom years, Moonta's population was exceeded in SA only by Adelaide's. However, only 1350 residents remained soon after the mines closed in 1923.

Information

The main tourist office for the Copper Triangle is in the old train station on Kadina Rd (☎ 8825 1891, fax 8825 2930, tourism@kadina.mtx.net.au). It opens daily except Christmas Day from 9 am to 5 pm.

The booklet *Discovering Historic Moonta* includes self-guided tours that take you to over 60 places of interest around the mines and township. You can get a copy at the tourist office.

Things to See & Do

The best place to discover local mining history is out at the **Moonta Heritage Site**, on the Arthurton road about 1km from town. This was the site of the Moonta Mine and an early mining village. Its relics include stone chimneys and enginehouses: these massive structures housed the engines that provided power for pumping and crushing operations. Several sites have been developed with walking tracks and information signs.

The impressive **Moonta Mines School** (1877) once had 1100 students on its roll, but these days is a National Trust museum (admission $3). Its cavernous rooms are filled with interesting displays including the story of Elizabeth Woodcock, the only woman ever to be executed in SA. It opens daily from 1.30 to 4 pm (on Sunday, and public and school holidays, from 11 am).

Nearby is the **Moonta Mines Methodist Church** (1865), an austere building that can seat 1250 people. Services are held on Sunday mornings, with the original organ still in use. Also nearby, the fully restored **Miners Cottage** (1870) is a romantic Cornish dwelling with period furnishings. Both church and cottage are open to the public, and the tourist office can give times.

Many of Moonta's finest historic buildings are features of the **Moonta Heritage Walk**, described in *Discovering Historic Moonta*. Outstanding examples are the Gothic-style **Methodist Church** (1873) and the contrasting Italian-style **Bible Christian Church** (also 1873). They're almost side by side in Robert St.

Nearby **Port Hughes** and **Moonta Bay** are quiet seaside resorts with sandy beaches. The best swimming beach is just south of the jetty at Port Hughes.

Organised Tours

A section of the 1980s **Wheal Hughes** mine, about 3km from town on the Wallaroo road, has been reopened for tourists. One-hour tours run daily (usually at 1 pm) and cost $12 – book at the tourist office. This is *not* one of the early mines.

Every weekend, and daily during public and school holidays, a tiny tourist train takes passengers on a 50 minute circuit ($2.50) of the heritage site, passing Moonta's photogenic train station (1908) en route. This is where you find the tourist office, which has train times.

Two-hour guided walks of Moonta cost $4 and leave from the rotunda in Queen Square every Saturday at 2 pm – also Wednesday during school holidays. For details contact the Pug 'n' Dabble Gift Gallery (☎ 8825 3003) on George St.

If you're interested in a serious **fishing trip**, Blue Fin Fishing Charters (☎ 8825 2880), Port Hughes Fishing Charters (☎ 8825 3388) and Copper Triangle Charters (☎ 8825 3814) operate out of Port Hughes. Each charges around $100 per person for a day's fishing, not including lunch, with minimum numbers from two to five.

Places to Stay

Moonta The *Royal Hotel (☎ 8825 2108, 2 Ryan St)* has basic pub rooms for $25/40 a single/double, including a light breakfast.

Moonta Bay Near the jetty, the friendly and attractive *Moonta Bay Top Tourist Park (☎ 8825 2406)* has tent/caravan sites for $13/15 and cabins with kitchens from $48.

Alternatively, the nearby *Moonta Bay Patio Motel (☎ 8825 2473, 196 Bay Rd)* has comfortable units for $58/69/75 a single/double/triple.

Port Hughes *Port Hughes Caravan & Tourist Parks (☎ 8825 2106)* has tent/caravan sites from $13/15 at two places: one on West Terrace overlooking the jetty, and the other a few minutes walk south on South Terrace, where the reception is. The latter also has cabins with private facilities from $51 ($61 with kitchen). Neither of these places has much shade.

Also near the jetty, *Blue Fin Apartments (☎ 8825 2880, 6 Dowling Drive)* has well-appointed holiday flats sleeping up to six. They cost from $140 a single or double (each extra adult is charged $20); there is a minimum stay of two nights.

Places to Eat

Locals are divided as to whether *Prices Bakery* of Kadina or the *Cornish Kitchen* on Ellen St in Moonta produces the best Cornish pasties in the Copper Triangle. I became fat doing research on this, but in the end decided in favour of the Cornish Kitchen. Its home-made soup and pasty for under $5 is a very satisfying lunch on a cold day.

Next door to the Cornish Kitchen, the *Shaft Steakhouse* is the most upmarket restaurant in town. It's reasonably priced for the standard, with mains starting at around $11.

The *Moonta Bakery (George St)* opens at 7 am daily and serves a good breakfast, among other things. Farther down the street, the *Moonta Pizza Cafe* is also recommended.

Tony's Chinese Takeaways, next to the BP service station on George St, has tempting lunch specials for $4 and $5.

KADINA
* **pop 4500**

The capital of Yorke Peninsula was founded in 1860 to service the Wallaroo Mine, which had been established earlier in the year. Kadina is from the Aboriginal words *kaddy-yeena*, meaning 'lizard plain', while Wallaroo is from *wadla-waru*, meaning 'wallaby's urine'.

The Wallaroo Mine reached its peak in the early 1870s, when it employed up to 1000 men and boys. Kadina's population plummeted after the mine closed in 1923, but while Moonta stagnated, it has managed to prosper as an agricultural, commercial and administrative centre.

Things to See & Do

The booklet *Discovering Historic Kadina* will take you to around 50 sites of interest. You can get one at the local newsagent or the Moonta tourist office.

Just off the Moonta road on the southern side of town, the National Trust's **Kadina Heritage Museum** (admission $4) features Matta House (1863), the restored home of the Matta Matta mine manager. Among its other features are the Matta Matta mine (one of several early small mines in this area), old farming machinery and a blacksmith's shop. It opens on Wednesday and weekends from 2 to 4.30 pm (during public and school holidays from 10 am).

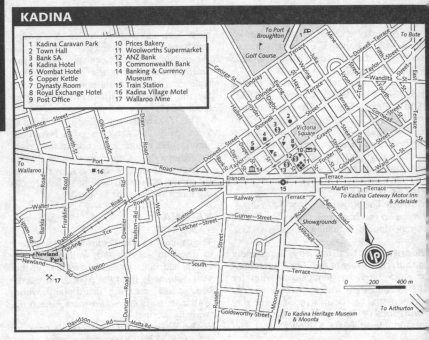

KADINA

1 Kadina Caravan Park
2 Town Hall
3 Bank SA
4 Kadina Hotel
5 Wombat Hotel
6 Copper Kettle
7 Dynasty Room
8 Royal Exchange Hotel
9 Post Office
10 Prices Bakery
11 Woolworths Supermarket
12 ANZ Bank
13 Commonwealth Bank
14 Banking & Currency Museum
15 Train Station
16 Kadina Village Motel
17 Wallaroo Mine

The **Wallaroo Mine** is about 1km west of town off the Wallaroo road. It takes half an hour to stroll around the site, which includes numerous shafts and the stone ruin of **Harvey's Enginehouse**, now a home for pigeons.

If you're interested in money (and who isn't?), the **Banking & Currency Museum** ($3) in the old Bank of SA building (1873) on Graves St has comprehensive displays. It opens daily except Friday and most Saturdays from 10 am to 5 pm, but closes during June. Guided tours are optional, and you can buy and sell coins there.

While not as rich in heritage as Moonta, the town still has many interesting old buildings. You can see them by strolling around the **Kadina Heritage Walk**, described in *Discovering Historic Kadina*. Included is the imposing **Royal Exchange Hotel** (1874) on Digby St; the prefix Royal was added after the Duke of Clarence stayed there in 1880.

Places to Stay

The **Kadina Caravan Park** (☎ 8821 2259, *Lindsay Terrace*) is mainly residential, bu does have a few lawned campsites for $13 and on-site vans for $32.

Locals recommend **Wombat Hote** (☎ 8821 1108, *19 Taylor St*) for simple good-value accommodation. The Womba charges $19 per person for its basic pub rooms, which includes a light breakfast. Alternatively, there is the **Kadina Hote** (☎ 8821 1008), which is a block away at No 29 Taylor St. This place has rooms with private bathrooms for which it charges $35/50 a single/double.

There are two motels on the outskirts o town. The **Kadina Village Motel** (☎ 882. 1920, *27 Port Rd*) charges from $44/54/66 single/double/triple, while the more luxuriou **Kadina Gateway Motor Inn** (☎ 8821 2777 *Adelaide Rd*) charges $69/72.

Places to Eat

The three local pubs serve excellent, cheap meals; they all have pokies, so competition for business is fierce. The *Royal Exchange Hotel* has the largest gaming room and the most imaginative menu.

There are a couple of *bakeries* and several *cafes*. Two dine-in and take-away places are the *Dynasty Room (4 Goyder St)*, which specialises in Chinese and Thai, and the *Copper Kettle (6 Hallett St)*. Both are open on Sunday night.

WALLAROO
- pop 2250

This was the port for Moonta and Kadina. It also had a huge copper smelter, said to be the largest in the southern hemisphere at that time – it contained 30 furnaces and produced 40 tonnes of copper each day. Unlike the mines, most of its employees were Welsh (although still Celtic).

The town's population had reached 5000 by the early 1920s, but crashed after the mines closed. The smelting works were demolished, leaving a single chimney which remains as a local landmark. It's now dwarfed by the banks of huge silos that advertise Wallaroo's modern role as a grain port.

Information

The post office (☎ 8823 2020), on the corner of Irwin St and Owen Terrace, has a range of brochures on the Copper Triangle. It opens weekdays from 9 am to 5 pm and Saturday morning; ask for information at Sonbern Lodge on John Terrace outside these times.

Things to See & Do

In the old post office, on Jetty Rd, there's the interesting **Heritage & Nautical Museum** ($3). It has displays telling of the windjammers that serviced this area from England, and the life story of Caroline Carlton, who wrote the words to *Song of Australia*. It opens on Wednesday, weekends, and public and school holidays, from 2 to 4 pm.

The museum is the starting point for a 9km heritage drive and a much shorter **walking trail** through the town's commercial

The Banking & Currency Museum, Kadina

centre. Both are described in *Discovering Historic Wallaroo*, which takes you to numerous places of interest around town.

Organised Tours

Alicia's Tours (☎ 8823 2682) offers a range of personalised tours in a 1975 'Silver Shadow' Rolls Royce and military jeep. Its three-hour heritage and sunset tours in the Rolls cost $75 per person, including chicken and champagne. Alternatively, you can take a jeep tour to remote beaches.

Wallaroo Bay Yacht Charters (☎ 8825 6235) does day sailing, fishing and diving trips from $60 to $100 per person (maximum six) including lunch. They also offer adventure cruises in the gulf for two people from two to eight days.

Places to Stay

Caravan Parks Near the jetty, the rather cramped and basic *Office Beach Holiday Cabins & Caravan Park* (☎ 8823 2722) has campsites from $12, on-site vans for $27, basic cabins from $32 and self-contained cabins with air-conditioning from $45.

A kilometre from town on Heritage Drive, the much more spacious *North Beach Caravan Park* (☎ 8823 2531) is by a good swimming beach. It has tent/caravan sites for $11/13 and well-appointed motel-style units on the beachfront from $57.

Hotels, Motels & Holiday Flats The grand old guesthouse *Sonbern Lodge Motel (☎ 8823 2291, 18 John Terrace)* has a marvellous old-world atmosphere right down to stained glass windows and a richly chiming grandfather clock in the hall. It has rooms with private bathroom for $40/55/63 a single/double/triple ($24/38/47 without private bathroom) and very tasteful motel units for $55/69/77.

The *Weerona Hotel (☎ 8823 2008, 4 John Terrace)* has basic rooms with ceiling fans for $20/30 a single/double. Otherwise the *Anglers Inn Hotel (☎ 8823 2545, 9 Bagot St)* has motel units for $45/55/65 a single/double/triple.

Mac's Beachfront Villas (☎ 8823 2137, 9 Jetty Rd) is a friendly place, and virtually on the beach. It has fully self-contained, two-bedroom units sleeping up to five for around $130 a night.

Places to Eat
The town's five pubs all have hearty counter meals for a good price.

There are several good take-aways, including Price's *Wallaroo Bakery (Owen Terrace)* and *Jetty Road Bakehouse* near the jetty. The *Wallaroo Cafe (Hughes St)* has a varied menu and a good reputation, while *Best Pizza (Irwin St)* is aptly named – its small pizzas are a substantial meal.

Down at the jetty, *Wallaroo Fisheries* sells fresh seafood as well as fish & chips. Upstairs is *Skinner's Jetty Fish Cafe*, considered the best seafood place in the triangle.

Flinders Ranges

A continuation of the spine of hills that forms the Mt Lofty Ranges, the Flinders Ranges begin near Crystal Brook and run north for 400km to Mt Hopeless, where they peter out in the Strzelecki Desert. There are no towering mountains here; the highest point, St Mary Peak, rises only 1170m above sea level. Even so, the often stark, semiarid scenery of rugged purple ridges, dramatic bluffs and gum-lined creeks is a spectacular highlight of SA.

As well as bushwalks and great views, there are numerous sites of cultural interest such as abandoned mines and settlements, and Aboriginal art galleries. The latter include rock paintings and petroglyphs, or rock carvings.

As in many other dry mountain regions of Australia, the vegetation is surprisingly diverse and colourful; tall river red gums are a feature throughout, while dark stands of native pine are more obvious in the north. The western flanks are in a rain shadow, so the vegetation here is much sparser than on the eastern side. In the south the hills are covered with large gums, while beyond Quorn the vegetation generally becomes scrubbier.

History

The Adnyamathanha, or 'hill people', have inhabited the Flinders Ranges for many thousands of years. In fact, the ranges and the people who lived there were an integral part of the long-distance trade routes that crossed the continent. Dotted among the hills and gullies are a number of archaeological sites, including ochre and stone quarries.

The first white people to visit the Flinders Ranges were members of the crew of HMS *Investigator*, who climbed Mt Brown (near Quorn) in 1802.

Next on the scene was Edward John Eyre. On two expeditions in 1839 and 1841 he travelled the length of the ranges from Crystal Brook to Mt Hopeless, which he named while in a despairing mood. After climbing it

HIGHLIGHTS

- Take in some of the state's major scenic and historical highlights along the 1200km Heysen Trail
- Explore the ranges on a horse or camel trek, or cycle the Mawson Trail
- Visit fascinating ruins and ghost towns, and see Aboriginal rock paintings and carvings
- Ride the Pichi Richi Railway and relive the romanticism of early train travel
- Photograph abundant wildlife, including euros, red kangaroos and yellow-footed rock-wallabies

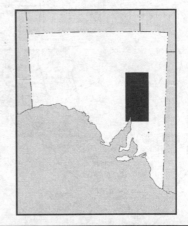

to view the surrounding country he became convinced that his way north was blocked by an impenetrable barrier of salt lakes.

A combination of remoteness and Eyre's unfavourable reports on the far north meant there was no land rush here as there was in the south. Even so, sheep runs were

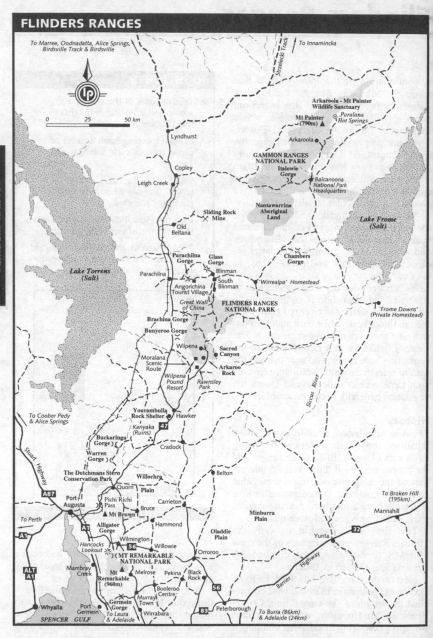

FLINDERS RANGES

To Marree, Oodnadatta, Alice Springs,
Birdsville Track & Birdsville

To Innamincka

Strzelecki Track

0   25   50 km

Lyndhurst

Arkaroola - Mt Painter
Wildlife Sanctuary

Mt Painter
(790m)

Paralana
Hot Springs

Copley

Arkaroola

GAMMON RANGES
NATIONAL PARK

Leigh Creek

Italowie
Gorge

Balcanoona
National Park
Headquarters

Sliding Rock
Mine

Nantawarrina
Aboriginal
Land

Lake Frome
(Salt)

Old
Beltana

Parachilna
Gorge

Glass
Gorge

Chambers
Gorge

Blinman

Parachilna

South
Blinman

'Wirrealpa' Homestead

Lake Torrens
(Salt)

Angorichina
Tourist Village

Great Wall
of China

FLINDERS RANGES
NATIONAL PARK

'Frome Downs'
(Private Homestead)

Brachina Gorge

Bunyeroo Gorge

Wilpena

Sacred
Canyon

Moralana
Scenic
Route

Arkaroo
Rock

Wilpena
Pound Resort

Rawnsley
Park

Siccus River

To Coober Pedy
& Alice Springs

Yourambulla
Rock Shelter

Hawker

Buckaringa
Gorge

Kanyaka
(Ruins)

47

Warren
Gorge

Cradock

The Dutchmans Stern
Conservation Park

Willochra
Plain

Belton

Stuart Highway

Quorn

A87

Pichi Richi
Pass

Bruce

Carrieton

Minburra
Plain

To Broken Hill
(195km)

Port
Augusta

Mt Brown

Hammond

Mannahill

To Perth

Alligator
Gorge

A1

Oladdie
Plain

Yunta

32

Hancocks
Lookout

Wilmington

Willowie

Orroroo

Barrier   Highway

ALT
A1

56

MT REMARKABLE
NATIONAL PARK

Mambray
Creek

Melrose

Pekina

Black
Rock

Mt
Remarkable
(960m)

Booleroo
Centre

56

Whyalla

Port
Germein

Germein
Gorge

Murray
Town

Wirrabara

Peterborough

To Burra (86km)
& Adelaide (24km)

83

SPENCER GULF

To Laura
& Adelaide

stablished around Wilpena Pound in 1851 and farther north at Mt Serle later in the decade. But overstocking, and the resulting destruction of pasture, combined with drought in the early 1860s, caused many runs to be abandoned.

Better rainfall years lured wheat farmers, who reached Hawker by 1880. For a time there were rich golden harvests on the vast Willochra Plain, and there was wild talk of cereal crops stretching all the way to the Northern Territory (NT) border. Eventually, however, the grim reality of drought sent the farmers packing to the relative safety of Goyder's Line (see the History section in the Facts about South Australia chapter).

Today, a number of early settlements lie in ruins, the sheep runs have long since been cut up into smaller blocks, and Quorn is the northern limit for cereal crops. Tourism is the chief means of survival for most of the smaller towns.

Information

Tourist Offices The main tourist office for the Flinders Ranges is in Port Augusta, with others at Hawker, Peterborough, Quorn and Wilpena. See the sections on these towns.

National Parks The National Parks & Wildlife Service (NPWS) head office for the central and northern Flinders Ranges is in Hawker (☎ 8648 4244, fax 8648 4242). You can write to them at 60 Elder St, Hawker 5434.

For the southern Flinders (between Telowie Gorge and Dutchmans Stern) contact the NPWS office in Port Augusta. See under Information at the start of the Outback chapter.

There are other NPWS offices at Wilpena Pound (in the Flinders Ranges National Park), the Mt Remarkable National Park, and the Gammon Ranges National Park. See the sections on these places.

The **Flinders Parks Pass** and the various NPWS statewide passes cover entry and camping fees (up to five nights in any location) in the Mt Remarkable and Flinders Ranges national parks. They do not include camping in the Wilpena Pound Resort. See National Park Offices in the section on Useful Organisations in the Facts for the Visitor chapter.

Books The Royal Automobile Association (RAA) publishes the comprehensive travel guide *Flinders Ranges & Mid North* ($15 members, $30 nonmembers).

Explore the Flinders Ranges, by the Royal Geographic Society of South Australia, is excellent. It includes general information, natural and social history, and details of numerous walking tracks, highways and byways.

For history buffs, Hans Mincham's *Hawker, Hub of the Flinders* gives an interesting historical account of Hawker and several now-vanished towns in the central ranges.

If you're keen to identify the local flora get hold of the pocket-sized *Wildflowers of the Southern Flinders* and *Wildflowers of the Northern Flinders* – both are widely available.

The leaflet *Interpreting Rock Art of the Flinders Ranges* (available from most information outlets) explains the meanings of many of the petroglyphs to be seen at Aboriginal art sites.

Maps Local experts reckon the most accurate touring map of the Flinders Ranges is published by Westprint; it includes a lot of information on local towns and attractions. The RAA map is also very good.

Organised Tours

There are lots of tours from Adelaide to the Flinders Ranges, with others mainly leaving from Port Augusta, Quorn, Hawker and Wilpena Pound. Many people unwisely leave booking their tour until they get to the ranges, where they discover that there's not a lot on offer.

Coach/4WD Tours The South Australian Tourism Commission (SATC) and the Port Augusta tourist office can provide details of most tour companies operating to and within the ranges. Check your hostel for tours that cater for backpackers and other budget travellers.

You can tour from Adelaide in a luxury coach with Premier Stateliner (☎ 8415 5566) and Adelaide Sightseeing (☎ 8231 4144), or look at more adventurous options with some of the smaller operators.

Groovy Grape, Heading Bush, Oz Experience and The Wayward Bus all visit the Flinders on their runs between Adelaide and Alice Springs. See the Bus section in the Getting There & Away chapter.

Gawler Outback Tours (☎ 8278 4467) does mainly accommodated 4WD trips ex-Adelaide. Their summer specials are worth investigating.

Operating from Quorn, Intrepid Tours does 4WD trips from half a day to six days ex-Quorn and Port Augusta. Wallaby Tracks, also of Quorn, does day trips as well as backpacker packages from Adelaide. See the section on Quorn for more details of these two operators.

Both the caravan parks in Hawker do 4WD tours, and there are other small operators scattered through the ranges north of Wilmington. You can do Aboriginal culture tours from Hawker.

Horse & Camel Rides Horse rides (generally day rides or shorter) are available at the Gammon Ranges National Park, Quorn and Rawnsley Park (near Wilpena). Camel rides and treks are on offer at Blinman. See the sections on these places.

Bushwalks & Cycling Several Adelaide-based operators do walking, climbing and/or cycling trips into the Flinders. For cycling enthusiasts, the Mawson Trail is a great challenge. See the Outdoor Activities chapter.

Accommodation
Hotels, motels, caravan parks, cottages, farms and stations offer a wide range of accommodation, particularly south of Blinman. As well as a couple of upmarket hotels and motels, there are numerous moderately priced and budget places, including bush campsites.

The tourist offices in Quorn and Hawker are agents for various remote homesteads, cottages and holiday flats. See the sections on these towns for contact details.

Generally, the busiest times in the Flinders Ranges are September, October and Easter, when you should book well in advance. Many places put their rates up during school and public holidays at these times, as well as the mid-year school break.

Getting There & Away
Port Augusta is the main transport hub for travel to and from the Flinders Ranges. See the Port Augusta section later in this chapter for details on air, bus and train services to that town.

Bus Premier Stateliner runs to Quorn, Hawker and Wilpena from Adelaide (twice weekly) and Port Augusta (three times weekly). They have four daily services up Hwy 1 from Adelaide to Port Augusta.

Bute Buses' Mid-North Passenger Service (☎ 8826 2346) visits Orroroo and Peterborough from Adelaide. See the sections on these towns for details.

Car The Flinders Ranges are reached by sealed roads leading off Hwy 1 and Main North Rd, both from Adelaide, and the Barrier Hwy from New South Wales (NSW).

As an alternative if you're coming from NSW, you can turn off the Barrier Hwy at Yunta and take gravel-surfaced back roads to Wilpena Pound, the Gammon Ranges National Park and Arkaroola.

Getting Around
Anyone planning to travel off the main roads, particularly in the north, should always be prepared for the shortage of drinking water, shops and service stations.

Most points of interest in the south are accessible from good sealed roads. Heading north, there are sealed roads from Port Augusta and Melrose to Wilpena Pound via Quorn and Hawker, but farther on the roads are gravel or dirt. The road skirting the ranges' western flank from Hawker via

Parachilna and Leigh Creek is sealed as far as Lyndhurst.

Depending on what you're used to, the region's unsealed roads are usually quite reasonable when dry, but they can be closed by heavy rain. For recorded information on road conditions phone ☎ 1300 361 033. Otherwise contact the various NPWS offices and hotels for a local update.

Southern Ranges

The southern Flinders Ranges district extends from just north of Crystal Brook to Hawker, and eastwards as far as Peterborough. It includes the Mt Remarkable National Park and several conservation parks, most of which are south of Quorn.

PETERBOROUGH
• pop 2300
Established in the 1870s, Peterborough was first called Petersburg after the German settler Peter Doecke, who owned the land it was built on. The anti-German hysteria during WWI resulted in its name being anglicised.

Although its beginnings were agricultural, Peterborough became an important railway junction – three gauges met here – and at one time over 100 trains passed through each day. Unfortunately for locals, the interstate gauges were standardised in the mid-1990s and, as a result, the prospects for future employment are not good.

The tourist office (☎ 8651 2708) is in the railway carriage near the imposing town hall, on Main St. It generally opens daily from 10 am to 3 pm.

Things to See & Do
There are a couple of ghost towns near Peterborough, the most interesting of which is Dawson, about 25km to the north-east. These agricultural centres closed down as farm sizes expanded and the transport system improved.

Steamtown, at the junction of West and Railway Terraces, is a working railway museum with steam locomotives, numerous freight and passenger vehicles, and an enormous railway roundhouse with turntable. Ask at the tourist office if you want to check it out.

On holiday weekends between April and October, narrow-gauge steam trains run between Peterborough and Orroroo or Euralia. The tourist office can tell you who to contact for bookings.

Peterborough has the state's only operating government gold battery; it's used to treat ore from goldfields to the north-east. Built in 1897, it's a 10-head gravity stamp battery powered by a diesel engine, and when the stampers are pounding up and down the din is terrific. Once again, contact the tourist office for access details.

Eric Rann's Museum, at 142 Moscow St, has an interesting collection of shiny stationary engines, while Ivan Ley's Museum, at 53 Queen St, has everything from antique dolls to barbed wire to butter churns. Both are open daily.

You can also visit St Cecilia, an impressive two-storey Edwardian mansion (1912) on Callary St. Originally a bishop's residence, it became a convent and boarding school for the Sisters of St Joseph of the Sacred Heart. The building is richly furnished with antiques, and is filled with Roman Catholic history and memorabilia. You can do tours ($5) by arrangement (☎ 8651 2654 or 8651 3246).

Early in February a rodeo on the national circuit usually attracts a good crowd.

Places to Stay & Eat
Caravan Parks & Hostels The friendly Peterborough Caravan Park (☎ 8651 2545, 36 Grove St) has tent/caravan sites for $10/13, on-site vans for $25, basic cabins for $33 and self-contained cabins for $39.

Also good value is the Budget Travellers' Hostel (☎ 8651 2711, 86 Railway Terrace), opposite the train station, which has beds from $13.

Hotels & Motels The town's oldest pub, the Peterborough Hotel (☎ 8651 2006, 195 Main St) has basic motel units for $44/48 singles/doubles.

The **Railway Hotel/Motel** (☎ *8651 2427, 221 Main St*) is somewhat more sophisticated. Its pub rooms with ceiling fans are $28/46/69 for singles/doubles/triples including breakfast, and it has pleasant motel units from $49/56.

Units at the **Peterborough Motor Inn** (☎ *8651 2078, 25 Queen St*) cost $49/56/70. Their restaurant enjoys a good reputation – it has a 'Sizzler'-style smorgasbord where you can fill up for $10.

The **St Cecilia Private Hotel** (☎ *8651 2654, Callary St*) has large, tastefully furnished rooms with share facilities for $38 per person, including a cooked breakfast. It's well known for its weekend 'murder mystery' banquets.

Getting There & Away
Bute Buses' Mid-North Passenger Service (☎ 8826 2346) visits Peterborough from Adelaide daily except Saturday and Monday ($24).

ORROROO
• pop 600

This pleasant little town began in 1864 as an eating house on the stage-coach route from Burra to Blinman and Port Augusta. From here you can continue north to Hawker via Carrieton, where the sealed road ends, or head west to Wilmington.

The **Yesteryear Costume Gallery** (admission $3) on Main St is a real surprise. Its fascinating collection of period costumes and accessories, dating from 1830 to 1930, can be viewed most days between 10 am and 5 pm.

Cellar Antiques, also on Main St, has several rooms filled with antiques, collectables and bric-a-brac. It opens Thursday to Sunday from 10 am to 5 pm.

On the way up to **Tank Hill Lookout**, which has a great view over the town and surrounding farmland, you'll pass the **Early Settler's Cottage**, on Fourth St. This evocative little dwelling of timber slabs, pug and stone has been expertly restored. It's definitely worth a visit, which you can arrange by phoning ☎ 8658 1264.

Lion's Park on Pekina Creek features a pleasant picnic area with a lawn and shady gums. From here you can walk upstream past Aboriginal **rock carvings** and return via a rock with a rather sad poem etched into it by an early settler.

Just out of town and north of the Wilmington road, there's a huge **river red gum** on the western bank of Pekina Creek. This magnificent specimen has a trunk 3m in diameter and a canopy 20m across. It's not the biggest tree in the world, but it's not bad for up this way.

Late in December each year at **Carrieton** (population 200), 37km north of Orroroo, a rodeo on the national circuit usually attracts a good crowd.

Places to Stay
The little **Orroroo Caravan Park** (☎ *8658 1444, 1 Second St*), at the Wilmington end of town, has tent/caravan sites for $9/12, on-site vans for $22 and basic cabins for $25. Otherwise the attractive **Commercial Hotel** (☎ *8658 1272, Main St*) has basic rooms for $35/55, including a light breakfast.

In Carrieton, the **Carrieton Hotel** (☎ *8658 9007*) has rooms with ceiling fans for $30/50, including a cooked breakfast.

Getting There & Away
Bute Buses' Mid-North Passenger Service (☎ 8826 2346) visits Orroroo from Adelaide via Burra on Wednesday and Friday ($27).

PORT GERMEIN
• pop 220

Founded after a road was built through nearby **Germein Gorge** in the 1870s, Port Germein became an important outlet for the wheat producers further east. Windjammers called in here to load grain for England as late as the 1940s, but these days this quaint little town survives mainly on holidaymakers.

Each New Year's Day there's the Festival of the Crab, which celebrates the blue swimmer crabs caught in abundance along the coast here.

Euros and yellow-footed rock-wallabies inhabit the steep hills and crags of the 2000 hectare **Telowie Gorge Conservation Park**, 10km east of town. The access road ends at a car park, from where a 20 minute stroll takes you up an attractive rocky creek into a gorge.

Premier Stateliner buses will drop you off in town on their daily services between Adelaide and Port Augusta.

Places to Stay & Eat

The basic *Progress Association Caravan Park* (☎ 8634 5266, Esplanade) has tent and caravan sites, on-site vans and cabins, while the venerable *Port Germein Hotel* (☎ 8634 5244, High St) has basic pub rooms – it also does counter meals.

Otherwise there's *Casual Affair* (☎ 8634 5242, High St), a friendly coffee shop, gallery and craft centre with backpacker accommodation. Dorm beds in a tranquil Japanese-style room cost $10; if you're staying there you can rent a bike for $15 per day. Meals are available, but you have to book.

There are a couple of *bush campsites* without facilities on the road into Telowie Gorge. They're about 1km before the carpark.

MT REMARKABLE NATIONAL PARK

This steep rugged park, which covers over 16,000 hectares, straddles the ranges between Melrose and Wilmington. Dramatic scenery, secluded gorges, a variety of plant and animal habitats, and some good bushwalks, including the Heysen Trail, are among its attractions.

Information

The park office at Mambray Creek (☎ 8634 7068) is usually attended between 8.30 am and 4.30 pm daily. You pay the entry fee ($5 per car) here or, if coming in from the north, at Alligator Gorge.

A number of walking trails from 2km to 18km are included in a brochure. For longer, more adventurous walks you'll need the Melrose and Wilmington 1:50,000 topographical maps produced by AUSLIG.

Things to See & Do

The park's main access points are at Wilmington to the north, Melrose to the east (walkers only) and Mambray Creek to the west.

Wilmington Area Turning off Main North Rd just south of town, an 11km gravel road, which offers tremendous views, ends at a carpark near colourful **Alligator Gorge**. There's a short but rather testing walk to this picturesque feature, where grey and red sandstone walls close in to just 2m apart.

From here you can walk to places such as **Kingfisher Flat** (two hours), **Hidden Gorge** (four hours) and **Mambray Creek** (seven hours).

Melrose Area A walking track climbs up from a carpark about 3km north of Melrose to the summit of 960m **Mt Remarkable**. You'll probably see euros, and there are stunning views from the top; allow four hours for the return walk. The Heysen Trail descends along the Mt Remarkable Range from the summit to Wilmington.

Mambray Creek The road into Mambray Creek turns off Hwy 1 about 21km north of Port Germein. Majestic red gums and tall native pines line the creek, and farther in is a scenic gorge where you might see euros and yellow-footed rock-wallabies. Red kangaroos are reasonably common on the plains, while noisy birdlife (particularly kookaburras, galahs and corellas) is a feature along the creek.

A number of **walking tracks** head off into the ranges from Mambray Creek. If you're really fit and well-prepared you can walk to Alligator Gorge, then across to the Mt Remarkable Range and on to Melrose via Mt Remarkable.

Premier Stateliner will drop you off at the Mambray Creek turn-off on Hwy 1.

About 15km north of the turn-off, the 7800 hectare **Winninowie Conservation Park** is another good spot to see kangaroos and many bird species including emus; its mangroves support breeding colonies of waders. Access is by a dirt road leading in to Miranda and Chinaman Creek.

Places to Stay
The bottom carpark near Alligator Gorge has a quiet picnic area. From here it's a 10 minute walk to *Longhill Camp* – this and other bushwalker campsites cost $3 per person.

If you don't have a Flinders Parks Pass (see under Information at the start of this chapter), vehicle-based camping at *Mambray Creek* costs $12 per car including the entry fee. The campground is by the creek and has many magnificent gums. You can also stay in a cabin with a kitchen and four bunk beds for $25 per person.

PORT AUGUSTA
- **pop 14,600**

Matthew Flinders, who came ashore here and sent an exploring party into the nearby ranges, was the first European to set foot in the area. Called *kurdnatta* (heaps of sand) by the Aborigines, initial discouraging reports on the surrounding country kept settlers away.

The need for an outlet for the new agricultural districts to the east and north-east resulted in the port being established in 1854. Shipping boomed until the early 1880s, when it began to decline as the new railways took trade elsewhere. Port Augusta was ultimately saved from extinction when it became the headquarters for the Transcontinental Railway to Perth.

Today, this busy modern town is a major crossroads for travellers. From here, main roads head west across the Nullarbor to Western Australia (WA), north to Alice Springs and Darwin, south to Adelaide and east to Broken Hill and Sydney. The *Indian Pacific* and *The Ghan* trains both pass through Port Augusta.

Information
Tourist Offices The tourist office is in the Wadlata Outback Centre at 41 Flinders Terrace. It's the major outlet for information on the Flinders Ranges and Outback

regions, and also has a good selection of material on the Eyre Peninsula. The office is open weekdays from 9 am to 5.30 pm and weekends from 10 am to 4 pm. You can contact the office on ☎ 8641 0793, 1800 633 060 toll free, fax 8642 4288, info@flinders.outback.on.net.

The NPWS office for the southern Flinders Ranges and far north is in the SGIC building at 9 MacKay St. See Information at the start of the Outback chapter.

Money The Commonwealth Bank, Bank SA, National Bank and Westpac are all on Commercial Rd in the town centre.

Shopping The town's main supermarkets – Coles and Woolworths – are open daily from 7 am to midnight (10 pm on Sunday). Both are in the town centre.

Laundry There are seven-day launderettes behind Ian's Chicken Hut (on Hwy 1) and at 74 Stirling Rd (next to the Pampas Motel about 2km from the town centre).

Dangers & Annoyances Locals warn against walking by yourself at night near any of the town's hotels.

Things to See & Do
The acclaimed **Wadlata Outback Centre** (admission $7) has many excellent exhibits tracing the Aboriginal and European history of the Flinders Ranges and Outback. The place is under-utilised, probably because most travellers are in a hurry to get somewhere else – a pity as it really is worth a visit. It opens the same hours as the tourist centre.

A brochure from the tourist office details a two hour **heritage walk** that takes in numerous historic sites. They include **AD Tassie's house** (1864), the **Troopers Barracks** (1860) and the Corinthian frontage of the **Town Hall** (1887).

There are tours ($2) of the **School of the Air**, at 59 Power Crescent, at 10 am on weekdays. Tours also operate at the **Royal Flying Doctor Service** base, 4 Vincent St, on

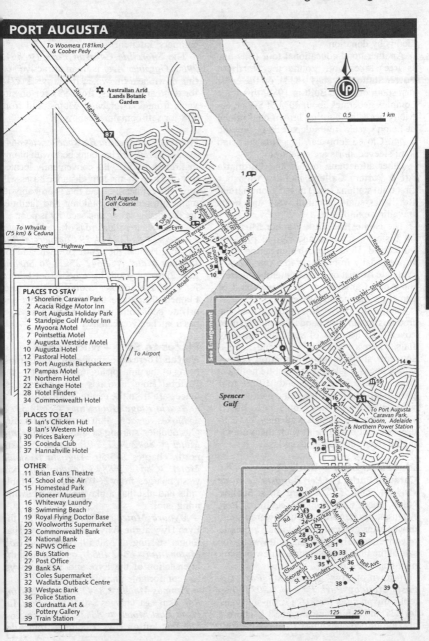

PORT AUGUSTA

FLINDERS RANGES

To Woomera (181km) & Coober Pedy

Stuart Highway

87

Australian Arid Lands Botanic Garden

Port Augusta Golf Course

To Whyalla (75 km) & Ceduna

Eyre Highway

A1

To Airport

Spencer Gulf

See Enlargement

To Port Augusta Caravan Park, Quorn, Adelaide & Northern Power Station

A1

0   0.5   1 km

PLACES TO STAY
1 Shoreline Caravan Park
2 Acacia Ridge Motor Inn
3 Port Augusta Holiday Park
4 Standpipe Golf Motor Inn
6 Myoora Motel
7 Pointsettia Motel
9 Augusta Westside Motel
10 Augusta Hotel
12 Pastoral Hotel
13 Port Augusta Backpackers
17 Pampas Motel
21 Northern Hotel
22 Exchange Hotel
28 Hotel Flinders
34 Commonwealth Hotel

PLACES TO EAT
5 Ian's Chicken Hut
8 Ian's Western Hotel
30 Prices Bakery
35 Cooinda Club
37 Hannahville Hotel

OTHER
11 Brian Evans Theatre
14 School of the Air
15 Homestead Park Pioneer Museum
16 Whiteway Laundry
18 Swimming Beach
19 Royal Flying Doctor Base
20 Woolworths Supermarket
23 Commonwealth Bank
24 National Bank
25 NPWS Office
26 Bus Station
27 Post Office
29 Bank SA
31 Coles Supermarket
32 Wadlata Outback Centre
33 Westpac Bank
36 Police Station
38 Curdnatta Art & Pottery Gallery
39 Train Station

0   125   250 m

weekdays between 10 am and 3 pm; admission is by donation.

Another good educational tour (this one is free) takes you around the **Northern Power Station** (☎ 8641 1633), on the coast just south of town. Built in 1985, this huge complex generates about 40% of SA's electricity needs by burning brown coal mined at Leigh Creek. Tours depart at 11 am and 1 pm. Closed footwear, long trousers and long-sleeved shirts are essential.

Other attractions include the **Curdnatta Art & Pottery Gallery**, in Port Augusta's first train station (1887) at 105 Commercial Rd. It has some beautiful work and hosts travelling exhibitions.

The **Homestead Park Pioneer Museum**, on Elsie St, features an original pine-log homestead (1850s) furnished in period style. It opens daily from 10 am to 5 pm ($2.50).

In late August or early September there's the Apex Camel Cup, a fun weekend of camel racing and novelty events.

On the Stuart Hwy just north of town, the free **Australian Arid Lands Botanic Garden** covers 250 hectares of sandhills and clay flats. There's a pleasant cafe and a good souvenir shop in the information centre, which opens weekdays and public holidays from 9 am to 5 pm (weekends 10 am to 4 pm). Small black ants infest the pathways in warm weather – they don't bite, but if you're wearing sandals you may have to use repellent if you don't want them crawling all over your feet and ankles.

Places to Stay – Budget

Caravan Parks The *Port Augusta Caravan Park* (☎ 8643 6357, 9 Brook St) at Stirling North, about 6km from the centre of Port Augusta, has powered and unpowered sites, on-site vans and cabins, including a couple of converted railway carriages. It was up for sale at the time of this update – new owners may improve things.

In town on Hwy 1, the leafy *Port Augusta Holiday Park* (☎ 8642 2974) has tent/caravan sites for $16/17, on-site vans for $37 and cabins starting at $39. There's also a four bed bunkhouse ($12 per person,

no fans or air-con) with an adjacent campers' kitchen.

The *Shoreline Caravan Park* (☎ 8642 2965, Gardiner Ave) is in an attractive setting down near the water. It charges $12/14 for tent/caravan sites, from $23 for on-site vans, from $32 for basic cabins, and from $38 for self-contained cabins.

Hostels *Port Augusta Backpackers* (☎ 8641 1063, 17 Trent Rd) has bunk beds with lumpy mattresses for $15. It's conveniently located just off Hwy 1 – the long-distance buses will drop you off nearby – but this is probably its major attribute. The building and facilities are decidedly weary, and security is poor.

A much better standard is offered by *Hotel Flinders* (☎ 8642 2544, 39 Commercial Rd), which is right in the centre of town, and the *Pampas Motel* (☎ 8642 3795, 76 Stirling Rd), 2km out. Both have beds (not bunks) for $15. Backpacker rooms in the Hotel Flinders sleep three and have TV, fridge and private bathroom, while the Pampas Motel has a kitchen you can use.

Places to Stay – Mid-Range

Motels There are a number of motels, most being of the uninspiring transit variety – the Pastoral Hotel also has motel units. Distances are from the centre of town.

Acacia Ridge Motor Inn (☎ 8642 3377, 33 Stokes Terrace), 4km north-west, has singles/doubles starting at $46/52. *Poinsettia Motel* (☎ 8642 2411, 24 Burgoyne St), 3km north, charges $45/50. *Augusta Westside Motel* (☎ 8642 2488, 3 Loudon Rd), 1km west, charges from $64/70 for comfortable units and also has a playground and swimming pool.

Myoora Motel (☎ 8642 3622), on the Eyre Hwy at the Whyalla end of town, has rooms starting at $50/59. *Standpipe Golf Motor Inn* (☎ 8642 4033), on Daw St at the intersection of the Eyre and Stuart Hwys, has comfortable units for $75/80.

Pampas Motel (☎ 8642 3795, 76 Stirling Rd), 2km east, charges $40/50. The *Port Augusta East Motel* (☎ 8642 2555), 5km east (the first left on Hwy 1 coming from Adelaide), charges $50/55, while *Port Augusta Hiway One Motel (☎ 8642 2755)*, the second left coming from Adelaide, has large units starting at $56/62 and a swimming pool.

Hotels Several hotels in or near the town centre have accommodation. Unless otherwise stated the following rates are for rooms with shared facilities.

Augusta Hotel (☎ 8642 2701, 11 Loudon Rd) has renovated single/double pub rooms for $25/35, while the renovated pub rooms at the *Pastoral Hotel (☎ 8642 2818)*, on the corner of Stirling Rd and Carlton Parade, are $30/40 and motel units $75/80.

The *Commonwealth Hotel (☎ 8642 2844, 73 Commercial Rd)* has rooms for $25 per person. In the same street, the *Hotel Flinders (☎ 8642 2544, 39 Commercial Rd)* has renovated rooms with en suite facilities $42/55/62.

Northern Hotel (☎ 8642 3906, 4 Tassie St) charges $25/35 for basic pub rooms and $45/55 for renovated rooms with en suite facilities; prices include a light breakfast. The *Exchange Hotel (☎ 8642 2522)*, at No 2 Tassie St charges $25 per person including a light breakfast.

Places to Eat
There are plenty of places to eat, including most of the hotels, motels and roadhouses. As always the pubs are generally good value, as is the *Cooinda Club* on Commercial Rd in the town centre. It does pub-style lunches and dinners most days. *Port Augusta Hiway One Motel*, *Myoora Motel* and *Standpipe Golf Motor Inn* have decent restaurants, but are not for the budget-minded.

Most of the take-away places on Hwy 1 are pretty ordinary. *Ian's Chicken Hut*, just east of the Stuart Hwy intersection, has an excellent reputation.

On Commercial Rd, in the centre of town, *Prices Bakery* and the bakery in *Woolworths* supermarket are both good. *The Outback Tuckerbox* in the Wadlata Outback Centre is popular for lunches, and there are several coffee shops and cafes in the town centre.

Entertainment
The tourist office can tell you what's happening in town; you can also check the local weekly newspaper, the *Transcontinental*, for events and venues.

For films there's the *Brian Evans Theatre*, on Carlton Parade in the town centre. It opens daily except Thursday, and screens films mainly in the evenings from 8 pm.

On Friday night there's usually a rock band at one of the *football clubs*, and a DJ at the *Augusta Hotel*. For video clips of your favourite star, try *Pete's Bar* in the Pastoral Hotel on Wednesday, Friday and Saturday nights.

Getting There & Away
Air Airlines of SA (bookings ☎ 13 13 13) flies weekdays to Adelaide ($120) and Leigh Creek ($100), and Wednesday and Thursday to Woomera ($80).

On Saturday (returning Sunday) you can take the mail plane to Boulia in outback Queensland, stopping at Innamincka and Birdsville en route; for details check with Airlines of SA (☎ 8642 3100). A twin-share package ex-Adelaide is $955 (leaving Friday); a single fare including accommodation and meals is $970 ex-Adelaide and $740 ex-Port Augusta.

Bus The bus station (☎ 8642 5055) for Premier Stateliner and Greyhound Pioneer is at 23 Mackay St – you can book with Premier Stateliner here, but not Greyhound. McCafferty's picks up and drops off at the Shell Meteor Roadhouse, on Hwy 1 on the Adelaide side of town.

Premier Stateliner (☎ 8642 5055) runs daily to Adelaide ($29), Port Lincoln ($41), Ceduna ($54) and other places on the Eyre Peninsula. It visits Quorn, Hawker and Wilpena Pound three times a week – see the sections on these places.

Greyhound Pioneer (bookings ☎ 13 20 30) travels daily to Perth ($199), Alice Springs ($147), Darwin ($270) and Sydney via Adelaide ($123). McCafferty's (☎ 8212 5066) travels daily to Alice Springs, Darwin and Sydney for the same prices.

FLINDERS RANGES

Train From Port Augusta you can get to all mainland capitals except Darwin by train (call ☎ 13 21 47 for inquiries and bookings). All 1st-class sleeper tickets include meals.

To Sydney (32 hours) an economy seat costs $185, an economy sleeper $362, and a 1st-class sleeper $545.

It's 33 hours to Perth and an economy seat/economy sleeper/1st-class sleeper ticket is $224/467/704.

To Alice Springs the train takes 16 hours. An economy seat/economy sleeper/1st-class sleeper ticket costs $136/295/500.

Adelaide ($33) is four hours away.

Getting Around
There is no bus service to the airport, but you can ring Augusta Taxis (☎ 8642 4466) from the phone box there – it costs about $10 to the centre of town.

A town bus service operates daily except Sunday. Ask at the tourist office for a route map and timetable.

Hire cars are available from Budget (☎ 8642 6040), at 16 Young St.

LAURA TO MELROSE
Heading north from Adelaide along Main North Rd you officially enter the Flinders Ranges region at **Stone Hut**, 10km north of Laura.

Nine kilometres farther on is **Wirrabara** (population 250), a friendly town showing the faded prosperity of former times. About 7km to the west, the **Wirrabara Forest** was once noted for its huge river red gums – these were a valuable source of jetty timbers and railway sleepers – and the majestic **King Tree** has been preserved as an example. There are some good walks including the Heysen Trail.

About 10km north of Wirrabara you can turn left and travel through the scenic **Germein Gorge** towards Port Germein. On Main North Rd just beyond the intersection is tiny **Murray Town**, where there's a pub.

Places to Stay & Eat
Wirrabara Heritage B&B (☎ 8668 4018, Main North Rd) is a large 1895 house at the northern end of town. It's a homely sort of place with comfortable rooms sleeping up to six for $25/45 for singles/doubles, including a substantial light breakfast. A backpacker room sleeps three for $20 per person.

Alternatively, the 1870s *Wirrabara Hotel* (☎ 8668 4162, Main North Rd) has air-con rooms for $20/30, and does counter meals daily. Otherwise you can camp at the sports ground, where sites cost $5 ($10 with power) – the Horseshoe Cafe on Main North Rd has a key.

The *Wirrabara Forest (forest headquarters ☎ 8668 4163)* has a basic campground close to the Heysen Trail. Also in the forest, and 7.5km from Wirrabara township, the *Wirrabara YHA Hostel* has beds costing $12 for members. For contact details phone the YHA office in Adelaide on ☎ 8231 5583.

Vondon Homestead (☎ 8666 4209) near Murray Town has friendly farm-style accommodation. Their standard package costs $240 for two people for two nights, including all meals and a farm tour. The turn-off is about 1km south of Murray Town.

MELROSE
• pop 200

Established in 1853 when a copper mine was opened nearby, this pretty little town is the oldest settlement in the Flinders Ranges. It's in a great setting right at the foot of **Mt Remarkable** (960m) and is just outside Mt Remarkable National Park. If Melrose has a down side it's being woken early in the morning by the screeching clouds of corellas that feed in the wheat paddocks close to town.

The caravan park is the best place to go for tourist information.

Things to See & Do
There are a number of interesting old buildings including several pug-and-pine settler's cottages and two photogenic hotels. The 1860s police station and courthouse now houses a National Trust **museum**, open daily from 2 to 5 pm ($2).

Judging by the old cemetery in **Paradise Square**, life here definitely wasn't all beer and skittles in the early days. Used between 1858 and 1880, it contains a depressing number of children's graves.

You can explore Mt Remarkable's lower slopes on a pleasant 3km marked trail which starts at the caravan park. It leads up to a **war memorial**, where there's a nice view, then back via the abandoned **copper mine**, the reason for Melrose's existence.

About 15km to the south-east, **Booleroo Centre** (population 300) has a museum with the largest collection of stationary engines in SA. The Booleroo Steam & Traction Engine Society's rally, held annually in late March, is worth attending if you're in the area.

Melrose is a good base for walks in **Mt Remarkable National Park** – see the earlier section on the park for details.

Heading north from Melrose on Main North Rd, you'll notice many magnificent gnarled gums, some with large hollows at the base of their trunks. Apparently these were used as shelters by Aboriginal people, who created them with the clever use of fire. Such trees are common throughout the ranges.

About 14km north of Melrose, a turn-off on the left will take you to the old **Spring Creek Mine**. Copper was discovered here in 1860 and the deposit was worked off and on until 1916. All that's left today are some crumbling stone ruins in a lovely valley.

Places to Stay & Eat

Down by a pretty creek with huge river red gums, the *Melrose Caravan Park* (☎ 8666 2060) has bush campsites ($10), powered sites ($13), on-site vans with air-con ($30) and self-contained cabins ($40). Bunk beds in a well-appointed bunkhouse cost $10.

You can also stay at the *showgrounds* (caretaker ☎ 8666 2154) off the Wilmington road, which has good campsites scattered among gum trees. Facilities are very basic, which is reflected in the rate of $2 per person ($5 extra per site with power).

Mt Remarkable Hotel (☎ 8666 2119, Stuart St) has mobile motel-style units for $35/50 singles/doubles and self-contained cabins for $58 singles and doubles.

More interesting (if more basic) accommodation is provided by the *North Star Hotel* (☎ 8666 2110), at the southern end of Stuart St. Its rooms, which have shared facilities including a kitchen, are across the road in the National Trust-owned Exchange Hotel. They cost $30/50 including a light breakfast.

There are several holiday cottages and flats in the area and you can get details from the caravan park. They include *Eders Holiday Flat* (☎ 8666 2174) – the turn-off is 6km north of Melrose – which sleeps up to four people, charging $30 for two and $40 for four; linen extra. The friendly owner is German-speaking. From here it's an easy 2km walk along the back fence to connect with the Mt Remarkable walking trail.

Both pubs do great meals. *Bluey Blundstone's Blacksmith Shop* in Stuart St does lunches Friday to Monday, and also offers highly rated B&B.

WILMINGTON
• **pop 250**

Originally called Beautiful Valley, Wilmington is a somewhat stark and dusty contrast to its near neighbour, Melrose. It grew around a pub and Cobb & Co staging post in the 1860s and soon became an important agricultural centre. Although the town is pretty quiet these days, the **Wilmington Hotel** (1879) is a reminder of more prosperous times.

Things to See & Do

From here it's an easy drive to the **Alligator Gorge** section of Mt Remarkable National Park – see the earlier section on the park for details.

Stan Dawes' Museum on Second St features a huge collection of minerals, fossils and shells. It opens most days from 1 to 5 pm.

On the road to Port Augusta, the 7km detour to **Hancocks Lookout** turns off 3.5km from town. The views en route, and the expansive panorama over the western foothills to Spencer Gulf once you get there, make it worthwhile.

Continuing on over scenic **Horrocks Pass** towards Port Augusta, the barren western scarp is a dramatic contrast to the steep gullies and big trees on the eastern side.

If you're heading for Quorn, the **Gunyah Rd scenic route** is an excellent if winding and dusty alternative to the bitumen farther east. It takes you through the eastern foothills of **Mt Brown**, with many beautiful views along the way.

Another alternative route goes via the ghost town of **Hammond**, on the vast Willochra Plain 23km north-east of Wilmington.

Places to Stay

The well-shaded *Beautiful Valley Caravan Park* (☎ 8667 5197) is just south of town on Main North Rd. It has attractive bush campsites for $11 (the ground is as hard as nails in summer), powered sites for $15, on-site vans for $28 and air-con cabins starting at $35.

About 4km to the east off Amyton Rd, the *Wilmington Caravan Park* (☎ 8667 5002) has tent/caravan sites for $12/14, on-site vans starting at $25 and air-con cabins at $35. It's in a very pleasant bush setting on the banks of a creek.

In the centre of town, the *Wilmington Hotel* (☎ 8667 5154, Main St) has basic rooms (some with air-con) for $25/40 for singles/doubles.

Out of Town Off Gunyah Rd 16km from town, *The Gunyah* (☎ 8667 5199) is a remote stone farmhouse in a beautiful setting in the foothills of Mt Brown. During the week it costs $30 for the first two people and $10 for extras; on weekends and school holidays it's $50 and $10 (the complex has 21 beds). The Heysen Trail is nearby and there's plenty of potential for other walks.

QUORN
* pop 1400

A picturesque town on the edge of the Outback, Quorn is about 330km north of Adelaide and 50km north-east of Port Augusta. Wheat farming began in the area in 1875, and the town was surveyed three years later with the arrival of the Great Northern Railway from Port Augusta.

The railhead moved north in 1880 and soon after the town was linked to the main line from Adelaide to the eastern states. Quorn thus became an important railroad junction and service town for the surrounding farms and stations. Although the railroads have long since closed, it retains a strong flavour of its early boom days.

Quorn is within 50km of a number of attractions such as Dutchmans Stern, Mt Remarkable National Park and the Kanyaka ruins.

Information

The Flinders Ranges Visitor Information Centre (☎ 8648 6419, fax 8648 6001, tourism@flindersrangescouncil.sa.gov.au), on Seventh St, opens daily except public holidays from 9 am to 5 pm. At the time of writing they were talking about relocating to the nearby train station.

Outside the times given above you can try Quornucopia (on Railway Terrace) or the caravan park.

Things to See & Do

One of Quorn's most appealing features is the evocative **Railway Terrace** streetscape across from the train station. The almost unbroken line of two-storey hotels and shops, which dates from the late 19th century, is an impressive reminder of busier times. You can easily picture a horde of thirsty passengers erupting from the train to slake their thirst in the four pubs across the road.

In the same street there's an old **flour mill** (now a motel and restaurant), built in 1878, and an elaborate stone **town hall** (1891). The tourist office has a brochure that takes you on a self-guided walk past these and other sites.

Ask at the train station about tours ($5) of the large **railway workshop**, which normally operate on train days (see the following section on the Pichi Richi Railway). There's a mind-boggling collection of around 20 steam and diesel-powered locomotives as well as numerous carriages, freight wagons, brake vans and sundry items. Most are in working condition.

Art Galleries There are several good art galleries. The **Carine Turner Studio Gallery**, on First St, has a good selection of fine arts, leadlight, batik, antiques and bric-a-brac, while **Sue's Art Studio Gallery**, on Seventh St, has some beautiful paintings.

Quornucopia on Railway Terrace is an old-style emporium which has a range of crafts and gifts.

Artist Val Francis displays many marvellous pieces including paintings of wildlife and landscapes at her **Junction Art Gallery**, about 20km north of town and off the scenic route (see the following section). There's a nice walk from the gallery to the top of the Ragless Range, where you get good views.

Buckaringa Scenic Drive The 56km unsealed road heading north from Quorn along the eastern foothills has plenty of interest. First up is the 3500 hectare **Dutchmans Stern Conservation Park**, which features a bold bluff shaped like the rear end of an 18th century Dutch sailing ship. The Heysen Trail runs through the park, and you can get to the top of the bluff via an 8km walking track. The park turn-off is 7km from Quorn.

About 9km farther on is the turn-off to the **Junction Art Gallery** (see Art Galleries, above).

Continuing on you'll pass **Warren Gorge**, **Buckaringa Gorge** and **Middle Gorge**, all of which are small but picturesque. There's a pleasant bush camping area at Warren Gorge, with a good rock-climbing spot – you may see **yellow-footed rock-wallabies** here as this area is one of their strongholds.

FLINDERS RANGES

Meet Petrogale Xanthopus

Found in the rocky hills of the Barrier, Flinders and Gawler ranges of SA, the large yellow-footed rock-wallaby (Petrogale xanthopus) is easily identified by its brown-and-orange banded tail. This is one of the prettiest of Australia's marsupials, its coat being richly ornamented with reddish-brown, black, grey and white. At one time it was hunted so enthusiastically for its skin that extinction was feared. It was protected in SA in 1912, but hunting for the fur trade continued for some time after that.

The total population of yellow-footed rock-wallabies was estimated at 10,000 in 1981 and significantly less than that in 1995. It is now classified as 'vulnerable' to extinction. There are around 200 known colonies, with most consisting of six to 12 animals but some being as large as 40. The main threat comes from foxes, which seem to prevent the recovery of local populations after drought. Another major threat is competition from introduced grazing animals, particularly sheep, goats and rabbits.

All is not lost, however. Since the early 1990s the NPWS has been baiting foxes in selected areas, including the Flinders Ranges National Park and adjoining stations, and local wallaby populations appear to have doubled as a result. Also, goats are no longer present in the ranges in such huge numbers as previously, while rabbits have sharply declined thanks to the calici virus.

The wallabies' preferred habitat is steep rocky slopes with overhangs and boulders where their young can shelter from wedge-tailed eagles. There are a number of places in the Flinders Ranges where they can often be seen. Probably the best are the gorges around Warren Gorge north of Quorn, and Brachina and Wilkawillana gorges in the Flinders Ranges National Park. Early morning and late afternoon are the best times to see them.

Denis O'Byrne

Buckaringa Sanctuary, which encompasses Buckaringa and Middle gorges, lies 30km north of Quorn. An ecotourism venture in the style of Warrawong Sanctuary in the Adelaide Hills is planned for the area – contact the tourist office for an update.

The scenic route continues on past the **grave** of Hugh Proby, Kanyaka's founder – see the section on Kanyaka, following – before meeting the main road to Hawker about 34km from Quorn.

Other Outlying Places For $15, the Quorn Mill Motel will hire you a key to gain access to private **4WD tracks** around Devils Peak and Mt Brown East. At both places you'll find great spots for picnics, bush camping and walks; it's a tough, two hour return trek to the top of Devils Peak, but the views are terrific.

Rugged **Mt Brown Conservation Park** is reached by a walking trail from the end of the road near **Olive Grove** Homestead, about 14km south of Quorn. Allow five hours for the 12km return walk via **Waukarie Falls** to the top of Mt Brown (970m). The walk is described by an excellent brochure, available at the tourist office.

Starting at Woolshed Flat in Pichi Richi Pass, the **Waukarie Creek Trail** follows Waukarie Creek to meet the Heysen Trail near Olive Grove Homestead; there's plenty to see, so allow at least five hours for the return walk of about 9km.

Pichi Richi Tourist Train Part of the long-defunct Great Northern Railway line has reopened as the Pichi Richi Railway, which runs through the scenic Pichi Richi Pass between Quorn and Port Augusta. Most trains run to Woolshed Flat, 16km south, while others continue on about 4km to Saltia; the 13km section between Saltia and Stirling North, near Port Augusta, was expected to open late in 1999.

The train, which is often pulled by a vintage steam engine, makes the 2½ hour return trip to Woolshed Flat for $24. It operates from April to October inclusive, running fairly frequently during school and public holidays and at other times mainly on alternate Sundays. The tourist office can give you a timetable and advice on how to make a booking.

Organised Tours

Specialising in 4WD natural history trips, **Intrepid Tours** (☎ 8648 6277, intrepid@ dove.net.au) have been around a long time. Tours depart Port Augusta and Quorn daily, costing $47 ex-Port Augusta for a half day tour and $85 for a full day to the Wilpena area or Blinman. It also has weekend and extended tours throughout the ranges and as far afield as Lake Eyre.

Wallaby Tracks Adventure Tours has day tours to the northern ranges around Wilpena from $79 and to the southern ranges including Alligator Gorge for $65. Its packages include two/three day tours for $249/279 ex-Adelaide. It can be contacted through Andu Lodge (see the Places to Stay section).

The **Quorn Mill Motel** does half-day 4WD trips to Dutchmans Stern for $44.

Pichi Richi Saddle & Pack Horse Treks (☎ 8648 6074) has a range of day and half-day rides in the hills around Quorn as well as extended treks (up to five days) in the Wilpena area. Its overnight trek to Devils Peak costs $150 per person if there's a group of four.

Places to Stay

Shaded by huge gums populated by kookaburras, parrots, galahs and little corellas, the *Quorn Caravan Park* (☎ 8648 6206, Silo Rd) is one of the nicest parks in the Flinders. It's just behind the train station, and has tent/caravan sites (starting at $11/14), on-site vans without air-con ($28) and self-contained cabins with air-con ($46).

In the old hospital, *Andu Lodge* (☎ 8648 6655, 1800 639 933 toll free, headbush@ dove.net.au, 12 First St) is a very good hostel with excellent facilities. Beds in spacious dorms cost $15, and there are also single ($28), twin ($36) and double rooms ($38). You can hire mountain bikes ($20 per day) and Mick, the owner, can tell you all about the bushwalks and rides around town – places such as Devils Peak and Dutchmans Stern are within easy cycling distance. Transfers from Port Augusta can be arranged ($6 each way).

The *Transcontinental Hotel (☎ 8648 6076, 15 Railway Terrace)* is the pick of the town's four hotels for accommodation. It's a friendly place with standard rooms (no air-con) for $29/45 singles/doubles, including a light breakfast.

At the east end of Railway Terrace, *Quorn Mill Motel (☎ 8648 6016)* has comfortable units starting at $62/75.

Out of Town The tourist office acts as the agent for a number of holiday homes, flats and cottages in the area.

The *Pichi Richi Holiday Camp (☎ 8648 6075)* in Pichi Richi Pass has a fully self-contained cottage sleeping up to eight. It charges from $80 per day for the cottage.

You can hire the homestead and shearers' quarters at *Dutchmans Stern Conservation Park* (Port Augusta NPWS ☎ 8648 5300) for $35 for up to four people and $5 per extra person. The complex has 15 beds.

Places to Eat

Quorn's four hotels offer counter and dining room meals, with the *Transcontinental Hotel* having the best reputation. For something more upmarket there's a very good restaurant in the *Quorn Mill Motel*, where main courses start at $13.

Alternatively, the cosy *Quandong Cafe* on the corner of First and Sixth Sts opens daily for coffee, snacks and lunches. It has wonderful gourmet pies including kangaroo and claret, and quondong.

The *Old Willows Brewery Restaurant* (☎ 8648 6391) in Pichi Richi Pass has a menu which will really get the juices working. Specialising in gourmet-style bush tucker, it offers treats such as kangaroo Wellington, damper with acacia seeds, and quandong pie. It opens for dinner from Thursday to Sunday, and for lunch on weekends.

Getting There & Away

Premier Stateliner (☎ 8415 5555) buses travel from Port Augusta on Wednesday, Friday and Sunday, costing $37 from Adelaide and $6 from Port Augusta.

KANYAKA

The ruins of several early settlements are scattered along the road between Quorn and Hawker, with the most impressive being those at Kanyaka, 41km from Quorn. Here, by a gum-lined creek about 500m off the road, are the substantial remains of the 16 room **Kanyaka Homestead** and various stone outbuildings. Founded in 1851, the station ran 50,000 sheep and employed 70 families before it was devastated by drought and overstocking in the 1860s. The homestead was finally abandoned in 1888, after which the property was subdivided.

Kanyaka's founder, **Hugh Proby** (third son of the Scottish Earl of Carysfort), is buried under an imported granite tablet beside the Buckaringa scenic route 12km north-east of Buckaringa Gorge. He drowned in a flash flood in Willochra Creek in 1852, aged 24 years.

From the homestead ruins you can take a 10 minute walk to the old woolshed. The track continues about 1.5km to a beautiful waterhole, which is overlooked by a massive boulder known locally as **Death Rock**. According to one story, local Aborigines once placed their dying kinsfolk here to see out their last hours.

If you're coming from Wilpena Pound, don't be confused by the sign that indicates the old Kanyaka town site (surveyed 1863); the clearly marked turn-off to the homestead ruins is 4km farther on.

Northern Ranges

Much more remote and undeveloped than the southern ranges, the sparsely populated area between Hawker and the Strzelecki Desert contains three of the state's finest conservation areas: the Flinders Ranges and Gammon Ranges national parks, and the Arkaroola Wildlife Sanctuary.

The road from Hawker to Marree is sealed as far as Lyndhurst. To get to the

Gammon Ranges National Park and Arkaroola from this direction you take the gravel road from Copley, just north of Leigh Creek. Alternatively, you can go from Wilpena Pound via Wirrealpa Homestead and Chambers Gorge.

HAWKER
• pop 490

Hawker is 55km south of Wilpena Pound and, like Quorn, owes its existence to the now-defunct Great Northern Railway. It was established in 1880, by which time the surrounding Willochra Plain was gaining a reputation as one of the colony's finest wheat-growing areas. Optimism was high, but the uncertain seasons eventually brought a decline that culminated in the last significant harvest taking place in 1947.

Information

The main tourist information outlet is in Hawker Motors (☎ 8648 4014, fax 8648 4283, hawkmts@dove.mtx.net.au) on the corner of Wilpena and Cradock Rds. It sells a good range of books on the Outback and Flinders Ranges.

You can send and receive email here.

Things to See & Do

Hawker Motors has a brochure which takes you on a self-guided walk around the town's oldest buildings.

The Jarvis Hill Lookout, about 6km south-west of Hawker, gives nice views over the Willochra Plain to Hawker and north to Wilpena Pound.

There are Aboriginal rock paintings 12km south of Hawker at Yourambulla, where three sites are open to visitors. They're among overhangs and cliffs high up on Yourambulla Peak, a half hour walk from the carpark. The name means 'two men' and refers to the twin peaks just east of the art sites.

Organised Tours

The Hawker Caravan Park offers various 4WD tours into scenic station country and the gorges of the Flinders Ranges National

Park. These cost $50 for a half day and from $75 for a full day – you can tag along in your own vehicle if you want.

The Flinders Ranges Caravan Park does a half day 4WD tour to spectacular Arkaba Station for $65.

Fray Cultural Tours (☎ 8648 4182/22) offers a range of Aboriginal cultural tours from one to six days to places between Hawker and Arkaroola – it's owned and operated by Aboriginal people. The overnight trips can be camping or accommodated, and there's a tag-along option. Rates are available on application.

Places to Stay – In Town

The *Hawker Caravan Park* (☎ 8648 4006, Chaceview Terrace) at the Wilpena end of town has tent/caravan sites for $12/15 (powered sites with private facilities $5 extra), on-site vans with air-con for $30, and self-contained cabins from $65.

About 1km out on the Leigh Creek road, the friendly *Flinders Ranges Caravan Park* (☎ 8648 4266) has similar facilities for similar prices – it has a good campers' kitchen, and lots of trees.

The *Hawker Hotel/Motel* (☎ 8648 4102, Elder Terrace) charges $30/40 singles/doubles for basic hotel rooms (some with air-con) and $50/60 for motel units.

The *Outback Chapmanton Motel* (☎ 8648 4100, 1 Wilpena Rd) charges $55/65/75 for its motel units and holiday flats.

Places to Stay – Out of Town

Hawker Motors acts as the agent for a number of holiday homes, flats and cottages in the northern Flinders.

Merna Mora Station (☎ 8648 4717), off the Leigh Creek road 46km north of Hawker, has holiday flats for $50 singles and doubles and $10 each extra adult (they sleep up to six). The property has beautiful scenery and plenty of wildlife. You'll find the turn-off at the intersection of the Leigh Creek road with the Moralana Scenic Route.

Edeowie Station (☎ 8648 4713) is 12km past the Merna Mora turn-off. Its old shearers' quarters are more basic, but in peak times it's a quiet contrast to Merna Mora. There are some great walks you can do, including the trek into the ranges to spectacular Edeowie Gorge – experienced walkers can continue from here into Wilpena Pound. It charges from $39 for doubles ($10 per extra adult) in the quarters, or you can camp in the bush for $5 per car.

Places to Eat
There are several eateries including the reasonably priced *Old Ghan Restaurant*, in the train station. Travellers recommend the *Elder Terrace Cafe*, which is open daily for breakfast, lunch and dinner. They have an imaginative menu as well as more basic fare such as gourmet pizzas and roo burgers.

Getting There & Away
Premier Stateliner buses travel from Port Augusta on Wednesday, Friday and Sunday, costing $48 from Adelaide and $17 from Port Augusta.

HAWKER TO WILPENA
There are increasingly compelling views of the rugged **Elder Range** and **Rawnsley Bluff**

as you head towards Wilpena Pound. **Rawnsley Lookout**, about 41km from Hawker, has magnificent views of bold bluffs and soaring cliffs to the north-west and the **Chace Range** to the south. Rawnsley Bluff marks the southern end of the Flinders Ranges National Park.

Arkaba Station, 21km north of Hawker, offers 4WD tours into the Elder Range. See Organised Tours in the Flinders Ranges National Park section.

A little farther north, the unsealed 28km **Moralana Scenic Route** runs between the Wilpena and Leigh Creek roads. It takes in magnificent scenery between the Elder and Wilpena Pound Ranges, and is well worth doing. The turn-off is 24km from Hawker on the Wilpena road (46km on the Leigh Creek road).

Friendly **Rawnsley Park**, 35km from Hawker and 21km from Wilpena, offers a range of activities. These include sheep-shearing demonstrations, trail rides ($30/100 for one/eight hours), 4WD tours ($50/80 for a half/full day) and good bush-walking; phone ☎ 8648 0030 or 8648 0008. Premier Stateliner passes three days a week and will drop you at the front gate – you can

FLINDERS RANGES

Local Legends

The 'spirit of place', almost palpable in the Flinders, has inspired a rich heritage of Aboriginal 'Dreaming' stories. Many of these legends – some secret, but others related by Adnyamathanha elders – explain the creation of the landscape and the native fauna that inhabits it.

Arkaroola comes from *Arkaroo*, the name of a Dreamtime serpent ancestor. Suffering from a powerful thirst, *Arkaroo* drank Lake Frome dry, then carved out the sinuous Arkaroola Creek as he dragged his bloated body back into the ranges. *Arkaroo* went underground to sleep it off, but all that salty water had given him a belly ache. Now he constantly moves about to relieve the pain, which explains the 30 to 40 small earth tremors that occur in the area each year.

Another story relates that the walls of the pound are the bodies of two *Akurra* (giant snakes), who coiled around *Ikara* (Wilpena Pound) during an initiation ceremony, creating a whirlwind during which they devoured most of the participants.

In another story, the bossy eagle *Wildu* sought revenge on his nephews, who had tried to kill him by building a great fire. All birds were caught in the flames, and, originally white, they emerged blackened and burnt. The magpies and willy wagtails were partially scorched, but the crows were entirely blackened, and have remained so to this day.

arrange to be picked up, or walk the 2km to the homestead.

Arkaroo Rock, 40km from Hawker, is another Aboriginal art site. It features reptile and human figures executed in yellow and red ochre, charcoal and bird lime on the underside of a huge fallen boulder. This is one of the Flinders' most important Aboriginal cultural sites, and was used for initiation ceremonies as late as 1940. The return walk from the carpark, where there's a pleasant picnic area among native pines, has views of towering cliffs and takes about one hour.

Places to Stay
Arkaba Station (Wilpena visitor centre ☎ 8648 0048) has a two bedroom cottage that sleeps seven. It costs $100 for a double and $15 per extra adult. There is bush camping near the homestead for $10 for doubles.

Rawnsley Park (☎ 8648 0030 or 8648 0008) has tent/caravan sites for $10/17, onsite vans (no air-con) for $36 and basic cabins for $44. The views to nearby Rawnsley Bluff are stunning.

FLINDERS RANGES NATIONAL PARK
This 94,500 hectare park has many attractions including rugged gorges, saw-toothed ranges, gum-lined creeks, abandoned homesteads, Aboriginal sites, abundant wildlife and, in early spring, carpets of wildflowers. Most areas of interest are readily accessible from a network of dirt roads and walking tracks.

The best-known feature in the entire Flinders Ranges is the natural basin known as **Wilpena Pound**. Covering about 80 sq km and ringed by steep ridges, it's accessible only through a narrow gorge near the Wilpena Pound Resort. On the outside the **Wilpena Wall** soars 500m high, while inside the basin slopes relatively gently away from the peaks.

Standing up on the rim, you can see why the Adnyamathanha people consider it to be the joined bodies of two snakes, *akurra*, with the head of one being St Mary Peak. (*Wilpena* is their word for 'bent fingers'.)

The visitor centre *(☎ 8648 0048, fax 8648 0092)* is on the entrance road into the Wilpena Pound Resort. Open from 8 am to 5 pm daily, it has a wealth of information on the park and surrounding district. It also sells the **Flinders Parks Pass** as well as entry and camping permits – see Information at the start of this chapter.

Things to See & Do
You could easily spend two or three days at Wilpena doing tours and walks, or longer if you wanted to explore farther afield.

For natural history enthusiasts there's the 20km **Brachina Gorge Geological Trail**, which you follow in your car. It features an outstanding geological sequence of exposed sedimentary rock, covering 120 million years of earth history. An excellent brochure and information signs along the way explain it all.

You can make the geology trail part of a 110km round trip from Wilpena, taking in the scenic **Bunyeroo Valley**, Brachina Gorge, **Aroona Valley** and **Stokes Hill Lookout** – the latter has some interesting information on Aboriginal culture. The trail starts at the junction of the Brachina Gorge and Blinman roads, so if you want to follow it logically you'll have to do the round trip in an anticlockwise direction. Take the time to do some short walks (allow a full day for the trip) and make sure to stop at **Bunyeroo Valley Lookout** for its spectacular views.

Wildlife is plentiful. Euros and red kangaroos are often seen, and yellow-footed rock-wallabies are reasonably common in Brachina Gorge. Wallaby numbers are on the increase now that goat and fox populations are controlled and the good old calici virus has devastated local rabbits.

Just outside the park's south-east corner, **Sacred Canyon** has galleries of Aboriginal petroglyphs featuring abstract designs and animal tracks.

The resort is powered by Australia's largest off-grid **solar electricity system**, with 400kWh of battery storage. You can view it from a lookout, where there are information signs.

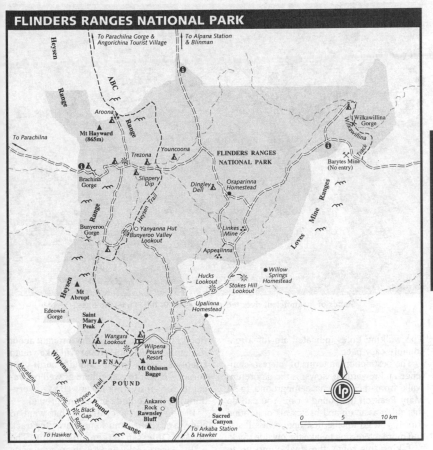

FLINDERS RANGES NATIONAL PARK

To Parachilna Gorge &
Angorichina Tourist Village

To Alpana Station
& Blinman

Heysen

ABC

Range

Range

Aroona

Mt Hayward
(865m)

To Parachilna

Trezona

Youncoona

FLINDERS RANGES
NATIONAL PARK

Wilkawillina
Gorge

Wilkawillina

Barytes Mine
(No entry)

Brachina
Gorge

Slippery
Dip

Dingley
Dell

Oraparinna
Homestead

Loves Mine Ranges

Range

Bunyeroo
Gorge

Heysen Trail

Yanyanna Hut

Bunyeroo Valley
Lookout

Linkes
Mine

Appealinna

Heysen

Mt
Abrupt

Hucks
Lookout

Stokes Hill
Lookout

Willow
Springs
Homestead

Edeowie
Gorge

Saint
Mary
Peak

Upalinna
Homestead

Wangara
Lookout

Wilpena
Pound
Resort

WILPENA

Mt Ohlssen
Bagge

POUND

Moralana

Wilpena

Scenic

Route

Heysen Trail

Black
Gap

Range

Ankaroo
Rock

Rawnsley
Bluff

Sacred
Canyon

To Hawker

To Arkaba Station
& Hawker

0   5   10 km

FLINDERS RANGES

Bushwalks If you're planning to walk for more than three hours, fill in the logbook at the visitor centre – and don't forget to 'sign off' when you return. Searches are no longer initiated by the rangers, so make sure someone responsible knows the details of your walk. Remember that this is arid country – carry plenty of drinking water.

There are numerous walking tracks marked (sometimes not very clearly) by blue triangles; sections which incorporate the Heysen Trail are indicated by red markers. The NPWS has a leaflet with brief descriptions of around 20 walks. In addition, the Royal Geographic Society of South Australia (RGSSA) has excellent pamphlets on several walks. Topographical maps at 1:50,000 are available for $8.30 from the visitor centre.

Most of the walks around Wilpena start from the campground. They vary from short walks suitable for parents with small children, to longer ones taking a day or more.

RICHARD I'ANSON

FLINDERS RANGES

Stands of magnificient river red gum preside in the Flinders Ranges

The walking times indicated are for a reasonably easy pace.

The best option, in terms of interest, challenge and rewarding views, is the day return walk from the Wilpena campground to **St Mary Peak** on the pound's rim. You can do this either as an up-and-back walk or a round trip. If you go for the first option, it's faster and more interesting to take the outside track.

Taking this route, the final climb up to **Tanderra Saddle** is fairly steep and the stretch to the top of the peak is a real scramble. However, the views are superb; the white glimmer of Lake Torrens is visible off to the west and the Aroona Valley stretches away to the north.

Descending back to the saddle you can return to the resort by the same direct route or take the longer, but very pleasant, walk through native pines and mallee on the pound floor. The pound was a wheat farm between 1902 and 1914, and you'll pass the old **homestead** near the end; ironically, it was

flood rather than drought that brought about its demise. A detour en route will take you to **Edeowie Gorge** in the pound's north-west corner – if you're going there as well be prepared for an overnight stay (BYO everything) at the **Cooinda** bush campground.

If you don't have all day, but want to enjoy a challenge and some views, the track up **Mt Ohlessen Bagge** might suit. The walk – steep, rocky and tough going in parts – takes about three hours return from the Wilpena campground. A stunning panorama awaits at the summit.

A good short walk is the one hour return trip to the old homestead inside the pound. En route you walk through scenic **Sliding Rock Gorge**, the only break in the pound's rim. If you go in the early morning or late afternoon you should see euros.

Organised Tours

Nearby Arkaba Station can be explored on a **4WD tour** costing $55/75 for a half/full day, and there's a tag-along option. Tours include a barbecue/vegetarian lunch and sweeping panoramas from high ridge tops. Book through the Wilpena visitor centre.

Scenic flights over the pound and surrounding ranges cost $50/60/85 for 20/30/45 minutes; prices are based on three passengers. You can also fly up to Arkaroola and do their famous Ridgetop Tour, or take a flight over Lake Eyre and **Marree Man** (see the Marree section in the Outback chapter). Book through the Wilpena visitor centre.

Sky Trek is an exhilarating 4WD route on Willow Springs Station, 21km north-east of Wilpena. You can take a tour with several operators in the area, or drive yourself for $30 (self-drive bookings ☎ 8648 0016). The trip takes about six hours and includes the summit of Mt Caernarvon (923m), said to be the highest vehicle access point in the ranges.

Places to Stay & Eat
Unless you have a tent there is no cheap accommodation at Wilpena Pound itself. The *Wilpena Pound Resort* (☎ 8648 0004, 1800 805 802 toll free, wilpena@adelaide.on.net) has a campground where an unpowered/powered site costs $11/17. You purchase your permit at the visitor centre, which has a store selling essential grocery lines and takeaway food.

Within the national park (ie outside the resort) are bush camping areas with very basic facilities for $5 per car per night; you can purchase a permit from either the visitor centre or roadside stands along the way. The nicest places are *Trezona*, *Aroona* and the east end of *Brachina Gorge*, all of which have tranquil creek-bank sites among big gum trees; remote *Wilkawillana Gorge* in the north-east is the quietest.

BLINMAN
* pop 50

This quaint hamlet owes its existence to the shepherd 'Peg Leg' Blinman, who discovered copper here in 1859. A mine was soon operating, but things didn't really get moving until 1903, when a smelter was built on the site. Four years later the town had a

population of 2000, but soon after went into decline as a result of falling copper prices and dwindling reserves. The mine closed in 1918, having produced 10,000 tonnes of copper.

Today, Blinman's main distinction is the fact that it's the state's highest town: 610m above sea level. Most of the structures at the **old copper mine** – it's on a small hill about 1km to the north – have long been demolished. However, the site has been developed with lookouts, walks and information signs, and you can view the surface workings through a safety fence.

The Bush Safari Company (☎ 8543 2280, goodfellow@riverland.net.au) does **camel treks** through remote and rugged station country east of Blinman. You can do day rides, but their five/eight day treks for $685/985 are the most popular.

Places to Stay
The *Blinman Hotel* (☎ 8648 4867) has a real Outback pub flavour, with the beer being particularly flavoursome. Its renovated air-con rooms cost $35/60 for singles/doubles ($45/70 with en suite), and there's a good dining room. They also have campsites (dusty ones) and a backpacker bunkhouse with a kitchen ($13 per person).

Down at the mine, the heritage-style *Captain's Cottage* (☎ 8648 4844) is a restored stone house dating from the 1860s; originally it was the mine manager's quarters. It sleeps up to eight and starts at $100 for the first two people ($25 per person after that).

AROUND BLINMAN
There are several day trips you can do on the network of generally good dirt roads around Blinman town. These include a loop through the Flinders Ranges National Park via Aroona Valley and Brachina Gorge.

Alpana Station, 5km south of Blinman on the Wilpena road, has half and full day **4WD tours** to stations, old mines and gorges in the area. It also does guided bushwalks – if you're experienced you can go off by yourself around the property. See the following Places to Stay & Eat section.

About 7km farther on is the **Great Wall of China**, a low ridge topped with a wall-like layer of sandstone. Don't get excited as it's not a patch on the real thing.

Chambers Gorge

Chambers Gorge is accessible by a rough track that turns off the Arkaroola road about 64km from Blinman. It features huge gum trees, dramatic tan-coloured dolomite cliffs and galleries of **Aboriginal rock carvings**.

To reach the carvings, park your car and walk up the little gorge on your left 8.3km from the main road; the first major gallery is 350m upstream and on your left just before a small waterfall. Most of the carvings were produced by 'pecking' at the surface with a hard rock.

You can get as far as the carvings in a conventional vehicle, and a 4WD with good clearance will take you into the main gorge. It's a scramble to the top of **Mt Chambers**, the highest point on the right just inside the gorge, but the view is worth it. You can see over **Lake Frome** to the east and all the way along the ranges to **Mt Painter** in the north and Wilpena in the south.

The SA Museum's *A Field Guide to Chambers Gorge*, by Graham Medlin, is a useful reference that describes numerous walks.

Parachilna

There's some really inspiring scenery on the 31km drive from Blinman down through **Parachilna Gorge** to tiny Parachilna, on the vast saltbush plain west of the ranges. As well as beautiful views most of the way down, you'll find good camping and picnic spots along the creek. There's a great pub in Parachilna.

The northern end of the Heysen Trail is in Parachilna Gorge 2.6km past the **Angorichina Tourist Village**, 15km from Blinman. Other walks from Angorichina include the 11km Blinman Pools trail, considered one of the best in the Flinders.

Having reached Parachilna, you can head south to Brachina Gorge or north on the Marree road to the **Beltana Roadhouse**. From here a bush road heads east for 8km to historic Old Beltana (see the following section).

Ask at the hotel in Parachilna about 4WD tours and scenic flights in the area. There are several trips: you can see red desert dunes and **Lake Torrens** (a huge mainly dry saltpan), and do station tours.

Places to Stay & Eat

Angorichina Tourist Village (☎ 8648 4842) in Parachilna Gorge boasts a beautiful setting with steep hills all around. It has campsites ($8), on-site vans ($20/30 for singles/doubles, no air-con), backpacker beds ($13) and self-contained units (from $48). The store sells and repairs tyres.

The friendly owners of Parachilna's *Prairie Hotel* (☎ 8648 4844, ab@flinders .outback.on.net) have worked hard to create an oasis of comfort in this sleepy spot, and they've been very successful. They offer a huge range of accommodation – tent sites for $5 per person, powered sites for $15, basic cabins (some with air-con) starting at $40 singles and doubles, very tasteful hotel rooms at $70/80 singles/doubles and executive suites for $165/180.

They also have an imaginative menu featuring reasonably priced, gourmet bush tucker (emu paté on damper, for example). This is one of the few pubs in SA where you can get a meal at any time of the day.

Close by, the *Old Schoolhouse* (☎ 8648 4676) has bunks and a kitchen for $12 per person.

Station Accommodation
A number of station properties in the Blinman area have tourist accommodation.

Angorichina Station (☎ 8648 4863), 9km east, is the booking agent for several places near town. All have beds for $15, with a minimum booking of $80. Angorichina in particular has excellent walks near the homestead.

Alpana Station (☎ 8648 4864), 5km south, has beds in the shearers' quarters (minimum booking $75).

Gum Creek Station (☎ 8648 4883), 15km south, charges $8 in the shearing shed and

$12 in the shearers' quarters – there's a minimum charge of $60 in the quarters. They also have a miners' cottage in Blinman.

Nilpena Station (Prairie Hotel ☎ 8648 4844) near Parachilna has self-contained shearers' quarters ($15 per person, minimum $50) and two small cottages ($50 for singles and doubles). You can do 4WD station tours and there's good birdwatching around natural springs.

OLD BELTANA

Once a busy centre on the Great Northern Railway, Old Beltana was home to over 400 people in the 1880s and 1890s, when it had 70 houses as well as a train station, telegraph station and hotels. These days it is only saved from being a ghost town by a handful of people seeking to escape the rat race. It's a fascinating spot with a number of ruins and old stone buildings surrounded by saltbush; ask at the Beltana Roadhouse about the booklet *Beltana Trails*, which gives a **self-guided tour** of the old township.

Continue east from Old Beltana for about 23km and you come to the **Sliding Rock copper mine**, by beautiful Sliding Rock Creek. Opened with feverish optimism in the early 1870s, it produced about 1000 tonnes of copper before being closed by flooding in 1877. There are some interesting **ruins**, including the Rock Hotel, a couple of tall stone chimneys and the inevitable graveyard. In its heyday the mine supported a population of 400.

Historic *Beltana Station (☎ 8675 2256)*, between the Beltana Roadhouse and Old Beltana, has beds in the shearers' quarters for $15 per person.

LEIGH CREEK
* **pop 1400**

Coal was discovered at Leigh Creek in 1888, but mining operations didn't get under way until 1943. Since then the field has produced 60 million tonnes of hard brown coal for use in the power stations at Port Augusta; the current annual production is about 2.5 million tonnes. All operations are controlled by Flinders Power (FP).

The present township was developed in 1980 when the original town was demolished to make way for mining. Landscaping and tree planting have created a pleasant, leafy environment in dramatic contrast to its stark surroundings.

The *Opencut Cafe* in the town centre has tourist information – and good coffee.

FP offers two-hour **guided tours** of its mining operations; for an update on schedules contact ☎ 8675 4320.

Leigh Creek's water supply comes from scenic **Aroona Dam**, 10km to the southwest, where there's a pleasant picnic spot and a small campground operated by FP.

Spotless Catering (☎ 8675 2025) runs a *motel* on Black Oak Drive in the town centre, where comfortable units are $50/60 for singles/doubles (they have more basic rooms for $30/40). Their *caravan park* has tent/caravan sites for $10/15 – the amenities are very good but the ground is like concrete.

They also have a *tavern* (next door to the motel) which has reasonably priced meals and bar facilities.

COPLEY
* **pop 100**

Just 5km north of Leigh Creek, this little township is at the turn-off to the Gammon Ranges National Park (99km) and the Arkaroola Wildlife Sanctuary (129km). The drive into these areas is extremely scenic, but the road winds about and it's easy to come to grief if you're not careful.

At first glance Copley doesn't have much going for it, but hidden away on the main street is a real gem: *Tulloch's Bush Bakery & Quondong Cafe*, the home of the gourmet pies I mentioned back at Quorn. Always expect the unexpected!

You can stay in an air-con room at the pleasant old *Leigh Creek Hotel (☎ 8675 2281)* for $30/46, including a light breakfast.

GAMMON RANGES NATIONAL PARK

Covering 128,200 hectares, this remote park has deep gorges, rugged ranges and beautiful gum-lined creeks – you'll see many kangaroos in the late afternoon and (sadly) even more feral goats. Most of the park is difficult to get to. It's certainly not the place for anyone who isn't prepared for the isolation and lack of facilities.

The ranger's office (☎ 8648 4829) is at **Balcanoona Homestead**, 99km from Copley. Contact the NPWS office in Hawker if no-one answers your call.

Things to See & Do

On the drive in from Copley you pass through **Nepabunna** Aboriginal community in the park's south-west corner, after which it's 22km to scenic **Italowie Gorge**. RM Williams, the famous bush clothing and footwear designer, made his first pair of riding boots while camped here in the 1920s.

At Balcanoona, information signs in the big old shearing shed give you some details of the park's cultural and natural history. Included is the story of a murder at **Grindells Hut**, an old outstation in the park's central pound.

Grindells Hut is in a very pretty area with commanding views and stark ridges all around. You can reach it on a 4WD track off the Arkaroola road, or by walking through **Weetootla Gorge**. The hike is worthwhile, but it's 13km return; if you leave early in the morning you've a good chance of seeing yellow-footed rock-wallabies. Check with the ranger before attempting to drive or walk in this area.

The RGSSA has informative brochures detailing several walks you can do from Grindells Hut.

An interesting 4WD round trip of about 160km from Balcanoona passes Grindells Hut, **Idnina** outstation, **Yankaninna** Homestead, **Owieandana** Homestead and Nepabunna Aboriginal community. En route you can make a 5km detour to climb **Arcoona Bluff** in the park's extreme west. It's not a hard climb if you're fit, and the views are fantastic.

Operating from Balcanoona, Aboriginal ranger Gil Coulthard leads two-hour to full-day **trail rides** with a cultural emphasis (book through Arkaroola).

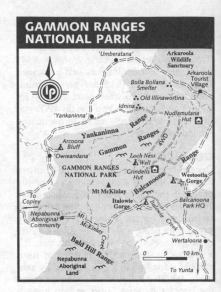

Places to Stay

There are **bush camping areas** at Italowie Gorge, Grindells Hut, Weetootla Gorge and Arcoona Bluff. You can purchase camping permits at Balcanoona; permits cost $5 per car.

Grindells Hut sleeps eight and costs $40 per night for exclusive use – if you're going during the winter or spring school holidays you'll need to book a year in advance. You can also hire the *Nudlamutana Hut*, which sleeps five, for $25. Beds in single and twin rooms in the shearers' quarters at *Balcanoona* cost $10.

ARKAROOLA-MT PAINTER WILDLIFE SANCTUARY

Once a sheep station and now a privately operated wildlife sanctuary, complete with a self-contained tourist village, Arkaroola is in a remote and scenically spectacular part of the Flinders Ranges. The sanctuary was established in 1968 by Reg and Griselda Sprigg. They introduced strict conservation measures – 96,000 feral goats have been shot or trapped since 1974 – and the previously

Sir Douglas Mawson

One of Australia's greatest geologists, scientists and explorers, Douglas Mawson was born in Yorkshire in 1882 and migrated to Sydney as a child. In 1905 he became a lecturer in mineralogy and petrology at Adelaide University, where he developed an interest in glacial geology.

During this period Mawson investigated the mineralogical potential of the Barrier Ranges, which stretch from the northern Flinders through Broken Hill, and discovered Australia's first major radioactive deposit – Radium Hill near Olary. His explorations of this remote and rugged area were largely carried out on a bicycle. Observing the huge amount of ancient glacial sediment in the ranges, he became determined to see first-hand a glacier at work.

In 1907, Mawson was appointed as a scientific assistant on Sir Ernest Shackleton's Antarctic expedition. The following year he and a companion became the first people to climb Mt Erebus (3960m) and reach the vicinity of the South Magnetic Pole.

Mawson returned as leader of the Australasian Antarctic Expedition (1911-14), which mapped over 1500km of coastline, penetrated 500km inland and collected a large amount of scientific data. His account of a 1912 trip, *Home of the Blizzard*, which told of his 160km solo trek following the death of his two companions, became a classic in the annals of polar exploration.

Mawson led two further polar expeditions between 1929 and 1931, which confirmed the existence of a land mass below the ice cap. Although the Antarctic earned him fame he never lost his fascination for the northern Flinders Ranges, returning often with his students to study the geological diversity of the Arkaroola area. Described as having 'infinite resource, splendid physique and astonishing indifference to frost', Mawson was knighted in 1914 and died in Adelaide in 1958.

The 800km cycling trail through the Flinders Rangers commemorates Mawson's contribution to exploration science (see the Mawson Trail under Cycling in the Outdoor Activities chapter).

Denis O'Byrne

degraded 61,000 hectare property is well on the way to recovery.

For information and bookings contact either the Arkaroola Travel Centre (☎ 8431 6900, 1800 676 042 toll free, admin@ arkaroola.on.net) in Adelaide, or ring the resort direct on ☎ 8648 4848.

Things to See & Do

The resort has an interesting **information centre** with displays on the area's natural history, including a scientific explanation of the frequent earth tremors that occur here; there's a seismological recording station in the centre.

You can take guided or tag-along **tours**, or do your own thing on over 100km of graded, generally single-lane tracks. Most places of interest are accessible to conventional vehicles, with some hiking involved.

For something more physical there are a number of excellent **bushwalks**. The RGSSA has detailed brochures covering four walks ranging from six to 15km, all leaving from the tourist village.

One of Arkaroola's highlights is the four hour **Ridgetop Tour**, along a 4WD track through wild mountain country. It's not for the faint-hearted as there are some adrenaline-pumping climbs and descents. Apart from the sweeping panoramas you may see wedge-tailed eagles, euros and yellow-footed rock-wallabies. The tour costs $60 and is well worth it.

Another excellent tour, which has the entertaining Doug Sprigg as your guide, allows you to view the heavens through a high-powered telescope at the **Arkaroola Astronomical Observatory**. This one costs $22 and lasts 1½ hours.

FLINDERS RANGES

Other attractions include scenic gorges and waterholes with euphonic Aboriginal names such as **Nooldoonooldoona** and **Barraranna**. The area has received plenty of attention from prospectors and miners; relics include the ruins of the **Bolla Bollana** copper smelter.

Paralana Hot Springs, about 28km from the tourist village, is the 'last hurrah' of Australia's geyser activity. A small hot pool – the water is heated by the radioactive decay of underlying granite – was used as a health spa for a short time in the 1920s. Ironically, those who came to be cured of their aches and pains probably overdosed on radon. It's not worth a special trip unless you're particularly interested in geology.

You can do **scenic flights** with a geological and botanical emphasis over the ranges for \$55/90 per seat for 35/75 minutes, provided there are at least two passengers. The longer flight shows you the dramatic contrast between the ranges and Lake Frome. Other flights take you to places such as Andamooka or Innamincka.

Places to Stay & Eat

The resort has a caravan park and a motel complex. Campsites in the dusty hilltop caravan park and along the creek (much more enticing) cost \$10, as do beds in spartan huts. Comfortable cabins (shared facilities and no air-con) start at \$29 per person twin share, while motel units with air-con start at \$49 for singles and doubles.

There's a small shop where you can buy basic supplies, and a decent restaurant with main courses from \$12.

Eyre Peninsula & West Coast

The vast, triangular Eyre Peninsula is bounded by Spencer Gulf to the east, the Great Australian Bight to the west, and the Gawler Ranges to the north. It takes its name from Edward John Eyre, who, in 1841, made the first overland crossing between Port Augusta and Albany, Western Australia (WA).

Apart from low ranges in the east, and some scattered hills and granite outcrops elsewhere, the peninsula is mainly flat to gently undulating. Superphosphate and trace elements have made its infertile soils suitable for cereal crops, and as a result it now produces about 40% of the state's wheat crop. There's a large gypsum mine near Penong, and deposits of iron ore are mined in the Middleback Ranges.

Fishing and tourism are other important industries. The coastline is dotted with small ports and resort towns, with the sheltered bays between Cowell on the central east coast and Coffin Bay in the south the most popular with summer holiday-makers. Port Lincoln is home to the state's tuna fleet, and here are lucrative rock lobster, abalone and prawn fisheries. Oyster farming is practised at several places.

The coastline from Port Lincoln to the WA border is exposed to the full fury of the Southern Ocean; the Great Australian Bight is one of the roughest stretches of water anywhere in the world. Here you find surf beaches, spectacular coastal scenery and breeding grounds for southern right whales, Australian sea lions and great white sharks (some scenes for *Jaws* were filmed here).

Information

The main tourist offices are in Whyalla (☎ 8645 7900), Port Lincoln (☎ 8683 3544) and Ceduna (☎ 8625 2780); the Wadlata Outback Centre (☎ 8641 0793) in Port Augusta also has quite a bit on the peninsula. See the sections on these towns for further details.

HIGHLIGHTS

- Dangle as shark-bait in a submerged cage and watch the great whites near their breeding grounds at Dangerous Reef and Neptune Island
- Watch bus-sized southern right whales from the clifftops at Head of Bight
- Hire a dinghy and try your luck fishing for the succulent King George whiting, or go crabbing in the open season
- Try world-class surfing at Cactus Beach on the West Coast
- Detour off the Eyre Highway and experience the awesome emptiness of the Nullarbor Plain

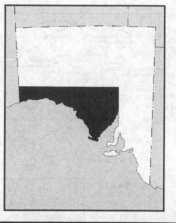

National Parks Most conservation areas south of the Eyre Highway between Port Augusta and Ceduna are administered by the National Parks & Wildlife Service (NPWS) office at 75 Liverpool St, Port Lincoln (☎ 8688 3111, fax 8688 3110).

The NPWS office at 9 MacKay St in Port Augusta (☎ 8648 5300, fax 8648 5301) looks after areas east of Ceduna and north of the Eyre Hwy.

For the far west of the state, including the Streaky Bay area, contact the NPWS office at 11 McKenzie St, Ceduna (☎ 8625 3144, fax 8625 3123). You can write to them at PO Box 569, Ceduna 5690.

The annual **Eyre Parks Pass**, which costs $40 per car, entitles you to unlimited entry and camping (up to five nights at any one location) at all Eyre Peninsula's conservation areas, excluding the far west. You can buy it from the NPWS office in Port Lincoln, the Environment Shop in Adelaide and from other outlets

For information on the **Great Australian Bight Marine Park** contact either the NPWS office in Port Lincoln or Environment Australia's Marine Group (☎ 02-6274 1721, fax 02-6274 1771) in Canberra.

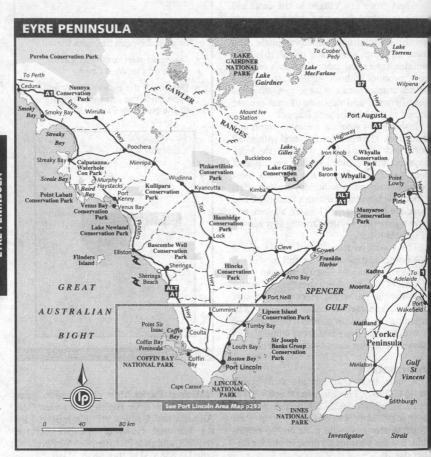

For bushwalkers at remote and difficult Gammon Ranges National Park, one full moon is reward enough.

JOHN ARMSTRONG

JOHN ARMSTRONG

Sand dunes in the Coorong

RICHARD I'ANSON

The campfire colours of evening in the spectacular Outback

DENIS O'BYRNE

The Nullarbor Plain is as empty as its etymology suggests: in Latin *nullarbor* means 'no tree'.

DENIS O'BYRNE

Fishing on the surf beaches near Talia Caves, north of Elliston, on the west coast of Eyre Peninsula

Books & Maps The best reference book is the Royal Society of South Australia's *Natural History of Eyre Peninsula*. It includes plenty of social history as well.

The Royal Automobile Association (RAA) has two good touring maps: *Lower Eyre Peninsula* and *Upper Eyre Peninsula & Far West Coast*. Carto Graphic's *A Tourist Map of the Nullarbor Plain (Perth to Adelaide)* is an attractive souvenir and guide.

Organised Tours

Bus/4WD Tours Great Australian Bight Safaris (☎ 8682 2750, gabs@terra.net.au) offers tours and safaris, including local sightseeing, bush camping and fishing, mainly around Port Lincoln. It also does whale-watching tours along the Eyre Peninsula coast; its five day camping trip from Port Lincoln to Head of Bight costs $750, and it has two and three-day accommodated trips ex-Ceduna.

Outback n' Coastal Tours (☎ 8250 2911, oca@webscene.com.au) has 4WD safaris to the west coast beyond Ceduna between July and early October. Attractions include fishing and whale watching. Outback's five day camping tour costs $640, all inclusive ex-Adelaide.

Shorecatch Fishing Safaris (☎ 8854 5311) has 4WD tours of up to 10 days along the coast west of Ceduna. It provides everything including tuition, and rods and reels if you don't have your own.

Operating from Wudinna, Gawler Ranges Wilderness Safaris (☎ 8680 2020, 1800 243 343 toll free) does tailor-made 4WD safaris from one to seven days. You can tour the Gawler Ranges and the Eyre Peninsula coast, and visit the far west coast for whale watching. They charge from $150 to $190 a day, depending on whether you're camping or staying in homesteads.

The Nullarbor Traveller (☎ 8364 0407, 1800 816 858 toll free, nullarbor@kem .com.au) offers leisurely trips between Adelaide and Perth. Options include visits to the Gawler Ranges, Streaky Bay, Cactus Beach and Head of Bight. See the Bus section in the Getting There & Away chapter.

Boat Charters/Cruises There's a good choice at Port Lincoln, where several operators offer diving, fishing and sightseeing charters. See Organised Tours in the section on Port Lincoln. Otherwise there are fishing and sightseeing charters at Baird Bay, Ceduna, Coffin Bay and Tumby Bay.

You can swim with the sea lions and dolphins at Baird Bay; some of the tour operators mentioned earlier include this option in their itineraries.

Accommodation

Eyre Peninsula has a good range of accommodation, particularly on the Spencer Gulf coast. Most towns south of Cowell have holiday flats, but book early if you're heading that way over January or Easter.

West of Coffin Bay there are fewer places to stay, although all towns along the coast have at least one caravan park and there are plenty of spots where you can camp without facilities. There's a backpacker hostel at Mt Dutton Bay, near Coffin Bay.

Most townships along the Eyre Hwy between Port Augusta and Ceduna have transit-style motels and caravan parks, as do the roadhouses west of Penong.

Several privately owned islands, such as Boston Island off Port Lincoln, have accommodation – mainly for extended stays.

Getting There & Away

Air Mostly daily services link Adelaide with Ceduna, Cleve, Port Lincoln, Whyalla and Wudinna. See the sections on these towns.

Bus Premier Stateliner (☎ 8415 5555) has daily services from Adelaide and Port Augusta down the east coast to Port Lincoln, and via the Eyre Hwy to Ceduna and Streaky Bay (see the sections on these towns for details). There is no public transport along the coast between Port Lincoln and Streaky Bay.

Getting Around

The Eyre Hwy (Hwy 1) from Port Augusta to WA cuts across the northern part of the peninsula to Ceduna, then follows the coast to the border. It's 468km from Port Augusta to Ceduna and another 482km to the WA border.

The much more interesting coastal route around the peninsula is in two parts: the 344km Lincoln Hwy runs between Port Augusta and Port Lincoln; and the 402km Flinders Hwy runs from Port Lincoln to Ceduna.

Eastern Eyre Peninsula

Between Whyalla and Port Lincoln are the popular resort towns of Cowell and Tumby Bay. These and other small ports were busy shipping points in the days before heavy motor transport, and they retain the character of those times.

WHYALLA
* **pop 23,400**

The largest city in the state after Adelaide, industrial Whyalla was established in 1901 when mining giant BHP constructed a 55km tramway from Hummock Hill on the coast to its new iron ore mine at Iron Knob. Just a shipping point at first, the town grew slowly until 1938, when the threat of war caused a dramatic expansion in industrial activity. A deep-water port was dredged and a blast furnace and five-berth shipbuilding facility were built. A pipeline bringing water from Morgan on the Murray River was completed in 1944, resulting in further development in steel-making and ship-building.

Economic difficulties and the loss of markets to overseas competition caused the shipyards to close in 1978. The town's population reached a peak of 33,400 in 1976, but steadily declined through the 1980s and 1990s due to the continuing recession in the South Australian manufacturing sector.

Each year Whyalla produces around 1.2 million tonnes of raw steel and 1.5 million tonnes of pellets from ore mined in the nearby Middleback Ranges.

Information

The Whyalla Tourist Centre (☎ 8645 7900, fax 8645 3620, ic3tour@plain.sa.gov.au) is on the Lincoln Hwy at the northern approach to town. It is open weekdays from 9 am to 5 pm, Saturdays and public holidays from 9 am to 4 pm, and Sundays from 10 am to 4 pm. You can't miss it – it's beside a large naval vessel sitting high and dry beside the road.

Things to See & Do

On the highway 10km north of town, the 1100 hectare **Whyalla Conservation Park** has stands of myall and saltbush. Euros, grey and red kangaroos, and over 70 species of birds can also be seen here. There's a walking trail to the top of **Wild Dog Hill**, a prominent sandstone outcrop in the park's north-west corner.

Next to the tourist office, the **Maritime Museum** features the 650 tonne WWII corvette HMAS *Whyalla*. It opens daily from 10 am to 4 pm, with guided tours leaving on the hour between 11 am and 3 pm for $6.

Tours of the **BHP steel works** ($8) leave from the tourist office at 9.30 am on Monday, Wednesday and Saturday. They take 2½ hours and cover everything from where the ore comes in to where the steel goes out. Long trousers, long-sleeved shirts and closed footwear are essential. Cameras are not permitted.

Hummock Hill Lookout gives a good view of the town, BHP complex and Spencer Gulf. The concrete fortifications housed a WWII anti-aircraft battery which was supposed to protect the shipyards from Japanese attack; there were only four guns (one is still there), so it's a good job there were no air raids. The distant jetty to the east is at **Point Lowly**, where ships are loaded with natural gas piped from Moomba in the state's north-east.

The historic **Mt Laura Homestead**, on Ekblom St, is now a museum. It has a variety of displays – including an old locomotive and a rose garden – and is open Sunday, Monday and Wednesday from 2 to 4 pm and Friday from 10 am to noon. Admission is $4.

Set in attractive bushland 7km south of town, the informal **Whyalla Wildlife & Reptile Sanctuary** is the state's largest wildlife park outside the Adelaide area. It has a good collection of native reptiles, over 50 species of native mammals and a huge walk-through aviary. It opens daily from 10 am to dusk; allow at least two hours for a visit. Admission is $6.

The town's major entertainment venue is the **Middleback Theatre** on Nicholson Ave. There's usually something happening, whether it be film screenings, an art exhibition, live theatre or variety entertainment. The tourist office has programs.

Places to Stay
Two kilometres from the town centre, and with a lovely beach frontage, the *Whyalla Foreshore Caravan Park* (☎ 8645 7474) on Broadbent Terrace has tent/caravan sites for $11/14, on-site vans with air-con for $24, basic cabins starting at $28 and self-contained cabins at $35. If you're keen, you can hire rakes for crabbing during the open season.

A friendly Finnish couple own *Hillview Caravan Park* (☎ 8645 9357), off the Lincoln Hwy 5km south of town. The rates are similar to those given above, except for the self-contained cabins which start at $43.

All rooms in the town's four hotels have air-con, TV and an en suite bathroom. The *Bayview Hotel* (☎ 8645 8544, 11 Forsyth St) charges $25/45 for singles/doubles, and *Hotel Eyre* (☎ 8645 7188), on the corner of Playford Ave and Elliott St, charges $30/40. *Hotel Spencer* (☎ 8645 8411, Forsyth St) has rooms at the same price and the *Lord Gowrie Hotel* (☎ 8645 8955, 10 Gowrie Ave) has rooms for $33/44.

Cheapest by far of the six motels are the *Sundowner Hotel Motel* (☎ 8645 7688, Lincoln Hwy) and the *Whyalla Country Inn* (☎ 8645 0588, 95 Playford Ave). Both have units for around $45/50. The Sundowner is near the airport, 5km from town towards Port Lincoln.

The tourist office has full details of all hotels and motels.

Places to Eat
There are plenty of places to eat in Whyalla. The pubs are good, as always; the smorgasbords at the *Hotel Eyre* and *Hotel Spencer* are considered the best value in town.

Vega's Bar & Bistro, in the Westland Hotel/Motel on MacDouall Stuart Ave, has a salad bar and hearty specials. Also in the Westland, the *Bottle & Bird* is very popular with locals; you line up on one side for your booze, and on the other for take-away chicken.

Lam Inn (167 Jenkins Ave) and *City Pearl* (Jenkins Ave) are both reasonably priced Asian restaurants.

Memories Coffee Lounge (31 Playford Ave) has a good atmosphere and is recommended for light lunches and coffee.

Getting There & Away
Kendell Airlines (☎ 13 13 00) and Whyalla Airlines (☎ 1800 088 858 toll free) fly daily from Adelaide for $127 and $95 respectively.

Premier Stateliner has daily buses from Adelaide ($33) and Port Augusta ($12) to the bus station at 23 Darling Terrace.

Getting Around
There is no bus service to the airport, but Des's Cabs (☎ 8645 7711) charges around $8 for the airport to town centre run.

Hire cars are available from Avis (☎ 8645 9331), Budget (☎ 8645 5333) and Hertz (☎ 8645 3354).

Public buses operate around town. Ask the tourist office for a map and timetable.

COWELL
• **pop 700**
Once an important port, this pleasant little town is on mangrove-fringed **Franklin Harbor**. It was settled in the 1850s when the McKechnie brothers emigrated from Scotland and established Wangaraleednie Station.

In the nearby Minbrie Range is a large **jade deposit** with several mines. Local jade products are sold at the Jade Motel, on the highway at the northern end of town.

EYRE PENINSULA

There is a small but interesting **folk museum** in the old post office on Main St (it's next door to the 'new' post office). Entry costs $1 and you can get a key from the council office next door.

Oysters are farmed locally, and you can buy them from several outlets for as little as $5 a dozen. Otherwise the best **fishing** is off the beach near Point Gibbon.

Cleve (population 750) is an attractive farming centre 42km inland from Cowell and near the scenic Minbrie Range. The town has a National Trust **museum**, which is opened on request.

Places to Stay

Two kilometres north of town, the *Harbour View Caravan Park* (☎ 8629 2216) has tent/caravan sites for $10/12, on-site vans start at $26 and air-con cabins at $30.

Close to the town centre, the attractive and shady *Cowell Foreshore Caravan Park* (☎ 8629 2307, The Esplanade) charges $11/13 for tent/caravan sites, while on-site vans start at $32 and cabins at $35. You can also hire dinghies here, which go for $60 per day.

There are two lovely old pubs on Main St: *Franklin Harbour Hotel* (☎ 8629 2015) at No 1 and the *Commercial Hotel* (☎ 8629 2181) at No 24. Both charge $20/30 for singles/doubles.

The *Jade Motel* (☎ 8629 2002) on Lincoln Hwy charges $50/55.

For something more homely try *Schultz Farm* (☎ 8629 2194), where spacious rooms cost $45 per couple, including a cooked breakfast. It's on Smith Rd about 1km south-west of town.

At Cleve, the *Cleve Hotel/Motel* (☎ 8628 2011, Fourth St) charges $50/65 for its motel units.

Getting There & Away

Whyalla Airlines (☎ 1800 088 858 toll free) has daily services from Adelaide to Cleve ($90).

Premier Stateliner buses call in daily at Cowell, costing $48 from Adelaide and $19 from Port Augusta.

SOUTH OF COWELL
Elbow Hill

The first township south from Cowell is tiny Elbow Hill, 15km away. From here you can drive to **Point Gibbon** (6km), which has cliffs and beautiful beaches. En route you'll pass four concrete **bunkers**, the remains of a WWII communications facility.

The *Elbow Hill Inn* (☎ 8628 5012) has a great atmosphere, with lots of timber and antique furnishings. It provides light lunches and gourmet dinners, averaging around $14 for a main course. You can stay in a double room with en suite facilities ($70 for couples), or in a renovated church ($80).

Arno Bay
* pop 300

Forty-three kilometres from Cowell, Arno Bay has a safe **swimming beach** and a fishing jetty.

You can stay at the fairly basic *Arno Bay Caravan Park* (☎ 8628 0085) or in the town's grandest building, the *Hotel Arno* (☎ 8628 0001).

Port Neill
* pop 200

Turn left 33km south of Arno Bay to picturesque Port Neill, which boasts two good **swimming beaches**.

The town has some interesting exhibits, including vintage engines and motor vehicles at **Vic & Jill Fauser's Museum**, opposite the caravan park. It opens daily – just knock on the house door, or get a key from the caravan park.

Places to stay include the *Port Neill Caravan Park* (☎ 8688 9067) and the *Port Neill Hotel* (☎ 8688 9006).

Tumby Bay
* pop 1100

Named by Matthew Flinders in 1802, the bay is graced by a very attractive town with a wonderful seaside atmosphere. Its long, curving white-sand beach is one of the peninsula's finest.

Hales Mini Mart (☎ 8688 2584) at 1 Bratten Way (the Port Lincoln road) has tourist information and hires outboard powered tinnies from $35 per day (you'll need a boating licence).

Tumby Bay has a number of interesting old buildings, including the original school house on Lipson Rd. This now houses the National Trust's **CL Alexander Memorial Museum**, open Friday and Saturday from 2.30 to 4.30 pm, entry $2.

About 5km south-east of town, **Ski Beach** is a popular swimming and picnic spot. From here you can wade out to **Tumby Island Conservation Park** – the water is knee-deep at low tide. It's a rookery for several bird species, including Cape Barren geese. There's good fishing on the gulf side.

The **Sir Joseph Banks Group of Islands**, 25km south-east of town, form a marine conservation park, with bird rookeries, sea lion colonies and excellent scuba diving.

An old homestead and scattered implements are evidence of past farming activity.

At **Koppio**, a farming centre in picturesque hills 25km south-west of Tumby Bay, the National Trust's excellent **Koppio Smithy Museum** is open daily, except Monday, from 10 am to 5 pm. It has an extensive collection of memorabilia, including a pioneer hut and numerous restored vintage tractors.

Tumby Bay Charters (☎ 8688 2811) offers half and full day fishing, diving and sightseeing **boat charters,** including trips to the Sir Joseph Banks group. It is $95 per person for a day trip (with a minimum of three passengers). A couple of operators based in Port Lincoln also offer charters to the islands (see Organised Tours in the Port Lincoln section).

Premier Stateliner calls daily, charging $56 from Adelaide and $35 from Port Augusta.

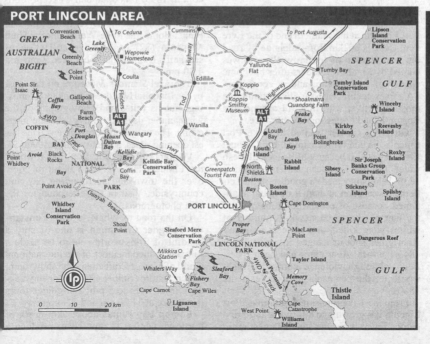

PORT LINCOLN AREA

EYRE PENINSULA

Places to Stay & Eat On the foreshore, the *Tumby Bay Caravan Park (☎ 8688 2208, Tumby Terrace)* has tent/caravan sites for $12/14, on-site vans for $30 and self-contained cabins starting at $45.

The *Sea Breeze Hotel (☎ 8688 2362, Tumby Terrace)* and the somewhat grander *Tumby Bay Hotel (☎ 8688 2005, North Terrace)* charge around $19/29 singles/doubles for their rooms.

Tumby Bayside Holiday Units (☎ 8688 2087, Yaranga Ave) is a friendly place with basic but clean and well-appointed units a short walk from the sea. They charge from $40 for two people to $70 for eight (linen is $5 extra per bed).

Both the pubs do counter and dining room meals, and there are several takeaways and a good bakery in town.

At Louth Bay, 31km south of Tumby Bay, there's a *camping area* with toilets close to a sandy beach.

PORT LINCOLN
• **pop 13,000**

Port Lincoln, at the southern end of the Eyre Peninsula, is 662km from Adelaide by road but only 250km as the crow flies. It was named by Matthew Flinders after his home county of Lincolnshire and is considered SA's finest natural harbour. It's certainly the most attractive, with hills all around and Boston Island protecting the entrance.

Governor Gawler wanted to make Port Lincoln the site for the capital, but Colonel Light rejected it because of its lack of fresh water. The first European settlers arrived in 1839. While they made a good start, the settlement was soon in danger of being abandoned because of economic problems and the fear of Aboriginal attack. A number of whites were killed, and at least as many Aborigines shot or hanged in reprisal. By 1845 the local Aborigines had been 'pacified', although violence continued elsewhere on the peninsula until at least the 1860s.

From these unpromising beginnings, Port Lincoln has grown into a thriving and prosperous town. It has the state's largest grain exporting terminal and most of its tuna fleet. Fishing is big business; there are numerous **tuna farms** in Boston Bay and the town has several seafood-processing factories.

Information
The very helpful Port Lincoln Visitor Information Centre (☎/fax 8683 3544, 1800 629 911 toll free) is at 66 Tasman Terrace. It is open from 9 am to 5 pm daily.

For national parks offices, see the Information section at the start of this chapter.

Things to See & Do
The Old Mill on Dorset Place was built in 1846 as the tower for a flour mill that was never completed. You can climb to the lookout for nice views out over the bay.

On the Flinders Hwy, **Mill Cottage** is a historic homestead (1866) in an attractive park. It houses many artefacts belonging to the Bishop family, who came to Port Lincoln in 1839. It is open daily, except Monday, from 2 to 4.30 pm, and entry is $2.

Next door, at the Eyre Peninsula Old Folk's Home, the **Rose-Wal Memorial Shell Museum** ($2) has a huge collection of seashells. It opens daily between 2 pm and 4.30 pm.

The **Axel Stenross Museum**, on the coast by the Lincoln Hwy, doesn't look too promising, but its relics and photographs of the windjammer days are said to be quite interesting. The tourist office can give you the latest opening times, and entry will cost you $2.

Winters Hill Lookout, 5km from town off the Flinders Hwy, gives a beautiful view over the town and surrounding bay and countryside. Visit in the afternoon for the best photographs.

On the road to Whaler's Way, **Constantia Designer Craftsmen** is one of only a handful of firms worldwide to be made a fully accredited member of the International Guild of Master Craftsmen. The showroom, which features timber crafts, is open weekdays from 9 am to 5 pm; and guided tours take place at 11.30 am and 2.30 pm.

Boston Bay Wines about 6km north of the town centre, is reputed to produce a

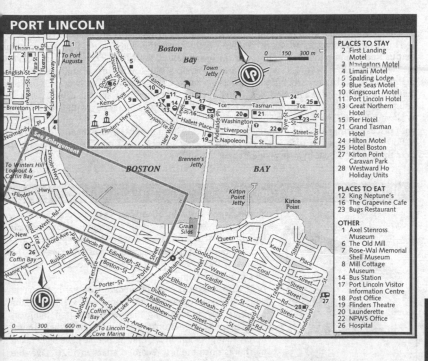

PORT LINCOLN

Boston Bay
Town Jetty
0   150   300 m

BOSTON   BAY

Sea Enlargement

To Port Augusta

To Winters Hill Lookout & Coffin Bay

Brennen's Jetty

Kirton Point Jetty

Kirton Point

Grain Silos

To Coffin Bay

To Coffin Bay

To Lincoln Cove Marina

0   300   600 m

PLACES TO STAY
2 First Landing Motel
3 Navigators Motel
4 Limani Motel
5 Spalding Lodge
9 Blue Seas Motel
10 Kingscourt Motel
11 Port Lincoln Hotel
13 Great Northern Hotel
15 Pier Hotel
21 Grand Tasman Hotel
24 Hilton Motel
25 Hotel Boston
27 Kirton Point Caravan Park
28 Westward Ho Holiday Units

PLACES TO EAT
12 King Neptune's
16 The Grapevine Cafe
23 Bugs Restaurant

OTHER
1 Axel Stenross Museum
6 The Old Mill
7 Rose-Wal Memorial Shell Museum
8 Mill Cottage Museum
14 Bus Station
17 Port Lincoln Visitor Information Centre
18 Post Office
19 Flinders Theatre
20 Launderette
22 NPWS Office
26 Hospital

decent chardonnay. It is open for tastings 11.30 am to 4.30 pm on weekends and public/school holidays, and throughout December and January.

Special Events
The annual Tunarama Festival, which runs over the Australia Day weekend in January, celebrates the tuna-fishing industry. Entertainment includes tuna and wheat-sheaf tossing, keg rolling, slippery-pole climbing, a boat-building race, stalls and bands.

Organised Tours
Port Lincoln has a good variety of land and sea tours, and all can be booked through the tourist office. The following will give you an idea of what's available.

Great Australian Bight Safaris (☎ 8682 2750, gabs@terra.net.au) has an excellent range, including a town tour ($25), a town

tour plus Whalers Way ($65), 4WD day tours to Memory Cove ($65) and the Coffin Bay Peninsula ($80), a five day sail-and-4WD safari ($750) and fishing trips (that start at $75).

Yacht Away (☎ 8684 4240 or 0408 083 529, yachtway@basshams.com.au) has a very good reputation thanks to its personable skippers and comfortable craft. It does twilight, half-day, full-day and extended **yacht cruises** to off-shore islands, the yachts sleeping up to eight passengers. Prices are very reasonable at $90 per person for 24-hours all-inclusive (except liquor) for a minimum of four passengers.

LEP Boat Charters (☎ 8682 6111) does half-day, full-day and extended tours, including diving, fishing and sightseeing trips to nearby reefs and islands. Prices vary, but you can expect to pay around $75 for a half day and $120 for a full day, provided there are at least six passengers. It specialises in the Sir Joseph Banks group off Tumby Bay.

Thirty-one kilometres offshore is **Dangerous Reef**, an important breeding area for the white pointer or great white shark. Sightings of sharks are rare, but you'll normally see plenty of Australian sea lions. Cruises to the reef can be arranged through Westward Ho Holiday Units (☎ 8682 2425), with prices starting at $55.

For a real adrenaline rush you can hang over the side of a boat in a suspended cage, from where you can view **great white sharks.** The sharks are (hopefully) attracted by burleying, and I'm told the success rate is around 65% to 70%. There are four local operators; the tourist office will give you details. As an example, Westward Ho has four and five-day live-aboard diving trips for $450 per person per day with a minimum of four divers.

Alternatively, a cruise out into Boston Bay to see the tuna farms costs around $27.

All the Better to Eat You With

Sharks were around 150 million years before dinosaurs, having evolved from a group of armour-plated animals known as placoderms. There are 375 known species worldwide, about 30 of which live in South Australian waters. The largest of these is the great white shark, or white pointer, which grows to 8m.

One of the most efficient predators on earth, the great white roams the oceans of both hemispheres. However, the primitive fear and loathing that we have for anything capable of biting large chunks out of us has given them an undeserved reputation. In SA, only 12 people have been taken by sharks since the first recorded attack in 1926. Over the same period more than 1200 people have drowned!

Until recently the popular attitude to great whites was 'the only good shark is a dead one', and decades of unrestrained slaughter have seriously depleted their numbers. Today, there is a growing awareness that these are magnificent creatures with an essential role to play in their environment.

With some estimates placing the global population of great whites as low as 2000, the SA government has now joined California, Florida, the Maldives, Namibia and South Africa, as well as the Australian states of Queensland, Western Australia and Victoria, in protecting them. It has banned game-fishing of the species and imposed restrictions on the shark-viewing industry; observing great white sharks from boats and submerged cages is popular in Port Lincoln, which is close to global 'hot spots' at Dangerous Reef and the Neptune Islands.

Although commercial fishing of great whites was banned in SA in 1994, many juveniles are thought to die each year after becoming entangled in nets. Two species of shark – gummy and school shark – are commercially fished in SA, with an annual catch of around 1000 tonnes. Called 'flake', their meat once ended up in take-away fish & chips, but is now more likely to be found in restaurants. With Asian diners prepared to pay up to $20 for a bowl of shark-fin soup – not to mention the increase in demand for powdered shark cartilage as an aphrodisiac and health remedy – there seems little likelihood that shark-netting will end in the near future.

Denis O'Byrne

Places to Stay

On Hindmarsh St, 3km east of the town centre, *Kirton Point Caravan Park (☎ 8682 2537)* has nice views of Boston Bay. It costs $6 per person for a campsite, $16 for powered sites, basic cabins start at $25 and newer, better ones at $46.

There are five hotels in the town centre. For a room with shared facilities you can expect to pay $22/42 singles/doubles at the *Hotel Boston (☎ 8682 1311, 19 King St)*, or $32/48 for a room with en suite bathroom. At the *Grand Tasman Hotel (☎ 8682 2133, 94 Tasman Terrace)* singles start at $55, double and twin share are $65, and an executive suite is $80. All hotels have en suites.

Great Northern Hotel (☎ 8682 3350, 34 Hallett Place) has basic pub rooms for $25/38 for singles/doubles, and the *Port Lincoln Hotel (☎ 8682 1277, 16 Tasman Terrace)* has rooms with shared facilities for $20/35 and with en suite bathroom for $25/45. The *Pier Hotel (☎ 8682 1322)*, also on Tasman Terrace, has rooms with en suite facilities for $35/40.

The town's seven motels are generally of a good standard, but vacancies are often hard to come by – hence the prices. If you're on a budget, the *First Landing Motel (☎ 8682 2919, 11 Shaen St)*, 2km north, charges from $48/54.

There are a number of holiday flats and the tourist office has details.

For budget travellers, *Westward Ho Holiday Units (☎ 8682 2425, 112 London St)* charges from $45/55 for singles/doubles. If there are six of you, and you have your own linen, you can get a flat for $63 outside holiday periods.

The more upmarket *Spalding Lodge (30 Lincoln Hwy)* has modern, very well-appointed two-bedroom units sleeping up to four adults for $55 off-peak and $90 peak. Book at the tourist office.

The tourist office also has details of the numerous B&Bs around town. These include several traditional places where you can stay in a family home and eat with your hosts. Prices start at $65 for doubles.

Places to Eat

Bugs Restaurant (Eyre St) and *King Neptune's (5 Light St)* are good for pasta, pizza and seafood. You can also get good value meals at *The Grapevine Cafe* in the Civic Centre Arcade, at 60 Tasman Terrace, near the tourist office.

All the pubs have substantial counter and dining-room meals; probably the best is the *Great Northern*, which is noted for seafood. The *Grand Tasman* has a bistro and an à la carte restaurant, as well as take-aways.

Entertainment

For details of entertainment check the *Port Lincoln Times*. The *Flinders Theatre (3 Hallett Place)*, has film screenings daily (usually afternoon and evening) except Monday and Tuesday.

Invariably, there's a live rock band at one of the pubs on Friday and Saturday nights.

Getting There & Away

Kendell Airlines (☎ 13 13 00) and Airlines of SA (☎ 13 13 13) fly several times daily from Adelaide, and charge $128 and $95 respectively.

Premier Stateliner buses run daily from Adelaide via Cummins or Tumby Bay to the bus station at 24 Lewis St, in the city centre ($58). From Port Augusta it's $41.

Getting Around

There is no bus service from town to the airport, but Lincoln City Taxis (☎ 8682 1222) do the trip for around $15.

Public buses run weekdays and Saturday morning on five routes around town. Ask at the tourist office for a route map and timetable.

The local hire-car agencies are Avis (☎ 8682 1072), Budget (☎ 8684 3668) and Hertz (☎ 8682 1933).

AROUND PORT LINCOLN

At the entrance to Boston Bay, **Boston Island** is a sheep-grazing property. You can have the entire island to yourself for $200 per person per week (minimum five people). Contact the tourist office for details.

There are several **surfing and diving** spots around town. For information about the best areas, contact the Port Lincoln Skin-Diving & Surfing Centre (☎ 8682 4428), at 1 King St. Licensed divers can hire scuba diving equipment.

Cape Carnot, better known as **Whalers Way**, is 32km south of Port Lincoln. It features rugged coastal scenery with 120m cliffs; poignant memorial plaques recall the anglers and others who've been swept off the rocks by king waves. At **Fishery Bay** are the remnants of a whaling station, abandoned in 1842. Spectacular **Cape Wiles** has fur seals. The area is privately owned, but you can visit by obtaining a permit ($15 plus key deposit) from most petrol stations or from the tourist office in Port Lincoln. The permit is valid for 24 hours and allows you to camp at Redbanks or Groper Bay.

En route to Whalers Way you pass **Sleaford Mere**, a large brackish lake with waterbirds and stromatolites. A little farther on is **Sleaford Bay**, which has beautiful beaches.

Continuing on towards Whalers Way is **Mikkira Station**, the first sheep station on Eyre Peninsula. You can visit its **koala sanctuary** with a permit, available from most petrol stations or the tourist office for $8. This place is best in winter and spring.

Lincoln National Park

South of Port Lincoln, this 29,100 hectare park has a magnificent coastline of quiet coves, sheltered beaches and sheer cliffs. Apart from some cleared areas showing past farming activity, most of the park is covered by thick mallee scrub.

There's a good network of unsealed roads and tracks, over 60% of which are suitable for conventional vehicles. You will definitely need a 4WD to get to the huge **Sleaford and Wanna dunes**, in the southwest, and to tranquil **Memory Cove**, in the south-east about 50km from Port Lincoln.

At Memory Cove is a **memorial** to the two officers and six crew who drowned off Cape Catastrophe during Matthew Flinders' 1802 expedition. There are a number of tall rugged islands off the coast here, and some

are visible as you drive along the clifftops towards Memory Cove. Flinders named eight of them after the missing men.

By following the **Investigator Trail** you can walk from Port Lincoln to places such as Sleaford Bay, Pillie Lake, Cape Donington and Taylors Landing. The 109km trail runs mainly along the coast from about 15km north of Port Lincoln to various points in Lincoln National Park. The tourist office has brochures.

There's a fully furnished *holiday cottage* at Spalding Cove ($25 per person) and several *bush campsites*, some with caravan access. If you don't have an Eyre Parks Pass or other relevant pass you'll need to obtain camping and/or entry permits at the park entry station. Entry costs $5 per car and there's an additional $5 per car per night if you're going to camp. The tourist office in Port Lincoln can give you a key for the Memory Cove track.

Western Eyre Peninsula

The Flinders Hwy from Port Lincoln to Ceduna will take you past a number of popular summer holiday destinations, including Coffin Bay, Elliston and Streaky Bay. Scattered between them are smaller resorts and beautiful surf beaches where you can ride the waves or go fishing.

PORT LINCOLN TO STREAKY BAY

The most scenic part of the entire coastal route from Port Augusta to Ceduna is the section from Port Lincoln to beyond Coffin Bay. For about 75km you drive through rolling farmland with beautiful gums and occasional freshwater lakes and brooding hills, then it's back to the dreariness of stunted mallee and wheat paddocks.

Coffin Bay

Ominous-sounding Coffin Bay (named by Matthew Flinders to honour Sir Isaac Coffin, a British Lord of the Admiralty) is a large and attractive estuary with many quiet beaches. There's also good fishing, particularly for the revered King George whiting.

Coffin Bay township (usual population of 400) literally bursts at the seams in January, when holiday-makers descend in droves. From here you can visit wild coastal scenery along the ocean side of Coffin Bay Peninsula, which is entirely taken up by the 28,100 hectare **Coffin Bay National Park**. Entry to the park costs $5 per car, payable at the ranger station (☎ 8685 4047).

Access to conventional vehicles is limited within the park; you can get to scenic **Point Avoid** (20km) and adjoining **Gunyah Beach** quite easily, but otherwise you'll need a 4WD. If you're experienced in soft sandy conditions try the 50km track to **Point Sir Isaac**, taking care with tide times on **Seven Mile Beach**. Allow a full day for this trip.

For something less arduous, the 1780 hectare **Kellidie Bay Conservation Park**, east of the township, is good for birdwatching (113 species). You may see some unusual migratory species such as the buff-banded rail and the wood sandpiper.

Oysters are grown locally and you can buy them for $6 a dozen from several outlets around town.

The caravan park hires out Suzuki 4WD vehicles (five hours and 100km costs $50), and you can rent **dinghies** and **runabouts** nearby at Hire Boat Haven; a 4m dinghy with 8hp motor costs $65 per day plus fuel, and you won't need a boating license (though you will for larger craft).

Clarky's Charters (☎ 8683 3441) does **fishing trips** from $75 per person for a day.

Places to Stay & Eat The *Coffin Bay Caravan Park* (☎ 8685 4170, Shepperd Ave) is the only place in town where you can camp ($11). It also has on-site vans for $25 and cabins for $38, as well as plenty of lawn and shade.

Alternatively, *Coffin Bay Motel* (☎ 8685 4111, Shepperd Ave) has units starting at $50/60 for singles/doubles.

There are also a large number of holiday flats, homes and cottages. The best people to ring about bookings are Century 21 Real Estate (☎ 8685 4063) in Coffin Bay.

Bush camping (no drinking water and generally difficult access) is allowed at several places in the national park. Permits cost $5 per car per night, payable at the ranger station.

The motel does counter meals, and there are a couple of basic take-aways. *Sea-K's Cafe & Restaurant (61 The Esplanade)* is recommended for light lunches and evening meals – it serves Chinese and pasta dishes and is very good value.

Coffin Bay to Elliston

At the fading hamlet of **Wangary**, on the Flinders Hwy 14km past the Coffin Bay turn-off, a gravel road leads to **Farm Beach**. This is a popular boat-launching spot – you'll know it by the old tractors that are used to pull boats into the sea. You can camp here, or stay at the well-appointed *Mt Dutton Bay Woolshed* (☎ 8685 4031) on the road in. B&B is $80 for couples and there's a backpacker bunkhouse with kitchen, TV room and laundry for $15.

Farther north is the rugged stretch of coastline known as **Gallipoli Beach**, so called because it was the location for Peter Weir's film *Gallipoli.*

Near **Coulta**, 18km from Wangary, gravel roads lead to **Convention Beach**, **Greenly Beach** and **Coles Beach**, all popular surfing and surf-fishing spots.

If you don't want to camp rough near the beach, the friendly *Wepowie Ostrich Farm (☎ 8687 2063)*, off the Edillilie road about 5km north of Coulta, has pleasant campsites and also does B&B.

Cummings Lookout, 47km from Coulta, is worth stopping at for its dramatic coastal views. Seven kilometres farther on, the restored 1850s **Lake Hamilton Eating House** is an evocative reminder of the pioneering days.

Turning off 67km past Coulta, the road to Sheringa Beach will take you past huge white dunes and Round Lake, which has excellent windsurfing and sheltered campsites. The beach is another good surfing spot – the breaks here are suitable for all classes, including beginners. You can buy fuel, basic provisions and take-aways at the Sheringa Store on the highway.

Spectacular **Locks Well Beach**, 23km past the Sheringa turn-off, is a famous salmon-fishing spot. There's a long steep stairway from the carpark down to the beach.

Elliston
* **pop 240**

On tranquil Waterloo Bay, 167km from Port Lincoln, Elliston was created in the 1860s as a shipping point for wool. It has a beautiful swimming beach and (allegedly) one of the best jetties in SA for catching tommyruff.

Just north of town, take the unsealed 7km loop road to **Salmon Point** and **Anxious Bay** for some dramatic ocean scenery. En route you'll pass **Blackfellows**, which has some of the best surfing breaks on the west coast. From the clifftop you can see distant **Flinders Island**, where there's a sheep station and tourist accommodation.

Places to Stay The *Elliston Caravan Park* (☎ 8687 9061), on the Flinders Hwy, about 1km north of town, has tent/caravan sites for $10/12, on-site vans for $20 and basic cabins starting at $25. It's popular with visiting surfers.

In town, the attractive *Elliston Waterloo Bay Caravan Park* (☎ 8687 9076) charges similar prices, but has better facilities. It has self-contained cabins for $45.

At the *Elliston Hotel* (☎ 8687 9009, Fifth St) rooms with en suite bathroom start at $35 for singles and doubles. The nearby *Ellen Liston Motel & Holiday Flats* (☎ 8687 9028, Beach Rd) has motel units with kitchen for $50/55/63/71 (for one person to four) and more basic holiday units for $40 for singles and doubles ($5 for each extra person).

Flinders Island Holidays (☎ 8626 1132) in Streaky Bay can tell you about accommodation on Flinders Island.

North of Elliston

The 8400 hectare **Lake Newland Conservation Park** starts about 20km north of Elliston. With huge white dunes, wetlands and yet another long surf beach, it continues a farther 20km up the coast to **Talia Caves**. Here you can explore colourful low cliffs, collapsed crevices and sinkholes.

Seven kilometres beyond the Talia Caves turn-off a road will take you to **Mt Camel Beach**, another good salmon spot. Just to the north on Venus Bay are the sleepy resorts of **Venus Bay** and **Port Kenny**, both with caravan parks and fishing jetties.

There's 4WD access into the 1650 hectare **Venus Bay Conservation Park** (ranger office ☎ 8625 5110) on the northern side of the bay. The park has kangaroos, prolific birdlife (including ospreys, pelicans and migratory waders) and marvellous coastal scenery.

Baird Bay Area

Between Port Kenny and Streaky Bay, gravel roads will take you by various routes to **Point Labatt**, where there's a large colony of Australian sea lions. You can view the animals from the clifftop – they're usually lazing about at least 100m away from the viewing platform, so binoculars are recommended.

At **Sceale Bay**, 23km north of Point Labatt (28km south of Streaky Bay) there are cliffs and a long sandy beach where you can swim, surf and fish. There's also the *Sceale Bay Caravan Park* (☎ 8626 5099), which has powered and unpowered sites, on-site vans and cabins. Jenny, the owner, can arrange fishing charters.

Based at **Baird Bay**, a small fishing village 50km south of Streaky Bay, Baird Bay Charters (☎ 8626 5017) does sightseeing, fishing and diving charters from $20 to $50 – one of their trips allows you to swim with the bay's sea lions and dolphins. They also rent outboard powered dinghies ($35/50 per half/full day).

Back on the Flinders Hwy, the road to the west 21km past Port Kenny (39km from Streaky Bay) will take you to Point Labatt

Return of the Bettong

At the time of European settlement, the brush-tailed bettong (*Bettongia penicillata*) was wide-spread in the open forests and woodlands across southern Australia. It is now rare, having vanished in the wild apart from a few scattered populations on islands and the WA mainland.

One of a group generally referred to as 'rat kangaroos', the bettong has an average length, including its tail, of about 65cm. It appears to eat mainly the fruiting bodies of underground fungi, supplementing this with roots and insects. Its nest is a domed affair made of grass and shredded bark, which it carries to the site using its tail.

Prior to its extinction on the SA mainland the bettong was one of many marsupial species that inhabited the Venus Bay area, on the west coast of Eyre Peninsula. In 1994, the NPWS decided to attempt a reintroduction program. A rabbit-proof fence was built across the neck of the peninsula in the Venus Bay Conservation Park, and the foxes and feral cats were reduced by baiting and trapping. Finally, 67 bettongs were released.

At the time of writing the bettongs were doing nicely, although feral cats have accounted for a number of them. In fact the population has increased to the point where some of them are to be transferred to Lincoln National Park. The exercise is proving the theory that if only foxes and cats can be controlled, the potential to reintroduce native animals to their former range is almost unlimited.

Denis O'Byrne

via **Murphy's Haystacks**. These tall, colourful weather-sculpted granite tors stand on a hilltop about 2km from the highway.

A farther 12km towards Point Labatt on this road is the south-east corner of the **Calpatanna Waterhole Conservation Park** (3600 hectares). You can camp at Wedina Well, in the park's north-east corner.

STREAKY BAY
* **pop 1000**

This attractive little fishing and agricultural centre gets its name from the 'streaks' of seaweed Matthew Flinders saw in the bay. Established as a wool port in 1865, when it was called Flinders, it soon boasted a hotel, a store, a couple of cottages and an Aboriginal ration station; a small oyster cannery was built in the 1870s.

The main tourist information outlet is in the Shell Auto Mart (☎ 8626 1126) at 15

Alfred Terrace. It opens daily from 8 am to 6 pm. Out the back is the cast of a 5.5m great white shark, caught in 1990.

Things to See & Do

Across from the information outlet, the **Restored Engine Centre** has numerous engines dating from 1904. It opens on Tuesday and Friday from 2 to 4 pm and at other times by arrangement.

On Montgomery Terrace, and open much the same hours, the National Trust's **Old School Museum** ($2) has many interesting exhibits, including a restored pioneer's pug-and-pine hut complete with period furnishings.

The coastline near Streaky Bay has some outstanding scenery as well as surfing and fishing spots. **Cape Bauer**, about 5km north-west of town, has high, colourful cliffs. To the south, **Back Beach** is good for surfing and salmon fishing, as is **High Cliff** farther on. **Yanerbie**, at the northern end of Sceale Bay, has white Sahara-like dunes and a swimming beach.

Oysters are farmed in Streaky Bay and you can buy them for $5 a dozen from various outlets, including the caravan park.

The Streaky Bay Apex Camel Cup is held on the Sunday before the Melbourne Cup (which is on the first Tuesday in November). It's a fun day of camel races and novelty events such as donkey racing.

Streaky Bay Air Charter (☎ 8626 1385) offers **scenic flights**; a 30 minute flight along the coast costs $135 for up to five passengers.

Places to Stay & Eat
About 1km from town, and by a safe swimming beach, the attractive *Foreshore Tourist Park (☎ 8626 1666)* has tent/caravan sites starting at $11/16 and cabins at $34. The adjoining *kiosk* does good take-aways.

Streaky Bay Motel (☎ 8626 1126, 7 Alfred Terrace) has well-appointed units with kitchenette for $46/54 for singles/doubles.

Just up the road at No 35, the comfortable *Streaky Bay Community Hotel/Motel (☎ 8626 1008)* has standard pub rooms for $25/30, pub rooms with en suite bathroom for $55/65, and motel units for $50/60.

Headland House (☎ 8626 1315, 5 Flinders Drive) has a very good reputation. It offers B&B in tastefully furnished rooms starting at $50/60.

You can get good meals at the *Shell Auto Mart* and the pub. The *Terrace Bakery (Alfred Terrace)* is also recommended.

SMOKY BAY
- pop 100

There's not much to do in Smoky Bay but fish, swim or lie on the beach contemplating your navel, and that's what attracts most visitors. There's a gravel road to scenic **Point Brown**, 26km south-west; a whaling station operated at nearby **Point Collinson** between 1850 and 1860. The town **jetty** offers good fishing for tommies, garfish and trevally.

Twenty kilometres north of Smoky Bay towards Ceduna, the 267 hectare **Laura Bay** **Conservation Park** has mallee scrub, rocky headlands, mangroves and tidal flats, making it an excellent spot for birdwatching. There are carparks by the shore.

Places to Stay & Eat
The very friendly *Smoky Bay Caravan Park (☎ 8625 7030)* is right on the foreshore, with tent/caravan sites for $9/12 and basic cabins starting at $20.

You can buy fresh oysters for $5 a dozen at the *general store*, which has a bottle shop as well as fuel and provisions, and a caravan park.

Eyre Highway & West Coast

PORT AUGUSTA TO CEDUNA
The Eyre Hwy's first 140km will take you through semiarid station country to near Kimba, where the wheat paddocks begin. These will keep you company all the way to Ceduna, with a string of small agricultural service centres and grain terminals in between.

There's not a huge amount of interest on this route apart from the Iron Knob mine and some granite outcrops near Wudinna and Minnipa. A more adventurous, if longer and slower, alternative is to leave the highway at Iron Knob and take gravel roads to Wudinna or Minnipa via the scenic Gawler Ranges.

Iron Knob
- pop 275

Iron Knob, 62km south-west of Port Augusta, was Australia's oldest working mine until it closed in 1998. BHP commenced mining the iron ore deposits here in 1899, and built a tramway to its port at Whyalla two years later. Mining is still carried on in the area – mines in the Middleback Ranges produce 2.8 million tonnes of iron ore annually for processing at Whyalla.

Guided tours of the huge open cut leave from the tourist office (☎ 8646 2129) at 10 am and 2 pm weekdays, except public holidays. Tours last about one hour and cost $3; closed footwear is essential. The tourist office has a mining museum and an informative video on mining and steel-making.

You can camp for free at the tourist office, or there's the basic *Iron Knob Roadhouse Motel (☎ 8646 2058)* out on the highway.

Beside the highway 40km from Port Augusta, *Nuttbush Retreat (☎ 8643 8941, nuttbush@dove.net.au)*, on Pandurra Station, has backpacker beds for $18, single/twin rooms for $30/40 and grassy tent/caravan sites for $13/15. This place is clean and friendly, and has good facilities – there's a campers' kitchen, or you can buy station-style meals. They have a variety of 4WD station tours on offer.

Gawler Ranges

Consisting of steep granite hills and ridges, the Gawler Ranges commence about 30km north-west of Iron Knob and run westwards for 200km. There is plenty of interest here, including picturesque scenery, unusual rock formations, historic ruins, wildlife and, in early spring, magnificent wildflowers.

Mt Ive Station (☎ 8648 1817), in the central ranges, sells fuel and has a store, tent sites for $15, bunkhouse accommodation for $20, or $45 if you want linen and blankets, and a communal kitchen. The 84,000 hectare sheep property is 125km from Iron Knob. Its attractions include bushwalks, birdwatching (70 species) and access to **Lake Gairdner National Park**, another huge mainly dry saltpan.

Kimba
- **pop 680**

The local Aboriginal word for 'bushfire', Kimba is the largest of the peninsula's northern wheat towns. Apart from grain silos, its most obvious feature is the **Big Galah** (ho hum!). The 8m-high, steel-and-fibreglass likeness of the bird stands in front of a shop selling carved emu eggs and other novelties.

On the highway 18km east of town, the 45,100 hectare **Lake Gilles Conservation Park** has diverse habitats, including salt lakes, granite outcrops, sandhills and tall mallee. There's 4WD access to Lake Gilles in the north, where you can camp.

Between Kimba and **Koongawa**, 57km to the west, the highway passes close to the southern boundary of the 127,150 hectare **Pinkawillinie Conservation Park**. Consisting mainly of jumbled sand dunes covered by mallee scrub, it's accessible off the Koongawa-Buckleboo road.

The *Kimba Motel Roadhouse (☎ 8627 2040, Eyre Hwy)* has a caravan park and motel units.

In town, the pleasant *Kimba Community Hotel/Motel (☎ 8627 2007, High St)* has pub rooms for $20/35 and motel units from $40/60/67 singles/doubles/triples. It does counter meals daily except Sunday.

Tod Highway

Turning off the Eyre Hwy at **Kyancutta**, a tiny grain terminal 88km west of Kimba, the Tod Hwy south to Port Lincoln passes through **Lock** (population 220) at 55km. Named after a local farmer who was killed in action in Belgium in WWI, Lock is central to three large conservation parks: **Hambidge** (38,000 hectares), **Hincks** (66,300 hectares) and **Bascombe Well** (31,300 hectares). The parks preserve tracts of the mallee scrub that originally covered most of Eyre Peninsula. Bascombe Well, which has stone ruins, old wells and stands of beautiful red gums, is probably the most interesting.

For places to stay, Lock has a very basic *caravan park (caretaker ☎ 8689 1192)*, the *Lock Hotel/Motel (☎ 8689 1181)* and the *Boomerang Motel (☎ 8689 1193)*.

Wudinna
- **pop 570**

This little township's main attraction is **Mt Wudinna**, 10km north of town. While interesting, this large granite inselberg is nowhere near as spectacular as the local tourist industry would have you believe. A **tourist drive** links Mt Wudinna with other granite outcrops in the area.

Places to Stay The *Gawler Ranges Motel & Caravan Park (☎ 8680 2090, Eyre Hwy)* has tent/caravan sites for $12/16, on-site vans from $23, cramped motel units for $45/50 and larger ones for $63/72.

There's also the *Wudinna Hotel/Motel* (☎ *8680 2019, Burton Terrace)*, which has single pub rooms for $18 and motel units for $39/49/57 singles/doubles/triples.

At Minnipa, 37km west, the *Minnipa Hotel/Motel (☎ 8680 5005)* charges $25/45 in the pub and $40/58 in the motel.

Tiny Poochera, 35km farther on, has a *pub (☎ 8626 3025)* with an adjoining caravan park.

CEDUNA
• **pop 3600**

Just past the junction of the Flinders and Eyre Hwys, Ceduna is at the start of the long, lonely drive across the Nullarbor Plain into WA. The town was founded in 1896, although there had been a whaling station on St Peter Island, off nearby Cape Thevenard, back in 1850.

Ceduna is the service and administrative centre for the west coast, as well as a major export terminal for cereal grains, salt and gypsum – the deep-water port is at nearby Thevenard. Ceduna's fishing fleet keeps three seafood-processing factories in business.

Information

The tourist office, open weekdays from 9 am to 5.30 pm and Saturday morning, is in Traveland Ceduna (☎ 8625 2780, 1800 639 413 toll free) at 58 Poynton St. If you get tired of waiting for a lift you can visit Traveland, the local agent for Greyhound Pioneer, and purchase an onward ticket.

Money There are branches of the ANZ Bank and Bank SA (both have an ATM), a Commonwealth Bank agency in the post office, and an EFTPOS cash-withdrawal facility (maximum $500) in the Foodland Supermarket. All are on McKenzie St.

Laundry There's a seven-day launderette on the corner of South Terrace and Poynton St. Next door is a same-day drycleaners.

Quarantine Ceduna has a quarantine check point for vehicles entering SA from WA. You'll be asked to declare all fresh fruit and vegetables, which will be confiscated.

Things to See & Do

The National Trust's **Old Schoolhouse Museum**, on Park Terrace, has pioneer exhibits as well as artefacts and newspaper clippings from the British atomic weapons program at Maralinga. There's also the cast of a huge basking shark which was washed up at Fowlers Bay. It opens daily except Sunday and admission is $3 – check with the tourist office for times.

Each October long weekend the town's population doubles, thanks to Oysterfest. The three days of fun and games includes oyster-eating competitions.

The **Sea Dragon Gallery** on Day Terrace has some fine examples of local arts and crafts.

Off the coast between Ceduna and Smoky Bay, the **Nuyts Archipelago** and **Isles of St Francis** are home to sea lions, little penguins and greater stick-nest rats – the latter have vanished from the mainland and are considered endangered. Millions of short-tailed shearwaters nest here each year before their winter migration to the northern hemisphere.

Just 28km north of town, on the edge of the **Great Victoria Desert**, you'll enter the arid emptiness of the adjoining **Pureba Conservation Park** (144,400 hectares), **Yellabinna Regional Reserve** (2.5 million hectares) and **Yumbarra Conservation Park** (327,600 hectares). This vast area is best suited to experienced Outback travellers, so seek advice from the NPWS rangers in Ceduna before going there.

Denial Bay, 14km west of town, has several oyster farms. Most are open to the public and their produce sells for as little as $5 a dozen; the tourist office has a sketchmap. The bay was the site of **McKenzies Landing**, the district's first farming settlement.

Organised Tours

Ceduna Boat Charter (☎ 8625 2654 or 014 643 519) does fishing and diving charters in

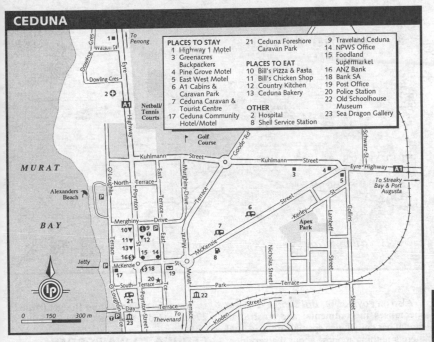

CEDUNA

PLACES TO STAY
1 Highway 1 Motel
3 Greenacres Backpackers
4 Pine Grove Motel
5 East West Motel
6 A1 Cabins & Caravan Park
7 Ceduna Caravan & Tourist Centre
17 Ceduna Community Hotel/Motel
21 Ceduna Foreshore Caravan Park

PLACES TO EAT
10 Bill's Pizza & Pasta
11 Bill's Chicken Shop
12 Country Kitchen
13 Ceduna Bakery

OTHER
2 Hospital
8 Shell Service Station
9 Traveland Ceduna
14 NPWS Office
15 Foodland Supermarket
16 ANZ Bank
18 Bank SA
19 Post Office
20 Police Station
22 Old Schoolhouse Museum
23 Sea Dragon Gallery

the area, as well as sightseeing trips out to Nuyts Archipelago.

Places to Stay

Best of the local caravan parks is attractive *Ceduna Foreshore Caravan Park* (☎ 8625 2290, *South Terrace*) in the town centre. It has tent/caravan sites starting at $13/15 and six-berth cabins at $35 (extra adults $3).

A1 Cabins & Caravan Park (☎ 8625 2578, *41 McKenzie St*) has basic cabins for $25 and self-contained cabins from $40.

Greenacres Backpackers (☎ 8625 3811, 017 165 346, *12 Kuhlmann St*) is basic, but clean and friendly. You'll find Vaughn, the owner, very helpful and obliging. Beds in small dorms and private rooms (some with fans) cost $15, including a substantial dinner, or you can camp out the back.

The *Ceduna Community Hotel/Motel* (☎ 8625 2008), on the foreshore on

O'Loughlin Terrace, has pleasant pub rooms with shared facilities starting at $25/29 for singles/doubles ($35/37 with en suite facilities). Motel units start at $58/63.

Other motels include the *East West Motel* (☎ 8625 2101, *67 McKenzie St*), with units from $60/65, and the *Highway 1 Motel* (☎ 8625 2208, *Eyre Hwy*), which charges from $46/51.

Places to Eat

There are plenty of places to eat in Ceduna. The *Pine Grove Motel* (*49 McKenzie St*) has a small bar and does substantial dinners from $7, while the *Ceduna Community Hotel/Motel* has good-value counter and bistro meals.

Poynton St has some good eateries. *Ceduna Bakery* and *Country Kitchen* are popular for coffee and cake – the latter also does home-style cooked breakfasts and lunches.

WEST COAST

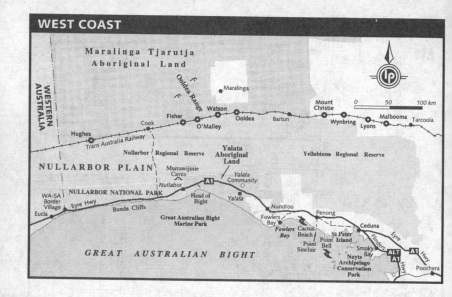

WEST COAST

Also on Poynton St, *Bill's Pizza & Pasta* specialises in continental and Australian fare. It has daily lunch specials from $4, and there's nothing modest about the servings. *Bill's Chicken Shop* is good for cooked chooks and fresh fish.

Getting There & Away
Kendell Airlines (☎ 13 13 00) flies daily, except Saturday, to Ceduna ($217).

Premier Stateliner (☎ 8415 5555) has daily bus services running from Port Augusta ($54) and Adelaide ($68). Its terminal is at the Shell Service Station on McKenzie St, from where you can purchase tickets.

Greyhound Pioneer buses pass through Ceduna daily, calling in at the Pine Grove Motel. Greyhound tickets are available from Traveland Ceduna (☎ 8625 2780) at 58 Poynton St.

Getting Around
There is no bus service from town to the airport, but A1 Cabs (☎ 015 977 944) will run you there for around $6.

You can rent a car from Budget (☎ 8625 2742) or Ceduna Rent-a-Car (☎ 8625 2085).

CEDUNA TO WA BORDER
Wheat and sheep paddocks line the highway to Nundroo, 150km from Ceduna, then it's attractive eucalypt woodland until 50km past Yalata. Here the gums start to become more sparse before petering out altogether in a flat sea of shrubby bluebush 20km later. From here it's the true **Nullarbor Plain** (the name is derived from the Latin for 'no trees'), which elsewhere is mainly north of the highway.

There's quite a bit of interest on this section. You can detour to good **surf beaches** between Ceduna and Penong, and visit the historic township of Fowlers Bay. Past Yalata there's whale watching at Head of Bight and some great lookouts on the Nullarbor Cliffs.

Penong
• **pop 250**
This fading township has a large, historic shearing shed (1865), now an interesting

Juggernaut of the Nullarbor: the *Indian Pacific* pictured at Cook

RICHARD I'ANSON

museum and craft shop, open daily except Tuesday. The turn-off to popular surfing and surf-fishing spots at **Point Bell** and **Rocky Point** is 54km from Ceduna (19km east of Penong).

Penong is the jumping-off point for **Point Sinclair**, 21km to the south. On the ocean side of the point, **Cactus Beach** is one of Australia's most famous surfing spots. It has a number of strong breaks including left and right-handers, as well as waves suitable for beginners.

Ron Gates, manager of the *Point Sinclair Camping Ground (☎ 8625 1036)*, is a mine of information on local surfing. You can camp here for $6 per person ($36 per week) and there's a 12 week limit. Ron supplies bore water for showers (use it sparingly) and firewood, but you must bring your own drinking water in summer.

In town, you can stay at the *Penong Hotel (☎ 8625 1050)*, which has pub rooms for $30/40 singles/doubles.

Penong to Head of Bight

The turn-off to **Fowlers Bay** is 34km west of Penong, and it's another 31km to this almost ghost town. Established as a wool port in the 1860s, Fowlers Bay was once the most isolated settlement in SA, and several interesting old buildings remain from that era. There's good fishing as well as impressive coastal dunes.

The modest *Fowlers Bay Caravan Park (☎ 8625 6143)* has a small shop which sells basic take-aways and provisions.

Continuing west on the Eyre Hwy there are basic caravan parks and motel-style accommodation at the *Nundroo Hotel/Motel (☎ 8625 6120)*, 78km from Penong, and the *Yalata Roadhouse (☎ 8625 6807)* 51km farther on. Nundroo has a 24-hour fuel stop and a restaurant.

You can buy Aboriginal arts and crafts at Yalata, which is owned by the nearby Yalata Aboriginal community. There are some good beach fishing spots south of here – ask at the Roadhouse for a permit.

Head of Bight

This is a major breeding area for **southern right whales**. Between 20 and 30 calves are born here between June and October, and most times from July to September you'll

The southern right whale is at home along the South Australian coastline

see up to six adults at a time. There are excellent lookout points, but it's best if you have binoculars.

The breeding area is afforded a measure of protection by the 20,000 sq km **Great Australian Bight Marine Park**, which runs along the coast from about 40km west of Fowlers Bay to the WA border. This is the world's second largest marine park after the Great Barrier Reef.

Entry permits for the observation area at Head of Bight (it's on Aboriginal land) cost $7 per adult; you can get permits and information from the Yalata Roadhouse and the warden's hut on the access road. The turn-off is 78km west of Yalata and 14km east of the Nullarbor Hotel/Motel, and it's 12km from there to the viewing area. Keep an eye out for bare earth mounds beside the access road – they often show where wombats have been burrowing.

Head of Bight to Border Village

At the Nullarbor Hotel/Motel you enter the 558,300 hectare **Nullarbor National Park**, which follows the coast to the WA border.

While the plain's surface is dry, flat and featureless, it's a different story under-

ground – there are world-class limestone cave systems on both sides of the border. These are off-limits to casual visitors but you can inspect the **Murrawijinie Cave**, an overhang behind the Nullarbor Hotel/Motel. See the Caving section in the Outdoor Activities chapter.

From the motel you can drive north into the vast **Nullarbor Regional Reserve** and experience the awesome space, silence and solitude of the treeless plain. It's obvious why the Mirning Aboriginal people call it *Undiri* ('bare like a bone').

There are several signposted **lookouts** along the spectacular 80m-high Bunda Cliffs, where the plain nosedives into the Bight between the Nullarbor Hotel/Motel and Border Village. Locals recommend the lookout 70km west of Nullarbor as having the most extensive views.

The ***Nullarbor Hotel/Motel Inn*** (☎ *8625 6271*) and ***Border Village*** (☎ *08-9039 3474*) – the latter is at the SA-WA border – have caravan park, motel and restaurant facilities. Border Village has a 24-hour service station.

There's a fruit and vegetable quarantine check point just beyond Border Village for vehicles entering WA.

Outback

The wide open spaces of SA's arid Outback stretch from Port Augusta to the Western Australia (WA), Northern Territory (NT), Queensland and New South Wales (NSW) borders. This mainly flat to gently undulating region covers about 80% of the state and has 1% of the population. Thanks to its low rainfall (from less than 150mm to 250mm annually) and high evaporation there is no agriculture here; apart from a few isolated waterholes, the only permanent water is a chain of mound springs around the western rim of the Great Artesian Basin. About half the region consists of sandy and stony semidesert and dry salt lakes. Most of the western portion is Aboriginal land, with the remainder (where suitable) being used for low-intensity sheep and cattle grazing.

The Outback contains most of the state's mineral wealth: the Moomba oil and gas field is a major contributor to state coffers, as is the Roxby Downs copper and uranium mine. Opals are mined at Andamooka, Coober Pedy and Mintabie, and promising gold discoveries are being investigated in the Tarcoola area north of Ceduna. Although it's often difficult to travel through without a 4WD vehicle (or a camel), the Outback has plenty of interest. You can't help but be fascinated by the opal towns, while the natural and social history of the Oodnadatta Track are equally compelling. For an experience in remote touring, the Birdsville Track is unforgettable – as is a 4WD crossing of the Simpson Desert.

In keeping with its wide horizons, the outback's conservation areas are *big*. Witjira National Park is in the western Simpson Desert, and Lake Eyre National Park includes (yes!) Lake Eyre; other parks cover the dry beds of Lake Torrens and Lake Gairdner. The Simpson Desert, Strzelecki and Innamincka regional reserves all sprawl across the map. Most are best reached in a 4WD, although parts of Witjira

HIGHLIGHTS

- Cross the vast emptiness of the Simpson Desert in a 4WD and camp in splendid solitude on a lonely sandridge

- Contemplate the desperate isolation of explorers Burke and Wills; visit Innamincka, where their ill-fated expedition reached its tragic end

- Explore the many historical and geographical features of the remote Oodnadatta Track

- Be amazed by the optimism of the outback pioneers at the huge 120-stand Cordillo Downs shearing shed, one of the state's outstanding pastoral relics

- Experience the lunarlike desolation around the opal-mining townships of Andamooka and Coober Pedy

- Admire the vivid carpet of wildflowers that spring up in late winter after good rains

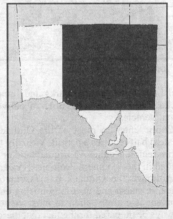

OUTBACK

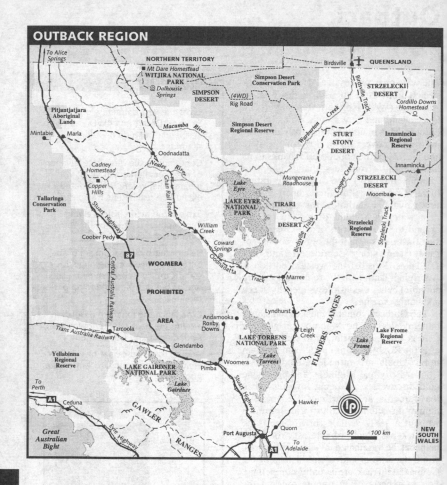

OUTBACK REGION

and Lake Eyre national parks and Innamincka Reserve are accessible to conventional vehicles.

Public entry to most of the Outback's western half requires a permit. Virtually this entire region is either Aboriginal land or included in the Woomera Prohibited Area.

Although the Outback is a fascinating place, its harsh and uncompromising environment is entirely alien to most visitors. Always be prepared for the fact that there is little drinking water and there are very few

facilities of any kind apart from a few isolated towns and roadhouses.

European History

The first reports on the Outback from explorers such as Edward John Eyre (1839) discouraged settlement. Twenty years later, however, John MacDouall Stuart was impressed by the grazing potential he found in the Lake Eyre Basin. His efforts in the region included an epic south to north crossing of the continent in 1862.

Following Stuart's success, and his favourable reports on the country he'd travelled through, the SA government decided to construct an overland telegraph line from Port Augusta to Darwin. The line, which took two years to build and was completed in 1872, became a conduit for white settlement of the Outback; enormous stations had been established all the way to the NT border within a year or two of its completion. In the 1870s and 1880s, more land was settled up to the north-east as far as the Queensland border.

In 1867, Lutheran and Moravian Brethren missionaries established mission stations among the Dieri people on Cooper Creek, but fierce opposition from the Aborigines forced them out four years later.

The Lutherans returned in 1877 and revived their mission on Lake Killalpaninna, which they ran as a sheep station with Aboriginal labour for the next 25 years. In 1914, when the once numerous Dieri had declined to 150, the mission closed for good.

The second major development was the Great Northern Railway from Port Augusta, which reached Marree in 1883. Set on a barren stony plain, Marree became the trucking point for the huge mobs of cattle then being driven down the Birdsville and Oodnadatta tracks.

Marree was one of Australia's largest bases for the legendary 'Afghan' cameleers. These men, most of whom actually came from the region of India that is now Pakistan, supervised the long strings of camels that supplied the outback's far-flung stations and other settlements with everything from flour and corrugated iron to glass windows and pianos. Oodnadatta became another important cattle-trucking point and camel centre when the railhead reached there in 1889.

The Great Northern Railway (by now called the 'Ghan' after the cameleers it had replaced) eventually arrived at Alice Springs in 1929. Although it was a brave statement of optimism, the line had been built 'on the cheap', and delays running into weeks were often experienced when storms washed out the tracks. After 50 years of financial losses and inefficiency the Commonwealth decided to build a new line farther to the west. The 'New Ghan' to Alice Springs opened for business in 1980, following which the 'Old Ghan' line was closed.

Information

Tourist Offices The main tourist office for the region is in Port Augusta (see the section on this town in the Flinders Ranges chapter).

National Parks The National Parks & Wildlife Service (NPWS) has its northern regional headquarters at 9 MacKay St in Port Augusta (☎ 8648 5300, fax 8648 5301); you can write to them at PO Box 78, Port Augusta SA 5700. The Desert Parks Hotline (☎1800 816 078 toll free) can give details of all Outback parks except those in the far west (Unnamed Conservation Park is managed from Ceduna).

A NPWS ranger is based permanently at Innamincka, and there are seasonal rangers at Dalhousie Springs in Witjira National Park.

Radio Communications If you're going to drive SA's remoter tracks you should have a 50-watt (minimum) high frequency radio with Royal Flying Doctor Service (RFDS) frequencies – and know how to use it.

Regardless of where you go you'll need the frequencies of the Port Augusta RFDS base (☎ 8642 2044, call sign VNZ – Victor November Zulu). It uses 8165 kHz between 7 am and 5 pm, or 4010 and 6890 kHz between 7 am and 9 pm daily; its after-hours alarm frequencies are 2020 and 4010 kHz.

For the far northern areas it's a good idea to also have the frequencies for Alice Springs (☎ 8952 1033, call sign VJD – Victor Juliet Delta). You can reach the base on 5410 and 6950 kHz on weekdays (except public holidays) between 7.30 am and 5 pm; for after-hours emergencies use 2020 and 5410 kHz.

Give the radio a long-range test before you leave civilisation, making sure that the emergency alarm button is operational. Telephone the RFDS radio operators (or better still call

OUTBACK

in personally) for a friendly chat and to familiarise yourself with their services.

Books Lonely Planet's *Outback Australia* gives a detailed rundown on the Stuart Highway, the Simpson Desert and the Birdsville, Oodnadatta and Strzelecki tracks. The Royal Automobile Association's (RAA) comprehensive *Outback South Australia* travel guide includes the Alice Springs region and the parts of WA, Queensland and NSW that adjoin SA.

The Royal Society of SA's *The Natural History of the North East Deserts* (now out of print) is an essential reference for keen naturalists.

Localised references are mentioned where applicable.

Maps The RAA has the best regional road map. Westprint's *Desert Parks* shows how to get around the parks and reserves in the north-east of the state.

Meant more as a souvenir than a road guide, *Outback Central & South Australia*, published by the SA Department of Lands, is an excellent tourist map with lots of interesting information.

For more localised coverage, Westprint has several popular maps, all with text giving a wealth of information. They form part of your Desert Parks Pass package (see the following section).

National Park Permits

To visit most of the Outback's conservation areas you must have a Desert Parks Pass, which costs $60 per vehicle and covers entry and camping fees. It's valid for a year and includes an excellent information booklet and detailed route and area maps.

Desert Parks Passes are available in many places, including: Adelaide (the RAA and the Environment Shop), Birdsville (Birdsville Auto), Coober Pedy (Underground Books), Innamincka (Trading Post), Marree (Marree General Store), Mt Dare Homestead, Oodnadatta (Pink Roadhouse), Port Augusta (Wadlata Outback Centre) and William Creek (William Creek Hotel). Port Augusta's NPWS office can advise on other outlets.

If you just want to visit Cooper Creek in the Innamincka Regional Reserve, Lake Eyre in the Lake Eyre National Park or Dalhousie Springs in the Witjira National Park, you need buy only a day/night permit for $15 per vehicle. These are available from Mt Dare Homestead, the Pink Roadhouse in Oodnadatta, the William Creek Hotel, the Marree General Store, and the rangers at Innamincka and Dalhousie Springs.

Organised Tours

You can do town and mine tours at Andamooka, Coober Pedy and Roxby Downs, and visit the rocket-firing ranges at Woomera. If you've got a day to spare, the mail-run tours to remote settlements from Coober Pedy and Cadney Homestead are great value. Camel treks leave from a couple of places on the Oodnadatta Track. For details see later sections in this chapter.

If you want to visit the Pitjantjatjara people of north-western SA and learn something of their culture, Desert Tracks (☎ 02-6680 8566, dsttrks@nor.com.au) is your best bet. It has regular monthly tours from March to November inclusive, and at the time of writing was the only operator visiting the area.

Outback n' Coastal Tours (☎ 8250 2911, oca@webscene.com.au) has 4WD safaris along the Oodnadatta, Birdsville and Strzelecki tracks for around $130 per day all inclusive (tours are from seven to 10 days). It also has a five day opal tour for $695.

Groovy Grape, Heading Bush, Oz Experience and The Wayward Bus all include the Oodnadatta Track and Coober Pedy on their runs between Adelaide and Alice Springs. See the Bus section in the Getting There & Away chapter.

Dick Lang's Desert-Air Safaris (☎ 8264 7200, 1800 803 200 toll free) does round trips from Adelaide via Lake Eyre, the Simpson Desert, Birdsville, Innamincka and the Flinders Ranges. You stay overnight at Birdsville and land at the 'Dig Tree' for land tours – the three day tour also lands in the Simpson Desert. Tours cost $749/849 per person all-inclusive for two/three days, with a minimum of five passengers.

You can fly with Airlines of SA on the mail run from Port Augusta to Birdsville and Innamincka. See Port Augusta's Getting There & Away section in the Flinders Ranges chapter.

Scenic flights over Lake Eyre leave from Cadney Homestead, William Creek and Marree; most operators in the Flinders can also fly you around the Outback.

Accommodation

The roadhouses scattered along the Stuart Hwy have caravan park and motel facilities. There's an excellent range including backpacker hostels in Coober Pedy, which has more accommodation than the rest of the Outback put together.

Otherwise there is very little apart from what you find at the few small centres such as Oodnadatta and Innamincka. The midyear school holiday period sees heavy booking, so always check ahead if you don't want to camp.

There are countless good bush campsites near the Outback's main routes, although you may need a 4WD to get off the road. In warm weather the bushflies and mosquitoes can be troublesome; mosquito netting (or a tent with plenty of insect-screened ventilation space) is pretty well essential at such times. Large areas of the Outback are devoid of firewood, so either carry some in your car or use a gas stove.

Always carry plenty of drinking water (the bore water on the Oodnadatta and Birdsville tracks is mainly undrinkable), and *never* camp near or pollute stock watering points.

Getting There & Away

Air Kendell Airlines flies daily from Adelaide to Coober Pedy and Roxby Downs, while Airlines of SA flies most days to Woomera. See the sections on these towns for details.

Bus Premier Stateliner services Woomera and Roxby Downs from Adelaide and Port Augusta. Greyhound Pioneer and McCafferty's go up the Stuart Hwy to Coober Pedy and continue on to Alice Springs and Darwin.

Stuart Highway

The Stuart Hwy was named after the explorer John MacDouall Stuart, whose expeditions in SA and the NT took him through much of the country traversed by the road. You reach the NT border 930km from Port Augusta, after which it's 294km to Alice Springs.

The highway passes through Coober Pedy; if you want to visit the other opal towns you can detour from Pimba through Woomera to Andamooka, and from Marla to Mintabie. There are several minor roads from the highway across to the Oodnadatta Track.

Fuel and accommodation facilities for travellers are scattered along the highway at Pimba (171km from Port Augusta), Glendambo (285km), Coober Pedy (535km), Cadney Homestead (689km), Marla (771km) and Kulgera in the NT (949km). Pimba, Coober Pedy and Marla have 24-hour fuel sales.

WOOMERA
* **pop 1000**

Established in 1948, Woomera was used during the 50s and 60s to launch experimental British rockets and conduct tests in an abortive European project to send a satellite into orbit. In its heyday it housed 7500 people, but these days its main role is as a service town for the mostly US personnel working at Nurrungar, a communications facility at nearby Island Lagoon. Rocket launches and defence exercises are still carried out in the area.

A small **heritage centre** in the centre of town has several interesting displays on Woomera's past and present roles. Outside is a collection of old military aircraft, rockets and missiles. Except during summer, when it's closed, the centre is open daily from 9 am to 5 pm.

Olympic Dam Tours (☎ 8671 0788) has a 3½ hour tour that takes in places such as

OUTBACK

the Koolymilka camp, the main operational area at Range E, and the old Blue Streak launching site at Lake Hart. The tours cost $46 (minimum four passengers) and are subject to range availability (there are no tours during summer).

Fuel at Woomera's two service stations is up to 9c a litre cheaper than at nearby **Pimba**, on the highway. Pimba is a dramatic contrast to neat, leafy Woomera – stranded on a saltbush-covered plateau, it's one of SA's most visually unappealing towns.

Places to Stay & Eat

The friendly *Woomera Travellers' Village (☎ 8673 7800)*, near the town entrance, has backpacker accommodation for $15/20 singles/doubles with ceiling fans ($17/24 with air-con), grassed campsites ($5 per person), air-con cabins (from $45) and budget motel units ($45).

Alternatively, the *Eldo Hotel (☎ 8673 7867, Kotara Ave)* has comfortable rooms with shared facilities from $33 per person; rooms with private facilities cost $70/105/132. You can get counter meals for around $6 and restaurant meals averaging $12 for a main course. ('Eldo' is the acronym for the European Launcher Development Organisation).

In Pimba, *Spud's Hotel/Motel (☎ 8673 7473)* has units for $25 per person.

Getting There & Away

Air Airlines of SA (bookings ☎ 13 13 13) flies from Adelaide daily except Friday and weekends for $180, and from Port Augusta on Wednesday and Thursday for $80.

Missiles & Bombs

Woomera (an Aboriginal term for a spear-throwing tool) was established by Britain and Australia as a base for international space research and the testing of guided missiles. In its heyday in the 1950s and 1960s over 3000 rockets were launched, including a major program of test firings of the 32m Europa rocket.

Things have been fairly quiet since, although a resurgence in activity in 1995, when the American space agency NASA fired a number of rockets, seems to have sparked a rebirth. At the time of this update, there was a proposal to launch several satellites from Woomera, and various countries such as Japan, Malaysia and Russia were showing interest in using the facility.

Farther west, on the northern edge of the Nullarbor Plain, the British exploded atom bombs at Emu in 1953 and Maralinga in 1956 and 1957; Maralinga is an Aboriginal word for thunder. The largest explosion, equivalent to a 26.6 kilotonne conventional bomb, was detonated on a balloon about 300m above ground level.

Between 1960 and 1963 the British conducted a number of 'safety tests' with simulated bombs containing plutonium at Maralinga. These were detonated with conventional explosives to discover whether or not nuclear weapons would release nuclear energy in the event of an accident.

Prior to the tests, most of the nomadic Aborigines who lived in the area were moved to Yalata, west of Ceduna. Concerns about the effects of the tests on local Aboriginal people prompted a Commission of Enquiry in the mid-1980s. It found that they had suffered greatly because of the tests and that the bomb sites were still contaminated. The commission also suggested that it was Britain's responsibility to clean up the mess. Finally, in 1998, after years of argument and stalling, a $104 million operation (40% funded by the British Government) cleaned up much of the contaminated area.

Denis O'Byrne

Bus Woomera is 7km off the Stuart Hwy from Pimba. The long-distance bus lines pass through Pimba daily and will drop you off at Woomera, while Premier Stateliner passes through Woomera daily except Saturday on its run to Roxby Downs.

ANDAMOOKA
* **pop 470**

Off the Stuart Hwy, and 110km north of Woomera by sealed road via Roxby Downs township, Andamooka is a rough-and-ready opal-mining centre with a strong frontier flavour; if you think Coober Pedy is barren and moonlike, wait until you see this place! Despite its Wild West 'badlands' appearance, the local residents are friendly and welcoming, as a rule. Unfortunately for them, the ground generally isn't safe enough to have dugouts in which to escape the searing summer heat, and air-conditioning is a luxury in a place where water often has to be trucked in.

Information
The post office, by Duke's Bottlehouse in Opal Creek Blvd, is the best place for information.

Organised Tours
For an educational **mine tour** call in at the Treasure Chest, by the tall gums at the entrance to town. Tours ($5) leave at 2 pm daily and you drive yourself.

Olympic Dam Tours (☎ 8671 0788) has a three hour tour of the town and mines departing from Roxby Downs ($54) and Andamooka ($28). There are no tours over the summer months.

Duke's Bottlehouse runs one hour walking tours ($10), visiting several historic dugouts and an underground mine.

Places to Stay & Eat
You can camp (from $14) or stay in an on-site van or cabin without air-con (both $30) at the dusty *Andamooka Caravan Park* (☎ 8672 7117, 94 Government Rd). There's not much shade here – not that there is anywhere else, either!

Right in the town centre, the *Andamooka Opal Hotel/Motel* (☎ 8672 7078, Main Rd) has units starting at $55/65. Also central, *Duke's Bottlehouse* (☎ 8672 7007, 275 Opal Creek Blvd) charges $45/65 for its motel units.

The best place to eat is the *Tuckerbox Restaurant*, next to Duke's Bottlehouse, which sells hearty meals for reasonable prices. You can also eat at the hotel.

ROXBY DOWNS
* **pop 2000**

Just 30km from Andamooka, but a world away in appearance, Roxby Downs is the dormitory and service centre for the huge **Olympic Dam** uranium, copper, gold and silver mine. The ore body was discovered in 1976 and the town developed in 1988 after much public soul-searching on the question of uranium mining. Plentiful underground water and better soil than Andamooka have allowed the whole town to be pleasantly landscaped.

There's a National Bank branch with an ATM in the town centre.

Surface **tours** of the mine and town cost $26 and last 2½ hours. Except during summer, when they close, tours leave daily at 9.45 am from the Olympic Dam Tours office (☎ 8671 0788), next to the BP service station. They also do **4WD charters** to places such as Lake Torrens, a huge, mainly dry saltpan near Andamooka.

Places to Stay
The *Roxby Downs Caravan Park* (☎ 8671 1000, Pioneer Drive) has lawned tent/caravan sites for $10/12 and on-site vans with air-con for $34.

In the town centre, the *Roxby Downs Motor Inn* (☎ 8671 0311, Richardson Place) charges $85 for its units.

Getting There & Away
Kendell Airlines (bookings ☎ 13 13 00) flies in daily to Roxby Downs from Adelaide ($216) and Coober Pedy ($112).

Premier Stateliner has buses daily except Saturday from Adelaide ($63).

OUTBACK

GLENDAMBO
* pop 20

Glendambo is 114km north-west of Pimba and 253km south of Coober Pedy. It was created in 1982 as a service centre on the new Stuart Hwy to replace the township of Kingoonya, which was bypassed. Glendambo has a good pub, a motel, two roadhouses and a caravan park. Fuel is available from 6 am to midnight.

The township howls on the last weekend of November, when the annual Bachelors & Spinsters Ball is held out at the racetrack. Early in October, the Glendambo Races & Ball makes for another wild weekend.

From Glendambo you can take the unsealed road west to fast-fading Kingoonya (43km), then south to the Gawler Ranges and on to the Eyre Peninsula coast. Alternatively, keep going west from Kingoonya for another 80km to the old gold-mining centre of **Tarcoola**, where *The Ghan* and *Indian-Pacific* trains part company. There are numerous historic relics to explore here.

If you're heading north, there are no fuel stops between Glendambo and Coober Pedy.

Places to Stay & Eat

The ***Glendambo Tourist Centre*** (☎ 8672 1030) has bars, a restaurant and 60 motel units each sleeping up to five people. Rooms cost from $72/74 for singles/doubles and $12 for each extra person.

Right next door, the ***BP Roadhouse & Caravan Park*** (☎ 8672 1035) has a basic backpackers bunkhouse (no air-con) with beds costing $12; tent/caravan sites cost $12/15 and there are on-site vans without air-con.

In Tarcoola you can stay in an air-conditioned room at the very charming old *Wilgena Hotel* (☎ 8672 2042) for $30/40.

COOBER PEDY
* pop 3000

On the Stuart Hwy, 535km north of Port Augusta, Coober Pedy is one of Australia's best-known Outback towns. The name is Aboriginal and supposedly means 'white fellow's hole in the ground'. This aptly describes the place, as about half the population lives in dugouts to shelter from the extreme climate: summer temperatures can soar to over 50°C and winter nights are freezing. Apart from the dugouts, there are over 250,000 mine shafts in the area. Keep your eyes open!

Coober Pedy is in an extremely harsh area and the town reflects its environment; even in the middle of winter it looks dried out and dusty. It's not as ramshackle as it used to be, and these days there are even a few gardens, but there's no way you could describe it as attractive. In fact, to many visitors the town looks a bit like the end of the world – which is probably why much of *Mad Max III* was filmed here. Others love it!

Coober Pedy is also very cosmopolitan, with about 40 nationalities represented. Greeks, Serbs, Croats and Italians form the largest groups among the miners, while the gem buyers are usually from Hong Kong.

The town has a reputation for being volatile: since 1987 the police station has been bombed twice, police vehicles have been blown up, the courthouse has been bombed once and the most successful restaurant (the Acropolis) was demolished by a blast. Hundreds of thousands of dollars worth of mining equipment has gone the same way.

But for visitors Coober Pedy is by and large a friendly place. However, you should remember that this is a town where people value their individuality. Some of those involved in tourism aren't as sophisticated as everyone would like, but this is part of the fabric of the place.

Information

The tourist office (☎ 1800 637 076, fax 8672 5699) is in the council offices diagonally opposite the Ampol Roadhouse at the entrance to town on Hutchison St. It opens from 9 am to 5 pm on weekdays only. Outside these times you can ask at Underground Books (☎ 8672 5558), on Post Office Hill Rd.

There are plenty of opal shops, however banking facilities are limited: there are several EFTPOS cash-withdrawal facilities, a

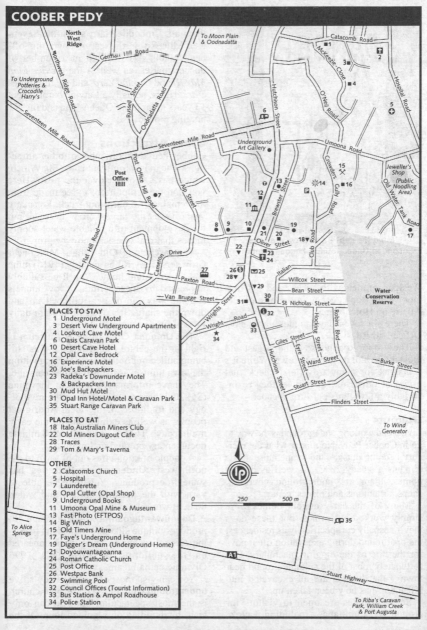

COOBER PEDY

PLACES TO STAY
1 Underground Motel
3 Desert View Underground Apartments
4 Lookout Cave Motel
6 Oasis Caravan Park
10 Desert Cave Hotel
12 Opal Cave Bedrock
16 Experience Motel
20 Joe's Backpackers
23 Radeka's Downunder Motel
& Backpackers Inn
30 Mud Hut Motel
31 Opal Inn Hotel/Motel & Caravan Park
35 Stuart Range Caravan Park

PLACES TO EAT
18 Italo Australian Miners Club
22 Old Miners Dugout Cafe
28 Traces
29 Tom & Mary's Taverna

OTHER
2 Catacombs Church
5 Hospital
7 Launderette
8 Opal Cutter (Opal Shop)
9 Underground Books
11 Umoona Opal Mine & Museum
13 Fast Photo (EFTPOS)
14 Big Winch
15 Old Timers Mine
17 Faye's Underground Home
19 Digger's Dream (Underground Home)
21 Doyouwantagoanna
24 Roman Catholic Church
25 Post Office
26 Westpac Bank
27 Swimming Pool
32 Council Offices (Tourist Information)
33 Bus Station & Ampol Roadhouse
34 Police Station

OUTBACK

RICHARD l'ANSON

'Mind the gap' – a new twist on the
London Underground's famous mantra

Westpac branch with ATM, and a Commonwealth Bank agency in the post office.
All are on Hutchison St.

There's a seven day launderette on Post
Office Hill Rd.

The Ampol Roadhouse is the largest and
most modern of its genre in town. While it's
a magnet for many travellers, check fuel
prices at other outlets first as they're invariably a few cents per litre cheaper.

Dugouts

Living and working underground is the way to
go in Coober Pedy. No matter what the mercury is doing outside, the temperature inside
remains a steady 23°C. As well as dugout
homes, there are underground churches,
shops, restaurants and places to stay.

Many of the early dugout homes were
simply worked-out mines, but these days
they're usually cut specifically as residences;
the opal found during excavation often pays
for the hire of the digging machinery. Unfortunately most of the suitable ground near
town – the dugouts are all excavated into
hillsides – has now been taken up.

Several homes are open to visitors for
around $3 admittance, including **Faye's**,

Digger's Dream and, the most eccentric of
them all, **Crocodile Harry's**. On the Seventeen Mile Rd north-west of town, this off-
beat dugout has featured in a number of
documentaries, as well as the movies *Mad
Max III* and *Ground Zero*, and the miniseries
Stark. Harry, actually a Latvian baron, spent
13 years in far north Queensland and the NT
hunting crocodiles.

Other Attractions

Coober Pedy has a number of other attractions. The most prominent is the **Big Winch**,
which has a lookout over the town. Here
you find the sculpture of a tree made from
the remains of a burnt-out truck. For many
years it was the largest 'tree' in town, but
the development of a reliable water supply
means that real trees can now be grown.

The fascinating **Old Timers Mine**, near
Crowders Gully Rd, is an early (1916) mine
and underground home. You'll be suitably
impressed by its labyrinth of low tunnels
and the way the diggers climbed up and
down the shafts. It's open from 9 am daily
for self-guided tours ($5).

The **Umoona Opal Mine & Museum** is
right in the centre of town; opal was still
being pulled out of here until mining within
the town limits was banned some years ago.
They have informative tours of the mine
($5), and there are displays on the mythology and traditions of the local Aboriginal
people, as well as exhibitions on the early
mining days. There's an excellent 18 minute
documentary on opal and mining.

A couple of kilometres out of town to the
north-west, **Underground Potteries** has
some fine products. You may be able to
yarn with the friendly potters and watch
them at work.

Doyouwantagoanna, on Hutchison St,
produces unique silk-screen designs featuring Australian fauna. Their work appeared
on the uniforms of Australia's 1996
Olympic netball team.

You can visit most of Coober Pedy's five
underground churches. The serbian church
is the most spectacular, but you can only
visit this building on a guided tour. Of the

remainder, the Catholic church is probably the most interesting.

Opal

The first opals were discovered by 14-year-old Willie Hutchison in 1915. Today there are literally hundreds of working mines in the various opal fields that lie scattered over the barren saltbush plain around town. Coming up the highway you see the first diggings 38km before town and the last ones 34km after it.

There are no big operators in opal mining, and the claims, which measure 50m by 50m and 100m by 50m, are limited to one per person. This means that when somebody makes a find on new ground, dozens of miners home in like bees around a honeypot. You'll take one look at the large areas of virgin salt-bush between the diggings and wonder at the vast quantities of opal still waiting to be found here.

Several specialised items of opal-mining equipment have been developed. They include automatic hoists (these work off a car differential), tunnelling machines and giant truck-mounted vacuum cleaners known as 'blowers'. If you see columns of white dust rising like smoke above the waste dumps you'll know that a blower is at work.

Keen fossickers can have a go themselves, but note that wandering around on the outlying opal fields is discouraged – the safest area is the **Jeweller's Shop** field in the north-east corner of town. Fossicking through the mullock (waste) dumps for opal is called 'noodling'. You can rent or buy sieves from several outlets around town.

There are numerous reputable – and some not so reputable – opal outlets in town. It's best to shop around and be wary of anyone offering discounts over 30% (there's a 30% sales tax on opal, so discounts of much more than this usually indicate that the opal is overpriced). Some of the best buys are found at the **Opal Cutter** on Post Office Hill Rd.

The Opal Festival is a fun day held every Easter Saturday. It features games, competitions and stalls, and visitors can get together and form their own teams – for events such as the dirt-shovelling competition, for example.

Organised Tours

There are several sightseeing tours that take you into an opal mine, underground home and various other places in and around town.

The tour offered by Radeka's Downunder Motel ($25) is popular with budget travellers – it includes noodling in an open cut. Alternatively, the Desert Cave Hotel has a good sightseeing tour for $36.

The 2½ hour Opal Quest tour ($25; ask at Underground Books) is the only one to visit a working mine.

Also good is an informative 'star tour' ($15) where you explore the heavens from the Moon Plain, a barren table-like plain just outside Coober Pedy on the Oodnadatta road – an appropriate venue. Book at Radeka's for this one.

On Monday and Thursday you can travel with the mail truck along 600km of dirt roads as it does the round trip from Coober Pedy to Oodnadatta and William Creek. This is a great way to get off the beaten track and visit remote homesteads. The backpackers' special price is $67, not including lunch; other passengers pay $89. For details, call ☎ 1800 069 911 toll free or contact Underground Books.

Places to Stay – Budget

Caravan Parks There are four caravan parks in and around town. None are visually inspiring – there's no lawn but plenty of dust, and the ground is as hard as nails.

Reasonably central to the action is **Oasis Caravan Park** (☎ *8672 5169, Seventeen Mile Rd*). It has the best shade and shelter, as well as an undercover swimming pool in a big old storage tank. Campsites cost $5.50 per person, on-site vans are $35 and self-contained cabins cost from $58; small twin rooms with air-con cost $26.

Also central is the **Opal Inn Caravan Park** (☎ *8672 5054, Hutchison St*), beside the Opal Inn, which has tent sites (from $9) and caravan sites ($15).

OUTBACK

Colour in Opal

It's thought that opal was formed by the hardening of a silica-rich gel which collected in cracks and other spaces in the sandstone, such as those left by the breakdown of organic material like shells and bones. Look through an electron microscope and you'll see that opal is made up of spheres of silicon dioxide, much like a bag of oranges, with the spaces filled with water.

A piece of opal in which the spheres are regular in size, shape and arrangement acts like a three-dimensional diffraction grate, splitting white light into the different colours of the spectrum. Large spheres produce all the colours (violet, indigo, green, blue, yellow, orange and red), intermediate ones produce violet to yellow and small ones produce violet only. However, in most cases the spheres are irregular in size, shape and arrangement. This scatters the white light and produces milky or white potch.

The patterns seen in precious opal depend on variations in the size, regularity and arrangement of the spheres. Created during the opal's formation, these variations commonly consist of horizontal banding and the bending of those bands; others include the irregular presence of trace elements.

Buying an Opal

Precious opal exhibits a play of colour. It comes in several varieties, including jelly (transparent opal with little colour), crystal (jelly with more colour), white, milky (somewhere between crystal and white) and black (transparent to opaque opal with a dark background colour). Potch is opal without a play of colour and hence has no value.

Cut opal comes in various forms: solids are natural stones that have been cut and polished but otherwise not interfered with; doublets are thin slices of precious opal glued to backs of dark potch or synthetic material; and triplets are doublets with a layer of clear glass, potch or quartz cemented to the face. Domed opals are generally more attractive than flat ones because of their greater depth of pattern and play of colour.

Whichever type you decide to buy, there are several characteristics that determine the stone's value. Number one is brilliance – a brilliant stone is far more attractive than a dull stone, hence it is more valuable.

Second is pattern. Large patterns are better than small ones, and if it is an interesting one or has some definable shape (such as a flower, bird or cross) so much the better.

Third is colour. A stone with a dominance of strong red is most valuable, followed by orange, green and blue, in that order.

The best opals are beautiful when seen from any angle and in any light, whether it be direct sunlight, semishade, shade or artificial light. Some look best in particular types of light – an opal may show brilliant colour in shade, but not in direct sunlight.

Another consideration is shape. Unless the opal is valuable, choose a standard shape so that it won't need a special (and costly) mounting.

Finally, faults or flaws such as sand, cracks or areas of potch all reduce the value of a stone. The easiest way to detect sand and cracks is to hold the opal up to the light.

OUTBACK

The **Stuart Range Caravan Park** (☎ 8672 5179, Hutchison St) is the largest in town and has the best facilities, including a swimming pool. Its self-contained cabins ($50) are more like motel rooms; it also has backpacker beds ($10).

Riba's (☎ 8672 5614), on the William Creek road 5km from town, has above-

Coober Pedy's answer to Rome's Church of the Catacombs

Windsurfers near Port Lincoln

Coober Pedy's lunar landscapes provided a backdrop to the movie *Mad Max III*.

Siding ruins lie forlorn in the Gibber Plains along the old Ghan route, Pedirka.

Wildflowers and steam mark Purni bore, north-west of Oodnadatta in the Simpson Desert.

Don't be deceived by the beauty: many have died thirsty in the area around Sturt Stony Desert.

ground sites for $4.50 per person (underground $8 per site) – showers are free, unlike the other places. It does an interesting one hour evening tour ($10, which includes the above-ground camping fee if you're staying there).

Hostels There are four backpacker places, all underground. The best standard is offered by *Radeka's Backpackers Inn* (☎ 8672 5223, 1800 633 891 toll free, Hutchison St), at Radeka's Downunder Motel. It has underground bunks in open alcoves for $14, including linen and showers; if you want more privacy, the renovated twin and double rooms with share facilities cost from $40. It has a very good kitchen as well as a bar, barbecue facilities, restaurant, games room and laundry, and the staff also do free transfers. The office is open for bookings from 7.30 am to 1 am.

Joe's Backpackers (☎ 8672 5163, Oliver St), in the town centre, has two-bedroom, apartment-style bunkhouses each sleeping 10 for $14 per person including linen and showers. There's no laundry, but the launderette is only a short walk away. The staff do free transfers from the bus station and airport.

The very basic *Opal Cave Bedrock* (☎ 8672 5028, Hutchison St) has four-bed alcoves opening off a wide central passageway – curtains provide a measure of privacy here. Beds cost $12 including linen and showers. It's a fair hike to the toilets and showers, particularly for the males, and kitchen facilities are limited.

The *Umoona Opal Mine* (☎ 8672 5288, Hutchison St), has beds in basic, two-bunk rooms for $10, including shower (bed linen is $5 extra). Its kitchen facilities are reasonably limited.

Hotels & Motels The *Umoona Opal Mine* (see Hostels) has basic singles/doubles for $20/25.

The *Opal Inn Hotel/Motel* (☎ 8672 5054, Hutchison St) has basic pub rooms with air-con and fridges for $25/35 singles/doubles and motel units starting at $40/45/50 singles/doubles/triples.

Places to Stay – Mid-Range
Motels There are a number of motels in the mid-range and all offer a good standard. Most are underground.

Desert View Underground Apartments (☎ 8672 3330, Shaw Place) has comfortable, spacious units with kitchen and laundry facilities sleeping up to nine for $65/80/100.

The underground *Experience Motel* (☎ 8672 5777, Crowders Gully Rd) is probably the homeliest place in town. It has very pleasing rooms with shared facilities for $80 singles and doubles ($90 with private facilities), and there's a backpacker room sleeping six for $100.

There's an excellent lookout on the hilltop above the *Lookout Cave Motel* (☎ 8672 5118, 1800 632 251 toll free, McKenzie Close), which charges $65/75/85.

One of the friendliest places is the *Mud Hut Motel* (☎ 8672 3003, 1800 646 962 toll free, St Nicholas St), which has rammed-earth units for $70/84/104 singles/doubles/triples. It has two-bedroom apartments costing $110 for singles and doubles.

Opal Dreaming Underground Cottage (☎ 8672 5985) is very well appointed (apart from the fact that there's no flush toilet) and has stunning views of the wide open spaces. It charges $70 for doubles and you can book at the Underground Art Gallery in Hutchison St – the cottage is about 4km from town at Black Point.

Another nice place, with a beaut panorama towards the Breakaways, *The Underground Motel* (☎ 8672 5324, 1800 622 979 toll free, Catacomb Rd) charges $75/85 including a large, self-cooked breakfast.

Radeka's Downunder Motel (☎ 8672 5223, 1800 633 891 toll free, Hutchison St) charges $90 for its underground family room, which sleeps six. Its other units (above and below ground) cost $50/70/75.

Places to Stay – Top End
Hotels *Desert Cave Hotel* (☎ 8672 5688, reserve@desertcave.com.au, Hutchison St) has luxurious rooms above and below ground for $148 singles and doubles.

OUTBACK

Places to Eat

There are plenty of places to eat in Coober Pedy, although most won't suit a tight budget.

Tom & Mary's Taverna and *Traces* are Greek places on Hutchison St, and both are popular in the evenings (Traces stays open until 4 am). Both do platters – an economical meal for three people.

The *Breakaways Cafe*, under Traces, is popular for lunch. They make their own bread and cakes.

If you crave Italian, the *Italo Australian Miners Club (Italian Club Rd)* has good value dinners on Wednesday and Saturday.

For Chinese food try *Opal Inn Chinese (Wright Rd)*. Main courses start at $8. You can also get a reasonably priced counter meal in the pub's lounge bar – Thursday and Friday are 'specials' nights.

The *Old Miners Dugout Cafe (Hutchison St)* has simple but tasty dinners from $10. Similar prices are charged by the nearby *Opal Run Restaurant*, which specialises in continental cuisine – its steaks are reputed to be the best in town.

Alternatively, there's the more expensive *Umberto's* in the Desert Cave Hotel; actually its prices are quite reasonable given the quality of the food and service.

Getting There & Away

Air Kendell Airlines (bookings ☎ 13 13 00) flies from Adelaide to Coober Pedy daily for $274. The Desert Cave Hotel handles reservations and operates the airport shuttle bus ($5 one way). Most of the hostels will meet you if you ring ahead.

Bus Greyhound Pioneer charges $76 from Adelaide and $75 from Alice Springs. The buses stop at the Ampol Roadhouse on Hutchison St.

McCafferty's, which stops at Radeka's Downunder Motel, charges $76 from Adelaide and $69 from Alice Springs.

Getting Around

Coober Pedy Tours (☎ 8672 5333) runs the local taxi service. The Desert Cave Hotel is an agent for Thrifty, and it can arrange one-way rentals into the NT.

The Opal Cave (next to the Opal Cave Bedrock hostel) rents mountain bikes for $8 per day.

AROUND COOBER PEDY

The **Breakaways Reserve** is a stark but colourful area of arid hills and scarps about 33km by road north of Coober Pedy – you turn off the highway 22km from town. You can drive to a lookout in a conventional vehicle and see the white-and-yellow mesa known as the **Castle**, which featured in the films *Mad Max III* and *Priscilla, Queen of the Desert*. Entry permits ($2 per person) are available at the tourist office or Under-

The Breakaways punctuate the Outback's vast open space.

Getting there and Outback!

ground Books in Coober Pedy. Late afternoon is the best time for photographs.

An interesting loop of 70km on mainly unsealed road from Coober Pedy takes in the Breakaways, the **Dog Fence** and the table-like **Moon Plain** on the Coober Pedy-Oodnadatta road. Underground Books has a leaflet and 'mud map' for $1; check road conditions before attempting this route.

CADNEY HOMESTEAD
On the Stuart Hwy 82km south of Marla and 151km north of Coober Pedy, *Cadney Homestead Roadhouse (☎ 8670 7994)* has tent/caravan sites for $12/17, basic twin-share rooms with air-con for $25 (linen extra) and motel rooms for $77 singles and doubles.

The roadhouse offers scenic flights over the aptly named **Painted Desert** – an area of colourful mesas – between March and October inclusive. These take about one hour and cost $80/100 per passenger for three/two passengers; you can go further if you wish.

You can visit this interesting area weekdays on the mail run from Cadney towards

Oodnadatta. The tour takes around six hours and costs $50 per person, including lunch and a one hour walk in the Painted Desert. Ask at the roadhouse for details.

If you're heading for Oodnadatta, turning off the highway at Cadney gives you a shorter run on dirt roads, rather than going via Marla or Coober Pedy. You pass through the Painted Desert en route, and there are cabins and bush camping at *Copper Hills (☎ 8670 7995)*, about 32km east of the roadhouse.

MARLA
• **pop 150**
In mulga scrub about 180km south of the NT border, Marla replaced Oodnadatta as the official regional centre when the Ghan railway line was rerouted in 1980. Fuel and provisions are available here 24 hours a day; there's also an EFTPOS cash-withdrawal facility.

The small, frontier-style **Mintabie** opal field is on Aboriginal land 35km to the west of Marla. It has a general store, restaurant and caravan park.

OUTBACK

Marla Travellers Rest (☎ 8670 7001) has lawned tent/caravan sites for $10/15, very basic twin rooms with air-con for $19/28 (linen extra), and comfortable motel rooms from $59/65/70 – a TV and phone in the room are $10 extra. They also do meals.

Outback Tracks

The Birdsville, Oodnadatta and Strzelecki tracks are minor, unsealed routes which are tracks in name only these days – unless, of course, it rains. However, they'll appeal to the more adventurous traveller by virtue of their loneliness and lack of facilities, and the fact that they cross some of Australia's most inhospitable country. Most times you can do them in a conventional vehicle provided it's robust and has good ground clearance.

If you want to be even more daring there's the **Rig Road** (4WD only) across the Simpson Desert from Mt Dare Homestead to Birdsville. Alternatively, you can take the **Old Andado Track** (also 4WD only) from Mt Dare to Alice Springs via Old Andado Homestead.

All these tracks are covered in detail in Lonely Planet's *Outback Australia.* They are summarised only briefly in this book.

LYNDHURST
* pop 20

Squatting among low, barren hills at the southern end of the Strzelecki Track, Lyndhurst is at the end of the bitumen 300km north of Port Augusta. About 1km out along the track is the eccentric home and workshop of Cornelius Alferink, otherwise known as Talc Alf. He produces interesting abstract carvings from lumps of local talc.

You can get fuel and meals daily at the local roadhouse. The *Lyndhurst Hotel (☎ 8675 7781)* has rooms for $25/40 and does counter meals.

STRZELECKI TRACK

The Strzelecki Track runs for 460km to the tiny outpost of Innamincka, close to the Queensland border. Once just a two-wheel track meandering through the sandhills of the Strzelecki Desert, the route was substantially upgraded after the discovery of huge oil and gas deposits near **Moomba** in the 1960s. However, the amount of heavy transport travelling on it means the surface is often badly corrugated.

The track skirts the northern Flinders Ranges at first, coming to the ruins of historic **Blanchewater** Homestead on Mac-Donnell Creek, 157km from Lyndhurst. Established in 1857, it became the largest horse-breeding enterprise in Australia, but was abandoned after a huge flood devastated the homestead in 1940. The station is associated with the exploits of the famous cattle duffer Harry Redford, who pioneered the route with a stolen mob from Queensland in 1870.

There are no facilities of any kind between Lyndhurst and Innamincka. Tourists are not permitted to enter Moomba except in an emergency.

INNAMINCKA
* pop 10

At the northern end of the Strzelecki Track, Innamincka is on Cooper Creek close to where the ill-fated Burke and Wills expedition of 1860 came to its tragic end. One of Innamincka's major attractions is the famous **Dig Tree**, which marks the site of the expedition's base camp – the word 'dig' is no longer visible, but the expedition's camp number can still be made out.

While the Dig Tree is on the Queensland side of the border, the memorials and markers where Burke and Wills died, and where King, the sole survivor, was found are downstream in SA. There is also a memorial where Howitt, who led the rescue party, set up his depot on the creek. For a moving account of the Burke and Wills expedition, read Alan Moorehead's *Cooper's Creek.*

Cooper Creek flows only rarely – it takes big rains in central-west Queensland to bring it down in flood – but has deep, permanent waterholes and the semipermanent **Coongie Lakes**. These lakes are significant habitats for aquatic fauna and water birds, and are a major reason why the surrounding **Innamincka Regional Reserve** (1.4 million hectares) was created.

The restored **Australian Inland Mission** hospital in Innamincka now has the NPWS ranger's office (☎ 8675 9909) and informative displays on the regional reserve.

You can take a conventional vehicle over the unsealed road to Birdsville via **Cordillo Downs** Homestead. Built in 1883, the station's huge stone shearing shed, which had stands for 120 shearers, is one of SA's most outstanding pastoral relics.

Places to Stay & Eat

The *Innamincka Hotel (☎ 8675 9901)* has motel-style rooms with air-con sleeping five for $40/60/80 (extra persons $10). It does takeaways and has counter meals in the evenings; its Wednesday night 'Beef-and-Creek' and Sunday night roasts are both good value at $10 for all you can eat.

Alternatively, the *Innamincka Trading Post (☎ 8675 9900)* has three very modest two-bedroom cabins sleeping up to four for $40/60/85/100. Fuel and provisions are available here.

Otherwise there are plenty of nice places to camp among the coolibahs along the Cooper Creek system – see the ranger about a permit ($15 per vehicle per night). However, there are no facilities here apart from the odd toilet. (For a donation to the Progress Association you can use the shower, toilet and laundry facilities outside the Trading Post.)

LYNDHURST TO MARREE

About 5km north of Lyndhurst, the **Ochre Cliffs** are exposures of red and yellow ochre in a low breakaway. Be there in the late afternoon to get the best photos of its striking colours.

The ghost town of **Farina** is 25km from Lyndhurst. Established in 1882 as a farming centre on the Great Northern Railway (the name is Latin for flour), the little township survived well into this century but is now in ruins. The only substantial remains among the scattered chimneys and debris are those of the Transcontinental Hotel and post office.

Nearby is Farina Homestead (☎ 8675 7790), which offers 4WD **guided tours** of the station. These take you to rugged breakaway country and some interesting saltwater springs.

You can stay in the homestead's *shearers quarters* for $15, or camp at a pleasant *bush camping area* among large river red gums 500m north of the ruins; sites are $3 per person and you pay at the honesty box. Go through the campground to get to a sad old **cemetery**, which is on a desolate gibber rise 2km away. The Afghan section is off to the north by itself.

MARREE
* pop 80

At the junction of the Birdsville and Oodnadatta tracks, 380km north of Port Augusta, sleepy Marree has managed to survive several hard blows: first was the replacement of the camel teams (1930s) and drovers (1960s) by motor transport, then came a knockout punch with the closure of the Great Northern Railway in 1980.

Although it is now a shadow of its former self, there are still signs of the town's former prosperity. By far the grandest building in town is the two-storey **Great Northern Hotel**, built in the 1880s, and the railway complex complete with old locomotives is still more-or-less intact. A couple of date palms and a large sundial in the shape of a squatting camel (it's made from railway sleepers) recall the camel teams of earlier days.

Thanks to its isolation the town has a good range of facilities, including a small hospital, fuel sales and minimarkets. The Commonwealth Bank agency and post office are in the Marree General Store; both it and the Oasis Cafe have EFTPOS cash-withdrawal facilities. The latter has the Bank SA agency.

Marree comes to life during the winter tourist season, but really fires up in July on odd-numbered years when the Marree Australian Camel Cup is held the first Saturday of the month. There's an Aboriginal **heritage museum** in the Arabanna Centre.

Worth doing is the Muloorina (pronounced mu-LOO-rinah) **scenic drive**, which takes you to Lake Eyre and a beautiful deep waterhole in Frome Creek. Allow a day for the round trip; the Oasis Cafe can give you a mud map.

Book at the Oasis Cafe for scenic flights over Lake Eyre, Cooper Creek, the Flinders Ranges and other places – these include **Marree Man**, the 4km-long outline of an Aboriginal warrior etched into the desert sands near Lake Eyre. A one hour flight costs from $100 per person.

Places to Stay & Eat

In town, the *Oasis Caravan Park (Oasis Cafe ☎ 8675 8352)* has little shade but there are lawned campsites for $5 per person, and self-contained cabins with air-con for $20 per person, including linen.

The somewhat dustier *Marree Caravan & Campers Park (☎ 8675 8371)* is at the start of the Birdsville Track about a kilometre south of town. It has campsites from $5 per person, on-site vans with no air-con for $25 (air-con $30), and basic twin rooms with air-con for $12/20. There's a campers' kitchen, and the park sells fuel and tyres (as well as repairing them).

Alternatively, the *Great Northern Hotel (☎ 8675 8344)* has standard rooms costing $30/50 – the family room, which sleeps five, costs $80. Counter meals are available daily.

BIRDSVILLE TRACK

For nearly 80 years from the early 1880s, huge mobs of cattle from south-west Queensland were walked down the 520km Birdsville Track to Marree. Here they were loaded onto trains for the last part of their journey to the Adelaide markets. Motor transport took over from the drovers in the 1960s, and these days the cattle are trucked out in road trains.

There are some fascinating books on the Birdsville Track. *Mail for the Back of Beyond* by John Maddock (Kangaroo Press) is an inspiring account of the early motor

mail service – if you reckon the track is tough today, read this book. Eric Bonython's *Where the Seasons Come and Go* (Illawong) is an absorbing read covering history, lifestyles and adventure on the Cooper up to the 1950s.

In Australia you won't find country much harsher and drier than the land which lies along the Birdsville Track. The route more or less follows the boundary between the sand dunes of the Simpson Desert to the west and the desolate gibber wastes of Sturt Stony Desert to the east. At one point it touches the fearsome **Tirari Desert**, the closest thing Australia has to true desert. Despite its desolate appearance, you pass scattered homesteads as well as various scant ruins, while artesian bores gush boiling-hot, sulphurous water at several places.

Like most of the Lake Eyre Basin, you don't need to travel across this country to feel thirsty – just looking at a few pictures is usually sufficient. Dozens of people have perished of thirst along the track, the last being a family of five in December 1963. Their vehicle broke down and, having failed to take adequate water, they paid the ultimate price for their lack of preparation. Several travellers have had lucky escapes since then.

At **Clifton Hills**, about 200km south of Birdsville, the track splits, with the main route swinging around the eastern side of Goyders Lagoon; the 4WD 'Inner Track' crosses the lagoon (actually a vast seasonal swamp) and is the more interesting way to go, except when it's wet!

Although conventional vehicles can usually manage the main road without difficulty, it's worth bearing in mind that traffic is anything but heavy – particularly in summer, when days can go by without a vehicle passing.

Petrol, diesel, minor mechanical repairs, meals, accommodation and a campground are available at *Mungeranie Roadhouse (☎ 8675 8317)*, about 205km north of Marree and 315km south of Birdsville. It also sells lovely cold beer.

Birdsville, just across the Queensland border, has an excellent range of facilities,

The Birdsville Mail Run

Heading north on the Birdsville Track you cross Cooper Creek and enter a world of high yellow dunes which, for the next 20km, roll away on either side like ocean waves. Known as the Natterannie Sandhills, they mark the convergence of the Strzelecki Desert to the east and the Tirari Desert to the west.

Provided you stay on the road there is little likelihood that you'll become bogged in this frightful country, but it wasn't always so. In the droving days, before the track became a road, the Natterannie Sandhills were a nightmare for anyone travelling in a motor vehicle. Even the famous mail-driver, Tom Kruse, who became an expert in taking heavy vehicles through soft sand on his fortnightly trips up the track, found them tough going.

There was little chance of not getting stuck on this section, and because each bog meant unloading the truck then loading it again, it usually took Kruse eight hours to get through the worst section of 12km. The tyre-deflation method could rarely be used because the effort involved in pumping up the tyres put the driver at risk of heat exhaustion, or worse.

The innovative Kruse tried various strategies in his efforts to defeat the sandhills. Any truck fitted with dual rear wheels carried 6m lengths of 75mm bore casing. These were laid on the sand in the direction of travel so that the rear wheels could grip them and hopefully find traction.

Alternatively, the sand in front was covered with heavy iron sheets to provide a solid surface; great care had to be exercised as the sheets were liable to fly up and damage the underside of the truck if tackled at speed. Kruse even tried using conveyor belts to create a half-track vehicle, but with limited success. Mostly, it was a case of charge up the dune as far as he could, get out, unload the truck and start digging.

Denis O'Byrne

---

including a police station, small hospital, hotel, vehicle repairs, caravan park and general store.

OODNADATTA TRACK

Reeking with history, the 615km Oodnadatta Track from Marree to Marla is a fascinating and adventurous alternative to the Stuart Hwy. Between Marree and Oodnadatta, the road closely follows the route of the old Overland Telegraph Line and the Great Northern Railway; here, the evocative ruins of fettlers huts, railway sidings and telegraph stations excite the imagination. You can also detour to Lake Eyre (the world's sixth largest lake) and to various mound springs, the natural outlets for the Great Artesian Basin.

There are several routes across to the Stuart Hwy. These include the roads from William Creek to Coober Pedy; and from Oodnadatta to Coober Pedy and Cadney Homestead.

Fuel, accommodation and meals are available at Marree, William Creek (204km from Marree), Oodnadatta (406km) and Marla.

Coward Springs

The very basic *Coward Springs Camp Ground* (☎ 8675 8336) is 130km from Marree at the old Coward Springs railway siding. Shaded campsites cost $12 a vehicle, and there's a hot pool you can soak in; be prepared for mosquitoes if you're camping here in warm weather. In the cooler months you can do **camel rides** and, if you've got more time, a five day camel trek to Lake Eyre. There's a wetland with numerous water birds behind the campground.

A few kilometres back down the road towards Maree, the **Wamba Kadurba Conservation Park** includes artesian mound

SIMON ROWE

'Sheilas', aka the ladies' toilet, at Curdimurka, near Coward Springs

springs such as the Bubbler and Blanche Cup.

William Creek

The weather-beaten *William Creek Hotel* (☎ *8670 7880)* has a dusty campground ($3 per person), pub rooms ($20 per person), modest motel-style units with air-con ($45/60) and a bunkhouse without air-con ($12). It also sells fuel, cold beer, basic provisions and meals, and sells and repairs tyres.

The pub can arrange **scenic flights** costing from $35 per person with two passengers; an hour's flight over Lake Eyre costs $90/130 with three/two passengers.

Also operating from William Creek, SA Outback Research (☎ 1800 064 244) has **camel treks** with a historical and biological emphasis. They cost $95 per person per day all-inclusive, and not surprisingly are closed during summer.

OODNADATTA
• **pop 200**
This little outpost is at the point where the main road and the old railway line diverged. It was here that in 1912 the Reverend John Flynn, who later founded the Royal Flying Doctor Service, established the first hospital in the Australian outback.

These days – and despite losing most of its population when the railway closed – it has an excellent range of services, including a police station, small hospital, vehicle repairs, general store and pub.

For travellers, the gathering place at Oodnadatta is the **Pink Roadhouse**, an excellent source of information on track conditions and attractions in any direction. The owners, Adam and Lynnie Plate, have spent a great deal of time and effort putting in road signs and kilometre pegs all over the district – even in the Simpson Desert you'll come across signs erected by this dedicated pair! They've also produced a series of mud maps to make it even easier.

Across from the general store, the old train station (by far the most impressive building in town) has been converted into an interesting little **museum**. The pub, store and roadhouse have keys.

From Oodnadatta you can head northwest to Marla (209km) or north to the 771,000 hectare **Witjira National Park** (245km), on the western fringes of the Simpson Desert. The park contains **Dalhousie Springs**, a large group of artesian springs which are of great significance as the only permanent surface water in a vast area. Talk to Phil Hellyer at **Mt Dare Homestead**, within the national park, before attempting the 4WD routes to Alice Springs and Birdsville.

If you're heading up to Dalhousie and the Simpson Desert, a couple of very interesting references are *Simpson Desert* by Mark Shephard and *Natural History of Dalhousie Springs* (SA Museum).

Places to Stay & Eat

The *Oodnadatta Caravan Park* (☎ 8670 7822), attached to the Pink Roadhouse, has a range of accommodation: campsites cost $13 ($17 with power), basic twin-share

motel-style rooms are $40, self-contained cabins are $70, and there's a self-contained backpacker unit sleeping seven for $10 each. Most units have air-con.

Alternatively, there's the *Transcontinental Hotel* (☎ 8670 7804), which has air-con pub rooms for $30/55. You can get meals at both the pub (dinner only) and the roadhouse.

Lonely *Mt Dare Homestead* (☎ 8670 7835) provides the only facilities in Witjira National Park; it's the last place to fuel up before heading for Birdsville across the Simpson Desert, or Alice Springs via the Old Andado Track. It has basic accommodation in the old homestead and a campground – book ahead if you want a room or casual meals.

LONELY PLANET

Phrasebooks

Lonely Planet phrasebooks are packed with essential words and phrases to help travellers communicate with the locals. With colour tabs for quick reference, an extensive vocabulary and use of script, these handy pocket-sized language guides cover day-to-day travel situations.

- handy pocket-sized books
- easy to understand Pronunciation chapter
- clear & comprehensive Grammar chapter
- romanisation alongside script to allow ease of pronunciation
- script throughout so users can point to phrases for every situation
- full of cultural information and tips for the traveller

'...vital for a real DIY spirit and attitude in language learning'
– *Backpacker*

'the phrasebooks have good cultural backgrounders and offer solid advice for challenging situations in remote locations'
– *San Francisco Examiner*

Arabic (Egyptian) • Arabic (Moroccan) • Australian *(Australian English, Aboriginal and Torres Strait languages)* • Baltic States *(Estonian, Latvian, Lithuanian)* • Bengali • Brazilian • British • Burmese • Cantonese • Central Asia • Central Europe *(Czech, French, German, Hungarian, Italian, Slovak)* • Eastern Europe *(Bulgarian, Czech, Hungarian, Polish, Romanian, Slovak)* • Ethiopian (Amharic) • Fijian • French • German • Greek • Hill Tribes • Hindi/Urdu • Indonesian • Italian • Japanese • Korean • Lao • Latin American Spanish • Malay • Mandarin • Mediterranean Europe *(Albanian, Croatian, Greek, Italian, Macedonian, Maltese, Serbian, Slovene)* • Mongolian • Nepali • Papua New Guinea • Pilipino (Tagalog) • Quechua • Russian • Scandinavian Europe *(Danish, Finnish, Icelandic, Norwegian, Swedish)* • South-East Asia *(Burmese, Indonesian, Khmer, Lao, Malay, Tagalog Pilipino, Thai, Vietnamese)* • South Pacific Languages • Spanish (Castilian) *(also includes Catalan, Galician and Basque)* • Sri Lanka • Swahili • Thai • Tibetan • Turkish • Ukrainian • USA *(US English, Vernacular, Native American languages, Hawaiian)* • Vietnamese • Western Europe *(Basque, Catalan, Dutch, French, German, Greek, Irish)*

LONELY PLANET

Lonely Planet Journeys

J OURNEYS is a unique collection of travel writing – published by the company that understands travel better than anyone else. It is a series for anyone who has ever experienced – or dreamed of – the magical moment when they encountered a strange culture or saw a place for the first time. They are tales to read while you're planning a trip, while you're on the road or while you're in an armchair in front of a fire.

These outstanding titles explore our planet through the eyes of a diverse group of international writers. JOURNEYS books catch the spirit of a place, illuminate a culture, recount a crazy adventure or introduce a fascinating way of life. They always entertain, and always enrich the experience of travel.

ISLANDS IN THE CLOUDS
Travels in the Highlands of New Guinea
Isabella Tree

This is the fascinating account of a journey to the remote and beautiful Highlands of Papua New Guinea and Irian Jaya: one of the most extraordinary and dangerous regions on the planet. Tree travels with a PNG Highlander who introduces her to his intriguing and complex world, changing rapidly as it collides with twentieth-century technology. *Islands in the Clouds* is a thoughtful, moving book.

SEAN & DAVID'S LONG DRIVE
Sean Condon

Sean and David are young townies who have rarely strayed beyond city limits. One day, for no good reason, they set out to discover their homeland, and what follows is a wildly entertaining adventure that covers half of Australia.

'a hilariously detailed log of two burned out friends' – *Rolling Stone*

DRIVE THRU AMERICA
Sean Condon

If you've ever wanted to drive across the USA but couldn't find the time (or afford the gas), *Drive Thru America* is perfect for you. In his search for American myths and realities – along with comfort, cable TV and good, reasonably priced coffee – Sean Condon paints a hilarious road-portrait of the USA.

'entertaining and laugh-out-loud funny' – *Alex Wilber, Travel editor, Amazon.com*

BRIEF ENCOUNTERS
Stories of Love, Sex & Travel
edited by Michelle de Kretser

Love affairs on the road, passionate holiday flings, disastrous pick-ups, erotic encounters . . . In this seductive collection of stories, 22 authors from around the world write about travel romances. Combining fiction and reportage, *Brief Encounters* is must-have reading – for everyone who has dreamt of escape with that perfect stranger.

Includes stories by Pico Iyer, Mary Morris, Emily Perkins, Mona Simpson, Lisa St Aubin de Terán, Paul Theroux and Sara Wheeler.

LONELY PLANET

Lonely Planet Travel Atlases

Lonely Planet has long been famous for the number and quality of its guidebook maps. Now we've gone one step further and produced a handy companion series: Lonely Planet travel atlases – maps of a country produced in book form.

Unlike other maps, which look good but lead travellers astray, our travel atlases have been researched on the road by Lonely Planet's experienced team of writers. All details are carefully checked to ensure the atlas corresponds with the equivalent Lonely Planet guidebook.

- full-colour throughout
- maps researched and checked by Lonely Planet authors
- place names correspond with Lonely Planet guidebooks
- no confusing spelling differences
- legend and travelling information in English, French, German, Japanese and Spanish
- size: 230 x 160 mm

Available now: Chile & Easter Island ● Egypt ● India & Bangladesh ● Israel & the Palestinian Territories ● Jordan, Syria & Lebanon ● Kenya ● Laos ● Portugal ● South Africa, Lesotho & Swaziland ● Thailand ● Turkey ● Vietnam ● Zimbabwe, Botswana & Namibia

---

Lonely Planet TV Series & Videos

Lonely Planet travel guides have been brought to life on television screens around the world. Like our guides, the programs are based on the joy of independent travel, and look honestly at some of the most exciting, picturesque and frustrating places in the world. Each show is presented by one of three travellers from Australia, England or the USA and combines an innovative mixture of video, Super-8 film, atmospheric soundscapes and original music.

Videos of each episode – containing additional footage not shown on television – are available from good book and video shops, but the availability of individual videos varies with regional screening schedules.

Video destinations include: Alaska ● American Rockies ● Australia – The South-East ● Baja California & the Copper Canyon ● Brazil ● Central Asia ● Chile & Easter Island ● Corsica, Sicily & Sardinia – The Mediterranean Islands ● East Africa (Tanzania & Zanzibar) ● Ecuador & the Galapagos Islands ● Greenland & Iceland ● Indonesia ● Israel & the Sinai Desert ● Jamaica ● Japan ● La Ruta Maya ● Morocco ● New York ● North India ● Pacific Islands (Fiji, Solomon Islands & Vanuatu) ● South India ● South West China ● Turkey ● Vietnam ● West Africa ● Zimbabwe, Botswana & Namibia

The Lonely Planet TV series is produced by: Pilot Productions
The Old Studio
18 Middle Row
London W10 5AT, UK

LONELY PLANET

Lonely Planet On-line

Whether you've just begun planning your next trip, or you're chasing down specific info on currency regulations or visa requirements, check out Lonely Planet On-line for up-to-the minute travel information.

As well as mini guides to more than 250 destinations, you'll find maps, photos, travel news, health and visa updates, travel advisories, and discussion of the ecological and political issues you need to be aware of as you travel. You'll also find timely upgrades to popular guidebooks which you can print out and stick in the back of your book.

There's also an on-line travellers' forum where you can share your experience of life on the road, meet travel companions and ask other travellers for their recommendations and advice.

And of course we have a complete and up-to-date list of all Lonely Planet travel products including travel guides, diving and snorkeling guides, phrasebooks, atlases, travel literature and videos, and a simple on-line ordering facility if you can't find the book you want elsewhere.

Lonely Planet Diving & Snorkeling Guides

Known for indispensible guidebooks to destinations all over the world, Lonely Planet's Pisces Books are the most popular series of diving and snorkeling titles available.

There are three series: **Diving & Snorkeling Guides**, **Shipwreck Diving** series and **Dive Into History**. Full colour throughout, the **Diving & Snorkeling Guides** combine quality photographs with detailed descriptions of the best dive sites for each location, giving divers a glimpse of what they can expect both on land and in water. The **Dive Into History** series is perfect for the adventure diver or armchair traveller. The **Shipwreck Diving** series provides all the details for exploring the most interesting wrecks in the Atlantic and Pacific oceans. The list also includes underwater nature and technical guides.

LONELY PLANET

Guides by Region

L onely Planet is known worldwide for publishing practical, reliable and no-nonsense travel information in our guides and on our Web site. The Lonely Planet list covers just about every accessible part of the world. Currently there are nine series: travel guides, shoestring guides, walking guides, city guides, phrasebooks, audio packs, travel atlases, diving and snorkeling guides and travel literature.

AFRICA Africa – the South ● Africa on a shoestring ● Arabic (Egyptian) phrasebook ● Arabic (Moroccan) phrasebook ● Cairo ● Cape Town ● Central Africa ● East Africa ● Egypt ● Egypt travel atlas ● Ethiopian (Amharic) phrasebook ● The Gambia & Senegal ● Kenya ● Kenya travel atlas ● Malawi, Mozambique & Zambia ● Morocco ● North Africa ● South Africa, Lesotho & Swaziland ● South Africa, Lesotho & Swaziland travel atlas ● Swahili phrasebook ● Tanzania, Zanzibar & Pemba ● Trekking in East Africa ● Tunisia ● West Africa ● Zimbabwe, Botswana & Namibia ● Zimbabwe, Botswana & Namibia travel atlas
Travel Literature: The Rainbird: A Central African Journey ● Songs to an African Sunset: A Zimbabwean Story ● Mali Blues: Traveling to an African Beat

AUSTRALIA & THE PACIFIC Australia ● Australian phrasebook ● Bushwalking in Australia ● Bushwalking in Papua New Guinea ● Fiji ● Fijian phrasebook ● Islands of Australia's Great Barrier Reef ● Melbourne ● Micronesia ● New Caledonia ● New South Wales & the ACT ● New Zealand ● Northern Territory ● Outback Australia ● Papua New Guinea ● Papua New Guinea (Pidgin) phrasebook ● Queensland ● Rarotonga & the Cook Islands ● Samoa ● Solomon Islands ● South Australia ● South Pacific Languages phrasebook ● Sydney ● Tahiti & French Polynesia ● Tasmania ● Tonga ● Tramping in New Zealand ● Vanuatu ● Victoria ● Western Australia
Travel Literature: Islands in the Clouds ● Sean & David's Long Drive

CENTRAL AMERICA & THE CARIBBEAN Bahamas and Turks & Caicos ● Barcelona ● Bermuda ● Central America on a shoestring ● Costa Rica ● Cuba ● Dominican Republic & Haiti ● Eastern Caribbean ● Guatemala, Belize & Yucatán: La Ruta Maya ● Jamaica ● Mexico ● Mexico City ● Panama
Travel Literature: Green Dreams: Travels in Central America

EUROPE Amsterdam ● Andalucía ● Austria ● Baltic States phrasebook ● Barcelona ● Berlin ● Britain ● British phrasebook ● Canary Islands ● Central Europe ● Central Europe phrasebook ● Corsica ● Croatia ● Czech & Slovak Republics ● Denmark ● Dublin ● Eastern Europe ● Eastern Europe phrasebook ● Edinburgh ● Estonia, Latvia & Lithuania ● Europe ● Finland ● France ● French phrasebook ● Germany ● German phrasebook ● Greece ● Greek phrasebook ● Hungary ● Iceland, Greenland & the Faroe Islands ● Ireland ● Italian phrasebook ● Italy ● Lisbon ● London ● Mediterranean Europe ● Mediterranean Europe phrasebook ● Norway ● Paris ● Poland ● Portugal ● Portugal travel atlas ● Prague ● Provence & the Côte d'Azur ● Romania & Moldova ● Rome ● Russia, Ukraine & Belarus ● Russian phrasebook ● Scandinavian & Baltic Europe ● Scandinavian Europe phrasebook ● Scotland ● Slovenia ● Spain ● Spanish phrasebook ● St Petersburg ● Switzerland ● Trekking in Spain ● Ukrainian phrasebook ● Vienna ● Walking in Britain ● Walking in Italy ● Walking in Ireland ● Walking in Switzerland ● Western Europe ● Western Europe phrasebook
Travel Literature: The Olive Grove: Travels in Greece

INDIAN SUBCONTINENT Bangladesh ● Bengali phrasebook ● Bhutan ● Delhi ● Goa ● Hindi/Urdu phrasebook ● India ● India & Bangladesh travel atlas ● Indian Himalaya ● Karakoram Highway ● Nepal ● Nepali phrasebook ● Pakistan ● Rajasthan ● South India ● Sri Lanka ● Sri Lanka phrasebook ● Trekking in the Indian Himalaya ● Trekking in the Karakoram & Hindukush ● Trekking in the Nepal Himalaya
Travel Literature: In Rajasthan ● Shopping for Buddhas

LONELY PLANET

Mail Order

Lonely Planet products are distributed worldwide.They are also available by mail order from Lonely Planet, so if you have difficulty finding a title please write to us. North and South American residents should write to 150 Linden St, Oakland, CA 94607, USA; European and African residents should write to 10a Spring Place, London NW5 3BH, UK; and residents of other countries to PO Box 617, Hawthorn, Victoria 3122, Australia.

ISLANDS OF THE INDIAN OCEAN Madagascar & Comoros • Maldives • Mauritius, Réunion & Seychelles

MIDDLE EAST & CENTRAL ASIA Arab Gulf States • Central Asia • Central Asia phrasebook • Iran • Israel & the Palestinian Territories • Israel & the Palestinian Territories travel atlas • Istanbul • Jerusalem • Jordan & Syria • Jordan, Syria & Lebanon travel atlas • Lebanon • Middle East on a shoestring • Turkey • Turkish phrasebook • Turkey travel atlas • Yemen
Travel Literature: The Gates of Damascus • Kingdom of the Film Stars: Journey into Jordan

NORTH AMERICA Alaska • Backpacking in Alaska • Baja California • California & Nevada • Canada • Chicago • Florida • Hawaii • Honolulu • Los Angeles • Louisiana • Miami • New England USA • New Orleans • New York City • New York, New Jersey & Pennsylvania • Pacific Northwest USA • Puerto Rico • Rocky Mountain States • San Francisco • Seattle • Southwest USA • Texas • USA • USA phrasebook • Vancouver • Washington, DC & the Capital Region
Travel Literature: Drive Thru America

NORTH-EAST ASIA Beijing • Cantonese phrasebook • China • Hong Kong • Hong Kong, Macau & Guangzhou • Japan • Japanese phrasebook • Japanese audio pack • Korea • Korean phrasebook • Kyoto • Mandarin phrasebook • Mongolia • Mongolian phrasebook • North-East Asia on a shoestring • Seoul • South-West China • Taiwan • Tibet • Tibetan phrasebook • Tokyo
Travel Literature: Lost Japan

SOUTH AMERICA Argentina, Uruguay & Paraguay • Bolivia • Brazil • Brazilian phrasebook • Buenos Aires • Chile & Easter Island • Chile & Easter Island travel atlas • Colombia • Ecuador & the Galapagos Islands • Latin American Spanish phrasebook • Peru • Quechua phrasebook • Rio de Janeiro • South America on a shoestring • Trekking in the Patagonian Andes • Venezuela
Travel Literature: Full Circle: A South American Journey

SOUTH-EAST ASIA Bali & Lombok • Bangkok • Burmese phrasebook • Cambodia • Hanoi • Hill Tribes phrasebook • Ho Chi Minh City • Indonesia • Indonesia's Eastern Islands • Indonesian phrasebook • Indonesian audio pack • Jakarta • Java • Laos • Lao phrasebook • Laos travel atlas • Malay phrasebook • Malaysia, Singapore & Brunei • Myanmar (Burma) • Philippines • Pilipino (Tagalog) phrasebook • Singapore • South-East Asia on a shoestring • South-East Asia phrasebook • Thailand • Thailand's Islands & Beaches • Thailand travel atlas • Thai phrasebook • Thai audio pack • Vietnam • Vietnamese phrasebook • Vietnam travel atlas

ALSO AVAILABLE: Antarctica • Brief Encounters: Stories of Love, Sex & Travel • Chasing Rickshaws • Not the Only Planet: Travel Stories from Science Fiction • Travel with Children • Traveller's Tales

LONELY PLANET

FREE Lonely Planet Newsletters

We love hearing from you and think you'd like to hear from us.

Planet Talk

Our FREE quarterly printed newsletter is full of tips from travellers and anecdotes from Lonely Planet guidebook authors. Every issue is packed with up-to-date travel news and advice, and includes:

- a postcard from Lonely Planet co-founder Tony Wheeler
- a swag of mail from travellers
- a look at life on the road through the eyes of a Lonely Planet author
- topical health advice
- prizes for the best travel yarn
- news about forthcoming Lonely Planet events
- a complete list of Lonely Planet books and other titles

To join our mailing list, residents of the UK, Europe and Africa can email us at go@lonelyplanet.co.uk; residents of North and South America can email us at info@lonelyplanet.com; the rest of the world can email us at talk2us@lonelyplanet.com.au, or contact any Lonely Planet office.

Comet

Our FREE monthly email newsletter brings you all the latest travel news, features, interviews, competitions, destination ideas, travellers' tips & tales, Q&As, raging debates and related links. Find out what's new on the Lonely Planet Web site and which books are about to hit the shelves.

Subscribe from your desktop: www.lonelyplanet.com/comet

Index

Text

Bold indicates maps.

Bold indicates maps.

Boxed Text

MAP LEGEND

BOUNDARIES

. . . . International
. . . . State

HYDROGRAPHY

. . . . Coastline
. . . . River, Creek
. . . . River Flow
. . . . Lake
. . . . Intermittent Lake
. . . . Salt Lake
. . . . Spring, Rapids
. . . . Swamp
. . . . Waterfalls

ROUTES & TRANSPORT

. . . . Freeway
. . . . Highway
. . . . Major Road
. . . . Minor Road
. . . . Unsealed Road
. . . . City Highway
. . . . City Road
. . . . City Street, Lane

. . . . Pedestrian Mall
. . . . Tunnel
. . . . . . Train Route & Station
. . . . Metro & Station
. . . . Tramway
. . . . . . Cable Car or Chairlift
. . . . Walking Track
. . . . Ferry Route

AREA FEATURES

. . . . Aboriginal Land
. . . . Beach
. . . . Cemetery

. . . . Marine Park
. . . . . National Park, Gardens
. . . . Urban Area

MAP SYMBOLS

☼ **CAPITAL** . . . . National Capital
◉ **CAPITAL** . . . . State Capital
● **CITY** . . . . City
● **Town** . . . . Town
● **Town** . . . . Small Town
○ . . . . Point of Interest

■ . . . . Place to Stay
▲ . . . . Camping Ground
ᗟ . . . . Caravan Park

▼ . . . . Place to Eat
🍴 . . . . . . Pub, Entertainment
▣ . . . . Picnic Area

✈ . . . . Airport
✝ . . . . Airfield
❸ . . . . Bank
🧍 . . . . Beach
⌂ . . . . Cave
. . . . Church
. . . . Cliff or Escarpment
⛳ . . . . Golf Course
✚ . . . . Hospital
🗼 . . . . Lighthouse
❋ . . . . Lookout
✕ . . . . Mine
⚑ . . . . Monument
▲ . . . . Mountain
🏛 . . . . . . Museum, Art Gallery

🅿 . . . . Parking
)(. . . . . Pass, Chasm, Gap
★ . . . . Police Station
✉ . . . . Post Office
❖ . . . . Shopping Centre
🏛 . . . . Stately Building
🏄 . . . . Surf Beach
🏊 . . . . Swimming Pool
☎ . . . . Telephone
🚻 . . . . Toilet
ℹ . . . . Tourist Information
☕ . . . . Transport
🏠 . . . . Trekking Hut
🍷 . . . . Winery
🦘 . . . . Zoo

Note: not all symbols displayed above appear in this book

LONELY PLANET OFFICES

Australia
PO Box 617, Hawthorn 3122, Victoria
tel: (03) 9819 1877 fax: (03) 9819 6459
e-mail: talk2us@lonelyplanet.com.au

USA
150 Linden St, Oakland, CA 94607
tel: (510) 893 8555 TOLL FREE: 800 275-8555
fax: (510) 893 8572
e-mail: info@lonelyplanet.com

UK
10a Spring Place, London, NW5 3BH
tel: (0171) 428 4800 fax: (0170) 428 4828
e-mail: go@lonelyplanet.co.uk

France
1 rue du Dahomey, 75011 Paris
tel: 01 55 25 33 00 fax: 01 55 25 33 01
e-mail: bip@lonelyplanet.fr

World Wide Web: www.lonelyplanet.com *or* AOL keyword: lp
Lonely Planet Images: lpi@lonelyplanet.com.au